History of Education in India

History of Education in India

SURESH C. GHOSH

RAWAT PUBLICATIONS

Jaipur • New Delhi • Bangalore • Mumbai • Hyderabad • Guwahati

ISBN 81-316-0161-7

Published by
Prem Rawat for **Rawat Publications**
Satyam Apts, Sector 3, Jawahar Nagar, Jaipur 302 004 (India)
Phone: 0141 265 1748 / 7006 Fax: 0141 265 1748
E-mail: info@rawatbooks.com
Website: www.rawatbooks.com

New Delhi Office
4858/24, Ansari Road, Daryaganj, New Delhi 110 002
Phone: 011 2326 3290

Also at Bangalore, Mumbai, Hyderabad and Guwahati

Typeset by Rawat Computers, Jaipur
Printed at Chaman Enterprises, New Delhi

Contents

Preface

This is an authentic and comprehensive account of the history of education in India from the beginning of the third millennium B.C. (Indus Valley Civilisation) to the end of the second millennium A.D. The absence of such a work on the subject till date is not surprising in the light of the scant regard meted out to the discipline of the history of education in this country. The work is based on my own research on the subject during my career with the Jawaharlal Nehru University, New Delhi which has resulted in the occasional publication of papers abroad as well as in the three monographs earlier relating to the three periods of Indian history – ancient, medieval and modern.

In 'Modern India' in the work I have treated Independent India as an extension of British India, since until very recently not much change in the colonial education could be seen either in its structure or in its content. While presenting my subject, I have in my mind not only the needs and requirements of the students of higher learning institutions but also of a larger audience interested in the subject. I have, therefore, avoided footnotes, except on a few occasions, for a smooth reading. Finally, I wish to thank Shri Rajiv Gosain for the meticulous care and immense pains he has taken in preparing the manuscript for publication and Shri Pranit Rawat of Rawat Publications for his keen interest in the subject and its prompt publication.

Suresh C. Ghosh

Introduction

The Indian history is said to have begun with the Indus Valley Civilisation which existed in the North-West India, now mostly in
Pakistan, some 3000 years before the beginning of the Christian era
with the birth of Jesus Christ. The highly developed state of civilisation among the people of the Indus Valley presupposes an existence
among them a system of education which had probably little to do
with the religion of the Indus Valley people. This, however, cannot
be said about the civilisation created by the Aryans who replaced the
Indus Valley people and gave shape to the history and culture of the
sub-continent stretching from the Himalayas to the Bay of Bengal and
the Arabian Sea and variously known as 'Bharatavarsha, Jambudvipa,
Brahmarshidesha, Brahmavarta or Aryavarta. Education among the
Aryans did not exist for its own sake, just as it does today, and
therefore had no independent identity. It was essentially an integral
part of the religion of the Aryans. It is therefore necessary to have a
look at the different stages in the development of Aryan religious
beliefs and practices so that we can understand our subject in Ancient
India properly.

The religion of the Aryans was first revealed in the Rigveda
presumably composed orally between 1500 and 1000 B.C. The oldest
religious text in the world consisted of some 1028 mantras or hymns
recited at the Yajnas or sacrifices performed by the Aryans to please
the 33 gods and goddesses who were assigned to the three levels of the
Cosmos or the universe: the Celestial, Intermediate and Terrestrial.
The Cosmos or the universe mystified the Aryans as it does mystify

us till today. And they tried to explain it by assigning its different parts to different deities till they arrived at, towards the end of the Rigvedic period, the conception of a Supreme Creator or Brahma who was later identified with the Brahman in the Upanishads.

Yajnas or sacrifices formed the centre of the Aryan religion. No deities could be worshipped without the performance of the sacrifices. Sacrifices were complex rites, involving much preparation, the slaughter of numerous animals and the participation of the several well-trained priests as well as offerings by the worshippers of milk, ghee, grain, flesh and juice of the soma plant. In the days of the Rigveda such sacrifices were generally organised and financed by the chiefs and the wealthier tribesman to gratify the gods in order to obtain boons from them. The gods descended to the sacrifical venue, ate and drank with the worshippers, and duly rewarded them with success in war, progeny and long life and almost in everything asked for. The worshippers, inebriated with the som juice, saw wonderous visions of the gods; they experienced strange sensations of powers; they could reach up and touch the heavens; they became immortal and gods themselves. The worshippers came to possess a magical power, a sort of supernatural electricity identified with the Brahman in the Rigveda by uttering the sacred mantras or hymns. The possessor of this Brahman became known as Brahmana, the tribal priest and magician. The supernatural power of the Brahmana lay in the words of the hymns he uttered as in the alphabets 'OM' which contains the essence of the Vedas and is pregnant with the utmost power and mystery.

By the end of the Rigvedic period it was believed from the mystical identification of god, victim and sacrificer that the universe itself arose from the primeval sacrifice involving the god Prajapati, the Lord of Beings, later called Brahma, the masculine from the neuter Brahman. In the "Hymns of the Primeval Man", Prajapati was thought of as a primeval man or Prusha who existed before the foundation of the universe and who was sacrificed presumably to himself by the gods who were apparently his children. The universe came into existence out of the divine victim.

With the sacrifice of the primeval man, a new attitude to sacrifice gradually developed. It now became a supernal mystery. By means of it the priests mystically repeated the primeval sacrifice and the world was born anew. All cosmic processes would cease, and chaos would return without such regular sacrifices. The order of nature was ultimately dependent not on gods but on the Brahmanas who by the magic of the sacrifice maintained and compelled them. And so, the Brahmanas were more powerful than any earthly kings or gods, who could by the slightest variation of ritual, turn the sacrifice against the patrons and destroy them.

With the passage of time and contact with the new people eastwards and southwards the domination of the Brahmans came to be challenged by the ascetics who were worshippers of the less prominent gods of the Rigvedic period like Siva or Rudra, Vishnu or Vasudeva and the meaning of the term, Brahmana, came to acquire a new significance. It now meant not the power to create or destroy, favour or disfavour a thing on a person but the knowledge to liberate oneself from the samsara or transmigration, that is, the cycle of birth and death. The doctrine of samsara or transmigration was first propounded in the Brihadranyaka Upanishad and by the end of the sixth and the beginning of the fifth centuries B.C., it had gained wide currency and universal acceptancy among the Aryans. The doctrine was however, propounded in a very crude and primitive form stating that the souls of those "who have lived the lives of sacrifice, charity and austerity first go to the World of Fathers, then after a period of bliss, go to the moon and from moon they go to the air and descend to earth in the rain. On earth they become food... and are offered again in the altar fire what is man to be born again in the fire of woman. And those who have failed to live their lives righteously are reincarnated as worms, birds or insects. In whatever form, the doctrine of transmigration was developed it involved belief in the repeated passage of the soul from life to life, either for all eternity or for an inestimably long period of time for all forms of life".

Life, with or without sorrows, was one of acute suffering and the prospect of having to die innumerable times to be born again was not only dreaded but was also terrible and painful. A way had to be found to escape the cycle of birth and death and this was provided by the Upanishads in the form of the knowledge of Brahman or Absolute and of Atman or Self. The Absolute was not subject to change but the individual was. The Upanishads stated that it was the individual who died and not the Absolute. And so the individual must merge with the Absolute to escape from change, decay and dissolution. Selfishness or Individualism resulted from the pursuit of objective knowledge which connected the mind with the worldly matter. When one was able to stop those activities which connected the mind with worldly matter, one was able to know one's Atman or Self and thus became a part of Brahman or Absolute. One then became free from the Samsara or the cycle of birth and death. One achieved what Buddha called later, Nirvana.

And how could the merger of the Atman or the Self with the Brahman or the Absolute be realised. It could be achieved through sravana, manana, and nididhyasana. Sarvana means listening to the words or texts as they are uttered by his Guru or teacher, Manana means deliberation or reflection or the topic taught and nididhyasana means yoga or meditation through which truth is to be realised. The Rishis or Sages achieved their liberation through these stages. And so did Mahavira and the Buddha. The Buddha was taught the doctrine of Nirvana by his guru, Alara Kalama who was so used to meditation that "he would not, sitting on the roadside, be conscious of a caravan of 500 carts rattling past him".

Since the chief aim of education in Ancient India was to achieve emancipation or liberation, it may be argued, that it had little to do with the material development of the Aryan society. British officials who reported on the education in Ancient India, and following them, Western and Indian scholars who have written on the history of education in British India have always maintained that education in Ancient India was spiritual and classical, and not practical or vocational. Nothing, however, can be more farther from the truth than such belief.

In Ancient India while the Brahmanas or the priestly class took care of the spiritual needs of the people of the society, there were three other groups or classes – the Kshatriyas, the Vaisyas and the Sudras – who looked after their basic needs and requirements. This division of the Aryan society into four groups or classes had religious sanction in a hymn in the Rigveda. It described that when the universe came into existence out of the sacrifice of the primeval man, his mouth became the Brahmana or the priest, his arms the Kshatriya or the warrior, his thighs the Vaisya or the trader and out of his feet was born the Sudra whose job was to serve the first three groups though in the Rigvedic age a Sudra could have access to the study of the Vedas. The Sudras were said to be the original descendants of the Indus Valley people vanquished by the Aryans and though at the beginning left out of the Aryan society as Anaryas or Dasas, were later accommodated as its members.

While the Kshatriyas after a study of one of the four Vedas specialised in administration and protection of the tribesmen, the Vaisyas similarly added to their prosperity by participating in trade and agriculture, commerce and industry. The Sudras specialised in the arts and crafts including painting, music, dancing, magic spells and Ayurveda or indigenous medicine which could be traced to the fourth or the last Veda, the Atharvaveda. As with the study of the Vedas, the apprentice had to live with his guru, the master craftsman, to learn the secrets of his work, assimilate his sprit and method, not revealed in any final manner at all. A hymn in the Rigveda throws light on the kind of profession pursued by the four classes of the Aryan society: "We different men have different tastes and pursuits. The carpenter (takshaka) seeks something that is broken (rishtam), the physician (bhishaj), a patient (rulam), the priest (Brahmana) some one who will perform sacrifice (savantamichchati)". However, castes were not always rigidly observed in the pursuit of professions. In a family where the mother was a grinder of corn or housewife, the father was a bhishaj and the son was the composer of hymns or a sage.

The shaping of the Aryan schools of learning and of its various disciplines was conterminous with the shaping of the Aryan political organisation from tribal to monarchical. These were the years which saw the composition of the Rig, Sama, Yajur and Atharva Vedas, Brahmanas, Aranyakas and Upanishads as well as the coming into existence of a variety of ascetic movements, the most important of which was Buddhism which offered a serious challenge to Brahmanism, in achieving Nirvana or salvation. The Brahmanism rejuvenated itself through the works of the Sutrakaras to meet the challenge of Buddhism but in the process the Sutrakaras canonised learning which adversely affected the growth and development of original and creative ideas in future. The succeeding centuries after the beginning of the Christian era were characterised more by a desire to preserve, explain and comment on the wisdom of the past than by any serious attempt to broaden and widen the horizon of learning by discovering a new philosophy or idea not in conformity with the canonised scriptures. Thus an age of intellectual freedom, when the Aryan Society used to successfully reconcile its reverence for the past with its regard for the new frontiers of knowledge was followed by an age of preservation of the past wisdom when the philosophers could only explain and comment on it.

In the beginning when Brahminism was the sole dominant religion, the Brahminical centres of learning received the exclusive patronage of the kings who were mostly Kshatriyas. With the emergence of Buddhism as a dominant religion through the support provided by the Mauryan emperor Asoka, the Buddhist centres of learning began to dot the various parts of the Asokan empire. In the subsequent centuries till the coming of the Islam to India, the fate of the two systems of learning, the Vedic and the Buddhist which more or less peacefully coexisted, depended partly on the royal patronage extended to them and partly on the frequent internecine warfare among the kings and monarchs for supremacy and almost incessant intrusions of the foreign invaders through the North-West, both of which threatened the peace and stability of the Aryan kingdoms so vitally needed for the growth and development of learning and culture in a country.

In Ancient India education was religion, and religion education but not so was the Islamic education in Medieval India. Islamic education came into existence after the Prophet Muhammad had started giving discourses on the acquisition of knowledge in science and literature to the Arabs after the fall of Mecca and a host of foreigners from Persia, Greece, Syria, Iraq and Africa came and gathered around him at Medina to hear him. In a sense the prophet's teachings on the subject of knowledge formed "the nucleus of an educational institution, which after years grew into universities at Baghdad and Salaerno, at Cairo and Cordova". In Islam, quite in keeping with the philosophy of the Prophet's life and teachings, acquisition of knowledge came to be looked upon as the fulfilment of the Islamic religion which also meant the spread of the religion in the non-Islamic lands or Dar-ul-harb.

In Medieval India Islamic education which replaced the existing Vedic and Buddhist education to meet the growing needs of the Islamic administration and of an increasing Islamic community fulfilled its goals admirably, and in more ways than one, it resembled and anticipated English education in colonial India. For the first time in thousand years since the fall of the Guptas the Islamic rulers built up an empire with a central administration where bureaucracy took orders from Delhi and Agra in Persian which was the medium of instruction in the Islamic educational institutions of higher learning in Medieval India. Persian was not merely the language of the court, but also of public business, of diplomacy and public society. Persian tastes and ideas came to profoundly influence arts and letters in contemporary India. Hindus from the vanquished ruling classes as well as from the affluent families began to learn Persian from the sixth century onwards for a foothold in the Islamic administration and with a common language, a common taste in arts and letters, a common etiquette, along with the Muslim officials, formed one of the invisible pillars of Islamic rule in Medieval India. In short, Persian language, the language adopted and patronised by the Islamic rulers in Medieval India came to acquire a position similar to the one achieved by the English in colonial India.

When Islam came to India and established its own rule, the Muslim rulers imported their own system of education consisting of Maktabs, Madrasahs, Mosques and Khanqahs to meet the needs of a growing Islamic administration as well as to cater to the needs of a growing Muslim community. Muslim rulers from Qutab-ud-din-Aibak onwards as well as Muslim nobles and officials, both at the Centre and in the provinces, became a pivot upon which the Islamic system of education revolved in Medieval India. While Islamic education spread to the remote parts of their extensive dominion, Hindu learning survived in Muslim India through Guru-Shishya-Parampara and thrived in the Hindu kingdoms in the North and flourished in those across the Vindhyas. While in many respects Islamic education emphasised the continuities from the past, it also created new conditions for the further development of vernaculars and village schools as well as for the birth of a new language, Urdu, which many years later was to become the *lingua franca* of the Muslim community in India.

By the time the British came to India as traders of the East India Company, only two systems of education belonging to the Hindus and the Muslims were in existence. Demolition of the Buddhist Viharas from the very beginning of the Muslim rule in Medieval India had led to the disappearance of the Buddhist system of education. And the British officials who reported on the Hindu and the Muslim system of education in the provinces, scarcely talked about the Buddhist Viharas and the Buddhist system of education. However, they made an error in describing the Muslim education along with the Vedic education as an indigenous one, for, the Muslim system of education was not certainly born in India but was imported from outside India to meet the needs and requirements of an expanding Muslim administration and an ever-increasing Muslim community.

In the beginning, the British as traders, though interested in the classical and spiritual education of the Hindus and of the Muslims were reluctant to take an interest in the education of the people of the country under their rule till 1813. However, events at home including fresh demand for raw materials for a blooming Industrial Revolution in England and Europe and pressures from the utilitarians for the introduction of a Western system of education in India while transformation of the British traders and merchants into rulers of the country forced their hands. In 1835, English was introduced as the official language replacing Persian in the administration and in 1854 in an education despatch from London, was laid down the foundation of a modern system of education in the country. The despatch provided for the setting up of universities on London model, opening up of departments of education in the provinces and instituting the system of grants-in-aid to encourage private enterprise in education in India.

Encouraged by the despatch, many Indians came forward to setting up schools to further the cause of education. However, the Indian educated under the new system of education soon found that the British administration was unable to meet their hopes and aspirations and became increasingly discontented with it. In 1885, Allan Octavium Hume founded the Indian National Congress to help them to let their steam of discontent out but soon a section of them was drawn to militant nationalism. By that time the British officials had realised their blunder of introducing English education in India and they took several measures to stop its spread further but in vain. However, with the outbreak of the Second World War in 1939, the British Raj found it difficult to stick to its position in India and after the close of the war and a change of government at home, the British decided to quit, which they did in August 1947.

After the departure of the British, leadership in India naturally fell to the Western educated Indians. Unfortunately, they found their hands too preoccupied with other problems to give much attention to the renovation of the existing education structure to suit national needs and aspirations. However, they soon found that it would be best to continue the existing system as left by the British with some minor alterations. There were indeed some attempts at renovating the education system in the country but they did not bring much success. Meanwhile, with the rise of the Dalits, the Scheduled Castes and the Scheduled Tribes and the other socially backward classes, who had now the benefit of a liberal education, a new element entered into the Indian political scene and they now challenged the leadership of the Western educated Indians. With the change of leadership at the Centre and in many provinces, education which empowers person has now become a battlefield among different groups holding power in the administration. And with the waves of globalisation hitting the shores of India the educational scene in the country has not only become further aggravated but also confused by the end of the second millennium A.D.

II

It is a pity that Indian scholars till date have not been much attracted to the discipline of history of education. Consequently very few works exist on the subject and those that exist are mostly periodical – Ancient, Medieval and Modern. We may select here a few known works and have a look at them.

In Ancient India there are two widely read works, though both of them were published in colonial India, that is, before independence. The first authored by A.S. Altekar candidly admits in his preface to the second edition of the works entitled, *Education in Ancient India:* "Particular attention has been given to the method of teaching and curricula that prevailed in the different period of Ancient Indian History... This method of treatment no doubt enables the reader to get a clear idea of the development of each theme, but does not give him the picture of the educational education as a whole of the different epochs of Indian history". The bulk of the materials of the second work entitled, *Ancient Indian Education* by Radha Kumud Mookerji was collected as early as in 1918-20 but for various reasons could not be published as a monograph before 1947. And by that time much of its theme had already appeared in various learned journals. When the book was brought out, it consisted of the articles already published earlier. In such a work the continuity and discontinuity of the changes in education could not be observed as they did not relate to the changes in the contemporary Aryan Society. To put in a nutshell, both the works by Altekar and Mookerji give us an impression of the growth and development of education in a vacuum. And we all know that nature does not only abhor vacuum but also does not allow anything to happen in a vacuum.

Similarly in Medieval India there exist two works on the subject – one by Narendra Nath Law and the other by S.N. Jaffar. Law brought out his work entitled, *Promotion of Learning in India during Muhammadan Rule* in 1915 to highlight the contributions made by Muslim rulers, chiefs, and private individuals "to promote learning and diffuse education among the people of the country".

Law has divided his work into two broad sections, Book-I and Book-II. While Book-I relates to the pre-Mughal period, Book-II deals with the Mughal period. The Book-I is again divided into eight chapters – each chapter dealing with a particular theme. The Book-II which relates to the Mughal period is subdivided into six chapters, of which the first five, excepting the second on Sher Shah are devoted to the collection of materials on the promotion of learning by the Mughal emperors and the last chapter gives us an insight into the education of the females belonging to the royal families.

It is unfortunate that Law has not attempted to bring out the significance of the information on the subject either by analysis or by interpretation. Nor has he tried to relate the efforts of the Muslim rulers towards promotion of learning to geography and chronology which are the twin eyes of history. His work gives the impression of a clinical surgery separating Muslim learning from the realities of Muslim rule in India. His inability to relate historical developments to time and space has often led him to misjudge many a contemporary observation such as the one made by Babar in his Memoirs which was presumably written between 1526 and 1530. Babar has said: "The people of Hindustan have no good horses, no good flesh, no grapes or musk-melons, no good fruits, no ice or cold water, no good food or bread in their bazaars, no baths or colleges, no candles, no torches, not a candle-stick". This is, no doubt, an observation of an exile who missed the place he had left behind and longed to be there and is certainly an exaggeration as it is indeed difficult to form an impression of a country within a short period of four years spent in constant wars with the Rajputs and the Afghans. Yet Babar's observations on Hindustan depicts a hopeless state of the country which was a natural sequel to its distracted condition which had begun in 1398 when Timur landed in Delhi and continued for more than a hundred and twenty-eight years through the rule of the Sayyids and the Lodis till it was further aggravated by Babar's wars in India in 1527 and 1529 before his death in 1530. Yet Law's work is important not only in its pioneering approach to the subject of Muslim education and learning and in its use of contemporary Arabic and Persian sources but also in casting doubt on Akbar's illiteracy, which has been accepted by almost all European scholars on Akbar including Count Von Noer, H.Beveridge and Vincent Smith as *fait accompli*. S.M. Jaffar's work entitled, *Education in Muslim India, 1000-1800 A.D.* was published in 1936. Both in collection and processing of materials from the contemporary sources on Muslim learning in Medieval India, Jaffar seems to have blindly followed Law's work published much earlier in 1915 and as such his work suffers from all the limitations of the former's monograph just discussed above. However, while Law's work is characterised by an impartial and unbiased approach in his treatment of the subject, Jaffar's work cannot be said to have possessed this attribute. The bias and partiality of the author are evident in almost all pages of his work where he speaks highly of the endeavour of the Muslim rulers towards promotion of Muslim learning but keeps mum not only on the destruction of Hindu and Buddhist seats of learning – temples and viharas – but also on the harming of Muslim education by the Muslim rulers themselves. For example, Jaffar has not bothered to say about Ala-ud-din's 'firman' depriving Muslim educational institutions of their endowments or about the neglect of Muslim education by the weak successors of Firuz Tughluq or Aurangzeb, who solely devoted themselves to the pleasures of life, particularly wine and women. And finally despite the title of his work as *Education in Muslim India, 1000-1800*, he has not cared to speak about non-Muslim, Hindu or Buddhist learning during his period. We all know that Hindu learning continued in Muslim India through the priestly families who organised their Sanskrit schools in various parts of the country and often received patronage not only from the tolerant Muslim rulers of the provinces but also from the *petite* Hindu chieftains of small principalities who survived by paying allegience and tributes to their Muslim masters.

As a matter of fact, Jaffar's work betrays his ignorance about education in Ancient India. Had Jaffar carefully studied the history of education in Ancient India, he would have realised that the domestic or residential system of teaching, village schools, literary assembly or parishad and libraries are not at all innovations in India under the Muslim rule as he would have us believe. His failure to understand the subtle current of continuity beneath the past historical developments has led him to strongly endorse Abdul Qadir's observation on institution of libraries in his article in the January 1936 issue of the *Journal of the Royal Asiatic Society:* "The libraries which came into existence in

India as a result of the love of learning of many of its Muslim rulers were a great help to the cause of learning". Every student of Ancient Indian history knows about the existence of excellent libraries not only in the Hindu temples but also in the Buddhist Viharas which draw a lot of Chinese and other scholars including Fa-hien in the Fifth Century A.D. Hiuen-Tsang and I-Tsing in the Seventh Century A.D. to study and copy the Buddhist manuscripts in Sanskrit and Pali kept in their custody.

Finally, it is obvious that Jaffar's work suffers from the fallout of the contemporary Muslim politics in India in the 1930s. His book was written and published in 1936 on the eve of the election recommended by the Government of India Act of 1935, which returned Muslim governments to four out of eleven provinces in British India. Otherwise, he would not have argued, after crossing the limit of his period at 1800 A.D. by 136 years, about the superiority of the Muslim education to the prevalent English education or about the adoption of Urdu as the *lingua franca* of India in place of English!

In Modern India the history of education book that still holds the ground among those who are ignorant of the recent progress made in the research on the subject is the work jointly authored by S. Nurullah and J.P. Naik and was first published in 1945 under the title, *History of Education in India during the British Period.* Nurullah who held an M.Ed. degree from Leeds University in England was a distinguished member of the Bombay Education Service. J.P. Naik served the Bombay Education Department before becoming an Adviser in the Ministry of Education in 1959.

The popularity of Nurullah and Naik's book could be gauged from the fact that within three decades after the first year of publication, it underwent six editions, the last being in 1974 when J.P. Naik (Nurrullah since expired) added a chapter to update the educational history to 1973. There is no doubt that Nurullah and Naik's work gave us for the first time an idea of the educational development in colonial India and an insight into the nature of printed official documents utilised to obtain this information. Unfortunately for us, the work instead of encouraging further research in the subject, became instantly a handy, stereotyped model for the educationists and scholars in the country to follow. And consequently, there has been until recently no apparent advancement in knowledge on the subject.

Yet, it is difficult to describe Nurullah and Naik's book as a good piece of historical research. The book is mainly based on available printed selections of official records and reports and other printed works on education that they could lay their hands on to the exclusion of contemporary printed sources such as memoirs, diaries, letters, pamphlets, newspapers as well as non-printed manuscript sources including private papers of important government officials. It is absolutely necessary to consult and compare all the available sources before processing them for interpretation. Otherwise, the presentation is bound to become lopsided and unreliable. And so in Nurullah and Naik's book, it is mostly the government which does all the talking. Secondly, both the authors being members of the educational service of the British Raj, it is indeed difficult for them to view from within the educational developments in colonial India objectively. Thirdly, it is further difficult for Naik who participated in the Freedom Movement in India to write about the educational developments in British India dispassionately and without any bias. The book was written during the high noon of the Freedom Movement and as such it reflected the spirit of the time. Finally, the title of Nurullah and Naik's book, *History of Education in India during the British Period*, is a misnomer because it scarcely says anything about any education other than the British.

III

The works discussed above are the leading ones in the history of education in Ancient, Medieval and Modern India. What is common to them is not only an absence of historical research methodology in the treatment of the subject but also of an interpretation of the evidences showing how changes in education relate to changes in the socio-economic and political structure of the society. These works also ignore the fact that all educational activities, however small, emerge from the top and filter down to the people. In Ancient India, as well as in Medieval India to a great extent, it is the religion of the rulers and the ruling class which directed such activities while in British India it is mostly and largely the imperial and the commercial interests of the rulers and the ruling class which gave shape to them.

In all these periods there were large groups of people who could not participate in the educational programmes of the country initiated by the rulers and these groups remained less empowered and more backward. In Ancient India education was dominated by the priestly class and the last two classes, the Vaishyas and the Shudras remained mostly deprived of it. In Medieval India, domination of education by the priestly class of Ancient India was pushed to the background with the introduction of an Islamic system of education by the Muslim rulers which benefited the ruling class only. The priestly class as well as the three other classes of the Ancient Indian Society could not participate in the Muslim educational programmes in the country, and without state patronage from the Muslim rulers whatever remained of the Vedic education in Muslim India began to wither gradually. And, consequently there may be many among the priestly class who joined the rank of those deprived of education. In British India, a rising middle class living in urban areas monopolised Western education while the bulk of the people living in areas spreading from the rural and the desert areas to the hilly and the other inaccessible areas could not participate in the educational programmes introduced by the British. And, naturally India remained largely illiterate and by the time India achieved independence in 1947, her literacy rate stood at less than 13 per cent[1] among a population of nearly 350 million.[2]

In Independent India since 1947, this disparity in educational opportunities among different groups of people living in different parts of the country has not only increased but also has created major tensions among them. This has now become a serious cause for concern among the elected rulers of the country, whose educational activities are often guided and shaped by their own political ideologies, irrespective of the wishes and the interests of the people under their rules.

Based on varied sources, both primary and secondary, as related to the subject in the different periods of Indian history,[3] the present work not only attempts to meet the deficiencies in the earlier works in Ancient, Medieval and Modern India but also seeks to provide to the reader for the first time a comprehensive and authentic account of the history of education in India from the beginning of the third millennium B.C. to the end of the second millennium A.D.

Notes

1. P.N. Tyagi, *Education for All: A Graphic Presentation*, p. 22.
2. *Ibid.*
3. See bibliography.

Part I

Ancient India, 3000 B.C. – 1192 A.D.

1

Indus Valley Civilisation

In the introductory chapter we have spoken about the highly developed state of civilisation which flourished among the people of the Indus Valley some five thousand years ago from now. Only some seventy years ago we have come to know the existence of this civilisation from the archaeological excavations carried out under John Marshall between 1924 and 1931 at Mohenjo-Daro in the Larkana district, Sind and at Harappa in the Montgomery district, Punjab. This civilisation flourished at the same period which witnessed the growth of ancient civilisations in Egypt, Assyria and Babylonia. However, while we know a great deal about these civilisations from the successful deciphering of the written material on stone or on Papyrus scrolls left in the tombs of their dead, we know very little about the Indus Valley Civilisation, handicapped as we are by our inability till now to decipher the letters engraved on some 2,000 seals discovered at the sites.

An Advanced State of Professional Knowledge

Yet, what little we know of this civilisation on the basis of various finds at the sites of excavations, it is quite impressive and tends to strengthen the belief that this glorious civilisation was created and sustained by a very advanced state of professional knowledge. The people who built up this civilisation knew the art of building towns and cities and enjoyed to a degree, unknown elsewhere in the ancient world, not only the sanitary conveniences but also the luxuries and comforts of a highly developed municipal life. The numerous dwelling houses vary in size from a small house with two rooms to a palatial structure and are made of well burnt and good quality bricks. The big houses have two or more storeys and are furnished with paved floors and courtyards, doors, windows, narrow stairways, wells, drains and bathrooms. The most imposing structure in the city is the Great Bath, 180 feet long and 108 feet wide, consisting of a large open quadrangle in the centre with galleries and rooms on all sides. In the centre of the quadrangle there is a large swimming enclosure. The Great Bath has a flight of steps at either end and is fed by a well situated in one of the adjoining rooms. The water is discharged by a huge drain with a corbelled roof more than six feet in height. One can not but marvel at the engineering skill that went into the making of the Great Bath which has successfully withstood the ravages of five thousand years.

What is more – the people who built up this Great Bath displayed an amazing skill in various facets of life. Mainly an agricultural people, they knew the art of cultivating wheat, barely and palm date and of rearing animals like goats and pigs, fish and birds for domestic consumption. The weavers among them knew how to produce dress out of cotton fabrics and wool; the jeweller, the goldsmith and the ivory-worker produced ornaments worn by both men and women in various shapes and designs out of gold, silver, ivory and copper using both precious and semi-precious stones like jade, crystal, agate, carnelian and *lapis lazuli*. The potters knew how to produce vessels of copper, bronze, silver, porcelain and of earth which were either plain or painted. From the discovery of toy wheeled carts and chairs, we can infer that they were actually in use and the people knew how to make them. The blacksmith knew how to produce weapons of war out of copper and bronze like axes, spears, daggers, maces and slings though certainly not swords, shields and helmets or any other defensive armours which are conspicuous by their absence. The discovery of more than 2,000 small seals, made of terra cotta, depicting animals, both real and mythical, with brief inscriptions, suggests that they were probably used in their trading activities not only with different parts of India but with many countries of Asia which fetched them many of their metals and both precious and semi-precious stones. They are further important in telling us that the people worshipped Siva and Sakti, both in human and symbolic forms as well as stones, trees, notably the pipal, and animals, particularly the bull in the belief that these are abodes of spirits, good or evil and we all know that these are also the elements in our present religion absorbed in Aryan religion since the beginning of the seventh century after the fall of the Guptas.

The Genesis of this Knowledge is yet to be traced

How did the Indus Valley people acquire this highly advanced technical knowledge as indicated by potter's wheel, kiln-burnt bricks, boring of hard substances like carnelian and the casting and alloy of metals as well as the highly advanced aesthetics sense as shown by beautiful designs of ornaments, the superb relief figures on seals and the execution of fine stone statues? Did they acquire this knowledge from outside or develop it from within, through their own families or through some indigenously developed organisations? The Indus Valley Civilisation was contemporary to the two other civilisations developed in the river valleys of the Nile and the Euphrates and there are striking similarities between the Indus Valley Civilisation and the civilisations in Sumer and Mesopotamia proper. The developed city life, use of the potter's well, kiln-burn bricks, and vessels made of copper and bronze, and, above all, the pictorial writings are some of the common and distinctive features of all the three civilisations. Since the Indus Valley Civilisation flourished in the North-West only, the proverbial gateway to the subcontinent for all foreign invaders before the British who came by sea, it can be reasonably surmised that the people who built up this civilisation came from outside, as did the Aryans later. However, the fate of such speculation, despite its being a logical one, depends on the identification of the scripts of the pictorial writings on the seals, which still remains an outstanding puzzle among us.

2

Composition of the Four Vedas and the Birth of the Vedic Schools

The Coming of the Aryans

The Aryan invasion of India was not a single concerted action, but one covering centuries and involving many tribes, perhaps not all of the same race and language. There were frequent internal conflicts among these tribes as well as prolonged struggles with the non-Aryans or the survivors of the Indus Valley Civilisation and kindred peoples of the Punjab and the North-West described as Dasas or Dasyus, a dark-skinned, flat-nosed race who spoke a tongue unintelligible to the Aryans and possessed forts and herds of cattle coveted by the new-comers. In the campaign against the Dasas, the Bharatas among the Aryan tribes were ably supported by their rivals, the Purus, one of whose kings bore the significant name of Trasadasyu or Terror to the Dasyus. The geographical area eventually occupied by the Aryans is clearly indicated by the mention of certain identifiable rivers which implies the possession by them of a considerable portion of the country stretching from eastern Afghanistan to the upper valley of the Ganges. The major part of this area came to be known as Sapta Sindhu – the Land of the Seven Rivers. However, the whole of the extensive tract of land could not have been occupied entirely by Aryan tribes but also by the clans of the Dasas who must have occupied some part of this territory as their supersession and later absorption was a very slow and gradual process.

The Aryan Society

These Dasas or Dasyus were later given a place in the Aryan society. When the Aryans entered India, there was already a class division in their tribal structure as in the use of the terms, Kshatra or the nobility, and the Vis or the ordinary tribesmen. As the Aryans settled among the darker aboriginals, they laid greater stress than before on purity of blood, and class divisions hardened, to exclude those Dasas who had found a place on the fringes of Aryan society, and those Aryans who had intermarried with the Dasas and adopted their ways. While both these groups sank in the social scale, the priests whose sacrificial lore was becoming more and more complicated and who therefore required greater skill and training, were arrogating higher privileges to themselves. By the end of the Rig Vedic period the Aryan society was divided into four great classes, and this fourfold division was given religious sanction in the Hymn of the Primeval Man where the four classes are said to have emanated from the dismembered primeval man, who was sacrificed by the gods at the beginning of the world – the Brahmana grew out of his mouth, the warrior or the Kshatriya out of his arms, the Vaishya out of his thighs and the Shudra was born out of his feet.

The Composition of the Rig Veda

As said above, the Brahmanas or the priests were the most powerful groups in the society. They were the possessors of 'Brahman', a supernatural electrical power, which they had derived from their composition and uttering of Mantras or hymns addressed to gods and sung at the sacrifices performed by tribal chiefs or kings to ensure the prosperity and success of their tribes in peace and war. The Brahmanas belong to the tribes, chief of which was that of the Bharatas, who had settled mainly in East Punjab and in the region between the Sutlej and the Yamuna which later became known as Brahmavarta. The hymns composed by their priests in their new home were carefully handed down by word of mouth, and early in the first millennium B.C. were collected and arranged. They were still not committed to writing, but by now they were looked upon as so sacred that even minor alterations in their text were not permitted, and the priestly schools which preserved them devised the most remarkable and effective system of checks and counterchecks to ensure their purity. Even when the art of writing was widely known in India the hymns were rarely written but, thanks to the brilliant feats of memory of many generations of Brahmanas, and the extreme sanctity which the hymns were thought to possess, they have survived to the present day in a form which, from internal evidence, appears not to have been seriously tampered with for nearly three thousand years. This great collection of hymns is the Rig Veda, the most sacred of our numerous sacred scriptures.

The Contents of the Rig Veda

The Rig Veda is divided into ten Mandalas or Sections. Six Mandalas from II to VII are attributed to the six Rishis or Seers and form their family books and serve as the nucleus of the whole Rig Veda. These six Rishis are: Gritsamada, Visvamitra, Vamadeva, Atri, Bharadvaja and Vasishtha. Mandalas I, VIII and X are later, especially parts of X while IX Mandala was compiled by extracting the hymns to the god Soma from the other parts of the Rig Veda. In this way the whole compilation came to include 1,028 hymns and 10,580 verses in 70,000 lines (including 5,000 which are merely repetitive) of 153,826 words. The European scholars who have worked on the Rig Veda are all agreed that Rig Veda as we know today has been long in the making. Macdonell points out: "Some hundreds of years must have been needed for all the hymns found in the Rig Veda to come into being". This has been strongly endorsed by Winternitz: "Centuries must have elapsed between the composition of earliest hymns and the Samhita of the Rig Veda". The agreed dates for the composition of the Rig Veda have been fixed at between 1,500 and 1,000 B.C.

The Genesis of the Vedic Schools

The hymns in the Rig Veda present the worship of 33 gods divided into three groups of 11 each and assigned to the three planes of the universe – Dyuloka or the celestial, Antariksha or the intermediate and Bhurloka or the terrestrial. These hymns are the outcome of the pursuit of the highest truth and of its direct realisation by the seeker through ascetic austerities and concentrated contemplation and meditation called Tapas, which marks out or makes a Rishi or a Seer. Rita and Satya, truth of thought and speech, are regarded as the fruit of Tapas and the whole creation is conceived as the result of the Tapas of Brahma. When highest knowledge was thus built up by these Rishis and revealed and stored up in the hymns often after discussion at the assemblies held on some sacrificial occasions, there were necessarily evolved the methods by which such knowledge could be acquired, conserved and transmitted to the posterity. Thus, every Rishi was a teacher who would start by imparting to his son the texts of the knowledge he had personally acquired and such texts would be special property of his family. Each such family of Rishis was thus functioning like a Charana or Vedic School admitting pupils for instruction in the literature, texts or hymns in its possession. The number of such Charanas or Vedic Schools increased proportionately to the number of Rishis composing new hymns as well as to the number of successful students who on their return home after completion of studies set up their own Vedic schools in their residences or areas.

The Coming of the Three More Vedas

The hymns of the Rig Veda were thus the first course of study for students admitted to the Vedic schools. In the succeeding three centuries, the Rig Vedic religion showed considerable developments of ceremonial and priesthood out of their beginnings in the Rig Veda. These developments centred on the fixed order of sacrifices. However, the order of the hymns in the Rig Veda had nothing to do with the order of the sacrifices while it included many hymns which had no use for any sacrifices. The need was felt for the composition of new hymns which could be exclusively used for purposes of ritual application and in course of time, say by 600 B.C., three more Vedas, Sama, Yajur and Atharva, came to be compiled.

How ritualistic the religion of the Aryans had become since the days of the Rig Veda could be seen in an increase in the number of personnel of priesthood participating in sacrifices. The Rig Veda mentions only 8 priests including Hotri, Udgatri, Adhvaryu and Brahman, each with an assistant, besides the institutor of the sacrifice. Now the number of assistants under each of the four categories of priesthood had increased from one to three so that the priesthood had a personnel of sixteen members to participate in sacrifices. The Hotri priests specialised in the recitation of hymns; the Udgatri priests specialised in the chanting of hymns, which required a special training, the Adhvaryu priests specialised in the actual performance of sacrifice involving a number of operations and material details and the Brahmana priests had to acquire such a proficiency and knowledge in the whole matter that they could detect and correct errors in the performance of the different parts and operations of sacrifice and pass judgements on all doubtful points and disputes, thereby laying the beginnings of the systems of Nyaya and Mimamsa.

The Sama Veda

The Sama Veda is the compilation of all the hymns recited on the occasion of the Soma Yajna. While the Udgatri priests have contributed 78, out of 1,549 verses, the bulk of the verses have been taken out of the VIII and IX Mandalas of the Rig Veda. These verses have been classified into two parts the Archika of 585 single stanzas or riks and the Uttararchika comprising of 400 chants, mostly of three stanzas each. The text of the Sama Veda is tailored to the learning of melodies. The student who wanted to be trained as an Udgatri priest had first to learn the melodies with the aid of the Archika where he is given only the text of the first stanza of each song as an aid to the recollection of the tune. While a stanza can be sung to various melodies and one melody can be applied to different stanzas, certain stanzas are marked out and fixed as the texts or Yonis for certain melodies. The Uttararchika gives the stanzas, out of which are formed the Stotras to be sung at the sacrifices, to the tunes which the Archika teaches. While Sama Veda can give only the texts as they are spoken, their melodies are taught by oral and instrumental rendering. Music is known to the Rig Veda as also the instruments producing music by means of percussion, wind, and string such as drum, lute, and lyre or harp with its seven notes recognised and distinguished, together with the flute of reed called Nadi.

The Yajur Veda

The Yajur Veda is the prayer-book of the Adhvaryu priest just as the Sama Veda is the song book of the Udgatri. Prayers were accompanied by sacrificial acts about which differences of opinion were more likely to arise leading to the formation of numerous schools, the number of which was 101 in the time of Patanjali (C. 200 B.C.) as stated in his Introduction to his Mahabhashya. The Yajur Veda consists of two divisions the Black or Krishna and the White or Shukla. The White Yajur Veda contains only the Mantras or hymns, the prayers and sacrificial formulae which – the priest has to utter, while the Black Yajur Veda contains the Mantras in verse and also a portion in prose, presenting the sacrificial rites that go with the Mantras along with discussions thereon, anticipating the later Brahmana literature. The Yajur Veda has thus made a material contribution to the creation of a prose literature which later culminated in the literary masterpieces of Upanishads. The Yajur Veda fixes the religious life of the Aryans in the course of ceremonies it prescribes. It prescribes various sacrifices such as those for the new and full moon, the fathers or Pinda-pitri-yajna, fire or Agnihotra to be performed both morning and evening, seasons or Chaturmasyas to be performed every four months, Rajasuya for kings only, Asvamedha for a king of kings and Agnichayana or building the fire-altar lasting an year and possessing a mystical significance.

The Atharva Veda

While the Sama Veda and Yajur Veda came into existence to meet the highly complex religious requirements on sacrifices, the Atharva Veda to meet largely the daily needs of the Aryans including kings and chieftains. It is also more original than the Sama and the Yajur Vedas in the sense that the majority of its mantras or hymns have not been adapted from the Rig Veda. Only 1,200 stanzas out of 6,000 have been derived largely from I, VIII and X Mandalas of the Rig Veda. The Atharva Veda consists 731 Mantras divided into twenty books. A large part of the Atharva Veda refers to appropriate herbs as remedies against diseases like fever, leprosy, jaundice, dropsy, scrofula, cough, opthalmia, baldness, impotence, and surgical ailments like fractures and wounds, bite of snakes and other injurious insects, and against poison in general, mania, and other complaints. The Atharva Veda is the earliest work on medical science in the country. Its ninth book anticipates astronomy by its mention of the lunar mansions. It also deals with domestic rites at birth, marriage and death, thereby anticipating the later Griha Sutras. Along with spells for warding off evil, it also contains spells for securing good, such as harmony in family and village life, reconciliation of enemies, long life, health, prosperity, safety on journeys and luck in gambling. Finally, there are also hymns in the Atharva Veda which give us an insight into the economic, political and philosophical life of the contemporary Aryan society. To put in a nutshell, the Artharva Veda is mainly a collection of songs, spells and incantations for the healing of disease, restoration of harmony and the exorcism of evil spirits.

The Vedas as the Courses of Studies

The subject of learning in the Vedic Schools by 600 B.C. was thus the hymns of the four Vedas. The Vedas were composed orally and taught orally by recitation involving correct pronunciation of Chhandas or metres made of Padas or divisions and which in turn were made of Aksharas or words. A spiritual benefit flows from the observance of the strict order of word of the hymns recited and unless this is done, its meanings could not be comprehended by the reciter. The Rig Veda holds those to ridicule whose knowledge is confined only to repetition of its words without an insight into their meaning by constant and concentrated contemplation: "He who does not realise the ultimate Truth behind the Rik and Akhara (word and letter) in which rest all gods – what will he do by merely reciting and repeating the Riks?" Thus the Rig Veda attaches great value and potency to the very sounds of the letters and syllables of the hymns uttered and describes learning without understanding as cramming or "like dry wood on ashes, which can never blaze".

The Vedangas

It is the lips of the teacher who are uttering the hymns – in other words the Guru is giving the Veda to his pupil by uttering it. This is Siksha which is from the root Siksh, to give. Secondly the hymns are to be uttered correctly bringing out their meaning clearly. The first comes Chhanda while giving Veda to a pupil by his Guru and then Vyakarana or grammar and Nirukta or etymology to convey its meaning correctly. And all these subjects, Siksha, Vyakarana and Nirukta had to be studied as aids to the comprehension of the meaning of the Vedic text upon which so much stress was laid. A mere crammer of Vedic texts was compared to an ass carrying a load of sandal wood without sensing its sweet and fragrant smell but only feeling its weight.

Again, the hymns correctly learnt are to be uttered by the Adhvaryu priests who are fully in the actual performance of the sacrifices. The operational aspect of the sacrifices means measuring the ground, building the altar and platform and ascertaining proper seasons and moments for them. It is also necessary to cultivate a knowledge of the parts of the bodily frame of the animals to be immolated at sacrifices. The Adharyu priests had to learn Kalpa and Jyotisha in discharging their responsibilities imposed on them by the Yajur Veda. As far as Jyotisha is concerned, it finds expression in the recognition of an immutable cosmic order or laws of nature as Dhata, Satya and Dharma. While Dhata refers to accomplished fact like the tree growing from a seed, the sun rising in the east, Agni consuming objects thrown to it, Satya refers to the law by which a tree grows out of a seed, the sun rises in the east and Agni gives heat, Dharma is that which holds in the midst of change.

These subsidiary studies or auxiliary sciences Siksha, Kalpa, Vyakarana, Nirukta, Chhanda and Jyotisha – were developed in the Vedic Schools as aids to the study of the Vedas and are known as Vedangas or the limbs of the Vedas. In course of time, say, by the time of the Sutra Age (C. 400-200 B.C.), we shall see that they have given birth to a number of independent and allied sciences like Philosophy and Yoga, Grammar and Philology, Anatomy and Physiology, Arithmetic, Algebra and Geometry, Astrology and Astronomy, Music and Songs while still serving the ends of Aryan religion.

In the next few centuries since 1000 B.C., the four Vedas and the six Vedangas were offered as courses in Vedic schools, where students after having gone through an Upanayana or initiation ceremony at the age of 12 were admitted after an enquiry into their Vamsha or family of birth, individual merits and capability to serve their teachers called Gurus, Acharyas or Preceptors. As a matter of fact, teachers at the Vedic schools were forbidden to admit such persons as students who were jealous, wanting in simplicity and straightforwardness and devoid of any self-control. The students after admission through the Upanayana ceremony were known as Dvija or twice-born; at the second birth they had as parents their teachers who pierce their ears with needles of truth and knowledge without causing them any physical pain or injury.

The Vedas as Sruti

The Vedas were always described as Sruti which should appeal to the ear and not to the eye. And the texts of the Vedas were imparted to the learners by recitation. Everyday the students started recitation of the Vedic texts before the birds started chirping, announcing the break of the day. The air in and around the Vedic schools resounded with the recitation of the hymns and it was the sight of such a familiar phenomenon that inspired the composition of a hymn in the Rig Veda which compared the monotonous recitation at a Vedic school to the croaking of frogs exhilarated by the advent of rains after summer.

The Brahmacharis and the Brahmacharya

And how did the students spend 12 years of their lives at such Vedic schools? They spent these 12 years in studying Vedas, leading self-controlled lives and serving their Gurus in lieu for free board and lodging. They were known as Vratacharis or Brahmacharis and the period of their studentship at such schools was known as Brahmacharya. In a long hymn, the Atharva Veda, the last of the four Vedas, gives us an insight into the rigorous discipline that was Brahmacharya.

A Brahmachari had to undergo a two-fold course of discipline, physical and spiritual. The physical discipline comprised of wearing the Kusha girdle and deer skin, letting his hairs grow, collecting firewood and tending the household fire and begging alms. The spiritual discipline included offering fuel to Agni and worshipping him twice daily, controlling senses, practising austerities, living a dedicated life and satisfying the teacher who was variously extolled as Yama, Varuna, sun and moon as the givers of light and happiness, by gifts acceptable to him. While undergoing through his rigorous course of discipline, the Brahmachari would pray for his success in his study of the Vedas without any interruptions[1] as well as for his faith, insight, progeny, wealth, longevity and immortality.

The system of Brahmacharya also covered the women who were admitted to the Vedic schools after the performance of the Upanayana ceremony. They were given prescribed courses of study in the Vedas to enable them to assist their husbands in the sacrificial offerings. The ambition of a father was often to see his daughter grow into a Vidushi or a learned woman and get a comparably suitable husband in Manishi or a learned man. The Age of the four Vedas produced many women sages called Rishikas and Brahmavadinis like Romasa, Lopamudra, Apala, Kadru, Visvavara, Ghosa, Juhu, Jarita, Urvasi, Yami, Indrani, Savitri, Devajani, Nodha and Gaupayana.

Thus, Brahmacharya at the Vedic schools was characterised by Srama or self-restraint, Tapas or penance and Diksha or consecration. It was the outcome of a discipline and detachment that have created and sustained the universe. The Supreme Being was a prime Brahmachari and all creations, great or small, are outcome of his Brahmacharya and Tapas: "Through these, a king protects his kingdom. Through these, Gods have conquered death... All creatures which have sprung from Prajapati (Brahma) have breath separately in themselves; all of these are preserved by Supreme knowledge (Brahma) which, is produced in the Brahmachari". For those students who wanted to enter family life, the period of Brahmacharya formally came to an end with the completion of their courses at the

Vedic schools. But for those who wanted to pursue knowledge like a sinking star beyond the utmost bound of human thought, Brahmacharya continued as before.

Were the Vedic Schools Open to the Non-priestly Classes?

We have seen that the courses offered at the Vedic schools were the hymns of the four Vedas. These hymns were composed by the priestly class. They were uttered by the priestly class at the sacrifices. The priestly class possessed a mystical power, Brahman, by composing and uttering these hymns. The Vedic schools therefore were there to crystallise their domination over the Aryan society. The priestly class would therefore, naturally like to restrict the study of the Vedas to their own class, their own progeny, their own sons and daughters. In the light of this it will be relevant to ask the question: Were Vedic schools open to the other classes, Kshatriyas, Vaishyas and Shudras, of the Aryan society?

We have already seen that the division of the Aryan society into four classes had got religious sanction in the Hymn of the Primeval Man – the Brahmanas were his mouth, Kshatriyas arms, Vaishyas thighs and Shudras feet. We also learn from a study of the Rig Veda that there was hardly any taboo on intermarriage, change of occupation or commensality. While we have instances of marriages of Brahmanas with Rajanya women, and of the union of Arya with Shudra, and of families who were not wedded to a particular profession, we have no evidences to suggest that there was a ban on the taking of food cooked by the Shudras and that impurity was communicated by the touch or contact of the inferior castes. On the other hand, we have evidences to show that Rishis or seers in the days of the Rig Veda were not exclusively monopolised by the priestly class or Brahmanas. The Rig Veda, besides including Visvamitra, a Kshatriya under the Mandalas II to VII, as one of the six Rishis, preserves the names of several Rishis like Ambarisha, Trasadasyu, Tryaruna, Asvamedha, Prurmilha, Ajamiiha, Sindhudvipa, Sindhukshit, Sudas, Mandhata, Sibi, as well as Pratardana of Kashi who were originally kings or Kshatriyas. They had become Rishis or seers by acquiring supreme knowledge, Brahman, through Tapas or Yoga or meditation. The Rig Veda also tells us of five peoples who offered sacrifice to Agni and these 'five peoples', according to Yaska's Nirukta included the four castes and the Nishadas or non-Aryan and depressed classes who remained at that particular period of time outside the pale of the Aryan society as Dasas or Dasyus. As a matter of fact, the Yajur Veda enjoins the imparting of Vedic knowledge to all classes, Brahmanas and Rajanyas, Shudras, Anaryas and Charanas or Vaishyas not to speak of women. In the same catholic spirit the Vajasaneyi Samhita or the Atharva Veda states that "all classes have an equal right to study the Veda".

We can therefore assert that the Kshatriyas, Vaishyas and the Shudras had access to the study of the Vedas in the Vedic Schools. Unlike the Brahmans who mastered the four Vedas, they were possibly instructed in the same way as the women were, to participate in the religious life of the Aryans. They all had to perform the Upanayana ceremony while entering the Vedic schools and had to observe Brahmacharya as long as they stayed there studying the Vedas. The Kshatriyas further learnt the art of warfare and adminis- tration, the Vaishyas trade and commerce and the Shudras agriculture and animal husbandry. And perhaps it was the priestly class or the Brahmanas alone who stayed at the Vedic schools till they obtained complete mastery of the four Vedas. They learnt not only the hymns of the Rig Veda, the ritualistic details of sacrifices of the Sama Veda and Yajur Veda as well as the hymns of the Atharva Veda throwing light on diseases and their cures, domestic rites at birth, marriage and death as well as spells for warding off evils and for securing good to the Aryan society.

A Recapitulation

Thus, in the Age of the four Vedas, the education system comprised of small domestic schools each of which was run by a teacher who admitted to his instructions, pupils who had to live with him for a considerable period of time under prescribed disciplines or vows as Vratachris or Brahmacharis. In the primary stage, the school would be marked by noisy recitation and repetition of Vedic texts by pupils lustily croaking like frogs at the advent of rains after summer. In the second stage, the collective work of the pupils ceased and their individual work commenced. Each had to achieve for himself by his individual effort, by his own Tapas or Yoga, the truth of the texts taught to him by recitation. It was at this stage that differences in mental aptitudes soon manifested themselves, like tanks or ponds of varying depth, among the sakhas or class-mates and the more unfit among them were weeded out, sent back to the plough or the loom or the family professions as they were not meant for higher learning and spiritual life. However, many among the students of higher learning had an unlimited thirst for knowledge. They would roam about the country in search of Guru for further learning after completing their studies at the Vedic schools, engaged themselves in debates and discussions in assemblies or Parishads held on some sacrificial occasions and win approval for their contributions to the advancement of knowledge, thereby acquiring the right to set up their own Vedic schools. Thus, in the Age of the four Vedas, knowledge is created, preserved and transmitted to the posterity by Rishis, sages or seers who mostly belonged to the priestly class among the Aryans and known as Brahmanas, possessors of 'Brahman' or supreme knowledge of the Brahma or the universe through Tapas or Yoga or meditation.

Note

1. Under the shade of trees, within sight of green barley and hearing of cattle, Vedic study was forbidden. Holidays, as observed in the Vedic schools, were those on the occasions of cloudy or windy weather.

3

Change and Reaction within the Vedic Schools: Composition of the Brahmanas, Aranyakas and the Upanishads

Changes in Education in the Wake of the Changes in the Life of the Aryans

In the next two centuries since the composition of the last of the four Vedas, the Atharva Veda, the structure of the system of education as thrown up by the Rig Veda continued. There were however substantial changes, additions and alterations, which came to be introduced in it in response to the changes in the life of the Aryans at all levels.

We have seen that the Aryans had spread over the whole country from the Kabul to the upper Ganges, built up small hereditary kingdoms which were surrounded by the non-Aryans. There were internecine strifes among some of the Aryan tribes. The most powerful among them absorbed the weaker ones and guided by the priests to cause Agni, the fire god, to taste new lands through sacrifices, went on an adventurous career towards the East, down the river Ganges and the river Yamuna as well as towards the South beyond the Vindhyan forest and established powerful kingdoms, in the Deccan to the North of the Godavari. Thus, from dhruvamadhyama – dis or firm middle – country stretching from the Sarasvati to the Gangetic Doab which was occupied by the Kurus who succeeded the Bharatas and the Purus, the Panchalas and some adjoining tribes, the Aryan influence spread to the outer provinces, to the land of the Koshalas and the Kashi drained by the Sarayu and the Varanavati, and to the valley of the Wardha occupied by the Vidarbhas. Beyond them lived the tribes of mixed origin like the Angas of East Bihar and the Magadhas of South Bihar, as well as Dasyus or aboriginal folk like the Pundras of North Bengal, the Pulindas and Savaras of the Vindhyan forest, and the Andhras in the valley of the Godavari.

As the Aryans settled down in the conquered territories, they adapted their culture to the changed geographical conditions. They organised themselves into little kingdoms with permanent capitals and invented a rudimentary administrative machinery to rule them and in the process the power of their tribal organisations gave way to the rising autocracy of the kings limited only by the power of the priests, the weight of tradition and the force of public opinion. The popular assemblies, Sabha and Samiti, were replaced by the relatives, courtiers, and palace officials of the king, collectively known as Ratnins or jewel-bearers. The latter were considered so important that special sacrifices were performed at the king's Rajasuya or royal consecration to ensure their loyalty to him. After Rajasuya the king could perform Vajapeya or drink of strength to revitalise an aging health and Asvamedha to raise his status from a mere Raja to that of a Samrat or emperor, receiving allegiance of all kings subordinate to him.

This transformation took a couple of centuries since the Atharva Veda to materialise and the Aryans had by now nearly all the ingredients of an Ancient civilisation. They cultivated a large range of crops, including rice, and they understood something of irrigation and manuring. Where the Rig Veda speaks only of gold and copper or bronze, there is now reference to tin, lead, silver and also iron. In place of the few occupation in the Rig Veda, specialised trades and crafts including jewellers, goldsmiths, metalworkers, basket makers, rope makers, weavers, dyers, carpenters and potters had appeared. They had a variety of domestic servants and a host of professional entertainers like acrobats, fortune-tellers, flute players and dancers which the Atharva Veda describes as Deva-Jana-Vidya. However, class distinctions were becoming rigid and change of caste was becoming difficult, if not impossible. The higher classes were still free to intermarry with the lower orders, though marriages with Shudras were not much approved. The ranks of Shudras were constantly swelled by the admission of new aboriginal tribes into the Aryan society. The Shudras were not infrequently grouped with the

Vaishyas, and the two together were set against the priests and the Kshatriyas who enjoyed privileges which were denied to the former. It was at this period that the seeds of untouchability began to be sown when the touch of a carpenter, usually a Shudra, is said to impart ceremonial impurity and the Shudras in general were not allowed to touch the milk needed for oblations to the Agni or fire god. The power and prestige of the Brahmanas who claimed themselves to be gods on earth and the protectors of the realm had increased immensely. They had developed a unique system of memory-training for transmission of the Vedic texts to a chosen few and they possibly zealously guarded their unique privilege and so frowned upon writing which was certainly known in some rudimentary form or other in the Age of the Buddha.

The Genesis of the Brahmanas, Aranyakas and the Upanishads

The spirit of the age is reflected in the output of further religious literature of the Aryans: the Brahmanas, Aranyakas and the Upanishads. We have already seen in the preceding chapter that the two Vedas, Sama and Yajur, are concerned with the practical aspect of religion as exemplified in the external worship of individual deities by means of Yajnas or sacrifices led by a priesthood consisting of sixteen members under the supervision of Hotri, Udgatri, Adhvaryu and Brahmana priests though it was the last group of priests, the Brahmanas, who supervised all aspects of sacrifices, and gave judgement in doubtful points. With the changed circumstance in the life of the Aryans, religion now began to concentrate more and more on Yajnas or sacrificial ceremonies, the details of which were more and more elaborated and called for suitable texts by which they could be regulated, fixed and conserved. A new type of religious literature, came into existence to meet the demands of the Brahmanas in Yajnas or sacrificial ceremonies where ritualism runs riot.

Thus, the Brahmanas are works that deal with the worship of the Brahma, that is, devotion and prayer. They are text books for rituals or treatises on the science of sacrifice and are composed in prose to explain the relations between the Vedic texts and their corresponding ceremonials as well as their symbolic meaning with reference to each other. An Aranyaka or forest portion is annexed to each of these Brahmanas for study in the sylvan solitude of the forests by those sages who had become its denizens and were not required to perform sacrifices. It is also possible that Aranyaka portion was added to the

Brahmanas to cover the Vratyas, who though Aryans, did not observe the sacrificial religion and led a nomadic life. The Brahmanas group themselves around the three Vedas which thus determine their subject matter. Thus, while the Brahmanas of the Rig Veda are concerned with the task of collecting hymns suited to a particular occasion as its Shastra or canon by the Hotri priests, the Brahmanas of the Sama and Yajur Vedas occupy themselves with the duties of the Udgatri and Adhvaryu priests.

The Upanishads as a Reaction to the Brahmanas

Thus, an age of creation is now succeeded by an age of conservatism and orthodoxy. Poets and Rishis or seers of the Rig Veda are now replaced by priests and theologians. Soon a reaction against the Brahmanas began from within the priestly class as the latter only knew the art of oral composition, and this expressed itself in the birth of the Upanishads which revived the atmosphere of abstraction and pure thought of the days of the Rig Veda.

The term Upanishad literally means 'a session' sitting at the feet of a teacher who imparts secret or esoteric doctrines in discourses to select band of pupils towards the end of their studentship or towards the end of the study of the Vedas. In the beginning the priestly class shunned the Upanishads because of their opposition to the sacrificial cult but later accommodated them as an end part of the study of the Vedas. The Upanishads thus came to be known as the Vedanta or the end of the Vedas.

There are said to be 108 Upanishads. The earlier Upanishads, like the Brihadaranayaka and Chandogya are in prose and consist of a series of short expositions of some aspect of the new doctrines, often in the form of questions and answers. The later Upanishads, like the Katha and the Svetasvatara are in verse and their contents are more closely integrated. In the Upanishads, one entity, often called Brahman, the term used in the Rig Veda to mean the magical power of the sacred word of hymns, fills all space and time. It is Brahman that pervades the ground beyond and below all forms and phenomena and from it the whole universe, including the gods themselves, has emerged. The knowledge that the Upanishads impart lies not in the mere recognition of the existence of Brahman, but in continual consciousness for it. For Brahman resides in the human soul – indeed Brahman is the human soul, is Atman, the Self. When a man or woman realises this fact fully, he or she is wholly freed from transmigration. The soul of the person becomes one with Brahman, and the person transcends joy and sorrow, life and death.

The sages of the Upanishads used imagery of every possible kind to express the idea of Brahman. Sometimes, Brahman is described as tiny manikin in the heart or the breath or the mysterious fluid which flows in the veins but often is thought of as quite incorporeal and immeasurable as in the Chandogya Upanishad where the father of Svetaketu the sage Uddalaka Aruni thus taught his son:

" 'Fetch me a fruit of the banyan tree.'
'Here is one, Sir.'
'Break it.'
'I have broken it, Sir.'
'What do you see?'
'Very tiny seeds, Sir.'
'Break one.'
'I have broken it, Sir.'
'Now what do you see?'
'Nothing, Sir.'

'My son, the father said, 'what you do not perceive is the essence, and in that essence the mighty banyan tree exists. Believe me, my son, in that essence is the Self of all that is. That is the Truth, that is the Self, and you are that Self. And you are that Self, Svetaketu".

As a matter of fact, the identity of the souls of the individual and the universe is reiterated throughout the Upanishadic literature with varying emphasis, and interpretations on the nature of the identity and the character of the universal soul.

Education as Revealed in the Upanishads

Let us now have a look at the system of education. As in the age of the four Vedas, students were admitted to the Vedic schools after performance of the Upanayana ceremony at the age of 12 and spent as many years at the residences of their teachers as Brahmacharis. The students started the study of the Vedas, which involved a knowledge of the pronunciation of its texts with all that it implied, a knowledge of phonology, metrics, elementary grammar and etymology. Simultaneously they served their teacher by begging alms for him, collecting fuel from the forest for the sacrificial fires and looking after the cattle grazing on the pasture.

The external duties in the form of services to the teacher were meant to instil in the student those mental and moral attributes which would help him to receive the highest knowledge, the knowledge of the Brahman, the special subject matter of the Upanishads. The Upanishads require that before the knowledge of the Brahman was taught to the Brahmacharin, the Brahmacharin should show that he was calm and composed, self-restrained and self-denying, patient and collected and could fulfil the vow of the head which indicated either the rite of carrying fire on the head or as Deussen suggests in his *Philosophy of the Upanishads*, that of shaving the head bare.

Teachers

What kind of teachers could instil in the mind of his students the qualities as were required of them to achieve the knowledge of the Brahman? A teacher was to possess the highest moral and spiritual qualifications and to be well versed in the sacred lore and dwelling in the Brahman or the Brahmanishtha. He was to illuminate the inner beings of his pupils with his own spiritual enlightenment – otherwise it would be like the blind leading the blind. A teacher should teach his pupils the truth exactly as he knew it and it was the natural desire of every teacher that the truth he had discovered should live after him in his pupils through a succession of teachers, Guru Paramparya, and thereby would contribute to the continuity of knowledge. As a matter of fact, every teacher was anxious to assure the continuity of his school of thoughts and ideas through his pupils. If a teacher found that he was not quite fit to teach any of his students on a particular subject, he considered it to be his duty and responsibility to send him to a fitter teacher. Similarly, if a teacher found that the student was not fit to acquire the knowledge he came for, he could withhold his instructions on it to him. He was also free to learn a secret subject and reveal his knowledge only to special persons capable of receiving it.

Normally and usually as in the days of the four Vedas, the teachers were all Brahmanas and came from the priestly class. Among the hosts of such Brahmana teachers, the more important names were: Asvala or Auddalaki, Gargi Vachknavi, Gotama, Rahugana, Kamalayana, Krishna Devakiputra, Maitreyi, Narada, Raikva, Satyakama, Javala, Saunaka, Sukesi, Bharadvaja, and Yajnavalkya. Aurneya Svetaketu's father, Uddalaka Aruni and grandfather, Aruna Aupavesi Gautama were a family of reknowned teachers of the time. Patanchala Kapya was another famed teacher who hailed from the

South, across the Vindhyas. However, as in the days of the four
Vedas, the attainment of divine knowledge or the knowledge of the
Brahma could elevate the status of a Kashtriya, usually a king, to that
of a Brahmana teacher and we have examples of learned kings who
had acquired supreme knowledge or knowledge of the universe who
acted as teachers even to Brahmana students. We know the case of five
learned Brahmanas who came to the Kshatriya king Asvapati Kaikeya
"with fuel in their hands" and became his pupils. Similarly the
Kshatriya kings – Janaka of Videha, Ajatasatru of Kashi, Pravahana
Jaivali of Panchalas – were regarded as Brahmanas as possessors of
supreme knowledge and acquired the right to provide instructions to
deserving students in the religious texts.

However, these Kshatriya kings acted as Brahmana teachers on a
few special occasions when they were approached by really learned
students for supreme knowledge. Otherwise the Vedic schools were
manned by teachers from the priestly class. And, what were the
subjects taught by them to their students? There were a variety of
courses offered by the Vedic schools to meet the demands of the time.
Besides the four Vedas and the six Vedangas and the Brahmanas such
courses now included Naya and Mimamsa, Ithihasa-Purana, Gatha,
Rasi, Daiva, Nidhi, Kayana and a whole range of Vidyas including
Kshatravidya, Nakshatravidya, Bhutavidya, Sarpavidya, Devavidya,
Brahmavidya and Deva-jana-vidya, many of which could be traced to
the Atharva Veda, the last of the four Vedas. The Deva-jana-vidya or
the arts affected by the lesser gods such as the making of the perfumes,
dancing, singing, playing on musical instruments and other fine arts
was highly popular as it met the needs of a contemporary Aryan
civilisation.

Students

And who benefited most from a study of these courses offered by the
Vedic schools? Certainly the Brahmanas who belonged to the priestly
class of the Aryans. They not only studied and mastered all the
religious scriptures till date but also the various 'vidyas' known to the
contemporary Aryan mind. Narada, a Brahmana, listed the subjects
as studied by him which included all the courses offered by the Vedic
schools. They were "the Rig Veda, Yajur Veda, Sama Veda, the
Atharva Veda as fourth, the epic and mythological poems as fifth
Veda,[1] grammar, necrology, arithmetic, divination, chronology,
dialectics, politics, theology, the doctrine of payer, necromancy, the

art of war, astronomy, snake charming and the fine arts". And one can logically assert that all Brahmana students studied the subjects listed by Narada. The Brahmanas represented the intellectual and spiritual interests of the community and they were required not merely to practice their own culture but also to give others the advantages of their skills either as teachers or as sacrificial priests or as Purohitas guiding the kings in administering their kingdoms. Admittedly the close connection between the Brahmanas and the kings rested chiefly on the support provided by the former in the performance of the three special sacrifices, Rajasuya, Vajapeya and Asvamedha where the latter had to take an active part with the officiating priests in the uttering of various Mantras or hymns.

This might have led the kings to study the Vedas and there are also few isolated and selected kings who mastered the Vedas and subsequent religious scriptures and discharged some priestly functions in those days when functions did not determine professions but the average Kshatriya kings were normally and principally concerned with those subjects of study like Kshatravidya or the science of the ruling class which included a study of polity and administration, Ekayana or Nitisastram and Dhanurvidya or the use of bow and arrow which would later help them in their professions. However, not all Kshatriyas were kings who had kingdoms or territories to govern or members of the royal families and one wonders whether the Vedic schools were open to them.

Agriculture and animal husbandry, spinning and weaving (which were of ten described in the religious scriptures as 'the plough and the loom') which were not taught in the Vedic Schools were the whole time occupations of the people belonging to the Vaishya and the Shudra classes. The goad of the plougher was the mark of a Vaishya in life and death and probably the trade of the country was in his hands as the vanij or vanijya was known to the age and his chief ambition in life was to become a Gramani or a village headman which he regarded as the summit of his prosperity. Thus a Vaishya's position was little better than a Shudra whose touch was regarded as impure. However both could be 'oppressed at will' by the two higher classes, the Brahmanas and the Kshatriyas and the Vaishyas and Shudras were often required to take part in wars under the Kshatriya kings. Unlike the Brahmanas and the Kshatriyas, the religious literature of the age did not throw any light at all on the intellectual attainment of these two classes. They had now, unlike the age of the four Vedas, no or

little access to the religious scripture of the time though most of them
were given opportunities to learn Deva-jana-vidya which included
some of the contemporary arts and crafts like dancing, singing,
playing on musical instruments, perfumery, dyeing and the like.

Here again, the teachers were the Brahamanas. In the
Chandogya Upanishad, Narad describes himself as a teacher or master
of some of these subjects. This has been confirmed by the Satapatha
Upanishad which describes the Brahmana as the teacher of similar
subjects to pupils who included usurers,[2] snake-charmers,
bird-catchers[3] and men unlearned in the scriptures, which definitely
means the Vaishyas and the Shudras as these classes did hardly have
any access to the study of the Vedas.

Vedic Schools unable to teach Brahman

We have been till now discussing the accessibility of the courses
offered at the Vedic schools to the different classes of the Aryan
society. In the words of the Upanishads such courses are Apara Vidya
as they could not throw any light on the Brahman or the knowledge
of the Supreme Being. As the Katha Upanishad forcefully points but
"Not by the Veda is the Atman attained, nor by intellect, nor by
much knowledge of books". The Vedic schools could not teach Para
Vidya or the knowledge of the Brahman, known as Vedanta, which
was the final and highest stage of the Vedic wisdom. However, the
Brahmacharya or studentship at the Vedic schools was preparatory to
the realisation of the knowledge of Brahman. With the passing of the
Aranyakas in the Upanishads the conception of the scope of
Brahmacharya is widened to include not merely the student period
but the entire course of life regulated by the disciplines of its four
successive Asramas or stages as the way that leads to the Brahman.
The students as Brahmacharis passed the first stage at the Vedic
schools. The second stage as Grihasthas or householders began when
they entered family life. The third stage of Vanaprastha started when
in well advanced middle age they left their homes for the forest to
become hermits and in the final stage as Sannyasins they became
homeless wanderers with all earthly ties broken. In this context the
address of the teacher at the Vedic school to his student who was
about to leave it after completion of his study is highly relevant. First,
the teacher enjoined upon the student fatherhood as a compulsory
religious duty to continue his race. Second, he asked him to continue
the study and teaching of the Veda so that the continuity of the
culture could be maintained by transmitting learning from age to age.

Third, he asked him to honour and respect his parents, teachers, guests and superiors as gods and to perform sacrifices and, in all doubtful cases to accept the judgement of approved authorities. Finally, he also asked his student to look after his health and worldly possessions.

In the light of his teacher's advice, the student who returned home and entered family life could still achieve Brahmavarchasa or knowledge of the Absolute or Brahma. This he could do by Svadhyaya or self-study, first by going to a place outside the town or village, north or north-east, from where only the roofs of the houses could be seen and secondly by reciting the Vedas at that place from sunrise till sun set when he returned home and offered a gift. The importance of such Svadhyaya has been pointed out by Satapatha Brahmana which regards it as a form of sacrifice to the Brahman by which an imperishable world is gained – one becomes calm in mind, independent of others, the best physician for himself with his restraint of the senses, uniformity of mental attitude, growth of intelligence, fame and power of perfecting the people.

Both the Katha Upanishad and Mundaka Upanishad emphasise the indispensability of a teacher for a student who did not go for self-study to acquire the knowledge of the Brahman. A teacher is needed, explains the Chandogya Upanishad, to disperse the mist of empirically acquired knowledge at a Vedic school from the eyes of a student. The Maitrayana Upanishad forbids communication of this most secret doctrine to anyone who is not his son or his pupil. Thus, Svetaketu learnt this esoteric doctrine from his own father, a Rishi or a seer, after his return from the Vedic school where he had spent 12 years. So did Bhrigu from his Brahmana father, Varuna. There are indeed many such cases where the students had obtained the knowledge of the Brahman from their fathers.

However, for those who did not possess Rishis as their fathers, they had to search for Gurus to obtain this secret knowledge and this could involve them in travelling from one part of the country to another. In the Chandogya Upanishad we have the classic example of Narada who after learning all the subjects offered in a Vedic school found himself "not learned in the Atman" or Atma-vid and approached Sanatkumara who had known Atman with a request to teach him this knowledge. "Yet have I heard from such as are like you that he who knows the Atman vanquishes sorrow. I am in sorrow – lead me then over, I pray, to the farther shore that lies beyond sorrow".

And how is the knowledge of Atman taught to a Shishya or a disciple by a guru or a teacher? By discourses, dialogues, questions and answers. In short, the method of teaching was catechetical which anticipated the method of the great philosopher, Socrates, in Ancient Greece. In these discourses were found utilisation of all the familiar devices of oral teaching such as apt illustrations, stories and parables. The use of discussion as a method of teaching later led to the development of logic called Vakovakyam or Tarka-Shastra or the Science of Disputation.

In these discourses the need for contemplation and introspection on the part of the student was never overlooked. Manana or cogitation as a means of convincing oneself of the truth of learning was specially prescribed. Thus, Svetaketul's father who was teaching his son how the functions of the mind and its faculties were dependent upon the body, how psychological conditions were bound up with the physiological, put him through a course, of actual fasting so that he could achieve a direct perception of the truth by his own experiments and experiences. The father first made him fast for 15 days, cutting of all food except drinks of water, to show that Prana or life depended on water. After this fast, the father asked him to recite the Vedas and the son found, to his surprise, that the knowledge of Vedas had vanished from his mind. And it began to dawn on his mind as he started taking food. By this experiment, Svetaketu realised the truth that Manas or mind depended on Anna or food and that it could not function in a famished body. Similarly, the Vak or the faculty of speech depended upon Tejas or heat of the body. His father thus made the concluding observation: "Just as by covering it a piece of straw or Trina, one make a single small spark or Khadyot left in it to blaze up, so is it with you".

However, the knowledge of the Atman could not be gained simply by mere study and speculation but only by revelation which leads to emancipation. We know how the sage Yajnavalkya about to take the life of an ascetic taught his wife Maitreyi on the subject of immortality where there was no consciousness of anything other than self or Atman; how this knowledge could be acquired. The acquisition of this knowledge involves annihilation, of all desires and illusions of a manifold universe or consciousness of plurality through Sannyasa and Yoga. While by Sannyasa one is able to cast oneself off from one's home, family and possessions which stimulate desire, by Yoga one is able to shake oneself free from the world of plurality and to secure union with the Atman through one's withdrawal of the organs from the objects of sense and desire leading to concentration on the Self. The Self or the Atman is thus awakened and the knowledge of the Brahman is realised. Once this is achieved, one achieves liberation or emancipation of soul from transmigration.

Eclipse of the Kuru-Panchala Countries

Towards the end of our period (C. 800-600 B.C.) the Aryan culture had firmly taken its root in Kashi, Koshala, Videha and Maghada and were about to eclipse the Kuru-Panchala countries, the original seats of Aryan culture, as centres of Aryan learning. Ajatasatru, the learned king of Kashi, used to envy Janaka, the king of Videha with its capital at Mithila for lavish patronage of learning. Janaka collected at his court the literary celebrities of the Kuru-Panchala countries – much as the intellects of Athens gathered at the court of Macedonian princes. In the literary congress held by Janaka on a sacrificial occasion he invited the entire body of the Kuru-Panchala Brahmins, but the wisest person to emerge out of the philosophical debates was Yajnavalkya, a Videhan scholar who had trained himself earlier as a pupil of Aruni, a Panchala Brahmana. Farther off from the centres of Aryan culture of Koshala and Videha were those of Magadha. Magadha embracing the districts of modern Patna and Gaya in the southern part of Bihar were the home of powerful non-Aryan chieftains in the Age of the four Vedas. Among them Kikatas were noted for their wealth of kine coveted by the Aryan invaders. The Aryans during our period were not able to Brahmanise Magadha thoroughly and the Magadhan Brahmanas were held in light esteem. Soon the eastern part of India consisting of Kashi, Koshala, Videha, Vrijian confederacy and Magadha was to revolutionise the Aryan civilisation and culture.

Notes

1. As far as we know there is no "fifth Veda". Description of the epic and mythological poems as "fifth Veda" by Narada suggests their religious importance and these may be Mahabharata and Ramayana. We shall discuss them in an appropriate place in a chapter subsequently.
2. Probably Vaishyas.
3. Probably Shudras.

4

Challenge to the Vedic Schools: The Age of Asceticism

The Genesis of Asceticism

In the eastern parts of the Gangetic basin, particularly in the region around Videha and to its south, Magadha, Brahmanism was not so deeply entrenched as in the western parts and non-Aryan current of belief flowed strongly. Aryan penetration was not however solely confined to the both banks of the river which were then probably thick swampy jungle, but along the Himalayan foothills including the regions of the Sakyas of Kapilavastu, the Mallas of Kushinagar, the Bhargas of Sumsumara Hill and the Mauryas of Pipphalivana and the Vrijian State in North Bihar formed by the union of several clans including the Lichchhavis and the Jnatrikas, all of which had a republican constitution, each known as Gana. The peoples of these regions including those of Magadha were not, as said before, fully Aryanised but bands of nomadic renegade Aryans who did not follow the Vedic rites and roamed about with their flocks and herds. They were the followers of a variety of cults including those of Siva and of his consort, Durga, in her various manifestations as Uma Haimavati and Vasini. Siva and the Mother Goddess were the two deities of the people of the Indus Valley Civilisation and it is possible that the superficially Aryanised people of the eastern parts of the Gangetic basin were originally the survivors of the earlier civilisation who had taken the most convenient and easiest routes of escape by the rivers, Yamuna and Ganges, to their present habitations. The rulers of the people of these regions were described in derisive term as Vratyas or degraded Kshatriyas in the Vedic texts.

In the middle of first millennium B.C., despite the great growth of material civilisation, a deep feeling of insecurity was overtaking the hearts of many people of these regions. This resulted from an expansionist policy pursued by the kings of Koshala and Magadha at the expense of their neighbours. Chieftains were overthrown, their courts dispersed and their lands and tribesmen absorbed in their kingdoms. The break-up of the old tribal units led to the disappearance of the feeling of group solidarity among the people who now stood face-to-face with the world, with no refuge in their kinsmen. They became alone, lonely and isolated and many of them turned to asceticism as a means of their salvation from worldly life now preached by the Upanishads.

Asceticism was known to the Rig Veda

It will however be a mistake to suggest that asceticism emerged with the Upanishads. It has been known to later part of the Rig Vedic days as a class of holy men different from the Brahmanas as Munis or silent ones who wear the wind as a girdle, and who, drunk with their own silence, rise on the wind, and fly in the paths of the demigods and birds, can read all men's thoughts as they have drunk the magic cup of Rudra, which is poison to ordinary mortals. However, there is no doubt that by the time of the Upanishads asceticism had become very widespread and it was through the ascetics rather than the orthodox sacrificial priests that the new teachings were further developed and spread often through debates and discussions, as in the courts of the King Janaka of Videha and Ajatasatru of Kashi, both of whom were patrons of new learning and probably lived in the sixth century B.C.

Nature of Asceticism

Most of the new developments in thought came from ascetics of less rigorous regimen, whose chief practices were the mental and spiritual exercises of meditation. While some of these dwelt alone on the outskirts of towns and villages, others lived in groups of huts under the leadership of an elder. Still others often wandered in groups, begging alms, proclaiming their doctrines to all who wished to listen, and disputing with their rivals. Some were completely naked, while others wore simple garments.

However, there were some ascetics who were solitary psycho-paths, dwelling in the depths of the forests, and suffering self-inflicted tortures of hunger, thirst, heat, cold and rain. Others dwelt in 'penance-grounds', on the outskirts of towns where like some of the less reputable holy men of later times, they would indulge in fantastic self-torture, sitting near blazing fires in the hot sun, lying on beds of thorns or spikes, hanging for hours head downwards from the branches of trees, or holding their arms motionless above their heads until they atrophied.

The original motive of most of these ascetics was the acquisition of magical power, already possessed by the Brahmanas by virtue of their birth and training as sacrificial priests. By the time of the Upanishads the wealthy patrons of sacrifices thought of them as a means of obtaining prosperity, long life, and rebirth in heaven rather than of sustaining of cosmos. The ascetic through his most severe penance rose far above the heights achieved by the sacrificial priest. Once he had injured his body to pain and privation immeasurable joys awaited him – honour and respect which as an ordinary man he could never hope for, and complete freedom from worldly cares and fears. As he advanced in self-training, the hermit acquired powers beyond those of ordinary mortals. He could see past, present and future; could mount heavens and meet gods and could crumble mountains into the sea. If offended, he could burn up his enemies with the glance of his eye, or cause the crops of a whole village to fail. If respected, he could protect a great city, increase its wealth, and defend it from invasion, famine and pestilence.

If asceticism had its charms even for less spiritual, they were still greater for the questing souls who took to a life of hardship from truly religions motives. And going "from darkness to darkness deeper yet", he understood, fully and finally, the nature of the universe and of himself, and he reached a realm of truth and bliss, beyond birth and death, joy and sorrow, good and evil. And with this transcendent knowledge came another realisation – he was completely, utterly, free. He had found ultimate salvation, the final triumph of the soul from the cycle of death and birth. In the early days of the Magadhan ascendancy the most important religious concept was assigned to the doctrines of Samsara and Karma, that is, a belief in repeated transmigration and the law of the deed. The whole world is conceived as "perpetual process of creation, destruction and rebirth filling eternity with an everlasting rhythm" and the entire scheme is placed under the law of Karma which secures that every individual shall reap the fruit of deeds performed in antecedent existence.

The Vishnu Bhagavatas

The new doctrine is preached among others by the Vasudevakas, later called Bhagavatas. They teach Bhakti in Vasudeva, also known as Krishna Devakiputra, who is identified in an Aranyaka with Vishnu and Narayana. The religious and philosophical views of the followers are expounded later in the Bhagavat Gita which forms part of sixth book of the Mahabharata known to Panini, the great grammarian of the Sutra Age.

The Siva Bhagavatas

In the wake of the appearance of the devotees of Krishna, appeared the devotees of Siva, later called the Siva-Bhagavatas, Mahesvaras or Pasupatis. In one of the later Upanishads, the Svetasvatara, Siva is the lord (Isa or Isana) of the universe – the object of devotion to the faithful. By devoting oneself to him, ignorance is dispelled, the nooses of death are snapped and eternal peace is attained. As a matter of fact, in the succeeding age the idea that the universe was created and maintained through sacrifice gave way to the firm belief that the universe depended on the penances of the great god Siva, meditating forever in the fastnesses of the Himalayas, and on the continued austerities of his human followers.

However, the new theistic sects while preserving their distinct individuality did not make a complete break from Brahmanism and attempts at a synthesis were made in the epics and later literature, whereby the gods of the Bhagavatas were recognised as emanation of the supreme divinity of Brahmanism. This leads to enunciation of the doctrine of Trimurti which in its mature form belongs to a much later age.

Humanitarian and Theistic Movements in Eastern India

In eastern India, with the growth of free speculation presaged in the Upanishads, humanitarian and theistic movements thus began to gather momentum and the spiritual leadership passed from the hands of priestly theologians and sacrificers to ascetics and wanderers called Sramanas or Parivrayakas. They believed in the doctrine of transmigration and the law of the deed but rejected the authority of the Vedas and of the Vedic priests. They denounced the blood sacrifices that

constituted so large a part of the Brahmanic ritual and even the
existence of god and consequently the efficacy of divine grace. They
laid the utmost stress on non-injury to living beings and the cessation
of craving for the material things of the world and declared that the
only way of getting out of the meshes of Samsara and Karma was
through right conduct and this right conduct included, among others,
the practice of Ahimsa or non-injury to living beings.

Among the wandering teachers were Vardhamana Mahavira and
Gautama Buddha, the scions of Kshatriya clans, like the lord of the
Bhagavatas, who created history as founders of new religions, Jainism
and Buddhism. Mahavira came from the Jnatrika clan of Kundapura
or Kundagrama near Vaisali in North Bihar and Gautama Buddha
from the Sakya clan of Kapilavastu near Rummindei in the Nepal
Tarai.

Mahavira

Mahavira's mother was Trisala, a Kshatriya lady related to the ruling
families of Vaishali and Magadha and his father was Siddhartha, a
Jnatrika chief. He married a princess named Yasoda and after leading
a life of a pious householder, he renounced the world at the age of
thirty and roamed as a naked ascetic in several countries of eastern
India. He practised severe penance for nearly 12 years and spent the
first halt of it with a mendicant friar named Gosala who subsequently
left him and became the founder of the Ajivika sect. In the thirteenth
year of his penance, Mahavira repaired to the northern bank of the
river Rijupalika outside Jrimbhikagrama, and attained the highest
spiritual knowledge called Kevala-jnana. He now became a Kevalin or
omniscient, a Jina or conqueror and Mahavira or a great hero. He
now became the head of a sect called Nirgranthas or free from fetters,
known in later times as Jainas or followers of Jina. For thirty years he
wandered as a religious teacher and died at Pava in South Bihar at the
age of 72 in C. 528 B.C.

Gautama Buddha

The original name of Gautama Buddha was Siddhartha and the first
name Gautama was derived from his gotra or family. He was born in
566 B.C. as the son of Suddhodana, a Raja of Kapilavastu and of Maya,
a princess of Devadaha, a small town in the Sakya territory. Maya
died at childbirth and Siddhartha was brought up by his aunt and
stepmother, Prajapati Gautami. At the age of 16 he was married to

Gopa, probably a niece of Maya. After his marriage, Siddhartha grew up amidst the luxurious surroundings of the palace till at last the vision of old age, disease and death made him realise the hollowness of worldly pleasures and he decided to leave his home and family after the birth of his son, Rahula, at the age of 29. For six years, he lived as homeless ascetic, seeking instructions first from the Brahman, Alara Kalama at Vaisali, with a following of 300 disciples, who taught him the successive stages of meditation and the doctrine of Atman from which Siddhartha turned back dissatisfied as it did not answer his quest "How shall I in this world of suffering be delivered from suffering?" He then attached himself to Uddaka, the disciple of Rama and the sage of Rajagriha with 700 pupils but as Asvaghosha, the author of Buddha-charita, says: "he gained no clear understanding from his treatment of the soul". He then came to "Uruvela a delightful spot with an enchanting grove of trees and a silvery flowing river, easy of approach and delightful, with a village near by in which to beg" where he settled down to a life of austere penance and engaged himself for the attainment of the knowledge which had been eluding him for the past six years.

However, he soon realised that "truth cannot be attained by one who has lost his strength". And so he resumed care of his body, persuaded himself to take some milk offered by Nandabala, the daughter of the head of the herdsmen of the neighbouring village. Thinking that Siddhartha had returned to the world when he took milk, the "five mendicants, desiring deliverance" who had attached themselves to him for the last six years, deserted him just as, in the words of Asvaghosha, "the five elements leave the wise soul when it is liberated". He then took a bath in the river Nairanjana and sat under a pipal tree and attained at last the supreme knowledge and insight, and became known as the Buddha or the Enlightened One, Tathagata or one who had attained the truth and Sakya Muni or the sage of the Sakya clan. He then proceeded to Sarnath near Kashi or Benares and began to preach his doctrine. And for the next forty-five years he roamed about as a wandering teacher and proclaimed his gospel to the princes and people of Magadha, Koshala and some adjoining territories till he died at the age of eighty at Kusinagara in Gorakhpur. And when he was about to achieve Nirvana, he made the last exhortation to his weeping disciples: "Decay is inherent in all component things. Workout your salvation with diligence".

Preachings of Mahavira and the Buddha

And what did Mahavira and the Buddha preach? It must be said at the beginning that the religious teachings of both were based on their own personal experiences and aimed at delivering human souls from Samsara and Karma. They rejected the authority of the Vedas, denied or doubted the existence of Brahma or Supreme Creative Spirit and inculcated reverence for saints who had attained supreme knowledge. However, unlike Mahavira, the Buddha did not acknowledge the existence of an immortal soul and did not like the idea of discarding garments and rejected the idea of rigid penance which Mahavira did not. The Buddha considered rigid penance to be as useless as indulgence in sensual pleasure.

For the Buddha the supreme knowledge was not the knowledge of Atman and Brahman but the knowledge about the miseries and sufferings of the human beings and it took him nearly six years to acquire it after renouncing the world. He now knew the four noble and universal truths relating to the nature of suffering, the cause of suffering, the destruction of suffering and the way that led to the destruction of sorrow. To him that way did not lie either in the habitual practice of sensuality or in the habitual practice of self-torture. There was a Middle Path called the Noble Eight-fold Path through Right Views, Right Aspirations, Right Speech, Right Conduct, Right Livelihood, Right Effort, Right Mindedness and Right Contemplation which "opened the eyes, bestowed understanding, led to peace of mind, to the higher wisdom, to full enlightenment, to Nirvana".

The Genesis of the Buddhist Viharas

In his religion the Buddha borrowed and adapted much from the popular beliefs of the region. Its simple ritual was not at all based on sacrificial Brahmanism but on the cult of chaityas or sacred spots. Such sacred spots were often small groves of trees, or a single sacred tree, on the outskirts of villages, and possibly included tumuli, such as those in which the ashes of chiefs were buried. These chaityas were the abodes of earth-spirits and genii who, to the simpler folk of the time, were more accessible and less expensive to worship than the great gods of the Aryans. Unorthodox holy men often made their homes in or near the chaityas and by doing so could easily obtain alms from the worshippers of the chaityas. The Buddha respected these local shrines and encouraged his lay followers to revere them. Soon after the death of the Buddha, many communities of his followers gave up the practice of constant travel except in the rainy season, and settled permanently on the outskirts of towns and villages, often near the local chaityas. With time many of these local habitations near the chaityas of the followers of the Buddha grew in size and importance with the support from a sympathetic laity and came to be known as the Buddhist Viharas.

5

The Age of the Buddha and of the Birth of the Buddhist Viharas

The Buddhist Viharas represent organised centres of learning among the Buddhists, aimed at Nirvana or the deliverance of human souls from the sorrows and sufferings of the world, through enlightenment. As such, they could very well be compared with the last two Asramas or stages of life in the days of the Upanishads – the Vanaprastha and the Sannyas meant for those who renounced the world after the first two Asramas as Brahmacharis and Grihasthas.

The Buddhist Scriptures

As in the Brahmanical system, the Buddhist system of learning was based on the religious scriptures of the Buddhists, which grew out of the teachings of the Buddha classified as Vinaya or Conduct, Sutta or Sermon and Abhidhamma or Metaphysics. The religious scriptures of Buddhism grew by a long process of development of accretion, spreading over several centuries. And the process started with the meeting of the followers of the Buddha who were asked by the Buddha to diligently work out their salvation, shortly after his Nirvana, at Rajagriha, the capital of Magadha where Upali recited the Vinaya rules as he recalled having heard them from the lips of the Buddha and another disciple, Ananda recited the Sutta or the Buddha's sermons on matters of doctrine and ethics. A century later, the second council which met at Vaisaii, condemned disputes on Vinaya and revised the scriptures. The third council met at Pataliputra, 236 years after the death of the Buddha, under the patronage of Ashoka and made a final compilation of the scriptures and the fourth was held under Kanishka at Purushapura or Peshawar and prepared elaborate commentaries, Upadesha Shastras and Vibhasa Shastras, on the sacred texts, in the first century A.D.

The Buddhist Order of Monks

The nucleus in the Buddhist system of learning was the Order of monks, Shramanas and Bhikkhus and in his last 45 years of life, spent as a preacher of his doctrines, the Buddha himself gave shape to its development. The Order was thrown open to all the castes, though at the beginning its membership was mostly confined to the Brahmanas and the Kshatriyas. However, slaves, soldiers, debtors and other persons under obligation or in tutelage were debarred from entering it without the permission of their superiors. Youths who wanted to join it had to obtain prior permission of their parents – this restriction was first introduced by the Buddha at the request of his father who grieved over the loss of all his male heirs by the adoption of the Order by all of them including his grandson, Rahula. In the beginning women were not allowed to join the Order because of the vow of the Neshthika Brahmacharya or life long celibacy of the monks but were later permitted by the Buddha to enter it as contact with them was found unavoidable in the daily round of a Buddhist monk begging for food.

Once a person was admitted to the Order, he lost his previous caste and identity and became member of an organisation characterised by the principles of equality and fraternity. As the Buddha himself has observed: "As the great streams, 0 disciples, however many they may be, the Ganga, Yamuna, Achiravati, Sarabhu, Mahi when they reach the great ocean, lose their old name and their old descent, and bear only one name, the great ocean, so also, my disciples, those four castes: Nobles, Brahmans, Vaisya, and Sudra[1] when they, in accordance with the law and doctrine which the Perfect One has preached, forsake their home and go into homelessness, lose their old name and old paternity, and bear only the one designation, Ascetics, who follow the son of the Sakya house".

Admission to the Order

How were they admitted to the Order? The admission was open to the children from the age of eight upwards, but they could only qualify for full membership at the minimum age of twenty after a long course of study. So the complete admission of the Order was through two stages. The first or the preparatory ordination was known as Prabrajya or Pabbajja and the final one as Upasampada. The first ordination rites involved putting on the three yellow or orange robes of the Order, ceremonially shaving the head and pronouncing the three jewels, that is, Buddham Sharanam Gachchami[2], Dhammam Sharanam Gachchami[3], Sangham Sharanam Gachchami[4] and the Ten Precepts or Commandments imposing one to refrain from: (a) harming living beings, (b) taking what was not given, (c) evil behaviour in passion, (d) false speech, (e) sura, meraya and majja which caused carelessness, (f) eating at forbidden times, (g)dancing, singing, music and dramatic performances, (h) the use of garlands, perfumes, unguents and jewellery, (i) the use of high or broad bed and (j) receiving gold and silver. The ceremony over, the novice now called Shramana was committed to the care of his elder or preceptor who brought him up till he was fit for the higher or final ordination.

In the first ordination the Shramana would go to his preceptor and with folded hands utter these words: "You are my preceptor". However, the final ordination was performed with the consent of the majority of the monks – ten monks of not less than ten years standing – at a function before all the monks after the necessary training or instruction had been imparted to him for the purpose. The Shramana having dressed himself as a monk, with the alms bowl in hand and upper robe covering only one shoulder sat down in squatting posture bowing down to other monks and entreating them three times to confer initiation on him "out of compassion". The initiation was conferred on him by the assembly of monks after his providing satisfactory answers to questions on disqualifications and other requirements by a senior monk other than the instructor.

In this way the Shramana became a full monk or Bhikkhu and chose his Upajjhaya or Upadhyaya who taught him the four Nissaya or Requisites and the four Akaraniyani or Interdicts of the monastic life. The four Requisites were: (1) eating of the food collected in the alms-bowl only, (2) wearing robes made of rags collected, (3) lodging at the root of a tree and (4) using cow's urine as medicine. The four Interdicts were: (1) sexual intercourse, (2) theft, (3) taking life and, (4) boasting of super human powers. Infringements of any of the prohibitions was punished by expulsion from the Order. At the same time an ordained monk could seek separation from the Order if he felt the promptings of the flesh, "if his father, mother, wife or the daughter and the jest, the pleasantry of his old days are in his thoughts". This he could do by declaring his weakness before a witness, be he a monk or not, that he renounced the Buddha, the Doctrine and the Order.

Education of the Monks

The ordained monk was then placed under the charge of two superiors qualified by learning, character and standing who were called the Acharya and Upadhyaya. In the Buddhist system the Upadhyaya who, according to Buddhaghosa, was to be a monk of ten years' standing occupied a higher place than the Acharya, normally a monk of some six years' standing. The Upadhyaya was entrusted with the duty of instructing the young Bhikkhu in the sacred texts and doctrines while the Acharya assumed responsibility for his conduct and tutorial work.

The normal period of Nissaya or training was ten years, though for a learned and competent Bhikkhu the period could be reduced to five years after which he was allowed to give a Nissaya to others, or receive pupils as an Acharya. The relationship between the Acharya who was called Nissaya-da or giver of protection and his protege who was called Nissaya-antevasika or pupil-in-dependence was described by Mahavagga as that between a father and a son and similar relationship existed between the Upadhyaya and the Saddhiviharika or the ordained monk.

The curriculum of the monks included what are termed Vinaya, Sutta or Suttanta and Abhidhamma together with Suttas and Sutta Vibhanga which were taught mainly orally. The art of writing was certainly developed by the time of the Mauryas and the Buddhists never considered the writing of their sacred texts as a sacrilege as the Brahmins did – the disuse of writing as pointed out by both Rhys Davids and Oldenberg was more probably due to the scarcity of any convenient practical material on which the known characters might be inscribed. Since the Bhikkhus came from different parts of the country with different dialects, there was a proposal from two very brilliant Brahmin Bhikkhu brothers to adopt the Vedic Sanskrit as the common language but the suggestion was overruled by the Buddha: "I allow you, O Bhikkhus, to learn the word of the Buddhas each in his own dialect". Thus, Buddhism gave an impulse and impetus to the study of local dialects and vernaculars which facilitated its spread later. The Bhikkhus therefore did not learn through the medium of Sanskrit and were not also allowed to study several subjects of study, as for example, the Lokayata system together with the "low arts" of divination, spells, omens, astrology, sacrifices to gods, witchcraft, and quackery. However, the Bhikkhus were allowed facilities in their very monasteries for training and practice in the handicrafts such as spinning, weaving and stitching.

The Bhikkhus as students were assigned to different classes according to their progress in studies. The lowest class consisted of students "who were repeaters of the Suttantas", the next class consisted of students who mastered Vinaya by discussing it with one another, the next higher class of Bhikkhus trained themselves up as teachers of the Dhamma by talking over the subject with one another before they could preach it to others. And lastly, the Bhikkhus of the highest classes were given to meditation of the four Jhanas. Besides these classes of students some Bhikkhus were distinguished and classed as Epicurians, being "wise in worldly lore and abounding in bodily vigour". Thus, we see that in the Buddhist system of education from the very beginning, emphasis was laid on debates and discussions so that the Bhikkhus got the necessary training for the spread of Buddhism by winning converts from other religions. As a matter of fact, the Buddha's whole career of forty-five years of ministry was practically a continuous round up of debates and discussions with the exponents of other schools of thought, Brahamanism and Jainism or answering of questions put to him at the assemblies of his own disciples. The places of such important discussions which marked cultural and religious life in those days were public halls which were called in Pali texts Santhagaras or Samayappavadasalas erected mainly in Sravasti, Vaisali Champa and Rajagriha[5].

Besides the regular teachers, the Upadhyayas and the Acharyas, arrangements were also made for the imparting of instruction by distinguished teachers who were acknowledged authorities and specialists in their subjects. Thus Upali was such a specialist in the Vinaya, the Vinayadhara that "many Bhikkhus, old and middle-aged and young, learnt the Vinaya from the Venerable Upali". Besides Upali, the texts tell us of the names of some of those distinguished teachers who were known as the Thera or senior Bhikkhus who were often invited to deliver lectures or discourses in different parts of the country. Some of them were Devadatta, Sariputta, Maha-Moggailana, Maha-Kachchana, Maha-Kotthitat, Maha-Kappina, Maha-Chunda, Anuddhal, Revata, Ananda and Rahula.

Duties and Obligations of the Buddhist Monks to their Teachers

The Buddhist system, like the Brahmanical, enjoined upon the pupil the duty of serving his preceptor as a part of education. The pupil was to rise early from bed often at the crowing of domesticated crows at some places kept for the purpose and gave his teacher teeth-cleanser and water to rinse his mouth with, then, preparing a seat for him, served him rice-milk in rinsed jug and, after his drinking it, washed the vessel and swept the place. Afterwards, he was to equip him for his begging round by giving him fresh undergarment, girdle, his two upper garments, and his alms-bowl rinsed and filled with water and then he was to dress and equip himself if he wanted to accompany his teacher but must not walk too far from or near him. In returning the pupil must get back ahead of the teacher to be ready with necessary things and help him to change his clothes. Then, after serving him with some food, if required, he was to help him in bath by getting him cold or hot water as desired and if the pupil was to bathe himself, he must finish it quickly so as to be ready in time to receive his teacher out of the bathroom with water for washing his feet, a footstool and a towel. After bath, came an interval of teaching in the form of answering questions or delivering a discourse. The pupil was to sweep and clear the Vihara where his teacher lived and was also to clean out other compartments of Vihara such as store-room, refectory, fire-room and was required not to do anything including travel without the permission of the teacher. And finally, if his teacher fell sick, he must nurse him till his death or recovery. A pupil without any great affection, inclination, reverence and devotion for his Upajjhaya and without any shame for his lapses was likely to be expelled. Similarly, the Nissaya also ceased when the teacher was away, or had returned to the world or had gone over to a schismatic faction or had died.

Duties and Obligations of the Buddhist Teachers to their Students

In return, the teacher had to give the Bhikkhu under his charge all possible intellectual and spiritual help and guidance "by teaching, by putting questions to him, by exhortation, and by instruction", helped him with necessary articles such as an alms-bowl or a robe out of his own if the pupil did not have them and nursed him when he was taken ill. Such duties demanded of the teacher some special qualifications besides his intellectual attainments, like: "self-concentration, wisdom, emancipation and the knowledge and insight thereto, and the like as described in the Mahavagga and without these no monk was allowed to give Nissaya or ordain a novice".

Admission of Women to the Buddhist Order

We have already said in the beginning that the Buddha permitted women to join the Order, though according to the philosophy of his teachings women were to be shunned. In the Aryan society, women controlled the households and in their daily round of begging, the Bhikkhus could not but come in contact with women as the givers of alms. The permission by the Buddha in fact was given under pressure from his foster-mother, Mahaprajapati and his favourite disciple, Ananda. Like the monks, they also had to renounce the world and to go through the two stages of ordination before they could become Bhikkhunis or nuns. However, the rules for regulating their life kept them in complete subordination to the monks. For example, the first of the eight chief rules stated that "a Bhikkhuni even of a hundred years' standing" must look up to a Bhikkhu "if only just initiated". The rules enjoined strict separation between monks and nuns though a monk specially selected by the brotherhood was to impart instructions and admonition to the nuns twice every month in the presence of another monk. The discipline and duties of daily life were the same for monks except that the solitary life was practically forbidden for them.

The Buddha's foster-mother was one of the firsts to enter the Order with nearly 500 Sakya ladies. Many ladies from royal and distinguished families became nuns such as Soma, daughter of Purohita or chief-priest of Bimbisara, king of Magadha; Anupama, a peerless beauty who was the daughter of a very wealthy parents. Similarly Sujata who was the wife of a very rich husband joined the Order in search of the ideal for its own sake, renouncing the happy conditions of life.

In the Order of Nuns, many distinguished themselves as teachers or Theris. The Chullavagga tells us about the Bhikkhuni Uppalavanna who was a teacher and in Manorathapurani Buddhaghosha speaks of thirteen ladies who entered the order as teachers and earned the appreciation of the Buddha as Theris – one of them, Dhammadinna, even taught her husband when he became a monk. However, the Order of Nuns did what it was intended to do – to provide solace and comfort to many ladies who had suffered the miseries of the world either through separation or bereavement. Thus, Champa unable to bear the pangs of separation from her husband who had become a monk joined the Order, so did Kisa Gotami who lost her infant and the rich heiress Sundari whose brother died and she was left alone in the world. In the first volume of the Ninth Oriental Congress Report, C.A. Foley cited the case of a bereaved mother Patadhara, who solaced some 500 bereaved mothers as well as that of Sukka, another nun, who was heard not only by the members of her Order but also by the people at large.

The Order of Nuns led to Social Service

Thus, the Order of Nuns opened up avenues for education and social service to a remarkable extent and was able to attract the sympathy and generosity of many an influential lay lady from the contemporary Aryan society such as Visaka and Ambapali of Vaisali and Suppiya of Kasi. Whatever may be the opinion of the Buddha on the womanhood, he was always responsive to the offers of hospitality and financial generosity coming from a host of women with religious zeal.

In this context we shall not, however, forget that social service or social reform was never the intention of the Buddha who was only seeking deliverance of the human beings from the miseries of the world. He never failed to accord prominence to the Brahmana and Kshatriya members of his Order. Lalitavistara, almost a contemporary of the Buddha, asserts that "a Buddha can be born only as Brahmana or as a Kshatriya and not in low family such as that of a Chandala or of a basket-maker or of a chariot maker or of a Pukkasa". Himself a product of the Brahmanical system of learning, he placed himself under two successive gurus, Alara Kalama at Vaisali and Uddaka at Rajagriha who were both Brahmana sages but who could not satisfy his quest for knowledge, not about the doctrine of Atman but about the miseries and sufferings of the human beings. Had he encountered a more capable exponent of the Vedantic philosophy like a Janaka or a Yajnavalkya, the history of the religion of Ancient India would have been probably different. Nevertheless, there can be no doubt that though the Buddha may not be a social revolutionary, his teachings form the basis of a social philosophy which we know today as humanism. In other words, Buddhism is the first starting point of the history of humanism in the world. It is also possible that

Buddhism influenced the early tenets of Christianity. In their book, *The Original Jesus*, Elmar R. Gruber, an eminent psychologist and Holger Kersten, an authority on religious history, offer interesting and compelling evidence of extensive Buddhist influence on the life and teachings of Jesus.

The Buddhist Viharas

Thus, we see the unit of the Buddhist educational system was the groups of young Bhikkhus or monks living under the guardianship of a common teacher, the Upajjhaya or Acharya who was individually responsible for their health and studies, manners and morals and their spiritual progress. Unlike the Brahmanical system these groups did not exist as isolated and independent units but federated themselves into a larger unit called the Vihara or monastery. The Vihara was originally the name for the private apartment of a single Bhikkhu which lay near one another in numbers. Later the term came to denote a larger building with apartments for many monks. In the beginning the monks were devoid of any dwelling-house properly so called. They "dwelt now here, now there – in the woods, at the foot of trees, on hillsides, in grottoes, in mountain caves, in cemeteries, in forests, in open plains, and in heaps of straw". Seeing them coming from all such places, a rich Setthi of Rajagriha offered to erect fixed dwellings for them and the offer was accepted by the Buddha. With the passage of time Viharas came to mean detached houses or as Aramas, Prasadas or storied houses, elaborately equipped with all kinds of dwelling – assembly halls, dining halls, structures for warm baths and ablutions, and council-chambers, and equipped also with furniture of diverse kinds satisfying every need of health and life.

During the time of the Buddha, the best example of a Vihara that was constructed for the Samgha was by the merchant prince Anathapindika in the Arama made in the garden of Prince Jeta which was situated as the Buddha himself indicated, "not too far from the town and not too near, convenient for going and for coming, easily accessible for all who wish to visit him, by day not too crowded, by night not exposed to too much noise and alarm, protected from wind, hidden from men, well fitted for a retired life". Besides the Jetavana Vihara at Sravasti, there was another Vihara constructed for the monks called Purbarama. Besides these Viharas at Sravasti, there were Viharas at Rajagriha called Yashtivana, Venuvana, and Sitavana; at Vaisali called Mahavana Kutagara Hall and Mango-grove; at

Kapilavastu called Nigrodharama; at Kausambi called Ghoshitarama and finally at Pava called the Mango-grove of Chunda the Smith.

The Management of the Buddhist Viharas

The management of these elaborately equipped establishments where so many monks lived together naturally called for a numerous and varied staff of officials with a well worked-out differentiation of functions. The Samgha staff included (1) the apportioner or distributor of lodging places, (2) the regulator or apportioner of rations, (3) the overseer of stores, (4) receiver of robes, (5) distributor of robes, ungey or fruits, (6) distributor of dry foods, (7) disposer of trifles like needle, pairs of scissors, sandals and braces, girdle, filtering cloth, regulation strainer and the like, (8) receiver of undergarments, (9) receiver of towels, (10) Aramikas or those who kept the grounds of the Aramas in order, (11) superintendents of Aramikas to look after their work and (12) superintendents of Shamaneras to keep them to their duties.

These offices show that the monks had to engage in various kinds of practical, secular work instead of being constantly or exclusively occupied in purely religious or spiritual exercises. Thus, there were ample opportunities for business training or education in the practical arts and crafts for their inmates. Bhikkhus were often deputed to serve as "building overseers" to take charge of building operations on behalf of a lay donor so that the buildings might be in accordance with "the rules of the Order as to size, form and object of the various apartments" of a Vihara. Besides supervising constructions and repairs of the Viharas, Bhikkhus were required to prepare their own robes and keep them in fit conditions with the help of all necessary weaving appliances.

However, these officials though Bhikkhus, could not take any decisions regarding the management of a Vihara – these rested with the committee of elder monks and important decisions, such as the admission or expulsion of members could only be made by the committee and not by the chief. The chief monk or abbot was not appointed from above or nominated by his predecessor but held office by the suffrage of all the monks in the monastic parish. Thus, the constitution of a Vihara as laid down by the Buddha himself had elements of democracy about it and was perhaps modelled on the constitution of one of the republican tribes, the Sakyas to whom the Buddha himself belonged, which then existed in the foothills of the

Himalayas in Nepal Tarai. As a matter of fact, Buddhist monastic affairs were managed by a general meeting of the monks, with a regular system of procedure and standing orders, not very different from that of the business meeting of a present day society. The Buddhist Chapter differed from the modern committee, however, in that all decisions needed the unanimous consent of the assembled monks. Differences which could not be settled were referred to a committee of elders.

The monks assembled every fortnight on the evenings of the full and new moons for Upavasatha, an act of general confession. The long list of monastic rules from the Vinaya Pitaka was read and each monk confessed any breaches which he had committed during the preceding fortnight. If his fault was serious, his case was referred to a committee of elders, which might impose penance or expel him from the Order. The ceremony concluded with the preaching of sermons, to which the pious lay folk of the vicinity listened.

However, there was no central authority to regulate the many monasteries and enforce uniformity; each was a law unto itself guided only by the precepts of the Buddha as it had received them, and as it interpreted them. Since the monastery was a federation of individual educational groups or schools, the efficiency of its organisation depended upon the federal principles of administration which aimed at three distinct objects: (a) the independence and efficiency of each constituent group of pupils bound to an individual teacher, (b) the adjustment of relations between the different constituent groups, (c) the framing of laws governing them.

The Buddhist Viharas depended on a Friendly Neighbourhood

The Buddhist Viharas were built and maintained with the support of people around them. That is why the Buddha always insisted that they should be erected at places which were neither very near nor very far off from any village or town to facilitate not only the monks' daily round of begging but also their daily requirements without which they could not maintain themselves as they could not generate them after renouncing the world.

The friendly neighbourhood consisted of those people who believed in Buddhism but did not choose to belong to the Order or the monastery and be ruled by its discipline. Nevertheless, Buddhism was very vitally interested in the growth of a believing and pious laity and framed certain rules, which were more observed in breach than in compliance, for the regulation of their life. For example, the laity were required to formally declare their refuge with the Buddha, the Dhamma and the Samgha though it was never insisted upon as it might go against the interests of a Vihara with the laity as its neighbour. This means that those very people who were supporting a Buddhist Vihara could be followers of Brahmanism or Jainism, Saivasim or Vaishnavism or any other sects. People with sympathy for Buddhism were called Upasak[6] and Upasika[7]. They might belong to any religion but Buddhism insisted, according to Rhys Davids, that as householders they should perform right conducts and right duties – parents should educate their children, who should honour and obey their teachers and the teachers in turn should show ample affection and responsibility for their well-being. The monks were also often requested to instruct them as Bimbisara asked the overseers of 80,000 townships over which he held his rule to wait upon the Buddha for "instruction in the things of eternity". Thus, the laity had to depend on the monks who were experts in the knowledge of the sacred lore for instruction in religious education but for education in areas including medicine which helped them to earn their living they obviously had to go to Brahmanical schools.

The Buddhist Viharas vis-à-vis the Vedic Schools

As a matter of fact, the Buddhist Viharas formed the chief mark of difference between the Buddhistic and Brahmanical schools of education in Ancient India. And the history of the Buddhist system of education is practically the history of the Buddhist Viharas or Order or Samgha. Buddhist education and learning thus centred round monasteries as Vedic culture centred round the sacrifices. The Vedic system of education was predominantly a domestic system of education under which the individual teacher's home was the school of the young admitted to it as pupils. The influence of the home was installed as an indispensable factor, though it was the home not of the natural but of the spiritual parents of the pupil. The students did not lose their past identity and culture to which they returned after completion of their studies and began their householder's life to fulfil their material as well as spiritual goals. They never lost their self identity till they opted for Vanaprastha and Sannyas. They were allowed to set up schools and transmit their knowledge to their own students who in turn could do the same when they returned home thereby preserving the continuity of their learning and culture.

The Buddhist system of education began with the destruction of home life as the starting point and superseded home by monastery which was organised on democratic principles. In the monastery all were equal except the respect and the privilege that was shown and accorded to the senior monks of several years' standing. They participated in its management by the power to vote in a meeting in which all members, seniors and juniors were present. Once a monk, always a monk and they could not return to the worldly life till they were expelled or they themselves renounced the monkhood. A monk's life thus bear close resemblance at least apparently, to that of an ascetic's life of Vanaprastha and Sannyas which a householder could enter in search of the supreme knowledge but while a Vedic ascetic led a life full of hardships and penances, such was not the case with the monks in the Viharas who lived with all sorts of admissible comforts – as Rhys Davids has pointed out in his *Buddhism*, "the body is to be decently draped, cleansed and massaged, regularly fed, sheltered in the rainy season, rested during the noonday heat, and medically treated when ailing". Such medical treatment often came from outside when a disease was serious as the monks in the Viharas knew only the uses of some medicinal herbs and cow's urine when they fell ill, say from sun's stroke or excessive cold.

This brings us to a further point of difference. The Viharas only specialised in spiritual and religious training and taught no other subjects which characterised the Brahamanical system of learning. The scope of the subjects taught in the Vedic system to attain supreme knowledge gradually became wider and wider with the passage of time since the days of the Rig Veda in response to the changing times which saw the emergence of new branches of learning – this was never the case with the Buddhist Vihar as though some changes crept into the courses later but basically they remained the same as they were in the days of the Buddha.

Yet, it was the Buddhist Viharas and not the Vedic Gurukulas which now began to attract the novices in large numbers since the days of the Buddha. The doors of the Buddhist Viharas were always open to all castes and creeds and they offered no struggle for existence within the Order which lived on the charity of the laity or the Upasakas and the Upasikas who supported the brotherhood as a religious duty. Indeed the easy life within the Order drew many to it – the Vinaya texts tell us many stories of people's entering the Order to solve their problems of survival. The parents of Upali who later became a famous monk trusted by the Buddha, anxious for his life of ease after their death, decided upon his monkhood as the best occupation for that purpose in preference to all other usual occupations of the times such as lekha or writing at which "his fingers will become sore", ganana or arithmetic at which "his breast will become diseased by too much thinking" or rupam or drawing at which "his eyes will suffer".

However, the Upali anecdote should not minimise the importance of the Buddhist system of learning. It did what the Brahmanical system of learning could do only at the last two ascetic stages of life to people belonging to the higher castes only. It offered solace to many, many people, irrespective of their castes, cults and religion, who had suffered the miseries of life. The case of Kisa Gotami illustrates this point very clearly. She came to the Buddha with the dead child in her arms and entreated him to restore it to life. The Buddha replied that he could do it if she was able to fetch him a little mustard seed from a house which had not suffered any death. Kisa Gotami searched desperately for a mustard seed from such a house but was unsuccessful and returned to the Buddha with the realisation that death was the inevitable and common lot of all and that nobody could escape it. The Buddha consoled her and at her request, admitted her to the Order of the Nuns. Thus, while the Brahmanical system of learning appealed more to the head than to the heart, the Buddhist system of learning did just the reverse by appealing more to the heart than to the head and gradually began to win millions to its fold, at least, in eastern India.

Notes

1. Buddha admitted Upali, the Barber, in his Order.
2. I take refuge with the Buddha.
3. I take refuge with the Religion.
4. I take refuge with the Order
5. See p. 60 for names of the Buddhist Viharas in these places.
6. Male Worshipper.
7. Female Worshipper.

6

Reaction to the Challenge of the Buddhist Viharas: The Age of the Sutras

Challenge of the Buddhist Viharas to the Vedic Schools and the Latter's Reaction

It was Buddhism rather than Jainism that threw a challenge to the dominant Brahmanism. In Jainism the layman was a definite member of the Order, encouraged to undertake periodical retreats, and to live as far as possible the life of the monk for specified periods. The saints and prophets of Jainism were not altogether different from those of Brahmanism and the Jainas did not altogether dispense with the worship of the old deities or the services of the Brahmanas at their homes on occasions like birth, death and marriage. As long as Buddhism was concerned with the settlement of mere theological and speculative issues, there was no confrontation with Brahmanism. However, a struggle for self-preservation and self-assertion for Brahmanism began when Buddhism addressed itself to the practical points of religion, worship and life and soon developed itself into an easily accessible system of religion among the Aryans. The doors of Buddhism were thrown open to all members of the Aryan society and anyone seeking relief from sorrows, and sufferings of the world could join it by renouncing the world. On the other hand, the extravagant and elaborate ritualism of Brahmanism and its complex and difficult religious scriptures which could be mastered only by the priestly class had alienated many among the Aryans belonging to all the four classes of the Aryan society. In this circumstance, Brahmanism was forced to forge a suitable weapon of defence against the onslaught of Buddhism by making Brahmanism easily accessible to all through compilation, codification and simplification of the existing religious scriptures. This new literary activity in Brahmanism which emerged under the changing times to meet the challenge of Buddhism is known as Sutras and their authors as Sutrakaras.

Nature of the Sutras

The Sutras represent the quintessence of all the knowledge previously acquired and accumulated through study and meditation spreading over several centuries. And their authors, the Sutrakaras generally claimed no originality or inspiration for themselves except perhaps credit for making the religious scriptures of the past centuries more easily accessible to all. They adopted a business like style and condensed the vast mass of literary material of the past within the smallest possible compass.

Thus, the soul of the new literary creation was brevity and as Patanjali, one of the Sutrakaras who came towards the end of Sutra period, observes in his Mahabhashya, "an author rejoiceth in the economising of half a short vowel as much as in the birth of a son".

Forms of the Sutras

Among the various forms of Sutras, Shrauta Sutras were the first to come into existence and may be said to be continuation of the Brahmanas on their ritual side. Next came the Griha Sutras which deals with the various domestic ceremonies of birth, marriage and death and are also known as Smriti or that which is the subject of memory as distinguished from Sruti or that which is the subject of hearing. The third form of Sutras is known as the Dharma Sutras. They deal with various customs and manners of social life and are therefore the earliest legal literature of the Aryan society. The last form of the Sutras is the Sulva Sutras which deal with the various practices of the time such as measurement required for the construction of the Vedi or altar. They may be regarded as our earliest mathematical treatise incorporating an advanced knowledge of geometry and algebraical propositions.

The Beginning of the Sutra Age

The Sutra Age which is presumed to start with the composition of the standardised Sanskrit grammar by Panini (C. 400 B.C.) and end with the commentary on Panini's work by Patanjali (C. 200 B.C.) roughly covers two centuries. During this period the Brahmanical education system as it developed in the past continued, though here and there some changes and innovations were introduced to adjust it to the needs of the changing time. It will be more fruitful for us to concentrate on these changes and alterations instead of entering into the details of the education system which was not basically different from that of the previous ages.

Changes in Education in the Sutra Age

One such change relates to the beginning of a child's education or Vidyarambha which now started at the fifth year of his age. The ceremony of Vidyarambha consisted in the child offering worship to the deities, Hari, Lakshmi and Sarasvati or the goddess of learning as well as to the Vidya cultivated by his family, the Sutrakaras of that particular Vidya and the Vidya or subject of his choice. As in the past, the Vidyarambha ceremony which introduced a child to the alphabets was restricted only to the three upper castes of the Aryan society. A few years after the Vidyarambha ceremony, the Upanayana ceremony was performed after Chudakarama or tonsure of head. The normal age for Upanayana was now 8 for a Brahmana, 11 for a Kshatriya and 12 for a Vaishya. The corresponding maximum age for it was 16 for a Brahmana, 22 for a Kshatriya and 24 for a Vaishya. The ages were fixed in accordance with the different capacities and aptitudes for learning which varied from caste to caste. Usually, the Upanayana ceremony was performed for all the castes in the five months from Magha (12 January-12 February) as these months constituted the auspicious portion of the year known as Uttarayana. As a part of the Upanayana ceremony, a Brahmacharin had to observe the rules of the Savitri Vrata for three days which was followed by the performance of the Medhajana rite invoking gods for the development of his mental powers. The Medhajana rite ended the Upanayana ceremony.

Courses of Studies and their Durations

In the Sutra Age the Brahmacharin had to spend 12 years at the residence of his teacher under prescribed conditions as before for learning each Veda. If the Brahmacharin wanted to master all the four Vedas, he had to spend nearly 48 years and this was usually done by a Brahmacharin belonging to the priestly class who monopolised the learning profession in the Aryan society. The course of study not only included "the Whole Veda" or the four Vedas with the six Angas or the ritualistic treatises on Siksha or phonetics, Chhanda or prosody, Vyakarana or grammar, Nirukta or etymology and Jyotisha or astronomy but also the Rahasyas or the esoteric treatises such as the Aranyakas or the Upanishads. Before starting a course, a Brahmacharin had to observe some special Vratas for a certain period of time. While Savitri Vrata introduced him to Savitri verse, Sukriya Vrata to the study of the main portion of the Veda, Aruvachana Vrata to the mode of this study and finally Sakvara Vratika and Aupanishada Vratas each lasting for a year to the study of the different portions of Aranyakas. By observing these Vratas a Brahmacharin sought to develop his inner faculties to comprehend his graduated course of studies which he pursued at the residence of his teacher or a Vedic school.

School Sessions

The school term opened solemnly with the performance of a special ceremony called Upakarman on the full moon of the month of Shravana, (July-August) and continued until the full moon of the month of Pausha (December-January) when it was solemnly closed by the performance of the Utsarjana ceremony after which the Brahmacharin had to leave off learning the Veda. However, the Brahmacharin had to recapitulate what he had learnt from his teacher in the next five or six months till the school term opened again in the month of Shravana. According to the Sutrakar Manu after the performance of the Utsarjana ceremony the Brahmacharin was to study the Veda in the bright fortnight of each month and all the Vedangas and the rest in the dark fortnight of each month until the full moon of Shravana when the school term opened in order to fix in his mind the part already learnt. With the opening of the new session of the school when the names of those who had contributed most to the study of the Vedas and the allied subjects were gratefully recalled, the Brahmacharin began to learn from his teacher a fresh part of the Veda and other subjects.

Teachers: Acharya and Upadhyaya

In the Sutra Age there seems to have emerged a gradation of teachers known as Acharya and Upadhyaya. Acharya who was ten times more venerable than the Upadhyaya was the chief among all gurus or teachers. Manu defines Acharya as one who initiated a pupil and taught him the Veda, together with the Kalpa and the Rahasyas. Upadhyaya is defined as one who taught only a portion of the Veda or the Angas to his students "for a fee" or "for his livelihood" according to Manu. However, the Acharya could accept a fee in the form of a gift only from a pupil whose instruction under his charge was completed. In fact, it was one of the obligations of the Brahmacharin to bring to a close the period of his formal pupilage by making presents to his teacher, though in the majority of cases such gifts were not certainly any adequate remuneration for the amount of labour and expense involved in supporting and educating a student for a minimum period of 12 years. Such parting gifts to the Acharya which depended on the economic ability of a student and his parent often took shape, in the words of Manu, of "a field, a cow, a horse, a parasol and shoes, a seat, grain, even vegetables" and when any one of these were presented to a teacher, it gave immense pleasure to him.

It is possible that many of the Upadhyayas who taught "for a fee" or "for livelihood" could have come from the class other than the Brahmanas for some of the Sutrakaras of the Age mention existence of non-Brahmana teachers. The Sutrakara Baudhayana permits "study under a non-Brahman teacher in times of distress" and so do the Sutrakaras Apastamba and Gautama who assert that "in times of distress a Brahmana may study under a Kshatriya or a Vaisya". Such a non-Brahmana teacher was to be paid due honour by the Brahmana student throughout the long period of his studentship – for example, as Manu says, "he must walk behind him and obey him". This shows that teaching as a profession was attracting classes other than the Brahmanas and that as in the Rig Vedic age the adoption of a profession was not determined by the caste in which a person was born. This relaxation of rule of the previous ages in education was possibly due to the challenge of Buddhism which could boast of teachers coming from different classes of the Aryan society. In the Sutra Age everybody except perhaps the Shudra was required to go to a Vedic school. As Manu says "An Aryan must study the whole Veda together with the Rahasyas, performing at the same time various kinds of austerities and the vows prescribed by the rules of the Veda". The rules of studentship applied not only to the boys but also to the girls of the Aryan society. Both the Srauta Sutras and the Griha Sutras mention that Vedic Mantras or hymns were to be uttered by the wives along with their husbands at religious ceremonies. The

Sutrakara Hemadri says that "Kumaris, unmarried girls, should be taught Vidya and Dharmaniti. An educated Kumari brings good to the families of both her father and husband. So she should be married to a learned husband (or manishi) as she is a Vidushi".

Samavartana

We have already spoken about the occasion when a gift was presented to the Acharya by his student who was about to return home after completion of his studentship at the Vedic school. The returning home of the student is known as Samavartana and he had to perform or go through several activities signifying the end of his Brahmacharya or studentship before he left his school. In the first place the Brahmacharin was confined in a room in the morning lest his superior lustre put to shame the Sun who shines in the lustre borrowed of him. At mid-day, he came out of the room, shaved his head and beard and took a bath accompanied by the use of powder, perfumes, ground sandalwood and the like – all presented to him by his friends and relatives and then threw into the water all the external signs of his Brahmacharya such as the upper and lower garments, girdle, staff and skin. After the bath he became a Snataka or one who had taken a bath, wearing new garments, two earrings, and a perforated pellet of sandalwood overlaid with gold which was to bring him gain, superiority in battles and assemblies, at its aperture. Dressed in new garbes and ornaments the Snataka prayed that he should be dear to all, kings, Brahmanas, Kshatriyas, Vaishyas and Shudras. He then became Samavritta or one who had returned home where a sacrifice was performed with a prayer that the Snataka could become a successful teacher. He then in his new dress, paid a visit, in a chariot or an elephant, to the local Parishad or learned assembly where he was introduced as a full-fledged scholar by his teacher.

Parishad

In the Sutra Age a Parishad which was an academy of learned and religious men consisted of ten members, as the Sutrakara Gautama informs us. Among them, four would be scholars who had studied the four Vedas, three would come from the three Asramas, or stages of life, that is, a student, a householder and an ascetic and the last three would be well versed with the Dharma Sutras or three different institutes of law. Such a Parishad was intended to be an academy of experts who provided authoritative interpretations and decisions on doubtful points in the sacred texts. And the decisions of the Parishad were intended to be as binding on the local community as the sacred texts themselves. It was from such a Parishad situated either at a famous learned centre or an imperial capital that an author who wanted to have his work accepted in all parts of the country, had to obtain its approval as Panini did for his grammar from the Parishad at Pataliputra travelling all the way from Salatura near Peshawar to the imperial capital.

Study of Law: Dharma Sutras

In the Parishad the last three members were to be specialists in three different institutes of law. Study of law or customs and manners of the Aryans formed part of the curricula at the Vedic schools for a pretty long time but such study, like most of the Vedangas, had gradually parted company with them to further its own development. In the Sutra Age special law schools grew up and these schools found plenty of materials for such special studies as the two Dharma Sutras of Vasishtha and Baudhayana. Most of the materials related to the detailed rules, though not systematically arranged, on the moral duties of the Aryans. They also relate to the legal procedure on civil and criminal law but the treatment is not satisfactory except that of the law of inheritance and partition. Since the Vedic schools were more concerned with matters spiritual, a detailed and orderly treatment of legal matters was irrelevant and a mere smattering of the knowledge of local customs was sufficient for such posts as Dharmadhikarins or legal advisers or judges. In the Sutra Age specialists who now studied the sacred law tried to do away with these deficiencies in the past works on the subject mostly by remodelling them into works which claimed the allegiance of all members of the Aryan society. In law the chief surviving representatives of the age are the Dharma Sutras of Manu and Yajnavalkya.

The Vedangas emerging as Independent Disciplines

Many of the Angas of the Vedic schools were also fast becoming independent disciplines in the works of the Sutrakaras. Kalpa or ritual reached large dimensions as seen in the Sutras of Baudhayaniyas and Apastambiyas. Similarly Vyakarana or grammar developed as an independent science as reflected in Panini's Ashtadhyayi or eight chapters which laid down the rules applicable to the language of the Vedas, which now became known as Sanskrita or refined. Finally in both Gargi Samhita and Vasishtha Samhita which was composed later. Astronomy shows no connection with the Vedic schools except that the authorship is attributed to Rishis or descendants of their families.

In philosophy, as in law and Angas, the Sutra Age represents a tremendous growth and development. In the Rig Veda a sense of diversity expresses itself in the creation of a richly varied pantheon of gods like Agni, Indra, Varuna and Vayu but behind this variety is the underlying conception of the One, extending as a god to the gods from afar and embracing this universe, who is called in his different aspects as Hiranyagarbha, Prajapati, Visvakarma, Brihaspati or Brahmanaspati, the god of all gods, culminating in Brahman and Atman. The Upanishads themselves are the products of an intense philosophical activity in which all including Satyakama Jabala of an unknown parentage and Raikva, a Shudra made their mark. It became a fairly national pursuit extending from the solitary hermitages in the forests to the kings' courts in the capitals. If the dawn of philosophy is to be discovered in the hymns of the Rig Veda, the Upanishad shows its meridian in its uses of terms like Brahman and Atman, Dharma and Vrata, Yoga and Mimamsa.

Thus, long before the rise of the philosophical Sutras, there had been an accumulation of philosophical thought which was orally handed down to the succeeding generations. And what the philosophical Sutrakaras did was to systematise and codify the speculation contained in the existing religious scriptures. The result was a multiplicity of schools of thought, of which six systems have held their own as the most typical and representative of them all. These six systems of philosophy have come to be distinguished as orthodox systems from the heterodox philosophical systems of the Buddhists, Jains and Charvakas, as they are somehow reconcilable with the Vedic system of philosophy. They are (1) the Samkhyha of Kapila, (2) Yoga of Patanjaii, (3) Nyaya of Gautama, (4) Vaiseshika of Kanada, (5) Karma or Purva Mimamsa of Jaimini and (6) Sariraka or Uttara Mimamsa or Vedanta of Badarayana. As said before, the philosophers of these systems were not necessarily their originators but gave final form to the Sutras which themselves refer to earlier philosophers. Some of the Sutras again refer to the opinions of other Sutras thereby indicating the existence of different philosophical schools before their final redaction.

The foundations of these six different schools of philosophy rest on a common system of discipline, known as Varnasramadharma or the regulations belonging to the different castes and Asramas or stages of life in the Aryan society. These comprise the various Samskaras or sacraments prescribed for different stages of life: Upanayana, Brahmacharya, and Samavartana for its first stage; and various sacrifices prescribed for the householder's life in the second; the rules for the gradual detachment from the world in the third stage of the forest dwelling hermit and finally various forms of meditation prescribed for the wandering mendicant in the last stage. Thus, in the Aryan society the study of philosophy aimed at the attainment of the supreme truth or mukti – emancipation through different stages of life or experience, each representing a specific degree of conquest achieved over the physique and the material world. To put in a nutshell, a system of philosophy ultimately becomes a system of release. And this is something which cannot be learnt from mere books but has to be lived, like religion, to realise the truth.

Emergence of New Disciplines

We have been till now focussing attention on the independent development of those disciplines which have cut off their umbilical cord from the Vedic schools. The Sutra Age also saw emergence of some new disciplines to meet the needs and requirements of a particular class in the society. Since such disciplines developed independently of the Vedic schools which centred round the Aryan religion, these could be termed as non-religious or secular. One such subject is the study of statecraft or treatise on governance and the most outstanding work of the age is Kautiliya Arthasastra. Kautilya whose original name was Chanakya was the Brahmana scholar who helped Chandragupta Maurya to usurp the last of the Nanadas and capture the Magadhan throne between C 324 and 318 B.C. Kautiliya Arthashastra which compares well with Machiavelli's, *The Prince* in modern times deals with the education and training of the monarch and provides the necessary guidelines for him in successfully administering a kingdom. Kautilya himself served Chandragupta Maurya who founded the illustrious Maurya dynasty at Pataliputra as his minister and it is possible that many of his experiences were embedded in his work.

According to Kautilya the education of a prince consisted of four divisions – Anvikshaktit, Trayi, Varta and Dandaniti. While the first two divisions relate to the course on religious and philosophical subjects, the third on subjects like agriculture, cattle-rearing and trade under practical experts, the fourth relates to the science and art of governance. The studentship of the prince is to continue only up to his sixteenth year when he should marry. This is indeed a very short time since the Dharma Sutras of the age prescribe the eleventh year as the age for the beginning of the studentship of a Kshatriya. As a king he is to have the company of his Purohita who should come from a family well versed in traditional learning. The Purohita should be fully educated in the Vedas, the six Vedangas, the science of portents and omens, the art of administration and be able by his knowledge and application of the Atharvan remedies to ward off calamities due to divine and human agencies.

Contributions of Taxila to the Sutra Age

Many of the Sutrakaras including Panini and Kautilya were the products of Taxila. Founded by king Bharata and named after his son, Taksha, Taxila lay in Gandhara to the east of the river Indus and on the highway connecting Central and Western Asia to the interior of India by way of the river Ganges. From C 558 B.C. onwards it came under the influence of the Persians when it became a part of the most prosperous and populous twentieth satrapy of the Achamenid empire of Persia and from 326 B.C. onwards the Persian influence was replaced by the Greek when it became part of the Macedonian empire in the North-West India of Alexander the Great. Thus, the Aryans in Taxila were exposed to both Persian and Greek influences which enriched the city as a famed centre of learning and by the time of our period the fame of Taxila had risen to the pinnacle of its glory. And students from different parts of India, especially from Kashi, Rajagriha and Mithila of eastern India which was then fast coming under the spell of Buddhism flocked to Taxila for higher learning.

Taxila's system of education during the Sutra Age was not different from the system prevailing in other parts of India. It was like the Vedic schools, a domestic system of education where individual teachers sometimes admitted upto 500 students who had completed 16 years of age and who came from all classes of the Aryan society. Tuition was imparted either on payment of 1,000 pieces of coin in advance or on rendering services to the teacher concerned. A teacher admitting some 500 students had to depend on senior students as his assistants and had to seek public help and charity in running his school since only the rich among the students could pay him an advance fee and the rest constituting the majority of his students offered their services for free board and lodging. However, residence with the teacher was not compulsory as in the case of the Prince Junha of Kashi who attended his school from his own house at Taxila.

The duration of studentship at Taxila was normally seven years and the subjects offered for study were vast and varied: Vedatrayi, Vedanta, Vyakarana, Ayurveda, eighteen Sippas or Arts, Astronomy, Agriculture, Commerce, Law and Military Science. Choice of a subject did not depend upon the class or caste of a student and we have numerous cases of Brahman boys who instead of opting for Vedas or liberal arts chose such ecstatic subjects as archery, magic charms, charms for commanding all things of sense, divining from signs of the body[1] and hunting. As Taxila came under the Greek influence from 326 B.C. onwards in our Age, Greek language, Greek Military Science and Greek Art were also included in the courses offered at Taxila.

From the evidences in Jatakas it may be said that except in religious scriptures, lessons were imparted from written works and most of the lessons taught were followed up by practical applications.

While the practical application in some subjects like medicine, where search for medicinal plants and surgery was to be conducted under the careful eye of the teacher, in other subjects the practical course was left to be completed by the students themselves after they had left Taxila. Thus, we read of a Brahmana student "of a market town in the north country" who went as far as Andhra to practise his skill in archery learnt at Taxila. Similarly the five Pandava brothers of the Mahabharata "travelled about with the idea of mastering local customs" after learning them at Taxila. And finally, a Kashi student who returned home after learning eighteen Sippas or Arts at Taxila was asked by his parents to demonstrate his knowledge in them.

Benares or Kashi noted as a Brahmanical centre of learning in the days of Ajatasatru was fast receding into the background in the Sutra Age and no serious student from Benares would have regarded his higher education complete without a visit to Taxila more than a thousand miles away which took months of hazardous and risky journey to reach the place. In this context it is interesting to note from the Jatakas or birth stories about the Buddha, the story of Brahmadatta, the king of Benares, who sent his son to Taxila for higher learning.

One day the king called his son, also named Brahmadatta and now 16 years old, gave him one-soled sandals, a sunshade of leaves and a thousand pieces of money and said to him "My son, get you to Takkasiia, and study there". The boy obeyed his father. Arriving at Taxila, he searched for the teacher of his choice and when he spotted him after a lecture walking up and down at the door of his house, he took off his sandals, closed his sunshade and with a respectful greeting stood still where he was. The teacher welcomed the weary lad, gave him food and asked him after he had taken some rest:

"Where have you come from?"
"From Kashi."
"Whose son are you?"
"I am the son of the King of Kashi."
"What brings you here?"
"I come to learn."
"Well, have you brought a teacher's fee? Or, do you want to attend on me in return for teaching you?"
"I have brought a fee with me."

And with this the Prince of Kashi laid at the feet of his teacher his purse containing thousand pieces of money and was admitted to the school for study in his chosen subject for the next seven years.

Most students from Kashi to Taxila on their return home set themselves up as teachers of subject like magic charms, divinations and other esoteric subjects which they had learnt at Taxila. In the Sutra Age, Kashi specialised in certain subjects like music and we read of a School of Music presided over by an expert who was "the chief of his kind in all India". However, traditional subjects like the Vedas, Vedangas and the Rahasyas retained their importance in Kashi despite the emergence of Buddhism and Jainism in eastern India and we read of a very famous teacher at Kashi who had in his school 500 young Brahmana students maintained by the generosity of the "Benares folk".

Extent of Knowledge by the Time of the Sutra Age

Since the Aryans came to India in the early part of the second millennium B.C. the best brains of their priestly class were deeply absorbed in the mysteries of the universe as expressed in their compositions of the hymns of the Rig Veda. The search for supreme knowledge or Brahman continued throughout the succeeding centuries and in the process they unravelled the mystery of many a natural phenomenon of the universe. By the time of the Sutra Age the Aryans knew about the existence of the seven planets through observation with the naked eye and added two more to the list, Rahu and Ketu, the ascending and descending nodes of Moon. The seven planets are Surya or Sun, Chandra or Moon, Budha or Mercury, Sukra or Venus, Mangala or Mars, Brihaspati or Jupiter and Sani or Saturn. They also knew the 27 Nakshatras or stars which formed the constellations of these seven planets. They knew further through Greek influence that the zodiac was divided into 12 parts – Mesha or Aries, Vrishabha or Taurus, Mithuna or Gemini, Kataka or Cancer, Simha or Leo, Kanya or Virgo, Tula or Libra, Dhanus or Sagittarius, Makara or Capricornus, Kumbha or Aquarius and Mina or Pisces. With their achievement in mathematics, the Aryans, however, outdistanced the Greeks in their knowledge of astronomy which they considered sufficient by the time of the Sutra Age for the purpose of settling the dates and times at which periodical sacrifices were to be performed and never used their knowledge for prognosticating the future which they used to do by the Art of Divination taught in the Vedic schools, particularly at Taxlia.

For purposes of calculating the date and time of a sacrifice, the Aryan priestly class mainly relied on the moon. It was the Tithi or lunar day which formed the basic unit of such calculations. Approximately thirty Tithis formed a lunar month of 29½ days. A Tithi or a lunar day might begin anytime of the solar day and the Tithi current at sunrise was taken into consideration for the whole day which was given its number for the Paksha, there being two Pakshas, Sukla and Krishna, which divided a lunar month into two halves of fifteen Tithis each. A year consisted of 12 lunar months which was again divided into six seasons of two months each – Grishma or summer, Varsha or rains, Sarad or autumn, Hemanta or mild winter and Sitha or extreme winter.

The Aryan priestly class also knew by the time of the Sutra Age that the universe was classified by five elements – earth, air, fire, water, and Akasha or ether. These five elements were thought of as medium of five sense impressions: earth of smell, air of feeling, fire of vision, water of taste, and ether of sound. The Brahmanical and the Buddhist schools of thought believed that all the elements other than ether were atomic and therefore eternal. Pakudha Katyayana, an older contemporary of the Buddha used to teach on this subject[2] which was further developed by the Vaishesika school during the Sutra Age. According to this School the atom or Anu which was quite invisible to the human eye was a mere point in space, completely without magnitude. A single atom had no qualities, but only potentialities, which came into play when the atom combined with others. And before coming to form any material objects, atoms made primary combinations of diads and triads. Thus, the Vaishesika School of Philosophy was the School of Atomism par excellence.

In many other similar areas related to the study of the Vedangas in the Vedic schools, search for further knowledge had led to its substantial advancement by the time of the Sutra Age but in their conception of the structure of the universe, the Aryan minds faltered. They believed that the universe was shaped like an egg and called it Brahmanda. It was divided into twenty-one zones or regions, of which earth was seventh from top. Above the earth were six heavens of increasing beatitude and below it the seven stages of Patala, the nether world which was abode of Nagas and other mythical beings and below Patala lay Naraka which was again divided into seven zones of increasing misery and inhabited by souls in torment. The universe hung in empty space and was virtually isolated from other universes. They postulated earth as a flat disc of enormous size with mount Meru in its centre round which sun, moon and stars revolved. Around Meru were four Dvipa or continents separated from it by oceans, and named according to the great trees which stood on their shores opposite Meru. The southern continent, on which human beings dwelt, had a Jambu as its distinctive tree and was therefore called Jambudvipa. The southern zone of this continent separated from the rest by the Himalayas was "the land of the sons of Bharata", Bharatvarsa. Jambudvipa is separated from the next continent, Plakshadvipa, by an ocean of salt. Plakshadvipa in turn forms a concentric circle round Jambudvipa, forming seven circular continents, each divided from its neighbour by an ocean of different composition of treacle, wine, ghee, milk, curds and fresh water respectively. This fantastic geographical scheme of the universe and the earth held by the Aryan priestly class was really amazing in view of the fact that the kings who led their armies thousands of miles on their campaigns, the merchants who carried their wares from one end of India to the other end and beyond it, the sailors who sailed the ocean from Socotra to Canton or from Sopara to Alexandria and the scholars who travelled from one place to another, say, from Kashi to

Taxila in search of further knowledge as well as the pilgrims who visited the Buddhist sacred places and stupas all over India had a far greater and wider practical knowledge of geography than the Aryan theologians.

The Sutra Age was essentially an Age of Retrogression

Thus, geography remained an Achilles' heel in the otherwise remarkable knowledge accumulated by the Aryans since the days of the composition of the Rig Veda. The Sutrakaras who collected this knowledge from the past religious scriptures and put it in the framework of their Sutras wanted to leave it as the ultimate authority to the posterity for any judgement in any sphere of life. While they thus did a great service to us by preserving knowledge and culture from oblivion, they equally did us great harm by discouraging any further search for knowledge in areas where doubts about the truth existed. Thus, the astronomers who knew through Greek influence the conception of a flat earth to be an incorrect one, had to accept the theologians' conception of the flat earth nevertheless and adjust it to their correct knowledge of a spherical earth by making Meru the earth's axis, and the continents zones on the earth's surface. Similarly, there was little development in the Sanskrit language later since any such development was to be within the framework of Panini's grammar, Ashtadhyayi which he composed at the beginning of the Sutra Age. As late as the eighth century A.D., the great religious reformer Sankaracharya had to spend a lot of energy and time to prove that his philosophy of Advaitaism or Monism was in conformity with the teachings of the Upanishads. Thus, the Sutrakaras imprisoned learning and threw cold water on future creative thinking leading to its future stagnation.

In other ways also the Sutrakaras did great harm to the progress of the Aryan society, as for example, their Dharma Sutras not only introduced rigidity into the caste system relegating the Vaishyas and the Shudras to a further interior and despicable position in the Aryan society but also put a stop to the progress in surgical knowledge in Ayurveda by imposing a taboo on touching a corpse and by providing ceremonial purification for the violators. Again Dharma Sutras of Yajnavalkya and Manu provided for the discontinuance of the Upanayana ceremony for girls for Vedic studies as many of them could not utter the hymns correctly and advised for their early marriage as soon as they reached puberty, thereby making the women almost equal in status to that of the Sudras in respect of learning in the succeeding centuries. All these were retrograde steps, no doubt, and put the clock back on progress and creativity. Yet the Age of the Sutrakaras is remembered not merely as an age of compilations and codifications but also an age of creations and innovations. The Age gives us not only Panini and Patanjali, Manu and Yajnavalkya, Kapila and Gautama but also Kanada[3] and Kautilya – all products of the Vedic schools at Taxila. In defence of this galaxy of these Sutrakaras who are still revered and remembered respectfully, we can say that some of the retrograde steps, as for example in the case of women, were considered necessary to preserve the purity of the Aryan race and culture against the successive influx of foreigners or Mlechhas through the North-West and that the momentum in creative thinking proportionately declined to the momentum of progress in the material prosperity of the Aryan civilisation through the flourishing of various arts and crafts which added comforts and leisures to their lives in the succeeding centuries. We now propose to discuss the emergence of various vocations which acted as great diversions to the pursuits of intellectual knowledge in the next chapter.

Nots

1. Or the Art of Divination which the Aryans used in predicting future.
2. It was the Aryan philosophers who first propounded their theory on atom. The Greek Philosopher Democritus who first thought of atom in Europe came much later after the time of the Buddha.
3. Uluka Kanada the founder of the Vaishesika School of Philosophy, who was more interested in physics than in theology as his Sutras indicate.

7

The Vedic Schools and the Vocations: The Development of the Ingredients of a Prosperous Civilisation

Education to meet the Non-religious Needs of the Aryan Society

In the previous chapters we have analysed and discussed education as revealed in the religious literatures of the Aryans. We have also seen that such education includes a list of subjects which met the various non-religious needs and requirements of the contemporary Aryan society. They were, for example, Ayurvedic medicine, military science and various arts and crafts. The method of study of these subjects was different from the method of study of the religious scriptures and they required performance of a different kind of Upanayana ceremony or training by the students before these could be taught to them. The genesis of many of these subjects could be traced to the metrical hymns of the Atharva Veda which was presumably composed around 600 B.C. By that time the Aryans had started expanding eastwards down the Ganges and the basic elements in the Aryan civilisation had also started taking its shapes.

Ayurvedic Medicine

The foremost among these subjects as indicated above was the Ayurvedic medicine. The interest in the subject may be traced partly to the sacrifice where a knowledge of the anatomy of the physique of the animal for sacrifice was required to be known by the sacrificer at the time of its performance as well as partly to the Yoga or meditation where a knowledge of human physiology was imperative for its practitioner. As said before, we first come across with the Ayurvedic science in the Atharva Veda, the last of the four Vedas. The Atharva Veda gives us a list of contemporary diseases like fever, leprosy, jaundice, dropsy, scrofula, cough, opthalmia, baldness, and impotence. Among the surgical ailments mentioned by the Atharva Veda are fractures and wounds, bite of snakes and other injurious insects. It also prescribes appropriate herbs as remedies against these diseases as well as against the incidence of mania and insanity, the effects of poisons and other complaints. Thus, Atharva Veda reveals anatomical, physiological and pathological views which were neither magical nor religious.

We have already seen in the previous chapter that Ayurvedic medicine was one of the important programmes of study at the Vedic schools at Taxila. Admission to this programme was through a special Upanayana ceremony where deities like Brahman, Prajapati, the two Asvins and Indra and sages associated with the development of Ayurvedic science like Dhanvantari, Bharadvaja and Atreya were invoked. The study of Ayurvedic medicine including a six months probationary period according to Susruta Samhita lasted nearly seven years and was open to all classes including the Shudras. However, all candidates for admission to this programme were required to be physically fit with well-formed limbs such as eyes, nose, ears, tongue and teeth and mentally sound with good morals and manners such as courage, intelligence, patience, tenacity, capacity, humility and generosity. At the end of the seven-year programme of study, the students who came out successful through an examination were delivered an address by their teachers which reminds us of the Hippocrates Oath in modern medical profession. This is how Charaka who taught Ayurvedic medicine in the first century A.D. at Taxila advised his students after the completion of their training: "If you want success in your practice, wealth and fame, and heaven after your death, you must pray everyday on rising and going to bed for the welfare of all beings, especially of cows and Brahmanas, and you must strive with all your soul for the health of the sick. You must not betray your patients, even at the cost of your own life. You must not get drunk or commit evil, or have evil companions. You must be pleasant of speech and thoughtful, always striving to improve your knowledge. When you go to the home of a patient you should direct your words, mind, intellect and senses nowhere but to your patient and his treatment, Nothing that happens in the house of the sick man must be told outside, nor must the patient's condition be told to anyone who might do harm by that knowledge to the patient or to another".

It is also clear from the address of Charaka to his successful Ayurvedic students that around the birth of Jesus Christ the teachers of Ayurvedic medicine had developed the ethical codes including the duties and responsibilities of the practitioners in Ayurvedic medicine to such an extent as to lay claim to its professionalisation. And, as a matter of fact, Ayurvedic medicine became a highly reputed and lucrative profession of many a brilliant student belonging to the four classes of the Aryan society. A king's license or authorisation from him was required before one could start practising medicine – a quack or an unsuccessful student in medicine practising it without an authorisation was liable to be punished by the king. It is obvious that such authorisation was issued only on the recommendation or the certification by a teacher of his student who had successfully followed a prescribed course in Ayurveda under him.

By the time of the Buddha there were many practitioners in Ayurvedic medicine in the capital cities of Kashi, Koshala, Magadha and Avanti. However, the most outstanding among them was the son of a Rajagriha courtesan, Salavati, who as an infant was thrown away on a heap of dust. Prince Abhaya of Rajagriha rescued him, brought him up and sent him to Taxlia to study Ayurveda. He was Jivaka Komarabhachcha who on his return from Taxila cured the Magadhan king Seniya Bimbisara of his fistula by an ointment and became his personal physician. Under the orders of king Bhimbisara, he had to look after the health of the members of the royal family as well as that of the Buddha and his followers. Jivaka was stationed in the Magadhan capital Rajagriha but had to often attend calls from such distant places as Saketa, Kashi, and Ujjayini. At Kashi, Jivaka performed a very difficult operation on the son of a Setthi or merchant, who had got his intestines entangled by a gymnastic or acrobatic feat. As a result, the son of the Setthi "could not digest anything nor could he ease himself in the regular way, and looked discoloured with the veins standing out upon his skin". Jivaka "cut through the skin of the belly, drew the twisted intestines out and showed them to his wife." He then "disentangled the twisted intestines, put them back into their right position, stitched the skin together, anointed with salve". The Setthi gave Jivaka 16,000 Karshapanas[1] when his son came round. The Mahavagga which records this incident also tells us how Jivaka had cured a Setthi at Rajagriha of his head disease by surgical operation and the king Pradyot of Avanti of his jaundice by administering him boiled ghee "with various other drugs" so that it could take "the colour, smell and taste of an astringent decoction", as the patient had a great aversion to ghee. The successful career of Jivaka indicates the proficiency which Ayurveda had attained by the time of the Buddha. We may now ask the question how was this course of Ayurvedic medicine studied? Ayurveda had two aspects – theory and practice and both aspects were studied simultaneously under the careful eye of a teacher. The Ayurvedic medicine consisted of diverse disciplines – pathology, medicine, toxicology, blood test, bones, snake-bite and surgery. Specialisation was encouraged and the students were expected to master the different branches of learning from different experts. Whether there were provisions of hospitals as in modern times for studying the practical aspect or Prayoga of Ayurvedic medicine we do not know. However, the existence of charitable dispensaries where persons were treated free was noted by Fa Hien as late as fifth century A.D. in big cities like Pataliputra, could possibly fill in the gap. Since the theory aspect or Shastra could only be learnt from works written in Sanskrit, students were required to be proficient in it. As in Vedic schools, students were also required to understand the meaning of Slokas and Padas while memorising them.

The whole conception of Ayurvedic medicine was based on Dosa or humours and the Ayurvedic teachers maintained that health was maintained through the even balance of the three vital fluids of the body – wind, gall and mucus and connected them with the scheme of the three Gunas or universal qualities associated with virtue, passion and dullness respectively, However, they never realised, despite their awareness of the existence of microscopic forms of life that these might cause diseases. Nevertheless, they insisted on scrupulous cleanliness as they understood it and recognised the therapeutic value of fresh air and light. Their Pharmacopoeia was quite large and comprised animal, vegetable and mineral products and by the end of our period many Ayurvedic drugs were known to the outside world in Europe through Persian, Greek and Arabic contacts such as the oil of the Chaulmugra tree traditionally used in curing leprosy, still the basis of its modern treatment.

In surgery which was an empirical one, the Ayurvedic science reached a degree of excellence which was unique among the contemporary civilisations of the world. The students were first taught how to hold and use their surgical instruments including knives on fruits like pumpkins, cucumbers, and watermelons. They were taught how to puncture the veins of dead animals, to hold the probe on dry Alabu fruits, and to do scarification on stretched pieces of leather covered with hair. They also learnt how to do sewing on thin pieces of cloth or skin, how to apply bandages on stuffed human figures and how to use caustics on soft pieces of flesh. The novice was then gradually initiated to use his skill in extracting darts, cleansing wounds as well as in cutting the diseased parts of the body which could not be healed. Corpses used to be decomposed in water and surgery students were required to dissect them and visualise the nature of skin, muscles, arteries, bones and internal organs of the human body. As a matter of fact, despite the taboo imposed by the Sutrakaras on contact with dead bodies, by the end of our period, the Ayurvedic surgeons were experts in caesarian operation, bone-setting and in repairing noses, ears and lips, lost or injured in battle or by judicial mutilation. It will not be out of the way to mention here that the skill of our Ayurvedic surgeons in the art of rhinoplasty reached such an excellence that the surgeons of the East India Company in the Eighteenth Century were not ashamed to learn it from their modern successors.

It is not merely in the case of human beings but also in the case of animals, Ayurvedic science developed considerably through the expertise of families closely associated with agriculture and animal husbandry. Agriculture could not be done without draught animals, wars could not be fought without horses and elephants and so a knowledge about their diseases and remedies was imperative. In the Mahabharata, Nakul and Sahadev, the two Pandava brothers were said to be experts on the diseases of horses and Ashoka took pride in the fact that he had not only provided medicine for men but also for animals and the doctrine of non-violence encouraged the endowment of animal refuges and homes for sick and aged animals.

Military Science

The skill of a surgeon must be in frequent demands among the Aryan chiefs and tribes who were not only occupied with subjugating the non-Aryans or Dasas but also in constant internecine warfare among themselves. Each village was asked to learn the art of defending it against the attack of a hostile tribe and as kingdoms arose, each king, began to maintain a huge army consisting of infantry, cavalry, chariots and elephants to defend his kingdom against the attack of his jealous neighbours. The Asvamedha sacrifice through which a king could proclaim and establish his supremacy over his neighbours and become a Samrat or emperor often meant fierce warfare among themselves. In the prevailing situation in Ancient India warfare opened up new avenues for employment to classes other than the Kshatriyas, particularly the Vaishyas and the Shudras. And we often come across with evidences when enterprising persons organised military training and supplied the kings and chiefs with trained soldiers in return for lands, money and horses.

However, courses on warfare, as we have already seen, were regularly taught at Vedic schools at Taxila which was open to Persian and Greek influences of military art. Elephant lore, horsemanship, cavalry training, and use of contemporary weapons including bows and arrows[2] were taught at Taxila. In one such school at Taxlia 103 princes from different parts of India could be seen receiving training in different branches of the military science. According to Dhanurveda Samhita of Vasishtha, an Upanayana ceremony had to be performed by the candidate for admission to military training, who was given a weapon while his preceptor uttered a Vedic Mantra or hymn. The weapon given varied from class to class – a Brahmana was given a bow, a Kshatriya a sword, a Vaishya a lance and a Shudra a mace. The preceptor or the teacher was required to be an expert in the use of seven weapons, that is, the bow, the disc, the sword, the spear, the mace, the arms and the Kharika. The completion of the military training was marked by Chhurikabandhanam, whereby a dagger was tied to the dress of a pupil.

However, the military schools at Taxila required a fee[3] which only the members of the royal families and affluent classes like merchants and traders could afford. It is therefore obvious that the majority of the Aryans who were willing to take up this profession but were unable not only to pay the required fees but also to undertake and expensive and hazardous journey to the extreme North-West, were trained locally by experts and it is these persons who often swelled the rank of infantry men of a local chieftain or king.

Arts and Crafts

We have already stated earlier that the list of curricula at the Vedic schools includes besides Ayurvedic science and military art, various arts and crafts which required considerable practical training. It is on – the principle of practical training involved that the Jatakas rightly differentiate between the religious subjects like the Vedas and the Silpas proper which could not be learnt properly without some practical skills. However, the Brahmanical list as well as that of Milinda Panha which was probably inspired by the former do not make any such difference. According to the Brahmanical list the Vedic schools at Taxlia by the end of the Sutra Age used to teach eighteen Sastras comprising four Vedas, six Vedangas, four Upangas consisting of Purana, Naya, Mimamsa, Dharmasastra and four Upavedas consisting of Ayurveda, Dhanurveda, Gandharvaveda and Sthapatya or, according to some, Arthasastra while the Milinda Panha in the first century A.D. gives us a list of nineteen Sippas or Silpas, Holy Tradition and Secular Law; Samkhya, Naya, Vaiseshika; arithmetic, music, medicine, four Vedas, Puranas, Ithihasas; astronomy, Spells, Hetuvidya; magic; military art; poetry; and conveyancing.

The contemporary religious literatures of the Aryans, both Brahmanical and Buddhist, put the total number of arts and crafts described as Kalas at 64. These 64 arts and crafts cover all aspects and all needs and requirements of the emerging Aryan civilisation. While at the one end these include painting, music, dancing, architecture, sculpture, carpentry, smithery, pottery, jewellery, tannery, weaving and spinning, constructing ships, chariots, carts, weapons, tanks, wells, grafting of trees for abnormal fruits, at the other they cover such daily activities like cooking, preparing drinks from flowers, fruits and plants, wrestling, gambling, dressing, bedding, washing and even shaving!

Agriculture and animal husbandry were the traditional occupations of the Aryans and these cut across their castes and classes. We know that in the Vedic schools those pupils who were found unfit for higher learning were sent to the plough or to the loom and that their Brahmana teachers used to keep fields and cows which were attended to by the students residing at their teachers' houses as Brahmacharins. We also know that the Kshatriya king Janaka discovered Sita, later the wife of the legendary Rama, at the furrow of his plough while cultivating his field.

Many of the arts and crafts which related to agriculture and animal husbandry were learnt through families while those related to Ayurvedic medicine like a knowledge of metals, minerals and herbs or of extracting arrows and spears stuck in human and animal bodies and of incising open wounds and blood-vessels as well as those related to Military science like the art of forming an army into Vyuhas or groups in the battlefield, of using a bow and arrow or of driving a chariot, elephant and horse were taught as allied to their main subjects of study in the Vedic schools.

Guru-Shishya Parampara

However, for most of the crafts there was the traditional system of learning through Guru-Shishya Parampara which at present goes by the name of apprenticeship among us. Narada, in the Age of the Sutras, who along with many other subjects studied some arts and crafts and himself taught these to his students later, has thus vividly described the method of teaching them in his Dharmasastra:

> If a young man wishes to be initiated into the art of his own craft, he must first obtain the sanction of his relations and then proceed to live with his master, after previously fixing the period of his training or apprenticeship. Then the master must impart to his pupil his training at his own house where he is to provide his board and lodging. He must not make the apprentice perform other work but must treat him like a son. If the apprentice deserts his master who duly instructs him and is not at fault in any way he should be compelled by forcible means to stay with his master and will be liable to corporal punishment and confinement. In case the training of an apprentice is completed before the stipulated time, he should not leave, but continue at his master's place upto the limit of the stipulated time and all the fruits of his work done during this time will be his master's. When the apprentice has mastered the art of his craft within the stipulated time, he should make gifts to his teacher according to his means and then take leave of him. An apprentice after graduation may have his services retained by his master who will then have the right to employ him after settling his remuneration with reference to his qualifications. In such a case the pupil should not seek service with others.

The rules of apprenticeship as given by Narada indicate that admission to a craft was free and open to all. In the Aryan society economic ends were not ends in themselves but must subserve the higher religious and spiritual ends of life and so different castes were to pursue different crafts in consonance with the ideals and values of each caste. While deviations often occurred in the earliest time of our period, the situation later changed with the elevation of the Brahmanas and Kshatriyas at the cost of the Vaishyas and the Shudras. Manual arts and crafts began to be held in low esteem leading to their boycott by the Brahmanas and the Kshatriyas. However, this happened towards the end of our period.

The apprenticeship system under which a pupil lived and worked at his master's house was significant in that it enabled him to closely observe his master at work – his skill, his secrets and his method which led him to imbibe his master's talent and become successful as a craftsman. While the home of the artisan functioned as the school, the collective interests of the craft as a whole in a particular area or region were administered by an organisation called Shreni or guild. Each guild had its own rules to administer its craft. According to Gautama, the important guilds belonged to those of cultivators, herdsmen, traders, money-lenders and artisans to which Brihaspati adds, the guilds of artists and dancers. Thus all these guilds may be taken to function like schools of fine arts and crafts in those days.

Centralised Control

By the time of Chandragupta Maurya (C. 323-299 B.C.) the activities of the 64 arts and crafts had expanded to such an extent that they called for a centralised control. Thus, the Kosadhyaksha looked after the business in pearls, gems and diamonds as well as in sandalwood, cotton and silken clothes such as Dukuia or fine, Kshauma or coarse, Kauseya, or silk, Chinapatta or Chinese. The Akaradhyaksha supervised the metallurgical industry and was required to be proficient in knowledge of copper and other minerals as well as in the art of distillation and condensation of mercury. He was assisted by a staff of experts in mineralogy, mining labourers and equipped with necessary apparatus. The Lohadhyaksha dealt with the manufacture of copper, lead, tin, mercury, brass, bronze or bell-metal, sulphate of arsenic, and the like. There were besides the above, a Department of Salt which leased the salt fields, a Department of Gold and Silver, a Department of Agriculture, a Department of Navigation which looked after traffic and transport by water and finally a Department of Gambling under Dyutadhyaksha which supervised the gambling halls which had to be licensed and hired. Thus, Kautiliya Arthsastra which gives account of these departments under Chandragupta Maurya is an important authority on the flourishing of various Kalas or arts and crafts in India nearly three hundred years before the birth of Jesus Christ.

Guilds

By the first century A.D. these various arts and crafts had crystallised into well-defined vocations in the form of Shreni or guilds, embracing almost all trades and industries, in every important town. The artistic skill of the craftsman could be seen not only in the production of semi-transparent silks and muslin, excellent jewellery, the bright hard polish of the type of pottery usually called "northern black polished ware" but also in the enormous monolithic pillars on which Ashoka engraved his edicts, stupas and monasteries including the famous tower of Kanishka at Purushapura or Peshawar and numerous caves hewn out of solid rocks in different parts of the country. It is, however, more in sculpture than in architecture that the artist trained in the Kala left his mark: several important schools of sculpture including those at Bharhut, Bodh Gaya, Sanchi, Mathura and Gandhara, and Amravati flourished in different parts of India. The Gandhara School of Sculpture as well as that of Mathura which were lavishly patronised by the Scythian kings are famous for images of the Buddha with great and meticulous attention of the accuracy of their physical details. The religious motifs in such arts show that material prosperity is not an end in itself but is an essential means to the achievement of emancipation of soul.

Trade and Commerce as an Index to the Material Prosperity of Aryan Civilisation

When arts and crafts flourished, trade and commerce also prospered. By the time of the Buddha, recognised trade-routes covered most of northern India, and by the Mauryan times similar routes existed in the southern India. The great rivers like the Ganges and the Indus in the northern India and the Narmada and the Godavari in the southern India with their branches and tributaries were used to carry both goods and passengers in vessels, large and small. Luxury articles like spices, sandalwood, gold and gems from the South, silks and muslins from Bengal and Benares, musk, saffron and yaks' tails from the hills and metals like iron from South Bihar, copper from the Deccan, Rajasthan and western Himalayas and salt from the sea-coast and from various rock-salt deposits, notably in the Salt Range in the Punjab, formed the chief items of long-distance trade.

Many of the luxury items of the inland trade were exported to the countries, east and west of India. In the east, the Ganges Basin was served by the river port of Champa, from which ships sailed down the Ganges and coasted to the South and Ceylon. By Mauryan times with the eastward expansion of Aryan culture, Tamralipti became the main seaport and from the beginning of the Christian era, ships from Tamralipti sailed to South-East Asia and Indonesia. In the west the chief sea ports were Bhrigukaccha, Supara near Mumbai and Patala on the Indus delta. Since the invasion of Alexander the Great in 326 B.C. the land route from India to the Mediterranean coast running through Persia and the shores of the Caspian Sea to Syria and Asia Minor had become more familiar. The trade with Rome and other Western countries was carried through the port of Alexandria where goods, carried by sea up to the Red Sea coast, were transported either by land or by small boats through canals of the Nile. The merchants and seamen of Roman Egypt knew India well, and there survives a remarkable seaman's guide, compiled in Greek by an anonymous author towards the end of the first century A.D., *The Periplus of the Erythraean Sea*. The main requirements of the West were spices, perfumes, jewels and fine textiles, but lesser luxuries such as sugar, rice and ghee were also exported, as well as ivory, both raw and worked. Iron, dyestuffs such as lac and indigo as well as animals like elephants, tigers, lions and buffaloes which the Roman emperors and provincial governors needed for their wild beast shows, were also exported from India. Smaller animals and birds such as monkeys, parrots and peacocks found their way to Rome in even larger quantities as pets of wealthy Roman ladies. India imported pottery and glassware, wine and fig which was mainly popular among the members of the royal families as well as tin, lead, coral and slave-girls. The balance of trade was very unfavourable to the West and resulted in a serious drain of gold from the Roman empire as noted later by Pliny who, while inveighing against the degenerate habits of his day, computed the annual drain to the East as 100 million sesterces, "so dearly we pay for our luxury and our women". No doubt with the aid of surplus gold, Kanishka was able to add the institution of a gold coinage to the existing medium of exchange of copper and silver coins.

Thus, by the beginning of the Christian era with the ascendancy of Magadha over the neighbouring kingdoms of Kashi, Koshala, Videha and Avanti and the subsequent building up of the Mauryan empire with its contact with outside world in Asia and Europe, the Aryan civilisation was poised for a grandiose take off. There is no doubt about the contribution of the various vocations or Kalas taught and trained in the Vedic schools to the material prosperity of the Indian civilisation and thereby it leads to the demolition of the much accepted myth that the education in Ancient India was highly spiritual and classical, and not practical at all.

Notes

1. Copper coins, each weighing a little more than 146 grains.
2. We know from the Mahabharata and the Ramayana how devastative and destructive such weapons could became in a war.
3. Normally thousand pieces of coin, silver or copper.

8

The Ascendancy of the Vedic Schools and of the Buddhist Viharas

Ascendancy of the Vedic Schools immediately after the Sutra Age

In one of the preceding chapters we have seen how the Brahmanical system of learning after having rejuvenated itself through the works of the Sutrakaras reasserted itself to meet the challenge of Buddhism. And in this respect it was largely successful for nearly two hundred years after the Sutrakaras had begun their work of simplification and compilation of the Vedic scriptures and other religious works mainly because of the patronage extended to it by the kings of Magadha and Videha in eastern India.

In the death of Bimbisara who is said to have been assassinated by his own son Ajatasatru in 493 B.C., the Buddha lost a great friend and patron. Bimbisara, as we have already seen, helped the Buddha with his own personal physician Jivaka, erected a Vihara for him and asked the officials of his kingdom to be instructed by the Buddha and his followers. The Buddha survived the death of Bimbisara only by seven years till 486 B.C. when he achieved his own Nirvana but the last seven-year period of his life as well as that of his disciples in Magadha was often marred and embarrassed by Ajatasatru, the new king of Magadha at the instigation of Devadatta, the schismatic cousin of the Buddha.

It is obvious that Buddhism did not receive the friendly and sympathetic support under Ajatasatru as it did under his father,

Bimbisara. Besides, Ajatasatru, as we already know having come across his name in the religious scriptures of the time, was a great scholar and patron of Brahmanical learning. The Kaushitaki Upanishad informs us how the Brahmana scholar, Gargya Balaki "well read in the Veda" was silenced by the display of superior knowledge on every topic by Ajatasatru and how the greatly impressed Balaki approached Ajatasatru "with fuel in hand" to become his student..." Let me attend thee as thy pupil", Balaki had said to Ajatasatru.

However, Ajatasatru had a rival in the patronisation of Brahmanical learning in eastern India in king Janaka of Videha, the legendary father-in-Law of Rama, the hero of the great epic, Ramayana. Janaka performed Asvamedha, patronised Yajnavalkya and gathered in his court most of the celebrities of the Kuru Panchala countries "much as the intellects of Athens gathered at the court of Macedonian princes". The Brihadaranyaka Upanishad mentions that the literary patronage of Janaka made his contemporary Ajatasatru admit that he could hardly find any learned man to patronise, because all of them were running after Janaka and settling down at his court.

In one respect Ajatasatru outdid the king Janaka and this was in extending his political ascendancy over the neighbouring territories. He defeated his aged maternal uncle, Prasenjit, the king of Koshala and annexed Kashi to Magadha. He went to war with the tribal confederation of the Vrijis on the north bank of the Ganges and annexed their lands including the capital city, Vaishali and to prevent the Vrijians from descending in sporadic raids on the Magadhan capital, Rajagriha, he fortified the village Pataligrama on the confluence of the Ganges and the Sone. He thus laid the foundations of the famous fortress which within 100 years of his reign developed into the stately city of Pataliputra and became the imperial capital of the Mauryas and the Guptas later. Ajatasatru also annexed Koshala when its king Virudhaka who had earlier deposed his father Prasenjit, the maternal uncle of Ajatasatru, mysteriously died soon after massacring the Sakyas, the tribes of the Buddha, in the Himalayan foothills. Ajatasatru later fought Pradyota, king of Avanti, one of the four great kingdoms of the time and though he was not successful in capturing Avanti, he was at least able to certainly create the most powerful empire of Magadha unknown to contemporary India, controlling both banks of the Ganges from Benares to the borders of Bengal which remained beyond the pale of Aryan civilisation at that time.

Under Ajatasatru and his successors Darsaka and Udayi, Brahmanism and Brahmanical system of learning was certainly dominant in the Magadhan empire and continued to be so under Nandivardhana and Mahanandin of the Saisunaga dynasty, the last of whom is said to have had a son, by a Shudra woman named Mahapadma or Mahapadmapti Nanda, with whom began a line of Shudra or semi-Shudra kings. The new king, though of humble origin, was a vigorous ruler who exterminated all Kshatriyas and became sole monarch and held sway in Kalinga or southern Orissa and the contiguous part of the Northern Circars. Mahapadma was succeeded by his eight sons, of whom the last was named Dhana Nanda.

He owned a vast treasure, and commanded a huge army of 20,000 cavalry, 200,000 infantry, 2,000 chariots and no less than 3,000 elephants. The rule of the Nandas roughly cover a period of 100 years and it is obvious that the Brahmanas and the Kshatriyas, the two most powerful groups in the Aryan society could not be happy under a line of Shudra kings. Added to this, the conduct of Dhana Nanda towards his subjects was so 'low' that he was detested and held cheap by them. The disaffected element found a leader in Chandragupta, who, with the help of the Taxilan Brahmana scholar Kautilya alias Chanakya, overthrew him and laid the foundation of the illustrious family of the Mauryas.

With Chandragupta Maurya as emperor and Kautilya as his Purohita, Brahmanism recovered its lost supremacy, probably obscured under the Nandas, and extended its influences as far as Afghanistan which became a part of the Maurya empire when Chandragupta Maurya defeated Alexander's general Seleucus Nicator who was left in charge of Alexander's Indian conquests after his invasion of India in 326 B.C. Chandragupta entered into a matrimonial alliance with Seleucus who later sent an ambassador Magasthenes to reside at the Mauryan Court at Pataliputra. Chandragupta remained a firm believer in Brahmanical faith till his last years when he was drawn to Jainism, abdicated his throne in favour of his son, Bindusara, and fasted to death like a Jaina monk at the great Jaina temple at Sravana Belgola in Karnataka. Bindusara who maintained his hold over his father's empire and possibly added to it parts of the Deccan followed his father's Brahmanical faith and maintained at Pataliputra a court of learned persons. He was keen to add a Greek Sophist to it and requested Antiochus 1, the Selucid king of Syria to send one along with a present of figs and wine. The latter obliged Bindusara by sending him figs and wine only, with a reply that the Greek philosophers were not for export. In 269 B.C. Bindusara was succeeded by his son, Ashoka, the greatest and the noblest ruler India has ever known and indeed one of the great kings of the world, whose reign of 36 years became a turning point in the history of religion in the world, not to speak of India only.

Ascendancy of the Buddhist Viharas

With Ashoka the stars of the Buddhism and of the Buddhist Viharas were ascendant though in the first eight years of his reign he was a traditional inheritor of a king's devotion to Devas or gods and the Brahmanas. The sight of misery and bloodshed following his conquest of Kalinga smote his conscience and awakened in his breast sincere feelings of repentance and sorrow. In one of his oldest inscriptions probably drafted by Ashoka himself, the monarch says: "Just after taking of Kalinga the beloved of the Gods began to follow Righteousness, to love Righteousness, to give instructions in Righteousness". He became a lay worshipper or Upasaka of the Buddha, and went out to Bodh-Gaya and established intimate relations with the Buddhist Samgha or Order. This apparently galvanised Ashoka into greater exertions for the cause of religion and morality. He made a deep study of the Buddhist scriptures and undertook Dharma-Yatra in place of Vihara-yatra of his ancestors. In the course of these tours he visited the people of the country instructing them in Dharma and questioning them about Dharma. At the end of 256 nights spent on tour, Ashoka was satisfied about the influence of Dharma on them. Ten years after the first tour, he undertook a similar one and in the course of the second tour, he visited the birth place of Sakyamuni and that of a previous Buddha and worshipped at these holy spots.

Two years after his first tour, Ashoka requisitioned the services of important officials like Rajukas,[1] Pradesikas[2] and Yuktas[3] to help him bring the message of Dharma to the doors of all his subjects in the remotest corners of his far-flung empire. He ordered his officers to publish rescripts on morality and set out on tours every five years to give instructions in morality as well as for ordinary business. The rescripts and proclamations were to be engraved on rocks, existing stone pillars and on Dharma Stambha or "pillars of morality" which were to be set up. These orders must have taxed the capacity of the official severely for Ashoka soon realised that these could better be executed by special functionaries in charge of religion. These new officials, called Dharma Mahamatras, were employed in the imperial capital as well as in the outlying towns and tribal territories, especially on the western and north-western border of his empire. They busied themselves with the affairs of all sects and people including prince and princess, householders and their servants, jailed prisoners and homeless ascetics. Ashoka posted reporters everywhere to keep him informed of the activities of his officials and subjects. Thus, Ashoka gave up the old policy of chastisement of turbulent forest tribes and troublesome neighbours and evolved a new policy of peace and forbearance, of conquest by morality – "the reverberation of the war-drum" was to become "the reverberation of the law" – "Bherl Ghosha" gave way to "Dhamma Ghosha".

Thus, Ashoka geared his entire administration to implementing moral principles based basically on the Buddhist scriptures in different parts of his empire and he created an example by practising what he preached – he banned animal sacrifices, at least in his capital, regulated the slaughter of animals for food, completely forbidding the killing of certain species as well as the holding of festive gatherings to prevent loss of life or the practice of immorality, developed the cultivation of medicinal herbs which with other drugs, were supplied to men and animals alike and finally improved communications by planting fruit trees along the roads to provide shade and food, digging wells at intervals, and setting up rest houses for weary travellers.

However, Ashoka's Buddhism, though enthusiastic, was not exclusive. More than once he declared that all sects were worthy of respect and he dedicated artificial rock-cut caves to the sect of Ajivikas, the followers of Gosala and were among the chief rivals of the Buddhists. He continued to style himself the "Beloved of the Devas or Gods" and never became an enemy of the Devas and the Brahmanas or any other religious fraternity. He laid special emphasis on concourse and the guarding of speech and warned people against the evil consequences of using harsh language in respect of other sects.

Ashoka thus imbibed the true spirit of Buddhism the virtues of compassion and liberality and there is no doubt that both by precepts and deeds he made Buddhism a living force regulating the lives of his subjects in his empire. He was not only keen in the exposition of the Buddhist Dharma but was equally keen to see that it endured for many, many years to come. He impressed upon the monks the need of a correct exposition of the true doctrine as well as maintaining the integrity of the Buddhist Viharas. With that end in view, a great council of the Buddhist monks was held at Pataliputra at which the Pali canon was finally codified and after which missions were sent throughout the length and breadth of India and beyond. Thus, it was in Ashoka's reign that Buddhism ceased to be a simple Indian sect and began its career as a world religion. In one of his inscriptions, Ashoka said that his policy of Dharma-Vijaya met with phenomenal success, and he claimed to have made, a spiritual conquest of the realms of his Hellenistic, Tamil and Ceylonese neighbours. It was however in Ceylon that the mission headed by prince Mahendra, a son or brother of Ashoka who became a Buddhist monk, was most successful in converting the ruler, Devanampiya Tissa and his subjects into Buddhism.

Ashoka ruled for 36 years and of these 36 years, 24 years were spent in providing active support to the spread of Buddhism. When the emperor, his family members and his officials were firm believers in Buddhism, the people at large could not but choose otherwise – and the Buddhist Viharas now came to dot different parts of the empire now stretching from Afghanistan to Andhra and Karnataka and from Gujarat to Bengal. One such Vihara which had its birth in the days of Ashoka was at the village of Nalanda near Rajagriha, old Magadhan capital, where Sariputta, a favourite disciple of the Buddha was born. Taranath in his *History of Buddhism* asserts that when Ashoka went to see his Chaitya, he added a temple to it, though Nalanda did not become educationally important before the rise of the Mahayana or the Great Vehicle of Buddhism at the beginning of the Christian era. Thus, whatever its position in the Buddha's lifetime and immediately after it, in Ashoka's days Buddhism was a distinct religion and the Buddhist system of education through Viharas was a dominant force and had gained sufficient prominence and strength even to attract a Brahmana scholar well-versed in the Vedas to it.

This is illustrated by the career of Nagasena, an esteemed Buddhist philosopher. At seven years of age Nagasena, a Brahmana boy, was sent to a Brahmana teacher with thousand pieces of coin to learn the three Vedas and other subjects. After gaining mastery over these, Nagasena's thirst for knowledge drove him to approach Rohana the Buddhist monk who lived at his hermitage at Vattaniya. However, Rohana would not instruct Nagasena unless and until he entered the Buddhist Order. When Nagasena entered it after obtaining permission from his parents, Rohana taught him Abhidhamma. And when Nagasena fully mastered Abhidhamma, he was sent by his teacher on an educational tour for discussion and discourses on the subject in the same way as the Vedic scholars used to do in the days of the Vedas and the Upanishads.

The Collapse of the Ashokan Empire deprived the Buddhist Viharas of Royal Support

However, when Ashoka died about 232 B.C., his empire began to fall apart and the governors of the important provinces, usually members of the royal families, established their virtual independence. The collapse of the empire may be partly because of the antagonism of the Brahmanas who had been relegated to a position of secondary importance after Ashoka's patronisation of Buddhism and partly because of the demoralisation of the Maurya army in view of the fact that Ashoka not only gave up military conquests and royal hunts, making the army nearly inactive for the most parts of his reign but also called upon his sons and other descendants not to think of fresh conquests but to take pleasure in "conquest by morality".

Revival of the Vedic Schools

However, for some fifty years Mauryan kings continued to rule in Magadha until, about 183 B.C., when Pushyamitra Sunga, a Brahman general of Brihadratha, the last Mauryan king, succeeded in gaining power by a palace revolution. Pushyamitra was a supporter of the orthodox faith and revived the ancient Vedic sacrifices in a grandiose scale, including the horse-sacrifice and he ruled from Vidisa[4], and not from Magadh surrounded by a circle of vassal states, small and great in varying degrees of subservience but some evidently autonomous enough to issue their own coins. Beyond the realm of Pushyamitra much of the old Mauryan empire was now independent and though little was known of Magadh the chief scene of the activities of the followers of the Buddha, there was no doubt about the flourishing state of Buddhism as attested by the remains at Bharhut and the stories of Pushyamitra's persecution of the Buddhist monks were probably exaggerated by sectarian tradition.

Foreign Invaders: The Greeks

However, contrary to Ashoka's expectations his Hellenistic contemporaries in the West Asia were not much impressed by the message of

Buddhism on non-violence. And as soon as the strong arm of Ashoka "who possessed the power to punish in spite of his repentance", was withdrawn, the Greeks poured once more into the Kabul valley, the Punjab and even the Gangetic region and threw all these provinces into confusion. The first invaders were the Bactrian Greeks. Demetrius, the son of successor of Euthydemus who had usurped Diodotus' son Diodotus II, governor of Bactria, early in the second century B.C., pressed further into India beyond the North-West Frontier which had probably broken away from the Mauryan empire. He and his successors occupied most of the Indus Valley and the Punjab and led great raids far into India, at least one of which, perhaps led by king Meanander, king of Sialkot in Punjab, reached Pataliputra. The Greek domains in India were divided into several petty kingdoms – those of the Kabul Valley and the district of Taxila chiefly ruled by kings of the line of Eucratides, who later usurped the Bactrian Greeks though the descendants of Euthydemus continued to rule in the Punjab and parts of the North-West.

Attitude of the Greek Kings towards Indian Religion

What was the attitude of the Greek kings towards the contemporary Indian religion, particularly Buddhism and Brahmanism? The Greeks while introducing Western theories of astrology, medicine and literature[5] to enrich Indian culture and though not completely merging with the Indian population, soon felt the impact of the Indian ways of thought and culture and made many compromises with their own culture to such an extent that Manu describes them as degenerate Kshatriyas or members of the warrior class and thus gives them a place in the contemporary Indian society. Many supported the orthodox creeds of Brahmanism as the Besnagar column which was erected by the Greek ambassador, Heliodorus in honour of the early Vaishnavite deity Vasudeva shows. Still many more became the followers of Buddhism and one of them is still specially remembered by Buddhism as the patron of Nagasena, the Brahmana philosopher, who became a Buddhist monk later. This was Milinda or the king Meanander who, as said earlier, ruled at Sialkot in the Punjab. His long discussions with the sage Nagasena were recorded in a well-known Pali text, "Milinda Panho" or "the Questions of Milinda". We can therefore say that the flourishing state of Buddhism reached under Ashoka as well as the Buddhist system of learning continued more or less unhampered.

The Sakas

However, the Greeks in Bactria were soon replaced by the Scythains under pressure from a nomadic people called by the Chinese Yuch-chih who also occupied Bactria. The Scythains, known as Sakas in India, moved on from Bactria to attack first the Parthian rulers of Iran and then the Greeks in India and as a result by the middle of the first century B.C. only a few petty Greek chiefs still ruled in India and the power of the Sakas reached as far as Mathura though for a brief period towards the end of the first century B.C., a line of kings with Iranian names, usually known as Pahlavas which included such important name as Gondophernes to whose kingdom St. Thomas first brought the knowledge of Christianity gained the suzerainty of North-West India.

The Kushans

The Pahlavas were in turn conquered by the Yuch-chih of Turki origin, who spoke an Iranian language like the Sakas. The various autonomous tribes of the Yuch-chih were consolidated by Kujula Kadphises of the tribe of Kushans and at some time in the first century A.D. Kujula and his son Vima Kadphises between them gained control of North-West India. Vima Kadphises was succeeded after a short interregnum by Kanishka who controlled all the western half of Northern India and at least as far as Benares and whose dominions in Central Asia were very extensive. The Chinese annals speak of a Kushana king, either Kanishka or one of the Kadphises who was soundly defeated by the great general Pan Chao for his arrogance in demanding the hand of a princess of the imperial house of Han.

We all know Kanishka to be a great patron of Buddhism – what about the Sakas who ruled North-West India before him? The Sakas continued the earlier practice of issuing coins with inscriptions in Greek on the obverse and in Prakrit on the reverse. As Prakrit was the language adopted by the Buddhist followers for ready access to the masses, it could be reasonably surmised that Buddhism continued to remain in the flourishing state and received a great impetus for further development under Kanishka.

Heydays of the Buddhist Viharas back again

Kanishka's administration was a very important one in the history of Buddhism. Numerous remains testify to the importance and popularity of Buddhism at the time, and it was now that it began to spread to Central Asia and the Far East. Some informations of the Indian religion had already reached China, but it exerted no real influence until now, when the Kushans and Chinese empires were in close contact. It was during his reign that the Gandhara School of Art became influential not only in India but also indirectly in the Far East. A patron of Asvaghosha, author of the Buddha Charita at his court at Peshawar and founder of an era, known as the Saka era (78 A.D.) though Kanishka was not strictly speaking, a Saka, his reign after Ashoka, became the most important landmark in the spread of Buddhism and Buddhist Vihara in and outside India.

Kanishka patronised the holding of the fourth great council in Kashmir[6] which codified the Sarvastivadin doctrines which were very strong in Mathura and Kashmir in a summary, the Mahavibhasa. It was chiefly among the Sarvastivadins, but also in the old schism of the Mahasanghikas that new ideas developed, which were to form the basis of the division of Buddhism into the "Great" and "Lesser Vehicles" known as Mahayana and Hinayana. In the North-Western India the rule of the Greeks, the Sakas and the Kushans had thrown open the gates to the West, and ideas from Persia and beyond entered India in greater strength than before while the Brahmanas and their lay supporters had by now largely turned from the older gods worshipped with animal sacrifices towards others who were worshipped with reverent devotion. In these conditions the Buddhist philosophers and teachers like Nagarjuna in the early Christian centuries gave to Buddhism a wholly new outlook and claimed to have found a new and great vehicle which would carry many souls to salvation, while the Sthaviravadins whose Pali canon emanated from the great monastery near Sanchi, and the kindred sects had but a small one. The Great Vehicle became rapidly popular in many parts of India, for it fitted the mood of the times and the needs of many simple people better than did the Lesser Vehicle, which soon began to lose ground. In Ceylon, however, the Lesser Vehicle resisted all the attacks of the new sects and thence it was taken to Burma, Siam and other parts of South-East Asia, where it became the national religion while the Great Vehicle though later riven by various schisms, remained predominant in India and was carried by a succession of Buddhist monks to China and thence to Japan.

The successors of Kanishka continued to rule in North-West India but their empire was soon much reduced about the middle of

the third century, when Vasudeva, one of Kanishka's successors, was
fully defeated by Shapur I of the new Sasanian dynasty of Persia, and
from now on the North-West came much under Iranian influence. In
the North-West Deccan the Satavahanas who were driven by the
Sakas of the clan of Ksaharata returned to their seat of power under
Gautamiputra Satakarnin about 130 A.D. and another Saka dynasty
known as Western Satraps remained in control of Kathiawar and
Malwa till about 388 A.D. and by the third century A.D. all India east
of the Punjab and Malwa was in the hands of small Indian kings and
tribal chiefs, many of whom were foreign invaders though by this
time they had become thoroughly Indianised, patronising either
Buddhism, or Saivaism, Vaishnavaism or Jainism.

The Guptas

In A.D. 320 a new Chandra Gupta, arose, whose successors in great
measure restored the splendour of the Mauryas. He owed his rise to
power largely to his marriage with a princes Kumaradevi, of the tribe
of the Lichchhavis, who now, reappear on the scene eight centuries
after the defeat by Ajatasatru. Chandra Gupta I possessed fairly large
domains, including the reigns of Magadha and Koshala. Under his
successor, Samudra Gupta (C. 335-376 A.D.) Pataliputra once more
became the centre of a great empire. Samudra's power reached from
Assam to the borders of the Punjab. He aimed at the establishment of
a closely knit empire of the Mauryan type.

Samudra Gupta's main effort was in the direction of the west,
where the Sakas had ruled for over 200 years and the land was
enriched by the lucrative Western trade. It was Chandra Gupta II (C.
376-415), the son of Samudra and younger brother of the shadowy
Rama Gupta, who finally defeated the Sakas, soon after 388 A.D.
Thus, he became the paramount sovereign of all Northern India, with
the exception of the North-West; and he had some control over much
of the Northern Deccan, thanks to the marriage of his daughter
Prabhavati with Rudrasena, king of the Vakatakas, who ruled a large
kingdom in the modern Madhya Pradesh and Hyderabad.

The reign of Chandra Gupta perhaps marks the high watermark
of ancient Indian culture. Later Indian legend tells of a great and good
king Vikramaditya, who drove the Sakas out of Ujjayini, and ruled
over all India which in his reign was most prosperous and happy.
Vikramaditya was certainly one of the titles of Chandra Gupta II and
the legend seems therefore to refer to him. Kalidasa, the greatest of

India's poets and dramatists is traditionally associated with Vikramaditya, and the internal evidence of his works points to the fact that he wrote at about this time.

Revival of the Vedic Schools

The Guptas – Chandra Gupta II, his father Samudra Gupta and his grand father Chandra Gupta I as well as his successors – were followers of the Brahmanical faith and revived some of the Vedic rites that had been in abeyance for a long period. However, Brahmanism in the days of the Guptas became more gentle and more humane than 700 years earlier in the days of the Mauryas. In place of the old sacrificial Brahmanism, Hinduism had appeared now, in a form not greatly different from that of recent centuries. Bhakti, that is, intense devotion to God conceived of as personal, a saviour worthy of trust and ready to be gracious, is an important element of Vaishnavism and Saivism as expounded in the Gita and the Svetasvatara Upanishad: "He who with unwavering practice of devotion does god service has crossed beyond the strands" and is fit for salvation. The growing importance of Bhakti or loving faith in God and the love of fellow-beings found expression in benevolent activities and toleration of the opinions of others. The wide prevalence of a feeling of toleration is well illustrated by epigraphic and literary references to the employment by Vaishnava kings of Saivite and Buddhist officials and the affection felt by Jainas for Brahmanas and by Brahmanas for the Tirthankaras and the Buddha. Soon harder and more primitive elements were to re-emerge but by the time of Chandra Gupta II (376-415 A.D.) Indian civilisation and culture had reached a perfection which it was never again to attain.

The Buddhist Viharas not only survived but flourished under the Tolerant Guptas

In this circumstance it will not be unreasonable to surmise that both the Brahmanical as well as the Buddhist systems of learning did not only flourish but also reached their apogee under the Guptas. While there is no doubt that Brahmanism and the Brahmanical centres of learning received the most favoured treatment under the Guptas we have evidence to show that Buddhism and Buddhist centres of learning also flourished under them. And this is attested by none other than a Buddhist scholar from China, Fa-Hien whose travels through different parts of India in search of Vinaya texts for the

Buddhist Viharas in China roughly coincided with the last fifteen years of the reign of Chandra Gupta II or the first decade and a half of the fifth century A.D.

En route from Udyana or modern Swat on the North-West to Tamralipti on the East, Fa-Hien saw an abundance of Buddhist Viharas or monasteries, inhabited by monks who were either followers of Hinayana or Mahayana form of Buddhism and was pleased to find that "the Law of Buddha was very flourishing" in the Doab between the Ganges and the Yamuna as well as in the Buddhist heartland of Magadh. In these monasteries he found some eighteen schools of Buddhist thought, each following the views and decisions of its own master though he mentioned only three of them. They were – the Mahasamghika, the Sabbatthivada and the Mahimsasaka. He further observed that these monasteries were maintained by the endowments of the laity, including kings and merchant-princes, "the heads of the Vaisyas". They "built Vihars for the priests and endowed them with fields, houses, gardens and orchards, along with the resident populations and their cattle". These grants were "engraved on plates of metal" and were "handed down from king to king without anyone daring to annul them". The monks in each of these monasteries had erected 'topes' or Chaityas in honour of the sacred characters of Buddhism like Sariputra, Mahamaudgalyayana, Anand and Rahula where they offered their worship. Sramanas made their offerings to the tope of Rahula while Bhikkshunis made these to that of Ananda "because it was he who requested the world-honoured one to allow females to quit their families and become nuns". At the Pataliputra monastery where Fa-Hien stayed for three years "learning Sanskrit books and the Sanskrit speech and writing out the Vinaya rules", he met two Mahayana Buddhist teachers. They were both Brahmanas, named Radhasami and Manjusri and respected not only by the inmates but also by the people outside the monastery at Pataliputra. It was only in the Mahayana monastery at Pataliputra and later at Tamralipti out of numerous monasteries visited by him that he could copy the manuscripts of sacred texts – in the various monasteries of North India he had found the master transmitting orally the rules of the sacred texts to another, but no written copies he could transcribe as he did at Pataliputra and Tamralipti. We can infer that the writing of the sacred Buddhist texts first started in the Buddhist heartland of Eastern India.

Fa-Hien did not go beyond the Vindhyas or the Godavari. Nor did he speak of Taxila which figured so largely in the Buddhist Jatakas as a centre of learning or of Nalanda which was yet to attain the celebrated status as a Buddhist centre of learning as it did in the succeeding centuries. Yet there is no doubt about the flourishing state of the Buddhist centres of learning in India by the end of the reign of Chandra Gupta II. Fa-Hien was much impressed by the observance of non-violence, the essential creed of Buddhism, by the whole community except the outcastes and by the benevolence and righteousness of the people of the Ganges valley, who not only directed their attention to the ceremonial side of the religion but also to the practice of charity.

Contributions of the Age of Ascendancy to various Disciplines, Arts and Crafts

Thus, the Age of Ascendancy of the Vedic schools and of the Buddhist Viharas which started with the supremacy of the Brahmanical centres of learning through the works of the Sutrakaras, gave way to the domination of the Buddhist Viharas under Ashoka and his successors and after a brief spell of a mild Brahmanic reaction under Pushyamitra Sunga and his successors arrived at the rule of the Guptas when both systems were respectful and tolerant of each other and when both contributed to the making of the Gupta Age as the golden period in the history of Ancient India. The characteristic of this Age which enjoyed a long innings of peace and stability was not so much in the creation of any new area of study or philosophy in the field of learning but to preserve, explain, comment and refine the earlier creative knowledge since stored in the Sutras.

Yet in some areas of learning significant and outstanding contributions were made as in astronomy and mathematics, arts and letters.[7] In the fourth century A.D., the anonymous author of a surviving mathematical text, "Bakshali Manuscript" first devised the simplified system of writing numerals and in 499 A.D., Aryabhatta in his terse "Aryabhatta" suggested the existence of zero or infinity which has since revolutionised the world of mathematics and has later indebted Europe to us through the Arabs who came and settled in Western India since the beginning of the eighth century A.D. The earliest Indian inscription recording the date by a system of nine digits and a zero with place notation for the tens and hundreds, comes from Gujarat, and is dated 595 A.D. However, Aryabhatta's suggestion probably under Greek influence that the earth revolved round the sun and rotated on its axis failed to affect the prevailing astronomical practice of using the planetary system as geocentric for the purpose of fixing the dates and times at which periodical sacrifices were to be performed and for other purposes of astronomical calculations.

In the field of metallurgy the age reached its apogee in the Iron Pillar, first erected as a memorial to Chandra Gupta II (C. 376-415 A.D.) on a hill near Ambala and later transferred to Mehrauli in Delhi where the Kutab Minar now exists. We do not know how this pillar which is 23 feet high and consists of a single piece of iron was made but it must have demanded immense care and labour and great technical proficiency in preparing and heating the metal. The metallurgical skill of the age could be seen in the fact that though it has weathered the torrential rains of over 1,595 monsoons, it shows no sign of rusting and until a century and a half ago it would have been difficult for the best European foundry to manufacture a similar piece made of wrought iron.

As in metallurgy, so in painting and sculpture the age stands out as unique in the contemporary ancient civilisations of the world. The fine fresco-paintings on the walls and ceilings of the Ajanta Caves as well as the carvings of the Ellora Caves are among the finest sculptures in India and have extorted the unstinted admiration of the whole world. In sculpture, the age saw the perfection of the past techniques spreading over several centuries in the execution of the stone and bronze images of the Buddha at Sarnath, Mathura and other places as well as in the sculpturing of the images of Siva, Vishnu and other Brahmanical gods at the temple at Deogarh and elsewhere. A sublime idealism, combined with a highly developed sense of rhythm and beauty in their design and execution characterise the sculptures of the age which not only remain as models of Indian art for all times to come but inspired in the past the sculptures of the Indian colonies in the Malay Peninsula, Sumatra, Java, Annam, Cambodia and Celebes. The sculptures of the age still remain as expressions of deep religious experience as sermons in bronze and stone on the oneness of the universal soul, taught by the Upanishads.

Notes

1. District judges and survey officials
2. Revenue collectors and police officials.
3. Secretaries and clerks.
4. Malwa in Madhya Pradesh.
5. Mainly drama and play.
6. Exact date is not known – it may be either towards the end of the first century, or at the beginning of the second century, A.D.
7. See Chapter 10 for details

9

The Decline of the Vedic Schools and of the Buddhist Viharas

The reign of Chandra Gupta II did not only represent the climax of the Gupta empire but also its climacteric. Within fifty years after the death of Chandra Gupta II the glory of the Gupta empire began to disappear and there were signs of degeneration and of dissension in the imperial line itself, and the devotion of the more loyal feudatories could not save the empire from its impending doom.

The Coming of the Hunas: The Beginning of the End

However, in the first fifty years the empire was ruled ably by Kumara Gupta I, the successor of Chandra Gupta II who ascended the throne in 415 A.D. He assumed the title of Mahendraditya and maintained his hold over the vast empire now extended from North Bengal to Kathiawar and from the Himalayas to the Narmada and if the numismatic evidence was to be believed, the empire at one time extended further southwards possibly as far as the Satara district of the Deccan. The achievements of Kumara Gupta I were sufficiently remarkable to entitle him to perform the famous rite of the horse-sacrifice which he did. However, in his last days the emperor faced troubles – one emanating from the Narmada valley where a people called Pushyamitras reduced the imperial government to such straits that a prince imperial had to spend a whole night on bare earth; the other came from the proverbial North-West – the Hunas. They were a Central Asian people, known to Byzantine writers as white Hunas and usually considered a branch of the group of Turko-Mongol people who were then threatening Europe. The Hunas had occupied Bactria some time before and now, like the earlier Greeks, Sakas and Kushans; they crossed the mountains and attacked the plains of India. In 455 A.D., Kumar Gupta I died in his wars with the Hunas and was succeeded by Skanda Gupta. Skanda Gupta succeeded in repelling the early invasions of the Hunas and recovering most of the imperial provinces, which were placed under special wardens of the Marches. Proud of his success against the barbarians, Skanda Gupta assumed the title of Vikramaditya and the memory of his achievements is popularly reserved in the story of Vikramaditya, son of Mahendraditya, narrated in the Kathasaritsagar.

In 467 A.D., Skanda Gupta died and on his death the great days of the Guptas were over. The empire continued but the central control weakened, and local governors, usually members of the royal family, became feudatory kings with hereditary rights. Beyond Magadha and Pataliputra, the Gupta emperors exercised little more than titular control.

A fresh inroad of the Hunas towards the close of the fifth century further weakened the Gupta empire, when there was no Gupta emperor of the calibre of Skanda Gupta to repel them. And for some thirty years from 500 A.D. onwards Western India was in the hands of the Huna kings, two of whom, Toramana and his son, Mihiragula were apparently mighty monarchs. The Hunas were supporters of Saivism and some of them like Mihiragula were fierce persecutors of Buddhism. The memories of the sadistic tyranny of Mihiragula in Kashmir, one of the centres of his power, were still alive in the twelfth century, when they were recorded by the historian Kalhana in his Rajtarangini. Mihiragula retained his hold on Kashmir and parts of the North-West after being driven away from the plains of the Ganges by Narasimha Gupta and from the Western India in 530 by Yasodharman, an energetic king of Mandasor, who built a large kingdom which did not survive his death. Petty Huna chieftains continued to rule over a circumscribed area in the North-West India and Malwa waging a perpetual warfare with the indigenous princes till they were absorbed into the Rajput population. The Huna power never again seriously threatened India.

The Rise of the Maukharis: Harshavardhana

However, by 500 A.D., the Gupta empire completely vanished and another kingdom, that of the Maukharis who claimed descent from

Asvapati of epic fame, rose to prominence, north of the Ganges and its capital, the city of Kanyakubja or Kanauj, became the cultural centre of Northern India until the coming of the Muslims. In the war with the Guptas who were aided by Sasanka, king of Bengal, both Grahavarman of Kanyakubja and his brother-in-law Rajyavardhana of Sthanvisvara or Thaneswar whose family claimed descent from the illustrious Pushyabhuti, a devoted worshipper of Siva, were both killed. The former died without any heir, and the two kingdoms were combined under Harshavardhana or Harsha who was brother of Rajyavardhana and at the same time was brother-in-law of Grahavarman. Harsha ascended the throne in 606 A.D. and was destined to revive the imperial memories of the Gupta epoch and obtain recognition as the lord paramount of the whole of Northern India from Kathiawar to Bengal, even from his bitterest enemies. Only in the Deccan, Harsha could make no progress and was checked by the Chalukya king Pulakeshin II.

A follower of Saivism, he was equally a patron of Buddhism and in his last days he fell increasingly under the influence of the latter. He travelled ceaselessly from one province to another, both in his own domains and in those of his feudatories and was accompanied by a tremendous train of attendants, courtiers, officials, Brahmans and Buddhist monks. A lover of philosophy and literature, he was fantastically generous to those whom he favoured and while his court was adorned by some famous scholars and poets like Bana, he himself found time to compose three very competent dramas.

The Buddhist Viharas Coexisted with the Dominant Vedic Schools: Evidence of Hiuen Tsang

Under such a monarch as Harsha, both Brahmanism and Buddhism flourished and so did the two systems of learning associated with these two religions. However, since the Guptas were followers of Vaishnavism and their successors including the intruders Hunas were those of Saivism, it is not unreasonable to expect that Brahmanism and the Brahmanic system of learning received a favoured treatment and were in a more flourishing state than Buddhism and the Buddhist system of learning. This is endorsed by no other person than Hiuen Tsang, a Chinese Buddhist scholar who came to India to visit Buddhist religious shrines and collect Buddhist religious documents, towards the end of Harsha's reign (629-645 A.D.). Despite his chief interest in Buddhist life and thought, Hiuen Tsang who enjoyed the patronage of Harsha, wrote a very valuable description of India, which, unlike the account of Megasthenes, has survived intact.

Hiuen Tsang noted that the general name for India was "country of the Brahmanas". He further observes: "Among the various castes and clans of the country, the Brahmans were purest and in most esteem. So from their excellent reputation the name 'Brahmana country' had come to be a popular one for India". The predominance of Brahmanism is further attested by the fact that Sanskrit, the language of the Vedas, had now become the language of the cultured classes including the famous Buddhist teachers. Hiuen Tsang regarded the Sanskrit language which was both written and spoken in "Mid-India" or Madhya-desa as at once the parent and the standard of all the dialects of "North India": "The people of mid-India are pre-eminently explicit and correct in speech, their expressions being harmonious and elegant, like those of the Devas, and their intonation clear and distinct, serving as rule and pattern for others". He then went on to describe the growth of numerous ascetic orders or sects, each distinguished by its own special garb as well as the Brahmanical system of education, the details of which are not required here to prove our assumption on the dominance of the Brahmanic system of learning. What will be more relevant here, is to know from the account of Hiuen Tsang how Buddhism and the Buddhist system of learning was faring in the presence of a dominant Brahmanism and a dominant Brahmanic system of learning.

Unlike Fa-Hien, Hiuen Tsang traversed widely from Kashmir to Kanchipuram and Negapatam, from Surat to Tamralipti and found Buddhist thought represented by a good number of schools, each of which claimed and counted many monasteries, specialising in the study of its doctrines and practices. He estimated the number of the active monasteries at 5,000 and the number of the monkish population at 2,12,130. Hiuen Tsang broke his journey at several monasteries which were renowned as seats of learning either for their teachers or for their collection of rare manuscripts. In one such monastery in Kashmir at the beginning of his journey through India, he spent two years in studying Buddhist scriptures and was helped by the king with twenty clerks under the guidance of the Buddhist teacher Bhadanta and his disciples to copy out as many manuscripts as he wanted to carry home. Similarly, he spent several months in studying and copying one of the works of the Buddhist teacher, Gunaprabha, in a monastery at Matipur where he also came across the disciple of Gunaprabha, Mitrasena by name, who was then 90 years old. It is thus clear now that within a lapse of 200 years since the time of Fa-Hien's visit, the art of writing had considerably developed in Northern India and the practice of putting religious scriptures to it had started among the Buddhist teachers and philosophers. However, the Buddhist scriptures, as seen by Hiuen Tsang were still transmitted orally like the Vedas in these monasteries.

These monasteries were in charge of higher education in Buddhist learning as confined within the limits of the Buddhist canon, whether Vinaya, Abhidhamma or Sutra but there were a few cases where these usual limits were transgressed by the inclusion of subjects usually taught in a Vedic school like Yoga, magical invocations or exorcisms. Hiuen Tsang noted that the Buddhist higher education in these monasteries was fed by a well-developed system of elementary education which appears to us to be more Vedic than Buddhist. A child was first introduced to a Siddham or Siddhir-autu (may there be success!) or a primer of twelve chapters giving the Sanskrit alphabet and the combinations between vowels and consonants. After Siddham, he was introduced at the age of seven to the "great Sastras of the Five Sciences", that is, Vyakarana or grammar, Silpasthanavidya or the sciences of arts and crafts, Chikitsavidya or the science of medicine, Hetuvidya or the science of reasoning, Naya or logic, and Adhyatmavidya or inner science, which according to Watters, author of Yuan Chwang or Hiuen Tsang, were "the metaphysical and argumentative treatises of the great Doctors of Abhidhamma". It is thus clear that at the time of Hiuen Tsang, the Buddhist education which originally started purely as a religious learning had come to acquire over the course of several centuries, elements of practical arts and crafts to help the recipients of Buddhist learning serve the humanity better.

Hiuen Tsang noticed that the studies and curricula adopted by a monastery would depend upon the particular sect of Buddhism with which it was connected and there were as many as eighteen sects of Buddhism, besides its division into the Great and Little Vehicles. Each sect had its own special literature bearing upon its characteristic tenets and practices associated with a host of Buddhist celebrities like Asanga, Vasubandhu, Parsva, Asvaghosa, Narayana-deva, Dharmatara, Isvara, Kumaralabdha, Deva, Nagarjuna, Madhyantika, Samghabhadra, Skandhila, Purna, Bodhila, Vinitaprabha, Katyaniputra, Gunaprabha, Srilabdha, Buddhadasa, Devasarman,

Gopa, Dharmapala, Gunamatit Sthiramati, Dinanaga, Bhavaviveka, Achara, Jinaputra, Bhadraruchi and Maha-Katyayana. Much emphasis was laid upon the ability to expound the texts in public meetings at a time when much of the intellectual life of the country was occupied with the controversies and discussions between the exponents of the different schools of thought. As Hiuen Tsang observed: "the tenets of these schools keep these isolated, and controversy runs high". Each school was always on the look out to establish its superiority over the other and organised public debates and discussions: "The Brethren are often assembled for discussion to test intellectual capacity to reject the worthless, and advance the intelligent," as Hiuen Tsang mentioned, that the emperor Harsha used to bring the Brethren together for examination and discussion and rewarded the meritorious.

Quite in line with the tradition of Vedic learning, a Buddhist scholar belonging to a particular sect would travel to a far-off place in another part of the country for such debates and discussions. Thus, the South Indian Buddhist scholar, Deva, with the permission of his master Nagarjuna, came to a monastery near Pataliputra called Kukkularama where he defeated all its Tirthikas in a discussion lasting twelve days. Another Buddhist scholar from South, Dinanaga who belonged to a Brahmin family at Kanchi, made the buildings of the Nalanda monastery in Magadh resound with his victorious discussions with the exponents of various schools of thought at Nalanda. The Pala king, Dharmapala representing the Buddhist school of thought at Vikramsila scored victory after seven days of discussions with 100 Hinayana Buddhist scholars at a monastery in Visoka.

Nalanda as the Coordinator of the Buddhist Viharas

Thus the intellectual life at the time of Hiuen Tsang's visit during the reign of Harsha was animated by controversies, debates and discussions and there was certainly a need for an umpire to pass judgements on them. And who else could do so but the monks at Nalanda? The monastery at Nalanda which had a very humble beginning at the time of Ashoka had now grown over the past several centuries through a continuous series of endowments in the form of lands and buildings from a succession of sovereigns into a huge complex of learning which according to Hiuen Tsang accommodated some 10,000 monks[1] including the 1,510 monks who belonged to the ranks of teachers. One thousand of the latter could explain "twenty collections of Sutras and Sastras", 500 "thirty collections" and perhaps 10 "fifty collections". The Nalanda establishments including the 1,510 teachers were presided over by Silabhadra, a Brahmin prince, unique in learning and character, who had renounced the world and become a Bhikkhu. He studied and understood the whole number of collections of the Sutras and the Sastras and his "eminent virtue and advanced age" had made him "the chief member of the community".

The range of studies at Nalanda was vast and varied including both Brahmanical and Buddhist learning. Primarily a Mahayana Centre of learning, Nalanda attracted students from Hinayana School also. All students at Nalanda studied' "the Great Vehicle, and also the works belonging to the eighteen sects, and not only, so, but even ordinary works, such as the Vedas and other books like the Hetuvidya, Sabdavidya, the Chikitsavidya, the works on Magic or Atharvaveda, the Samkhya, besides these, they thoroughly investigate the 'miscellaneous' works". Thus, Nalanda had the merit of collecting at one centre the available authorities on every subject of learning and every day as many as one hundred chairs or pulpits were arranged for the lectures or discourses by so many teachers living there "and the students attend these discourses without any fail, even for a minute". Thus, Nalanda had brought to its sprawling campus schools, whose "tenets would keep them isolated" and had become the meeting ground of the warring sects and creeds with their "possible and impossible doctrines" and an opinion approved and recognised at Nalanda would at once obtain universal currency: "those who stole the name of Nalanda brother were all treated with respect wherever they went". No doubt therefore the doors for admission to Nalanda comprising mainly "Schools of Discussion" were jealously guarded by the specialists and expert religious controversialists, who were always ready with difficult problems to try the claimants for admission. As Hiuen Tsang observed: "of those from abroad who wished to enter the Schools of Discussion, the majority, beaten by the difficulties of the problems, withdrew; and those who were deeply versed in old and modern learning were admitted, only two or three out of ten succeeding".

And Hiuen Tsang was one of the fortunate few from abroad who was able to get admission to Nalanda to study Yoga Sastra followed by a study of Nyaya, Hetuvidya, Sabdavidya under Silabhadra and spent nearly five years at Nalanda to learn all these subjects. Hiuen Tsang who was allowed the services of two attendants according to the status attained by him, received each day 120 Jambiras, twenty areca nuts, twenty nutmegs, an ounce of camphor, and a peck of the finest variety of rice called Mahasali rice which grew only in Magadha and was offered only to the king or to religious persons of great distinction – a rice which looked "as large as the black bean" and "when cooked, was aromatic and shining, like no other rice at all". He also received "every month three measures of oil, and daily, a supply of butter and other things according to his need".

Nalanda: Evidence of I-Tsing

Nearly forty years after the departure of Hiuen Tsang from Nalanda with his mastery of Mahayana Buddhism, came another Chinese Scholar I-Tsing, a follower of Hinayana, in 672 A.D. By that time Nalanda had grown further and had been visited in the interval by nearly fifty-six scholars from China, Japan and Korea, some of whom came by sea via Tamralipti and others by land via Khotan, Tibet and Nepal. I-Tsing studied at Nalanda which was then housing some 3,000 monks on the campus for a long period of ten years from 675 to 685 A.D., collecting some 400 Sanskrit texts of 500,000 Slokas from the library situated at Dharmaganja or mart of religion. The library comprised three huge buildings – Ratnasagara, Ratnodadhi and Ratnaranjaka – of which the first was a nine-storeyed one, specialising in the collection of rare sacred works like Prajnaparamita-Sutra and Taiitrika works like Samajaguha.

Political Instability as a Setback for the Buddhist Viharas and the Vedic Schools

It would seem from the accounts of HiuenTsang and I-Tsing of the Nalanda Vihara in Magadha that all was well with the Buddhist centres of learning in other parts of contemporary India. As a matter of fact, not only the Buddhist but also the Brahmanical seats of learning had begun to suffer a setback since the beginning of the Huna invasions of India in the middle of the fifth century A.D. The repeated incursions of the Hunas and their temporary rule for nearly thirty years in Western India did create havoc with the Buddhist monasteries there, as the Hunas were known persecutors of Buddhism. They adopted Saivism as their faith but this did not deter them from ravaging the excellent centres of learning in Taxila which along with Kashmir and other parts of the North-West was retained by them after being driven out from the plains of the Ganges. And when Hiuen Tsang came towards the end of Harsha's reign, he did not speak much about Taxila where Buddhist influences had firmly established themselves since the days of the Kushana king, Kanishka and found many Buddhist monasteries in North India, either dilapidated in ruins or deserted. Hiuen Tsang's estimate of the total number of monkish population of India including Ceylon at 212,130 was not certainly an indicator of the flourishing state of the Buddhist Viharas and pales into insignificance before the number of the militia men maintained by Dhana Nanda of Magadha nearly seven hundred years ago, which stood at 220,000. Unlike Fa-Hien who came in the early fifth century A.D., before the invasions of the Hunas, Hiuen Tsang faced enormous dangers and difficulties while travelling down the Ganges – he was twice robbed by bandits in Harsha's domains and on one occasion he was nearly sacrificed to the goddess Durga by river pirates in the very heart of Harsha's empire.

The deterioration in law and order in Harsha's time was an index to the degeneration that had set in, following the break-up of the empire of the Guptas in the Aryan society. The stability of the Aryan society in the Ganges valley deteriorated further when a severe struggle for supremacy among the neighbouring potentates ensued after Harsha's death in 647 A.D.: The bone of contention was the possession of Kanyakubja or Kanauj which in those days, was synonymous with the acquisition of power and culture in Northern India. In other words Kanauj was to the upspringing dynasties of the seventh, eight and ninth centuries A.D. "what Babylon was to martial races of Western Asia, what Rome was to the Teutonic barbarians and Byzantium to the mediaeval world of Eastern and Southern Europe".

First, a usurper, Arunasva, one of Harsha's minister, occupied Kanauj and seized a Chinese mission coming to Harsha's court. The latter with assistance from Tibet and Nepal, defeated him and took him to China to serve the Chinese emperor. After this, Harsha's old ally, Bhaskaravarman of Assam extended his power westwards and occupied parts of Magadha. From 672 A.D. onwards, Adityasena Gupta of the revived second Gupta dynasty of Malwa and Magadha became the most powerful sovereign in the Madhya-desa, who revived the ancient Vedic rites of horse -sacrifice, and was followed by three Gupta successors, Deva Gupta, Vishnu Gupta and Jivita Gupta II. Early in the eighth century, an upstart named Yasovarman established an empire at Kanauj, which for a while controlled much of the North, had diplomatic intercourse with the Chinese empire, and extended his patronage to the illustrious poets Bhavabhuti and Vakpatiraja. However, Yasvarman's empire soon fell to Lalitaditya, one of the few Kashmir kings to play an important part in the politics of the Gangetic plain.

In the following two centuries two great dynasties the Palas of Bihar and Bengal, and the Gurjara-Pratiharas of Kanauj divided the hegemony of Northern India between them. The Palas of Eastern India were the first to gain the ascendancy and for a while, in the early part of the ninth century, were the masters of Kanauj. The Pala kings are chiefly notable for their patronage of Buddhism which, in a rather corrupt form, flourished in their domains for nearly three centuries till they were succeeded by the Senas who originally came from the South and were followers of the Brahmanical faith. In the 9th and 10th centuries the Gurjara-Pratiharas, who probably originated in Rajasthan, were masters of Kanauj, and the most powerful kings of Northern India. They successfully resisted the Arabs, who, in 712 A.D., had occupied Sind after coming through the North-West and who for over a century made frequent attacks on their eastern neighbours. The two most powerful Pratihara kings, Mihira Bhoja (840-885 A.D.) and Mahendrapala (885-910 A.D.) pushed back the Palas, and were overlords of most of Northern India as far as the borders of Bengal. But they were weakened by repeated invasions of the Rastrakutas of the Deccan, who, in 916 A.D., temporarily occupied Kanauj. These repeated and persistent raids from the South seem to have turned the attention of the Pratihara kings away from the North-West, where new forces were gathering into a storm which, was ultimately to blow over the plains of the Northern India and herald the coming of a new religion and culture in the history of India.

The Flight of Creativity from a Society becoming more Conservative and Defensive under increasing Political Instability

Peace and stability so vitally needed for the growth and development of learning took its flight partly under frequent influx of the foreign invaders including the Arabs through the North-West and partly under the impact of an almost incessant warfare among the ambitious northern potentates for the prized possession of Kanauj. In this circumstance the Aryan society could not but become more firmly defensive than before and the relationship among the various groups of the society began to be governed more strictly by the rules of endogamy², commensality and craft-exclusiveness. In such a society creative thinking, and original ideas were likely to be buried under an obstinate desire to preserve, expound and comment on the outstanding works of the past since canonised. And reason and logic, truth and knowledge were likely to be sacrificed at the altar of popular beliefs and myths as endorsed by the theologians of the day. Thus, in the seventh century, Brahmagupta who attempted to measure the circumference of the earth as 5,000 yojanas and who knew well the reason behind eclipses of the sun and the moon, endorsed the popular belief in his Brahmasiddhanta that they were caused by Rahu and Ketu attacking and swallowing the luminaries! He even went further in denouncing both Aryabhatta and Varamihira, who came after the former for their beliefs that eclipses were caused by the shadow of the earth. However, in mathematics which was not as canonised as astronomy, the same Brahmagupta, followed by Mahavira in the ninth century A.D., was able to make several important discoveries which in Europe were not known until the Renaissance. Both understood the import of positive and negative quantities, evolved sound systems of extracting square and cube roots, and could solve quadratic and certain types of indeterminate equations.

It was also this age which saw the abandonment of the colonial activities of the Aryans, which in turn affected trade and commerce. There had been little progress in the Ayurveda since the discontinuance of dissection. And agriculture which was earlier so highly held in esteem by the upper classes now came to be the sole occupations of the Vaishyas and the Shudras. The worst affected were, however, the arts and crafts which now failed to attract the best brains of the Aryan society partly because of the rigidity of the caste system and partly because of the low esteem in which these professions began to be held now. Consequently, there were no flashes of genius as in the past age, except occasionally at places where they were still held in high esteem as shown by the construction of the Kailasanatha Temple at Ellora (C. 756-773 A.D.) and that of the Trimurti at Elephanta a century or two later. Indeed, the only silver lining in an Age of Decline is the South which not only saw the revival of Hinduism under Sankara, but also setting up of new centres of learning in Sanskrit and astronomy at Dhara and Devagiri respectively while in the far South the Pallava kings extended their traditional patronage to educational institutions at Kanchi and Bahur.

In the ninth century A.D., Bahur which was situated near modern Pondicherry was famous for the study of the Vedas, Vedangas, Mimamsa, Nyaya, Puranas and Dharmasastras[3]. And thus South kept the lamp of learning burning steadily while it was almost flickering in the Northern India.

The Gradual Extinction of the Buddhist Viharas

However, it was the Buddhist systems, rather than the Brahmanical system of learning which suffered most and almost came to the verge of extinction; though paradoxically it was also the age which saw two Buddhist Viharas set up by the Palas at Uddandapura and Vikramasila in Bihar. The decline of the Buddhist Viharas is significant, in as much as, it not only marks the decline of an organised institution of learning but also marks the coming of the middle ages with the advent of Islam in India. We may now analyse the factors which contributed to the withering of the Buddhist Viharas in India.

In the first place, the Buddhist Viharas which were open to all classes, castes and creeds had become, over the centuries, a haven for all kinds of people of the Aryan society who found in them an escape from various problems of life. The Buddhist brotherhood lived on the charity of the sympathetic laity or the Upasaks who supported the brotherhood as a religious duty. And so there was no struggle for existence within the Order and in many places the Buddhist Viharas failed to live upto the expectations which had brought them in existence. As Rhys Davids observes in his *Buddhism:* "When successive kings and chiefs were allowed to endow the society, not indeed with gold or silver, but with necessaries of the monkish life, including lands and houses, it gradually ceased in great measure to be the school of virtue and the most favourable sphere of intellectual progress and became thronged with the worthless and the idle". Looked at from this point of view, one can argue that the seeds of the ultimate decline of the Buddhist Viharas lie in themselves and sooner or later they would have died a natural death even without the attack of the Hunas or the Muslims.

Secondly, the Buddhist Viharas, composed as they were of a heterogeneous mixture of residents coming from different classes of the Aryan society with their own ideas and beliefs, and also exposed as they were particularly in the North-West to the ideas of Zoroastrianism, and the multifarious influences of the Greeks, Sakas, and Kushans, gradually began to make room for the development of theism in Buddhism. One such development was the doctrine of Bodhisattva. According to it, the Buddha in a long series of transmigrations as a Bodhisattva, wrought many deeds of kindness and mercy before achieving his final birth as the Sage of the Sakyas. Now, if there had been Buddha as before Gautama, there would be Buddhas after him and around the beginning of the Christian era, the cult of the future Buddha, Maitreya, was widespread among all Buddhist Sects. Since Maitreya and other unnamed Buddhas after him were yet to be born, there must be Bodhisattvas existing at present in the universe, who were working continuously for the welfare of all things living. These Bodhisattvas, though neither omniscient nor almighty, might be adored and prayed to without any misgiving, for it was part of their mission to answer prayer. The Bodhisattva doctrine which formed the hallmark of the Mahayana, the Great Vehicle, peopled the heavens with mighty forces of goodness, and presented Buddhism with a new mythology and brought Buddhism nearer to Hinduism. The Buddha came to be worshipped as a Hindu god with flowers, incense, waving lamps and deep devotion from the first century A. D. onwards as the carvings of the stupas of Bharhut and Sanchi indicate. With the deification of the Buddha and his gradual admission into the Vishnuite pantheon as an incarnation of Narayana-Vishnu, there was little to distinguish the Buddhist laity from their Brahmanical neighbours. The Great Vehicle which promised to carry many souls to salvation became rapidly popular in many parts of India as it fitted the mood of the times and the needs of many simple people better than did the Hinavana or the Lesser Vehicle, which however held its ground firmly in Ceylon from where it was taken to Burma, Siam and other parts of South-East Asia where it became the national religion.

Thirdly, there is a further development in the Mahayana form of Buddhism which brought it much nearer to the religious practices of the people of Eastern India. From the end of the Gupta period onwards religion in Ancient India became, more and more permeated with primitive ideas of sympathetic magic and sexual mysticism. With the coming of feminine divinities in the pantheon of the Great Vehicle, the Buddhas and Bodhisattvas who were thought of as male, now became like the gods of Hinduism, endowed with wives, who were the active aspect, the "force" or "potency" or "Sakti" of their husbands. The productive activity of the divine was thought of in terms of a sexual union, an idea as old as the Rig Veda, and led to the development of a third vehicle, "the Vehicle of the Thunderbolt" or Vajrayana in the eighth century A.D. in Eastern India where the Mahayana Buddhism was very strong and popular and it grew rapidly in Bengal and Bihar. It was this form of Buddhism, modified by primitive local cults and practices, which was finally established in Tibet, in the eleventh century A.D., as a result of missions sent from the great Vajrayana monastery of Vikramsila, in Bihar, when the Palas were ruling Eastern India. This development in Buddhism almost wiped away any substantial differences between it and Hinduism in Eastern India, the heartland of Buddhism.

Finally, in the ninth century A.D., when the growth of Tantricism had made the distinction between the Vajrayana Buddhism and certain forms of Saivism and Saktism purely nominal, a revived and reformed Hinduism began to travel northwards from Kerala when the great theologian Sankara travelled the length and breadth of India disputing with the Buddhists. An ardent Vedantist and the most powerful exponent of the doctrine of pure monism or Advaita which he elucidated in his commentaries on the Upanishads, the Bhagavad Gita and the Brahma Sutras of Badarayana, he organised monasteries at Sringeri in Mysore, Dwaraka in Kathiawar, Puri in Orissa and Badrinath on the snowy heights of the Himalayas. He died at a comparatively early age but left behind him an organised body of Hindu monks to carry on his work of spreading the message of devotional Hinduism which now made a vigorous appeal to the ordinary men and women.

However, no new messiah now turned up to revitalise Buddhism and to prevent its being swallowed up by Hinduism, now greatly reinforced by its revival in the South. And when in the eleventh and the twelfth centuries, in the first rush of the Muslim advance down the Ganges from Ghazni and Ghur, through the proverbial North-West, Nalanda and other great monasteries of Magadha, the Buddhist heartland of India, were sacked, libraries were burnt, and the monks were put to the sword, the last nail in the coffin of a dying Buddhism was driven by the Islam. The survivors fled I-led to the mountains of Nepal and Tibet and Buddhism in India was almost dead. In his last exhortation to his weeping disciples just on the eve of his death at Kushinagar, the Buddha had said "Decay is inherent in all component things". While it is acceptable that the Buddhist Viharas would have decayed one day, the kind of tragic decay that gradually overtook them was not perhaps visualised by the Sakya muni in 486 B.C. at the time of his Nirvana before his weeping disciples.

Notes

1. The archaeological excavations at Nalanda, however, show that there was a huge complex of Buildings at Nalanda, it could have hardly accommodated a thousand monks in comfort as described by Hiuen Tsang.
2. Prevents marriage from outside the group, class or caste.
3. For details about Vedic Learning in the South in Medieval India, see the second part of this work under Hindu Learning.

10

The Art of Writing, Language and Literature

We have already seen that the Vedic system of learning has emerged out of the four Vedas, Brahmanas, Aranyakas and the Upanishads. Similarly, the Buddhist system of learning has emerged out of the teachings of the Buddha later compiled and codified under Vinaya or conduct, Sutta or sermon and Abhidhamma or metaphysics. Both were composed and transmitted orally, while it was considered a sacrilege to commit the Veda to writing, no such stigma was attached to the writing of the Buddhist religious scriptures. Yet, the latter continued to be transmitted orally till the beginning of the seventh century A.D. The questions that we may now ask are: Was writing unknown to the Vedic and Buddhist India? If not, when and how did it develop? And secondly, if the contents and themes of the ancient systems of learning were basically religious, was there any development of secular literature during our period? In the following pages, we shall attempt to answer these questions.

The Art of Writing

In the Pali scriptures of the Buddhists as well as in the Sutra literature of the Hindus, there were references to writing. Mahavagga refers to it as a source of livelihood or an occupation while a passage in Kautiliya Arthashastra says how after the ceremony of Chudakarna a boy was to be taught Lipi or writing and Samkhyanam or counting and arithmetic. So writing was known to Ancient India at least four centuries before the birth of Christ. The usual writing material was the leaf of the talipot palm, or talapatra dried, smoothed, sized and cut into strips. The ink made from lampblack or charcoal which was applied with a reed pen, was the usual writing medium. In the South, instead of a reed pen, a stylus was used to scratch the letters on a palm leaf and after rubbing the leaf over with finely powdered lampblack, a fine sharp outline of the letters emerged. This method allowed the use of very small script and later probably encouraged the development of the angular forms of the Tamil alphabet. In the Himalayan districts where palm trees are not grown, palm leaf was replaced by the inner bark of the birch tree, which carefully pared and smoothed, served the purpose excellently. A book usually grew out of a number of such strips loosely held together by a cord passed through a hole in the centre of the leaf or in the case of large books, by two cords at either end. The book thus formed was usually strengthened by wooden covers and such covers were often lacquered and painted. Besides palm leaf and the inner bark of the birch tree, sized cotton and silk, and thin slips of wood or bamboo gradually came to be used and important documents, king's orders or instructions, came to be usually engraved on copper plates. We do not, however, have any evidences of the use of paper which was traditionally invented in China in the second century A.D., and was widely used in Central Asia during our period.

By the time of the Mauryas, writing was fairly developed and the Brahmi and Kharosthi scripts used on Ashokan edicts were the earliest important written documents known to us. While Brahmi which is normally read from left to right as in European script was most popular everywhere in India except North-West where Kharosthi was widely used as in Achaemenid Persia and is usually read from right to left. There were evidences of local variations of Brahmi script at the time of Ashoka and in the following centuries these differences developed further, until distinct alphabets evolved.

Languages: Prakrit and Sanskrit

What was the state of the language which was to be expressed now through writing? When the hymns of the Rig Veda were composed, its language was too archaic to be spoken by the people other than the priestly class. The ordinary Aryan tribesmen spoke a simpler tongue, more closely akin to classical Sanskrit. By the time of the Buddha (566-486 B.C.), the people were speaking languages which were much simpler than Sanskrit and these were known as Prakrits, which varied from region to region. Most inscriptions of the pre-Guptan times including those of Ashoka were in Prakrits and the men and women of the Sanskrit drama of the times were made to speak in formalised Prakrit of various dialects. One very important and early Prakrit was Pali, the language of the Sthaviravadan Buddhists. The Buddha who, as we have already seen, advocated preaching of his religion in local Prakrit dialect of a Bhikkhu, himself probably taught in Magadhi, but as his doctrines spread over India they were adapted to the local dialects.

While the people were thus speaking in Prakrits, the Vedic schools with their specialisation in the six Vedangas, particularly Vayakarana or grammar and Nirukta or phonetics were trying to preserve the purity of the Vedas in oral transmission. Out of these attempts came in the fifth century B.C., Yaska's Nirukta which explained obsolete Vedic words and by the fourth century B.C., Panini's great grammar, The Astadhyayi or Eight Chapters, which effectively stabilised the language of the Vedas, which could only develop now within the framework of Panini's rules. Panini, in all probability, based his grammar on the language as it was then spoken in the North-West. And with Panini, the language of the Vedas had virtually reached its classical form and thence forward it developed little except in its vocabulary. It was from the time of Panini onwards that the language of the Vedas began to be called Sanskrita or refined, perfected as opposed to the Prakritas which though unrefined developed naturally as popular dialects.

Since Panini's terse Sanskrit grammar could not be understood without the help of a suitable commentary, later grammarians fulfilled the need. In the second century B.C., Patanjaii composed his Mahabhasya or the Great Commentary followed by Kasika Vritti or Benares commentary composed by Jayaditta and Vamana. Sanskrit, already a lingua franca of the priestly class now came to be adopted by the kings and their courts. The first important dynasty to use Sanskrit was that of the Sakas of Ujjayini and the inscription of Rudradaman who ruled between 30 and 150 A.D. at Girnar is the earliest written Sanskrit document we possess, with the exception of a few inscriptions in Sanskrit, which are brief and unimportant.

Literary Works: Religious

It is natural that after the development of the art of writing and the refinement of the language there should be a spurt in literary activities. And indeed there had been great literary works which have survived the tests of time and quality of scholarship. We must however remember that no religious scriptures, Brahmanical or Buddhist, were ever put to writing as late as fifth century A.D. when Fa-Hien was hard put to it to find a copy of the Vinaya Pitaka and could only find it at Pataliputra and Tamralipti in Eastern India, though at the same time he could obtain Pali translations by his contemporary, Buddhaghosa of the old commentaries in Sinhalese Prakrit which were earlier committed to writing in Ceylon at the same time of the Pali canon of the Sthaviravadin School in the first century B.C. When Hiuen Tsang came in the second quarter of the seventh century, he could not only study the written copies of the Buddhist scriptures at Nalanda and elsewhere but also those of the Vedas presumably translated by those Brahmin Vedic scholars who later entered the Buddhist order and served as Acharyas or teachers in the Buddhist Viharas. It is possible that the writing of the Vedas by the Buddhist scholars could have provoked Kumarila Bhatta in the eighth century to condemn it as he has done in Tantra Varttika: "That knowledge of the truth is worthless which has been acquired from the Veda, if the Veda has not been rightly comprehended or if it has been learnt from writing".

Literary Works: Non-Religious

The earliest literature of a somewhat secular character is the two great epics, the Mahabharata and the Ramayana. These two epics blossomed out of many martial ballads sung on the occasion of great sacrifices like the Rajasuya and the Asvamedha. Among the sacrificers who performed Rajasuya and Asvamedha were many kings of the Kuru or Koshala realms. Some of the most famous lays and tales found in the Vedic texts celebrated the benevolence and prowess of Kuru kings like Parikshit and Janamejaya and of Ikshvaku and Koshalan monarchs like Harischandra and Para Atnara. Both Mahabharata and Ramayana though worked over by a succession of priestly editors give clear evidence of their origin as martial legends. Their religious importance lay at first in the royal sacrificial ritual, part of which involved telling stories of the heroes of the past. This put the martial ballads into the hands of the priesthood, who, in transmitting, often interpolated many long passages on theology, morals and statecraft.

Mahabharata

Traditionally the author of the Mahabharata consisting of more than 90,000 verses was the sage Vyasa, son of Parasara, who taught it to his pupil, Vaisampayana. The latter recited it in public for the first time at a great sacrifice held by king Janamejaya, the great grandson of Arjuna, one of the heroes of the story. Stripped of its episodes and interpolations the poem tells of the great civil war in the kingdom of Kurus, near modern Delhi, and the victory of the Pandus, helped by Krishna and the Panchalas over the Kurus proper, the sons of the blind king, Dhritarashtra Vaichitravirya.

The name of king Dhritarashtra Vaichitravirya, father of the Kurus has been mentioned in the Kathaka recension of the Yajur Veda and the ruin of the Kurus is hinted at in the Chhandogya Upanishad and one of the Srauta Sutras.

In the Chhandogya Upanishad, Krishna has been identified as the son of Vasudeva and Devaki and in the Taittiriya Aranyaka he is identified with the god Vishnu or Narayana. In the Satapatha Brahmana, Arjuna has been identified with Indra though in the epic he is the son of Kunti, wife of Pandus, by Indra.

It may be presumed that the Gupta Age saw the completion of the Mahabharata containing some 100,000 verses which has been mentioned for the first time in an inscription of the time. The Mahabharata is not merely a song of victory but a collection of old legends of high-souled kings and pious sages, of dutiful wives and beautiful maids like Sakuntala and Savitri, Nala and Sibi, Amba and Vidula.

Bhagavad Gita

Among the religious poems which form part of the Mahabharata, the most famous is Krishna's address to Arjuna, who was reluctant to fight his dear and near ones, which form the subject matter of the Bhagavad Gita, or the Song of the Lord – later bed-rock of Aryan theism. As the Upanishads represent the Vedanta or the essence of the Vedas, the Bhagavad Gita represents the essence of the teachings of the Upanishads when Krishna says to Arjuna that: "the soul is everlasting, it dwells in all things, firm, unmoving, eternal". In other words, Atman is Brahman. The essence of the teaching of the Bhagavad Gita may be summed up in the maxim: "Do your work without concerning yourself with its result"[1] In an organised society each individual has his special role to play and in every circumstance there are actions which are intrinsically right as laid down by the sacred law of the Aryan society. The right course must be chosen according to the circumstances, without any considerations of personal interest or sentiment. Thus man serves God, and in so far as he lives up to this ideal he draws near to God. As a matter of fact, the stern ethics of the Gita are clearly intended as a defence of the order of the Aryan society against the attacks of reformers and unbelievers. The virtue of the Brahman is wisdom, of the Kshatriya, valour, of the Vaishya, industry, of the Shudra, service. By fulfilling his class function to the best of his ability, with devotion to God and without personal ambition, a man will find salvation, whatever his class.

Ramayana

The author of the Ramayana a little more than the quarter of the size of the other epic was Valmiki, a contemporary of its hero, Rama, the eldest son of Dasaratha, a prince of the Ikshvaku family of Ayodhya, the capital of the old kingdom of Koshala. Rama married Sita, the daughter of Janaka, the celebrated king of Videha in North Bihar but had to leave his home and go into exile for a period of 14 years. Rama with the help of his half brother Lakshmana, Sugriva, Hanuman and other monkey chiefs of Kishkindhya in the Bellary region of South India, recovered his wife, Sita, from Ravana, (the Rakshasa king of Lanka who had kidnapped her) after slaying him and repaired to Ayodhya. However, he had to banish his faithful consort Sita to please his subjects to the hermitage of Valmiki where she gave birth to the twins, Lava and Kusa who subsequently returned to their ancestral home and succeeded to their heritage.

The names of Rama and Sita though met within the Vedic literature often as appellations of human beings are in no way connected in the Vedic texts with the illustrious lines of the Ikshvakus or the Videhas and the name of Ravana is absolutely unknown to Brahmanical or non-Brahmanical literature till we come to the epics themselves or to works like the Kautiliya Arthasastra. Whatever may be the kernel of historical truth underneath the Ramayana, there is no doubt that the Ikshavaku princes from Koshala kingdom played a leading part in the colonisation of the southernmost part of South India, as names of Ikshvaku kings figure prominently in the early inscriptions of Southern India.

Which was composed First – Mahabharata or Ramayana?

Both the Epic Poems were known before the Sutra Age and by sixth century A.D. their fame spread to far-off places like Cambodia. Both of them contain a good deal of pseudo-epic or didactic material which came to be included at a comparatively later date. The question that now may be asked is: Which one of the two saw the beginning of its composition first, Mahabharata or Ramayana?

Since both the epics were more or less contemporaries, worked over through years by a succession of priestly editors, it was always possible for them to interpolate materials from each other and these cannot be used as arguments for advancing the date of the composition of one over the other. For example, the Mahabharata contains as an episode the story of the Rama in a form which suggests the editor of the final version of the Mahabharata knew the Ramayana. Similarly, the Ramayana mentions Janamejaya and "Vishnu who upraised a mountain with his hands", that is Krishna.

However, the tale of the Pandus is known to the Jataka Gathas or the collection of folk-tales and other stories adapted to Buddhist purposes and is hinted at by the Greek writers of the fourth century B.C. in the confused legends about the Indian Herakles and Pandia. It is also known to Panini who composed his Sanskrit grammar, Astadhyayi by 400 B.C. and Asvalayana the author of Griha Sutra as well as the grammarians Katyayana and Patanjali. Patanjali who came towards the end of the Sutra Age and composed his commentary on Panini's grammar seems to be acquainted with the Kishkindhya episode of the Ramayana, which has never been mentioned by any of his predecessors.

Secondly, the style of the Ramayana is less rugged than that of the Mahabharata which contains occasional grammatical and prosodical errors and has a close relationship to that of classical Sanskrit poetry in post-Panini age.

Finally, the scene of the Mahabharata is the holy Brahmanical heartland of the Kuru-Panchalas where the Aryans settled first when they came to India and that of the Ramayana is Koshala in the eastern part of the Ganges Valley where the Aryans expanded later.

All these point to the fact that the main narrative portions of the Mahabharata, admittedly at first only about a quarter of its present size, are appreciably much earlier than those of the Ramayana.

Literary Works during the Sutra Age: Sanskrit and Prakrit

In literary outputs, the Sutra Age though mainly preoccupied with the task of compiling and codifying the existing religious scriptures produces remarkable works on the six auxiliary sciences of the Vedas, as well as discovers new frontiers of learning in such works as that of Kautilya's Arthashastra which we have already discussed at the appropriate place. The most important grammatical works that came through Vedic schools during the Sutra Age in the form of commentaries on Panini's Astadhyayi are Kalapaka or Kalantra by Sarvavarman, Brihat Katha by Bhadrabahu and finally Patanjali's Mahabhashya ascribed to the age of Pushyamitra Sunga the Brahmana general who usurped the last of the Mauryas.

The Age of Sutras whose main concern was to meet the challenge of Buddhism since 486 B.C. also saw the beginning of the composition of the Buddhist scriptures and the Pali Jatakas. The Buddhist Katha Vatthu and the Pali Jatakas whose characters are often talking birds and animals indicate the compositions in Prakrit had also started during the Sutra Age. Since the time of the codification of the Pali canon in the first century B.C., we have evidences of verses here and there which seem to catch echoes of folk song and oral literature. We know from a Chinese translation in 440 A.D., of that part of the Buddhist canon called Samutta Nikaya acquired by Fa-Hien in Ceylon in 411 A.D. – how a Buddhist monk who hears the singing of various secular songs, and converts them to Buddhist purposes by comparatively slight alterations, which in modern parlance may be described as a parody with a religious objective.

An important literary work in Prakrit is the Gatha Saptasati or Saptasataka of Hala, a Satavahana king who ruled in the Deccan in the first century A.D. This is a large collection of self-contained stanzas of great charm and beauty and though these economical and suggestive verses were mainly written for a highly educated literary audience, they contain certain simple and natural descriptions and references to the lives of peasants and the lower classes. About the same time in the North (first century A.D.), the semi-canonical Pali work, Milinda-panha or the questions of Meanander which is an account of the discussions of the Greco-Bactrian king, Milinda with the Buddhist monk Nagasena is written with such literary and dialectical skill that it has been suggested, without much evidence, that the author knew something of Plato. The end of the first century A.D. also saw the composition of the earliest surviving Sanskrit poetry, Buddhacharita, a metrical life of the Buddha by Asvaghosha, the court poet of Kanishka at Purushapura or Peshawar. The compositions such as celebrated astronomical work of Garga, the Paumachariya of Vimalasuri, portions of the Divyavadana as well as Lalitavistara and the Saddharma Pundarika also belong to the post-Maurya Age.

Literary Works during the Gupta Age

In literary activities the Gupta Age shines as the bright morning star. Samudra Gupta took delight in the title of Kaviraja or king of poets and kept himself in close touch with the learned men of his times. He is said to have put an end to the war between good poetry and prosperity by patronising many poets who were none too wealthy. The most notable poet of his court was Harisena who wrote the Allahabad Panegyric about him. One of the ministers of Chandra Gupta II, Vikramaditya, son of Samudra Gupta, was a poet named Virasena-Saba. Bhasa who flourished earlier than Kalidasa, the celebrated poet or the poet laureate of Chandra Gupta II's court, wrote perhaps the oldest complete plays of which thirteen, including Svapnavasvadatta, or the vision of Vasavadatta and Pratijnayaugand-harayana or the vows of Yaugandharyana have survived. Sudraka, probably a contemporary of Kalidasa wrote the play, Mrichchhakatika or the little clay cart, a very realistic Indian drama, unravelling a complicated story, rich in humour and pathos and crowded with action, of the love of a poor Brahman, Charudatta for the virtuous courtesan, Vasantasena. At the same time, Visakhadatta wrote a drama with political overtones Mudra Rakshasa or the Signet Ring of the Minister, which deals with the schemes of the wily Chanakya to foil the plots of Rakshasa, the minister of the last of the Nandas and to place Chandragupta Maurya firmly on the throne. And two of the most outstanding products of the Vedic schools, Aryabhatta and Varahmihira known for their immortal contributions to astronomy and mathematics are said to be the near contemporaries of Kalidasa. Another near contemporary of Kalidasa is Vatsyayana, one of the authorities on sexuality in Ancient India, whose work, *Kamasutra*, gives us detailed instructions on erotic technique, aphrodisiac recipes and charms. His detailed description of the courtship of the husband to win the love and confidence of his newly married wife is still relevant as in India most marriages are arranged ones where the bride has not met her groom before.

Kalidasa

Kalidasa is said to have flourished not only in the reign of Chandra Gupta II but also in that of his son Kumara Gupta I, who assumed the title of Mahendraditya and is considered to be the greatest among all the learned men who adorned the courts of these two kings. Kalidasa saw ancient Indian courtly culture at its zenith, which, like the murals of Ajanta, has been reflected in all his works. He wrote three plays – Malavikagrnimitra, Vikramorvasiya and Abhijnanasakuntala, two large or long poems – Kumarasambhava and Raghuvamsa and two small poems: Meghaduta and Ritusamhara. Meghaduta which is a work of little over 100 verses has always been one of the most popular of Sanskrit poems. It describes a Yaksa who dwells in the divine city of Alaka in the Himalayas, who offends his master Kubera and is banished for a year to the hill of Ramagiri in the Madhya Pradesh. He has left behind his beautiful wife and finds it difficult to bear his separation from her. So, at the beginning of the rainy season when he sees a large cloud moving northward to the Himalayas, he pours his heart out to it. And after a verse or two, the rest of Meghaduta, which seems to contain the quintessence of a whole culture, consists of the Yaksa's address to the cloud.

Among Kalidasa's plays, Abhijnanasakuntala is regarded as the masterpiece and is set in the days of legend, when gods and men were not so apart as they became later. While chasing a deer in the neighbourhood of a forest hermitage, king Dusmyanta falls in love with Sakuntala, the illegitimate child of the nymph Menaka now the foster-daughter of the chief of the hermits, the Sage Kanva who is not then at his home. Sakuntala reciprocates the love with due modesty and later sick and languid with love, confesses her feelings to her friends, Anasuya and Priyamvada who persuade her to write a letter to the king. The king who has not left the hermitage in the absence of the Sage Kanva, overhears the conversation from a nearby thicket appears before Sakuntala and marries her by Gandharva rite and gives her a ring before his departure for the capital. While Sankuntala is undergoing separation from her husband, a great and irascible hermit, Durvasa visits the hermitage and as a result of a fancied slight curses Sakuntala, saying that she will be forgotten by her husband until he sees the ring he has given her. Now Kanva who knows already of what has happened, decides on his return to the hermitage to send the now pregnant Sakuntala to the king and the king because of the curse of Durvasa fails to recognise her. The chief priest of the king wants to adopt Sakuntala till the birth of the child as he knows the prophecy of the sages that the first son of the king would be a universal emperor. The king agrees but Sakuntala is carried to heaven by her mother Menaka. Soon a fisherman finds the ring in the maw of the large fish he has caught and when it is shown to the king, the latter at once recognises it as the one he has given to Sakuntala. His memory returns and he is given to grief for he has lost his wife and he has no heir. Several years later when the king is returning victorious from the battle with the demons, where his help has been earlier sought by Indra, he meets a small boy nobly wrestling with a tame lion cub at the hermitage of the divine sage Maricha. The king stops his chariot to admire the strength and courage of the child and is told that he is Bharata the son of Sakuntala. He now reunites with Sakuntala and the play comes to an end.

When Goethe of the Faust's fame came to know of Sakuntala through the translation of Sir William Jones, the founder of the Royal Asiatic Society in Calcutta in 1783-84, and George Forster[2] he became an instant admirer of its author, Kalidasa. Considered to be Shakespeare of the East, Kalidas is regarded in India as the greatest of Sanskrit poets after the immortal composers of the two epics, the Mahabharata and the Ramayana. After Kalidasa, many other poets like Kumaradasa and Bharavi who composed Janakiharana and Kiratarjuniya respectively, tried their hands at long courtly poems but none of them was as successful and popular as those of Kalidasa.

Literary Works during the Age of Harsha: Bhatti and Bhartrihari

In the seventh century Bhatti wrote Bhattikavya to illustrate rules of grammar and Magha wrote a long poem, Sisupalavadha. However, the finest poet in the single stanza poems in the seventh century was Bhartihari, a Buddhist scholar, whose work, Bhartrihari-Sastra, a commentary on Patanjaii's Mahabhashya was taught at Nalanda at the time of the visits of Hiuen-Tsang and I-Tsings. Bhartihari, wrote on the subjects of worldly wisdom, love and renunciations. Probably his themes had much to do with his own life – as he became seven times a monk, and "seven times returned to the laity". And later wrote in self-agony or mortification: "Through the enticement of the world I returned to the laity./Being free from secular pleasures again I wear the priestly cloak./How do these two impulses/play with me as if a child"?

Harsha

However, seventh century or the Age of Harsha was known more for literary works in the fields of drama and of ornate prose developed under the Guptas than for those in the field of poetry. Harsha himself was credited with the authorship of three plays – Ratnavali, Priyadarsika and Nagananda or the Joy of the Serpents. The first two are charming harem comedies named after their heroines while the last one has a religious purport as shown by prince Jimutavahana who gives his own body to put a stop to the sacrifice of serpents to the divine Garuda. Among the monarchs in Ancient India, Harsha was perhaps the first king to achieve this distinction of producing, not one, but three works. When one remembers that the major part of his 40 years rule were spent in creating the hegemony of Kanauj in the Upper Ganges Valley and that he was constantly on the tour in the different parts of his empire to maintain his suzerainty, one can, however, reasonably doubt whether Harsha has actually authored these three works.

Bana

Harsha's court poet Bana produced Harshacharita and Kadambari in ornate prose style also known as Kayya developed under the Guptas. In this genre there were two other writers Dandin and Subandhu, all of whom including Bana lived in the late sixth and early seventh centuries. Dandin's Dasakumaracharita a collection of exciting and ingenious stories, held together by a framing narrative in a comparatively simple prose and all interwoven with great skill. In ornate prose Subhandhu's Vasavadatta tells of the vicissitudes of her love for the prince Kandarpaketu. Bana's style is similar to that of Subandhu but this work is much more vital and congenial to our taste. His two works where the personality of the author breaks through, show accurate and close observation of life both at the court and outside it. In Harshacharita, Bana gives us a fragment of autobiography unparalleled and perhaps unique in Sanskrit literature. Despite being born of a well-to-do Brahman family, Bana seems throughout his life to have transcended the bounds of orthodoxy and to have retained some of the unconventionality of his wild youth when, after the death of his father at the age of fourteen, he used to wander from city to city among the intellectual bohemians of the time, including ascetics of various sects, literary men, actors, musicians entertainers, doctors and humble members of poor and low castes. His works often show implicit sympathy for the last category of persons – a sentiment rarely found in ancient Sanskrit literature. He was not afraid to put forward his opinions which might have made him unpopular with his royal patron as it actually did when he kept himself away from Harsha's court till his reconciliation with the king many years later. He condemned the doctrine of royal divinity as gross sycophancy and attacked the doctrine of state craft associated with Kautilya as immoral and inhuman. While Harshacharita tells us of Harsha's rise to power with evident exaggeration and general authenticity but without circumstantial detail, Kadambari is perhaps a conscious attempt to improve on the romance as enshrined in Subandhu's Vasavadatta. While the first was apparently unfinished, the second one was completed by Bana's son.

Mahendravikramavarman

Harsha's royal contemporary in the South, the Pallava king Mahendravikramavarman, wrote a one-act play, Mattavilasa where a drunken Saivite ascetic, who loses the skull which he uses as a begging bowl, accuses a Buddhist monk of stealing it and after much satirical dialogue in which are involved other dissolute ascetics of both sexes and of various persuasions, it is found that the skull has been stolen by a dog!

Literary Works During the Post-Harsha Age

In the early eighth century, Bhavabhuti who lived at Kanauj and is regarded as next to Kalidasa in the art of writing plays, produced some important works, three of which, Malatimadhava, Mahaviracharita and Uttaramacharita – have survived. The first is an exciting and horrifying love story where heroine is more than once rescued from death, while the two latter plays, as their names suggest, tell the story of Rama.

After Bavabhuti the quality of writing both in Sanskrit drama and poetry began to decline though prose narrative of fables or folklore was becoming popular. One such collection of fables is the Panchatantra which is in fact a book of instruction in Niti or the conduct of one's affairs, especially intended for kings and statesmen. The little stories are contained in a framing narrative which tells how a king distressed at the evil and stupidity of his sons, entrusted them to a sage who reformed them in six months by telling them a series of fables. Panchatantra was translated into Pahlavi or Middle Persian in the sixth century A.D. and from Pahlavi into Syriac, and from Syriac into Arabic in the eighth century A.D. In various versions the Panchatantra appeared in Hebrew, Greek and Latin, and thus gradually found its way all over Europe.

Literary Works Across the Vindhyas

We have already noted the work of the Pallava king Mahendra Vikramavarman who was Harsha's contemporary in the South. The king's work betrayed penetration of Aryan influence in the South since the days of the Mauryas, which intensified with each successive Imperial Aryan dynasty trying to move beyond the Vindhya hills, Narmada or the Godavari. By the end of the sixth century Aryan influence had penetrated the whole of Tamil land, and her kings and chiefs worshipped and supported the gods of Hinduism, Jainism and Buddhism.

Tamil

Tamil tradition tells us of three Sangam or literary academies which met at Madurai. Nothing survives at the first Sangam attended by gods and sages, only Tamil grammar, Tolkappiyam survives at the second and out of the third Sangam comes Ettutogai or eight anthologies and these together with later poetic works, make up a very large body of poetic literature consisting of poems well over 2,000 ascribed to more than 200 authors. Under the influence of Sanskrit, Tamil poets took to writing long poems which they called by the Sanskrit name Kavya. The earliest and greatest of these is Silappadikaram or the Jewelled Anklet followed by its sequel Manimekalai where the heroine Manimekalai, the daughter of Kovalan, the hero of the Jewelled Anklet, by the dancer Madhavi became a Buddhist nun on hearing the death of her former lover. A third Tamil epic Sivaga-Sindamani describes the exploits of the hero Sivaga or Jivaka from the art of archery to that of curing of snake-bite, winning a new bride for his harem with every feat, only to become a Jaina monk at the end. By now Tamil poets took to translations and adaptations of many northern themes, the most notable of which is Kamban's Ramayana composed in the ninth century A.D. Kamban adapted themes as he thought fit and here and there added episodes of his own.

In his hands the demon Ravana frequently takes on the proportions of a heroic figure, and contrasts favourably with the rather weak and unimpressive Rama. Thus, Kamban's Ramayana as well as the other earlier epics come closer to the realities or the lives of the people and sharply contrast with those courtly epics produced in the Brahmanical and the Buddhist heart lands of the Northern India.

Telugu and Kanarese

Telugu and Kanarese which are spoken further north are naturally even more strongly influenced by Sanskrit; Kanarese first appears in inscriptions at the end of the sixth century A.D. and its earliest surviving literature goes back to the ninth. Telugu does not appear as a literary language until the twelfth century A.D. and became important later in the Middle Ages as the court language of the Vijayanagar empire. Malayalam very closely akin to Tamil became a separate language in the eleventh century A.D.

While these Dravidian languages had been flourishing for centuries, the modern Indo-Aryan groups of languages had not found any literary expression at the time of the Muslim invasion. In the Middle Ages, Apabhramsa or falling away achieved literary form in the poetic compositions of the Jaina writers in Gujarat and Rajasthan. Its chief characteristic is the further reduction of inflexions, which are in part replaced by post positions, as in modern Indian vernaculars. A few late Buddhist writers in Bengal used a similar degenerate Prakrit which is the ancestor of modern Bengali.

Thus, with the development of the art of writing and transformation of the crude language of the Rig Veda into Sanskrit, and the emergence of its six Vedangas or auxiliary sciences as independent disciplines during the Sutra Age, the use of Sanskrit language transcended the religious field and began to vividly portray in drama, prose and poetry the contemporary courtly life of the Aryans. There were however occasions when such writings touch the lives of ordinary men and women as in Sudraka's Mrichchakatika as well as anticipate future Muslim historical chronicles as in Bana's incomplete Harsha Charita.

Sanskrit literary writings which reached its climax under the Guptas began to show signs of its decline, both in quality and in quantity in the subsequent years except for a brief period under Harsha. And when the Muslim came to India and gradually settled down in the North, they ceased to receive the state patronage which had been so long enjoyed by them. With Sanskrit having been replaced by Persian as the language enjoying the patronage of the new rulers, the ground was thus prepared for the gradual refinement of the regional dialects as the vehicles of expression for the future writings in the Middle Ages.

Notes

1. This seems to be inconsistent with the doctrine of the Law of the Deed as believed by the Hindus. However, there is no inconsistency at all. By advising one not to expect the result of the work done, the Bhagavad Gita is actually teaching the Upanishadic doctrine of detachment as practised in the last two stages of the life of a contemporary Hindu.

2. Goethe read the German translation by George Forster, sent to him by Johann Gottfried Herder, a leader of the Romantic Movement in German literature, in 1791. After reading Shakuntala, Goethe wrote a poem on the drama in *Deutsche Monatsschrift* in the same year, which is now famous.

Part II

Medieval India, 1192 A.D. – 1757 A.D.

11

The Dramatis Personae

The Arabs

Islam entered India through the proverbial North-West which had in the past seen hordes of foreigners, the Greeks, the Sakas and the Hunas, coming to India, conquering our territories, settling down there and becoming members of the Indian society as "degenerate Kshatriyas"[1] after assimilating Indian religion and culture with their own. The Arabs were the first to come to India in the early eighth century taking advantage of the struggle for power among the Hindu dynasties in the North over the possession of Kanauj, the imperial capital which had become synchronised with power and culture after the fall of the imperial Pataliputra under the Guptas.

The Arabs were the hardy and sturdy people of Arabia. In Arabia, in the city of Mecca, sometime in 570 A.D. was born the Prophet Muhammad. It was he who founded a new religion called Islam which preached unity of God among the Arabs and roused the desert people to unbounded energy and enthusiasm. Under his successors, the Caliphs of Baghdad, the arms of the Islam advanced from 632 A.D. onwards in all directions, and the banner of Islam floated over many countries from Iran to Spain.

In 712 A.D. the Arabs under Muhammad-bin-Kasim overran Sind by defeating the Brahmana king Dahir, son of Chach, the founder of the ruling dynasty of Sind and captured the rich sea-ports of Western India. However, the further progress of the Arabs was resisted by the Chalukyas in the South, the Pratiharas in the East and the Karkotas in the North. Kasim's work was greatly facilitated by the treachery of certain Buddhist monks and renegade chiefs who deserted Dahir and joined the invader.

The Ghaznavids: Sabuktigin and Mahmud

A new scene soon opened with the foundation of the kingdom of Ghazni in Afghanistan by Alptigin in 962 A.D. Alptigin's son and successor, Sabuktigin carried fire and sword into the territory of Jaipal who belonged to the Hindu Shahiya dynasty of Waihand and whose kingdom extended from Lamghan to Kangra. In 997 A.D. Sabuktigin died and his successor, Mahmud, inflicted a crushing defeat on Jaipal near Peshawar in 1001 A.D. Jaipal burnt himself on a funeral pyre and was succeeded by his son, Anandapala. In 1008 A.D. Mahmud routed the troops of Anandapala under prince Brahmanapala at the battle of Waihand and penetrated further into the territory beyond the Punjab, capturing Thaneswar in 1014, burning the temple of Mathura, sacking Kanauj in 1018 A.D. and thereby extinguishing the once powerful empire of the Pratiharas. In 1022-23 A.D. he subdued Gwalior and Kalinjar and in 1025 A.D. he looted the celebrated temple of Somnath in Kathiawar. The fall of this temple synchronised with the extinction of the Hindu Shahiya kingdom of the Punjab.

Mahmud's expeditions were mostly in the nature of plundering raids and they resulted not only in the annexation of the Hindu Shahiya kingdom of the Punjab but in breaking down of the morale of the Hindu armies. However, between 1030 A.D. when Mahmud died and 1192 A.D. when the Muhammad of Ghur appeared on the scene, the Rajput powers of Western and Central India who had divided among themselves the imperial heritage of the Pratiharas remained comparatively immune from foreign invasions though there were occasional harassment by the Ghaznavid Sultans such as the one when one of their generals advanced up to Benares and sacked the holy city. However, the Ghaznavid occupation of the Punjab not only served as a key to unlock the gates of Indian interior but made big cracks in the Indian polity whose fall was only a question of time. It is true both the Arabs and the Ghaznavid Sultans could not succeed in adding India to the growing empire of Islam but there is no doubt that they paved the way for the eclipse of the Gangetic kingdoms soon.

The Ghurs

The successors of Sultan Mahmud were too feeble to maintain their position at Ghazni in the face of the rising power of the princes of Ghur, a small obscure principality to the south-east of Herat in the mountainous region of Afghanistan and of the Ghuzz tribe of Turkmans. The latter captured Ghazni by driving Khusrav Shah who fled to the Punjab, then the sole remnant of the wide dominions of his ancestors. Ghiyas-ud-din Muhammad, cousin and successor of Saif-ud-din who died while fighting against the Ghuzz Turkmans, drove the Ghuzz Turkmans from Ghazni in 1173 A.D., appointed his younger brother, popularly called Muhammad of Ghur, governor of that province and it was in that capacity that Muhammad of Ghur began his Indian campaigns in 1175 A.D. which led to the capture of Lahore and the final extinction of the rule of the Ghaznavids in the Punjab. The occupation of the Punjab by Muhammad of Ghur made inevitable a confrontation with the Rajputs, particularly with his neighbour, Prithviraj, the powerful Chauhan king of Ajmer and Delhi.

The political condition of Northern India at that time had changed considerably since the days of the Sultan Mahmud. A part of Bihar was in the possession of the Pala kings who were Buddhists but Bengal had passed under the control of the Senas who were followers of the Hindu faith. The Chandellas still controlled Bundelkhand but the Pratiharas in Kanauj had been replaced by the Gahadavalas. Jaichand, the Gahadavalas ruler of Kanauj, who lived mostly at Benares was considered to be the greatest king of India at that time but he was jealous of Prithviraj and did not ally himself with him when Muhammad of Ghur appeared on the scene in the winter of 1190-1191 A.D.

In 1191 A.D. in the first battle of Tarain near Thaneswar Prithviraj with the help of his fellow Rajput princes inflicted a crushing defeat on Muhammod of Ghur who retired to Ghazni. Next year Muhammad of Ghur returned with a strong army, met Prithviraj at the same battle site, defeated him and put him to death along with his brother. This victory of Muhammad at the second battle of Tarain was a decisive one – it did lay the foundation of Muslim dominion in India and the subsequent attempts of the relatives of Prithviraj to recover their lost power ended in fiasco.

After the battle of Tarain in 1192 A.D., Muhammad of Ghur left Qutb-ud-din Aibak who began his career as a slave and who rendered valuable services to him during the Indian expeditions in charge of his conquests. Qutb was left, in fact, "untrammelled not only in his administration of the new conquests but also in his discretion to extend it", and within the next few years, with the help of Ikhtiyar-ud-din Muhammad, he was able to conquer a considerable portion of Hindusthan, extending from the Indus in the West to the Ganges in the East. In 1206, after the assassination of Muhammad of Ghur on his way back from Lahore to Ghazni, his provincial viceroys established their own authority in their respective jurisdictions as there were no male heirs to Muhammad of Ghur. Thus Taj-ud-din Yildiz, Governor of Kirman, ascended the throne of Ghazni while Qutb-ud-din Aibak assumed the title of Sultan and was acknowledged as the ruler of the Indian territories by the Muslim officers in India like Ikhtiyar-ud-din of Bengal and Nasir-ud-din Qubacha of Multan and Uch.

Dynasties of Muslim Rulers

From 1206 to 1757, the end of our period, India was under the rule of Muslim rulers. The kingdom of Delhi under the dynasty of Qutb belonging to Ilbari Turks popularly known as the Slave dynasty, "was not a homogeneous political entity" though they ruled in India for about eight decades till 1290 A.D. The Khaljis ruled India from 1290 A.D. to 1320 A.D. followed by the rule of the Tughluqs which continued upto 1413 A.D. The Tughluqs were replaced by the Sayyids who ruled India till 1451 and were followed by the Lodis till 1526. From 1526 onwards began the rule of the Mughals which after going through a period of ascendancy began to decline in the eighteenth century and lingered on in some form or other till 1857, when it was replaced by the British Crown.

The Delhi Sultanate

The rulers belonging, to the, several dynasties before the Mughals, assumed the title of "Sultan" and owed allegiance to the Caliphs of Baghdad and of Egypt, the successors of the Prophet Muhammad. The authority of the Sultans was normally recognised in the territory roughly corresponding to the united provinces of Agra and Oudh, Bihar, Gwalior, Sind and certain parts of Central India and Rajputana. The Muslim Governors of Bengal were mostly inclined to remain independent of their control and the imperial hold over the Punjab by the Delhi Sultans was occasionally threatened by the Mongols from Central Asia. The fiefs on all sides of Delhi were indeed nuclei of Muslim influence though there were many independent local chieftains and disaffected inhabitants always inclined to defy the authority of the Central Government.

Imperial Period

It was under Ala-ud-din Khalji that "the imperial period of the Sultanate" began when the Muslim dominion over different parts of India witnessed a rapid expansion. The Hindu kingdom of Gujarat was conquered, so were the Rajput strongholds of Ranthambhor, Chitor, Malwa, Ujjain, Mandu, Dhar and Chanderi. The whole of Southern India including the Yadava kingdom of Devagiri, the Kakatiya kingdom of Telingana, the Hoysala kingdom of Mysore and the Pandya kingdom of Malabar came to be included in Ala-ud-din Khalji's empire by 1312. The reign of Ala-ud-din Khalji indeed represented the apogee of the Delhi Sultanate.

Dismemberment

However, dismemberment of the Delhi Sultanate began with Muhammad-bin-Tughluq. Endowed with an extraordinary intellect and industry, he lacked the essential qualities of a constructive statesman. His ill-advised measures and stern policy enforced in disregard of popular will, sealed the doom of his empire of twenty-three provinces. Under his successor Feroz Shah, the process of disintegration was further accelerated by such measures as the revival of jagir system, the extension of the institution of slavery, the persecution of the heretical Muslim sects and the imposition of jizya on the non-Muslims. While the impact of such administrative measures had been eating into the vitality of the Delhi Sultanate, the invasion of Timur in 1398 destroyed its coherence and increased the selfish intrigues of the nobility, who, like the feudal baronage of later Medieval Europe, plunged the whole kingdom into disorder and confusion. It was beyond the capacity of the weak Sayyids and the unsagacious Lodis to restore order and discipline in the kingdom. As soon as the central authority grew weak, the centrifugal tendencies, so common in the history of India, made headway. And a number of independent Sultanates like Bengal in the East, Jaunpur, Malwa, Gujarat and Kashmir in the North-West, Khandesh, Berar,

Ahmadnagar, Bijapur, Golkunda and Bidar in the South arose on the ruins of the Delhi Sultanate.

Among the Hindu kingdoms which appeared on the scene were the Vijayanagar empire, Orissa, Mewar, Kamarupa and Assam and finally Nepal on the Himalayas.

The Coming of the Mughals under Babar

It was the internal dissension in the Court of Ibrahim Lodi who succeeded Sikander Lodi in November 1517 that led to an invitation to Babar who represented Timur on his father's side and Changiz Khan on his mother's side to invade India. Babur who had inherited in 1494 from his father at the age of eleven, the small principality of Farghana in Turkestan cherished the desire of recovering the throne of Timur at Samarquand but was thwarted by his kinsmen and by the rivalry of the Uzbeg chief, Shaibani Khan. Having been deprived of his own patrimony of Farghana, he spent his days as a homeless wanderer for about a year when he formed the bold design of conquering Hindusthan like his great ancestor Timur, the story of whose Indian exploits he had heard from an old lady of 111 years, mother of a village headman who had once given him shelter. Taking advantage of a rebellion in another part of the dominions of the Uzbegs, whose rising power had kept off the Timurids from their principalities, Babar occupied Kabul in 1504. With the help of Shah Ismail Safavi of Persia, he tried to grab Samarquand for the third time in 1511 but the Uzbegs under Shaibani's successor finally defeated him in 1512.

When therefore the invitation from Daulat Khan Lodi, the most powerful noble in the Court of Ibrahim Lodi, reached Babar, he at once accepted it, entered the Punjab and occupied Lahore in 1524. When Daulat Khan and his ally, Alam Khan saw that Babar had no desire to give up his conquests, they turned against him and compelled Babar to retire to Kabul. Within a year Babar came back with reinforcements, captured the Punjab, and defeated Ibrahim Lodi, the nominal ruler of the shrivelled Afghan empire in the historic battle of Panipat in 1526 A.D. It is true that this victory did not at once give Babar the virtual sovereignty of the country because there were other strong powers like the Afghan military chiefs, and the Rajputs under Rana Sangha who also then aspired after political supremacy and were thus sure to oppose him but it did enable him to set his foot on the path of empire building in India and thereby marked the foundation of Mughal dominion in India. The battle of Panipat of 1526 is thus a turning point in the history of India.

Mughal Conquest of India

As a matter of fact, there were three phases in the history of the Mughal conquest of India. The first phase from 1526 to 1530 was occupied with the subjugation of the Afghans and the Rajputs under Rana Sangha. The second phase which lasted till 1540 commenced with the reign of Humayun in 1530, who made unsuccessful attempts to subjugate Malwa, Gujarat and Bengal, but was expelled from India by Sher Shah, the Afghan, which meant revival of the Afghan power for a brief period of fifteen years. The third phase which began in 1555 was marked by the restoration of the Mughal dominion by Humayun and its expansion and consolidation by Humayun's son and successor Akbar, who ascended the throne of Hindusthan after Humayun's death in 1556.

Mughal Rule in India

The establishment of the Mughal dominion in India may be regarded as "an event in Islamic and world history" as it meant a fresh triumph for Islam in India, at a time when its followers were gaining success in other parts of the world. Thus, the Turks had captured Constantinople in 1453 and one of their very successful rulers, Sulaiman the Magnificent who ruled Constantinople between 1520 and 1566, had extended the authority of the Turki empire over South Eastern Europe while in Persia, Ismail Safavi who ruled the country between 1500 and 1524 had laid the foundation of the famous Safavi empire.

Akbar

Babar who formed the link between Central Asia and India, between predatory hordes and imperial government, between Changiz Khan, Timur and Akbar, brought to his descendants the energy of the Mongol, the courage and capacity of the Turk, the culture and urbanity of the Persian and laid the first stone of the splendid fabric which his grandson Akbar completed. An intrepid soldier, a benevolent and wise ruler, a man of enlightened ideas, and a sound judge of character, Akbar launched himself on an annexationist career immediately after his accession to the throne of Agra in 1556 till 1601 when unforeseen and uncontrollable circumstances prevented him from carrying it further. "A monarch", as he held, "should be ever intent on conquest, otherwise his neighbours rise in arms against him". He brought under his control the whole of Northern and Central India and guided by the traditional policy of the past imperial governments as those of the Mauryas, the Guptas, the Khaljis and the Tughluqs as well as by his desire to drive the Portuguese out to the sea as he did not think it wise to allow them a share in the economic resources and politics of India, he sought to bring the Deccan Sultanates, Ahmadnagar, Bijapur, Golkunda and Khandesh, under his hegemony.

However, Akbar did not ignore the feelings of the conquered and trample on their rights and privileges with an eye only to self-aggrandisement. He correctly realised the soundness of not ill-treating the Hindus, who formed the overwhelming majority of the population, or of relegating them permanently to a position of inequality and humiliation, thereby showing his transcendental ability of Akbar as a statesman. He not only meted out fair treatment to the Hindus and appointed them to high posts but also tried to remove all invidious distinctions between the Muslims and non-Muslims. Thus, he abolished the pilgrim tax in the eighth year (1564) and the jizya in the ninth year (1565) of his reign, and inaugurated a policy of universal toleration.

Decline and Fall

Akbar thus built up and consolidated on his policy of religious toleration, a vast empire which continued in full glory till the end of Shah Jahan's reign. However, reversal of Akbar's policy by Shah Jahan's successor, Aurangzeb, a great grandson of Akbar, contributed to the decline of the Mughal empire, which was further hastened by a succession of weak rulers after the death of Aurangzeb in 1707, followed by the invasion of Nadir Shah in 1739 and of the four invasions of Ahmad Shah Abdali, the first of which took place in 1748. By the end of our period, that is, by 1757 when the battle of Plassey which marks the beginning of Modern India was fought in Bengal, the Mughal empire had virtually shrunk to a district around Palam as in the last days of the disintegration of the Delhi Sultanate, and the Mughal emperor, Aziz-ud-din, a great grandson of Aurangzeb, who had succeeded the Mughal emperor, Ahmad Shah, in

1754 under the title of Alamgir II, was desperately fighting to free himself from the control of his ambitious and unscrupulous Wazir, Ghazi-ud-din Imad-ul-Malk, a grandson of the deceased Nizam-ul-Malk of the Deccan.

Note

1. This is how Manu describes the foreign invaders who ruled in Ancient India. "Kshatriyas" were the ruling or the warrior classes of the Indian society in the past.

12

The Muslim State: Its Nature and Administration

The Muslim state in Medieval India under the Delhi Sultans and the Mughal emperors was a theocratic one and its existence was theoretically justified by the needs of religion. The heads of the state at times paid only ceremonial allegiance to the Caliphs of Baghdad and Egypt but they never owed their power and position to them nor to the will of the people of the conquered lands, which rested on their military strength. And this was understood and acquiesced in, not merely by the unthinking rabble but also by the soldiers and the intellectuals – the poets and philosophers, and the Ulemas of the age. They had to be constantly on their guard against the hostility of the Hindu States, the Hindu fighting communities and the foreign invaders through the north-west. This required a strong centralised government, which gradually made itself despotic, in the absence of a hereditary Muslim aristocracy which was conscious of its own rights and privileges and eager to assert these against royal despotism, of popular assemblies keen about constitutional liberty and of public opinion strong enough to oppose autocracy. The Ulemas, who exercised much influence in the state had not the courage to openly oppose the activities of the heads of state though the heterogeneous Muslim nobility sometimes played its cards in the choice of a successor as the succession to a deceased head of the state in Muslim India was not regulated by any recognised law or any definite principle of inheritance. He was the chief commander of forces; he was also the chief law-giver and the final Court of appeal. In theory the authority of the head of the Muslim state in religious matters was limited by the *Quran* but in practice he was a perfect autocrat, unchecked by any restrictions – his word was law and binding upon all. He was the Caesar as well as the Pope – both combined in one person.

However autocratic a ruler could be, it was difficult to manage the affairs of a large and unwieldy empire which rose to its apogee under Ala-ud-din and Muhammed-bin-Tughlaq in the time of the Sultanate and Akbar and his successors in the time of the Mughals, single-handed. He had to devise an administrative machinery with a regular hierarchy of officers in charge of various departments, who, however, did not in any way check his authority but rather carry out their respective duties according to the former's orders. In matters of administration both the Delhi Sultans and the Mughal emperors could consult their trusted friends and officers who formed a sort of advisory body or council but the latter's advice was not binding upon the former who selected their own personnel for administration. Under the Delhi Sultans as under the Mughal emperors the highest officer in the state was the Wazir who had control over the other departments such as those of Risalat or appeals: Arz or military; Insha or correspondence; Bandagan or slaves; Qaza-l-Mamlik or justice, intelligence and posts, Amar Kohi or agriculture (created by Muham-mad-bin-Tughluq), Mustakhraj or collection of arrears of revenues (created by Ala-ud-din Khilji); Khairat or charity (created by Firuz Shah Tughluq); Istihqaq or pensions as well as those of the mint, charitable institutions and the karkhanas. The chief departments of the state under the Mughals were (a) the imperial household under the Khan-i-Saman, (b) The exchequer under the Diwan, (c) the Military Pay and Accounts Officer under the Mir Bakshi, (d) the judiciary under the Chief Qazi; (e) Religious Endowments and Charities under the Chief Sadr or Sadr-us-Sudur, and (f) the censorship of Public Morals under the Muhtasib. The Diwan or Wazir was usually the highest officer in the state, being in sole charge of revenues and finance. Every officer of the state held a Mansab or official appointment of rank and profit, and, as such, was bound theoretically to supply a number of troops for the military service of the state. Thus, the Mansabdars formed the official nobility of the country, and this system was the "army, the peerage, and the civil administration, all rolled into one", Each of the chief officer of the departments was assisted by a number of subordinate officials. Thus, the Qazi-ul-Qazat or the principal judicial officer in the realm appointed Qazis in every provincial capital who made investigations into, and tried, civil as well as criminal cases of both the Hindus and the Muslims; the Muftis expounded Muslim Law; and the Mir Adls drew up and pronounced judgements.

In the days of the Sultanate the number of provinces rose from 20 to 25. The head of province was the Naib Sultan who exercised his executive, judicial and military functions, like a despot, subject only to the control of the central government, which varied according to the strength or weakness of the latter. The Naib Sultan subdivided his province into smaller portions which were placed in the charge of Muqtas or of Amils. These were further subdivided into smaller units under Shiqdars, whose jurisdiction did not often extend beyond a few miles. Similarly the number of provinces under the Mughals rose from 12 in the time of Akbar to 21 in the time of Aurangzeb. The head of the province often styled as the Sipah Salar or the Commander-in-Chief, Sahib Subah or Lord of the Province or simply Subadhar was officially described as the Nazim who was the head of the civil, and military administration, assisted by a staff of subordinate officers like the Diwan, the Bakshi, the Faujdar, the Kotwal, the Qazi, the Sadr, the Amil, the Qanungo, the Bitikchi, the Potdar and the Waqa-i-navis. The provincial head was paid from the revenue of his province and after meeting the cost of his administration he had to remit the surplus to the central exchequer. He maintained a local militia and had to render military aid, at times, to the centre. Normally members of the ruling families were appointed to the provinces as their governors or viceroys. Thus, the administration of the provinces under the Delhi Sultans as well as under the Mughals "was an exact miniature of the central government" or "a replica of the empire".

Needs of an Islamic Community and Administration

With the building up of a vast empire by the Delhi Sultans under Ala-ud-din Khalji and Muhammad-bin-Tughluq as well as by the Mughals under Akbar and his successors, a vast bureaucracy was needed to administer it both at the centre and in the provinces. Thus the need of the hour was a large number of qualified personnel trained in the Muslim rules of governance which could not be met by the existing systems of Hindu and Buddhist learning. Secondly, the Muslim community in India which was smaller in size in the beginning began to expand as the Muslims gradually settled down to rule partly through conversion of non-Muslims into their religion and partly through marriages with Indian women of non-Muslim religions helped by the Quranic allowance of four wives, as most of them, except perhaps the royals and the nobles, were not accompanied by their females. Their social and religious needs and interests could not be served by the Hindu or the Buddhist systems of learning. As a separate religious group, the Muslims in India were concerned with maintaining their own religious identity and, therefore, with transmission of basic knowledge about religion to the younger generations and with the production of experts in Hadith, Fiqh, Qurat, Hitz or Ulema in appropriate numbers, not only to lead congregational prayers in mosques but also to act as religious counsellors and even perform judicial and quasi-judicial functions. Finally, a study or a knowledge of the *Quran* was a must for every faithful follower of Islam and it was imperative upon his Muslim parent in Medieval India to provide sufficient education to his children to do so and to help him utter his prayers at namaz at the appropriate times in praise of the Allah.

All the needs and requirements of the Muslim administration, of Muslim community as well as of their individuals were met and supplied by their own system of education which the Muslim rulers gradually introduced in India. From a very humble beginning in 1206, it began to expand to cope with an expanding empire and gradually covered the Muslim empire in Medieval India with a network of maktabs and madrasahs, mosques and khanqahs, just as the Buddhist Viharas had dotted the empires of Ashoka and Kanishka in the hey-days of Buddhism in Ancient India.

13

The Structure and Nature of Islamic Education

In the previous chapter we have briefly analysed the history of Islamic rule in India. Let us now briefly discuss the structure of Islamic education so that we can subsequently understand the thrust provided by the Muslim rule to its spread in Medieval India.

The Quran as the Genesis of Islamic Education

The genesis of Islamic education is the holy *Quran*.[1] The *Quran* consists of words which came to Muhammad when in a state of trance and is never confounded with the Hadith or Sunnah of the Prophet, which consists of words he uttered when no physical change was apparent on him. The *Quran* is also known as *Al-Quran*, "The Reading", the Reading of the man who knew not how to read and who was bade to read despite his illiteracy by the angel Gabriel at Mount Hira where Muhammad used to retire with his family during Ramadan, the month of heat, every year, for meditation in a desert cave.

Thus the Surah-i-Iqra or the Al-alaq, that is, the first revealed version of the *Quran* opens with an injunction addressed to the Prophet Muhammad on the art of reading and of the art of writing as a religious duty. Without the knowledge of reading and of the art of writing, the *Quran* could not be studied, the Hadith and other sciences could not be understood and the truth could not be apprehended. As the Prophet Muhammad himself says: "Acquire knowledge because he who acquires it in the way of the Lord, performs an act of piety; who speaks of it, praises the Lord; who seeks it, adores God; who dispenses instruction in it, bestows alms; and who imparts it to its fitting object, performs an act of devotion to God". The Prophet further explains why he asks every follower of Islam to acquire knowledge: "Knowledge enables its possessor to distinguish what is forbidden from what is not; it lights the way to heaven, it is own friend in the desert, our society in solitude, our companion when bereft of friends; it guides us to happiness; it sustains us in misery; it is our ornament in the company of friends; it serves as an armour against our enemies. With knowledge the servant of God rises to the heights of goodness and to a noble position, associates with sovereigns in this world, and attains to the perfection of happiness in the next".

As a matter of fact the entire Islamic system of education is geared to the acquisition of knowledge without the rigours of a Brahmacharin as in a Vedic school or the renunciation of the world as in a Buddhist Vihara and is open to all the followers of Islam, rich or poor, orphan or destitute. In Medieval India there were usually three conduits through which this knowledge was acquired. These were maktab, madrasah and khanqah. While maktab was a place where elementary education was imparted, higher learning was pursued at a madrasah and religious education or theology was chiefly discussed at a khanqah, the birthplace of Sufism or spiritualism in Islam.

Maktab

Maktab occupies a very important place in the Islamic scheme of learning. As the Prophet had preached that acquisition of knowledge was essential for every true Muslim and had asked all his followers to seek knowledge from "the cradle to the grave", the building or identifying a place where this process of acquisition of knowledge could start was synchronous with that of a mosque or a place where Allah could be worshipped. The local boys whose parents could not afford to teach them at home, and their number was usually large, were sent to it for instruction. A maulavi or a religious preceptor was appointed either by the patron or the builder of the mosque where the maktab was situated. The offerings made at the shrine by the devotees as well as regular help from the patron or the builder of mosque contributed towards its maintenance including the financial support to the maulavi.

When a child was four years, four months and four days old, he was dressed in his best clothes and seated on a cushion in the presence of his family members and their friends. Placed before him were the alphabets, the form of letters used for computation, the Surah-i-Iqra or the Al-alaq, the *Quran* and he was asked to touch them in succession. If the child refused to oblige, he was made to pronounce Bismillah which answered every purpose and from that day his education was deemed to have begun. This compares favourably with the Upanayana ceremony of Hindu learning at the age of 5 years of the child in the Sutra Age onwards.

The child at the maktab was first taught the alphabet, with correct pronunciation, punctuation and signs of accents. After learning this, he was taught their combinations and then made to read and write short sentences where such combinations occurred. He was given some exercise daily, which he read and wrote on his takhti, an oblong board which could be washed clean after use. For correct pronunciation, the child was taught the Pandenamah of Sadi. Once the correct pronunciation was learnt, the art of writing was taught followed by the cramming of the Persian grammar. Four or five hours a day were devoted to the art of writing, as good writing was considered essential for all children attending a maktab. Afterwards, the Gulistan and Bostan of Sadi as well as such poetic works as Yusuf and Zulekha, Laila and Majnu and Sikandarnamah were taught, and the morals, if any, explained to them. Study of the holy *Quran* began at the age of seven and the child learnt by rote the thirtieth chapter of the *Quran* which contained verses of daily prayer and Fatiha or verses which were recited at the time of burial. As a matter of fact, the *Quran* was the first school in which children of Islam received their early education. Besides *Quran*, education in Khalikbari, Karimah and Mamkimah was given. Finally, instruction in elementary arithmetic, particularly acquaintance with the numerals, completed the curricula at the maktab stage where children learnt by rote and cramming was universal.

Madrasah

After the completion of his study at a maktab, one could be eligible for admission to a madrasah where instruction in higher education was given. A madrasah comparable to a college in pre-1854 days in Modern India was usually attached to a mosque and was built either by a Sultan or a Padshah, an Amir or an Omraha, an affluent or wealthy person who usually appointed the one or more erudite teachers for imparting instruction. Usually a land or some specific grant as charity was made available by the state or the builder or the patron for the maintenance of the madrasah including its teachers and students. Sometimes, prompted by religious and other sentiments a ruler or a patron could provide accommodation for the lodging and boarding of students and teachers.

While a comprehensive and profound study of the *Quran* and its commentary by noted theologians dominated the courses at a madrasah, other relevant subjects included agriculture, accountancy, astrology and astronomy, history, geography, mathematics, Islamic law and jurisprudence, and statecraft or the art of administration. The courses also included a critical study of the Arabic and the Persian languages and literatures and later, after Akbar had thrown the doors of a madrasah open to a Hindu student in pursuance of his policy of religious toleration, a study of Sanskrit and Hindu religious scriptures such as the Upanishads as Abul-Fazl informs us.

It is clear that the curricula at a madrasah took care of the contemporary socio-economic and political needs of Muslim India and aimed at empowering the students for improving their positions and prospects in the contemporary society. This is why years before the formal opening of a madrasah to a Hindu student in the days of Akbar, we come across a number of Hindus who were well-versed in Arabic and Persian and were occupying important positions in the Muslim administration – obviously they took pains to learn these subjects privately, sitting at the feet of a learned Muslim scholar or teacher. They usually came from the affluent sections of the Hindu society including Brahmins who could afford to pay the fees of a teacher engaged privately. The inclusion of the art of administration in the curricula is significant in the sense that in the Muslim India the study of this subject was not a close preserve of the princes and members of the royal families as it had been in Ancient India. At a madrasah no subject was forcibly thrust upon a student who could choose his own subject according to his aims and interests. It may be noted here that even after completing his study in a subject at a madrasah, a student could pursue further studies in it by engaging the services of a learned teacher in the field as was actually done by many well-known scholars of Medieval India such as Abdul Qadir Badaoni, Abul Fazl and his brother Faizi.

The duration of a course at a madrasah depended upon the calibre of a student in acquiring proficiency in it. It could be seven years or more at the end of which the teacher conducted an examination or a test to satisfy himself about the student's mastery over the subject. A successful student was often rewarded not only with sanads, imams, and tamghas but also with a suitable position in the state administration on the recommendation of his teacher.

Each madrasah was provided with a hostel for its students and apartments for its teachers. As said before the life of a student in a hostel was free from the hardships associated with the one in a Vedic school or a Buddhist Vihara. The students lived comfortably as could be seen from contemporary accounts such as those of Allam Shibli who says that students of a madrasah were not only provided with room, carpet, food, oil, pen and paper but also with sweets and fruits daily. Each student used to receive an Asharfi or a gold coin per month to meet his monthly expenses. Similarly Ibn Batuta who visited India during the reign of Muhammad-bin-Tughluq speaks about a big madrasah with 300 rooms for the residence of the students who daily studied the *Quran* and were provided with daily allowance for food and annual allowance for clothes. In another madrasah where he stayed for sixteen days on its campus, he marvelled at the beautiful and costly diet of its students. They were provided with four kinds of food daily that is, chicken loaves, 'Poloo' and 'Korma' which were special meat dishes and a plate of sweets. In Buddhist Viharas vegetarian food served to its resident monks varied according to their status and only the most important among the resident visitors were served food which was princely. Thus, Hiuen Tsang during his residence at Nalanda in the seventh century A.D. received each day 120 jambiras (a kind of fruit), twenty areca nuts, twenty nutmegs, an ounce of camphor, and a peck of the finest variety of rice called Mahasali rice which grew only in Magadha and nowhere else and was offered only to the king or the religious persons of great distinction. Besides the supply of these provisions, he received every month three measures of oil, and daily, a supply of butter and other things according to his need. In any case, meat never formed a part of diet of a student either at a Vedic school or a Buddhist Vihara. Thus the life of a student at a madrasah supported by grants of big jagirs, villages or estates was more comfortable and less rigorous than that of his counterpart in Ancient India.

Mosques and Khanqahs

Islamic education was diffused not only through maktabs and madrasahs but also through mosques which were founded by rulers and others, and khanqahs which were started by the heads of religious orders and other pious persons. The khanqahs which were comparable to the monasteries of Medieval Europe often grew out of the tombs of celebrated saints known as dervishes, who, on account of their profound knowledge, were loved and respected by the people at large as their murshids or spiritual preceptors. These dargahs which could be seen in different parts of Muslim India spearheaded Islamic education and culture among the common people and were associated with such venerable saints and scholars as Shaikh Ali Hajveri known as Data Sahib, Sayyid Hussain Zanjani, Khawajah Muin-ud-din Chisti who died at Ajmer in 1265 A.D., Shah Nizam-uddin-Auliya who hailed from Ghazni and died in Delhi, after living a long life, in the reign of Ala-ud-din Khalji in 1325 A.D., Hazrat Mahbub-i-Ilahi, Bawa Farid Ganj Shakar, Khwajah Baha-ud-din Multani and Hazrat Mujaddad Alf Sani. These dargahs and mosques were too numerous to be enumerated and many of them could still be seen today as from the very nature of their being places of divine worship, they were more permanent than maktabs and madrasahs. Needless to say, they greatly supplemented the educational work done at maktabs and madrasahs in Medieval India.

Nature of Islamic Education

Thus Islamic education was imparted to the followers of Islam through organised institutions such as maktabs and madrasahs which were endowed either by the rulers, their relations, friends and followers as well as by the wealthy and pious Muslims. In this respect they bear close resemblance to the Buddhist Viharas and the temple colleges of South India from seventh century onwards which were similarly founded and endowed for their upkeep. However, they vastly differed in their approach and treatment of the subject of education. Both had separate goals to reach – while for the Buddhist Viharas and the Brahmanical institutions education was religion and religion education which would help the followers to attain supreme knowledge and blissful liberation from the cycle of birth and death, the Islamic educational institutions prepared the followers for the present life and the life after death only. Consequently, in the scheme of Islamic education there had been no questions to explore the mysteries of the universe which had given birth to the Vedas and the Upanishads in Ancient India. In a sense, Islamic education was more practical than spiritual despite its Sufi philosophy.

The reason why Islamic education appeared to be more practical than spiritual was because of the inherent goal it had set up before itself. The followers of Islam were exhorted by the Prophet to convert the dar-ul-harb or non-Muslim lands into dar-ul-Islam or realms of Islam. While the initial stages could be completed by the Jihad or the holy wars, the final stages required the transmission of the knowledge of the Prophet and of the *Quran* to the newly converts. As a matter of fact, a course at the maktab was never completed for one who was not able to read the *Quran* and utter the prayers at the namaz. Secondly, the Muslims were called upon to rule in an alien environment, a people belonging to another religion and culture, who far out-numbered them. Unless and until they had adequate number of personnel with qualifications in Islamic education, law and jurisprudence, art of war and of administration, the foundations of their empire in India rested on quicksands. It was a chain of madrasahs which every ruler was keen to create that supplied the necessary qualifications needed for the required personnel. And until the days of Akbar these madrasahs which were attached to mosques or the vice versa were the close preserves of the Muslims, though occasionally instances could be found of a Hindu with a knowledge in the Persian or Arabic serving the army or the administration at a higher level under a tolerant ruler like Sher Shah.

It may be mentioned here that the British who virtually began to rule parts of India from 1757 onwards did exactly the same thing, though in a different perspective. They ruled India with their own men trained in their own education, though reluctantly from 1853 onwards they began to admit a few qualified Western educated Indians as member of the covenanted civil service. However, the difference between the British and the Muslims lies in the fact that while the former regarded India as a colony and looked upon themselves as mere birds of passage, the Muslims never did so. The latter accepted India as their new homeland and the rich among them were never allowed to remit wealth out of the country. Secondly, while the British discriminated the Indians on the basis of their colour, the Muslims never did so and we all know that one of the wives of the Prophet Muhammad was a coloured one. Finally, while the British liaisons with the Indian women from 1757 onwards gave birth to the Anglo-Indian community, who were neither accepted by the British nor by the Indians as members of their own societies: there was no such hybrid community that came into existence in the long span of nearly 650 years of Muslim rule in the country simply because of the Quranic allowance of four wives that a Muslim could take after conversion into Islam, which obviously they did in India.

However, the British, despite the presence of the Christian missionaries, never officially interfered with the religions of the Indians which the Muslims did in the past to fulfil the goals of Islam. The Muslim rulers looked upon themselves as Ghazis or Holy Warriors and the Mughal emperors from Jahangir onwards officially affixed Ghazi to their regal titles. As a matter of fact, the early years of the Islamic rule in India concentrated on increasing the number of converts from other religions often by force, coercion or persuasion and there is no doubt that a large number of people suffering from the various disabilities and restrictions of their own religions joined the new faith which was the faith of the new rulers. And they did so certainly not without any material advantages such as the exemption from the payment of the jizya tax imposed by the Muslim rulers except Akbar on 'unbelievers' in Islam. For these new converts as well as for the offsprings of the inter marriages maktabs were more important than the madrasahs, where, as we have already said, introduction to the knowledge of the *Quran* was made. Maktabs were always attached to mosques which could be seen dotting the different parts of the Muslim dominions, including villages where the Muslims often outnumbered the followers of other religions.

While maktabs with mosques could be constructed and maintained by the local Muslims or by the rich among them for congregational prayers, the construction and maintenance of a madrasah which called for more expenses was usually done by the rulers, members of the ruling families and by the wealthy officials and nobles not excluding the prosperous merchants and traders, petty landlords and chieftains. The contemporary Muslim chronicles are often strewn with references to the construction of madrasahs by these people and the usual sites for them were the imperial and provincial capitals, new cities and towns built by the rulers and important trading and commercial centres. It was to these institutions that students would often come from faraway places and would reside on the campus, attending instructions by distinguished teachers in advanced Islamic learning, in the morning and in the evening with a break at noon, for several years before they could empower themselves for a better life and prospect.

Relevance of Islamic Education

The question that we may ask now is how far the subjects taught at the maktabs and the madrasahs were relevant to the people and society of Medieval India under the rule of Islam? There is no doubt that the Islamic education catered to the needs of its rulers and its people and was geared to the fulfilment of its religion by spreading the message of Allah as revealed in the *Quran* and the Hadith. The courses offered and the themes taught were all Islamic and they hardly reflected the interests of religions other than Islam. The texts were Arabic and Persian and their authors were also Arabic and Persian though Muslim authors from Amir Khursrav onwards, with family connections in Central and Western Asia who composed their works in India, gradually came to be studied at the madrasahs. Yet the subjects the latter composed in India, particularly history and *belles-lettres* had little to do with interests outside their own rulers and communities and were therefore largely irrelevant to the needs of the society at large. It was, as if, a bit of Arabia and Persia was transplanted in the Indian soil through the maktabs and the madrasahs. And though Akbar tried to broaden the courses by including Hindu learning they continued to have little impact as the basic character of the Islamic education was not much altered. And if Bernier were to be believed, Aurangzeb was the first Muslim ruler of Medieval India to question the relevance of an education which did not enlighten one about the history, geography, politics, religions, culture and languages of the people of one's adopted homeland, that is, India.

Perhaps the nature of the Islamic education imparted at the Islamic institutions has something to do with what may be called 'colonialism' in modern parlance but it will be unjust to club it with the Western education of the British Raj later, which enlightened one more on England and Europe than on India. We must not forget that India was for the Muslims an adopted homeland which was a colony to the British. A correct and just interpretation will be in describing the Islamic education in Medieval India as the one reflecting only the interests of the ruling classes as in Ancient India when Brahmanical education gave way to Buddhist learning when the rulers from Ashok onwards shifted their interests in religion from Brahmanism to

Buddhism. Islamic education was therefore basically a religion oriented education which took care of the interests of the Muslim communities in Medieval India.

Indebtedness of Islamic Education to the Arts and Crafts of Vedic Schools

We have said earlier that the Islamic educational institutions were more practical than spiritual but they were not certainly so practical as to create new arts and crafts, from the scratch, which the Muslim invaders found in abundance to satisfy their's and their community's needs and interests when they came and settled down in Medieval India. The various arts and crafts including music, medicine, and painting which had contributed to the making of a glorious civilisation in the Age of the Guptas and which were taught not in Vedic schools but through apprenticeship or Guru-Shishya Parampara or through family connexions, where the father was often the teacher, came to be boosted greatly by lavish patronage and in course of time came to be influenced greatly by the tastes, ideas and interests of the Muslim rulers of Medieval India.

Inherent Vitality of Islamic Education

Yet the Islamic education in Medieval India possessed an inherent vitality which contributed to the growth and development of a homogeneous Muslim community in India. There is no doubt that courses taught at the maktabs and the madrasahs were not uniform and varied from place to place and often changed at the changing interests of the Muslim rulers but the medium of instruction in all these educational institutions, was the same, though it was not Turki, but Persian, the Court language of the Caliphs of Baghdad and Egypt, the successors and the descendants of the Prophet Muhammad. And the study of Arabic was compulsory as it was the language of the *Quran*, and without a knowledge of Arabic, no one could study the *Quran* which was a 'must' for every faithful follower of Islam, though Akbar tried to dispense with the study of the language of the Prophet in the context of the promulgation of his own religion, "Din-i-Ilahi".

It must be mentioned here that the study of Arabic and Persian was not peculiar to the Islamic educational institutions in the Medieval India alone but also common to their counterparts in other parts of the contemporary Islamic world. And this very fact had contributed to a great extent to the growth of a feeling of Islamic brotherhood among the Muslims of the world. This also contributed to the mobility of learned persons and scholars from one part of the Islamic world to another, thereby enriching the culture and learning of both. And Medieval India benefited most as a host of scholars from Central and Western Asia attracted by the wealth and munificence of its rulers came to reside at their Courts and ultimately made India their homeland, some of them acquiring Non-Muslim women as their wives, following the example of their patrons among the Delhi Sultans and the Mughal emperors. In the ultimate analysis it were the Delhi Sultans and the Mughal emperors and their nobles and provincial governors, many of whom later became independent, who acted as the pivot of the Islamic system of education in Medieval India. In the subsequent chapters we shall elaborate this point.

Note

1. All the Surahs of the Quran were recorded in writing before the Prophet's death and were committed to memory by many Muslims. Within two years after the death of the Prophet when a large number of those who knew the Quran by heart were killed, a collection of the whole Quran was made and put in writing.

14

The Age of Sultans

The Age of Sultans roughly covers a period of 320 years. It begins with the year 1206 when Qutb-ud-din Aibak became the recognised ruler of the Indian conquests of Muhammad of Ghur after his assassination without any male heir. The dynasty of Qutb-ud-din is, however, inaccurately described as Slave dynasty for none but three kings of this dynasty, Qutb-ud-din himself, Iltutmish and Balban were slaves and these three too were manumitted by their masters. Qutab-ud-din received a letter of manumission and a canopy of state from Sultan Ghiyas-ud-din Mahmud, the nephew and successor of his master, Muhammad of Ghur, before his elevation to the throne of Delhi and Iltutmish was freed even before his master Qutb-ud-din. He obtained his manumission during the campaign of Muhammad of Ghur against the Khokar and was elevated as Amir-ul-Umara. Balban who belonged to "forty Turki slaves of Iltutmish" got his freedom along with them. It is also incorrect to describe the members of Qutb-ud-din dynasty as Afghans or Pathans because all these rulers were neither Afghans nor Pathans, but Turks and belonged to the tribe of Ilbari in Turkestan.

The Ilbari Turks ruled in India for about eight decades, from 1206 to 1290, but under them the kingdom of Delhi "was not a homogeneous political entity". The authority of the Sultans was normally recognised in the territory corresponding to the United Provinces of Agra and Oudh, Bihar, Gwalior, Sind and certain parts of central India and Rajputana. The Bengal Governors were mostly inclined to remain independent of their control, and the imperial hold over the Punjab was occasionally threatened by the Mongols. The Ilbari Turks were succeeded by the Khaljis who ruled till 1320 when they were replaced by the Tughluqs. With the reign of Ala-ud-din Khalji which witnessed the rapid expansion of the Muslim dominion over different parts of India begins the imperial period of the Delhi Sultanate. The Tughluqs inherited from the Khaljis a kingdom which embraced within its sphere, the Doab, the plains of the Punjab and Lahore with the territories extending from the Indus to the coast of Gujarat in the north, the whole province of Bengal in the east, the kingdom of Malwa, Mahoba, Ujjain and Dhar in the central region, and the Deccan, which had been recently added to it. However, disintegration of the Delhi Sultanate began as a reaction to the fantastic projects of Muhammad-bin-Tughluq, which the successors of the Tughluqs, the Sayyids and the Lodis who ruled in India till 1526 could not stop.

Almost all the Delhi Sultans were devout Muslims, ruled India in the name of the successors of the Prophet, the caliphs of Baghdad and of Egypt and paid ceremonial allegiance to them, with two short breaks which happened under Ala-ud-din Khalji and Muhammad-bin-Tughluq. The two latter Sultans were certainly strong defenders and supporters of Islam but as both of them put the interests of the state before those of religion, they tried to rule independently of the Ulemas without obtaining any pontifical recognition from the Caliphs. It was only when Muhammed-bin-Tughluq was losing the loyalty and confidence of the people that he tried to restore it in them by obtaining a patent from the Abbasid Caliph of Egypt. It was however too late to do so for no one had questioned the Sultan's title to the throne but it was his policy and measures which were not to the liking of his subjects.

The Delhi Sultans looked upon their activities towards the spread of Islamic education and culture as an extension of their own religion, which reached its apogee under Firuz-shah-Tughluq. We propose to took at them from several angles: their patronisation of learned men, their endeavours to educate their children and finally their efforts to spread education institutionally among their subjects.

Patronisation of Learning and Learned Men

Quite in keeping with the observation of the Prophet that "he who favours learning and the learned honours me", the Delhi Sultans not only patronised learning but also learned men as a religious obligation. Attracted by the munificence of the Delhi Sultans, the learned men of the time came from far and wide and mostly from Central and Western Asia to reside at their Courts.

The first Sultan Qutb-ud-din Aibak known for his proficiency in Arabic and Persian and for his interest in science, hardly found any time to develop a Court of learned persons as he died after four years of his assumption of the title, in 1210. However, his son-in-law, Iltutmish who succeeded him and ruled for nearly two decades and half laid the foundations of such a Court through his patronisation of learned men despite his heavy preoccupation with the task of consolidating the Turki conquests in India. At that time Changiz Khan was plundering Central Asia and uprooted by the ravages, many scholars fled to Delhi and took refugee with the Court of Iltutmish. Thus, the famous Persian poet and philosopher Amir Kuhani fled from Bukhara when it was sacked by Changiz Khan and came to Delhi where under the patronage of Iltutmish composed some beautiful poems. Similarly came Nasir-ud-din, known for his popular collection of historical anecdotes in Persian, and made Iltutmish's Court his home. Also came Fakhr-ul-Mulk, formerly Wazir of the Caliph of Baghdad for nearly 30 years. Iltutmish appointed Fahr-ul-Mulk his Prime Minister for his known wisdom and learning.

The Persian influence at the Delhi Court increased further at the time of Nasir-ud-din Mahmud who succeeded Raziyya, the deposed daughter of Iltutmish in 1240. Nasir-ud-din who led the life of a student and of a hermit and was in the habit of purchasing his own food with the sale proceeds of the products of his penmanship, patronised the celebrated Persian historian, Minhaj-i-Siraj who had left for the posterity his famous work, *Tabaqat-i-Nasiri*, named after his patron and full of information on contemporary India and Persia.

However, it was during the reign of Ghiyas-ud-din Balban, who was earlier the Wazir of Nasir-ud-din and succeeded the Sultan who died without any male heir as his designated successor in 1266 that Persian influence rose to its great height at his Court. He was no doubt helped by Changiz Khan's ravages of Khurasan and other places in Central Asia which sent no less than fifteen princes including some of the most illustrious men of learning of the time to seek refugee with Balban's Court. Balban who assigned the uprooted princes suitable positions and allowances often prided himself on his generosity towards them. The uprooted learned men and princes came to the Court of Baban because they knew about his love for

learning. Balban ruled for nearly twenty years and though often busy
with the task of quelling rebellions which often took him out of
Delhi and with the hazardous job of checking the inroads of the
Mongols from Ghazni and Transoxiana, he had ample occasions to
demonstrate his love for learning. After his return from successful
Bengal campaigns spreading over a period of three years, he visited
the learned men at their own houses with gifts and presents and
honoured the Delhi Kotwal, Fakhr-ud-din who had taken care of the
capital in his absence. He was always on the look out for scholars and
learned men who could be a source of strength for his empire and in
this context the advice given by him to his son, Muhammad, is indeed
remarkable: "Spare no pains to discover men of genius, learning and
courage. You must cherish them by kindness and munificence that
they may prove the soul of your councils and instruments of your
authority". However, Balban's search for talented persons was not
limited to scholars from Central Asia – it was he who provided indigenous Amir Khusrav, the famous poet called "the Parrot of India"
with a prestigious and influential job as the tutor of his first son,
Prince Muhammad. Besides the local talent Amir Khusrav, Balban's
Court counted among its members such celebrated scholars as Amir
Hasan, Shaikh Shakarganj, Shaikh Baha-ud-din and his son, Shaikh
Badr-ud-din Arif of Ghazni, Sayyid Maula and Qutab-ud-din
Bakhtiyar Khaki. Thus, under Balban's patronage Delhi steadily rose
to become a rival of Bukhara, the great centre of learning of Central
Asia and inspired the composition of a few verses by Amir Khusrav in
his poem, 'Ashiqah'.

The two sons of Balban, Muhammad and Bughra Khan,
maintained their own Courts of learned persons in their palaces and
each of them heralded the birth of a new society in Medieval India.
While the Court of Muhammad which used to hold literary discussions regularly under the chair of Amir Khusrav developed the
concept of a literacy society, that of Bughra Khan frequented by the
musicians, dancers, actors and story tellers led to the development of a
society which compared favourably to that of an entertainment in
modern parlance. Following his father's advice, Prince Muhammad
used to gather to his Court learned men of the time. However his
attempt to bring Shaikh Usman Tirmizi of Turan and the famous
Persian poet, Shaikh Sadi of Shiraz did not succeed as the former did
not like the life of an exile in India and the latter who was to have in
Multan a khanqah or a monastery dedicated to him by Muhammad

could not come because of his old age. Sadi who was invited twice sent his apologies in verses and commended to Prince Muhammad the abilities of Amir Khusrav. In any case, the two societies of the princes created an example among the nobles and the wealthy residents of Delhi and, as Ferishta informs us, within a short time various societies were formed in every quarter of Delhi adding refinement to life and culture. The most important fallout of these societies was the Mushairas or the poetical symposiums held at the royal Courts and other important places where prominent poets invited from all parts of the country, enlightened the audience with their compositions in poetry.

Balban died in 1287 and the next Sultan Muiz-ud-din Kaiqubad who was placed on the throne by the nobles in disregard of the deceased Sultan's nomination, was a young man of seventeen or eighteen years. He destroyed what Balban and his two sons had built up over the past two decades, a refined Islamic culture which was Persian in nature through patronisation of learning, by giving himself up to profligacy. Despite his early education under tutors who "watched him so carefully that he never cast his eyes on any fair damsel, and never tasted a cup of wine", he succumbed to the temptations of wealth. And as both *Tarikh-i-Firuz Shahi* and *Tarikh-i-Ferishta* records, his ministers as well as the young nobles of his Court, his companions and friends, – all gave themselves up to pleasure. Their examples spread and all the ranks, high and low, learned and unlearned, acquired a taste for wine-drinking and amusements.

Kaiquabad ruled only for two years and he was replaced by the leader of the Khalji Party, Malik Jalal-ul-din Firuz who ascended the throne in June 1290 at the late Sultan's palace of mirrors at Kilokhri at the age of 70. Jalal-ud-din was not however liked by the nobles and the people of Delhi where the Turki Party was dominant but he soon won them over by his generosity and devotion. As he had a great taste for learning, he revived the literacy society of Prince Muhammad and often treated the renowned literary men in history, philosophy and poetry like Amir Khusrav, Taj-ud-din Iraqi, Khwajah Hasan, Amir Arsalan, Ikhtiyar-ud-din Yaghi, Baqi Khatir and Qazi Mughis of Jhansi to his private parties which were often full of music and songs. The Sultan who had a great respect for Amir Khusrav who would compose a poem or a song at ease on the occasions of his private parties would be rewarded on the spot, now gave him the charge of the Imperial Library, appointed him the Keeper of the *Quran* and raised him to the peerage and permitted him to wear white robes – a privilege which was only confined to the members of the ruling family and the nobles of the Court.

Jalal-ud-din's nephew and son-in-law, Ala-ud-din who ascended the throne of Delhi after deposing the late Sultan's son, Rukn-ud-din Ibrahim in 1296, had, according to Barni, "no acquaintance with learning" though according to Ferishta he learnt the art of reading Persian after his accession. Ala-ud-din was so arrogant that men of learning avoided his Court and kept their mouths shut in his presence. He neglected the education of his sons to such an extent that they were swept away by buffoons and strumpets. However, he showed favours only to a select group of literary men who were temporarily in the good graces of the whimsical Sultan or who had made themselves eminent by military prowess or administrative ability, and not by learning alone. Such persons included Qazi Maulana Khurami, Qazi Mughis-ud-din who used to explain Islamic law to the Sultan, Amir Khusrav, the Prince of poets who wrote as many as ninety-nine works on various subjects and who used to accompany Ala-ud-din or his general Malik Kafur on his campaigns, Amir Hassan called the Saadi of Hindusthan, Sadr-ud-din Ali, Fakhr-ud-din Khawas, Hamid-ud-din Rajah, Maulana Arif, Abdul Hakim, Shahab-ud-din Sadr Nashin as well as several historians and compilers of memoirs of the times. For the rest of the learned men who flocked to Delhi attracted by the capital's traditional munificence to learning, the Sultan appeared rather "cool and supercilious". Paradoxically, however, Delhi rose to its pinnacle of fame as a centre of learning during the reign of Ala-ud-din who was averse to patronising learning as the Delhi nobles came forward to support the steady "concourse of learned men from all parts" to the capital.[1]

The successor of Ala-ud-din in 1316 was his son Qutb-ud-din Mubarak who like Kaiqubad of the earlier ruling dynasty gave himself up to a course of the most degrading and odious debauchery and the Delhi Court as a centre of learning went through a period of retrogression. However, this retrogression did not last long partly because of the death of the Sultan soon, through assassination and partly because of the accession to the throne of Delhi by Ghazi Malik, the leader of the Alai nobles and the faithful Warden of the Marches, after replacing Khusrav, a low-caste convert from Gujarat who had earlier usurped and arranged for the murder of Mubrak in 1320. Ghazi Malik assumed the title of Ghias-ud-din Tughluq and became the founder of a new dynasty on the throne of Delhi. The new Sultan was fond of men of genius and learning and used to invite them to his Court, now "more austere than it had ever been except in the time of Balban". Amir Khusrav who continued to receive his monthly pension of one thousand tankas made substantial contribution to Islamic learning when he formulated a code of laws for the guidance of Ghias-ud-din Tughluq in his civil and military administration.

Ghias-ud-din's son and successor Prince Jauna who ascended the throne of Delhi, three days after his father's death in 1325, as Muhammad-bin-Tughluq was the most accomplished scholar among all the Muslim rulers of India. Endowed with a keen intellect, a wonderful memory and a brilliant capacity of assimilating knowledge, he was proficient in different branches of learning like logic, philosophy, mathematics, astronomy and the physical sciences. A perfect master of composition and style, he was a brilliant calligrapher. He had a vast knowledge of Persian poetry and quoted Persian verses in his letters. The science of medicine was not unknown to him. He was also well skilled in dialectics and scholars thought twice before opening any discussion with him on a subject in which he was well-versed. He also studied Greek philosophy. Immediately after his accession to the throne he held discussion with the learned men around him including the metaphysician Saad Mantaki, the poet Ubaid, Najm-ud-din Istishar and Maulana Zain-ud-din Shirazi. It is therefore not surprising that the Court of such a learned and accomplished Sultan would attract scholars and theologians from far and wide and as has been pointed out by Gibb in his translation of the travels of Ibn Batutah, the most energetic globe-trotter of Tangier, who came to Delhi in 1333, that Ibn Batutah himself came "to seek his fortune in India to which the boundless munificence of the reigning sovereign was attracting numbers of scholars and theologians from other countries". Yet, Delhi under Muhammad-bin-Tughluq did not prosper as a centre of learning as it had done in the days of Ala-ud-din and its "high standard of wisdom and erudition began to sink to an inferior level, and literature assumed quite another complexion". This is partly because of the irascible temper and uncontrollable rage of the Sultan, which put to death quite a number of holy and learned men for offences which did not merit such punishment and partly because of the transfer of his capital in 1327 from Delhi to Devagiri named Daulatabad which soon became "a monument of misdirected energy" after the Sultan shifted back his capital to Delhi which had now lost its former prosperity and grandeur.

With the sudden death of Muhammad-bin-Tughluq while chasing the rebels in Sind at Tattah in March 1351, the nobles asked Firuz, Muhammad's first cousin, the son of Ghiyas-ud-din's younger brother, Rajab, by his Bhatti wife, who was the daughter of Rana Mall, the Chief of Abuhar, to ascend the throne, which he did after some hesitation. Firuz was also an accomplished scholar *sans* his predecessor's whimsical temper and ideas. Fond of history, he authored his own autobiography, *Fatuhat-i-Firuz Shahi* and patronised the noted historians Zia-ud-din Barni and Shams-l-Siraj Afif, whose accounts of his reign under *Tarikh-i-Firuz Shahi* are invaluable for the posterity. Among the scholars who wrote on subjects other than history such as theology, Islamic jurisprudence, geography and philosophy under his fostering care were Maulana Jalal-ud-din Rumi, Maulana Alim Anandapati, Maulana Khawajgi, Qazi Abdul Qadir, Maulana Ahmad Thanisvari, Qazi Abdul Muktadir Shanihi, Aziz-ud-din Khalid Khani and 'Ain-ul-Mulk' who wrote a very popular work under the title Ain-ul-Mulk. Firuz was the first among the Delhi Sultans to show his interest in the preservation of the relics of Ancient India as well as its learning. He carefully transferred the two Ashokan Pillars – one in the village of Topra in Khizirabad in the hills and the other in the vicinity of Meerut – to Delhi at a huge cost and labour and he ordered the translation of some of the 300 volumes of Sanskrit manuscripts preserved in the temple of Jwalamukhi which fell to him when he captured Nagarkot, into Persian verses under the title of *Dalail-i-Firuz Shahi* by his Court poet Aazz-ud-din Khalid Khani.

Educating Princes[2] at Home

The next stage of the activities of the Delhi Sultans towards education was provided by the royal household where they endeavoured to provide their children, sons and daughters with "a good liberal education". And they followed the instruction of the Prophet who has said: "No present or gift of a parent, out of all the gifts and presents to a child" is superior to it and is certainly better than "a large measure of corn in alms" which he may bestow on a poor and needy person.

Qutb-ud-din Aibak who began his rule in India as the first Delhi Sultan as well as the other two Muslim governors Bakhtiyar and

Qabaicha, were Turki slaves of Muhammad of Ghur. Since Muhammad had no sons, he looked upon his Turki slaves as such and provided them not only with a sound literary education but also arranged for their instruction in the art of practical administration including war which was absolutely indispensable to prospective princes. When confronted by one of his courtiers on the absence of a male heir after his death, he told him indifferently that he had many thousand sons who would be the heirs of his dominions after his death and who would preserve his name in the Khutba throughout his territories. We all know how prophetic his words were as one of his Turki slaves, Qutb-ud-din Aibak, became the founder of the first Muslim dynasty to rule in India. We know very little about the efforts of Qutb in educating his children but his son-in-law, Iltutmish who succeeded him did provide a sound education to his son, Mahmud as well as to his daughter Raziyya who succeeded her father as the first women ruler or 'Sultana' to the throne of Delhi. Similarly Ghiyas-ud-din Balban of the Khalji dynasty took utmost care to educate his two sons, Muhammad and Bughra and appointed the celebrated poet and scholar of the day Amir Khusrav as the tutor of his first son, Muhammad.

Ghiyas-ud-din Tughluq, the founder of the Tughluq dynasty left no stone unturned in excellently educating his son, Jauna Khan who later ascended the throne of Delhi as Muhammad Tughluq after his father's death, as "the most learned man among the crowned heads of the Middle Ages". Muhammad Shah Tughluq in turn educated his cousin Firuz Shah Tughluq whom he wanted to be his successor and the latter as a father discharged his responsibility in educating his son Fath Khan. According to *Tarikh-i-Ferishta*, Fath Khan took lessons from his expert private tutors in grammar and military science and used to read and write at a maktab in his palace from early morning till breakfast time and from evening till late at night. Besides educating his son Fath Khan, Firuz took great care in educating his slaves as skilled artisans and craftsmen who regularly helped him in his various buildings activities. Firuz had under his care nearly 18,000[3] spread in different parts of his fiefs and as the historian of his reign, Barni informs us, 12,000 of them were trained as skilled artisans and craftsmen. These slaves were looked after by a department of officials organised under the Sultan's direct supervision.

Spreading Islamic Education Institutionally

Apart from patronising learned men in their Courts and providing for the education of their children at their palaces, most of the Delhi Sultans endeavoured to spread Islamic education through the construction of maktabs, madrasahs, mosques and khanqahs mostly in and around their capitals as a part of their religious activities.

The first Sultan, Qutb-ud-din Aibak, followed the example of his former master, Muhammad of Ghur at Ajmer, in raising mosques on demolished temples in various parts of his nascent empire and in the numerous mosques built by him, arrangement was made for instruction both in learning and religion. One of his military commanders, Bukhtiyar Khalji who proceeded as far as Bengal and Bihar destroyed the excellent Buddhist Viharas at Nalanda and Vikramshila and ravaged Nadia which was then political and cultural capital of Bengal. Needless to say, Bakhtiyar constructed numerous mosques and madrasahs in different parts of Bengal and Bihar to spread Islamic religion and education. Qutb's son-in-law Iltutmish built a madrasah in Delhi and his daughter, Raziyya, built another called 'Muzzi Madrasah' which was in such a flourishing state during her short reign that the heretics Karamathians mistook it for Jami Masjid and attacked it. Nasir-ud-din, a devout Muslim, who followed the example of his predecessors founded the 'Nasiriyya Madrasah' which took its name from the founder and appointed the celebrated historian Minhaj-i-Siraj as its principal. It is also probable that he had founded another madrasah at Jalandhar where his Prime Minister Ghiyas-ud-din Balban, and his followers offered their prayers on Id-ul-Zuha while returning to Delhi after a successful campaign. Balban who was more interested in raising the prestige and majesty of the Delhi Sultanate by introducing Persian etiquette and ceremonial and in ruling according to the provisions of the Shariat did not probably construct a new madrasah or a mosque but we know that his son, Prince Muhammad was interested in building a khanqah in Multan for the celebrated Persian poet Shaikh Saadi, which however, did not materialise.

Ala-ud-din Khalji who was not probably as devout a Muslim as his predecessors or as those who came after him, however never lost his faith in Islam. This is borne out by his retort to Qazi Mughis-ud-din of Biyana who often visited his Court and was an advocate of ecclesiastical supremacy: "Although I have not studied the science or the Book, I am a Mussalman of a Mussalman stock". According to Amir Khusrav, he "built anew by a profuse scattering of silver" all the mosques which lay in ruins. In 1311 he undertook the extension of the Qutb Mosque and the construction of a new Minar in the courtyard of the mosque of twice the size of the old Qutb Minar, which could not be completed in his lifetime. The inscription on the southern doorway of the Alai Darwazah, the incompleted Minar of the Sultan, describes him as "the strengthener of the pulpits of learning and religion and the strengthener of the rules of colleges and places of worships". Yet putting the interests of the state before those of religion, he did great harm to the Islamic education when in 1299 A.D. after the capture of Ranthambhor he directed his attention to the means of preventing rebellion and with this end in view, he attacked the institution of private property and not only appropriated to the state all pensions and endowments but confiscated all villages held in proprietary right (milk), in free gift (inam) and benevolent endowments (waqf). "So rigorous was the confiscation", as Barni informs us, "that beyond a few thousand tankas, all the pensions, grants of land and endowments in the country were appropriated". Some of the confiscated lands and endowments were restored to their original owners by Mubarak Shah, Ala-ud-din's son and successor but as "the Sultan attended to nothing but drinking, listening to music, pleasure and scattering gifts" during his short reign of four years and four months, the Islamic education could not achieve any further progress.

The Islamic education was put on its rails by Ghiyas-ud-din Tughluq who founded near Delhi the fortress city of Tughluqabad but suffered under his successor Muhammad-bin-Tughluq who, though an outstanding scholar, inspired by the example of Ala-ud-din Khalji "ignored the canon law" as expounded by the learned Ulemas and based his political conduct on his own experience of the world. However, he lacked practical judgement and common sense and, rather obsessed with his theoretical knowledge, indulged in lofty theories and visionary projects which, though sometimes showed flashes of political insight, were impracticable in operation and brought disaster on his kingdom.

In more ways than one the reign of Firuz Shah Tughluq, the successor of Muhammad-bin-Tughluq is remarkable in the history of education in Medieval India. Apart from patronising learning, fine arts and music, he endeavoured to diffuse Islamic education among the people who were mostly converts from other religions, particularly Hinduism, and were living at the periphery of his empire. By a royal decree, he encouraged learned men to reside in the different parts of his dominions for the sake of imparting religious education – a study of the *Quran* and its commentary and traditions of the Prophet Muhammad. Secondly, as he had a great passion for building new cities and renaming old ones, he founded the town of Jaunpur which was named after his cousin Jauna, Fatehabad, Hissar, Firuzpur near Badaun and Firuzabad, at a distance of ten miles from his capital, Delhi, as well as renamed Ikdala 'Azadpur' and Pandua 'Firuzabad' during his Bengal campaigns to chastise Hazi Iliyas, the independent ruler of Bengal who had styled himself as Sham-ud-din Iliyas Shah. He constructed a number of mosques, madrasahs, palaces, sarais, reservoirs, hospitals, tombs, baths, monumental pillars and bridges in each of the cities and town founded by him. As he says in his *Fatuhat-i-Firuz Shahi*: "Among the gifts which God bestowed upon me, his humble servant, was a desire to erect public buildings. So I built many mosques, colleges and monasteries, that the learned and the elders, the devout and the holy, might worship God in these edifices and aid the kind builder with their prayers". In Delhi also he built a madrasah with a mosque and reservoir attached to it in the vicinity of Qadam Sharif to perpetuate the memory of his son and heir apparent Fath Khan who had died in 1374. Thirdly, he repaired the madrasah built by Iltutmish and "furnished it with Sandal-wood doors". He also repaired the college which was attached to the tomb of Ala-ud-din, and which was most probably built by Ala-ud-din's son as a memorial to the deceased Sultan. Firuz met the expense of repairing and renewing these tombs and colleges from their ancient endowments and where such endowments were not there, he created new ones – "I had villages assigned to them, the revenues of which would suffice for their expenditure, in perpetuity". As a matter of fact, Firuz was the first among the Delhi Sultans to look into the question of endowing educational institutions and religious shrines since without any such endowments no institutions could survive for long.

What kind of madrasah did Firuz build to spread Islamic education in the country? We can answer this question from a description provided by Barni, of the madrasah, known as 'Firuz Shahi Madrasah' constructed by the Sultan in Firuzabad near Delhi. According to Barni, this madrasah was a commodious building, situated in an extensive and well-planned garden, with an adjacent reservoir which mirrored in its shiny and placid breast the high and massive house of study standing on its brink. As the students and the teachers resided in the campus, there was constant intellectual communion between them. It had separate apartments for the reception and accommodation of the travellers who, attracted by its reputation, visited it from distant countries. It also took care of the spiritual needs of its residents by providing within its campus a big mosque where the five compulsory and the extra prayers were regularly said, the former being performed in gatherings conducted by the Sufis, who at other times remained engaged in counting beads and praying for the well-being of the Sultan. While there was a suitable provision for the bestowal of stipends and scholarships upon the successful students by the madrasah, the masjid or the Mosque took care of the poor and the needy. Besides, every inmate of the madrasah, be he a student, teacher or traveller lodging there used to receive a fixed daily allowance for maintenance out of the sums of money set apart by the Sultan for charitable purposes. The teachers of the Madrasah came from such distant places as Samarqand. Among them the name of Maulana Jalal-ud-din Rumi[4] who used to lecture on theology – the *Quran* and its commentaries – was fairly well known.

How many madrasahs were built by Firuz Shah who encouraged his subjects, belonging to other persuasions "to embrace the religion" in which he himself found solace, in Firuzabad and other cities founded by him? Contemporary chroniclers differed from each other in their estimate of the total number – while Abdul Baqi and Faqir Muhammad estimated it at 50 and 40 respectively; Sujan Rai Khattri, Ferishta and Nizam-ud-din Ahmad gave it at 30. In any case the number of madrasahs built by Firuz could not be less than 30 – certainly a remarkable feat, which was without any parallel, in the diffusion of Islamic education and culture in the country which has not been achieved by any Muslim rulers of Medieval India, not to speak of the Delhi Sultans alone.

Decline and Fall of the Delhi Sultanate

However, the reign of Firuz Shah represents the climacteric in the history of Islamic education in Medieval India, for, immediately after his death in 1388 the Delhi Sultanate began to disintegrate. Firuz's revival of the Jagir system, extension of the institution of slavery, imposition of jizya on the non-Muslims, persecution of the heretical

Muslim sects and his indiscriminate generosity contributed no less to
the process of the disintegration of the Delhi Sultanate, which had
started since the days of Muhammad-bin-Tughluq whose various
ill-advised measures, enforced in disregard of popular will, proved
disastrous for his vast empire of 23 provinces. It hastened further
when Firuz was succeeded one after another by four weak successors
– Ghiyas-ud-din II, Abu Bakr, Nasir-ud-din and Mahmud – who
became mere puppets in the hands of some unscrupulous nobles
whose selfish intrigues largely fomented the civil wars among the
rival claimants to the throne of Delhi. The eunuch Malik Sarvar
founded the independent kingdom of Jaunpur; the Khokars revolted
in the north, the provinces of Gujarat, Malwa and Khandesh became
independent; Muslim principalities were established in Biyana and
Kalpi and a Hindu principality in Gwalior; the Chief of Mewat transferred his nominal allegiance from one prince to another at his sweet
will; and the Hindus of the Doabs were almost constantly in revolt.
When peace and stability of a kingdom is thus threatened, it is
obvious that the activities of the people including those in education
are bound to suffer and enter a period of retrogression.

Invasion of Timur Lang

The distracted and the chaotic condition of the Delhi Sultanate was
further aggravated when Amir Timur of Samarqand, tempted by the
wealth of India, invaded the country through the proverbial
North-West, the Achilles' heel of India, in 1398. He defeated Sultan
Mahmud in the outskirts of Delhi on 17 December and next day
entered the capital. After halting at Delhi for a fortnight when his
Turki soldiers looted, plundered and massacred the hapless inhabitants who could not flee the city, Timur returned through
Firuzabad, Meerut, Hardwar, Kangra and Jammu till he crossed the
Indus on 19 March 1399 "after inflicting on India more misery than
had ever been inflicted by any conqueror in a single invasion". Timur
appointed Khizir Khan to the government of Multan, Lahore and
Dipalpur before he left India with the artisans of Delhi as his captives
who were to build in Samarqand the famous Friday Mosque designed
by Timur himself.

The Sayyids

In March 1414, Khizr Khan marched against and defeated Daulat
Khan Lodi who had been acknowledged as the ruler of Delhi after the

death of Sultan Mahumd. Khizr Khan whose ancestors had hailed from Arabia, was regarded as a descendant of the Prophet and the dynasty founded by him has accordingly been styled as the Sayyid dynasty. During the rule of the Sayyids, the extent of the Delhi kingdom had been reduced to a smaller principality, and the authority of its ruler was limited to a few districts around Delhi. Yet the first two Sayyids – Khizr Khan and his son Mubarak – were known for their patronisation of learning and developed two formerly obscure cities, Badaun and Cuttair[5], as excellent centres of Islamic education. They possessed many mosques and madrashas which supplemented the educational works of Delhi and Firuzabad. The last Sultan of the Sayyid dynasty, Sayyid Ala-ud-din lived in Badaun, for nearly thirty years after Bahlul Lodhi had wrested Delhi from him.

The Lodhis

Bahlul Lodhi, founder of the Lodi dynasty, was not certainly a great literary man though he studied Muslim Law with great care and had a great reputation for dispensation of imperial justice impartially. He was, however, very fond of the company of the learned men whom he rewarded suitably. Abdul Baqi, the author of *Ma'asir-i-Rahimi*, informs us that he built some madrasahs in his kingdom to spread the knowledge of Islam. It was he who founded the new city of Agra which was soon to play an important part in the history of Muslim rule in India.

As a matter of fact, Bahlul's son Sikandar Lodhi transferred his capital from Delhi to Agra so that he could exercise more effective control over the rebellious provincial governors and refractory Hindu fief holders of Etawa, Biyana, Aligarh, Gwalior and Dholpur. Agra soon grew into prominence and began to draw towards itself the centre of gravity of the learned world, which had hitherto been at Delhi and Firuzabad. Himself a poet, he highly appreciated literary merit and gave encouragement to learning. Men of learning from Arabia, Persia and Bukhara as well as those of India came to Agra induced by the Sultan's munificence. They were provided with lands and other grants by the officials of the Sultan's administration in conformity with his orders or firmans. According to Abdullah's *Tarikh-i-Daudi*, the Sultan was always accompanied by "seventeen accomplished and learned men of tried merit". Among them were

Sayyid Sadr-ud-din of Kanauj, Miyan Abdur Rahman of Sikri and Miyan Aziz-Ullah of Sambhal.

Sikandar Lodhi was the first monarch in Medieval India to insist on the compulsory education of his military officers. His orders gave a new character to the profession of arms, in which military virtues had to be combined with literary qualifications. Secondly, he was also the first among the Muslim monarchs in India to systematically start the writing, translation and compilation of a number of standard authorities on various subjects in Arts and Sciences, thereby making outstanding contributions to our knowledge on them. He had a special department to do this job. As Rizqullah Mushtaqi, the author of the *Waqiyat-i-Mushtaqi*, informs us: "Miyan Bhudh succeeded to the late Khawas Khan and was confirmed in the dignity. He got together fine calligraphers and learned men, and employed them in writing books on every science. He brought books from Khurasan and gave them to learned and good men. Writers were continually engaged in this work".

One of the outstanding products of this endeavour was the compilation of an authoritative work in medicine which served as the foundation of the practice of the physicians of Hindusthan. The work was named after the Sultan and was known as *Tibb-i-Sikandari*. As Rizqullah Mushtaqi, the author of the *Waqiyat-i-Mushtaqi*, further adds: "He [Miyan Bhudh] assembled the Physicians of Hind and Khursan, and collecting books upon the science of medicine, he had a selection made. The book so compiled received the name of Tibbi-Sikandari and there is no work of greater authority in India".

However, Abdullah's *Tarikh-i-Daudi* asserts that *Tibb-i-Sikandari* was translated from the *Argar-Mahabedak* or the science of medicine and treatment of diseases, a standard Sanskrit work of Ancient India. Whatever may be the case, *Tibb-i-Sikandari* marks Sikandar Lodi out as a pioneer among the Delhi Sultans in the encouragement of the science of medicine in Medieval India.

It is, however, clear that both Hindus and Muslims during the reign of Sikandar Lodhi were learning each other's languages – the Muslims were acquiring a knowledge in Sanskrit and the Hindus in Arabic and Persian. Ferishta asserts that "the Hindus who had hitherto never learned Persian, commenced during this reign to study Muhammadan literature". In an article in the *Calcutta Review* entitled "A Chapter from Muhammadan History", Professor Blochmann endorses Ferishta: "The Hindus from the sixteenth century took so zealously to Persian education that before another century had elapsed they had fully come up to the Muhammadans in point of literary acquirements".

However, Sikandar Lodi was a bigoted Muslim and did not hesitate to further the cause of Islamic education by demolishing Hindu temples and building mosques and madrashas in their places. This he did at Narwar, according to Ferishta and according to Abdullah's *Tarikh-i-Daudi*: "He entirely ruined the Shrines of Mathura, and turned the principal Hindu places of worship into caravanserais and colleges". This is corroborated by Jan Jahan Khan's *Tarikh-i-Jan-Jahan* as well as by Adbul Baqi's *Maasir-i-Rahimi*. Sikandar's bigotry revealed itself on another occasion when in a religious discussion at Sambhal, participated by many learned Muslims, he put to death the lone Hindu debater Budhan who professed a religion similar to that preached by Kabir earlier and would not give up his views that all religions, whether Hindu or Muslim, were equally acceptable to God if followed sincerely.

After the death of Sikandar, his eldest son, Ibrahim ascended the throne at Agra on 21 November, 1517. A faction of the nobility set up his younger brother, Jalal Khan, on the throne of Jaunpur, who was however defeated and assassinated by the Sultan's orders. With a view to securing strength and efficiency, he unwisely embarked upon a policy of repression towards the powerful nobles of the Lahoni, Formuli and Lodi tribes who constituted the official class of the state. The discontent of the nobles was brought to a head by Ibrahim's unsympathetic treatment of Dilwar Khan, son of Daulat Khan Lodi, the semi-independent governor of Lahore. Daulat Khan Lodi and Alam Khan, an uncle of Sultan Ibrahim and a pretender to the Sultanate, invited Babar, the Timurid ruler of Kabul, to invade India. Thus, revenge and ambition, persecutions and disaffection brought about the final collapse of the Delhi Sultanate and paved the way for the establishment of a new Turki rule, that is the rule of the Mughals[6] which has its own magnificent contributions towards Islamic education and culture in the history of education in Medieval India.

Notes

1. For details, see Chapter 17.
2. We have discussed education of the princesses at an appropriate place. For details see Chapter 21.

3. The number of slaves under Firuz has been variously estimated by contemporary chroniclers. However, since all agree on the number of trained slaves which is 12000, 18000 seems to be a reasonable number.

4. In Medieval India there was another Maulana Jalal-ud-din Rumi who belonged to the twelfth century and was a mystic poet.

5. Khizr Khan also built Khizrabad after his own name. However Mubarak who wanted to follow the example of his father could not live to complete Mubarakbad as he was assassinated.

6. The Mughals actually belonged to a branch of the Turks named after Chaghatai, the second son of Changiz Khan, famous Mongol warrior, who came to possess Central Asia and Turkestan, the land of the Turks, in the thirteenth century.

15

The Age of Padshahs

Unlike the Delhi Sultans, the Mughals who ruled India for several centuries after 1526 did not belong to several dynasties but were members of the imperial family founded in India by Babar who possessed in his veins the blood of the two great scourges of Asia, Changiz Khan and Timur Lang. The Mughal rulers who called themselves Padshahs or emperors, ruled India, with one short break at the beginning of their rule between 1540 and 1555 when the fortunes of the Afghans were revived by Sher Shah, till the end of our period in 1757. They saw in the second half of the sixteenth century, the fulfilment of their rule under Akbar, grandson of Babar, who, being endowed with the farsightedness of a genius, built the political structure of the Mughal empire, and its administrative system, on the cooperation and goodwill of all his subjects. And when the wise policy of Akbar was reversed by his great grandson, Aurangzeb, the Mughal empire began to decline, which could not be checked by the weak successors of Aurangzeb after the latter's death in 1707. As in the Age of Sultans, so in the Age of Padshas we propose to analyse the activities of the Mughal rulers in the spread of Islamic education and culture in Medieval India under separate heads: patronisation of learned men, bestowing education on their children and on their subjects.

Patronisation of Learning, Learned Men and Scholars

Babar

When Babar came to India in 1526, he was already an accomplished scholar in Arabic, Persian and Turki, who had already composed a collection of Turki poems, a work on Turki prosody called *Mufassal* and a treatise on Turki music. In 1504 he had invented a new type of handwriting called 'Babari', with which he indicted a copy of the *Quran* and sent it to Mecca. In his early years as an author, he was greatly helped by the learned minister of Sultan Husain of Hirat who gave Babar the charge of his library with a valuable collection of contemporary manuscripts. Interested in astronomy, Babar found after coming to India the astronomical tables prepared by the Hindus in Ancient India at the observatory in Ujjain and Dhar in the kingdom of Malwa inferior to those prepared at the observatory at Samarqand in his times. He took with him all the specimens in painting he could collect from the library of his ancestors, which had a great influence on the subsequent development of the subject in India. His *Memoirs* written in Turki hold a high place in the history of human literature. Babar embellished his *Memoirs* with beautiful illus-trations of animals described in the text and this act of Babar became a trend-setter in illustration for subsequent Persian and Arabic monographs in Medieval India. Such an accomplished scholar as Babar could not but be a great patron of learned men, many of whom such as Ghiyas-ud-din Muhammad Khudamir, a Persian historian and author of many works including *Habibul-Siyar*, Maulana Sahab-ud-din and Mirza Ibrahim were members of his Court.

Humayun

Babar died at Agra at the age of 47 or 48 in December 1530 and was succeeded by his son, Humayun who did not possess the military genius, diplomatic skill and political wisdom of his father. Yet he was almost as great a scholar as 'Babar' and so deep was his attachment to books that while fleeing India as a fugitive after his defeat at the hands of Sher Shah at the battle of Kanauj, he took with him his librarian, Nizam, father of Lala Beg also known as Baz Bahadur as well as some of his favourite books including a copy of the history of Timur Lang. On his successful return to India, he converted the pleasure house of Sher Shah in the Purana Qilah, Sher Mandal, into his own library and stored it with books on astronomy and geography. He was deeply interested in the mysteries of the universe, wrote dissertations on the nature of elements and ordered the construction of terrestrial and celestial globes for his own use. He constructed seven halls for the reception of his audience and named them after seven planets. He divided the people of his empire into three classes – Ahl-i-Saadat,

Ahli-Daulat and Ahl-i-Murad – and included the learned men in the first group who were received by him in the hall named after Saturn and Jupiter on Saturdays and Thursdays as Saturn and Jupiter are planets which protect and preserve scholars and honourable persons. The learned men patronised by Humayun include such important names as Shaikh Husain, Jauhar who wrote *Tazkirat-ul-Waqiat* on private memoirs of Humayun, and the old Khudamir who after Babar's death became a favourite of his son and wrote the *Qanun-i-Humayun*. Khudamir accompanied Humayun to Gujarat where he died in 1534 and his body was carried back to Delhi where he was buried by the side of Nizam-ud-din Auliya and Amir Khusrav. Humayun invited Mir Abdul Latif, a great philosopher, theologician and historian who had written *Lubb-ul-Tawarikh* to his Court but before he could reach Delhi, Humayun died from an accidental fall, while descending at the time of namaz, from the roof of his library where he had gone to spot the planet Venus on the evening of 24 January 1556.

Sher Shah and his Son

It will be relevant here to see whether Sher Shah and his successor who replaced Humayun as arbiters of India were also learned in the tradition of the Muslim rulers of Medieval India. Educated at Jaunpur where Sher Shah served the Afghan Governor, Jamal and fond of poetry and history, he could repeat the works of Saadi and got by heart the *Sikandernamah*, the *Gulistan* and the *Bustan*. We are informed by *Tarikh-i-Sher Shahi* that he learnt Arabic to study the *Quran* and used to visit the khanqahs, dargahs and madrasahs for self-improvement by his association with the learned men of these places. Sher Shah's son, Jalal Khan who assumed the title of Islam Shah, used always to move in the company of the two most learned men of his time – Shaikh Abdul Hassan Kambu and Shaikh Abdullah Sultanpuri Maqdum-ul Mulk. *Muntakhab-ul-Tawarikh* informs us of another learned man of the time of Sher Shah, Shaikh Alai, who was an advocate of "continual learning with application and exertion" through "argument" by day and "repetition" by night!

Akbar

When Humayun died, Akbar was in the Punjab with his guardian Bairam, an old comrade of his father and was formally proclaimed on 14 February 1556, at the age of thirteen, as his successor. However, the Mughal supremacy over Hindusthan was still far from being assured and it was after defeating the Afghans under Himu who had occupied Agra and Delhi, at the second battle of Panipat in 1556 that Akbar was able to start the building of the Mughal empire in India. Despite his wars and annexations, conquests and consolidations, Akbar who inherited from his father Humayun a great love for books and a taste for their collection developed an excellent royal library in his palace at Agra partly by acquiring books through conquests as happened when he acquired the library of Itimad Khan, the vanquished ruler of Gujarat and partly by transferring the valuable collections of his learned Courtiers to his own library after their untimely demise as happened when Faizi, brother of Abul Fazl died, leaving behind a personal library of some 4600 manuscripts. Akbar provided for the good management of his library and after Faizi's death who was its keeper, he rearranged the classification of the books into three sections replacing the two earlier ones into science and history. The first section included books on poetry, medicine, astrology and music; the second books on philology, philosophy, Sufism, astronomy and geometry and the third books relating to the *Quran* – commentaries, traditions, theology and law. Every night at his leisure hours books were read out to him by some competent scholars and as Abul Fazl says that there was "hardly a work of science, of genius, or of history but was read to His Majesty; and he was not tired, with hearing them repeated, but always listened with great avidity".

There is no doubt that this habit of Akbar enabled him to be conversant with Sufi, Christian, Zoroastrian, Hindu and Jaina literature and later stood him in good stead when he held discussions with learned men "on all matters of worldly interest" at the Ibadat Khana in his newly constructed palace at Fatehpur Sikri in 1578 and out of such discussions held on Fridays, Sundays and holy nights with "Sufis, Doctors, Preachers, Lawyers, Sunnis, Shias, Brahmans, Jains, Buddhists, Charbaks, Christians, Jews, Zoroastrians and learned men of every belief" emerged his new religion, Din-i-Ilahi, 'compounded', as the Jesuit writer Bartoli informs us, "out of various elements, taken partly from the Koran of Muhammad, partly from the Scriptures of the Brahamanas, and to a certain extent, as far as suited his purpose, from the Gospel of Christ".

Din-i-Illahi was thus a synthesis of all religions and was based upon Akbar's philosophy of universal toleration. The seeds of such a toleration were sown in his mind partly by his mother, Hamida Banu, daughter of a Persian scholar and partly by his contact with Sufism during his stay in the Court at Kabul with his exiled father, Humayun, where many Sufi saints had fled Persia under the pressure of the Safavi persecution. Subsequently, the influence of his tutor, Abdul Latif and of his Rajput wives and his contact with Hinduism impressed his mind with sublime ideas and made him eager to "attain the ineffable bliss of direct contact with the Divine Reality". As Akbar's son and successor, Jahangir, mentions in his *Memoirs* that his father "in his actions and movements was not like the people of the world, and the glory of God manifested itself in him". Akbar never made any attempt to force his religion on others with the zeal of a convert or a religious fanatic but appealed to the inner feelings of men and as count Von Noer, the German historian of Akbar has correctly pointed out Din-i-Ilahi "will assure to him for all time a pre-eminent place among the benefactors of humanity – greatness and universal toleration in matters of religion".

In the ultimate analysis, it was Akbar's thirst for knowledge which he quenched from books read out to him every night that led him to took beyond the *Quran* whose authority he never denied. And he kept up his search for knowledge throughout his life. Most of the books which carried autographs of their respective authors were copied in beautiful hand, indicating the extent of excellency reached by the art of calligraphy during Akbar's time. Akbar encouraged penmanship, particularly the Nastaliq hand and some of the excellent persons of the time including Mulla Mir Ali and his son, Maulana were attached to his Court. The manuscripts in the collection of Akbar were not only written in beautiful hand but profusely embellished with beautiful illustrations such as the *Qissah Hamzah* or stories of Mir Hamzah of 360 Indian fables in twelve volumes which were illustrated with some 1400 paintings or sketches. There is no doubt that the art of painting which blossomed under his successor Jahangir had reached a new height under his patronage and his Court was the scene of the activities of the many eminent artists, both Hindu and Muslim, of the time who used to hold exhibition of their arts in the painting gallery established by Akbar. Among those who participated in such programmes were Khwaja Abdul Samad, Shirin Qalam Shirazi, Mukund, Madhu, Jagan, Mahes and Ram who were liberally patronised by Akbar. Besides painting, Akbar patronised music which also reached a new height in his reign. There were numerous musicians at his Court, Hindus, Iranis, Turanis, Kashmiris, both men and women, who were divided into seven groups, one for each day in the week, to regale Akbar. Besides Miyan Tansen, a Hindu convert to Islam, whose tomb at Gwalior has now become a place of pilgrimage among the Indian musicians and his two sons, Tantarang Khan and Bilas, Akbar's Court was attended by another father and son team in Ram Das and Sur Das who hailed from Lucknow. Baz Bahadur of Malwa who was employed in the service of Akbar was "the most accomplished man of his day in the science of music and in Hindi song".

The reign of Akbar reached its climax not only in the composition of works in Persian but also in the translation of Sanskrit works in it. Akbar maintained a Court of learned scholars and met all their wants to such an extent that some of them rose to affluence. Freed from the financial worries of life, they were able to devote their time to the cultivation of their chosen fields in arts and sciences. One of Akbar's contemporaries, Madhavacharya, a Bengali poet of Triveni, and author of *Chandimangal* bestows high praise on Akbar as patron of letters. Under the fostering care of Akbar, Abul Fazl, a poet, an essayist, a critic, and a historian rolled into one person, wrote *Akbarnamah* and *Ain-i-Akbari*; Mulla Daud *Tarikh-i-Alfi*; Abdul Qadir Badaoni, usually a critic of Akbar, *Muntakhab-ul-Twarikh*; Nizam-ud-din Ahmad *Tabaqat-i-Akbari*; Faizi Sarhindi *Akbarnamah* and Abul Fateh *Manshiat*. A number of famous poets or versifiers produced works of merit under the patronage of Akbar. The most important among them were Ghizali and Faizi, a brother of Abul Fazl. Other prominent poets were Muhammad Husain Naziri of Nishapur who wrote 'ghazals' of great merit, and Sayyid Jamal-ud-din urfi of Shiraj, the most famous writer of 'Qasidas' in his days.

Many important works in Turki and Arabic were translated into Persian under Akbar's care. Thus, Abdur Rahim Khan-i-Khanan, son of Bairam Khan, translated Babar's memoirs *Waqiyat-i-Babari* from Turki into Persian and a part of the Astronomical Tables of Ulugh Beg was translated from Turki into Persian by Amir Fathullah Shirazi. Abdul Qadir Badaoni translated *Jama-i-Rashidi* from Arabic into Persian and helped in the translation of *Muajam-ul-Buldan*, a charming geographical treatise from Arabic into Persian by other scholars. Similarly *Hayat-ul-Haiwan* was translated from Arabic into Persian and the *Shahnamah* was turned into prose from verse and Abul Fazl was charged with the task of translating the Gospel.

In translating Sanskrit works into Persian, Akbar took the help of Hindu scholars as in the case of *Mahabharata*, the *Ramayana* and the *Simhasana Battisi*. In 1582 Naqib Khan was placed in charge of scholars who were asked to translate the *Mahabharata* and Abdul Qadir Badaoni was asked to help Naqib Khan and when the translation was complete which was a sort of abstract of the Sanskrit work, under the title, *Razmnamah*, Abul Fazl wrote a preface, copies were made of it and the nobles were ordered to take them. After labouring for four years Abdul Qadir completed the translation of the *Ramayana* in 1589 as well as the *Simhasana Battish* into prose and verse under the title *Khirad-Afzanamah*. Haji Ibrahim Sarhindi translated the *Atharva Veda* into Persian; Faizi the *Lilavati*, a work on mathematics; Mukammal Khan Gujrati the *Tajak*, a treatise on astronomy, and Maulana Shah Muhammad Shahabadi the *Rajtarangini* of Kalhan. Similarly the *Haribansa*, the *Kishn Joshi*, the *Gangadhar* and the *Mahes Mahananda* were translated under Abul Fazl and the work delineating the love of Nala and Damayanti was translated into Persian verse after the model of Layala and Majnun. Nasrullah Mustafa and Maulana Husiani Qaiz translated *Panchatantra* into Persian under the title of *Kalilah-Damnah* as well as an easier adaptation of it under the title, *Ayar Danish*.

Needless to say, Akbar took great care to see that all the Persian works as well as the translations of Arabic, Turki and Sanskrit works were profusely embellished by ingenious artists and covered with excellent and ornamental bindings at huge cost and labour.

Was Akbar an Illiterate Person?

In the light of our discussion on Akbar's patronisation of learning and learned men of his time, let us now examine the question of his illiteracy. It was a Portuguese Christian missionary, A. Monserrat, who was at Akbar's Court from 1580 to 1582 first entered in his diary under 26 November 1582 his observations on Akbar's illiteracy: "He [Akbar] can neither read nor write, but he is very curious, and has always men of letters about him, whom he gets to discuss on sundry topics and tell him various stories". Another Portuguese Christian missionary, Jerome Xavier, who was also at Akbar's Court for few years wrote in a letter in 1598 that "The King [Akbar] is gifted with a wonderful memory, so that although he can neither read nor write, he knows whatever he has heard learned men discoursing about, or whatever has been read to him". Secondly, *Tuzak-i-Jahangiri* or the

Memoirs of Jahangir as translated by Rogers and Beveridge as well as by Lowe includes this observation of Jahangir which seems to corroborate the evidence of the Jesuit fathers on the subject of Akbar's illiteracy, Jahangir observes: "My father used to hold discourse with learned men of all persuasions, particularly with the Pandits and the intelligent persons of Hindusthan. Though he was *illiterate*,[1] yet from constantly conversing with learned and clever persons, his language was so polished that no one could discover from his conversation that he was entirely *uneducated*.[2] He understood even the elegances of poetry and prose so well that it is impossible to conceive of any one more proficient".

The evidences of the Jesuit fathers and the translations of Jahangir's *Memoirs* by Rogers and Beveridge and by Lowe have influenced historians of Akbar including Count Von Noer and Vincent Smith into accepting Akbar as an illiterate person or one who could not read and write.

Before presenting our arguments on the subject, let us first of all examine the evidences of Monserrat and Xavier. It is indeed difficult for the Christian missionaries who lived and moved in Akbar's Court in an environment of distrust and suspicion to get a first hand knowledge about Akbar's education. Monserrat's observations suffer from the same kind of inaccuracies which characterise the accounts left by the Catholic missionaries in Medieval India and by his own admission, Monserrat obtained most of his information on "the Mongols" [Mughals] indirectly. Secondly, against the translations of Jahangir's *Memoirs* by Rogers and Beveridge as well as by Lowe we can place the translation by Price entitled *Waqiat-i-Jahangiri* which only says that though Akbar was not profoundly learned, yet his conversation with the learned might lead one to believe that he was profoundly learned in every branch of science. Price's translation of Jahangir's *Memoirs* does not say that "he was illiterate" or "he was entirely uneducated". N.N. Law, an authority on the subject of learning in Medieval India has pointed out that the term 'Ummi' in *Tuzak-i-Jahangiri* which Beveridge and Rogers as well as Lowe have translated as 'illiterate' or 'uneducated' is capable of another meaning – 'taciturn' or 'reserved' and this meaning will be quite in accord with the context of the aforesaid passage.

As a matter of fact, with the evidences that we have at our disposal, it is difficult to accept the view that Akbar was an illiterate person. The first question that we may ask is: Did Humayun known for his love for learning neglect the education of his child? The answer is a positive no. According to Abul Fazl's *Akbarnamah*, Humayun with his knowledge of astrology fixed the lucky moment for the maktab ceremony of his son on 20 November 1547, when he was four years, four months, four days old and was placed under the charge of Maulana Azam-ud-din. Azam-ud-din was soon replaced by Maulana Bayazid, for his addiction to pigeon-flying, a taste which he might have communicated to his pupil also. Maulana Bayazid was followed by a number of teachers including Munim Khan who was entrusted with the task of training the future emperor in the military art. Humayun's solicitude for the education of his son could be seen also in his invitation to Mir Abdul Latif, a noted historian, philosopher and theologian of Hirat who arrived after the death of Humayun and was later appointed Akbar's tutor by his guardian and protector, Bairam Khan, an old comrade of his late father, Humayun. The appointment of Pir Muhammad Khan and Haji Muhammad Khan by Bairman Khan during his regency which lasted till 1560 as well as the many dismissals of tutors indicate that both Humayun and Bairam paid attention to Akbar's education. Besides Akbar's mother Hamida Banu Begam was the daughter of a celebrated Persian scholar, Shaikh Ali Ambar Jaini and Akbar's foster-mother Maham Anaga was an educated lady of her time. With such persons around him, it was indeed difficult for Akbar, however recalcitrant, idle and fond of sports he could be to systematically resist all attempts of his guardians at training him for at least twelve years and to come at the end of the period without a knowledge of the alphabets and of the art of writing. Since Akbar was very intelligent, a few months snatched out of the whole period of twelve years and devoted to studies under the fear of his guardians could have easily enabled him to read and write the alphabets.

Secondly, we refer to a passage in *Ain-i-Akbari*, Ain 34, p.115 which runs thus: "Whatever place [of the book], the reader daily reached, he [Akbar] wrote with his own jewelled pen numerical figures according to the number of leaves [read]. He paid the readers cash in gold or silver according to the number of leaves [read]". This translation of the passage which is taken from Gladwin's *Ain-i-Akbari* thus attributes to Akbar a knowledge of the numerical figures and their daily transcription with his own hand and pen on the pages of the books. It is a common practice to teach a boy how to learn and write the numerical figures along with or subsequent to the letters of the alphabets and Akbar as a child was no exception to it.

Finally, all contemporary sources including Jahangir's *Memoirs* and Abul Fazl's accounts confirm that Akbar appreciated abstruse controversies and elegances of literary compositions, took part in discussions with learned men, composed poetry, recited odes of Hafiz, was well-versed in history and philosophy and took meticulous care in supervising translations of classical works into Persian. Certainly all these scholarly capabilities imply a kind of knowledge that could never be the preserve of a person without the knowledge of the alphabets and of the art of writing!

Jahangir

A week after the death of Akbar in 1605, Salim as the only surviving son, succeeded to the throne of Agra at the age of 36 and assumed the title of Nur-ud-din Muhammad Jahangir Padshah Ghazi. A sincere believer in God, he was a desist at heart and would hold discussions with Hindu or Muslim saints and Christian preachers on Fridays, and valued religious pictures, notably of Christians but he never accepted the practices or rites of the Hindus, the Zoroastrians or the Christians and remained like his father a follower of Islam. Possessed of a fine aesthetic taste, he was himself a painter and known for "his hearty enjoyment of nature and his love of flowers". He inherited from Akbar his great love for books which were his constant companions and carried them on his campaigns or visits as he did when he visited Gujarat and presented the Shaikhs with his autographed copies of books from his library, mentioning the date of his arrival at the country as well as the date of its presentation. He was always on the lookout for acquiring a valuable manuscript for his library and would not hesitate to pay an exorbitant price for it as he did on one occasion when he collected a Persian manuscript for 3,000 gold mohurs – a sum equivalent to £10,000. Martin, author of *Miniature Painting and Painters of Persia, India and Turkey* comments that in his time[3] the manuscript for which Jahangir paid such a high sum would not fetch £2000 at an auction in Paris or London. Jahangir who knew Turki read the original copy of Babar's *Memoirs* and supplied the missing four sections in it by obtaining them from one of its copies writing in few lines in Turki to show that the addition was made by him. Like Babar, Jahangir wrote his *Memoirs* assisted by two reputed historians of the time – Muhammad Hadi and Mutamad Khan. He illustrated the frontispiece to his *Jahangirnamah* with the picture of his Court drawn by Abul Hasan, a celebrated painter of the time and its pages with the pictures of the animals brought to him from Goa by Muqarrab Khan as "actual likeness might afford a greater surprise to the reader than mere description" He presented the first copy of his *Memoirs* to his son, Shah Jahan.

Besides Muhammad Hadi, Mutamad Khan, his Court was adorned by Mirza Ghiyas Beg who was unrivalled in elegant composition and arithmetic; Naqib Khan, the most honoured Court historian since the days of Akbar; Nimatullah Khan, the historian of Afghanistan and Abdul Haqq Dihlawi who presented Jahangir with his work on the Shaikhs of Hindusthan and a number of poets as mentioned by *Iqbalnamah* – Fasuni Kashi, Mullah Naziri Nishapuri, Saada-i-Gilani, Baba Talib Isfahani, Shaida and Mullah Hayati Gilani – as well as a number of celebrated painters like Farrukh Beg and Mansur besides already mentioned Abul Hasan, who could copy in the words of Catrou, the author of *History of the Mughal Dynasty*, "the finest of our European pictures with a fidelity that might vie with the originals".

Shah Jahan

Shah Jahan who succeeded Jahangir in February 1628 under the lofty title of Abul Muzaffar Shihab-ud-din Muhammad Shahib-i-Qiran II, Shah Jahan Padshah Ghazi vastly added to the Mughal dominions by settling the affairs of the Deccan States after forty years of strife between 1545 and 1636. A zealous champion of his faith, he revived the pilgrimage tax and took steps not only to check the conversion of the Muslims to other faiths but also to add to their number. Besides his mother tongue Turki, he could speak Persian and Hindi and like his great grandfather Akbar, he heard books on travels, saints, prophets and former kings such as Timur and Babar read out to him when he retired to bed and encouraged learned men by rewards and stipends. Among the learned men who received his favours were Muhammad Amir-i-Qazwini who wrote the famous historical work at Shah Jahan's order, *Padshahnamah*, Abdul Hamid Lahori' author of another *Padshahnamah*, Sayyed Bukhari Gujrati, Sayyid Jamal-ud-din, Shaik Mir Lahuari, Shaikh Bahlul Qadiri, Shaikh Naziri, Mullah Shukullah Shirazi, and Mir Abdul Kasim.

Dara Shukoh

Shah Jahan was not, however, a scholar in the sense his predecessors were but in his son Dara Shukoh, the eldest of his four sons, the Mughal family possessed one of the greatest scholars that India has ever produced. Well-versed in Arabic, Persian and Sanskrit he was the author of some famous works including Persian translations of the *Upanishads*,[4] the *Bhagavata Gita* and the *Yoga Vasishtha Ramayana*; a calendar of Muslim saints; and several works on Sufi philosophy. In 1654 he completed the *Majma-ul-Bahrain*, a treatise on the technical terms of Hindu Pantheism and their equivalents in Sufi phraseology to reconcile the two religious systems – an act which has prompted one of his latest biographers to comment: "It is hardly an exaggeration to say that any one who intends to take up the solution of the problem of religious peace in India must begin the work where Dara had left it, and proceed on the path chalked out by that prince". Looking at the grave of Dara, William Sleeman, in his *Rambles and Recollections*, rightly points out that had he lived to occupy the throne, he would have "changed the destinies of India, by changing the character of education".

Aurangzeb

However, this was not to be as fate had decreed otherwise for Dara, Shah Jahan's nominee for the throne. In the war of succession that followed the illness of Shah Jahan in September 1657, Dara was defeated by Shah Jahan's third son Aurangzeb who ascended the throne at Agra in July 1658, under the title of Alamgir or conqueror of the world with the additions of Padshah or emperor and Ghazi or Holy Warrior. Next year in August 1659, Dara was beheaded on the orders of the Doctors of Muslim law, who condemned him on a charge of deviation from the Islamic faith.

As one who secured the throne as the champion of Sunni orthodoxy against the liberal Dara, Aurangzeb tried to enforce strictly the Quranic law, according to which it behoves every pious Muslim to "exert himself in the path of God", or, in other words, to carry on holy wars or Jihad against non-Muslim lands or dar-ul-harb till they are converted into realms of Islam or dar-ul-islam. This made him extremely puritanic in temperament, so that he took several steps to enforce "his own ideas of the morose seriousness of life and punctilious orthodoxy" by discontinuing Jharoka-darshan, Nauroz, the ceremony of weighing the emperor's body against gold and silver on his birthdays and by banning music, painting, poetry, astrology and astronomy at his Court and prohibited drinking of wine and bhang and visits at dancing girls and public women in his kingdom. He appointed Muhtasibs or Censors of Public Morals to "regulate the lives of the people in strict accordance with the Holy Law" and reimposed jizya tax on the 'unbelievers' in 1679.

Aurangzeb personally practised what he sought to enforce on others and he was regarded by his contemporaries as "a dervish born in the purple" and venerated by the Muslims as a 'Zinda Pir' or living saint. He used to study the *Quran* for two hours between 5 and 7 in the morning, copy it and study the works of Islamic saints between 2.30 and 5.30 in the afternoon. His last will revealed that he defrayed his personal expenses by selling copies of the *Quran* transcribed by him, as Nasir-ud-din of the Delhi Sultanate used to do some four hundred years ago. While his love for theology led him to augment the collection in the royal library by Fiqh, Tafsirs, commentaries on the *Quran*, works on Hadis and those of the Imam Muhammad Ghazzali, his love for the Quranic law led him to organise the compilation of the Islamic laws by eminent jurists or doctors of Muslim laws working under the supervision of Mullah Nizam under the title of *Fatawa-i-Alamgiri*, the only literary production which received his patronage and came to be regarded as "the greatest digest of Muslim law made in India".

Bestowing Education on Their Children

In this section we shall only concentrate on the efforts of the Mughal emperors in educating their sons who were groomed as future emperors. As far as the education of their daughters is concerned, we shall discuss it later at an appropriate place.

As we have said before, the Mughal emperors belonged to the imperial family of Babar, who ruled India in succession to one another and we have also some insight into the kind of education provided by Humayun to his son, Akbar. What kind of education did Humayun himself receive from his father, Babar or for that matter, did Akbar provide to his own sons? As in the case of the Delhi Sultans, the Mughal emperors often chose their successors and provided them with adequate education for their roles as prospective emperors, though in the absence of a law of succession this matter was often decided by the sword.

Babar and Humayun

We have little idea about Babar's education, who at the age of eleven inherited from his father the small principality of Farghana in Turkestan in 1494 and since that year he entered into a very difficult period of his life. Whatever education he received, and he must have received well for his remarkable attainments in languages, was during the time he had spent in Samarqand between the ages of 5 and 11. Similarly we know very little about the education of Humayun though we are informed by *Tazkirat-ul-Salatin* that when Humayun was four years, four months and four days old, he went through the maktab ceremony and was entrusted to the care of tutors. There is however no doubt that Babar must have made adequate arrangement for the instruction of his son, Humayun whom he wanted to succeed him to the throne of Hindusthan, along with his other sons, Kamran, Hindal and Askari and we all know that Humayun later married in 1542, Hamida Banu Begam who was the daughter of Hindal's preceptor, Shaikh Ali Ambar Jaini, a reputed Persian scholar.

Jahangir and his Brothers

We have already seen Humayun's endeavour to educate Akbar. His half brother, Mirza Muhammad Hakim who governed Kabul at the time of Akbar's accession to the throne of Hindusthan was similarly educated. Akbar in turn provided his sons, Salim, Murad and Daniyal, with an excellent education by appointing scholarly teachers for each one of them. Thus, Qutb-ud-din Khan, Abdul Rahim Mirza, Shaikh Ahmad and Maulana Mir Kalan Harvi who were Muhaddis of Herat were given charges of Salim, Faizi and Sharif Khan of Murad and Sayyid Khan Chagltai of Daniyal. Murad was also placed for some time under the instruction of the Jesuit father Monserrat "to be instructed in the sciences and religion of Europe", according to Hough's *Christianity in India*. According to Count Von Noer, Akbar placed one of his grandsons under the tuition of Abul Fazl and a Brahmana.

Shah Jahan, His Brothers and Sons

Shah Jahan similarly received from his father Jahangir a good education along with his other brothers, Khusrav, Parwez and Prince Shahryar. Shah Jahan who could speak Turki, Persian and Hindi, was trained by such eminent teachers as Mulla Qasim Beg Tabrezi, Hakim

Dawai, Shaikh Abdul Khair and Shaikh Sufi. Shah Jahan took great care for the education of his four sons, Dara Shukoh, Shuja, Aurangzeb and Murad. We have been already acquainted with the scholarly attainments of Dara Shukoh earlier – Shah Jahan appointed Mullah Shah, a native of Badakhshan who was very much respected by himself as the Murshid or spiritual guide of Dara. Mullah Shah was also the teacher of Aurangzeb who was earlier taught by Saadullah Khan who afterwards became one of the ministers of his father as well as by Mir Muhammad Hashim. Aurangzeb had a keen intelligence and quickly learnt what he read. He got by heart the *Quran* and the Hadis, could read and write Arabic and Persian with great facility, and had a mastery over Chaghtai Turki, the language of his remote ancestors.

Niccolao Manucci, a contemporary of Aurangzeb and author of *Storia do Mogor* provides us with an insight into the education of the Mughal princes. According to him, when the princes attained the age of five, they were taught to read and write their mother tongue, which was Tartar, or the old language of the Turks. Afterwards, they were placed under learned men and eunuchs who taught them the liberal and military arts. The teachers took care to regulate their amusements in such a way as to help them acquire a knowledge of the world and a taste for refined habits and culture.

Aurangeb's Dissatisfaction

Yet Aurangzeb did not seem to be satisfied with the kind of education, with its emphasis on Arabic and Persian reading and writing, grammar and literature that was traditionally imparted to a Mughal prince as a part of liberal package of education. It did not provide any knowledge of the country, history and civilisation of the country the Mughals were called upon to rule; nor did it acquaint a prince with the history and tradition of his own family to mould his future behaviour accordingly. If Bernier, a contemporary of Aurangzeb, is to be believed, he is said to have rebuked his old teacher[5] who went to congratulate Aurangzeb, in anticipation of some reward, when his old pupil ascended the throne of Hindusthan:

> Far from having imparted to me a profound and comprehensive knowledge of the history of mankind, scarcely did I learn from you the names of my ancestors, the renowned founders of this empire.... A familiarity with the languages of surrounding nations may be

indispensable to a king but you would teach me to read and write Arabic.... Forgetting how many important subjects ought to be embraced in the education of a prince, you acted as if it were chiefly necessary that he should posses, great skill in grammar, and such knowledge as belongs to a doctor of law; and thus did you waste the precious hour of my youth in the dry, unprofitable and never-ending task of learning words... Answer me, sycophant, ought you not to have instructed me on one point at least, so essential to be known by a king; namely on the reciprocal duties between the sovereign and his subjects? Ought you not also to have foreseen that I might at some future period, be compelled to contend with my brothers, sword in hand, for the crown, and for my very existence. Such, as you must well know, has been the fate of the children of almost every king of Hindusthan. Did you ever instruct me in the art of war, how to besiege a town, or draw up an army in battle array?

The military training to a Mughal prince was usually provided by an expert different from the teacher appointed to take care of his general education and Shah Jahan must have provided such teachers for their sons. Aurangzeb's address of the teacher as 'sycophant' and his charging him of his failure to provide him training in warfares do not seem to be justified in view of the traditional respectful relations existing between a prince and his teacher in the Mughal House. It is possible that Bernier has added some colour to the description of an episode which may be basically correct, to make it more attractive.

We also do not know positively whether Aurangzeb moulded the education of a royal prince according to his ideas on the subject and made it more relevant for him. What we do know for certain is the fact that Aurangzeb took extreme care in choosing a teacher for his third son Akbar, whom he designed as his successor, when the prince became 4 years, 4 months and 4 days old. He found time in the midst of the visit of the representatives of the ruling family of Ethiopia to summon his close associates and the learned men of his Court to select a teacher for Akbar. "He evinced upon this occasion", as Bernier informs us, "the utmost solicitude that this young prince should receive such an education as might justify the hope of his becoming a great man. No person can be more alive than Aurangzebe [sic] to the necessity of storing the minds of princes, destined to rule nations, with useful knowledge. As they surpass, others in power and elevation, so ought they, he says, to be pre-eminent in wisdom and virtue".

Spreading Islamic Education among the Subjects

We now come to the last and the most important stage of the activities of the Mughal emperors in the spread of Islamic education in Medieval India by carrying it to the subjects through construction of maktabs, madrasahs, khanqahs and monasteries.

Babar

During the four years Babar spent in Hindusthan, the Punjab, the territory covered by the modern United Provinces, and North Bihar, were conquered by him, and the leading Rajput state of Mewar also submitted to it. He had however hardly any time to enact new laws, or to reorganise the administration, which continued to retain its medieval feudal nature with all its defects created under the Delhi Sultanate. Yet so great was his zeal for the spread of Islamic education in Hindusthan where as he had lamented in his *Memoirs*, absence of colleges along with many good things of life, obviously in comparison with Kabul and Samarqand, made for the first time, construction of schools and colleges an organised activity of the existing administration. We learn from the *Twarikh* of Sayyid Maqbar Ali who was a minister of Babar that Babar ordered that along with the task of conducting postal service and of bringing out a Gazette[6], the Shuhrati Am or the Public Works Department should undertake the task of building maktabs and madrasahs and made adequate financial provisions for the purpose.

Humayun

Humayun who inherited from his father a monarchy which could be held together only by the continuance of warlike conditions was incapable of any sustained effort and after a moment of triumph would bury himself in his harem and dream away the precious hours in the opium-eater's paradise whilst his enemies were thundering at the gate. He lost the empire through his own weakness and indecision to Sher Shah in 1540, but by a favourable turn of fortune he was able to recover a part of what he had lost earlier after leading a life of exile for nearly fifteen years, in July 1555 but died soon in January next year. And yet, as we learn from Abul Fazl's *Ain-i-Akbari*, he could find time to build a madrasah in Delhi and appointed Shaikh Husain its teacher.

Akbar

A strong imperialist by instinct, Akbar followed a policy of conquest for more than forty years, for the expansion of his empire until the capture of Asirgarh in January 1601. He was not only able to achieve the political unification of nearly the whole of Northern and Central India but also able to extend the authority of the Mughal empire to the Deccan Sultanates which were organised into three subahs of Ahmadnagar, Berar and Khandesh under Prince Daniyal as its Viceroy.

The reign of Akbar is important not only for the administration he built up to consolidate his conquests but also for the spread of Islamic education in the different parts of his empire. There is no doubt the Public Works Department entrusted with the task of building schools and colleges was very active during the reign of Akbar. Akbar built many colleges at Agra, Fatehpur Sikri and other places. *Ain-i-Akbari* informs us of a very big madrasah at Fatehpur Sikri "on the hill, the like of which few travellers, can name". The madrasahs at Agra were under the charges of learned professors from Shiraj, the famous centre of Muslim learning in Central Asia, who were brought specially for the purpose of imparting higher education to their students. Lala Silchand, author of *Tafrih-ul-Imarat* informs us the existence of a very big madrasah under the charge of a philosopher from Shiraj, which flourished for a long time even after Akbar's death in 1605. In these madrasahs while stipends and scholarships were given to the deserving students, arrangements were made for the free tuition of the poor and the needy.

Not all madrasahs in Delhi and Agra were residential. Shaikh Abdul Haqq, who at twenty years of age mastered most of the customary branches of knowledge including *Quran* by heart informs us that he used to go twice a day to a college which was situated at a distance of two miles from his residence, morning and evening, in summer and winter. This he did to have his mid-day meal at home.

In education Akbar's reign marks a new epoch not merely in the construction of numerous maktabs and madrasahs but also in the introduction of various reforms which made education more relevant and useful not only to the needs of the students but also to those of the rulers. In keeping with his policy of religious toleration, he threw doors of the maktabs and the madrasahs open to the Hindus and appointed them to high posts as Sher Shah and his successors had done before him. And for the first time in the history of education in Medieval India, Hindus and Muslims were seen studying in the same schools and colleges and later aspiring for positions in the Muslim administration.

Akbar also introduced far-reaching changes in the curricula and the modes of study. For the first time Hindu learning was included in the curricula of a madrasah, thereby giving an opportunity to an interested Muslim student to learn it just as a Hindu student now had an opportunity to learn Arabic and Persian literature, jurisprudence, Islamic law and art of administration. Abul Fazl who was closely associated with such reforms has left for us a vivid account of them in his Ain 25 of *Ain-i-Akbari:*

> In every country, especially in Hindusthan, boys are kept for years at school, where they learn the consonants and vowels. A great portion of the life of the students is wasted by making them read many books. His majesty orders that every school boy should first learn to write the letters of the alphabet, and also learn to trace their several forms. He ought to learn the shape and name of each letter, which may be done in two days, when the boy should proceed to write the joined letters. They may be practised for a week, after which the boy should learn some prose and poetry by heart, and then commit to memory some verses to the praise of God, or moral sentences, each written separately. Care is to be taken that he learns to understand everything himself, but the teacher may assist him a little. He then ought for some time to be daily practised in writing a hemistich or a verse, and will soon acquire a correct hand. The teacher ought specially to look after five things, knowledge of the letters; meaning of words; the hemstitch; the verse; the former lesson. If this method of teaching be adopted a boy will learn in a month or even in a day what it took others years to understand, so much so that people will get quite astonished. Every boy ought to read books on morals, arithmetic, the notation peculiar to arith-metic, agriculture, mensuration, geometry, astronomy, physiognomy, household matters, the rules of government, medicine, logic, the *tabii*[7], *riyazi*[8] and *ilahi* sciences[9] and history; all of which may be gradually acquired. In studying Sanskrit, students ought to learn the Bayakaran[10], Niyai[11] Badanta[12] and Patanjal[13].

No one should be allowed to neglect those things which the present time requires.

The primary aims of these reforms, were to eliminate wastage of time and to make education more purposeful, and practical in the light of the requirements of the India of Akbar. Underlying these reforms, as we have already said before, is Akbar's principle of religious toleration and a mutual respect for each other's culture. In a reformed maktab or madrasah if a Hindu boy had an opportunity to partake of Islamic education, a Muslim boy had similar opportunity to learn Hindu education. Exposed to each other's education, culture and religion at the very beginning of their lives, the students were likely to develop an outlook which in modern parlance may be called "national".

We do not know for certain at what particular year of Akbar's reign these reforms were introduced. However, there is no doubt that these proved extremely beneficial and "shed a new light on schools, and cast a bright lustre over madrasahs". Abul Fazl who as we have already said, was closely associated not only with the formulation of these ideas of reforms but also with their implementation took a just pride on their success: "All civilised nations have schools for the education of youths; but Hindusthan is particularly famous for its seminaries".

With his remarkable sagacity and a large broad mindedness, Akbar thus not only sought to have education imparted to all classes of his subjects, rich or poor, irrespective of their race or religion, caste or creed but also to make it relevant and useful to the contemporary society. Akbar who had systematically and strategically curbed the influence of the Ulemas who, like the Popes in Medieval Europe, exerted "a parallel claim to the obedience of the people" delivered the final blows to them by changing the ideals and objectives of education from being strictly religious into purely political. Badaoni informs us and his information is corroborated by other contemporary sources that Akbar tried to make education secular by discouraging the study of the Arabic and Arabic Sciences. Standing on the threshold of the twenty-first century when we look back at the reign of Akbar, we find that it confronts us with the largest selection of educational ideas to estimate our thought in the educational reconstruction of an independent India.

Jahangir

Jahangir, whose "disposition towards his subjects appears to have been invariably humane and considerate" from the beginning to the end of his reign apparently followed Akbar's policy towards education. On his accession to the throne in 1605, he promulgated an ordinance proclaiming that whenever a well-to-do person or a rich traveller would die without any heir, his property would escheat to the Crown and would be utilised for building and repairing madrasahs, monasteries and other educational institutions. *Tarikh-i-Jan-Jahan* informs us that Jahangir made arrangements for the repairs of even those madrasahs which had been for the past thirty years the abode of birds and beasts and provided for the appointment of teachers and admission of students to them. In Jahangir's time the prosperity of Agra which had become an excellent centre of learning in the days of his father, Akbar, continued and as *Tuzak-i-Jahangiri* records: "The inhabitants of Agra exert themselves greatly in the acquirement of crafts and the search after learning. Various professors of every religion and creed have taken up their abode in the city".

Shah Jahan

Shah Jahan who founded Shah Jahanabad in Delhi and who was most interested in the construction of the magnificent buildings of his reign such as the Taj and the Pearl Mosque of Agra and the Diwan-i-Am, the Diwan-i-Khas and the Jama Masjid of Delhi, continued the work of his predecessors, Akbar and Jahangir, in education as confirmed by Lala Silchand in his work, *Tafrih-ul-Imarat*. He built the Imperial College at Delhi in the vicinity of the famous Jama Masjid and repaired the madrasah named Dar-ul-Baqa or the Abode of Eternity which had been entirely ruined. He appointed distinguished learned men as the professors of the College, now surrounded by two large reservoirs, a mosque, a hospital and a big bazaar which also met the needs of its residents and placed it under the charge of Maulana Muhammad Sadr-ud-din Khan Bahadur, formerly the Chief Qazi of Delhi.

Disruption of Islamic Learning towards the End of Shah Jahan's and the Beginning of Aurangzeb's Reign

There is no doubt that Shah Jahan despite his great interest in architecture and jewellery had not done anything to undo the educational work of his father and grandfather. Yet developments towards the end of his reign affected adversely the state of learning in the country. In September 1657 when Shah Jahan was seriously taken ill, Dara Shukoh alone of his four brothers were at Agra – and the three absentee brothers Murad in Gujarat, Shuja in Bengal and Aurangzeb in the Deccan suspected that their father had really expired and the news had been suppressed by Dara Shukoh. Shuja proclaimed himself emperor at Rajmahal, then capital of Bengal, Murad crowned himself at Ahmedabad in December 1657 and entered into an agreement with Aurangzeb at Malwa to partition the empire which was solemnised in the name of God and the Prophet. It is not necessary here to enter into the details of the fratricidal contest that followed Shah Jahan's illness – suffice it is to say that the next few years which saw the imprisonment of the emperor at Agra in June 1658 and of the prince Murad at Salimgarh as well as the accession of Aurangzeb to the throne of Delhi in July 1658, the execution of Dara Shukoh in August 1659 and the expulsion of Shuja to the jungles of Arakan in May 1660 plunged the entire country into chaos and disorder affecting peace and stability so vitally needed for the blossoming of arts and crafts which had already been affected by the misrule of the provincial governors and by the heavy burden imposed upon the farmers and the manufacturers resulting from the maintenance of an elaborate bureaucracy and a large army and the expenses incurred on the splendid architectural monuments during the reign of Shah Jahan. Education of the people in Mughal India could not but remain unaffected and it would seem that the good work in education so wonderfully started by Akbar, and continued by his son and grandson, was almost lost outside Delhi and Agra. As Bernier who travelled in the Mughal empire during and immediately after the War of Succession between 1656 and 1658 observes: "A gross and profound ignorance reigns in those states. For how is it possible there should be academics and colleges well founded? Where are such founders to be met with? And if there were any, where were the scholars to be had? Where are those that have means sufficient to maintain their children in colleges? And if there were, who would appear to be so rich? And if they would, where are those benefices, preferments and dignities that require knowledge and abilities, and that may animate youngmen to study?"

It must be mentioned here that it will be unjust to apply the observations of Bernier who remained mostly in the imperial capital during the twelve years he spent in India learning Persian and Sanskrit beyond the period from the end of the reign of Shah Jahan to the first decade of the reign of Aurangzeb.

Aurangzeb: Restoration of Islamic Learning under his Patronage

A zealous Sunni, Aurangzeb as we have already seen, was a critical scholar of Muslim theology and jurisprudence and as a champion of his faith, his mission was to carry the message of Islam into the hearts of the non-Muslims. This he sought to achieve partly by destroying the centres of non-Muslim learning and partly by spreading Islamic education and culture after bringing it in line with the tenets of his religion.

Thus, within a decade after his second accession to the throne with great eclat after his decisive victories at Khajwah and Deorai in June 1659, he issued imperial firmans to all his provincial governors to destroy the Hindu schools and temples and to put down their teachings and religions practices. At the same time he took steps to found "numberless colleges and schools" in different parts of his empire sometimes in confiscated buildings as he did in case of the Dutch in Firinghi Mahal in Lucknow and made them over to a local Muslim for a madrasah. Secondly, he sent imperial firmans to all provincial governors including Makramat Khan, the Diwan of Gujarat, that all students from the highest to the lowest standards reading Mizan and Kashshaf should be financially supported by the state with the sanction of the professors of the colleges and of the Sadrs of the places. According to *Mirat-i-Ahmadi*, he specially asked the Diwan of Gujarat to add three professors in Ahmedabad, Patana and Surat and forty-five students in Ahmedabad to the list of those receiving pecuniary help from his government. Thirdly, he took steps to reimburse the expenses of those pious Muslims who had set up madrasahs and maintained them at their own cost. Thus, in 1697 when the Sadr Akram-ud-din Khan built a college in Ahmedabad at an expense of Rs 124,000 and requested Aurangzeb for pecuniary help, the emperor gave him the jagirs of two villages in the parganas of Sanoly and Kari to defray his expenses involved in building and maintaining the madrasah. Aurangzeb similarly helped the construction of a madrasah in Bianah close to Qazium-ki-Masjid by Qazi Rafi-ud-din Muhammad. Finally, Aurangzeb also took care of the repair of the old madrasahs built earlier and now in ruins in different parts of his empire. Thus he sanctioned in 1678 a huge sum of money to repair the dilapidated madrasahs in Gujarat.

Aurangzeb used the machinery of his state not merely in constructing new madrasahs and repairing the old ones but also in educating the newly converts to Islam in different parts of his vast dominions. He was particularly keen about the education of the Bohras of Gujarat. He appointed teachers for them and asked the instructors to send regularly the results of monthly examinations to him. When some of the Bohras became troublesome, he ordered that the expense of their education which was made compulsory should be borne by the community itself.

Thus, the Islamic education with its theological overtones and proselytising zeals flourished under Aurangzeb, a zealous and orthodox Sunni Muslim as the emperor of India. And the system produced a large number of scholars who had specialised in theology and Islamic law, though *Farhat-ul-Nazirin* mentions only thirty-six including such distinguished teachers as Abdul Aziz, Abdullah and Abdul Karim.

The Decline and Fall

Paradoxically, the reign of Aurangzeb which witnessed the zenith of the Mughal empire and of Islamic education, also contained within it the seeds of their decline. In 1690, Aurangzeb was the lord paramount of almost the whole of India – from Kabul to Chittagong and from Kashmir to the Kaveri and everywhere the Islamic education was patronised by the provincial Muslim governors under his dictates. As we have said earlier, Aurangzeb was an ardent student of Muslim theology and an expert calligrapher who tried to "educate his children in sacred lore" as well as a pious Muslim who zealously and scrupulously followed the injunctions of the Holy Quran, abstaining himself from prohibited food, drink or dress.[14]

However, it is a pity that he seldom encouraged arts and letters. The only literary production which received his patronage as we have already said, was the *Fatawa-i-Alamgiri* which has been regarded as "the greatest digest of Muslim law made in India". It is also a pity that he failed to realise that the greatness of an empire depends on the progress of its people as a whole. In the intensity of his religious zeal he ignored the feelings of important sections of the people and thus roused forces hostile to the empire. While the first part of his reign which began in 1658 saw him fully occupied with the civil and military developments in the North, the second part which began in 1681 when Aurangzeb shifted to the South with his family, his Court and the bulk of his army saw him engrossed with the affairs in the Deccan. He was able to crush the Shia Sultanates of Bijapur and Golkunda but was unsuccessful in his struggles against the nascent nationalism of the Marathas under Shivaji, his sons and the Peshwas. His prolonged absence from the North plunged the Mughal administration into disorder and anarchy and his reversal of his predecessors' policy of religious toleration stirred the anti-imperial rebellions in the forms of the serious outbreaks by the Jats, the Bundelas and the Satnamis, the Sikhs and the Rajputs.

It was however the Deccan Ulcer which ruined Aurangzeb. The endless war in the Deccan exhausted his treasury and sapped the vitality of the empire which rested on the military strength of soldiers who, starving from arrears of pay, mutinied. Conscious of his failure and seriously apprehensive of the imminent disaster facing the empire, he wrote to his son, Azam: "I came alone and am going alone. I have not done well to the country and the people, and of the future there is no hope". And to his another son, Kam Bakhsh, he wrote "I carry away the burden of my shortcomings... come what may, I am launching my boat". Aurangzeb wrote these letters when he had already become worn-out in mind and body by heavy cares and hard toil. He died in March 1707 at the age of 89 "with the Muslim confession of faith in his lips" at Ahmadnagar, and was interred in the compound of the tomb of the famous Muslim Saint Burhan-ud-din.

Aurangzeb's advice to his rebellions sons to save the empire by partition went unheeded and immediately after his death the War of Succession that broke out among them saw the eldest son, Muazzam ascending the throne in 1708 under the little of Bahadur Shah and his death on 27 February 1712 was followed by a fresh War of Succession among his four sons, Jahandar Shah, Azim-us-Shan, Jahan Shah and Rafi-us-Shan. The last three were killed in course of the war, and Jahandar Shah secured the throne with the help of Zu'lfiqar Khan, who became the Chief Minister or Wazir of the State. "In the brief reign of Jahandar" observes Khafi Khan, "violence had full sway. It was a time for minstrels and singers and all the tribes of dancers and actors." Jahandar Shah who was completely under the influence of a favourite lady named Lal Kumari was deposed and strangled in the fort of Delhi under the order of Azim-us-Shan's son Farrukhsiyar who now proclaimed himself as emperor in 1713 A.D.

Farrukhsiyar owed his elevation to the throne to the two Sayyid brothers, Husain Ali, deputy governor of Patna, and Abdullah, governor of Allahabad, who henceforth began to exercise the real power in the state and placed one prince after another till they were removed by the anti-Sayyid group headed by Nizam-ul-Mulk of the Deccan during the reign of Rohsan Akhtar, son of Jahan Shah who had been earlier placed on the throne by the Sayyid brothers at the age of 18. Nizam-ul-Mulk became the new Wazir of Jahan Shah who had assumed the title of Muhammad Shah but as the atmosphere of the imperial Court did not suit his temperament, he soon left for the Deccan where he established a virtually independent kingdom, owing a nominal allegiance to Delhi.

The fall of the Sayyids, and the departure of the Nizam-ul-Mulk for the Deccan, did not however, serve to increase the power and prestige of Muhammad Shah who was "fond of all kinds of pleasures" and "addicted himself to an inactive life" to such an extent that it entirely enervated him. He was destined to have a long reign from 1719 to 1748 but "in utter unconcern he let the affairs drift in their own way, and the consequences was most fatal". Province after province – the Deccan, Oudh and Bengal – slipped out of imperial control; the Marathas established their power far and wide; the Jats became independent near Agra; the Ruhela Afghans founded the State of Rohilkhand in the North Gangetic Plain; the Sikhs became active in the Punjab; and finally the invasion of Nadir Shah of Persia in 1739 dealt a staggering blow to the Delhi empire. The next emperor, Ahmad Shah, son of Muhammad Shah, was unable to stop the forces of disintegration and the Mughal empire rapidly shrank in extent, being reduced only to a small district round Delhi within four decades of Aurangzeb's death.

The decline and fall of the Mughal empire dealt a lethal below to the Islamic education for hence forward there was to be no patronage, however small, at the centre while it was left at the mercy of the provincial Muslim rulers who were now occupied with their own internal squabbles and external rivalries with their immediate neighbours. Such a historical phenomenon had also occurred earlier at the time of the decline and fall of the Delhi Sultanate when its empire was similarly reduced in extent to the district around Palam – but while in the case of the latter the Islamic education was soon revived and strengthened through the coming of the another set of Islamic rulers in the form of the Mughals, there was now no such possibility for in

1757, after defeating the Muslim ruler of Bengal at the battle of Plassey, the East India Company had firmly entrenched itself in the Eastern India which was to soon serve as a launching pad for the inauguration of British rule in India, replacing Islamic education with Western, as had been done earlier by the Islamic conquerors of India replacing Hindu learning with Islamic, to suit its own imperial needs and interests.

Notes

1. Italics are mine.
2. Italics are mine.
3. In the first decade of the nineteenth century.
4. It is from the Persian translation of the Upanishads by Dara Shukoh that a Latin translation entitled, Oupnek'hat was made by a Frenchman Anquetil Duperron in 1801-02. And thereby Europe was introduced for the first time to the Indian religious thought which attracted a host of European scholars and philosophers in the nineteenth century.
5. Presumably Mullah Shah.
6. Obviously handwritten and should not be confused with the printed gazette of a government in modern times. The printing press came to India towards the end of the eighteenth century.
7. Tabii sciences are physical sciences
8. Riyazi sciences are those sciences which comprise mathematics, astronomy, music and mechanics
9. Ilahi sciences are divines sciences which comprise everything connected with theology, and the means of acquiring a knowledge of God.
10. Vyakarana – grammar.
11. Naya – logic.
12. Bedanta – Vedanta, end of the Vedas.
13. Patanjali, author of Mahabhasya, a commentary on Panini's Ashtadhyayi
14. The number of his wives "fell short even of the Quranic allowance of four" which was a praiseworthy restraint for an emperor in those days, though it was below the standard of Dara Shukoh and Khusrav.

16

The Age of Naib Sultans and of Nazims

In the preceding chapters we have highlighted the contribution made by the Delhi Sultans and the Mughal Padshahs to the spread of Islamic education in the different parts of their extensive dominions. While they mostly concentrated their endeavours on the imperial capitals of Delhi and Agra and other cities and towns they had founded around the former, the provincial governors mainly concentrated on their provincial capitals which acted as the spearhead of Islamic learning and culture in the interior of the extensive Muslim empire. The provincial governors who were officially known as Naib Sultans under the Sultanate and as Nazims under the Mughals usually followed the examples of their imperial bosses at Delhi and Agra. Yet when some of them became independent either at the time of the disintegration of the Delhi Sultanate or at the time of the decline of the Mughal empire, they made their own contributions to the spread of Islamic education.

Bengal

One of the earliest provinces to assert its independence long before the disintegration of the Delhi Sultanate was Bengal. Its distance from Delhi, and its profuse wealth often tempted its governors to rebel against the central authority, which caused much trouble to Iltutmish and Balban. Bengal became virtually independent under the weak descendants of Balban and was brought back under imperial control by Ghiyas-ud-din Tughluq who defeated Ghiyas-ud-din Bahadur Shah and to exhaust the power of the Bengal Sultan, divided Bengal into three independent administrative divisions with their capitals at Lakhnauti or Gaur, Satgaon and Sonargaon respectively. Soon after his accession, Muhammad bin Tughluq appointed Qadr Khan to the government of Lakhnauti, Izz-ud-din Azam-ul-Mulk to that of Satgaon, and restored Ghiyas-ud-din Bahadur Shah to the government of Sonargaon but associated with him his own foster-brother Tartar Khan, better known as Bahram Khan. It was Haji Iliyas, foster-brother of Ala-ud-din Shah of Northern Bengal, who united Bengal and made himself its independent ruler in 1345 under the title of Shams-ud-din Iliyas Shah. The reign of Iliyas who died at Pandua in 1357 was marked by peace and prosperity which "are attested by the inauguration of a national and typical coinage, and by the growth of a taste for the arts of peace, especially architecture".

The Bengal rulers, before and after Shams-ud-din Iliyas Shah, participated in the programme of spreading Islamic education, culture and religion in the various parts of their kingdom. Thus Ghiyas-ud-din Bahadur Shah who was a contemporary of Illutmish built a madrasah at Gaur; Iliyas Shah's son and successor Sikandar Shah who died in 1393, built the magnificent mosque at Adina and his son and successor Ghiyas-ud-din who died in 1460 was a corre-spondent of the famous Persian poet Hafiz; Nasir-ud-Din Mahmud who died in 1460 built a mosque at Satgaon and several buildings at Gaur and his son Rukn-ud-din Barbak Shah who was the first ruler in Hindusthan to maintain a large number of Abyssinian slaves as well as his son and successor in 1479 Shams-ud-din Yusuf Shah were known for their piety and patronisation of Islamic learning.

However, it was with the accession of Ala-ud-din Husain Shah, an Arab by descent, in 1493 that a new chapter in the history of education in Medieval India began. The dynasty of Husain Shah ruled Bengal for nearly half a century and made remarkable contributions to learning, both Islam and Hindu. Husain Shah who founded a madrasah as a memorial to the famous Saint Qutb-ul-Alam at Pandua and several at Gaur built of marble and granite, constructed mosques and alms-houses in different parts of his kingdom, making suitable endowments for their maintenance. It was he who appointed Maladhar Basu to translate the *Bagavat Purana* into Bengali and bestowed on him the title of Gunaraja Khan after the completion of his work. Husain Shah's son and successor in 1518, Nusrat Shah was a patron of art, architecture and literature. It was he who constructed two famous mosques, the Bara Sona Masjid or Large Golden Mosque and Qadam Rasul or Foot of the Prophet at Gaur and ordered the translation of the *Mahabharata* in Bengali. The great Bengali poet, Vidyapati, who was his contemporary immortalised him by dedicating to him one of his songs. Vidyapati also bestowed high praise on one of his predecessors, Sultan Ghiyas-ud-din Azam already mentioned earlier, who probably appointed Krittivas, whose Bengali version of the *Ramayana* has been regarded by some as the Bible of Bengal.

The last king of the Husain Shahi dynasty, Ghiyas-ud-din Mahmud Shah was expelled by Sher Shah whose successors ruled Bengal till 1564 when it came under the control of Sulaiman Kararani, governor of South Bihar, whose successor Daud was defeated and killed by the Mughal under Akbar in a battle near Rajmahal in July 1576. And thus, Bengal became a Mughal province and continued to be so till the end of our period. Murshid Quli Khan who was a contemporary of Aurangzeb and transferred his capital from Dacca to Murshidabad was known for his piety and learning. He used to copy the *Quran* every morning and used to send every year its copies and other valuable offerings to Mecca, Medina and other holy places. Alivardi Khan who replaced his grandson Sarfaraz Khan in 1740 and died in 1756, was according to Ghulam Husain, "a prudent, keen and a valorous soldier" possessing all the qualifications needed to become a good ruler. One of the learned men patronised by Alivardi was Mir Muhammad Ali who, if Ghulam Husain is to be believed, possessed a library of two thousand manuscripts.

Jaunpur

We have stated earlier that the city of Jaunpur was founded by Firuz Shah Tughluq to perpetuate the memory of his cousin and patron, Muhammad Jauna, later Muhammad-bin-Tughluq of Medieval India. In the confusion following the invasion of Timur, its ruler Khwaja Jahan threw off his allegiance to the Delhi Sultanate and founded a dynasty of independent rulers of Jaunpur, known as the Sharqi dynasty after his title "Mulk-ush-Sharq". We learn from the *Siyar-ul-Mulk* as quoted in the *Tazkirat-ul-Mulk* that Firuz set up many madrasahs and khanqahs there and people from the neighbouring district and areas used to flock there for free and liberal education under learned teachers.

Following the invasion of Timur, many uprooted scholars from Delhi and Firuzabad came to Jaunpur and adorned the Court of

Ibrahim Shah Sharqi who was the ruler of Jaunpur for nearly 38 years from 1402 to 1440. Among the learned men at the Court of Ibrahim were Qazi Shahab-ud-din Daulatabadi called the "King of Sages", Maulana Shaikh Ilahabad Jaunpuri, Zahir Dihlawi, Maulana Hasan Naqshi, Maulana Ali Ahmad Nishani and Nurul Haqq. Ibrahim granted them altamgahs and jagirs so that they could devote themselves entirely to the pursuits of knowledge. In the Jaunpur city during Ibrahim's reign there were hundreds of mosques and madrasahs and it earned such a great reputation as a centre of learning and culture that it outshone the Court of Delhi and earned for it the title of "the Shiraz of India".

The eminence of Jaunpur as a great centre of learning was not lost even after its annexation by the Delhi Sultan Buhlul Lodi and the demolition of many buildings including madrasahs there by Buhlul Lodi's son and successor, Sikandar Lodi and we know that Farid who later became the arbiter of Hindusthan as Sher Shah received his education in one of its madrasahs. When Jaunpur became a part of a Mughal Subah by 1560, it continued to be patronised by the Delhi emperors who sent firmans to its hakims asking them never to be amiss in their duties towards the many students and teachers of the madrasahs there. Fresh grants were made by the Delhi emperors whenever any madrasahs were in need of repairs. *Tazkirat-ul-Ulema* informs us that princes and amirs while passing by the city of Jaunpur, used to visit the madrasahs and donate liberally to please the Mughal emperors. However, the city of Jaunpur which had received the title, "Shiraz-i-Hind" from Shah Jahan, soon fell into bad days following the visit of Nawab Saadat Khan Nishapur who was the Subahdar of Oudh, Benares and Jaunpur. As no learned men and scholars turned up to greet him on his visit, he ordered confiscation of their stipends and jagirs and this dealt a fatal blow to the educational institutions at Jaunpur from which they failed to recover during our period.

Malwa

Annexed by Ala-ud-din Khalji in 1305 A.D., Malwa continued to be governed by Muslim chiefs under the authority of Delhi, till it became independent, like other provinces, during the period of disorder after the invasion of Timur. Mahmud Khalji was undoubtedly the ablest of the Muslim rulers of Malwa. He extended the limits of his kingdom up to the Satpura Range in the South, the frontier of Gujarat in the West, Bundelkhand in the east, and Mewar and Harauti in the north. The Caliph of Egypt recognised his position and he received a mission from Sultan Abu-Said. According to Ferishta, Mahmud devoted his leisure hours "to hearing histories and memoirs of the Courts of different kings of the earth". A great patron of learning, he gave encouragement throughout his reign of over thirty years to learned men like Shaikh Chand and many distinguished philosophers and maulanas who not only came from other countries but were also turned out by the many colleges including the one in Mandu opposite to the Masjid of Sultan Hushang that Mahmud founded in the different parts of his dominion. Ferishta asserts that in literary excellence, Malwa could bear a fair comparison with Shiraz or Samarqand. Mahmud's successor, Ghiyas-ud-din was though a devout Muslim, enjoyed the pleasures of life abstaining, however, from all intoxicants and prohibited articles of food. He appointed female teachers to educate some seventy ladies in his harem, who learnt *Quran* by heart and read it out to the Sultan while he was putting on his clothes. Baz Bahadur of Malwa who was noted for his taste for music devoted himself entirely to its cultivation to such an extent that he neglected the affairs of the state and paid a heavy price losing his kingdom to his contemporary, Akbar in 1561-1562.

Gujarat

The immense wealth of the province of Gujarat because of its active commerce through the rich ports of Cambay, Surat and Broach often drew upon her external invasions. Annexed to the Delhi Sultanate by Ala-ud-din Khalji in 1297 A.D., it was ruled for a long time by Muslim governors appointed by the Delhi Sultans till 1401 when Zafar Khan, son of a Rajput convert, who had been appointed governor of the province in 1391 A.D. by Muhammad Shah, the youngest son of Firuz formally assumed independence. Zafar lost his kingdom to his rebel son Tatar Khan but soon recovered with the help of Shams Khan and assumed the title of Sultan Muzaffar Shah. Zafar was succeeded by his grandson Ahmad Shah who ascended the throne after his death in 411 A.D. In his long reign of about 30 years, Ahmad Shah not only extended the limits of his kingdom, founded the beautiful city of Ahmedabad on the site of the old town of Asawal and adorned it with magnificent madrasahs and masjids and removed his capital to the newly-built city. He promoted learning with great zeal and according to Ferishta, men of letters from Persia, Arabia and Turkey found it worth while to settle in Gujarat in his liberal reign. Among his successors the most illustrious were Abul Fath Khan, a grandson of Ahmad Shah, who was commonly known as Mahmud Begarha and his grandson, Bahadur. Mahmud Begarha ruled vigorously without the influence of any minister or of the harem for about 53 years and as the leading Muslim historian of his country observes: "He added glory and lustre to the kingdom of Gujarat, and was the best of all the Gujarat kings, including all who preceded, and all who succeeded him, and whether for abounding justice and generosity... for the diffusion of the laws of Islam and of Mussalmans; for soundness in judgement, alike in boyhood, in manhood, and in old age; for power, for valour, and victory, he was a pattern of excellence". Bahadur was as brave and warlike as his grandfather but after he was treacherously put to death in 1537 by the Portuguese governor, Nunho da Cunha, confusion reigned supreme in Gujarat under his weak successors and was finally annexed by Akbar in 1572 A.D.

Sind

In Sind, the reigns of two monarchs, were important in the promotion of Islamic education. According to Ferishta, Nasir-ud-din Qabaicha who ruled at the beginning of the thirteenth century gave asylum to many learned men who fled Ghazni and Ghur under the ruthless ravages of Changiz Khan, and Shah Beg Arghun who ruled in the third decade of the sixteenth century was himself an author of many works and greatly promoted learning in his kingdom.

Multan

In Multan as in Sind, the reigns of two monarchs, Hussain Shah Langha and of Hussain Murza, were remarkable for encouragement of learning. While Hussain Shah built many colleges and appointed many distinguished scholars of the time as teachers, Hussain Mirza drew to his Court two well-known scholars – Sa'ad-ullah Lahori and Maulana Abdur Rahman Jami, who was an elegant composer of verses and had many learned men as his pupils. *Hadiqatul-Aqalim* informs us that once when Hussain Shah was told that Multan could not compete with Gujarat in erecting splendid buildings, his Wazir consoled him and said that "though Gujarat was noted for its buildings, Multan was superior to it in learning".

Kashmir

After travelling from Bengal, through Jaunpur, Malwa, Gujarat, Sind and Multan, we now arrive at Kashmir where Shah Mirza, a Muslim adventurer from Swat seized the throne of Kashmir in 1339, after the death of his master who was a Hindu, and assumed the title of Shams-ud-din Shah.

The most illustrious ruler of his dynasty was his grandson Sikandar who ascended the throne in 1394 A.D. Sikandar exchanged envoys with Timur though the two never met each other. He was generous towards the man of his own faith only, and many learned Muslim scholars flocked to his Court from Persia, Arabia and Mesopotamia. After his death in 1416 A.D., he was succeeded by Ali Shah who was overpowered by his brother Shahi Khan who ascended the throne in 1420 A.D. under the title of Zain-ul-Abidin. Shahi Khan was a benevolent, liberal and enlightened ruler. He recalled the Brahmanas who had left the kingdom during his father's reign, admitted learned Hindus to his society, abolished the Jizya and granted perfect religious freedom to all. Well-versed in Persian, Hindi and Tibetan besides his own language, he patronised literature, painting and music. Under his initiative, the *Mahabharata* and the *Rajatarangini* were translated from Sanskrit into Persian, and several Arabic and Persian books were translated into the Hindi language as well as many treatises on music were written. Thus, for all those qualities he has been justly described as "the Akbar of Kashmir", though he differed from him in a few traits of personal character. He died in 1470 A.D. which was followed by a period of anarchy till 1540 when Mirza Haidar, a relative of Humayun conquered Kashmir. In 1551 Mirza was overthrown by the nobles of Kashmir which was finally absorbed into the Mughal empire in the time of Akbar. *Maasiri Rahimi* informs us that during Akbar's reign, Husain Khan Wali built madrashas in Kashmir which were endowed with the paragana of Asapur.

Khandesh

Khandesh was a province of Muhammad bin Tughluq's empire in the valley of the Tapti river. Firuz Shah entrusted its government to one of his personal attendants, Malik Raja Faruqi, whose ancestors had been respected nobles of the Delhi Court in the reigns of Ala-ud-din Khalji and Muhammad-bin-Tugluq. In the period of confusion following the death of Firuz Shah, Malik Raja, following the example of his neighbour, Dilawar Khan of Malwa, declared his independence of the Delhi Sultanate. The kingdom of Khandesh during its existence as an independent principality found a patron of learning in its second ruler, Nasir Khan who ruled for about forty years. Nasir Khan founded a madrasha at its capital Burhanpur and was fortunate in having Shaikh Zainuddin, the disciple of a successor of Burhanuddin, as his priest. Both Sheikh Zainuddin and his preceptors were earlier principals of the madrasha at Daulatabad, the capital city founded by Muhammad-bin-Tughluq.

Bahamani Kingdom

Using Khandesh as the starting point for our search for Islamic learning in the Deccan, we first come across the Bahamani kingdom which arose on the ruins of the Delhi Sultanate. The nobles of the Deccan, driven to rebellion by the eccentric policy of the Delhi, Sultan Muhammad-bin-Tughluq seized the fort of Daulatabad and proclaimed one of themselves, Ismail Mukh, an Afghan, as king of the Deccan under the title of Nasir-ud-din Shah. Ismail Mukh, being an old and ease loving man, proved unfit for the office and voluntarily made room for a more worthy leader, Hasan, entitled Zafar Khan, who was declared king by the nobles on 3 August 1347, under the title of Abul-Muzaffar Ala-ud-din Bahman Shah. Hasan, contrary to Ferishta's account that he owed his position to prominence through the favour of his Brahmana master Gangu who was Muhammad-bin-Tughluq's astrologer, claimed descent from the famous Persian hero Bahman, son of Isfandiyar and the dynasty he founded thus came to be known as the Bahmani dynasty.

We do not know much about the literary accomplishments of Hasan, except that he knew Persian and took great care for the education of his sons, yet his dynasty produced two illustrious Sultans who made great contributions to learning. The first was Muhammad Shah II, and the second was Firuz, who assumed the title of Taj-ud-din Firuz Shah, who were both grandsons of the founder of the Bahmani kingdom, Ala-ud-din Hasan Bahmani. Muhammad who could speak Persian and Arabic fluently was himself a great poet and a great patron of learning. He invited learned men from Arabia and Persia who came to his Court and partook of his liberality. His invitation was even accepted by Hafiz, famous poet of Shiraz but because of a gale the ship carrying him had to return to the port of Ormuz and he abandoned the journey. In 1378 A.D. the Sultan, established schools for the education of the orphans in different parts of his dominion at Gulbarga, Bidar, Qandhar, Ellichpur, Daulatabad, Chaul, and Dabul and supplied them with ample endowments for their maintenance.

Firuz seized the throne of Gulbarga after the troubled and inglorious reigns of the two sons of Muhammad Shah-II. The author of *Burhan-i-Ma'asir* tells us that Firuz "was an impetuous and a mighty monarch, and expended all his ability and energy in eradicating and destroying tyranny and heresy, and he took much pleasure in the society of the *Shaikhs*, learned men and hermits", though he soon fell a victim to the common vices of his time as Ferishta has noted. A good poet who could compose extempore verses and a good linguist who could speak, as Ferishta informs, as freely with the ladies in the harem belonging to such diverse races as Arabians, Circassions, Gerogians, Turks, Europeans, Chinese, Afghans, Rajputs, Bengalis, Gujratis, Telinganese, Marhathtas in their own languages, he was well-versed in many sciences and very fond of natural philosophy. On Saturdays, Mondays and Thursdays he used to hear lectures on botany, geometry and logic either during the day or at night whenever he found leisure from his state works. A devout Muslim, he used to copy sixteen pages of the *Quran* every fourth day before he started his royal work. A great lover of astronomy, he started in 1407 building an observatory at Daultabad under the supervision of the astronomer Hakim Husain Gilani whose death put a stop to its completion. Firuz used to spend most of his time in the society of divines, poets, reciters of history and readers of the Shah-Namah and witty courtiers like Mulla Ishaq Sarhindi. He held the view that the king should draw around him the most learned men for help and advice and used to send ships every year from the ports of Goa and Chaul to different countries particularly to invite to his Court men celebrated for their learning.

Firuz was succeeded by his brother Ahmad Shah who carried on a terrible war with Vijayanagar to avenge the losses sustained by the Bahamani troops in his brother's reign. Ahmad Shah transferred the capital of his kingdom from Gulbarga to Bidar and though not endowed with such learning, he bestowed favour on some Muslim scholars like the poet Sheikh Azari of Isfarayin in Khurasan and Maulana Sharf-ud-din Mazandarani. Ahmad was succeeded peacefully by his eldest son under the title of Ala-ud-din II. Like other Sultans of the dynasty Ala-ud-din was a zealous champion of Islam and was benevolent towards the followers of his own faith. We know from Ferishta and the author of *Burhan-i-Ma'asir* that he "founded masjids, public schools and charitable institutions, among which was a hospital of perfect elegance and purity of style, which he built in his capital, Bidar, and made two beautiful villages there as a pious endowment, in order that the revenue of these villages should be solely devoted to supplying medicines and drinks".

Ala-ud-din died peacefully in 1457 and was succeeded by his eldest son, Humayun who was so cruel as to get the epithet of "Zalim" or the "Tyrant". After Humayun's death in 1461, people were freed "from the talons of his tortures" and had a new Sultan in his minor son, Nizam Shah. The Queen mother managed the administration of the state with the assistance of Khwaja Jahan and Khwaja Mahmud Gawan and on the sudden death of Nizam Shah in 1463, his brother aged only nine ascended the throne under the title of Muhammad III. Khwaja Jahan who aimed at a monopoly of power in the state was put to death through the machinations of the Queen mother and his place was given to Mahmud Gawan who received the title of Khawaja Jahan. Mahmud Gawan never abused his authority and by virtue of his conspicuous ability he served the Bahamani State with unstinted loyalty and brought the dominions of the Bahamanis "to an extent never achieved by former sovereigns". Mahmud Gawan appointed Adri-Jahan Shustari, a celebrated scholar as the tutor of the prince who made considerable progress in his studies and became the most learned king next to Firuz Shah Bahamani. However, being addicted to hard drinking, the Sultan became mentally unbalanced as years rolled on and took a suicidal step by passing the death sentence on Mahmud Gawan in 1481 at the instigation of the Deccani nobles who were jealous of his power and success. With the unjust execution of this old minister who led a simple and pure life, was fond of learning and the society of the learned and maintained a magnificent college and a vast library at Bidar, "departed", as Meadows Taylor rightly remarks, "all the cohesion and power of the Bahmani kingdom". The Bahamani kingdom was henceforth thrown into utter confusion after Muhammad III's death in 1482. The five weak successors of the deceased Sultan remained mere puppets in the hands of Qasim Barid-ul-Mamalik, a clever noble of Turki origin, and after his death in 1504, in those of his son Amir Ali Barid, "the fox of the Deccan". The last ruler, Kalimullah Shah, secretly tried to secure the help of Babar to restore the lost fortunes of his dynasty but was sadly disappointed. With his death in 1527, the Bahamani dynasty came to an end after about one hundred and eighty years' rule. Most of its Sultans employed themselves chiefly in terrible wars, many of them with their neighbour, Vijayanagar kingdom, and its internal politics were severely distracted by Court intrigues and civil strife. Among the eighteen kings of this dynasty, five were murdered, two died of intemperance, and three were deposed, two of them being blinded. Yet they were credited with patronage of learning and education according to their rights.

The Five Deccan Sultanates

On the break-up of the Bahamani kingdom five separate Sultanates arose in the Deccan, one after another and each one of them was known after the title of its founder – Imad Shahi dynasty of Berar, the Nizam Shahi dynasty of Ahmadnagar, the Adil Shahi dynasty of Bijapur, the Qutb Shahi dynasty of Golkunda and the Barid Shahi dynasty of Bidar. The first to secede was Berar, where Fathullah Imad Shah, a Hindu convert, declared his independence in 1484 A.D. and founded the Imad Shahi dynasty. Berar was absorbed by Ahmadnagar in 1574 A.D.

The history of those Sultanates is largely a record of almost continuous quarrel with one another and with Vijayanagar. Each aspired to the supremacy of the Deccan which was consequently turned into a scene of internal warfare, similar to what went on between the Chalukyas and the Pallavas in earlier days, or between Mysore, the Marathas and the Nizam in the eighteenth century. The disruption of the Bahmani kingdom, and the dissensions among the five Sultanates that rose on its ruins, seriously hampered the progress of Islam, political as well as religious, in the south, where the spirit of Hindu revival, that had manifested itself since the days of the Tughluqs, culminated in the rise and growth of the Vijayanagar empire.

Bijapur

Yet the kingdoms of Bijapur, Ahmadnagar and Golkunda produced some notable rulers who made substantial contributions to the spread of Islamic education and culture in the south. The foremost among them was Yusuf Adil Khan, Governor of Bijapur, who asserted his independence in 1489-1490 A.D. and ruled till 1510 A.D. According to Ferishta, he was the son of Sultan Murad II of Turkey who, after his death in 1451 A.D. was succeeded by his elder brother, Muhammad II and fled first to Persia, and then to India at the age of seventeen, to save himself from assassination ordered by Muhammad II. In India he sold himself as a slave to Mahmud Gawan. A poet and musician, he invited to his Court learned men and eminent artists from Persia, Turkistan and Rum to live under his patronage. Yusuf who married a Hindu lady – the daughter of a Marhatha Chieftain was not a bigot though he had a preference for the Shiah creed. Religion was no bar to securing offices in his government and many Hindus were appointed in his revenue department. His successor, Ismail Adil Shah (1510-34) was equally noted for his literary refinements and proficiency in the fine arts, particularly music and painting. Author of the *Nauras* or Nine Savours, he loved Turki and Persian music and language more than the Deccanese as a result of his education under the tuition of his aunt Dilshad who kept him away from the company of the Deccanese at his father's direction. His successor, Ibrahim Adil Shah I (1534-57) encouraged keeping public accounts in Hindi instead of Persian and many Brahmanas were appointed in charge of the accounts, so that they soon acquired a great influence in the government. The great historian, Muhammad Qasim, the author of the *Tarikh-i-Ferishta* lived in the Court of Ibrahim Adil Shah II (1579-96). The Adil Shahi dynasty of Bijapur not only established many maktabs and madrasahs where education was imparted free to the poor and the orphans but also built up an excellent library "some of its books are curious and interesting to any one acquainted with Arabic and Persian literature" – and though later "all the most valuable manuscripts were taken away by Aurangzeb in cart-loads", the remnant of the library still exists at Bijapur in the Asari Mahal.

Ahmadnagar

The first Sultan of Ahmadnagar, Ahmad Nizam Shah (1490-1508) who was educated as a captive by Ahmad Shah Bahmani was known for his eminence in Persian and Arabic literature as well as for his interest in single sword and wrestling and schools for these were set up in all quarters of the city of Ahmadnagar.

Golkunda

The kingdom of Golkunda grew up on the ruins of the old Hindu kingdom of Warangal which was conquered by the Bahamanis in 1424 A.D. The founder of the Qutb Shahi dynasty was Quali Shah, a

Turki Officer of the Bahamani kingdom under Mahmud Shah
Bahamani. Quali Shah declared his independence either in 1517 or
1518 and had a long and prosperous reign till he was murdered at the
age of 90 in 1543 by his son Jamshid, who reigned for seven years.
Quali Shah was a great patron of learning and was himself a poet. Ibn
Nishati who flourished under his fostering care wrote, *Tuti Namah*
and *Phulbar*, both of which are still considered as models in the
Deccanese dialect. He built in the centre of Hyderabad an elegant
masjid and the *Chahar Minar* – the latter structure being a quadrangle
with four arcades, each arch occupying the whole space between the
minarets at its corners. Over the middle there is a dome under which
a fountain plays with its jets of clear water. Each minar about 220 feet
in height contains apartments for the use of professors and students of
the college there. Thevenot who visited India in 1666 A.D. saw it and
admired it in Part III of his work, *Travels into the Levant*. Besides this
madrasah of Chahar Minar, the Sultan built several other colleges and
seminaries and appointed teachers with suitable remunerations for
instructing the students admitted there. One such college stood in the
vicinity of Hyderabad as Ferishta informs us. The reign of Quali Shah
is noted in Southern India for the emergence of the elementary
schools which were held in the houses of the masters providing
instruction in Arabic and Persian as well as in reading and writing on
paper mostly imported from China.

The three Shia Sultanates in the Deccan eked out a precarious
existence under the Mughals, first threatened by Akbar and then by
Shah Jahan until finally absorbed into the Mughal dominion as the
Deccan Subah by Aurangzeb. Following the disintegration of the
Mughal empire after Aurangzeb's death in 1707, Mir Qamar-ud-din
Chin Qilich Khan better known as Nizam-ul-Mulk, whose grandfather, Khawaja Abid Shaikh-ul-Islam came from Bukhara in the
middle of the seventeenth century and entered the service of
Aurangzeb, carved out an independent state out of the Deccan Subah
under the title of Asaf Jah, in October 1724. From this time may be
dated the Nizam-ul-Mulk's "virtual independence" for "seven and
thirty years" with which he governed an extensive tract in the Deccan
till his death at the age of ninety-one on 21 May, 1748, thereby laying
down, the foundation of the Hyderabad State.

Ma'bar

We now come to the kingdom of Ma'bar in the Southern most part of India which came into existence when Jalal-ud-din Ahsan Shah, the governor of Ma'bar, proclaimed himself independent of Muhammad-bin-Tughluq in 1335. The province of Ma'bar was originally created in 1311 when Malik Kafur as the Malik Naib of Ala-ud-din Khalji captured Madura, the capital of the Pandya king, Vira Pandya and collected an immense booty of elephants, horses and jewels. Jalal-ud-din Ahsan Shah who founded this independent kingdom comprising the entire area between the Malabar and the Coromandel coasts and from Cape Comorin up to Gulbarga was a patron of Islamic learning. And if Ibn Batutah who visited his kingdom during his reign is to be believed, there were nearly twenty-three schools for boys and thirteen for girls[1] in the capital of the kingdom at Hinawr or Hanaur. This Muslim kingdom of Madura existed till 1377-78, when it fell before the rising state of Vijayanagar which is said to have come into existence in 1336.

Note

1. In all probability these were schools which were run at private houses. For details, see Chapter 21.

17

Advancement of Learning by the Muslim Nobility

In the previous three chapters we have analysed the contributions made by the Delhi Sultans, the Mughal emperors as well as the Muslim governors and kings of provinces to the spread of Islamic education in Medieval India. However, such contributions were not confined to the royal families alone – the nobles who held important positions in the civil and the military administration as well as some of the learned men who gathered at the Courts often advanced the cause of Islamic education in the country by their deeds and acts.

The Muslim Nobility

We have already had some idea of the learned men who gathered at the Courts of the Delhi Sultans and the Mughal emperors – they mostly came from outside India attracted by the munificence of the latter. Most of the nobles also accompanied the Islamic rulers when they came to India or later joined them in search of their fortune in India. The depredations carried out by Changiz Khan and the frequent political changes in Afghanistan and the neighbouring countries in Central Asia led to the migration of many of the princes and the nobles who could not adjust themselves with the changing conditions at their places of birth. Thus, while the bulk of the nobles came from the class of their rulers who were Turks, there were nobles from other nationalities, like Arabs, Afghans, Abyssinians, Egyptians as well as Indians. The nobles who exercised a predominant influence in Muslim India as generals, administrators and sometimes as king-makers were not a hereditary, homogenous and well-organised body as was the case with the nobles of France or England in Medieval Europe. The nobles often occupied themselves with their mutual rivalries and pursued selfish interests at the cost of the state. A noble had only a life interest in his jagir, which escheated to the crown on his death; and the titles on emoluments could not usually be transmitted from father to son. The nobles led extravagant lives and squandered away all their money in unproductive luxury during their lifetime. Thus, the debased caricature of European feudalism in Medieval India prevented the country from having one of the strongest safeguards of public liberty and checks on royal autocracy, namely, an independent hereditary peerage, whose position and wealth did not depend on the king's favour in every generation and who could, therefore, afford to be bold in their criticism of royal caprice and their opposition to the royal tyranny.

It is therefore natural that the nobility would follow the examples of its masters in everything they did and would follow in their footsteps. There is no doubt that this tendency among the nobles often motivated by their own religion benefited Islamic education most. Let us first begin with the cases of those learned scholars and nobles at the Courts of the Delhi Sultans and the Mughal emperors who furthered the spread of Islamic education by setting up maktabs and madrasahs, mosques and khanqahs, libraries and literary societies in and around Delhi and Agra.

Sayyed Maula

Foremost among them was Sayyed Maula who adorned the Court of Ghiyas-ud-din Balban and founded a madrasah at Delhi. He saw the eclipse of the so-called Slave dynasty and accession to throne of Jalal-ud-din Khalji, the founder of the Khalji dynasty. By the time of Jalal-ud-din Khalji his reputation as a scholar soared high and he set up an alm-house to support the learned men, faqirs, travellers, as well as the poor who visited Delhi. So great was his reputation as a teacher that among his disciples were many nobles and princes. Jalal-ud-din's eldest-son, Khan Khanan, used to visit him frequently and describe himself as Sayyid's son. However, when Jalal-ud-din came to know that Sayyid was plotting against him with his disciples, he eliminated him.

The Nobility during the Reign of Ala-ud-Din

It is again nobles like Sayyid Maula who not only kept the flames of Islamic learning burning but helped them to rise further so that Delhi could become the rival of many a centre of learning outside India without the fostering patronage of Ala-ud-din Khalji who succeeded Jalal-ud-din. We have on record the names of such illustrious nobles as the Sayyids of Gardiz and of Bianah as well as the nobles of Nauhattah and the descendants of the Janjar family who were known for their munificence and greatly patronised different branches of Islamic learning such as Usul-i-Din[1], Fiqh[2], Usul-i-Fiqh[3], Nahw[4], Badi-o-Bayan[5] and Tafsir[6]. Besides these nobles, Ala-ud-din's Wazir or Prime Minister, Shams-ul-Mulk was a great patron of learning unlike his master and it is possible that there could be at the various levels of Ala-ud-din's administration officials who patronised learning. Shams-ul-Mulk is said to have counted among his pupils a great many scholars of the day.

The munificence of these nobles as well as the past reputation of Delhi as a great centre of learning continued to draw learned men to the capital city despite Ala-ud-din's failure to appreciate their merit. As Ferishta records: "Palaces, mosques, universities, baths, mausolea, forts and all kinds of public and private buildings seemed to rise as if by magic. Neither did there in any age, appear such a concourse of learned men from all parts. Forty-five doctors, skilled in the sciences were professors in the universities". Barni provides us with a long list of scholars living in Delhi at the time of Ala-ud-din, who had specialised in all branches of knowledge such as history, jurisprudence, logic, theology, music, astrology, medicine, grammar, commentaries on the *Quran* and Kathaks. The most famous among them were: Sayyid Taj-ud-din, Sayyid Rukn-ud-din, the brothers Sayyid Mughis-ud-din and Muntajib-ud-din in philosophy and poetry; Jamal-ud-din Shakbi, Ala-ud-din Maqri, Khwajah Ziki in the *Quran*; Amir Arslan in history; Kabir-ud-din whose *Fathnamahs* are spoken of very highly by Barni in belles lettres, Maulana Badr-ud-din Damashqi, Maulanana Sadr-ud-din, Juwaini Tabib, Alim-ud-din in the art of healing; Maulana Imad-ud-din Hasan, Maulana Hamid, Maulana Latif, Maulana Ziya-ud-din Sunnami and Maulana Shahab-ud-din Khalili in the art of Tazkirs. According to Barni, some of the scholars listed by him could surpass the most erudite of Bukhara, Samarqand, Baghdad, Cairo, Damascus, Ispahan or Tabriz.

Added to this list of galaxy of scholars, the names of few lucky learned persons like Amir Khusrav who continued to be patronised by Alauddin, Delhi certainly became "the envy of Baghdad, rival of Cairo and equal of Constantinople" as a centre of learning. And, as, Abdul Haqq Dihlawi observes: "During the time of Sultan Alauddin, Delhi was the great rendezvous of all the most learned and erudite personages, for notwithstanding the pride and hauteur, the neglect and superciliousness, and the want of kindness and cordiality with which the monarch treated this class of people, the spirit of the age remained the same".

It is interesting to note that the reign of Ala-ud-din who followed the principles of expediency rather than those of his religion in the matters of the statecraft and tried to ignore the Ulemas in his administration saw the blossoming of an interest in the study of theology and philosophy. Consequently such works on these subjects as *Qutah-ul-Qalib*, *Ihya-ul-Ulum* and its translation, *Awarif* and *Kashf-ul-Mahjub*, *Sharh-i-Tarif and Risalah-i-Qushiri* were in great demand. As a matter of fact, the khanqah of the saint Nizam-ud-din Auliya who flourished during this time and was a close friend of Amir Khusrav was one of the important centres of the time for imparting such lessons in religious education. Nizam-ud-din possessed an excellent library and had among his disciples such well-known scholars as Shaikh Usman, also known as Maqdum Siraj-ud-din. So popular was the study of theological subjects that Barni's list of scholars at the time of Ala-ud-din is dominated by no less than 46 specialists in Islamic law and religion and Ferishta also mentions "forty-five doctors, skilled in the sciences" who taught at the different madrasahs in the capital. The reason why such theological studies were popular among scholars is probably to record their discontent against Ala-ud-din who treated them with contempt and disregarded his religion in his administration, just as in our recent past, the people in Eastern Europe indulged more in religion than in politics to vent their protest against the communist rulers.

The Nobility after Ala-ud-Din

We have little evidences of the kind of contributions made to Islamic learning by the nobles as had been done by them in the days of Ala-ud-din Khalji till the coming of the Mughals. This may be partly because, of the fact that initiative for such acts was taken by the next dynasty, which has offered us Firuj Shah Tughluq and partly because of the steady decline of the Delhi Sultanate, which affected the fortunes of the nobles adversely.

Yet there were a few scattered examples to show the patronisation of Islamic learning by nobles and scholars. Thus, Amir Khusrav built on an isolated fortified hillock, called Nai-Ka-Qila or Barbar's Fort, a mile beyond Tughlaqabad, a madrasah for his retreat in the twilight of his life and career; Masnad Ali Husain Khan, a noble of Sikandar Lodi's time, was known for his proverbial generosity and as *Waqiati-Mushtaqi* informs us that if any one getting allowance from Masnad died, the nearest kin of the deceased continued to receive it and if there were none but the wife, she was made to adopt a son, whom the noble would send to school and would teach archery and riding. Another example was provided by Ghazi Khan, the Afghan noble of the Punjab who had invited Babar to India but later turned against him. When Babar defeated him, he found a library containing books on theology and other sciences in possession of Ghazi Khan, indicating his love for learning. Babar who "did not on the whole find so many books of value as from their appearance" he had expected to find, sent some of them to his sons, Humayun and Kamran, for their use.

The Nobility during the Mughals

The educational endeavours of the Mughal emperors were often reinforced remarkably by the educational activities of the Mughal nobility and the upper classes in and around Delhi. In the time of Humayun, lived Shaikh Zain-ud-din Hafi who could excel both in prose and verse to the emperor. According to *Muntakhab-ul-Tawarikh* he "was unapproachable in his age in the construction of enigmas and chronograms, in extempore versification and in all the minutiae of poetry and prose". He built a superb madrasah in Delhi where he was buried after his death in Chunar in 1534 A.D. Later a school was built on the side of the Yamuna, opposite to Agra, to perpetuate his memory.

Akbar's foster-mother Maham Anaga was one of the first female educationists who took a keen interest in spreading Islamic education. In 1561 A.D. she built a madrasah with a masjid attached to it. While the madrasaha was built of "rubble and plaster, with the ornamented parts painted by the use of red dressed stone and granite", the masjid inside "was profusely ornamented with coloured plaster and glazed tiles". The dilapidated cloisters of the madrasah which looked like a framed picture with its ornamented mosque can still be seen in front of the Western Gate of the Purana Qilah built by Sher Shah. Besides the madrasah of Maham Anaga, there was another built by Khwajah Muin in Delhi. One of the teachers at this madrasah was Mirza Muflis Samarqandi who taught there for three years between 1571 and 1574 A.D. Another noble who held an important position under Akbar's administration and who greatly patronised Islamic learning was Abdul Rahim Khan Khanan. Rahim was the son of Bairam Khan, Akbar's guardian who came from Balkh, a centre of Persian scholarship. Abdul Rahim could write volubly Persian, Turki, Arabic and Hindi and could compose poems. He presented to Akbar a Persian translation of the *Memoirs of Babar* in 1590 A.D. He gave good education to his son, Mirza Iraj and threw the doors of his personal library open to the learned men who used to come for study and self-improvement. Abdul Rahim was so learned that many came to study under him. According to the *Ma'asir-i-Rahimi* there were about 95 learned men who were favoured with his patronage in various ways. Similarly, Akbar's beloved friend and poet, Faizi, brother of Abul Fazl who passed away in 1595 used to throw the doors of his personal library consisting of some 4,600 manuscripts including 101 copies of poem "Nal Daman" open to learned scholars for enriching their knowledge further. Besides allowing the uses of their libraries, outstanding scholars of the time often provided further specialised knowledge to trained scholars like Abdul Qadir Badaoni, the historian of Akbar's reign, who lived and studied in the house of his preceptor, Mihr Ali Beg, at Agra, after leaving his own house at Basawar.

While we do not hear much about the contributions made by the nobles during the reign of Jahangir to Islamic education, we are informed by *Asar-ul-Sanadid* that Maulavi Muhammad Sadr-ud-din Khan Bahadur, Sadr-ul-Sudur or Chief Qazi of Shah Jahanabad, had the madrasah built by Shah Jahan in the vicinity of Jama Masjid transferred to him later. The Chief Qazi repaired the madrasah, made additions to the building and by his energy put new life into it.

It was the work of a group of learned scholars and nobles who kept Islamic learning alive during the reign of Aurangzeb who was averse to the patronisation of any kind of *belles lettres* and learning except the Quranic. Thus, Khafi Khan wrote secretly his history of Aurangzeb's reign, *Muntakhab-ul-Lubab*, Mirza Muhammad Kazim *Alamgirnamah*, Muhammad Saqi *Maasir-i-Alamgiri*, Sujan Rai Khatri

Khulasat-ut-Tawarikh, Bhimsen *Nushka-i-Dilkusha* and finally Iswar Das *Fatuhat-l-Alamgiri*. The last three were Hindu scholars and their Persian histories clearly indicate the extent of their remarkable knowledge not only in their subject but also in their language.

The Nobility during the Decline of the Mughal Empire

Such efforts mostly by the Muslim upper classes could also be seen in the days of the decline of the Mughal empire. Thus Ghazi-ud-din, as we are informed by Ali Muhammad Khan, the author of *Mirat-i-Ahmadi*, a favourite officer of Bahadur Shah I, constructed near the Ajmeri Gate at Delhi, a madrasah, a masjid and a mausoleum, all within the same enclosure, combining in one place, a house of worship, a tomb of the founder and a place of instruction, with a residence for those in charge of the whole establishment. Similarly, in 1711 A.D. Firoz Jang founded a madrasah at Delhi and Muhammad Wali-ullah, the author of *Tarikh-i-Farrukhabadi*, another at Farrukhabad. At the same time another madrasah called Fakr-ul-Marabi, where Maulvi Alim-ud-din and Maulvi Nasim-ud-din famous for their literary ability and attainments were educated, existed at Kanauj.

In the wake of the confusion in the administration of the country since the accession of Muhammad Shah to the throne of Delhi created by the two Sayyid brothers and the subsequent invasion of Nadir Shah, there was a brilliant impetus given to astronomy by the genius of Sawai Jai Singh, Raja of Amber and founder of the principality of Jaipur. He constructed observations not only in Jaipur, Ujjain, Mathura and Benares, but also in Delhi. His observatory in Delhi, the capital of the Mughal empire was built in 1724, in the fifth year of the reign of Muhammad Shah at his instance. Besides, in the reign of Muhammad Shah in 1722 Nawab Sharaf-ud-daulal constructed a madrasah and a mosque close to each other and if *Tabsirat-ul-Nazirin* is to be believed, Nadir Shah issued the order to pillage, plunder and massacre Delhi while he was seated within the "Madrasah of Raushan-ud-daulah". Assuming Raushan-ud-daulah was a different person from Sharaf-ud-daulah, there were, at the time of Muhammad Shah (1719-1748), three noteworthy educational institutions flourishing in Delhi.

The Nobility in the Provinces

We now come to the provinces to see how Islamic education in these places was fostered by the nobles and the affluent Muslims. As in the Age of Naib Sultans and of Nazims, let us begin with Bengal and travel through Jaunpur, Gujarat, Sialkot and Multan to the Deccan.

Bengal

In Bengal the most remarkable example of patronisation of learning occurred in the reign of Husain Shah. Husain Shah's general, Paragal Khan and his son Chhuti Khan have made themselves immortal by associating their names with the Bengali translation of a portion of the Mahabharata, Examples of Bengali translation of Sanskrit and Persian works at the instance of Muslim chiefs served to remove the supercilious spirit in which Bengali was looked upon by the Sanskrit loving Brahmanas and the Hindu Rajas. The latter imitated the Muslim rulers and chiefs in giving their patronage to Bengali writers and the institution of keeping "Bengali Court Poets" grew into a fashion. Many distinguished Bengali poets and writers had since adorned the Courts of Hindu Rajas, which raised Bengal to a high place in the estimation of the people and made it rival of the languages that had already established their footing. In 1479 A.D., Yusuf Shah issued a very large inscription at the village of Umarpur which mentioned him as the builder of a madrasah and a masjid. Both have since disappeared along with the madrasah built by Muslim chiefs at Asthipura or the place of bones where the bodies of all the slain in the 18 days' battle between the Kauravas and the Pandavas were said to have been collected and burnt. In the time of Murshid Quli Khan (1704-25 A.D.) a very liberal zamindar at Birbhum called Asadullah used to dedicate half of his income to the support of the learned men and other charitable works.

Jaunpur

In Jaunpur, in the fifteenth century, Munim Khan owned apartments near the big Jaunpur Bridge. The inner apartments housed a madrasah and the outer apartments were let out. The rent derived from them defrayed the expenses of the teacher and the taught. In the fifties of the fifteenth century Bibi Raji, wife of Mahmud Shah of Jaunpur constructed a Jama Masjid, a monastery and a madrasah and gave the name of Namazgah or place of worship and assigned stipends and scholarships to the teachers and students of the Madrasah. Similarly Rahim Dad of Gwalior built a madrasah there which was visited by Babar as he records in his *Tuzuk-i-Babari*: "Having visited these places, I mounted my horse and went to the college founded by Rahim Dad".

Gujarat

In Gujarat, Sadiq Khan who flourished in the sixteenth century founded a madrasah, where the learned Shaikh Wajih-ud-din Ahmad used to teach and when he died he was buried within this madrasah in 1589 A.D. In 1623 A.D., the Dewan Mahammad Safi founded quite a few madrasahs by the side of the madrasah of Sayit Khan and before Fort Irk. In 1697 Akram-ud-din, a contemporary of Aurangzeb, built a madrasah at Ahmedabad at a cost of Rs 124,000 and in response to his request was given two villages – Siha and Sundra – by Aurangzeb for its maintenance. In 1670 A.D., Qazi Rafi-ud-din made a madrasah at Bianah in the vicinity of Qazion-ki-Masjid. Maulavi Abdul Hakim also founded a school at Sialkot, of which his son, Maulvi Abdullah, became an eminent teacher.

Sialkot during Aurangzeb's time was a great seat of learning. Learned men from various parts of the country resorted to this place. Its eminence as a centre of learning rested partly on the voluntary efforts of the people and partly to the fact that paper was easily procurable there as it had a big manufactory of Mansinghi and silk paper, which was clean, durable and good in texture.[7]

Sind

During the Arab occupation of Sind, Multan grew into a flourishing city and gradually rose to be a centre of Islamic learning as could be seen by the presence of numerous tombs of Muslim saints and scholars. Multan had been an important asylum for the learned persons who had been ousted from their homes by the tyranny of their rulers. Shah Shans Tabrez whose tomb in Multan has now become a place of pilgrimage was the head of a religious order and a poet of sublime imagination. The patronisation of learning in Multan obviously came from its nobles as that in Rohri which came from the Sayyids and holy men who set up large madrasahs with minarets which add to the picturesque appearance of this part of Sind.

We now cross the Vindhyas and come to the days of the Bahamani kingdom. *Tuhfat-ul-Salatin* informs us that during the reign of Hasan Shah Bahmani (1347-1358), there was a learned scholar who

used to diffuse Islamic learning by teaching students at home, three
days per week on Mondays, Wednesdays and Saturdays. He imparted
lessons from his favourite books such as *Zahidid*, *Sharh-i-Tazkirah*,
Tahriri Uqlidas[8], *Sharh-i-Maqasid*[9] and *Mutawwal*[10].

During the reign of Firuz Shah Bahmani (1397-1427) Sadr-ud-din
Muhammad Hussaini, popularly called Banda Nawaz for his hospi-
tality and Gisu Daraz for his long locks, was a famous saint of
Gulbarga and a preceptor of Prince Ahmad Shah. Gisu Daraz had a
great fame for vast learning and authored a number of books like
Adab-ul-Murid, the *Wajud-ul-Ashiqin* and the *Asmar-ul-Asar*. After
Firuz Shah's death in 1422, when the Prince Ahmad Shah became
king, he gave several towns, villages and extensive lands near
Gulbarga in perpetuity to Sayyid Muhammad Gisu Daraz and built
for him a magnificent college near Gulbarga – an honour which Gisu
Daraz richly deserved as a lover of learning and promoter of
education.

Mahmud Gawan

The literary munificence of Mahmud Gawan, the Khwaja Jahan or
the minister of Muhammad Shah III of the Bahmani kingdom was the
most outstanding among the high officials of Medieval India. An
expert mathematician, he could compose prose and verse elegantly
and was the author of *Rauzat-ul-Insha*, the *Diwan-i-Ashar* and many
other works which could still be seen in some of the libraries of the
Deccan. He was so extremely learned that he corresponded regularly
with Maulana Abdur Rahman Jami, a celebrated poet, and some of
the letters written to him by the latter were reproduced in his books.
His literary beneficence was so extensive that there was scarcely a
town or a city the learned men of which had not derived advantage
from him. And this was not confined to the Bahmani kingdom only –
he used to send every year valuable presents to several learned men in
Khurasan and Iraq for which the princes of those countries bestowed
honours upon him.

Mahmud Gawan's name is preserved in history chiefly as the
founder of the celebrated madrasah, called Madrasah-i-Mahmud
Gawan in Bidar two years before his death in 1481. When Ferishta
saw it, it was so well intact as if it were just finished but in the second
half of the seventeenth century it lost much of its beauty through
mutilation by an explosion of gunpowder, which took place when
Aurangzeb used it as a magazine and a barrack. The college was

equipped with a library for the use of its students, containing some 3,000 volumes. It had a mosque attached to it in order that religion might go hand in hand in secular learning. Around the mosque there was a row of rooms for the residence of professors and students and distinguished scholars of distant countries were conveniently accommodated there and provided with all the necessaries of life *gratis*. Meadows Taylor thus describes the madrasah in his *History of India*: "The noble college of Mahmud Gawan in the city of Bidar was perhaps the grandest completed work of the period. It consisted of a spacious square with arches all round it, of two storeys, divided into convenient rooms. The minarets at each corner of the front were upwards of 100 feet high, and also the front itself, covered with enamel tiles, on which were flowers on blue, yellow and red grounds and sentences of the *Quran* in large Kufic letters, the effect of which was at once chaste and superb".

Initially, Gawan was interested in having the celebrated scholars of the time as teachers in his madrasah and issued invitations to them including Maulana Abdur Rahman Jami, most illustrious poet and scholar of Persia and Maulana Jalal-ud-din Davvani, the well-known author and teacher at the Madrasah-ul-Aitam of Shiraj but was disappointed when they could not come because of old age, strenuous journey and other inconveniences involved in accepting the invitations. Having failed to obtain the services of Maulana Abdur Rahman Jami for the post of the principal of his madrasah, his choice fell on Shaikh Ibrahim Multani, a well-known saint and scholar who happened to be staying at Bidar at that time. The Shaikh who fully repaid the confidence reposed in him was so learned that the princes of the Bahamani kingdom considered it an honour to be his disciples. In recognition of his learning and piety, he was later appointed as the Chief Qazi of the Bahamani kingdom.

Besides this madrasah at Bidar, Mahmud Gawan accomplished with his own resources a large number of public works, the remains of which could still be seen in the Deccan. Those works of Mahmud Gawan stand out as a brilliant example of what a single individual with his own unaided resources could achieve. He was involved with a spirit of such great self-sacrifice as is rarely met with, in a man. In many respects, Mahmud Gawan's character was far superior to any of his contemporaries. His income was very large, "equalling that of many kings" but his beneficence was so great that after his death only a small sum was left in his treasury. He lived the life of an ascetic, sleeping on a bare mat and using earthen utensils, thus combining plain living with high thinking – Murtaza Hussain has recorded in his *Haqiqat-ul-Aqlim* that after his death, 3,500 books were obtained from the house. It is indeed a great pity that such a saintly person fell a victim to the Court politics and had to die two years after the foundation of the college at Bidar through the sheer folly of Muhammad Shah III who in his later years had lost his sense of judgement being addicted to hard drinking and took the suicidal step by passing the death sentence on Mahmud Gawan.

Ferishta informs us that Mulla Abdul Karim Sindi has written the biography of the saintly scholar whose madrasah can still be seen in Bidar, though in a dilapidated condition. It is often through the work of a Mahmud Gawan, a Shams-ul-Mulk, a Nizam-ud-din Auliya, a Paragol Khan, a Muhammad Sadr-ud-din Khan or a Kafi Khan that when dynasties changed, kings died and their sons crossed swords, invaders came and looted the country or when the rulers withdrew their patronage from learning which often happened in Medieval India that Islamic education came alive to Modern India.

Notes

1. Theology
2. Jurisprudence
3. Logic
4. Grammar
5. History
6. Commentaries on the Quran and the Scriptures.
7. Paper came from China to Central Asia where a big manufactory existed at Samarqand and supplied paper to various countries of the East, including India. It was from Samarqand that paper was first brought into India about the tenth century of the Christian era.
8. Euclid (Mathematics)
9. Theology
10. Rhetoric

18

The Age of Vocations

Commerce in Medieval India

Islamic India inherited a prosperous internal and external trade from
Ancient India and since there had been no attempt at "any big
improvement in the method of production, a more equitable distribution of the economic wealth, or a better adjustment of the
economic position of the various social classes", trade and commerce
flowed on the traditional paths under the Muslim rulers. While her
large internal trade under the Delhi Sultans was occasionally thwarted
by the monopoly of the state or rigid administrative control, her
commercial relations with the outside world also expanded. As
before, the sea-route connected her commercially with the distant
regions of Europe, the Malay Islands and China, and other countries
on the Pacific Ocean; and she had now intensive intercourse through
land routes with Central Asia, Afghanistan and Persia as well as with
Tibet and Bhutan. In Mughal India there were two main land routes
for export trade on the north-west from Lahore to Kabul and from
Multan to Qandahar, while there were a few more in other parts. But
the traffic along these routes was restricted and insecure. The sea and
rivers were more advantageous for commercial purposes. The chief
ports of India were Lahori Bandar in Sind; the group of Gujarat ports
like Surat, Broach, and Cambay, Bassein; Chaul; Dabul in the
Ratnagiri district; Goa and Bhatkal, Malabar ports the most
important of which were Calicut and Cochin; Negapatam,
Masulipatam and a few minor ones on the east coast; and Satgaon,
Sripur, Chittagong and Sonargaon in Bengal. The chief imports were

articles of luxury for the richer classes and horses and mules; and the principal exports consisted of varieties of agricultural goods, and textile manufactures, the minor ones being tutenag, opium, indigo cakes. Some countries round the Persian Gulf were entirely dependent on India for their food supply. The ports of Bengal and Gujarat were then chiefly used for India's export trade. Barthema considered Bengal to be "the richest country in the world for cotton, ginger, sugar, grain and flesh of every kind." The important feature of the trade of India from the reign of Akbar was the commercial activity of English and the Dutch, who gradually established factories in widely distributed centres. As the demand for the costly European goods was confined to the wealthy, the European merchants had to import bullion from home to purchase Indian commodities in spite of strong criticism in England against this practice. This was the case earlier under the Delhi Sultanates when according to the author of *Masalik-ul-absar*: "Merchants of all countries never cease to carry pure gold into India, and to bring back in exchange commodities of herbs and gums".

Industry as the Source of Commerce

The reason why we have dwelt at some length on the commerce of India is to emphasise the existence of traditional industrial organisations which supplied the commodities for export after meeting the local demands. Though agriculture formed the occupation of the bulk of the people, there were some important industries in the urban as well as rural areas of the country. These were the textile industry, including the manufacture of cotton cloth, woollen cloth and silks, the dyeing industry and calico-painting, the sugar industry, metal work, stone and brick work, and the paper industry. The minor industries were cup-making, shoe-making, making of arms, especially bows and arrows, manufacture of scents, spirits and liquors. The excellence of Bengal goods has been highly praised by Amir Khusrav and foreign travellers, like Mauhan, who visited Bengal in 1406 A.D., Barthema, who came to India during the early part of the sixteenth century (1503-1508) and Barbosa, who came here about 1518 A.D.

By far the most important industry in India was the manufacture of cotton cloth. The principal centres of cotton manufacture were distributed throughout the country, as, for example, at Patan in Gujarat, Burhanpur in Khandesh, Jaunpur, Benares, Patna and some other places in the United provinces and Bihar, and many cities and villages in Orissa and Bengal. The whole country from Orissa and East Bengal looked like a big cotton factory, and the Dacca district was specially reputed for its delicate muslin fabrics, "the best and finest cloth made of cotton" that was in all India.

Pelsaert notes that at Chabaspur and Sonargaon in East Bengal "all live by the weaving industry and the produce has the highest reputation and quality". Bernier observes: "There is in *Bengale* such a quantity of cotton and silk, that the kingdom may be called the common store house for those two kinds of merchandise, not of Hindoustan or the empire of the *Great Mogul* only, but of all the neighbouring kingdoms, and even of Europe". The dyeing industry, too, was in a flourishing condition. Terry tells us that coarser cotton cloths were either dyed or printed with a "variety of well-shaped and well-coloured flowers or figures which are so fixed in the cloth that no water can wash them out." Silk-weaving limited in scope as compared with cotton manufacture, was also an important industry of a section of the people. Abul Fazl writes that it received a consid-erable impetus in the reign of Akbar due to the imperial patronage. Bengal was the premier centre of silk production and manufacture and supplied the demands of the Indian and European merchants from other parts of India, though silk-weaving was practised in Lahore, Agra, Fathpur Sikri and Gujarat. Shawl and carpet weaving industries flourished under the patronage of Akbar; the former woven mainly from hair, having originated from Kashmir, was manufactured also at Lahore, and the latter at Lahore and Agra. Woollen goods, chiefly coarse blankets, were also woven. Though India had lost her vigorous maritime activity, the ship-building industry did not die out at this time, and we have references to it from contemporary literature. Saltpetre, used chiefly as an ingredient for gunpowder in India and also exported outside by the Dutch and English traders, was manufactured in widely distributed parts of India during the seventeenth century, particularly in Peninsular India and the Bihar section of the Indo-Gangetic region. Bihar henceforth enjoyed a special reputation for the manufacture of this article and it was in high demand by the European for use in wars in their countries. Besides these major industries, we have testimony regarding the various crafts during the Mughal period. Edward Terry noticed that "many curious boxes, trunks, standishes (pen-cases), carpets, with their excellent manufactures, may be there had". Pelsaert also writes that in Sind "ornamental disks, draught-boards, writing cases, and similar goods are manufactured locally in large qualities; they are pretty, inlaid with ivory and ebony and used to be exported in large quantities from Goa, and the coast towns". Though encouraged by the state, the weavers were exploited by the middlemen who mostly financed them. The weavers also suffered from harsh treatment at the hands of the nobles and officers who forced them to sell their goods at low prices and exacted from them forbidden *abwabs*. This deprived the weavers and craftsmen of the benefit of economic profit from their occupations, though the taste of the nobles for high class manufactures kept up the tradition of their quality.

Skill underlying various Arts and Crafts

The skill that went into the making of these excellent articles for daily needs as well as for exports was not acquired overnight with the coming of Islam to India. It existed among the people from time immemorial and had contributed to the making of a glorious civilisation under the Mauryas as well as under the Guptas. The ancient religious scriptures inform us of 64 Kalas or arts and crafts which were taught either through Guru-Shisya Parampara or though family expertise where the father was often the teacher and the son student. While the people who specialised in such arts and crafts including agriculture, animal husbandry, medicine and military sciences came from a class other than the Brahmins, we have instances of the members of the priestly class often taking to such professions.

It is true that the fortunes of arts and crafts are affected when the political structure that acts as an umbrella to protect and nourish them declines. This is exactly what happened when the Gupta empire began to break up from the fifth century onwards and there ensued a keen and bitter rivalry among the potentates of Northern India for the possession of Kanauj which symbolised power and culture just as did the possession of Babylon to the martial races of Western Asia, of Rome to the Teutonic barbarians and of Byzantium to medieval Eastern and Southern Europe.

In those years the Deccan, which remained comparatively free from such chaos and disorder despite the occasional forays of its one or two dynasties into the affairs of the Northen India and bitter rivalries among its kingdoms, became an epitome of Indian cultures and civilisation in temple architecture, fine arts and crafts as well as in Vedic learning and religion.

The Magic Wand of Muslim Rule

Yet the skill among the people, just as the Vedic learning, which was transmitted through successive generations of families hardly died and remained dormant awaiting some magic wand to bring it back to life. And the Muslim rule in India as it began gradually to settle down in the country acted as this magic wand and the arts and crafts of the country began to flourish. They brought to India their own traditional ideas, religious motifs and personal tastes with which they profoundly influenced the skill of an indigenous artisan or craftsmen. The enormous building activities of the Delhi Sultans beginning with Qutb-ud-din who started Qutb-Minar reached its peak under Firuz who, in his words, possessed "Among the gifts which God bestowed upon, His humble servant, was a desire to erect public buildings". And the skill of the Indian artisan became so well-known outside India that when Timur in 1398 plundered and looted Northern India including Delhi and Firuzabad, he took care to send the captured Indian artisans to Samarquand where they helped Timur to build the famous Friday Mosque according to his own design. More than hundred years after this episode when Babar as the Mughal emperor wrote his *Memoirs* in Turki, he confirmed this deed of his famous ancestor: "A number of stone-cutters were brought from Hindusthan to work on it [Timur's Mosque]".

As a matter of fact, the art of stone-cutting in India is as old as the Buddha himself. Ancient India in the days of Ashoka is distinguished by its rock-cut caves and stone pillars and as the civilisation progressed from fifth century onwards rock-cut caves came to be adorned with beautiful sculptures and paintings as in Ajanta, Ellora and Elephanta and magnificent rock-cut temples began to emerge under the illustrious dynasties of Southern India such as the Pandyas, the Cholas and the Pallavas. Time kills everything – dynasties come and go, kingdoms appear and disappear – but it cannot probably kill the skill which flows through the generation of families for centuries. So when Babar came to India and laid the foundation of his imperial family in the country, he was surprised at the abundance of this particular skill of stone-cutting among the people and wrote about the stone-cutters in his *Memoirs*: "In Agra alone, and of stone-cutters belonging to that place only, I everyday employed on my palaces six hundred and eighty persons; and in Agra, Sikri, Biana, Dholpur, Gwalior and Koel [Aligarh] there were every day employed on my works one thousand four hundred and ninety-nine stone-cutters". It is this skill of Indian artisans which helped them to build their palaces and madrasahs, mosques and mausoleums which reached its climax under Shah Jahan in the construction of such magnificent architectural monuments of his times as the exquisite Taj and the Pearl Mosque at Agra and the superb Diwan-i-Am, Diwan-i-Khas and the Jama Masjid in Delhi, which now stand as the mute witness to the past splendour of Shah Jahan's reign.

The skill and craftmanship with which the stone-cutters built these architectural wonders also extended to fine arts and crafts such as painting, music, jewellery and daily needs of life. As Babar, an acute observer of his times, records in his *Memoirs*: "Another convenience of Hindusthan is that the workmen of every profession and trade are innumerable and without end. For any work, or any employment, there is always a set ready, to whom the same employment and trade have descended from father to son for ages". Nourished by the Hindu traditionality and Muslim ingenuity and boosted by the lavish patronage of the Mughal rulers and nobles who would not often hesitate to spend an amount which in modern times is equivalent to a fortune in acquiring an item of exquisite excellence and craftsmanship, these arts and crafts saw their hey-days under Akbar, Jahangir and Shah Jahan. Thomas Roe who visited Jahangir's Court was surprised to find that an Indian craftsman could produce an exact copy of a wooden couch made in England or a portrait drawn in Europe which he had gifted to Jahangir, within a short time. Barnier who came at the beginning of Aurangzeb's reign agrees with Thomas Roe when he observes: "Sometimes they imitate so perfectly articles of European manufacture that the difference between the original and copy can hardly be discerned. Among other things, the Indians make excellent muskets, and fowling-pieces, and such beautiful gold ornaments that it may be doubted if the exquisite workmanship of those articles can be exceeded by any European goldsmith". Travelling widely in different parts of Aurangzeb's empire he described the manufacture of shawls in Patna, Agra and Lahore, of Chintzes in Masulipatam, of silk and cotton cloth in Bengal and profusely admired the skill of the artisans and craftsmen of Kashmir: "The workmanship and beauty of their palkeys, bedsteads, trunks, inkstands, boxes, spoons, and various other things are quite remarkable, and articles of their manufacture are in use in every part of the Indus". They perfectly understand the art of varnishing, and are eminently skilful in closely imitating the beautiful veins of a certain wood, by inlaying with gold threads so "delicately wrought that I never saw anything more elegant or perfect. But what may be considered peculiar to Kachemere [sic], and the staple commodity, that which particularly promotes the trade of the country and fills it with wealth, is the prodigious quality of shawls which they manufacture".

Transmission of the Skill

The elegant buildings, the dazzling paintings, the sonorous music, the soothing medicine, the beautiful shawls, the costly carpets and the matchless muslin of Dacca indicate not only the flourishing of these arts and crafts but also the existence of a vocational knowledge which could not be taught in Medieval India, as in Ancient India, through formal educational institutions. Knowledge of these vocations was mostly hereditary and descended from fathers to sons through successive generations in such a way that in those days there was no generation gap among such families. In such cases where the sons were interested in trades other than their fathers', the former were apprenticed to experts who provided them free board and lodging during the duration of their training. Free from the artificiality of a classroom, the boys learnt the secrets of the trades by observing their masters and when their training was completed, they could either start their own workshops or assisted their masters in furthering their trade interests. The transmission of the knowledge of a craft from fathers to sons no doubt maintained the excellent quality of their crafts but at the same time aggravated the caste system by identifying the families with their products. In Medieval India such families of artisans and craftsmen comprised a large number of population, and were next only to those of peasants or farmers. They could be seen everywhere in the country as noticed by Bernier. The families work in their homes or in places of varying sizes known as Karkhanas or workshops. As Bernier observes: "Large halls are seen in many places, called Karkanays [sic] or workshops for the artisans. In one hall embroiderers are busily employed, superintended by a master. In another you see the goldsmiths; in a third painters; in a fourth, varnishers in lacquerwork; in a fifth, joiners, turners, tailors and shoemakers; in a sixth, manufacturers of silk, brocade, and those fine muslins of which are made turbans, girdles with golden flowers, and drawers, worn by females, so delicately fine as frequently to wear out in one night. This article of dress, which lasts only a few hours may cost ten or twelve crowns, and even more, when beautifully embrolidered with needlework".

Decline of Vocations

But for the lavish patronisation by the Muslim rulers, nobles and wealthy persons, who would often keep in their pay a number of artisans and craftsmen solely to work for them, these arts and crafts could not have reached the excellence as they had done before Aurangzeb. So when Aurangzeb who did not enjoy the good things of life and led a simple puritan existence, withdrew his patronage by royal proclamations, some like painting and music either disappeared from the capital or went underground. His incessant wars, particularly in the Deccan in the later part of his reign, led to a bankruptcy of the administration and the exhaustion of the exchequer, thereby affecting agriculture and industries which were managed by the Karkhanas adversely. During the years 1690-98 the English could not procure sufficient cloths for their shipping. "Thus ensued" observes Jadunath Sarkar, the historian of Mughal India, "a great economic impoverishment of India – not only a decrease of the 'national stock' but also a rapid lowering of mechanical skill and standard of civilisation, a disappearance of art and culture over wide tracts of the country". A succession of weak rulers, after Aurangzeb's death in 1707, who were mere puppets in the hands of some powerful nobles and who could not stop the disintegration of the Mughal empire, the Persian invasion of 1738-39, the rivalry among the European companies for the monopoly of the India trade involving oppression of the merchants and the weavers and of the artisans and the craftsmen, for the sake of a rich return on the huge investments of their companies, saw the beginning of the end of the glorious days of once magnificent arts and crafts which provided useful vocations and livelihood to millions of people among the Indians in Medieval India.

19
Hindu Learning

In the previous chapters we have seen how the patronage of the Delhi Sultans and the Mughal emperors have contributed to the expansion of Islamic education as well as arts and crafts in Medieval India. While Islamic education was an innovation in India by its Muslim rulers, not so was the arts and crafts which had a glorious past though unmistakably some of them like architecture, painting and music were profoundly influenced by Islamic culture and religion. We have also seen how Muslim rulers beginning with Firuz Shah Tughluq had begun to take an interest in Hindu learning which reached its climax under the great Mughal emperor, Akbar. In the context of all this, it will be relevant to examine the state of Brahminical and Buddhist learning in India under the Muslim rulers.

The Buddhist Learning

The Buddhist learning centred on the Buddhist Viharas where the Buddhist Shramanas and Bhikkhus lived and imparted instruction to the novices who had resigned the world and entered the Buddhist Order. In the early years of the history of Buddhism, these Viharas mainly concentrated on the teachings of the Buddha but as they became gradually exposed to a variety of influences, they splitted into two groups, the Greater Vehicle and the Lesser Vehicle leading to salvation. The first group absorbed in its courses many of the Brahminical courses and subjects including Sanskrit while the latter group retained its old philosophical identity. At the time of the Islamic invasion of India, there was a third group called the Vehicle of the Thunderbolt which moved Buddhism closer to Hinduism and almost wiped out its distinct identity as a separate religion. Most of the Buddhist Viharas of Eastern India belonged either to the group of the Greater Vehicle or to that of the Thunderbolt.

Between 1001 and 1027 Mahmud, son of the late Turki Chieftain of Ghazni in Afghanistan, made seventeen great raids on India which reached as far as the great shrine of Somnath in Kathiawar and the kingdom of the Candellas in Bundelkhand. Mahmud returned to Ghazni with enormous caravans of booties and slaves after annexing to Ghazni the North-West and the Punjab as well as the Arab kingdom of Sind which had long ceased to be a menace to the rest of India. For about a century and a half Northern India retained its independence till the coming of Muhammad of Ghur whose generals captured Delhi, over-ran Bihar and Bengal and occupied Bundelkhand by 1203.

While the first rush of Islamic invasions under Mahmud left the temples and Buddhist Viharas in the important cities of Northern India demolished, the subsequent raids by the generals of Muhammad Ghur like Muhammad-bin-Bakhtiyar razed them to the ground in Bengal and Bihar. The libraries at Nalanda and Vikramshila were burnt and the Buddhist monks were put to sword. The lucky ones who could escape the sabre of Islam fled to Nepal and Tibet. With the demolition of the Buddhist Viharas, Buddhist learning almost disappeared, though the Hindu learning continued as it never centred on the temples but on the Brahmanas, the priestly class of the Aryans, many of whom now migrated to Nepal or crossed the Vindhyas.

The Vedic Learning

When the Buddhist learning fell, the Cholas were the dominant power in the South, maintaining their hold on the region around Kanchi and Tanjore, the central part of their empire. By the thirteenth century the Cholas fell when their territory was shared by the Hoysalas of Mysore and the revived Pandya dynasty of Madura. It is in these Southern kingdoms that we have to look for the existence and continuance of the Hindu learning which lay mostly dormant in the North except in the ashrams of sages in remote areas or forests.

Such Hindu learning consisted, as in the past, of a study of the four Vedas, six Vedangas or auxiliary sciences such as Siksha, Kalpa, Vyakarana, Nirukta, Chhanda and Jyotisha and Upanishads. Long before the birth of Christ, each of the six auxiliary sciences had developed into an independent discipline, and of the numerous philosophies of the Upanishads six were dominant by the time of the coming of Islam. As in the past, students learnt at the residence of teachers who looked after their boarding and lodging in lieu of a nominal fee in the form of present or services to them by the students. The period of studentship lasted more than a decade, after which the students returned home to begin the next stage of their lives, that is, the life of a Grihastya or householder. However, there were many among them whose quest for supreme knowledge lasted till the last days of their final emancipation.

Emergence of the Mathas and the Temple Colleges

As in religion, so in education despite the occasional assembly of learned men to discuss the Vedas and the Upanishads, Ancient India did not believe in the external and mechanical methods of organisation and did not develop any religious or ecclesiastical institutions like the Buddhist viharas or Christian churches. The interests of religious life and spiritual growth were not handed over to any institutions and their regimented life of routine, but were left to be dealt with between the guru and his disciple in their personal relationship from which the whole world was excluded. Nevertheless, in the wake of the emphasis laid by Jainism and Buddhism upon organised brotherhoods in rock-cut caves and halls, viharas and monasteries, the Brahminical religion followed suit with similar institutions like mathas with regular colleges as centres of learning, from tenth century onwards following the revival of Hinduism by Sankaracharya.

Extent of Hindu Learning in South India

The extent of such Hindu learning concentrating on temples or mathas was widespread as could be gathered from the various inscriptions describing deeds of endowments in the Southern kingdoms of Hindu dynasties like the Rashtrakutas, Pallavas, Cholas, Hoysalas and Pandyas. The Sanskrit college at the temple of the Trayi Purusha founded by a minister of the Rashtrakuta emperor Krishna III at Salotgi in Bijapur District was heavily endowed to support twenty-seven hostels for residence of its students who hailed from different provinces. The Vedic college at Ennayiram in South Arcot District founded by Rajendra Chola I (C. 1023 A.D.) provided for the free board and tuition of 340 students and engaged ten teachers, three

for each of the two Vedas, Rig Veda and Yajur Veda, two for
Mimamsa and one each for other subjects. Besides this college, there
was another one attached to a temple where daily 506 learned
Brahmans were fed regularly and all surpluses of ghee, milk and curds
left after the worship were made over to the hostel housing some 340
students by the temple authorities. Five inscriptions on copper plates
of the Pallava king, Vijayanripatunga-Varman record the gift of three
villages to support a college, "like the Ganga supported by Siva on his
matted locks", which taught fourteen Ganas, comprising 4 Vedas, 6
Vedangas, 1 Mimamsa, 1 Nyaya, 1 Purana, and 1 Dharmasastra.
While an inscription records the endowment of another Sanskrit
college in 1048 A.D. which had 190 students and 12 teachers for its
Veda and 7 for Sastra Departments, another records the endowment
of some 410 acres of land for the construction of a separate hall for the
teaching of Panini's grammar and worship of God Vyakaranadana –
Perumal (Siva) in the temple at Tiruvorraiyur.

It is interesting to note here that the establishment of colleges
was not the close preserve of the monarchs in those days but castes
other than the Brahmans could participate in such endeavours. In
1062 A.D., as has been recorded by inscription 182 of 1915 in
Epigraphica Indica, an affluent Vaishya established a college for
teaching the Vedas, Sastras, Rupavatara (a grammatical work), a
hostel for its students and a hospital with one physician, one surgeon,
two servants for taking drugs, two servants to serve as nurses and a
general servant for the whole establishment to look after the health of
the students and teachers. The addition of a hospital to a temple
college which emphasised health with studies was an innovation and
the example was quickly followed by other colleges that came into
existence later. An inscription of 1068 A.D. records a similar triple
institution comprising a college, a hostel and a hospital. The
inscription on a pillar at Malkapuram in the Guntur District records
an endowment establishing a number of institutions, a temple, a
monastery, a feeding-house, colonies of Brahmins, schools of students
of Saiva Puranas and a maternity home and a hospital. The college not
merely looked after the spiritual needs but also physical requirements
of the community as could be seen from the categories of the staff
maintained by it. The staff of all these institutions included (a) three
teachers for teaching the three Vedas, (b) five for teaching logic, literature and the agamas, (c) one Physician (d) one accountant who could
be a Kayastha, (e) six Brahmana servants for the Matha and feeding

house (f) village guards called Vira-Bhadras, (g) village craftsmen called Vira-Mushtis to work as goldsmith, coppersmith, mason, bamboo-workers, blacksmith, potter, architect, carpenter, barber, and artisan. In the feeding house were fed at all hours men of all castes from Brahmana to Chandala – a remarkable instance of Saiva catholicity.

Besides the establishment of temple colleges, and colleges with hospitals and practical arts, arrangement was often made by specific endowment as can be seen in an inscription in 1122 A.D. which records the magnificent gift of 44 villages to a temple for the purpose of giving food and clothing to Vedic students, religious teachers, and ascetics. Moving upward, from the South to the North, we find, king Bhoja of Malwa (1018-60 A.D.) set up at his capital Dhara in 1034 A.D., a college appropriately located in a temple of *Vagdevi*, Goddess of learning whose image in stone is a masterpiece of Brahminical Sculpture.

Settlements of Learned Men

The cause of learning and culture was not, however, confined to these schools or colleges. It was recognised that learning should be a life-long pursuit and could not be confined either to the limits of study which a college could undertake within the time fixed for it. Accordingly, we find public benefactions establishing not merely the purely educational institutions where the foundations of learning were laid but institutions of wider scope, serving as centres of post-graduate, advanced study under savants devoting themselves completely to the pursuit of knowledge for its own sake. These endowments of higher learning and research sought to establish entire learned settlements or cultural colonies, made up of households of pious and scholarly Brahmanas in select areas. These learned settlements were centres of light and life, showing how theory and practice should go together, how precept should be supported by example, ethics by conduct, learning was to be lived, and truth or religion was to be realised in the activities of daily life. Sometimes, advantage was taken of these learned settlements or sabhas to judge of literary works of authors as stated in Inscription 198 of 1919. As late as 1158 A.D., an important centre of such learned settlements of Brahmana families, many of whom were earlier imported from the north, was at Talgunda near Belgame in Mysore and at the time of the Islamic invasion of the North, Mysore was abounding in such wider cultural institutions which were known in three distinct varieties, called Ghatika, Agrahara and Brahmapuri.

The colleges proper which sprang up as annexes of the temples received a wider scope not merely in the settlements of learned men but also in the mathas which served as an academy of arts and sciences. The mathas specially are indigenous Indian examples of educational organisation by which different and distant centres of culture and religious life, religious brotherhoods of different localities are affiliated to a central and common seat of authority at head quarters and regulated and controlled by it. The best example of this federal type of educational religious organisation is furnished by the Golaki Matha in the Kurnool district in the thirteenth century A.D. which exercised its spiritual influence and direction since its inception over as many as 3 lakhs of villages under a succession of its famous chiefs and teachers.

Thus, those kingdoms in the South kept the lamp of Brahminical learning burning when the North was reeling under the impact of the Islam. Once the Islamic rule settled down in the North, the Muslim arms crossed the Vindhyas in the reign of Ala-ud-din Khalji (1296-1315) under his eunuch general Malik Kafur, a convert from Hinduism, and for a time a Muslim Sultanate was even set up in the extreme South at Madurai. However, the Dravidians were not finally subjugated. Within a few years of Malik Kafur's raids, in 1336, an independent Hindu kingdom was founded at Vijayanagar, on the Tungabhadra River, which after desperately resisting the Bahamani Sultans of the Northern Deccan, established its hegemony over the whole Peninsula from the Krishna River southwards. Learning something of military strategy from their Muslim enemies, the kings of Vijayanagar maintained their independence until the middle of the sixteenth century, and, in a reduced form even later.

The Kingdom of Vijyanagar

It is the kingdom of Vijayanagar which for well nigh three centuries stood for the Hindu religion and culture of the country and saved these from being engulfed by the rush of new ideas and forces. By 1486, the Vijayanagar empire under the rule of its first dynasty, Sangama, extended over the whole of South India, reaching the shores of Ceylon, and attained the zenith of its prosperity as vouchsafed by the accounts of Nicolo Conti, an Italian traveller, and Abdur Razzaq, an envoy from Persia, who visited Vijayanagar in 1420 and 1443

respectively. Its prosperity rose further under Krishnadeva Raya of
the Tuluva dynasty. The reign of Krishnadeva Raya not only marked
the climax in the territorial expansion of the Vijayanagar empire, but
was also remarkable for the encouragement and development of arts
and letters. However, what characterises the Vijayanagar empire and
contributes to its stability for a considerable period of time was their
liberal attitudes towards all the prevailing four sects, Saiva, Buddha,
Vaishnava and Jaina as well as towards the alien creeds, Christian,
Jewish and Moorish. As Edoardo Barbosa who was present in
Vijayanagar in 1516 A.D. writes: "The King allows such freedom that
every man may come and go and live according to his own creed
without suffering any annoyance, and without enquiry, whether he is
a Christian, Jew, Moor or Hindu".

However, since the emperors were all zealous Hindus with
special devotion either to Saiva or Vaishnava, Hindu learning flourished tremendously in the Vijayanagar empire. Sayana, the famous
commentator of the Vedas, and his brother, Madhava Vidyaranya,
the celebrated Brahmana sage and scholar of the day, who flourished
during the early days of Vijayanagar rule were deeply attached to the
State. Madhava Vidyaranya has been described in an inscription of
Harihara II as "the supreme light incarnate", on whose advice,
Harihara and Bukka, two of the five sons of Sangama, laid the
foundation of the city and kingdom of Vijayanagar, on the southern
bank of the Tunghabhadra facing the fortress of Anegundi on the
northern bank.

Krishnadeva Raya

The reign of Krishnadeva Raya marked "the dawn of a new era in the
literary history of South India. Himself a scholar, a musician and
poet, he loved to gather around him poets, philosophers, and religious
teachers whom he honoured with munificent gifts of land and
money". He wrote his magnum opus, *Amukta-malyada* in Telugu. He
also authored five Sanskrit works which had been mentioned by him
in his introduction to the work in Telugu, which is not merely of
religious interest but also of great historical importance for his reign.
In his Court flourished the "Astadiggajas", or the eight elephants who
were celebrated Telugu poets and greatly supported Telugu literature.
His poet laureate, Peddana, enjoyed a wide reputation among Telugu
writers. The rulers of Aravidu dynasty which succeeded the Tuluva
dynasty to which Krishna Deva Raya belonged also patronised poets

and religions teachers, and Telugu literature flourished under them with "reinforced vigour". There were also authors among the petty chiefs and relatives of the emperors. Works on music, dancing, drama, grammar, logic and philosophy received encouragement from the emperors, their ministers and their feudatory chiefs and the Vijayanagar empire became a "synthesis of South Indian Culture".

It is not merely in theoretical learning but in practical education Vijayanagar empire shone brightly. The ruins of the old capital tell us that in the days of its glory, a distinct style of architecture, sculpture and painting by Indian artists evolved. According to Longhurst, the famous Hazara temple, built during the reign of Krishnadeva Raya is "one of the most perfect specimens of Hindu temple architecture in existence". The Vitthalasvami temple, also a fine example of Vijayanagar style, "shows the extreme limit in florid magnificence to which the style advanced", in the opinion of Fergusson. The art of painting attained a high degree of excellence, and the art of music rapidly developed. Some new works on the subject of music were produced. Krishnadeva Raya and the Regent, Rama Raya were proficient in music. People acquired proficiency in the manufacture of textiles, mining and metallurgy through apprenticeship and protected their interests through craftsmen's guilds – "the tradesmen of each separate guild or craft have their shops close to one another", writes Abdur Razzaq.

Decline and Fall of Vijayanagar

The Vijayanagar empire was severely jolted by its defeat at the battle of Talikota in January 1565 at the combined hands of the Deccan Sultanates of Bijapur, Golkunda and Ahmadnagar but the empire continued to exist till the early part of the seventeenth century under the rulers of the Aravidu dynasty, "before it got weakened and dismembered – weakened by the constant invasions from the north and dismembered by the dissatisfaction and rebellion of the viceroys within". The "insane pride, blind selfishness, disloyalty and mutual dissensions" of the feudatories of the Vijayanagar empire largely facilitated the conquest of the Hindu Deccan by the Muslim States of Bijapur and Golkunda while subordinate viceroys like the chiefs of Seringapatam and Bednur and the Naiks of Madura and Tanjore carved out independent kingdoms for themselves.

Besides the kingdom of Vijayangar in the South, Vedic learning received its royal patronage from the Hindu kingdoms which emerged at the time of the disintegration of the Delhi Sultanate and among such kingdoms were Orissa, Kamarupa and Assam in East and Mewar in the North.

Orissa

Orissa which was constantly threatened with extinction from its neighbours both Hindu and Muslim, maintained its existence till it was finally annexed by the Kararani Sultans of Bengal in 1568 A.D. Its glorious days of Hindu learning were under the reign of Purushottama (1470-1497 A.D.) and that of his son and successor, Pratapurudra (1497-1450 A.D.) who was a contemporary and disciple of Chaitanya.

Assam

At the time of the advent of the Muslims in Bengal in the early thirteenth century, the Brahmaputra Valley was parcelled out into a number of independent principalities under such tribes as the Chutiyas, Bodos, Kacharis, Bhuiyas, Khens, Koch and Ahoms who were at war with each other. Early in the fifteenth century a strong monarchy was established in Kamata by the Khens with their capital at Kamatapur, a few miles to the South of Cooch Behar. However, it was under the rule of the Koch tribe which was Mongoloid in origin since 1515 A.D., that the kingdom of Kamata or Kamarupa went through its prosperous days particularly under Nara Narayan. The latter, however was compelled to cede the portions of his kingdom to the east of the river Sankosh to his nephew Raghu Dev and the bickering between the two led in 1639 to the occupation of the Western and the Eastern States by the Muslims and the Ahoms respectively. The Ahoms gradually consolidated their position and established a strong monarchy which lasted for six centuries despite their frequent brush with their Muslim neighbours of Bengal.

Mewar

Some of the Rajput States were stirred with the spirit of revival on the dismemberment of the Turko-Afghan empire. The most prominent of these was the Guhila principality of Mewar, where the Rajput genius unfolded itself so brilliantly and which for generations produced a succession of brave generals, heroic leaders, prudent rulers and some brilliant poets. Mewar had its glorious days under Rana Kumbha who had, according to Tod, "Hamir's energy, Lakha's taste for arts, and a genius comprehensive as either or more fortunate, succeeded in all his undertakings". He was a great builder and built for the defence of Mewar, 32 including Kumbhalgarh out of 84 fortresses and created Jayastambha or Kirtistambha (Tower of Fame). Further the Rana was a poet, a man of letters and accomplished musician. One of his successors, Rana Sanga who ascended the throne of Mewar in 1509 A.D. fought successfully against Malwa, Delhi and Gujarat and organised the financial resources and military forces of Mewar with a view to building her supremacy on the break-up of the Delhi Sultanate which ended with the battle of Khanua in 1527.

Nepal

For more than two hundred years (1097-1326), the Karnataka king Nanyadeva of Mithila and his successors claimed, from their capital at Simraon a sort of loose sovereignty over the local princes of Nepal. In 1324 A.D. Harisinha of Tirhut, a descendant of Nanyadeva, invaded Nepal and subdued the reigning king of Nepal, Jayarudramalla. Harisinha who gradually extended his power over the whole valley from his headquarters at Bhatgaon, entered into diplomatic relations with China in the fourteenth century, left undisturbed the local rulers, who acknowledged their hegemony in the possession of the two other capitals, viz., Patan and Kathmandu. From 1376 A.D. onwards Nepal was ruled by the Malla kings, beginning with Jaya-Sthitimalla, grandson-in-law of the Malla king, Jayarudra (1320-1326). Nepal had its glorious days under the rule of Yakshamalla who ascended the throne in 1426 A.D., ruled for about half a century. However, he committed the mistake before his death around 1476 A.D. of partitioning his kingdom among his sons and daughters leading to the rise of the two rival principalities of Katmandu and Bhatgaon, whose quarrels ultimately led to the conquest of Nepal by the Gurkhas in 1768 A.D.

The break-up of the Mughal empire saw the revival of Hindu kingdoms in the North. Besides Mewar, two more Rajput states Marwar (Jodhpur) and Amber (Jaipur) tried to throw off their allegiance to the Mughal empire after the death of Aurangzeb in 1707. Ajit Singh of Jodhpur and Jay Singh-II of Amber played an important part in Delhi politics and either "by opportune aloofness or by adherence they had added to their possessions a large portion of the Mughal empire". The Sayyids tried to attach them to their party and they were rewarded with some appointments besides holding their dominions in full sovereignty. Ajit Singh remained governor of Ajmer and Gujarat till 1724. During the reign of Muhammad Shah, Jay Singh-II of Jaipur was appointed governor of Surat, and after the fall of the Sayyids, he received also the government of Agra. "In the way the country from a point sixty miles south of Delhi to the shores of the ocean at Surat was in the hands of the two Rajas, very untrustworthy sentinels for the Mughals on this exposed frontier."

The Marathas

The rise of the Maratha power introduced an important factor in Indian politics during the second half of the seventeenth century, as that of Vijyanagar had done in a previous age. The Marathas had brilliant traditions of political and cultural activities in the early Middle Ages of Indian history, when they upheld the national cause under the Yadavas of Devagiri. They lost their independence with the fall of the Yadava Ramachandradeva in the time of Ala-ud-din, but in forty years they began again to play an important part in the Bahmani kingdom and subsequently in the succeeding Sultanates. The seventeenth century saw them organised into a national state under Shivaji. Enclosed on two sides by mountains ranges like the Sahyadri running from north to south, and the Satpura and the Vindhya running from east to west, protected by the Narmada and the Tapti rivers and provided with numerous easily defensible hill forts, the Maratha country remained the bastion of Hindu culture and learning long before the time of Shivaji. The Marathi religious reformers, Ekanath, Tukaram, Ramdas and Vaman Pandit, preaching through successive centuries, the doctrines of devotion of God and of equality of all men before him, without any distinction of caste or position, and the dignity of action, had sown in their land the seeds of a renaissance or self-awakening which is generally the presage of a political revolution in a country. Ramadas Samarth, Guru of Shivaji, exerted a profound influence on the minds of his countrymen and inspired them with ideals of social reform and national regeneration through his disciples in maths (monasteries) and his famous work known as *Dasabodha*. The devotional songs of religious reformers were composed in the Marathi language, and consequently a forceful Maratha literature grew up during the fifteenth and sixteenth centuries to inspire the people of the land with noble aspirations. "Thus", observes Sir J.N. Sarkar, "a remarkable community of language, creed and life was attained even before political unity was conferred by Shivaji". What little was wanting to the solidarity of the people was supplied by his creation of a national state, the long struggle with the invader from Delhi under his sons, and the imperial expansion of the race under the Peshwas. Sincerely religious from his early life, Shivaji did not forget the lofty ideals with which he had been inspired by his mother and his guru, Ramdas, in the midst of political or military duties. He sought to make religion a vital force in the uplifting of the Maratha nation and always extended his patronage to Hindu religion and learning. "Religion remained with him", remarks a modern Marathi writer, "an ever fresh fountain of right conduct and generosity; it did not obsess his mind or harden him into a bigot". Tolerant of other faiths, he deeply venerated Muslim saints and granted rent free lands to meet the expenses of illumination of Muslim shrines and mosques, and his conduct towards the Capuchin fathers (Christian monks) at Surat, during its first sack by him, was respectful. Even his bitterest critic, Khafi Khan writes: "But he [Shivaji] made it a rule that whenever his followers were plundering, they should do no harm to the mosques, the Book of God, or the women of any one".

After Shivaji's premature death in April 1680 at the age of 53, the Marathas received a setback under his eldest son Shambhuji in March 1689 but they recovered quickly, and again began a war of national resistance to the Mughals, which ultimately exhausted the resources of the latter. For some time Rajaram, younger brother of Shambhuji and after Rajaram's death, his widow Tara Bai, a lady of masterly spirit guided the destiny of the Maratha nation at this juncture as regent to her minor son, Shivaji III. A protracted civil war followed following the release of Shivaji-II, better known as Shahu in 1707, the son of Shambhuji, which came to an end with the victory of Shahu with the help and advice of a Chitpavan Brahmana from the Konkan, named Balaji Viswanath who was appointed Peshwa or Prime Minister in 1713. By virtue of superior talents and abilities, Balaji Vishwanath and his illustrious son, and successor Baji Rao-I since 1720 made the Peshwa the real head of the Maratha empire, the Chhatrapati or the king in the course of a few years, being relegated to the background. Baji Rao-I who succeeded to his Peshwaship in 1720 followed a policy of expansion beyond the Narmada with a view to striking at the root of the imperial power. The Peshwaship came to be hereditary in the family of Balaji Vishwanath and aimed at supremacy on the dismemberment of the Mughal empire, preaching the ideal of

Hindu Pad-Padshahi or a Hindu empire which ended disastrously at the third battle of Panipat in 1761.

Hindu Learning in Muslim India

It will be a mistake to think that Hindu learning was confined only to Hindu kingdoms in the Medieval India. Islamic education and Islamic learning dominated Medieval India partly because of the patronage it received from its rulers and partly because of its democratic nature which made it accessible to all followers of Islam irrespective of their status in the society. When Islam came to India and settled down to rule the people, many among the Hindus suffering from caste and other disabilities accepted the religion of the Prophet Muhammad, while many upper class Hindus not only learnt Persian and Arabic to hold important positions in the administration but some of them converted themselves to Islam to do so. The history of Medieval India abounds in such examples of converted Hindus either holding high positions in Muslim administration or carving out important principalities for them in the provinces. Finally, while the Muslim rulers and the nobles when they first came to India were possibly accompanied by their women folk, the soldiers and officials of the Muslim armies came alone. Few of the latter brought their women from their native countries because of the expenses and travel hazards involved and found their wives from Indian women, mostly belonging to the castes and classes suffering from various religious and societal disabilities through easy marriage after their conversion into Islam.

Inner Strength of Hindu Learning

Yet Hindu learning survived because of its inner strength. It mainly concentrated on the priestly class who not only served as Purohitas to the kings but to their subjects on all social and religious functions including birth, death and marriage. In other words from time immemorial no socio-religious functions of a Hindu could be done without a priest uttering Vedic hymns and Mantras. The financial incentives involved in such assignments were sufficient to maintain them as they gradually came to be deprived of royal patronage under Islamic rule. So, it was in their own interest primarily as a means of survival that they had to keep their learning and trade alive and train their own descendants in it. This explains the presence of Vedic schools in the form of tolls and chathuspathis in various parts of the Medieval India under Islamic rulers who were tolerant and accounts for a considerable number of compositions in Sanskrit before the advent of the Mughals and these were mostly in defence of Hinduism against the onslaught of Islam, reminding us of the days of the Sutrakaras in Ancient India, who prepared elaborate treatises in defence of Brahmanism against the spread of Buddhism.

Compositions in Vedic and Hindu Learning

As the proselytising zeal of Islam gradually increased, conservatism in the orthodox circles of the Hindus also strengthened itself to fortify its position against the spread of the Islamic faith by increasing the stringency of the caste rules and by formulating a number of rules in the Smriti works. Thus Madhava of Vijayanagar wrote his commentary on one of the Smriti works of Parasara, entitled *Kalanirnaya* in between 1335-1360 A.D. and Visvesvara wrote another Smriti work entitled *Madanaparijata* for king Madanapala in between 1360-1370. The other famous Smriti works were by Kulika, a Bengali author belonging to the Benares School by domicile, who wrote his famous commentary on Manu and by Raghunandan of Bengal, who was a contemporary of Shri Chaitanya, the famous saint of Vaishnavism. As a matter of fact, not only Smiriti but also grammatical literature flourished during this period in Mithila besides Bengal and the most famous writers on these subjects were Padmanabha Datta, Vidyapati Upadhyaya and Vachaspati. Patharasathi Mishra wrote in 1300 A.D. several works on *Karma Mimansa*, of which *Sastra Dipika* was studied most widely. The period which saw the birth of some works expounding the doctrines of the Yoga, Vaiseshika and Nyaya systems of philosophy also saw a tremendous spur in the production of a mass of Jaina religious literature.

It will be a mistake to think that the period was characterised by a production of religious works in Sanskrit. Far from it. It also saw a continuation, however small, of literary works in Sanskrit from Ancient India. As before Sanskrit dramas stole the limelight and the most important among them were *Hammirmada-mardana* by Jay Singh Suri in between 1219-1229 A.D., *Pradyumnabhyudaya* by the Kerala prince Ravivarman; *Parata Rudra Kalyan* by Vidyanath in 1300 A.D., *Parvati Parinaya* by Vamana Bhatta Bana in 1400 A.D., *Gangadasa Pratapa Vilasa*, celebrating the fight of a prince of Champaner against Muhammad II of Gujarat, by Gangadhar, and *Vidagdha Madhava* and the *Lalita Madhava*, written about 1532 A.D., by Rupa Goswami, Minister of Husain Shah of Bengal, and author of no less than twenty-five works in Sanskrit.

It is interesting to note that some Muslim scholars came to possess a knowledge of Sanskrit who had helped Firuz-Shah Tughluq in arranging for the translation of the Sanskrit works captured at the temple of Jawalamukhi – Elliot mentions the translation of a Sanskrit work on astrology as well as another on veterinary sciences entitled *Salotar* in Persian, which he saw in the library of Nawab Jalaluddaulah at Lucknow. Such interest in Sanskrit language and literature which received a boost under Zain-ul-Abidin of Kashmir in the early fifteenth century and later under Akbar who not only arranged for the translation of many Sanskrit works into Persian and included Sanskrit in the curricula at the madrasahs, had been as a matter of fact, growing ever since the days of the Arab occupation of Sind when the Arab astronomer Abu Mashar went to Benares and studied astronomy there for ten years.

However, it must be admitted that in Muslim India, such interests in Sanskrit and its allied literature were purely academic – and be ordinary people other than the priestly classes had now ceased to the drawn to it, for, not only it did not enjoy the status of a Court language, having been replaced by the Persian but also faced a formidable rival in the refinement of the vernaculars, Hindi and Urdu in Medieval India.

20

Vernaculars and Village Schools

The development of vernaculars including Hindi and the emergence of Urdu, we have spoken of in the previous chapter, has lent its lustre to the history of education in Medieval India.

Prakrit or Pali

The vernaculars as the languages of the masses, with regional variations, have existed from time immemorial either in the form of Prakrit or Pali and we all know that the Buddha who used to preach in Magadhi asked his disciples to use their own regional dialects for the purpose. This is one reason why Buddhism quickly won the hearts of many and posed a serious challenge to Brahmanism whose scriptures were enshrined in Sanskrit, spoken mainly by the priestly classes among the Aryans. There is no doubt that the use of Arabic and Persian as the Court and official languages by the Islamic rulers for more than six hundred years till they were replaced by the English language gradually relegated Sanskrit to the background and made room for the rapid development of the vernaculars.

Contributions of the Religious Reformers

Yet the contributions of the religious reformers who were, with some differences in details, exponents of the liberal Bhakti Cult known to India since the days of the Upanishads, to this unique phenomenon cannot be underestimated. They preached before the unlettered masses themes like fundamental equality of all religions, the unity of God head, the dignity of man depending on his actions and not on his birth, protested against excessive ritualism and formalities of religion and domination of the priests, and emphasised simple devotion and faith as the means of salvation for one and all. The underneath current of Saivaism and Vaishnavism, that is devotion and love, which characterises the history of religion in Ancient India, continued its subtle flow in Medieval India. And a host of religious reformers preaching Bhakti, that is, faith and devotion, love and affection, as the means to salvation among the people appeared on the scene.

Among these religious reformers, the first in point of time was Ramananda though there are differences of opinion regarding the dates of his birth and death. Born at Allahabad in a Brahmana family of Kanyakubja or Kanauj, Ramananda travelled through the holy places of Northern India. A worshipper of Rama, he preached the doctrine of Bhakti in Hindi, to members of all classes and both sexes. Among his 12 principal disciples, one was a barber, another a cobbler and the third a Muhammadan weaver.

The next in point of time was the famous Vaishnava Saint Vallabhacharya who was an exponent of the Krishna cult. Born in 1479 A.D. of a Telugu Brahmana family near Benares where the latter had come on pilgrimage, he showed signs of genius in his early life. After finishing his education, he travelled to the Court of Krishnadeva Raya of Vijayanagar where he defeated some Saiva pandits in a public discussion. He advocated renunciation of the world and "insisted on the complete identity of both soul and world with the Supreme Spirit" – clearly a reflection of the teachings of Upanishads. His monism was known as *Suddha-Advaita* or Pure Non-Duality, which was however abused later by his followers to such an extent that Monier-Williams does not hesitate to write: "Vallabha-Charyaism became in its degenerate form the Epicureanism of the East".

However, the greatest and the most popular of the Vaishnava saints was Chaitanya (1485-1533). Born in a learned Brahmana family of Nadia in Bengal in 1485 A.D., Chaitanya displayed a wonderful literary acumen in his early life and his soul soon aspired to rise above the fetters of this world. At the age of 24, he renounced the world and spent the rest of his life in preaching his message of love and devotion – eighteen years in Orissa, and six years in the Deccan, Brindavan, Gaur and other places. His followers regarded him as an incarnation of Vishnu. Krishnandas Kaviraj, the author of *Chaitanyacharitamrita*, the famous biography of Chaitanya, thus brings out the essence of

Chaitanyaism: "If a creature adores Krishna and serves his *Guru*. he is released from the meshes of illusion and attains to Krishna's feet", and "leaving these [temptations] and the religious systems based on caste, [the true Vaishnava] helplessly takes refuge with Krishna". Thus he was opposed to priestly ritualism and preached faith in Hari. He believed that through love and devotion, and song and dance, a state of ecstasy could be produced in which the personal presence of God would be realised. His gospel was meant for all, irrespective of caste and creed, and some of his disciples were drawn from the lower strata of Hindu society and from among Muslims.

In Maharashtra the religion of devotion was preached by Namadeva; and among his followers a few were Muslim converts to Hinduism. Namadeva, who belonged to a caste of tailors or calico-printers, flourished probably either during the later half of the fourteenth or the first half of the fifteenth century. With his faith in the unity of God head, he did not set much store in idol-worship and external observances of religion. He believed that salvation could be attained only through love of God. "As the love between a child and his mother/so is my soul imbued in the God."

Kabir made the most earnest efforts to foster a spirit of harmony between Hinduism and Islam. His life is shrouded in a good deal of obscurity, and the dates of his birth and death are uncertain. He flourished either towards the close of the fourteenth century or in the first quarter of the fifteenth century. A legend tells us that he was born of a Brahmana widow, who left him on the side of a tank in Benares, and was then found and brought up by a Muhammadan weaver and his wife. He is represented by tradition to have been a disciple of Ramanada. Though, as Carpenter puts it, "the whole background of Kabir's thought is Hindu", he was also influenced to a great extent by Sufi saints and poets with whom he came in contact. Thus he preached a religion of love, which would promote unity amongst all classes of creeds. To him "Hindu and Turk were pots of same clay: Allah and Rama were but different names". It is needless to ask of a saint the caste to which he belongs. "The Hindus and the Mussalmans have the same Lord." A saint has no caste and God is accessible to all – barber, washerman, carpenter, Raidas and Rishis. Hindus and Moslems alike have achieved that end where remains no mark of distinction.

Kabir did not believe in the efficiency of ritual, or external formalities, either of Hinduism or of Islam; to him the true means of salvation was *Bhajan* or devotional worship, together with the freedom of the soul from all sham, insincerity, hypocrisy and cruelty. As he says: "It is not by fasting and repeating prayers and the creed/that one goeth to heaven; The inner veil of the temple of Mecca/is in man's heart, if the truth be known". He therefore preaches: "Make thy mind thy Kaaba, thy body its enclosing temples/conscience its prime teacher;/sacrifice wrath, doubt and malice;/make patience thine utterance of the five prayers".

Another great preacher of the time was Nanak, the founder of Sikhism and the reviver of the pure monotheistic doctrine of the Upanishads. He was born in a Khatri family of Talwandi, about thirty-five miles to the south-west of the city of Lahore in 1469 A.D. and spent his whole life in preaching his gospel of universal toleration, based on all that was good in Hinduism and Islam. As a matter of fact, his mission was to put an end to the conflict of religions. Like Kabir, he preached the unity of God head, condemned with vehemence the formalism of both Hinduism and Islam. As he writes: "Religion does not consist in mere words, in wandering to tombs or places of cremation or sitting in attitudes of contemplation or in wondering in foreign countries or in bathing at places of pilgrimage". The way to religion is to "abide pure amidst the impurities of the world" and to look upon "all men as equal". While advocating a middle path between extreme asceticism and pleasure-seeking, Nanak exhorted his followers to discard hypocrisy, selfishness and falsehood: "Make continence thy furnace, resignation thy goldsmith,/understanding thine anvil, divine knowledge thy tools,/the fear of God thy bellows, austerities thy fire,/divine love thy crucible, and melt God's name there in. In such a true mint the word shall be coined. This is the practice of those on whom God looked with an eye of favour".

Nanak's religion being a proselytising one, several Muslims were converted to it, and it gathered momentum under his successors.

Nature of the Contributions

These religious reformers, besides producing far-reaching social and religious effects, gave a great impetus to the development of Indian literature in different parts of India. While the orthodox scholars continued to write in Sanskrit, the religious reformers, with their aim of preaching before the uneducated masses, wrote and spoke in a medium which could be easily understood by them. Thus Ramananda and Kabir preached in Hindi and did much to enrich its poetry; and the *Dohas* and *Sakhis* of Kabir, permeated with devotional fervour, are brilliant specimens of Hindi literature. Mira Bai and some other preachers of the Radha-Krishna cult sang in *Brajabhasa*; Nanak and his disciples encouraged Punjabi and *Gurumukhi*; and Bengali literature owes a heavy debt to the Vaishnava teachers.

As in the fourteenth and the fifteenth, so in the sixteenth and the seventeenth centuries, the greater part of the poetical literature of the time was religious, marked by an exposition of either Krishna worship or the Rama cult. Many writers of the former faith flourished in the Brajabhumi, corresponding roughly to the Yamuna Valley, where it developed remarkably. Among the eight disciples of Vallabhacharya and his son Vithal Nath, grouped under the name of "Astachap", the most notable was Surdas, "the blind bard of Agra", who, writing in *Brajabhasa*, described in his *Sursagar* the sports of Krishna's early life, and composed many verses on the charm of Krishna and his beloved Radha. The other important poets of this school were Nand Das, author of the *Ras-Panchadhyayi*, Vithal Nath, author of the *Chaurasi Vaishnava Ki Varta* in prose, Paramananda Das, Kumbhan Das, and Ras Khan, a Muslim disciple of Vithal Nath, author of *Prema Varitika*. Among the writers of the Rama cult, the most illustrious was Tulsi Das (1532-1623 A.D.), who lived in Benares "unapproachable and alone in his niche in the temple of Fame". He was not merely a poet of a high order, but a spiritual leader of the people of Hindusthan, where his name has become a household word and his memory is worshipped by millions. The most famous of his works, known as *Ramcharitamanasa* or "the Pool of Rama's Life", has been justly described by George Grierson as "the one Bible of a hundred millions of people" of Hindusthan. Growse also observed in his translation of the *Ramayana* of Tulsi Das that "his book is in everyone's hands, from the Court to the cottage, and is read and heard and appreciated alike by every class of the Hindu community, whether high or low, rich or poor, young or old".

In Bengal the period was remarkable for brilliant outburst of the Vaishnava literature. Its various branches, such as the *Karchas* or notes, the *Padas* and songs, and the biographies of Chaitanya Deva, have not only saturated the minds of the people of Bengal with feelings of love and liberalism, but have also survived as a mirror of the social life of the province during that age. The most prominent Vaishnava writers were Krishnadas Kaviraj, born in 1517 A.D. of a Vaidya family of Jhamalpur in Burdwan, the author of the most important biography of Chaitanya, bearing the title of *Chaitanyacharitamrita*; Brindavan Das, born in 1507 A.D., the author of *Chaitanya Bhagavata*, which besides being a standard work on the life of Chaitanya Deva, is a storehouse of information concerning the Bengali society of his time; Jayananda, born in 1513 A.D. the author of *Chaitanya Mangal*, a biographical work giving some fresh information about Chaitanya Deva's life; Trilochan Das, born in 1523 A.D. at Kowgram, a village situated thirty miles to the north of Burdwan, the author of a very popular biography of Chaitanya Deva also known as *Chaitanya Mangal*; and Narahari Chakravarty, the author of *Bhaktiratnakar*, a voluminous biography of Chaitanya Deva, written in fifteen chapters and considered to be next in importance only to the works of Krishnadas Kaviraj. This period also saw the production of numerous translations of the great epics and the *Bhagavata*, and books in praise of Chandi Devi and Manasa Devi. The most important of these works were the *Mahabharata* of Kasiram Das and the *Kavi Kankan Chandi* of Mukundaram Chakravarti, which enjoys to this day as much popularity in Bengal as the famous book of Tulsi Das in upper India. Mukundaram's work depicts a graphic picture of the social and economic conditions of the people of Bengal of his time, and it is for this that Professor Cowell has described him as "the Crabbe of Bengal", and Grierson considers his poetry "as coming from the heart, and not from the school, and as full of passages adorned with true poetry and descriptive power".

Significance of the Contributions

The contributions of the religious reformers to the development of vernacular languages and literatures in our period are double-edged. These religious reformers not only preached and taught to the masses in their own dialects to reach their hearts but also wrote in them, composed songs and verses full of love and devotion, which at once appealed to the heart and mind of the people shaken by the socio-political disorder and chaos of the time. It will be seen that these religious reformers mostly belonged to the fourteenth and the fifteenth centuries which saw the disintegration of the Delhi Sultanate which had earlier supplanted Hindu rule in Ancient India. A feeling of social and political insecurity led the people belonging not only to the older religions but also to the new one of Islam influenced by such Sufi ideals and teachings as preached by Salim Chisti and Nizam-ud-din Aulia to seek shelter in the religion of love and devotion and of the oneness of the God echoing the Upanishads of Ancient India. Secondly, the disciples and followers of these religious reformers, in the subsequent centuries, kept up their work, wrote on their life and teachings and produced biographies and commentaries. And all such efforts, needless to say, greatly enriched the vernacular languages and literatures of Medieval India.

Patronage of the Provincial Muslim Rulers

It will be relevant here to emphasise also the patronage extended to their development by some Muslim provincial rulers and petty chieftains. Far away from Delhi and Agra, the seats of imperial power and position and consequently therefore from the routine influence of Arabic and Persian, these provincial rulers and their descendants in course of time, say roughly within 200 years since the establishment of Muslim rule in India, had become completely Indianised, patronising Indian arts and crafts and speaking provincial languages[1] and showing interest in Indian religion and culture though many of them still followed the manners and etiquettes of the Courts of Delhi and Agra which in turn looked to those of Baghdad and Cairo for inspiration and guidance. This explains why some provincial Muslim rulers and petty chieftains and high officials who were interested in Hindu religion and culture were commissioning translations of Hindu religious scriptures and literatures into provincial languages spoken and understood by them instead of Arabic and Persian as had been done by the Courts at Delhi and Agra under Firuz Shah Tughluq and Akbar.

Thus, Zain-ul-Abidin whose ancestors came from Swat and who ruled Kashmir from 1420 to 1470 could understand and converse in Hindi. It was he while arranging for the translation of the *Mahabharata* and *Rajatarangini* into Persian also got several Arabic and Persian works translated into the Hindi language. Similarly the Muslim rulers of Bengal engaged scholars to translate the *Ramayana* and the *Mahabharata* from Sanskrit into Bengali. It is widely believed that Krittivas whose Bengali version of the *Ramayana* has been hailed as the Bible of Bengal worked under the patronage of the Sultan Ghiyas-ud-din Azam who ruled Bengal from 1393 to 1410 and later eulogised by the Bengali poet Vidyapati. Sultan Husain Shah who reigned in Bengal from 1493 to 1518 patronised Maladhar Basu who translated the *Bhagavata* into Bengali and conferred on him the title of Gunaraja Khan in recognition of Basu's work. Husain Shah's

general Paragal Khan attempted a translation of the *Mahabharata* into
Bengali by the Bengali scholar Paramesvara also known as the
Kavindra. Paragal's son, Chuti Khan who became governor of
Chittagong, continued his father's work and employed the Bengali
poet Srikarana Nandi to translate the Asvamedha Parva of the great
epic. It is Husain Shah's son Nasir-ud-din Nusrat Shah, who
succeeded his father in 1518 and ruled Bengal till 1533, had the great
epic completely translated under his orders.

It is not merely the Muslim provincial rulers, their high officials
and petty chieftains who encouraged translations of important and
popular works from Sanskrit into a language which they spoke and
understood. Following their examples, many Hindu princes and
chiefs did the same. Thus, Vidyapati Thakur, who, though a native of
Mithila, is regarded as a poet of Bengal and his memory is still
venerated by Bengalis, was the Court poet of a Hindu chief named
Siva Simha. His contemporary, the famous Vaishnava poet
Chandidas who was born, probably towards the end of the fourteenth
century, in the village of Nannur in the Birbhum district of Bengal,
composed devotional lyrics and poems which are still popular among
the common folk of Bengal.

Around Delhi and Agra it was Hindi which received the
imperial patronage and the first writer of note after the coming of the
Mughals in 1526 was Malik Muhammad Jayasi, who in 1540 wrote
"the fine philosophic entitled the Padmavat, which gives the story of
Padmini, the queen of Mewar, in an allegorical setting". Akbar's keen
interest in, and patronage of, Hindi poetry gave a great stimulus to
Hindi literature. Among the courtiers of the emperor, Birbal, who
received from him the title of Kavi Priya, was a famous poet. Raja
Man Singh also wrote verses in Hindi and was a patron of learning.
The most distinguished writer among Akbar's ministers was Abdur
Rahim Khan-i-khanan, whose *Dohas* are even now read with interest
and admiration all over Northern India. Narahari, whom the
emperor gave the title of Mahapatra, Harinath and Ganj were also
noted writers of his Court. The peace and order secured by Akbar,
and the cosmopolitan ideas of the religious movements of the period,
preached by a band of saintly teachers in a language "understanded of
the people", stimulated the genius of the latter, which unfolded itself
in manifold petals. Consequently the sixteenth and seventeenth
centuries became "the Augustan age of Hindusthani literature".
However, with the withdrawal of the Court patronage, the growth of

Hindi literature received a setback during the reign of Aurangzeb. Nevertheless, Aurangzeb's successors like Bahadur Shah and Muhammad Shah revived royal patronage of men of letters who seemed to flourish more in the provincial capitals than in the imperial. In Bengal, for example, men of letters were patronised by Subedhars like Murshid Quli Jafar Khan and Alivardi Khan and Zamindars like Raja Krishnachandra of Nadia and Asadullah of Birbhum, though with the exception of the devotional songs of Ramprasad, the Bengali literature of the period was of a low tone and a vitiated taste.

The Flourishing of the Dravidian Languages

While the vernaculars in the North had not found any literary expression at the time of the Muslim invasion, the Dravidian languages have been flourishing for centuries past. Four of these languages have distinctive scripts and written literatures – Tamil, Canarese, Telugu and Malyalam. Of these Tamil is spoken in the South, from Cape Comorin to Madras (now Chennai), Canarese in Mysore and parts of Hyderabad, Telugu from Madras northward to the borders of Orissa and Malyalam in Malabar. Tamil is certainly the oldest of these languages, with a literature going back to the early centuries A.D. The earliest Tamil literature contains few Sanskrit-loan-words, and those it does contain are generally adapted to the Tamil phonetic system.

As Aryan influence penetrated whole of the Tamil land by sixth century A.D. and her kings and Chiefs worshipped and supported the Gods of Hinduism, Jainism and Buddhism, many words often in their correct Sanskrit form were borrowed by the Tamil literature. Telugu and Canarese, which were spoken further North were naturally even more strongly influenced by Sanskrit. While Malayalam, very closely akin to Tamil, became a separate language, in the eleventh century, Telugu did not appear as a literary language until the twelfth century and only became really important under the Vijayanagar empire, of which it was the Court language. We have already seen how under the patronage of the Vijayanagar kings, Telegu flourished. Since the rulers of the Vijayanagar empire as well as many among those of the Bahamani kingdom and the five Sultanates which later rose on its ruins, were tolerant, the development of the Dravidian languages which often enjoyed the patronage of local chieftains and rulers was the least affected in the entire history of the Medieval India.

The Emergence of Urdu

The Deccan Sultanates, particularly those of Bijapur and Golkunda, which patronised the regional vernaculars also helped in the development of a new language to its literary heights. This new language which did not belong to any particular region and was generally spoken by the successive generations of Muslims of Turki, and Afghan origins was Urdu – a language which represented the synthesis of Indo-Muslim culture in Medieval India.

India which had the tradition of completely absorbing the civilisation of the earlier invaders like the Greeks, the Sakas and the Hunas failed to do so in the case of the Turko-Afghan invaders of India who had definite social and religious ideas which differed fundamentally from those of Hindusthan and the political relations between the newcomers and the indigenous people were sometimes characterised by bitter strifes and struggles. However, when two types of civilisation come into close contact with each other and live side by side for centuries, both are bound to influence each other. The growth of the numbers of the converted Indo-Muslim community and inter-marriages between the Hindus and the Muslims as well as between the ruling members of the two which were often the result of compulsion, as a condition of conquest did much "to soften the acrimonious differences" between them and assist the transplanting of the customs of one to the fold of the other. Thus, some Muslims of aristocratic Hindu origin, or living in a Hindu environment, assimilated the Hindu customs of Sati and Jauhar and it was probably due to the existence of a feeling of friendliness that conversion of the Muslims into the Hindu fold, and reconversion of the Hindus to their original faith could be possible during our period.

As a matter of fact, both Hindus and Muslims had mutual admiration for each other's culture, since the early days of the advent of Islam into India, and one of the sources of Muslim mysticism was India. Famous Muslim scholars and saints lived and laboured in India during the Medieval period, and they helped the dissemination of the ideas of Islamic philosophy and mysticism in this land. The wholesome spirit of mutual toleration found expression in the growing veneration of the Hindus for the Muslim saints, particularly of the mystic school, and a corresponding Muhammadan practice of venerating Hindu saints, and it ultimately led to the common worship of Satyapir or the True Saint. It was out of the desire for mutual understanding that Hindu or Sanskrit religious literature was studied and translated or summarised in the Muslim Courts like those of Zain-ul-Abidin in Kashmir, Husain Shah in Bengal, Akbar in Agra and Dara Shukoh in Delhi. Further Muslim Courts and Muslim preachers and saints were attracted to the study of Hindu philosophy like Yoga and Vedanta and the sciences of medicine and astrology. The Hindu astronomers similarly borrowed from the Muslim technical terms, the Muslim calculations of latitudes and longitudes, some items of the calendar, that is, Zich and a branch of horoscope called Tajik, and in medicine the knowledge of metallic acids and some processes in iatro-chemistry. While some Muslims wrote in vernaculars on topics of Hindu life and tradition, as Malik Muhammad Jayasi did on Padmini, Hindu writers wrote in the Persian language on Muslim literary traditions, as Rai Bhana Mal did in his chronicles.

While the Muslim rulers, out of sheer necessity, had to retain the existing machinery of local administration – the Hindu headmen and accountants of the villages – they also employed a number of Hindus, well-versed in Persian, who became prominent in different branches of administration. While many of the official appointments might have been due more to political necessity than to any feeling of good will, there can be no doubt that they facilitated the growth of amity between the Hindu and Muslims. In fact, in different aspects of life – arts and crafts, music and painting, in the styles of buildings, in dress and costume, in games and sports – this assimilation between the two communities had progressed so much that when Babar came to India, he was compelled to notice their peculiar "Hindusthani Way".

While this assimilation between the two cultures and civilisations led to the springing up of new styles of art, architecture and music, "in which the basic element remained the old Hindu, but the finish and outward form became Persian and the purpose served was that of Muslim Courts", in the world of written and spoken words, it led to the growth of Urdu, of the mingling "out of Persian, Arabic and Turki words and ideas with languages and concepts of Sanskritic origin" as "a proof of the linguistic synthesis of the Hindu and the Muslims".

From the beginning of the eighth century A.D. the Arab occupation of Sind led to an exchange of ideas. The Arabs who lived side by side with their Hindu fellow citizens for many years on terms of amity and peace acquired from the Hindus, some new knowledge in Indian religion, philosophy, medicine, mathematics, astronomy and folklore and carried it not only to their own land but also to Europe. It is quite possible that they picked up Hindi and Sanskritic words and a scholar among them, the Arab astronomer, Abu Ma'shar went to Benares and studied astronomy for ten years, if Amir Khusrav is to be believed. Urdu as Rekhta or scattered and crumbled from Hindi, Sanskrit and Arabic and Persian words might have been in use among the Arabs and certainly Mas'ood-bin-Sa'ad is said to have written Rekhta or poems in Urdu.

The Turki element was introduced in Urdu since the beginning of the Muslim rule in Delhi with the rule of Qutab-ud-din Aibak in 1206 and it is generally believed that Amir Khusrav, the famous poet surnamed the "Parrot of India" who served the Courts of a number of Delhi Sultans beginning with Ghiyas-ud-din Balban through Ala-ud-din Khalji to Ghiyas ud-din Tughluq composed some of his poems in Urdu, not a few of which have come down to us to testify his use of Rekhta or Urdu in his poems.[2] Born and brought up in the Hindi belt of the Yamuna and the Ganges, trained in the maktab and the madrasah, Amir Khusrav was a prolific writer, whose genius unfolded itself in poetry, prose and music. A contemporary and close friend of the pious and learned scholar, Nizam-ud-din Auliya, Khusrav survived the former's death by a few years and died in 1324-1325 A.D. and was buried by the side of Nizam-ud-din's grave.

Urdu as the Rival to the Mother Tongue of the Muslim Rulers

It must be mentioned here that Arabic and Persian were not the mother tongues of the Delhi Sultans and the Mughal emperors, while Arabic was the language of the Prophet Muhammad and of the *Quran*, Persian was the language of the Court of Baghdad. The Delhi Courts which followed Persian manners, etiquettes and customs adopted Persian as the official language for purposes of administration as well as for polite conversations and scholarly transactions. The mother tongue of the Delhi Sultans and the Mughal emperors as well as the nobles and soldiers who accompanied them to India was Turki – so in a sense Arabic and Persian were foreign languages to them and had got to be learnt through a teacher either at the residence or at a maktab and a madrasah unlike Turki which they were born with. Set in the midst of a people who cherished their Sanskrit and Hindi for their own purposes of business or worship, Urdu emerged among the succeeding generations of the Delhi Sultans and the Mughal emperors and their followers who by that time had become Indianised through their births and upbringing, as a language for free intercourse among them. Urdu which is a word of Turki origin literally means 'camp' and indicates its popularity as a language spoken not only among the ruling classes at the imperial and the provincial capitals of Islamic India but also among their subjects including soldiers and the converts from Hinduism. In Shahjahan's time, for example, the capital of the Mughal empire, Shah Jahanabad in Delhi, came to be identified with Urdu-i-Mu'alla or high camp.

Urdu as a Literary Language

However, it was not the Courts at Delhi and Agra but those of Bijapur and Golkunda which provided necessary spur to Urdu as a literary language by their patronisation. The rulers of these two kingdoms were themselves poets and relished Urdu poetry. They patronised at their Courts such composers of verses in Urdu as Ibn Nishati and Nusrat who heralded the dawn of Urdu poetry. In the seventeenth century Urdu poetry received a definite standard of form at the hands of Shams Wali Allah, commonly known as Wali who was a resident of Aurangabad, and a contemporary and townsman of Siraj, another great scholar and poet. Wali significantly called "the father of Rekhta", has left a Diwan, which when first appeared at Delhi, set the whole literary city ablaze.

For the next hundred years till the middle of the eighteenth century, a new school of Urdu poets sprang up at Delhi, who drew inspiration from Wali. And by the middle of the eighteenth century when the Mughal empire was limited to the area around Delhi only, the literary centre of gravity shifted from Delhi to Lucknow where "Urdu Poetry" as writes S. Khuda Baksh in an article in Aligarh Muslim University Journal in July 1931, "put forth fresh blossom and bloom".

Urdu vis-à-vis other Vernacular Languages

Urdu is poetical in nature and so was it in Medieval India when it emerged, it followed the rules of Persian prosody. It borrowed its forms and conventions of diction such as Qasida or laudatory ode, Ghazal or love-song, Masnavi or narrative poem, Marsiya or derge, Rubai or quartain, Hajv or satire from Persian. However, while the forms and conventions of diction are Persian, the diction itself, or vocabulary is mostly Hindi. Its grammatical structure is almost entirely Hindi – most of its verbs are not only Indian but a large number of nouns are of Indian origin.

Yet in the context of the development of vernacular languages which became mother tongue of the people belonging to different parts of the country, for the Hindus, Urdu become a language like Sanskrit or Arabic and Persian which was to be learnt and cultivated. In Urdu the alphabet mostly consists not only of Arabic and Persian but the direction of reading and writing as in Arabic and Persian is from right to left, while the Hindus in India since the days of Ashoka were used to Sanskritised scripts and to reading and writing their languages from right to left as in Latin, Greek, English, French, German and other European languages. However, for the Muslim Sultans, particularly in the Hindi belt, who in course of time had lost touch with the mother tongue, Turki, Urdu which rested heavily on Hindi words, came to be spoken and written spontaneously. Similarly in the South in the Dravidian belt, Muslim Sultans of Turki origin found it much easier to patronise Urdu than a Dravidian language, say, Telegu, Tamil, Kanarese or Malayalam as next to their mother tongue.

It was the historical forces which led to the development of the vernacular languages including Hindi and the emergence of Urdu in Medieval India. Sanskrit which was driven by Persian from the Courts of Islamic rulers as the royal and official language was further challenged by the rising vernaculars both in the South and in the North while Arabic and Persian which had replaced Sanskrit in the Muslim Courts faced similar challenge in the rise of Urdu. Thus, the language situation in Medieval India remained a fluid one while preparing the grounds for the refinement of vernacular languages and literature in Modern India.

The Village Schools

The development of vernaculars largely facilitated the expansion of elementary learning – a knowledge of the three R's or a knowledge of reading, writing and arithmetic – at the village levels. From time immemorial the village school existed in some form or other to meet the educational requirements of the people other than the priestly classes who monopolised the Vedic schools where studies in Sanskrit religious scriptures were imparted. In Ancient India there had been since the days of the Mauryas village assemblies or functionaries under the village Pradhan or headman who managed the affairs of the village. In the post-Gupta period such a village assembly often consisted of the whole adult population or of Brahmanas or of a few great men of the village selected by a kind of ballot. The assembly whose work was supervised by royal officers or Adhikaries appointed committees to look after specific departments including tanks, temples, justice and provided for the appointment of a teacher to instruct in regional prakrits the children of the villagers who were usually peasants, artisans, craftsmen, small traders and merchants. The village teacher who imparted instruction in the three R's to them and usually received his fees in kind, kept his school open at all seasons of the year to admit them according to their convenience to his school which they left after they had picked up the necessary elementary knowledge, either to start their own work or to join their family professions. The children came mostly from the classes of the people who were generally debarred from joining the Vedic schools monopolised by the Brahmins and other higher castes who often distinguished themselves in the political, military, medical and economical activities of the kingdom.

With the coming of the Islam and setting up of its rule in India, most parts of the country came under its influence, though actual control was limited only to the imperial and provincial capitals and the adjoining areas. Large tracts of land had of necessity to be left in the hands of old Hindu chieftains, who were not interfered with the ruling of their ancestral territories so long as they sent their tributes and presents to Delhi and Agra. The village communities with their village schools remained unaffected by the establishment of a new government in the country which did not interfere with them as long as there was no violent crime or defiance of royal authority in the locality.

However, as Islam in the days of Ala-ud-din Khalji and Muham-mad-bin-Tughlaq and later under the Mughals penetrated the remote villages and as more and more converts from Hinduism began to join its ranks, numerous mosques with maktabs began to appear on the scenes. The new converts, began to receive their elementary education in a medium which was neither Arabic nor Persian though certainly they were required to learn these languages, particularly Arabic, to study the *Quran*. The maktab which was endowed and supported by a rich Muslim not only institutionalised the concept of education in a village but inspired others from the Hindu communities in the village to similarly come forward in support of the education of their children. Thus, Islam boosted to some extent the elementary education in the villages.

From the days of Akbar, the doors of a maktab were open to the Hindus and in such villages where there were no schools for the children of the Hindus, the latter often used to study in a maktab learning Arabic and Persian in a medium spoken and understood by the two communities. Conversely, children of the Muslim parents would often attend a Hindu school when there was no such maktab in a village which was dominated by the Hindus. Khurshid – Jahan – Namah asserts that at Silapur in Bengal there were some educational institutions where both Hindus and Muhammadens were taught Persian and Arabic – obviously in the medium of regional language which was, in this case, Bengali.

In the twilight of the Mughal rule in India there existed numerous such schools in the villages. Shoberl gives a graphic description of such a school in the Deccan in his *Hindusthan in Miniature*: "The pupils sit cross-legged on a bench or the floor. They write on paper with reed pens, or with tubes of some other kind. The paper mostly imported from China is not so good as that of Europe. It is smooth, very thin and easily tears. The *Quran* is chiefly read by the Mussalmans who also study the Persian language". It is possible Shoberl is referring to an advanced stage in elementary education where paper in elementary education was used chiefly for writing. Before this stage it was either the Slate or an oblong board which could be washed clean at the close of a session or banana and palm leaves were in use, as was the case in Bengal, by the end of our period.

The students at the village school as described by Shoberl were indeed fortunate but not so were those of the village schools lying in the remote parts of the country. Pietro Della Valle witnessed in 1623-24 while travelling through the Western Coast how the students learnt arithmetic by writing the number of figures on the ground with their fingers while reciting it rhythmically, without the aid of any paper, ink, slate or leaves!

Such village schools could be organised anywhere in a dilapidated mosque or a temple, under the shade of a tree or in an open field, in the Chandi Mandap where visitors were often housed or in the Baithakhana where village matters could also be discussed and were responsible for supplying not only the village professionals with some rudimentary knowledge but also the extreme lower rung personnel of Muslim administration such as Kharmarnavis, Patwari, Amin, Majumdar and Shumarnavis.

By the end of our period, village schools as distinguished from private domestic schools where teachers varied from a local Pujari Brahmin to a petty official flourished in the various parts of the Mughal empire. Apart from the surveys conducted after nearly three quarter of a century of our period, we have such evidences as to show that "almost all villages possessed schools for teaching, reading, writing and elementary arithmetic" and that every village with about a hundred houses had a school-master who taught "the children of the banias or shopkeepers and those of such cultivators, as choose". The age of the boys attending these schools normally varied from 8 to 14 and the duration of study could be from a few days to a few years by which time they could write letters on paper, compose grants, leases and other legal documents.

Such villages schools were not, however, attended by any girls who used to help their families in domestic chores though occasionally an affluent Hindu or a rich Muslim would care to teach their daughters at home to be able to read their religious scriptures or take care of their properties when they died without any male heirs. In the next chapter we shall analyse the education of girls and women in Medieval India.

Notes

1. In 1602-3 when Asad Beg Qazwini went to the Court of Ibrahim Adil Shah, the Sultan of Bijapur, with a proposal for the marriage of Akbar's youngest sonya Daniyal with the Sultan's daughter, he was surprised to find that Adil Shah spoke Marathi fluently, but could converse in Persian with great difficulty!

2. Amir Khusrav's use of Rekhta or Urdu in his poems could be seen in *Diwan-i-Amir Khusrau* edited by S. Yasin Ali at Delhi.

21

Education of Girls and Women

In the previous chapter we have said that the presence of girls, both Hindu and Muslim, was almost non-existent in the village schools. Let us now examine in detail the extent of education among the girls and women in Medieval India.

We know in Ancient India girls were encouraged to study religious scriptures so that after marriage they could assist their husbands in the discharge of social and religions responsibilities and we have also evidences of highly learned ladies like Gargi who could question the sage Yajnavalka in the Court of the king Janaka. All these however, relate to the years before Manu forbade girls going out to Vedic schools and advocated their early marriage as soon as they reached puberty. Manu did this mainly to preserve the sanctity of Aryan blood against the fresh inroads of foreign invaders through the North-West. The Islamic rulers placed in an alien and often hostile environment encouraged seclusion of women who had accompanied them to India and as they gradually settled down in India and the numbers of converts to Islam increased, the seclusion of women among them and the neo-converts through the system of *Purdah* became a common practice. And the girls of the Muslim ruling classes began to be educated at home as their Hindu counterparts.

The Muslim rulers while providing for the education of their sons also made adequate arrangement for the education of their daughters. While the boys were trained to be competent rulers, the girls were given adequate education including a knowledge of *Quran* to such an extent that many of them later distinguished themselves as authoresses of important works. We have the example of Raziyah who succeeded her father Iltutimish who could study *Quran* "with correct pronunciation, and in her father's lifetime employed herself in the affairs of the Government". Gulbadan Begum, daughter of Babar, who wrote the *Humayun-namah* which later inspired the composition of the *Akbar-namah* by Abul Fazl was a highly educated lady and possessed a library of her own containing valuable manuscripts. Salima Sultana, the niece of Humayun was a learned lady who used to write Persian poems under *nom de plume* of 'Makhfi' or 'concealed'. She became Akbar's wife after the death of her first husband, Bairam Khan. And we all know that Akbar's wet nurse or foster mother Maham Anaga was a learned lady who founded a madrasah in Delhi. Chand Sultana of Ahmadnagar who offered heroic resistance to Akbar's son, Murad, in 1576, was an accomplished lady who was noted for her skill on the lyre and for her melodious songs, could speak fluently Arabic, Persian, Turki, Kanarese and Marathi. Nur Jahan the celebrated wife of Jahangir who used to run his administration was well-versed in Persian and Arabic literature. Mumtaz Mahal, the beloved wife of Shah Jahan, was similarly well-versed in Persian and could compose poems in it. Her female Nazir, Satiunnisa, who used to recommend to Mumtaz Mahal the names of theologians and pious men for pensions and of poor scholars for donations to the marriage of their daughters could recite the *Quran* and Persian poems. She was appointed tutoress to Jahanara Begum, the eldest daughter of Shah Jahan. Herself a highly educated lady, Jahanara encouraged the learned men of the time with rewards and allowances. She was elevated by her father to the rank of the First-Lady and possessed managerial ability to regulate the affairs of the Imperial Harem as well as of the Women's Society in the capital. Known for humility and simplicity, she wrote her own epitaph in Persian which reads: "Except with grass and green things let not my tomb be covered; for grass is an all-sufficient pall for the graves of the poor". She described herself as "disciple of the saintly family of Chisti, daughter of Shah Jahan" and ordered that the epitaph should be placed on her tomb near that of Nizam-ud-din Auliya. Zebinda Begum, the fourth daughter of Shah Jahan, was a gifted poetess and composed a volume of mystical verses in Persian. Aurangzeb took great care in educating his daughters. The eldest one, Zeb-un-Nisa, who was well-versed in Persian and Arabic as well as proficient in the knowledge of the *Quran* and in the art of calligraphy was taught by Aurangzeb himself. She employed many learned men, poets and writers who dedicated their numerous compilations and original works to her. Aurangzeb's third daughter who knew the *Quran* by heart was not so well-educated as her eldest sister, Zeb-un-Nisa.

Such Muslim educated ladies in Medieval India would perhaps appear to pale into insignificance when compared with their educated counterparts in Spain such as Zainab, Hamda, Fatimah, Aishah and Maryum or in other parts of the Islamic World but there is no doubt that the education of the female members of the royal families was never neglected and the examples cited above clearly show the extent and care taken by the Islamic rulers in educating them.

An almost similar care was shown by some of the Muslim rulers in educating the ladies of their harems. Thus, Sultan Ghiyas-ud-din Khalji who ruled in Malwa between 1469 and 1500 A.D. established within his seraglio all the separate offices of the Court[1] and "among these were school mistresses, musicians, women to read prayers, and persons of all profession and trades". The very fact that he retained school mistresses in the harem indicates that the ladies in the palace were taught by them. Similarly, Akbar in his palace at Fathpur Sikri set apart certain chambers to serve as school for educating the ladies of his harem, who were then not less than five thousand in number.[2]

With so much care for the education of their daughters and ladies of their harems, it is indeed surprising that the Muslim rulers at the imperial capitals at Delhi and Agra did not do anything remarkable for the education of the females. Had they done so, this must have been recorded by their Muslim chroniclers who often gave minutest attention to details. Education of girls was treated by the Muslim rulers as extremely personal and left it to the wishes of their fathers and guardians. There is no doubt that the Muslim nobility followed the examples of their masters in educating their own daughters at their homes but there is doubt whether an ordinary Muslim subject could emulate it, as the appointment of a teacher who was to be presented with some gifts at the beginning and at the completion of their education was often expensive. However, since study of the *Quran* was incumbent upon all faithful followers of Islam, one could perhaps be justified in presuming that education of girls in ordinary Muslim houses was not neglected and they were either taught at home by their parents or sent to a local maktab in a private house. Many a Muslim widow considered it to be their sacred duty to impart religious education to their daughters and we learn from Leitner's work, *History of Indigenous education in the Punjab* that the number of such schools kept in private houses for the instruction of girls was numerous in the Punjab and Delhi.

It is in the light of the above we should try to understand Jafar Sharif's observation on the existence of schools for girls in Muslim India in his *Qanun-i-Islam* or when Ibn Batutah, the most energetic globe-trotter of Tangier spoke about the existence of 13 girls schools in Hinawr or Hanaur, the capital of the independent kingdom of Madura of Sultan Jalal-ud-din Ashan Shah, which comprised, at the time of Ibn Batutah's visit, the entire area between the Malabar and the Coromandel coasts and extended from Cape Comorin up to Gulbarga. Be that as it may, the examples set by the ladies of the ruling families in Islamic India were doubtless followed by the nobility and the higher classes of Muslims in India, though at the lower levels, the education of Muslim women might at best be extended to a study of the *Quran* since, as said earlier, engaging a teacher to continue education after it was certainly expensive in terms of gifts presented to the teacher called *Hadyah* after successfully completion of each course. At a further lower levels of the Muslim society where people were either poor or earned their living by very humble pursuits, it is doubtful whether the girls in their houses could have the privilege of being acquainted with the *Quran* also since in the absence of printing press hand written copies of the *Quran* were not only easily accessible but also too expensive to obtain one by a poor family either in a village or in a town. Since the number of such families vastly outnumber those belonging to the royal and affluent classes, it is reasonable to surmise that the overall picture of the education of girls and women in Medieval India is a dismal one and certainly not an encouraging one for the posterity.

Notes

1. Ferishta informs us that at one time the number of women in his palace reached fifteen thousand mark. Ferishta's observation is to be taken with a pinch of salt. It is really difficult to believe how a normal palace meant for the living of the royal family could accommodate such an huge and extraordinary number.

2. The archaeological remains of the palace at Fathpur Sikri also leads us to wonder whether such number as given by the contemporary Muslim chroniclers is a correct one.

Part III

Modern India, 1757 – 1999

22

The East India Company's Role in the Development of Education in India

Education in Pre-Colonial India

The remnants of the Vedic education as it survived through the priestly families in Muslim India as well as in Hindu kingdoms and the Islamic education as it was introduced by the Muslim rulers in Medieval India existed before the British as traders in the employ of the East India Company came to India. What was the nature of this education as it existed when the British came? It was communicated through the sacred classical languages of the Hindus and the Muslims, namely Sanskrit, Arabic and Persian. The subjects taught were the scriptures, grammar, logic and the classics which included codes of law and such scientific works as had come down to them from early times. While the Indian writers had been prolific in their production of philosophical and literary works, they paid little attention to the development of science which, though it had made some remarkable progress in early days, had now fallen in disgrace.

How was this learning imparted? Learning among the Hindus had been the monopoly of the high, especially of the priestly castes. The learned Brahmins gathered students from various parts of the country and in the homely atmosphere of their Tolls and *Chatuspathis* as these were known in Bengal and Bihar, imparted knowledge. Life in those places was pure and simple. The teachers not only received no fees but provided free board and lodging for their students. The course of studies extended from fifteen to twenty years and the hours of study were long and severe. There were also larger education establishments in the various religious centres, the most famous of which in the Ganges valley were Nadia, Tirhut (Tirabhukti or Mithila) and Benares. These were conducted by learned pandits, who were liberally patronised by the rulers and the aristocracy and were men of high character and immense learning and lived a simple life. The Muslim seats of learning called madrasahs were less spiritual and were smaller in number than the Hindu seats of learning and were meant chiefly for the training of law officers. Besides laws, instruction was also given in these institutions in scriptures, literature, grammar, penmanship, logic, rhetoric, natural philosophy and arithmetic and average duration of the study was ten to twelve years. One interesting feature was that the Hindus could also attend those seminaries meant primarily for the Muslims.

However, these institutions were not meant for education of an elementary kind. They were the highest seminaries of learning meant for the specialists. For primary education, there were in the villages pathsalas and maktabs where the gurus and the "maulavis imparted a knowledge of the three R's to the boys of the locality. These schools were not paying concerns and had to depend on the generosity of the people. Instruction in these schools was given in the vernaculars. The aristocracy did not send their children to these schools but preferred to educate them at home. There was no school for the education of the girls though the Zamindars often had their daughters educated at home. The majority of the Indians were unwilling to educate their girls on account of social prejudice and superstition, while the lower classes could not afford it.

What was the nature and extent of the elementary education as it existed in the late eighteenth and early nineteenth century?

Unfortunately, we do not have adequate sources of information to answer this question fully, but from a series of surveys carried out in elementary education by the officials of the East India Company between 1822 and 1838 we can fairly assume that elementary education was quite popular in the villages of British India. In a minute of 10 March 1826 Thomas Munro, the Governor of the Madras Presidency, observed that there were 12,498 schools with 1,88,650 pupils in the whole province out of a total population of 1,28,50,941 while a survey conducted in the Bombay Presidency by order of the Bombay Governor, Mountstuart Elphinstone in 1829 showed the existence of 1,705 schools with 35,153 pupils in a population of 46,81,735. In the Bengal Presidency the survey was conducted by a missionary, William Adam, appointed by the Governor-General, Lord William Bentinck, to report on the state of elementary education in the province. Adam submitted three reports between 1835 and 1838 – he estimated that at the beginning of the nineteenth century there were 1,00,000 schools in Bengal and Bihar or roughly two schools for every three villages. Assuming the population of these two provinces to be 4,00,00,000, there would be a village school for every 400 persons. He did not find any school for girls and as girls formed one half of the school-going population, Adam concluded that there was one elementary school, for every 32 boys. It must be mentioned here that these surveys, particularly those of Munro and Adam, included places of domestic instruction – the system of providing instruction at home – in their interpretation of the term schools and considering this, the figure of villages as offered by these surveys does not appear to be "a legend" or "a myth" as educationists like Philip Hartog would have us believe. From other sources also we are informed of the existence of a school in every village. William Ward, a Baptist Missionary based at Serampore, observed in his *A View of the History of the Religion and Mythology of the Hindus* that "almost all villages possessed schools for teaching, reading, writing and elementary arithmetic". Malcolm noted in his *Memoirs of Central India* that every village with about a hundred houses had a school-master who taught "the children of *the banians* or shop-keepers and those of such cultivators, as choose".

Village schools served a very useful purpose – they fulfilled the needs and requirements of the villagers, the petty Zamindar, the bania and the well-to-do farmer. The curriculum consisted of reading, writing and arithmetic (both written and oral). There were no printed books and the locally made slates and pencils were the only equipment the pupils needed. The hours of instruction and the days of working were adjusted to local requirements. There was no regular period of admission – a pupil could join the school at any time and leave it when he had acquired all that he desired to know. Such schools which were often without any buildings of their own were held sometimes in the home of a teacher or a patron, in a mosque or a temple, and not infrequently under the shade of trees. The number of pupils could vary from one to twenty but in bigger schools the senior pupils were appointed to teach the junior ones. This system attracted the attention of the Madras Chaplain, Dr. A. Bell, who introduced it in England as a cheap and efficient method of educating the poor and later it came to be known as the Monitorial or Madras System in England. The teachers for these schools, like their students, came from all classes including the depressed classes as Adam's analysis of castes shows and were paid either in cash or in kind according to the ability of the parents of the pupils. However, these schools which had shown wonderful adaptability to local environment and existed for centuries through a variety of economic conditions or political vicissitudes showed signs of decay at the coming of the British Raj. One factor which contributed to it was the gradual destruction of village crafts and industries and the growing impoverishment of the people following a series of economic reforms including the Permanent Settlement in the Bengal Presidency in the late eighteenth century.

British Interest in Oriental Education

It was the classical aspect of Indian education that first attracted the attention of a few high officials of the East India Company after the Company had stood forth as the Dewan in 1765 in the Bengal Presidency. Such officials though few in number had spent most of their career in India – they were not only able to survive the Indian climate but develop a taste for many things Indian. Foremost among them was Warren Hastings who came to India in the service of the East India Company as a writer in 1751 and by 1772 rose to be the Governor of Fort-William in Bengal. Hastings developed a great love for Indo-Persian culture. With his encouragement as Governor-General of Bengal, Nathaniel Halhed wrote *A Code of Gentoo Laws* in 1776 and *Bengali Grammar* in 1778 and in 1779 Charles Wilkins brought out his Sanskrit grammar; Francis Gladwin wrote *Institutes of the Emperor Akbar in 1783*. In 1781, he established the Calcutta madrasah at the request of a Muslim deputation. The main object was to "qualify the sons of the Mohammadan gentlemen for responsible and lucrative offices in the state even at that time largely monopolised by the Hindus". The institution was very popular and attracted scholars from far-off places. The period of study extended over seven years and the scholars received stipends to study the courses. The courses included natural philosophy, Quranic theology, law, geometry, arithmetic, logic and grammar – all on Islamic lines. The medium of instruction was Arabic. Hastings purchased a site and laid the foundation of the Madrasah on his own account and asked the Court of Directors to assign "the rents of one or more villages" near

Calcutta as an endowment for the institution. The Directors later sanctioned this and reimbursed Hastings.

Another high official of the East India Company who was greatly attracted to higher learning in India was William Jones. Unlike Hastings, Jones had not spent many years in India to develop a love for Indo-Persian culture. As a matter of fact, he was already an accomplished Persian scholar, whose *Grammar of the Persian Language* and translation of the work of Persian poets, published in 1771 and 1773 had won him a European reputation, when he came to India as a judge of the Supreme Court established by the Regulating Act of 1773 at Calcutta. He now applied his own enthusiasm to the organisation of scholarly efforts in Bengal but he soon realised that without "the united efforts of many" he could not achieve his ambition of knowing India *"better than any other European ever knew it"*[1] as he later told Lord Althorp. He had been elected a Fellow of the Royal Society in London in 1773 and had set out to create a similar learned society in Calcutta with the "enquiry into the history and antiquities, arts, sciences and literature of Asia" as its aim. The "Asiatick Society" of Bengal which was formed on 15 January 1784 to pursue this aim gave a great fillip to ancient learning in India by discovering, editing and publishing rare Sanskrit manuscripts, besides bringing out the journal, *Asiatick Researches,* containing scholarly contributions in Oriental learning. Jones himself developed a greater taste for Sanskrit learning and used to spend "three months every year" in Nadia, a pre-eminent centre for Sanskrit learning in Bengal, described by a contributor to the *Calcutta Review* in 1872 as the "Oxford of the Province", and used to converse fluently in Sanskrit with the Brahmins during his stay there.

Sanskrit learning in the Bengal Presidency received further impetus when in 1792 Jonathan Duncan, the Resident at Benares obtained the permission of Cornwallis, the Governor-General, to establish a Sanskrit College at Benares, for preserving and cultivating the laws, literatures and scriptures of the Hindus. In this college as in the Calcutta Madrasah, the students were not only taught gratis, but were also given stipends. Eight years later when Wellesley, the Governor-General, set up the Fort William College at Calcutta to train the servants of the East India Company as administrators of the vast territories acquired by the East India Company since 1765, he included courses on Oriental learning, including Sanskrit and Persian and appointed Pandits or Oriental experts to teach them.

These examples of patronisation of the classical learning by a few high officials of the East India Company do not in any way indicate the attitude of the Company towards education in India. For, both the Calcutta Madrasah and the Benares Sanskrit College were individual enterprises for preservation of ancient Indian culture and were attempts at reconciliating the feelings of the two major communities in India, while inclusion of Oriental learning in the courses at Fort William was an administrative expediency. Nor do these measures represent the attitude of the vast body of the employees of the East India Company in Bombay, Calcutta and Madras (now Mumbai, Kolkata and Chennai) towards education in India. Those who came to Bengal and elsewhere in India were just teenagers of good and influential connexions, with a good hand and knowledge of commercial arithmetic and bookkeeping. Since the employees were paid very lowly by the Company, they had to take to various irregularities to increase their earnings. For most of them the major concern was to make money and to enjoy it at home after retirement. Many who were able to survive the climate of Bengal, Madras and Bombay did return with a good fortune, purchased landed estates and became members of Parliament as well as of the Court of Directors and thus became an important factor in influencing the policy of the East India Company. Yet, these measures in classical learning particularly the creation of the "Asiatick Society" initiated by a few high officials of the East India Company had their impact later in raising a group of dedicated Oriental scholars who profoundly influenced the East India Company's policy towards education when it happened to have one in the second decade of the next century.

Charles Grant's Plan

Among those who were able to retire to a successful life in England after a career in India, Charles Grant shines as a bright star. The reason why Grant is singled out here for a special mention is because of his contributions to the development of a modern education system in India. Charles Grant's contribution to British rule in India has been investigated a few decades ago by Professor A.T. Embree but educationists in India generally tend to overlook his role in the introduction of Western education in India. We shall presently see that he was the first Englishman, at least four decades before Macaulay, to argue for the introduction of English education with a view to introducing Christianity in India. Grant was no missionary – so why did he want to proselytise the Indians? Grant who had come to India in 1767, acquired an immense fortune, and led a hectic life till 1786 when through family mishaps and close contact with the Chaplain David Brown and the Civilian George Udny, underwent a great change. He was appalled at the degeneration of the Indian society following the break-up of the Mughal empire in the late eighteenth century.

What was the state of the society in India as Grant saw it? In India, religion has always been a very strong spiritual force which binds the people together but at the time of Grant it had sunk into the grossest form of superstition. Every stone and every tree had acquired the importance of a deity and every phenomenon of nature was taken as a manifestation of the divine will. People had begun the practice of throwing children into the sea for propitiating the gods and of swinging the devotees in iron hooks during certain religious festivals. Over zealous devotees also practised various kinds of self-tortures such as *Dharna* in order to atone for their sins. The degenerated Brahmins had begun to impose their self-motivated interpretation of the scriptures upon the credulous simplicity of ignorant people, who looked upon their words as law which no one could contradict. Social life was degraded. Many abuses, some of the most gruesome nature, had crept into the society. Infanticide was widely practised in Central India, especially among the Rajputs. The custom of Sati or self-immolation of widows was widely prevalent and was looked upon as a sacred act. Caste, once based upon the functions of individuals, had become a rigid system which kept its various branches in watertight compartments, although the members had ceased to adhere to the functions originally assigned to them. Only the Brahmins had maintained their monopoly of priestly position. This had naturally led to grave abuses because it had given birth precedence over all other consideration and had consigned to the most degraded state of existence, some of the low caste people like the *pariahs* and untouchables, mere contact with one of whom was sufficient to make one lose one's caste. The aristocracy which had been hit most by the political instability, had degraded themselves in debauchery and dissipation. *Kulinism*, originally intended to maintain the purity of blood line of the higher classes, had degenerated into child marriage and polygamy. Where the higher castes had sunk to such low levels, the women could not have been expected to have a better fate. Married at quite an early age they got little, if any, opportunity of acquiring education and were kept in seclusion or *purdah*.

Grant felt that these abuses of the Indian society could be removed by the introduction of Christianity. So in 1790, when he returned home, he worked for it with greater vigour since the time for the renewal of the Company's Charter was drawing near, thus providing for an opportunity of bringing the case for evangelisation of India before the Parliament, and thereby also forcing the hands of the Directors who did not allow the missionaries to come to India for proselytisation. However, the idea had to be dropped when King George III, having been apprised of the scheme, was reluctant to support it chiefly in consequence of the alarming progress of the French Revolution and the proneness of the period to movements subversive of the established order of things. Wilberforce, MP for York, with whom Grant had been in contact before he came to London in 1790, then advised Grant to produce a paper showing a plan for the diffusion of knowledge in India, rather than for the propagation of Christianity. Grant picked up the suggestion and wrote: *Observations on the State of Society among the Asiatic subjects of Great Britain, Particularly in the Respect of morals And on the Means of Improving It.*

In his treatise which Grant wrote in 1792 and published at London in 1797, he charged the Hindus with dishonesty, corruption, fraud, mutual hatred and distrust, and described their customs such as *Sati* as barbarous; and the Muslims with haughtiness, perfidy, licentiousness and lawlessness and asserted that the intercourse of the two communities had led to the further debasement of both because each had imbibed the vices of the other. Grant blamed the East India Company for viewing those grave evils with apathy and contended that it was under no obligation to protect the creed of the Hindus which was monstrous and "subversive of the first principles of reason, morality and religion". As a remedy to all these evils, Grant suggested a "healing principle", namely, the supersession of the existing religions by Christianity through the dissemination of the science and literature of Europe, "a key which would at once open a world of new ideas" to them. Grant stated that the long intercourse between the Indians and the Europeans in Bengal rendered it feasible to use English as the medium of instruction. Moreover, he said, a knowledge of the English language would immediately place the whole range of European knowledge within their reach, while translation of English books into the Indian languages would take a long time and would be less efficacious. Grant also urged the substitution of English for Persian as the official language because that would induce the Indians to learn it. He urged the establishment of English schools under teachers "of good moral character", hoping that very soon the pupils taught in these schools would themselves become the teachers of English to their countrymen. In conclusion, he triumphantly asserted, "the true cure of darkness is light. The Hindus err because they are ignorant and their errors have never been fairly laid before them".

Grant's observations were reflections of the two forces at home, one unplanned, the other purposeful – the Industrial Revolution and the Evangelical Movement – in putting forward new social values. The Industrial Revolution created a new class of men with power and authority to set beside the old aristocratic, landowning leadership, where the latter had depended upon inheritance in a fixed hierarchical society and had set an example of grand, even extravagant living, the new men rose by personal effort, by hard work and by frugality. A new economic order developed a new code of social values and behaviour in answer to its unspoken need. Contemporaneously, a religious revival affected England which though it had its starting point in Vital Religion, in personal conversion, also served to promote such social virtues as frugality, sobriety and industry. Among the lower orders of society it was Methodism which inspired "the civilisation, the industry and sobriety of great numbers of the labouring part of the country". Among the upper classes the impulse was provided by the evangelicals and by such persons as Hannah More. They numbered in their ranks men such as Milner of Queen's College or Simeon of King's College, Cambridge, the merchant Zachary Macaulay, Wilberforce, Henry Thornton the banker and James Stephen, the lawyer, men of the class from which many of the Company's servants were drawn. In 1793, Wilberforce and Hannah More gathered round Joseph Venn, the Rector of Clapham and were there joined by Charles Grant, by Sir John Shore, Stephen, Thornton, Macaulay and others. These Claphamites were, perhaps, social conservatives in their acceptance of the order of the society, but they were radical in their determination to secure a reformation of manners and a new righteousness in the upper ranks of society.

When Henry Dundas, President of the Board of Control set up in 1784 by Pitt's India Act to supervise the activities of the Court of Directors, was shown Grant's manuscript containing his observations, he asked his Secretary, William Cabell, to write a note on it. Cabell emphasised the political advantages that could be derived from developing an education policy based on Grant's *Observations*. He mentioned that a common language would draw the ruler and the ruled into closer contact and the introduction of European education would lead to the removal of many abuses from which the people were suffering due to their "false system of beliefs and a total want of right instruction among them". However, when the subject was debated upon on the occasion of the renewal of the Company's Charter, the Attorney-General and the Solicitor General grouped the clauses into a Bill explicitly stating that the real end sought was to send missionaries and school masters to India for the ultimate conversion of Indians. And this was fully detrimental to the trading interests of the Company, dominated by men with long experience in India who considered that any such move would result in political unrest in that country.

They condemned the Bill and through some of their connections in both the Houses of Parliament manoeuvred to defeat it. And thus was lost Charles Grant's unique opportunity to become a pioneer in the introduction of Western education in India.

The Role of the Evangelists

The failure of Grant's plan of introducing Western education in India to facilitate conversion of Indians into Christianity did not mean an end to his effort to send evangelists to India. This he did indirectly. It was customary, at this time, for the Chairman of the Court of Directors to select Chaplains for Europeans in India, and Grant who subsequently came to hold the Chair, availed himself of this opportunity of sending out ardent evangelists like C. Buchanan and Henry Martin. There were also some among the retired officials of the East India Company who shared Grant's views on the introduction of Western education as a step towards proselytisation for the political benefits that it would accrue. For example, Sir John Shore after his retirement from the governor-generalship of Bengal observed: "Until our subjects there [India] shall be animated with us by a community of religious faith, we shall never consider our dominion as secure against the effects of external attack or internal commotion".

During the decade that followed, the Charter Act of 1793, the evangelicals in England focussed their attention towards finding some means of avoiding the restrictions imposed on the passage of missionaries to India by the terms of the Act. William Carey, a Baptist

Missionary and a shoemaker by profession was sent to India in 1793 in a Danish ship by the London Baptist Missionary Society and his example was followed in 1799 by two other missionaries who came in an American ship and settled down in Serampore, a Danish colony, not far away from Calcutta which was the headquarters of the East India Company in India. Carey had settled down with the help of George Udny in Dinajpore where he opened a free boarding school for poor children who were given instructions in Sanskrit, Persian and Bengali as well as in the doctrines of Christianity. In 1800, Carey joined Marshman and Ward in Serampore. With the help of a paper manufactory and the printing press which soon began to receive large commissions from the Company's establishments in Bengal, they carried on their work for the dissemination of education and propagation of Christianity among the people of Bengal.

As decided by Lord North's Regulating Act of 1773, the Charter Act of the East India Company was to be renewed every twenty years. Accordingly, when the term of the Company's Charter was due to expire in 1813, the missionaries were determined to make this occasion another trial of strength in Parliament with the Directors. In February 1812, a Committee was formed consisting of Wilberforce, Grant, Thornton, Stephen and Babington to arrange an interview on behalf of the various religious organisations in Britain. Soon there was dissension among the missionaries themselves due to the jealousy of the dissenters of the Church of England but Wilberforce managed to keep them together. He persuaded the Church of Scotland to take the lead of the Non-conformists and himself along with Grant interviewed Liverpool, the Prime Minister, who put them off with some vague promises. Moreover, Buckinghamshire, the President of the Board of Control and Castlereagh appeared cold and hostile and refused to countenance any change of the existing system.

The reluctance on the part of Castlereagh and Buckinghamshire was, however, related to the opposition of the Directors of the East India Company, who produced an imposing amount of evidence before the Committee of the House of Commons against the despatch of missionaries to India by important people who had long experiences of India and were esteemed highly by their countrymen. All emphasised the unfavourable political consequences that would follow the episcopal establishment in India. Malcolm's observations were representative of the views of the East India Company officials who deposed before the Committee. While admitting the blessings which Christianity would bestow on Indians, he warned the Committee that its introduction into India would have the most dangerous consequences for the stability of the empire which depended on the "general division of the great communities and their sub-division into various castes and tribes" because all these elements would then be united in a general opposition to any scheme which they might think would lead to their conversion.

It was at this stage, that Zachary Macaulay, encouraged by Wilberforce, organised a campaign calling on the missionary bodies to send petitions to the Parliament for the unrestrained despatch of missionaries to India. As a result between February and June 1813, no less than 837 petitions were presented. This extraordinary effort produced almost immediate effect. Liverpool and Buckinghamshire told Wilberforce that they were willing to establish a bishopric in India and to authorise the Board of Control to grant licenses to missionaries to proceed to India. In the House of Lords, the missionary question was not discussed at all, and none took the slightest notice of the vast body of evidence which the Directors of the East India Company had produced against them.

Charter Act of 1813

The new Act renewing the Company's privileges for a further period of twenty years was passed on 21 July 1813. An episcopate with archdeacons was set up in India and Board of Control was authorised to grant licenses to missionaries to proceed there. The question of dissemination of education among Indians was also taken up into consideration and a Clause to this effect was introduced in Parliament by a former Advocate General in Calcutta and was passed after a slight modification. This Clause (43rd) empowered the Governor-General to appropriate "a sum of not less than one lac of rupees" in each year out of "the surplus territorial revenues" for the revival and improvement of literature and the encouragement of the learned natives of India, and for the introduction and promotion of a knowledge of the sciences among the inhabitants of the British territories in India.

J.A. Richter, in his *History of Missions in India*, has suggested that the Clause 43 which spoke of the revival and improvement of literature and of the encouragement of the learned natives of India was created as "a reliable counterpoise, a protecting breakwater against the threatened deluge of missionary enterprise" enshrined in the

Charter Act of 1813. It is possible that the supporters of this Clause were influenced by the Orientalists in Calcutta who had been agitating for some time past for more funds for the maintenance of the Calcutta Madrasah and the Benares Sanskrit College, and for the revival and improvement of classical leaning of India. In March 1811, Minto, Governor-General of India between 1806 and 1813, had sent home a minute which definitely represented and endorsed the views of the Orientalists in India. In that minute, Minto spoke about the decay and the neglect of Indian classical learning and learned persons which could be traced to "the want of that encouragement which was formerly afforded to it by princes, chieftains and opulent individuals under the native governments". "It is seriously to be lamented", he had observed, "that a nation particularly distinguished for its love and successful cultivation of letters in other parts of the empire should have failed to extend its fostering care to the literature of the Hindoos, and to aid in opening to the learned in Europe the repositories of that literature".

While it is clear from the debates in the House of Commons and the House of Lords that by 'sciences' it was meant Western sciences, Clause 43 was otherwise quite vague. First, it is not clear what would be the maximum amount of expenditure on education and secondly, how to ascertain, in the absence of a proper financial machinery, the surplus in the territorial revenues. Since the Governor-General was the administrative head of the Presidency of Fort William only, the whole of the grant was likely to be appropriated for Bengal alone. Yet the Clause was important, inspite of its vagueness, in laying down for the first time that the dissemination of education among the people should be one of the tasks of the British Raj in India. It assumed more importance when one remembers that in those days education was not a state responsibility even in England, and except in Scotland, no public money was spent on elementary education, which was left mostly to the charity schools, the village dames, the private Sunday schools movement started by Robert Raikes and the personal efforts of individuals like Hannah More, "the bishop in petticoat" as she was then known to her contemporaries.

Note

1. Italics are Jones'.

23

Towards Education in the English Medium

The Court of Directors' Interpretation of the Clause 43 of the Charter Act of 1813

The Court of Directors informed the Governor-General of the provisions made by the Parliament for the diffusion of education among Indians on 6 September 1813, but did not send any specific instructions on the subject until 3 June 1814. In the first official despatch which showed the Court of Directors' conception of the nature and importance of the problem of education and the policy they wanted to pursue on the subject, they drew the attention of the Governor-General to the "two distinct considerations" presented by Clause 43 of the Charter Act of 1813, namely, "the encouragement of the learned natives of India and the revival and improvement of literature; secondly, the promotion of a knowledge of the sciences amongst the inhabitants of that country". They proposed to fulfil these considerations by encouraging the classical literature and sciences of the country through the long established Indian practice of giving "instruction at their own houses, and by encouraging them in the exercise and cultivation of their talents by the stimulus of honorary marks of distinctions, and in some instances by grants of pecuniary assistance". They discussed the question of establishing public colleges but summarily dismissed it as quite incompatible with the customs and mentality of the people, and asked the Governor-General Moira to gather information regarding the educational institutions of Benares, the traditional seat of Hindu learning and to devise means for their improvement. The Directors, significantly, did not make any observation on the subject of Western education but devoted the rest of the despatch to estimating the merits of Sanskrit literature which they considered to be rich in ethics and scientific works. They also hoped that "the study of these by the Europeans as well, will not only be profitable to them, but will also gradually make the Indians adopt the modern improvement in those and other sciences".

The despatch reached India at a very critical time. War had just broken out between the East India Company and Nepal and scarcely had the Company been able to conclude a victorious peace treaty with Nepal when it found itself embroiled in a war with the Marathas, then the most powerful of the Indian powers. Moira was therefore heavily preoccupied and the only thing he could do in education was to record a minute on his return from the North-Western Provinces in 1815, showing his "solicitude for the moral and intellectual condition of the Natives and his anxiety to see established and maintained some system of public education".

By 1821, the East India Company had emerged free from the prolonged series of wars which had started in 1814 and had established itself as the paramount power in India. This year also saw, for the first time, the "surplus territorial revenues" out of which Rs one lakh could now be employed for the purposes of education according to the Clause 43 of the Charter Act of 1813. The government first turned its attention to the probability of establishing the two Sanskrit Colleges as proposed by Minto in 1811 but soon gave up the idea in favour of Wilson's scheme proposing a Sanskrit College in Calcutta on the model of the Sanskrit College in Benares. This institution which would receive an annual grant of Rs 25,000 for its maintenance was to have a two-fold object, namely, "the cultivation of Hindu literature and the gradual diffusion of European knowledge through the medium of the sacred language".

Holt Mackenzie's Note on Education in the Bengal Presidency

Having enjoyed for the past three years, large surplus territorial revenues, the government decided to pursue a general policy towards educational matters in the Bengal Presidency and, therefore, took into consideration a note on the subject by Holt Mackenzie, Secretary to the Government in the Territorial Department, on 17 July 1823. In this note Mackenzie drew the attention of the government to the necessity of adoption of proper measures for the moral and intellectual improvement of the people. He suggested that the introduction of European science should form "an early part of the general scheme and should be authoritatively indicated by Government as such", and that "the Government should apply itself chiefly to the instruction of those who will themselves be teachers and to the translation, compilation and publication of useful works". When these objects had been achieved, the more immediate object of the government should be to support and establish "colleges for the instruction of what may be called the educated and influential classes" rather than "the support and establishment of elementary schools". He considered it impossible to provide for the education of the great body of people under the existing conditions. He advocated the formation of an "Association of Oriental learning with European Science and the general introduction of the latter, without any attempt arbitrarily to supersede the former". This implied the support and patronage of existing institutions as well as "a more positive encouragement to learned Natives, and consists well with the resolution to establish new institutions for the instruction of Natives in the learning of the East and of the West together". He preferred English as the medium of instruction, because its cultivation would facilitate the development of a community of language, and believed that the difficulties of introducing it had been greatly overrated. He finally proposed the establishment of a General Committee of Public Instruction for giving effect to his proposals, as well as for taking into early consideration the various suggestions made by the Madrassa Committee and the Management Committee for the establishment of the Calcutta Sanskrit College.

General Committee of Public Instruction

Mackenzie's proposal to establish a General Committee of Public Instruction was accepted by the Governor-General in Council to make use of the sum of one lakh rupees per annum in addition to such assignments as had been already made by the government and were likely to be made in the form of any endowments by individuals for the purposes laid down in the Clause 43 of the Charter Act of 1813. The Committee which was accordingly constituted with W.H. Harrington as President and H.H. Wilson as Secretary consisted of ten members. Most of these members were Oriental scholars of repute and the only wholehearted champion of "English Education" was Holt Mackenzie. Lumsden, a man of experience in educational matters and an advocate of the introduction of European science among Indians was not included in the Committee. All the members held high positions in the government and so they had little time or inclination to give much thought to their newly assigned and un-enumerative task. Moreover, none of them was particularly fit to determine an educational policy. They had spent practically the whole of their official career in the civil, medical or military service and now they found themselves suddenly elevated to the position of 'experts' on educational matters. Besides, their official experience had taught them to pay a great deal of consideration to the religious prejudices of Indians, which the government had always been at great pains not to rouse. The Committee, therefore, was ever apprehensive of hurting the sentiments of the people and never wanted to take any steps which might create antagonism. Consequently, as a rule it awaited rather than anticipated events. The Committee often carried this policy of conciliating Indian opinion far beyond reasonable limits even when the Indians themselves wanted the policy to be otherwise. Hence, the Committee's educational policy between 1823 and 1826 degenerated into a confused and confusing series of experiments which were often abandoned whilst still incomplete. Among such activities of the General Committee of Public Instruction were the recognition of the Calcutta Madrasah and the Benares Sanskrit College; establishment of a Sanskrit College at Calcutta and two more Oriental colleges at Agra and at Delhi; provision for financial assistance to some Tolls and Madrasahs; and finally employment of Oriental scholars to translate English books containing useful knowledge into Arabic, Persian and Sanskrit and undertaking the task of printing and publication of Oriental manuscripts.

Resistance to the General Committee of Public Instruction's Programmes

There is no doubt that the activities of the General Committee of Public Instruction formed in 1823 to disburse the grant on education were quite in keeping with the spirit of the interpretation of Clause 43 of the Charter Act of 1813 by the Court of Directors in their despatch of 3 June 1814 as well as by the Governor-General in his minute of 1815 but they certainly ran counter to the forces of history generated in India and England.

One such force generated in India was the impact created by the coming of the missionaries to India. Ever since the creation of the

East India Company in England in 1709, the missionaries were attracted to India for its prospects for the propagation of the Gospel. When the East India Company was just a trading concern, it used to permit and occasionally encourage such missionary activities in their areas. In South India by the late eighteenth century the Royal Danish Mission headed by such indefatigable missionaries like Ziegenbalg, Kiernander and Swartz had opened charity schools which taught Gospel to Indians through its translation in local vernaculars and had English classes attached to them not only for the children of the Company officials who could not afford to go to England, but also for the Eurasians and the Indian converts. After the Charter Act of 1813 had removed all restrictions imposed on the entry of the missionaries in India by the East India Company when it became a territorial power, many of the missionary organisations in Europe and America became active again. In Bengal, in 1818, the Baptist Missionary Society founded the Serampore College to train Indians, both Christians and non-Christians, in the arts and sciences of the West, and obtained a Danish Charter in 1827 for conferring degrees. The Serampore Mission established in 1816 the Institution for the Encouragement of Native Schools in India, and as directed by the Marquess of Hastings, extended its activities to Ajmer in Rajasthan. Under the auspices of the Calcutta Committee of the Church Missionary Society established in 1817, Captain James Stewart established schools at Calcutta, Burdwan, Khulna and Krishnanagar in Bengal and at Agra, Chunar and Meerut. The Church Missionary Society founded the Bishop College in 1820 at Shibpur (Howrah) in honour of Bishop Middleton, the first Bishop of Calcutta. The 36 schools, opened by the London Missionary Society between 1814 and 1818 and attended by nearly 3,000 children in and around Chinsurah, functioned well "as a joint Government-Missionary enterprise in the field of vernacular education in Bengal". Both the Church Missionary Society and the London Missionary Society extended their activities in vernacular schools to other parts of British India as well. In the Bombay Presidency, the London Missionary Society selected some towns in Gujarat while the Church Missionary Society was active in the districts of Poona (now Pune), Thane, Bassein and even in Sind. The American Marathi Mission started its work in 1813 and two years later opened a school for boys. In the Madras Presidency in 1817 the Society for Promoting Christian Knowledge established nine schools with a strength of 283 children and the Wesleyan Mission, starting its work in 1819, established two schools in the Madras city – one of them at Raypet which later grew to be the present Raypet College. Four years later in 1823 the same Mission established two more schools at Nagapattam.

The activities of the various missionary organisations received a new momentum and a new direction with the arrival of the Scottish Missionary, Alexander Duff, sent to India by the Church of Scotland in 1829. Hitherto, the missionary efforts – the major part of which was spent in compiling and publishing grammars and dictionaries of the different languages of India as well as translating the Bible – resulted in proselytisation only in the Indian lower classes. Duff held that the salvation of India depended on what the Bible could offer and hence the upper classes must be brought into contact with the missionaries through Western education, "inseparable from the Christian faith and its doctrines, precepts and evidence". With that end in view, he set up the General Assembly's Institution at Calcutta in 1830, out of which emerged the present Scottish Church College. Duff's institution imparted Western learning through the medium of English and made the study of the Bible a compulsory course for all who joined it.

The second force generated as a result of Clause 43 of the Charter Act was the emergence of a middle class in the capital cities of British India – Calcutta, Bombay and Madras. As English was fast becoming a language of the rulers, many Indians soon discovered that a capacity to speak and write English helped them materially. With increasing clerical posts in the growing British establishments, including some mercantile establishments which were fast coming up since the beginning of the nineteenth century, the knowledge of English proved to be useful. While the 'ordinary' men were concerned with the material benefits of the knowledge of English, some educated and liberal minded Indians, through their long interaction with the Europeans in Calcutta, had realised the futility of pursuing a system of exclusively classical education and the great possibilities which a knowledge of the language and literature of the West afforded. Hence, they were anxious for the diffusion of European education and English language among their countrymen. Of these the most prominent was Rammohan Roy, a retired Revenue Officer of the Company. Born in 1774 in an aristocratic and well-to-do Hindu family of West Bengal, Rammohan had, early in life, developed a profound detestation for the heathenism and gross superstition into which the Hindu religion had degenerated. When he was only 16 years old, he had written a pamphlet denouncing the existing forms of religion, which had resulted in his expulsion from home. Though temporarily reconciled to his family later, he could never accustom himself to the existing customs of the society. He, therefore, devoted himself to the study of the different languages of Asia and Europe and the scriptures of different religious system, in order to discover the "True Religion". Those studies together with his close connection with the Europeans and especially the missionaries, as well as persecution by his fellow religionists, ultimately led to his severance from the orthodox fold; and thenceforth he devoted himself to the teaching of Vedic Monotheism. He was thus admirably suited, not only to lead the advanced sections of the Indians but also to act as the intermediary between them and those Europeans like David Hare, a watch-maker by profession, who had come to India in 1800 and was solicitous of the well-being of the Indians. In 1815 Roy and Hare drew up a plan for an English institution at Calcutta and though Roy had to withdraw at the last stage because of opposition from orthodox Hindus to his professed religion, the school was opened on 20 January 1817, with 20 scholars receiving tuition in English, Bengali and Persian. A. Howell truly remarks in his *Education in British India prior to 1854 and in 1870-71* that "the foundation of this college marks an important era in the history of education in India, the first spontaneous desire manifested by the natives in the country for instruction in English and the literature of Europe". This was followed by the creation, through the combined efforts of the Indians, Europeans and the missionaries, of the Calcutta School Book Society and in 1819 the Calcutta School Society. The former was to promote "the moral and intellectual improvement of the Natives by diffusion among them of useful elementary knowledge", and the latter to open schools in Calcutta and its vicinity and to prepare teachers for the improvement of the indigenous schools. As early as 1821, the Calcutta School Society had 115 vernacular schools with a total strength of 3,328 pupils under its umbrella.

The third force emerged in England when, simultaneous with this development in vernacular and English education in British India, utilitarianism was fast becoming a dominant influence in British society in the second and third decades of the nineteenth century. In 1818, Sir Francis Burdett, at the zenith of his patriotism, applied to Bentham for assistance in framing a series of resolutions embracing the principles of radical reform which he wanted to place before the House of Commons. His resolutions were defeated but since that time Burdett became the spokesman of Bentham in and outside Parliament. And as Bowring observes: "Benthamism had in like manner been quickly carried off by less prominent characters and deposited unnoticed in public mind, there to strike root. He [Bentham] co-operated with the enemies of slavery in every land, with the humanizers of the penal codes, with the advocates of universal education. In his intellectual armoury were stored up implements fitted for the purpose of them all, and everyman was welcome to take and use". Young states that "in discipleship or reaction no young mind of the thirties could escape their [the utilitarians'] influence. Benthanm's alliance with James Mill, Mill's friendship with Malthus and Ricardo had created a party, almost a sect with formularies as compact as the Evangelical theology and conclusions no less exorable". The impact of the development of utilitarianism was seen on a number of young men who had just grown up into active employment and it was they who became the most efficient agents in the realisation of Bentham's principles. Many among them were now sent out to India in the employ of the East India Company. Secondly, it was James Mill, the faithful lieutenant of Jeremy Bentham who questioned the values of the Indian society and disagreed with Hastings, Jones, Wilkins and Wilson in their admiration of these in his *History of British India* which he undertook in 1806 and finished in 1817. The work obtained for him not only his reputation as a historian but also an appointment in the East India House, as well as of his more famous son, John Stuart Mill later, which led to the establishment of utilitarian influence in the headquarters of the East India Company. James Mill found nothing to praise in the Indian institutions, nothing to admire in the values of the Indian society and religion and saw almost nothing which appeared to him worth preserving. He considered Indian society to be static and stagnant. And so he suggested its reform on the Benthamite principles and pointed out that the key to progress lay in the introduction of Western science and knowledge.

These forces of change developing in India and in Great Britain soon began to resist the activities of the General Committee of Public Instruction. As soon as the proposal of the Committee to establish a Sanskrit College at Calcutta came to be known, it was opposed. In a letter to Lord Amherst, the Governor-General of Bengal, on 11

December 1823, Rammohan Roy pointed out that the proposed Sanskrit College "would impart such knowledge as is already current in India" thereby impeding the progress of the English education in India. He suggested that the proposal for establishing a Sanskrit College in Calcutta should be abandoned and the Government should "promote a more liberal and enlightened system of instruction: embracing mathematics, natural philosophy, chemistry, anatomy, with other useful sciences, which may be accomplished with the sum proposed by employing a few gentlemen of talents and learning educated in Europe and providing a college furnished with accessory, books, instruments and other apparatus". However, Rammohan Roy's protests bore no immediate fruit and the Government opened a Sanskrit College in Calcutta in 1824 and another College at Delhi for "instruction in the three classical languages of India".

A still more formidable attack on the Committee's work came from the headquarters of the East India Company in London. In a despatch of 18 February 1824, which bore Mill's stamp, the Directors wrote: "We apprehend that the plan of the institutions to the improvement of which our attention is now directed was originally and fundamentally erroneous. The great end should not have been to teach Hindu learning, but useful learning.... In professing, on the other hand, to establish seminaries for the purpose of teaching mere Hindu or mere Mohamadan literature, you bound yourselves to teach a great deal of what was frivolous, not a little of what was purely mischievous, a small remained indeed in which utility was in any way concerned".

The Committee which was in close touch with the view of the Pandits hesitated to embark on so large a measure of innovation and in a letter of 18 August 1824 informed the Governor-General that the Hindus and Muslims had vigorous prejudices against European learning; that Oriental literature was not to be summarily condemned and that it had a utility of its own; that the use of a classical language as a medium of instruction was unavoidable; that there were neither books nor teachers available just then to impart instruction in European sciences through such a medium; that the Committee was concentrating on the preparation of such books and the training of such teachers; and that before long the Directors' instructions would be fully complied with.

The Committee however went ahead with its work of promoting Oriental learning in India. The only fallout of the

Directors' letter at that moment was the addition of English classes to the Calcutta Madrasah in 1824 and following another from them on 5 September 1827 which stressed the need "to prepare a body of individuals for discharging public duties". English classes were also added to the Calcutta Sanskrit College (1827) and the Delhi College (1828). By 1828 however, a new Governor-General, Lord William Bentinck had arrived on the scene. He was undoubtedly affected by the contemporary utilitarianism in England. In a farewell dinner at Grote's house, just on the eve of his departure for India as Governor-General in December 1827, he had said to James Mill, "I am going to British India but I shall not be Governor-General. It is you, that will be Governor-General". A man of great energy and vigour, Bentinck utilised the long period of peace enjoyed by his government in tackling every problem that his administration faced in India – he was the person who made *Sati* illegal in 1829 and took steps to stop other social evils like *Thugi* and infanticide. In a letter to the General Committee of Public Instruction on 26 June 1829, he observed: "It is the wish and admitted policy of the British Government to render its own language gradually and eventually the language of public business throughout the country, and that it will omit no opportunity of giving every reasonable and practical degree of encouragement to the execution of this project". As a respect to the wishes of the Governor-General, the Committee added English classes to the Benares Sanskrit College in 1830 thereby providing for English classes in all the important Oriental institutions at Calcutta, Delhi and Benares. However, events outside the control of the Committee soon happened and they overtook the Committee's zeal for promoting Oriental Institutions and learning in India.

By 1830, the General Committee of Public Instruction which consisted of ten members had among them some young men who were profoundly influenced by the utilitarian ideas of James Mill and Bentham and were in no mood to support the Committee's work for promotion of Oriental culture and learning in India. With the departure of Horace Hayman Wilson from India in January 1833, the Orientalists lost one of their staunch supporters while the Charter Act of 1833 which renewed the Company's privileges for a further period of twenty years brought Macaulay as Law Member of the Council of the Governor-General of India to the shore of India on 8 June 1834. The Charter Act which bore the stamp of the age of English liberalism by its abolition of the commercial privileges of the

Company and by its declaration that "no native of India, nor any natural-born subject of His Majesty, should be disabled from holding any place, or employment, by reason of his religion, place of birth, descent or colour" increased the educational grant of rupees one lakh in 1813 to rupees ten lakh (£ 1,00,000) per year.

Macaulays Minute on 2 February 1835

Immediately after Macaulay's arrival in India, as the Law Member of his Council, Bentinck appointed him as the President of the General Committee of Public Instruction for his known intellectual attainments. Macaulay, whose interest in consolidating the British empire by the propagation of English laws and English culture began quite early in his life, grew up, being the son of Zachary Macaulay, in the circle of the Clapham Evangelists. Initially he did not take part in the controversy of the Committee. It was only when the Orientalists as well as the Anglicists decided to approach Bentinck after their failure to come to a decision on the future education policy of the government (occasioned by the question of converting the Calcutta Madrasah into an institution of Western learning as well as of reorganising the Agra College on the model of the Hindu College in Calcutta) that he drew up a long and elaborate minute championing the cause of English education in his usual characteristic prose marked by rhetoric and antithesis on 2 February 1835, at the suggestion of Bentinck.

Macaulay argued that the word 'literature' occurring under Clause 43 of the Charter Act of 1813 could be interpreted to mean English literature, that the epithet of a "learned native of India" could also be applied to a person versed in the philosophy of Locke or the poetry of Milton and that the object of promoting a knowledge of science could only be accomplished by the adoption of English as the medium of instruction. If this interpretation was not accepted, he was willing to propose an Act rescinding Section 43 of the Charter. He was against the continuance of institutions of Oriental learning and suggested that these should be closed as they did not serve any useful purpose: "We found a sanatorium on a spot which we suppose to be healthy. Do we thereby pledge ourselves to keep a sanatorium there if the result should not answer our expectations?"

On the subject of the medium of instruction, Macaulay pointed out that all parties agreed "that the dialects commonly spoken among the natives of this part of India contain neither literary nor scientific information, and are moreover so poor and rude that until they are enriched from some other quarter, it will not be easy to translate any valuable work into them. It seems to be admitted on all sides, that the intellectual improvement of those classes of the people who have the means of pursuing higher studies can, at present, be effected only by means of some language not vernacular amongst them". The choice of the medium of instruction was naturally left between Sanskrit and Arabic on the one hand and English on the other. Macaulay who admittedly did not have any "knowledge of either Sanskrit or Arabic" brushed aside the claims of these two languages to be the medium of instruction by observing that "a single shelf of a good European library was worth the whole native literature of India and Arabia". On the other hand, the claims of English could hardly be necessary to recapitulate. As he said, "It stands pre-eminent among the languages of the West.... whoever knows that language has already access to all the vast intellectual wealth which all the wisest nations of earth have created and hoarded in the course of ninety generations. It may safely be said that the literature now extant in that language is of greater value than all the literature which three hundred years ago was extant in all the languages of the world together.... In India, English is the language spoken by the ruling class. It is spoken by the higher class of natives at the seats of Government. It is likely to become the language of commerce throughout the seas of the East".

He referred to the alleged prejudices of the Indian people against English education and argued that it was the duty of England to teach Indians what was good for their health, and not what was palatable to their taste. He further pointed out that the Indians themselves preferred an English education to their own as the crowding of the Hindu College and the Scottish Church College in Calcutta and the comparative desertion of the Sanskrit College and the Madrasah in the same city inspite of its stipends showed. He also mentioned that while the Committee of Public Instruction was finding it hard to dispose of the Oriental publications, the English books of the Calcutta School Book Society were selling in thousands. "The question now before us", Macaulay observed, "is simply whether when it is in our own power to teach this language, we shall teach languages in which, by universal experience, there are no books on any subject which deserve to be compared to our own; whether, when we can teach European science, we shall teach systems which, by universal confession, wherever they differ from those of Europe, differ for the worse; and whether, when we can patronize school philosophy and true history, we shall countenance, at the public expense, medical doctrines which would disgrace an English farrier, astronomy which would move laughter in girls at an English boarding house, history abounding in kings thirty feet high and reigns thirty thousand years long, and geography made of seas of treacle and seas of butter".

Macaulay suggested that the government should not incur any heavy expenditure on the maintenance of Oriental institutions of learning which could be used for the promotion of English education. If Sanskrit and Arabic were essential as the languages of the law and religion of the people, government should start codifying Hindu and Muslim laws in English. In one respect Macaulay agreed with his opponents. He admitted that it was impossible to train the mass of the population. "We must, at present, do our best", he contended, "to form a class who may be interpreters between us and the millions whom we govern, a class of persons Indian in blood and colour, but English in taste, in opinions, in morals and intellect. To that class we may leave it to refine the vernacular dialects of the country, to enrich their dialects with terms of science borrowed from the Western nomenclature and to render them by degrees fit vehicles for conveying knowledge to the greater mass of the population".

Macaulay, however, was ready to respect some of the existing interest but would like to "strike at the root of the bad system which has hitherto been tolerated by us". He advocated that the printing of the Oriental works should be stopped, all Oriental colleges except that at Delhi and Benares – these being chief seats of Oriental learning – should be abolished and all stipends should be discontinued. Macaulay loosened his last shaft at Oriental education by declaring that "the present system stands not to accelerate the progress of truth but delay the natural death of expiring errors" and threatened to resign if his suggestions were not approved.

Bentinck's Decision on 7 March 1835

Bentinck gave his "entire concurrence" to the sentiments expressed by Macaulay despite Prinsep's note of 15 February answering some of the observations made by Macaulay on Oriental institutions and learning. In a resolution of 7 March 1835, Bentinck passed the following order:

First: His Lordship is of opinion that the great object of the British Government ought to be the promotion of European literature and science amongst the natives of India and that all the funds appropriated for the purposes of education would be best employed in English education.

Second: But it is not the intention of His lordship in Council to abolish any college or school of native learning while the native population shall appear to be inclined to avail themselves of the advantages it affords, and His Lordship in Council directs that all the existing professors and students at all the institutions under the superintendence of the Committee shall continue to receive their stipends.

Third: It has come to the knowledge of the Governor-General in Council that a large sum has been expended by the Committee in the printing of Oriental works. His Lordship in Council directs that no portion of the funds shall hereafter be so employed.

Fourth: His Lordship in Council directs that all the funds which these reforms will leave at the disposal of the Committee be henceforth employed in imparting to the native population a knowledge of English literature and science, through the medium of the English language.

And thus was taken the most momentous decision in the history of India – not to speak of the history of education in India.

Bentinck's order of 7 March 1835 came as a climax to the two important official steps he had already taken earlier – one was the decision to establish a Medical College at Calcutta to teach Medicine and Surgery according to the European system in English. This was more on the model visualised by Rammohan Roy more than a decade ago. The other was the appointment of William Adam, the Baptist missionary, to report on the state of vernacular education in Bengal, Bihar and Orissa.

An Estimate of the Part played by Bentinck and Macaulay in the Introduction of English Education in India

In India, Thomas Babington Macaulay is fully credited with the introduction of English education officially, though the necessary order on the subject was issued by Bentinck, the Governor-General of India, on 7 March 1835, after going through a long rhetorical minute written by the former on 2 February 1835 at the latter's request. Needless to say, in issuing this order on English education, Bentinck put his own political career in India at enormous risk. For, according to the rules of the East India Company, the Governor-General in India could not initiate any important action without first obtaining the approval of its executive body, the Court of Directors in London. Since Bentinck took the decision within a few weeks of receiving the papers from the General Committee of Public Instruction, it was clear that the Governor-General did not have the necessary time to obtain the required sanction of the Court of Directors. In those days of steamship navigation, a despatch from Calcutta used to take not less than three months to reach London. This simple fact does not need the scholarship of a Spear or a Ballhatchet to prove or disprove that Bentinck acted without the authority of the East India Company in London. Writing on the subject more than a hundred years later in *The Education of India* Arthur Mayhew argued that Bentinck took the decision without reading Macaulay's minute and was solely motivated by Macaulay's threat to resign. Such an argument is contrary to the image of Bentinck that has emerged through recent researches as a true child of his age.

Bentinck who came to India as the Governor-General in July 1828 was a firm believer in utilitarian principles. In a farewell dinner at Grote's house in December 1827 just on the eve of his departure for India, he had said to James Mill: "I am going to British India but I shall not be Governor-General. It is you that will be Governor-General", A man of great energy, vigour and action he utilised the long period of peace enjoyed by his government to tackle every problem that his administration faced in India – he was the person who made *Sati* illegal in 1829 and took steps to stop other social evils like *Thugi* and infanticide. He believed that it was English education alone which could cure Indian society of its various evils. In a letter to Metcalfe in September 1829 he described "the British language" [sic] as "the key of all improvements". Acting on his firm belief he took every step to widen the use of the English language in official work. He also persuaded young Indians to learn English by throwing open subor-dinate positions in judicial and revenue branches to the English educated young men though mainly as a measure of economy. In a letter to the General Committee of Public Instruction on 26 June 1829 he observed: "It is the wish and admitted policy of the British Government to render its own language gradually and eventually the language of public business throughout the country, and that it will omit no opportunity of giving every reasonable and practical degree of encouragement to the execution of this project". As a mark of respect to the wishes of the Governor-General, the General Committee of Public Instruction added English classes to the Benares Sanskrit College in 1830 thereby providing for English classes in all the important Oriental institutions in Calcutta, Delhi and Benares.

A gradual replacement of Persian by English in all official works as well as the spread of English language in educational institutions – these were the twin objects that Bentinck kept before him from the very beginning of his term as the Governor-General of India. His official position did not allow him to support the evangelists in India directly but he was sympathetic to those missionaries who took utmost care in the use of English in their educational institutions. He helped Alexander Duff, the Scottish missionary, to set up his General Assembly's Institution at Calcutta in 1830 which later grew to the still existing Scottish Church College. In 'a Private interview' given to Alexander Duff in February 1833, Bentinck "heartily approved of the design of giving a higher education to a select few, in preference to the plan of giving a common education to the many". He told Duff that "if there was one opinion on which he was more decided than another it was the expediency of teaching English in all our Higher Seminaries, gradually substituting it throughout every department of government business, instead of the Persian which ought as soon as possible to be abolished".

One reason why Bentinck was so keen on introducing English education was because he considered it not only to be a 'cure' for the kind of social evils that he had to deal with at the very beginning of his administration in India but also a key to the improvement of the country. In this respect he fully shared with James Mill the view that Indian society was decadent and the key to its regeneration lay in the introduction of Western knowledge and science. In a letter to Mancy on 1 June 1834, he explained: "General education is my panacea for the regeneration of India. The ground must be prepared and the jungle cleared away before the human mind can receive, with any prospect of *real*[1] benefit, the seeds of improvement... You will anticipate my entire dissent from those who think it better that the natives should remain in ignorance. I cannot regard the advantage of ignorance to the governors or the governed. If our rule is bad, as I believe it to be, let the natives have the means through knowledge, to represent their grievances and to obtain redress. If their own habits, morals or way of thinking are inconsistent with their own happiness and improvement, let them have the means provided by our greater intelligence of discovering their errors. I approve, therefore, of every plan by which the human mind can be instructed .and of course elevated..."

Such a plan came through Macaulay's minute of 2 February 1835 as an expert advice on the subject and Bentinck immediately acted on it. Macaulay, whose interest in consolidating the British empire by the propagation of English laws and English culture began quite early in life when he grew up as the son of Zachary Macaulay in the circle of the Clapham evangelists and gave evidence of it in his Parliamentary speech on 10 July 1833 on the occasion of the renewal of the East India Company's Charter, held similar views on the subject with Bentinck. And it will not be unreasonable to surmise that there had been earlier discussions on it either at the time when they were together in the Ootacamund in the Nilgiris in the summer of 1834 or at the time when Macaulay was appointed by Bentinck as President of the General Committee of Public Instruction in December 1834 at a time when the Committee was seized with the controversy on the future education policy of India. Assuming there had been no such occasions, it was still possible for Macaulay to know the Governor-General's mind through C.E. Trevelyan, a staunch Anglicist and a great favourite among Bentinck's officials, who was also married to Macaulay's sister. The threat of resignation held out by Macaulay if his recommendations on English education were not accepted was not a threat meant for Bentinck but a subtle challenge thrown to the opponents of English education in India.

The reason why Bentinck issued the order without obtaining the approval of the Court of Directors was because of the fact that following the return of the Tory Party to power in England Bentinck was contemplating his retirement as Governor-General of India by the end of March 1835. He did not want to leave the fate of a subject so dear to his heart to his successor and took immediate steps to decide on it on 7 March 1835. And he did so at a price – he earned the displeasure of the Court of Directors to such an extent that back home he withdrew from the affairs of the Company and led a secluded life. The Court of Directors on the other hand almost decided to reverse the order of 7 March 1835 by sending a despatch to Calcutta – the draft of the despatch was almost ready by October 1836 but was never sent as Hobhouse, the President of the Board of

Control, did not accept the draft despatch sent to him by Carnac, Chairman of the Court of Directors, under pressure from Auckland, the Governor-General of India.

Macaulay's minute became a secretarial sensation from the very moment of its composition on 2 February 1835. It shot him to further prominence in England and in India. Within four years large portions of the minute were made public by the zeal of Macaulay's brother-in-law, Charles Trevelyan and within hundred years, that is by 1935, it had been published either in full or in part on nine different occasions. The already great reputation of Macaulay assured the minute's notoriety in India,[2] and later his meridian fame secured its cordial reception in England. We must however remember that the minute did not initiate any new policy though it signalled the advance of a policy already pursued by Bentinck since 1829. It gave Bentinck the confidence to go forward on a subject in which he lacked the necessary intellectual, though certainly not moral, conviction.[3]

Significance of Bentinck's Decision

Bentinck's order of 7 March 1835 not only opened Europe to India but India to Europe and signalled the advent of far reaching socio-economic and political changes in India in a none too distant future and as said earlier, it became a milestone in the history of India. As a matter of fact, Bentinck's decision of 7 March 1835 contained within it the seeds of another development besides the promotion of Western education which he could have hardly foreseen at that moment. It was the development of vernacular languages which Bentinck's Resolution did not mention and the Orientalists who lost the battle with the Anglicists soon began to argue that European education could best be filtered to the masses only through vernacular education and began to clamour for financial support for its promotion. In a sense, therefore, Bentinck's decision of 7 March 1835 while cutting at the financial roots for Oriental learning, paved the way not only for the emergence of English as the most powerful language in British India but also for the development of vernacular languages which the missionaries had been popularising along with English in their schools while propagating the Gospel among Indians since 1813.

Notes

1. Italics are Bentinck's
2. During the freedom struggle in India, Macaulay's summary rejection and condemnation of Indian history, culture and civilisation in his minute of 2 February 1835 was used by the militant nationalist leaders to whip up anti-Raj feelings among the Indians.
3. For fuller details, see my article, "Bentick, Macaulay and the Introduction of English Education in India: in *History of Education*, London, 1995, Vol. 24, No. 1, pp. 17-24.

24

The Decade After 1835

Orientalists supported Petitions against Bentinck's Resolution of 7 March 1835

The Resolution of 7 March 1835 could not finally settle the disputes regarding the nature of education to be imparted to the Indians. Macaulay's minute, though kept a secret, had somehow leaked out, and "in three days a petition was got up and signed by no less than 30,000 people, on behalf of the Madrasah and another by the Hindus for the Sanskrit College". The Muslim petition written in Persian drew the attention of the government to the fact that it was its duty to encourage the learning of the people and warned it against the danger of vexing their spirit, stating that it was "necessary for the Government to enlist the goodwill and support of the Mussalmans, as it was through them and from them that the Government had got their Indian territories." In this the Orientalists were supported by a large number of Indians, both Hindus and Muslims who, though they had been in favour of English education before, now thought that the exclusive patronage of English education would be the first step towards the ultimate Anglicisation and conversion of the people. Moreover, however much they might have been anxious for English education, they were never in the least ready to see all patronage and support withdrawn from their own literature and science. Hence, they ceaselessly petitioned the government praying that the Resolution be modified.

The government, however, declared that the instructions imparted there would be adapted to future needs and expressed surprise at the needless alarm excited. It informed the Muslim petitioners that the Madrasah would be kept in its existing footing so long as the Muslims resort to it for educational purposes, and that "no one while he conducts himself with propriety will at any time be deprived of any stipend". The government also assured the students of the Sanskrit College on 8 April 1835, in reply to their petition, that the pecuniary grants would be continued to the present incumbents, although no new grants could be made in future.

Macnaughten's Minute on 24 March 1835

In a long minute of 24 March 1835, Macnaughten supported by H. Shakespeare and James Prinsep restated the Orientalist cause and declared that the falling off in the number of students was no criterion for the abolition of professorships and scholarships, because such a diminution might be of a temporary nature and if this criterion were adopted, it should apply to the English classes as well. He also pointed out that the government's reply to Muslims was inconsistent with the tenor of the Resolution of 7 March 1835, and observed that, inspite of the government's intention to abolish stipends they had been re instituted at the Calcutta Medical College. Macnaughten further advocated the importance of using Indian languages as the medium of education in order to conciliate the orthodox section of Indians and declared, "the grand object...to be kept in view in giving instruction in the English language is not so much that few who make themselves masters of its invaluable treasures should be enlightened, but that through their means the light should be diffused over the whole surface of the society". He therefore advised the government to approach the Directors for further grants with which schools and colleges should be established at all the large stations for both English and Oriental education, whereby a knowledge of the literature and science of Europe could be gradually engrafted upon Indians.

However, the government had no intention of reopening the question. Unable to persuade the government, Macnaughten resigned his membership of the General Committee of Public Instruction. His step was followed by James Prinsep who had supported Macnaughten. H.T. Prinsep, however, refused to let the matter drop here and carried on his agitation. Entirely concurring with Macnaughten in a minute of 20 May 1835, he bitterly accused

Macaulay and Bentinck of not allowing any reply to Macaulay's arguments to appear on record. He ended by indicting the late Governor General with making nominations, before his departure, to the General Committee in order to ensure a majority for the Anglicists. The government, now under the administration of Metcalfe, simply decided to send a copy of the minute to the Directors.

The Orientalists attempted to promote Vernacular Education

It was at this time that the General Committee of Public Instruction tried to establish a system of vernacular instruction in the provinces. During the heated discussions on the Anglo-Oriental controversy, the claims of the vernaculars had been summarily rejected, because they were not considered sufficiently developed to act as the medium of instruction. The Resolution of Bentinck also did not make any mention of the vernacular languages. The Committee, however, did not give up the idea of enriching and using them for educational purposes. In its report for the year 1835, it declared, "it would be our aim, did the funds at our command admit of it, to carry the... process on until an elementary school for instruction in the vernacular languages should be established in every village in the country". This was a deviation from the policy laid down in the Resolution of Bentinck and the Committee, therefore, tried to justify its policy. It pointed out that the main issue in the controversy was the rival claims of Oriental and English systems of education, and therefore, the government's decision did not prevent it from cultivating the vernaculars. The Committee also observed that even if the government had decided in favour of the former, the mass of the people would have to be educated through their own tongues, and declared "the formations of a native literature to be the ultimate object to which our efforts must be directed". To achieve this, they thought it necessary, for the time being, to cultivate "some learned foreign tongue" for improving the minds of the people, so that the best educated among them would be able to translate English words into the vernaculars. In pursuance of this object, the Committee attached teachers of vernacular languages to many of the institutions.

The General Committee of Public Instruction considered Adam's Scheme for the Improvement of Vernacular Education

Towards the end of 1838, the Committee took into consideration the three Reports of William Adam who was appointed by Bentinck in January 1835 to enquire into the state of vernacular education in Bengal, Bihar and Orissa. Adam had submitted his first report in 1835, second in 1836 and the third on 10 April 1838, giving a complete statistics of the number of schools in South Bihar, Tirhoot, Beerbhom, Burdwan and Murshidabad till 1838. In the last 119 pages of the third report, Adam submitted his scheme for the improvement of vernacular education. Adam considered it impossible to introduce compulsory education and also rejected the idea of instituting model schools on a graded system, beginning from the village schools and ending with the government Zillah schools. In order, therefore, to encourage education without compulsion, he recommended a plan of "payment by result". According to this system, rewards were to be given on results of examinations. The teachers were to be the first ones to be examined. For the examination of these teachers Adam suggested the appointment of examiners well-versed in European as well as Indian educational systems. All the teachers appearing for examination were to receive travelling allowances and the successful ones were to be given certificates of distinction, made eligible to enter normal schools, and finally appointed inspectors and examiners. Adam also suggested that each teacher should be allowed to recommend some of his pupils for examination and those students who would distinguish themselves in the highest class should become eligible for filling vacancies in the English school of the district. From his close investigations Adam had realised that want of discipline greatly handicapped the progress of the vernacular schools. To rectify this he suggested three methods, namely, written directions, practical examples in the examination of the teachers and their students and the precept and example combined in the normal schools. Adam also proposed the use of the vernacular classes of the English seminaries as normal schools. As a final reward, Adam suggested the endowment of each teacher suitably qualified under this system, after being recommended by two-thirds of the landowners, tenants and householders of the village to which he belonged, by a grant of land of an annual value not exceeding half the average annual income of a vernacular teacher of the district. A teacher might be deprived of his land on complaint of not less than one-fourth of the persons who had petitioned for the endowment after an independent government enquiry. Adam rejected the idea of introducing moral text-books. He declared that the best means of inculcating religious education without arousing apprehensions would be without employing any direct forms of religious inculcation to cause the spirit of religion, its philanthropic and devotional feeling to pervade the whole body of instruction on other subjects. Adam also proposed that the landowners and others should form a "village school association", which might develop as a nucleus for the "purposes of Municipal government, village police, local improvement and statistical knowledge", but he declared that before putting the scheme into operation the government should take a census and make an educational survey of the districts selected for the purpose.

The Committee found Adam's scheme of improving and extending the indigenous village schools impracticable and too expensive and opposed to the idea of filtrating education from the upper and middle classes to the masses. It, however, agreed to experiment with rural education on a limited scale in about 20 schools near Calcutta and suggested appointments of two inspectors to report on the progress of the schools. The Committee also suggested that the scheme be tried for three years after which, if no progress was witnessed, the scheme should be given up. But the government rejected the proposal, and Adam resigned his appointment and the Directors while endorsing the views of the government declared in their despatch of 23 February 1842 that when sufficient means had been provided for the education of the higher and middle classes and a complete set of vernacular textbooks had been prepared "then Mr. Adam's proposals might be taken up on a liberal and effective scale with some fairer prospect of success".

Auckland's Minute on 24 November 1839

Lord Auckland who, since his succession to Bentinck in March 1836 through Metcalfe as the Governor-General, had been watching these developments in education expressed his views in a minute of 24 November 1839. He frankly admitted:

> that the insufficiency of the funds assigned by the state for the purposes of public instruction has been amongst the main causes of the violent disputes which have taken place upon the education

question, and that if the funds previously appropriated to the cultivation of Oriental literature had been spread and then means placed
at the disposal of the promoters of English education, they might
have pursued their object aided by the good wishes of all.... The sum
immediately at command was limited. Parties wishing to promote
the diffusion of knowledge in different forms contended eagerly,
the one to retain, the other to gain, that sum for the schemes to
which they were respectively favourable, and had fresh sums been
at once procurable, no one might have objected to their
employment for a full and fair experiment on the new ideas which
began to prevail. The inference to which I would point from these
facts and observations is that a principle of wise liberality, not
stinting any object which can reasonably be recommended, but
granting a measured and discriminating encouragement to all, is
likely to commend general acquiescence and to obliterate, it may be
hoped, the recollection of the acrimony which had been so preju-
dicial to the public weal in the course of past proceedings.

Accordingly, Auckland restored the old grants sanctioned before
1835 to the Orientalists and desired that the funds for the Oriental
colleges be first appropriated for Oriental studies and then for English
instruction. He then guaranteed the maintenance of the Oriental
colleges and proposed to replace the stipends by scholarships to the
extent of one-fourth of total number of students on the rolls of the
Oriental institutions. He also sanctioned the preparation and publication of useful works for instruction in classical languages within the
limits of the prescribed funds. The Orientalists were more than
satisfied and Auckland could boast that with an additional expenditure of a meagre sum of Rs 31,000 per year, he could close a heated
controversy. Secondly, Auckland felt that the improvement of the
moral and intellectual condition of the people could be effected only
through the dissemination of European science and literature which,
he thought, could be done only through he medium of English
because the transmission of English education through translations
must necessarily be slow and limited in extent. He pointed out that
the chief inducement to acquire English education was still the
prospect of earning a good livelihood and referred to the question
already mooted of training and employing educated Indians as assistants to the zillah judges in the capacity of *moonsiffs*. Auckland who
was greatly influenced by the filtration theory impressed upon the

Committee that preference should be given "to rendering the highest instruction efficient in a certain number of Central Colleges, rather than employing funds in the extension of the plan of founding ordinary zillah schools". He selected Dacca, Patna, Benares or Allahabad, Agra and Bareilly as the places where the Central Colleges were to be established. These places were chosen because they had a large population and were conveniently situated. He suggested inclusion of the study of jurisprudence, government and morals and encouraged the use of college libraries. One of the objects of these colleges was to raise a class of "inferior schoolmasters". He further proposed to link these colleges with the proposed zillah schools by a comprehensive system of scholarships tenable for four years so that the ablest students of the latter might continue with the higher course of study without being hampered by financial consideration. He also remodelled the existing system of scholarships in the Hindu College so as to enable the students to stay there longer. Finally, he discussed the question of the utility and practicability of using the vernaculars as the medium of instruction in the zillah schools but considered such step to be rather premature because of the absence of suitable vernacular text-books and qualified teachers. It was on these grounds that he declared that Adam's plan should be undertaken only when a sufficient number of school books had been prepared and when the scheme could be laid under a liberal scale under proper managements.

Implementation of Auckland's Plan

The General Committee of Public Instruction communicated its sentiments on the minute of Auckland on 30 October, 1840. It submitted a detailed account of the institutions under its control, the expenses incurred in them and suggested various reforms and adjustments. It pointed out that in order to render the existing seminaries effective, and to extend their scope a further sum of Rs 1,40,471 per annum would be necessary. The Committee also stressed the necessity of recruiting suitable professors for ethics, political economy and jurisprudence which should be taught to start with at the Hindu (Anglo-Indian) College as the other institutions had not yet improved to the required extent. Since the Directors had not communicated their sentiments either on the Resolution of Bentinck or on the Minute of Auckland, Auckland adopted the measures without further delay and informed the Court accordingly.

The Court of Directors approved Auckland's Plan

Meanwhile, the Court of Directors were obviously watching the course of events in Bengal. In January 1841, still unaware of the measures taken by the government in Bengal, they communicated their approval of Auckland's suggestions. They deliberately refrained from reopening the controversy, but while ordering that the funds of the Oriental colleges should be used exclusively for those institutions, declared that the great object of the government should be to disseminate English education as laid down in the resolution of 7 March, 1835. They however refrained from expressing any opinion as to the best mode of doing this because they held that the experience hitherto gained did not "warrant the adoption of any exclusive system". But the Court of Directors approved the plan proposed by Auckland and authorised him "to give all suitable encouragement to translator of European works into the vernacular languages and also to provide for the compilation of a proper series of vernacular class books".

Importance of Auckland's Plan

The importance of Auckland's Plan which had hitherto received less notice cannot be underestimated. His minute of November 1839 on education was not written during a period of heated controversy. Auckland, through necessarily outside the controversies of 1835, had been able to watch dispassionately the working of the system established by Bentinck. The system was frankly based on the negation of the cherished tradition and desires of the people who although anxious to acquire a knowledge of the European arts and sciences, were not ready to see their own literature and learning excluded from the government seminaries. They also feared that the withdrawal of the government's patronage from Oriental education was only the first step to the ultimate interference with their customs, tradition and religion. Bentinck's government had grossly underestimated the difficulties which beset the path of English education and had paid no regard to the claims of the vernaculars and the necessity of providing for some type of pecuniary inducements for the students. It had not tried or claimed to lay down any comprehensive policy, but had simply settled the dispute between the rival claims of Oriental and English education. The government, however, tried to act according to this resolution and found that it could not be worked. It realised that the two systems of education should be kept distinct and cultivated separately, and abolished the English class in the Sanskrit College. It found that Indians were not ready to sacrifice their own system of learning, so it had to maintain the existing Oriental colleges and also on certain cases to continue the stipends on the former scale as happened in the case of the Madrasah. The authorities also had to assign an adequate share of the proposed scholarships to the Oriental colleges. Lastly, the government was convinced that it was not possible to spread education among the masses through the English language and that it could be done through vernaculars only.

Auckland watched those developments for four years and grasped the whole situation. Although just as desirous as, Macaulay and Bentinck to see the widespread diffusion of English education, he gave to Oriental education what was its due, and drew the Committee's attention to the necessity of developing the vernacular literature of the country. He reaffirmed the prospective abolition of stipends but substituted scholarships instead, because he realised that it was necessary to offer financial inducement to students. Auckland also realised that sporadic and unsystematic efforts would have but little effect on the development of education. He laid down a comprehensive and graduated system of education comprising of schools, to be set up in every district, and linked up by scholarships with the Central colleges, that were to be established in all important stations. He was thus the first Governor-General to set up a real and comprehensive educational policy which, with certain additions and alterations, (as we shall presently see) worked until 1854. Auckland, however, could not put his plan fully into operation because of the outbreak of the Afghan War and his departure from India, but he took care to see that his plan was adopted by the government and the necessary financial provisions made for the purpose.

The General Committee of Public Instruction was replaced by a Council of Education

In 1841 the General Committee of Public Instruction tightened its control over the local authorities in education, but itself soon underwent radical transformations. The increase of the activities of the Committee as well as of its funds, led the government to consider the possibility of bringing educational matters more directly under its control. The government therefore assumed in 1842 directly the general and financial business of the Committee which was later replaced by a Council of Education, whose main function was to be to advise the government on all matters relating to education. A newly appointed Deputy Secretary in the General Department was to act as the ex-officio Secretary of the Council of Education but the government changed its decision soon and appointed a Special Secretary to the Council. F.J. Mouat was selected for this appointment. While all schools and colleges in the Upper Provinces were transferred to the Government of Agra, the Council of Education was allowed to control all the institutions in Bengal. In 1842-43 the Council of Education drew the government's attention to the necessity of providing for proper inspection and supervision of the various institutions under government, and in 1844 an Inspector was appointed whose main functions included: (a) providing the means of diffusing a high standard of moral and intellectual education through English, (b) helping the students to acquire sufficient mastery of the vernaculars in order to enable them to communicate properly to the people the knowledge they acquired in the Central colleges, (c) extending the means of instruction in the districts by establishing vernacular schools, or improving the existing ones and preparing a complete series of vernacular text books, and finally, (d) introducing a uniform and systematic course of study in all government institutions.

The appointment of an Inspector and the transfer of the institutions in the Upper Provinces to Agra Government were the only important measures sanctioned by Ellenborough's Government for the development of education in Bengal. He was much too occupied, during his short tenure of office, with the war in Afghanistan and was glad to leave educational matters alone.

Educational Developments under Hardinge

But a great change came with the arrival of Hardinge as the Governor-General of India. Although distracted by war with the Sikhs, the last great political opponent of the Company in India, Hardinge was able to devote a great deal of attention to educational matters and to initiate reforms and innovations of far-reaching importance.

Auckland, in his minute of November 1839, had drawn attention to the importance of raising a trained body of teachers and the Committee had suggested a plan for the purpose. But nothing was done till 1847, when the Council's plan for a normal school for training the future teachers was sanctioned and a school, which was also to act as a normal school, was opened in Bowbazar in Calcutta but the school had to be closed within two years when it did not fulfil the expectations of the authorities mainly for want of funds.

Vernacular Education

Another failure of Hardinge was in the field of vernacular education. In October 1844, the Government of Bengal decided to establish 101 vernacular schools as the funds for education had shown a monthly surplus of Rs 3005.00. The government decided to make the collectors responsible for the supervision of these schools which were to be opened in towns or large villages, provided the inhabitants agreed to build a school and maintain it. The students were to be freely supplied with books and tuition and the Inspector of Schools and Colleges was asked to draw a detailed scheme of study. In vernacular education the government seemed to be influenced by the views expressed by B.H. Hodgson of the Company's Civil Service and Resident in Nepal during 1833-44. In a series of articles Hodgson had asserted that the issue was not between English and the classical languages of India, and gave it as his firm conviction that "if any scheme of public instruction were really to reach the Indian peoples, it must take as its basis their mother tongues". By July 1845, the scheme was made effective to a certain extent at Bhagalpur in Bihar and at Cuttack in Orissa, and by 1846, 12 out of the 17 schools allotted to the Jessore Division had been established. However, attendance in these schools was very poor as the neighbouring schools, particularly the missionary schools, absorbed large numbers of students. There was also a dearth of a better class of teachers as well as proper school books and by 1848 the government was hesitant to go ahead with these models for the mass of schools... "to extend generally an improved system of elementary instruction".

Higher Education

Higher education, however, advanced with rapid strides during Hardinge's time. Auckland had proposed to establish a comprehensive system of combined English and vernacular education comprising the formation of Zillah schools and Central colleges. In April 1845, Beadon drew a plan for its implementation providing for the establishment of five Central colleges at Krishnagar, Moorshidabad, Chittagong, Bhaugulpore and Cuttack and suggested that for recruitment of students for these colleges, schools should be established in every district in subordinate connection with these colleges which would attract the students by offer of scholarships. Hardinge who was keen on throwing open the public offices to educated Indians – not only to induce them to take advantage of educational institutions but also to raise a body of subordinate officials at a reasonably moderate cost – readily sanctioned the scheme, which was later approved by the Court of Directors in August 1847.

Plan for a University in the Bengal Presidency

In 1844-45 the Council of Education drew the government's attention to the necessity of establishing a university with faculties of Arts, Law and Civil Engineering and on 25 October 1845, C.H. Cameron, the President of the Council of Education, decided that "the present advanced state of education in Bengal Presidency... renders it not only expedient and advisable, but a matter of strict justice and necessity ... to confer upon the successful students some mark of distinction, by which they may be recognised as persons of liberal education and enlightened minds, capable of entering upon the active duties of life". A plan to establish a Central University on the model of London University set up in 1836, which would grant degrees in Arts, Science, Law, Medicine and Civil Engineering, and which would be "incorporated by a special Act of the Legislative Council of India and endowed with the privileges enjoyed by all Chartered Universities in Great Britain and Ireland" was forwarded in 1846 to the Government of Bengal with the request that royal assent should be procured for the scheme. The government, although it did not altogether think that the time for such a measure had come, wanted the scheme to receive the favourable attention of authorities at home. One of the main reasons which induced the government to favour the establishment of a university was "the great and increasing difficulty of providing suitable tests for the selection of candidates for public employment". In May 1846, the Governor-General recommended the scheme to the Court of Directors, but he admitted to them that the government would have to bear the initial expenses. Nevertheless, he hoped that the Directors would sanction the scheme. In their despatch of 22 September 1847, the Court of Director's refused their sanction without advancing any reason for the rejection of the plan for the university.

Summing up, the two most important developments in education during the decade after Bentinck's Resolution of 7 March 1835 were: first, the final settlement of the Anglo-Oriental controversy by Auckland and second, indications of the lines along which future educational developments in the country were to take shape.

25

Education in the Presidencies: Bombay, Madras and the North-Western Provinces

In the preceding two chapters we have concentrated solely on the educational developments in the Bengal Presidency, partly because Calcutta was the headquarters of the East India Company in India and partly because Bengal was given supervisory power over Bombay and Madras by the Regulating Act of 1773. The head of the Bengal Presidency was called the Governor-General and the heads of the Presidencies of Madras and Bombay were simply called Governors. This also means that any innovation or action in the Bombay or the Madras Presidency was first to be approved by the Governor-General in Bengal before being finally sanctioned by the Court of Directors at London. When the Charter Act of 1813 sanctioned one lakh rupees for the education of the people of India, the entire money was placed at the disposal of the Governor-General. This, however, does not mean that in the Madras or the Bombay Presidencies there were no educational developments during the period between 1813 and 1848, or that education developments in the Bengal Presidency were simply extended to either of them. However, the educational developments in both the Presidencies were in fact inspired by the Bengal examples and ultimately had to fit in with the general policy approved by the Court of Directors.

Bombay Presidency

Bombay Native Education Society

In 1818, after the overthrow of the last Peshwa at Kirkee, the Bombay Presidency was formed and Mountstuart Elphinstone, the Poona Resident, was appointed as Governor of the Presidency in November 1819. The Peshwa used to spend about Rs 5,00,000 a year in giving alms to the Brahmins. It was now decided to stop this expenditure and to use a part of, it in the promotions of Brahmanic learning. The Poona Sanskrit College was established in 1821, on the model of the Sanskrit College at Benares, established by Jonathan Duncan mainly to win over the Brahmins who had been adversely affected by the change of government. By 1822, the Bombay Education Society, established in 1815 by the Church of England originally to look after the education of Anglo-Indian children, found that its work for Indian children had grown considerably. Therefore, the special committee appointed in 1820 to further the cause of schools for Indian children was now formed into a separate society called the Bombay Native School Book and School Society or, since 1827, Bombay Native Education Society. This body was solely to look after the education of Indian children, while the parent society continued to look after the education of Anglo-Indian or European children.

Elphinstone's Minute on 13 December 1823

In 1823, the Bombay Native Education Society approached the Bombay Government for grants. Elphinstone took this occasion to record a minute on education on 13 December 1823, to outline the government policy towards education in the Presidency. He observed that the method of teaching in the existing native schools should be improved and their number increased. These schools should be supplied with books and the lower orders of natives be encouraged to join them. He also suggested the establishment of schools for teaching European arts and sciences and publication of books on moral and physical sciences in Indian languages. Elphinstone suggested a close cooperation between the government and private efforts as it was impossible for the government to take the entire responsibility of public education on itself. He therefore, advocated that while the government should assume the entire responsibility for opening and increasing the number of schools, grants should be given to private bodies like Bombay Education Society for the purpose of improving teaching in schools, for which the schools should lay their proceedings before the government. Elphinstone was thus the first British administrator in India to initiate a policy of state initiative and control in education, the need for cooperation between state and private efforts, and a system of grants-in-aid. However, he was opposed by Francis Warden, a member of his Council, who wanted to establish schools in every district for instructing children of higher and middle classes in English language and education. This difference of opinion between Elphinstone and Francis Warden was later to give rise to the Anglo-Vernacular controversy in the Bombay Presidency.

The Court of Directors approved the Activities of the Bombay Education Society

However, at that point the Court of Directors accepted the Bombay Education Society as the principal agent for the spread of education among the people and sanctioned a grants-in-aid to it. It was mainly because of the paternal interest shown by Elphinstone that the Bombay Native Education Society was able to give practical training to Indians in organising and conducting associations for the spread of education. By 1840, the Society was conducting four English schools at Bombay, Thane, Panval and Poona and 115 primary schools, aimed at the diffusion of Western knowledge and science through vernaculars, as the Society in its report of 1825-26 held that "these ideas will be most easily rendered comprehensible to them by means of the mother tongue of each scholar". In 1827, Elphinstone retired and the people of Bombay subscribed a fund of rupees two lakhs in order to commemorate his services to the Bombay Presidency. The Court of Directors contributed an equal amount and in 1834, the Elphinstone Institution was organised in Bombay to raise "a class of persons qualified by their intelligence and morality for high employment in the civil administration in India".

Replacement of the Bombay Native Education Society and the Beginning of the Anglo-Vernacular Controversy

The policy of the Bombay Native Education Society on the medium of instruction was continued to be held by the Board of Education which replaced the former in April 1840. The Board which consisted of seven members of whom three were to be nominated by the Society observed in its first report in 1840-41: "In a word, knowledge must be drawn from the stores of the English language, the vernaculars must be employed as the media of communicating it, and

Sanskrit must be largely used to improve the vernaculars and make them suitable for the purpose". However, this policy of the Board was challenged by Erskine Perry, a Judge of the Bombay High Court, when he became its president in 1843. He suggested that Bombay should follow the Bengal example and adopt English as the medium of instruction in higher education. This was at once challenged by Colonel Jervis and the three nominated Indian members of the Board. Unlike in Bengal, the controversy here was between English and the vernaculars. For two years the controversy dragged on till it was submitted to the Bombay Government for a decision. In April 1848, the Bombay Government passed its orders on the subject but they were extremely indecisive, and as Erskine Perry feared, "the different conflicting theories at the Board, which have already produced much inconvenience, will again be brought forward from time to time, and that each party will refer to this Government better as an authority for their views". It was this indecisiveness of the orders, coupled with the repeated pressure from Bengal that throttled the growth of education in Bombay in the mother tongue in those days when Bengal Government's sanction was necessary for expenditure on education in Bombay. English was adopted as the sole medium of instruction at the college level while vernacular was retained as the medium of instruction at the school level.

Madras Presidency

Munro's Minute on 10 March 1826

In 1822 Thomas Munro, the Governor of Madras, ordered an enquiry into the state of education in the Madras Presidency and when the report on the subject was submitted, he found it at a very low level on account of the poverty of the people and indifference of the government. In order to improve the situation, he proposed, in a minute of 10 March 1826, the establishment of two school – one for the Hindus and the other for the Muslims – in each collectorate and of one school in each tahsil (taluka) of the Presidency at an estimated expenditure of Rs 50,000 per annum. Munro died in 1827 and his successors lacked his vision and sympathy so that by 1830 only 70 tehsildaree schools had been established.

The Court of Directors disagreed

In September 1830, the Court of Directors asked the Madras Government to concentrate on the spread of English education rather than on an attempt to educate the masses. The scheme of mass education further received a setback when in 1836 the Bengal Government recommended the withdrawal of aid from the collectorate and tehsildaree schools and the establishment of an English college at Madras and of provincial English schools at some important places in the interior, if funds permitted.

Frequent Changes in the Administration of Education

In 1836 the Board of Public Instruction was reconstituted as a Committee of Native Education, later to be substituted by the University Board in 1841 which set up a high school called the University in Madras. The University Board was superseded by a Council of Education in 1845, which was dissolved at the instance of the Court of Directors in 1847, its duties being again undertaken by the University Board. Sir Henry Poffinger revived the Council of Education in 1848, only to replace it by a Board of Governors in 1851. It handed over its functions to the Department of Public Instruction formed as per the provision of the Education Despatch of 1854. A rolling stone gathers no moss, and as J.A. Richey has rightly observed in his *Selections from Educational Records, Part II*: "In view of the constant changes both in the policy of the local government and in the personnel of the authority whose duty it was to carry out that policy, it is not a matter for surprise that the educational activities of the Madras Government were not fruitful in results or that we find in 1852 but one single institution in the Presidency founded or under the immediate control of Government".

North-Western Provinces

Factors at work for the Improvement of Vernacular Education

In 1843, the control of the educational institutions was transferred from the Council of Education to the North-Western Provinces of Agra and Oudh when it became a separate provincial government. At that time the educational institutions consisted of three colleges at Agra, Delhi and Benares and nine schools maintained by the government. In 1845 James Thomason, the Lt. Governor of the North-Western Provinces, addressed circular letters to all the revenue collectors, calling their special attention to the low standard of vernacular education and to the factors at work for its improvement. These could be found in the new revenue settlement there, under which the right of every cultivator, whether land lord or tenant, had been ascertained and recorded, and for the protection of whose rights a system of registration of titles to land had been introduced. Of course, none but those able to read and write could avail themselves of the advantages they offered to an extent, while to the full enjoyment of them some knowledge of arithmetic and of the principles of land measurement was requisite. There was "thus a direct appeal and powerful inducement to the mind of almost every individual to acquire so much of reading, writing, arithmetic, mensuration, as may suffice for the protection of his rights", as pointed out by Thomason's Secretary. This stimulus was absent in the Lower Provinces of Bengal where the rights of the cultivators had been swept away by the Permanent Settlement in 1793 and consequently Hardinge's scheme of vernacular education became a failure.

Thomason's Plan

When in 1846 detailed statistics about the state of education in the North-Western Provinces were prepared, it was revealed that "on an average less than 5 per cent of the youth who are of an age to attend schools obtain any instruction and that instruction which they do receive is of very imperfect kind". Thomason proposed the establishment of a school in every considerable village to supply this grievous want but this was not supported by the Court of Directors. Not disappointed by the Court's rejection of his proposals, in April 1848 he submitted another scheme – to set up a model school in every tehsil or revenue district in addition to the ordinary village school at the general expense "to provide a powerful agency for visiting all the indigenous schools, for furnishing the people and the teachers with advice, assistance and encouragement, and for rewarding those school masters who may be found the most deserving". There would be a Zillah Visitor in each district and three Pargana Visitors and a Visitor-General were to be appointed from among the civil servants of the Company to supervise the working of the scheme. It was calculated that this scheme when put into operation would cost £ 20,000 (Rs 2,00,000) per annum. For the time being a partial experiment confining the scheme to eight districts only was to be made. Thomason sent his proposals to Lord Dalhousie, the newly appointed Governor-General of India, for recommendation to the Court of Directors for their approval.

26

Missionaries and Enlightened Indians

Before entering the age of Dalhousie which undoubtedly made the most important contribution to the development of an education system in India, let us have a look at the contributions made by the missionaries and the enlightened Indians before 1848. We have already noted in one of the preceding chapters how the missionaries and the educated Indians generated forces which resisted the activities of the General Committee of Public Instruction since 1823 in reviving and promoting Oriental literature and learning in British India. Between 1835 and 1848 they made further significant contributions towards the development of education in the country. It would be useful to discuss these briefly here.

Missionaries

Alexander Duff Model

The establishment of the General Assembly's Institution in Calcutta in 1830 by Alexander Duff marked the beginning of a new approach to proselytisation through education. Since the emergence of the utilitarians in the 1820s, the belief was gaining ground that conversion of the Indians to Christianity would be the ultimate result of the spread of Western education among them and so the missionary attempt since Duff centred round building up schools and colleges for imparting English education. Duff's faith in the potential power of English education as a means of proselytisation soon infected almost all the missionaries working in the field of Indian education and English schools conducted by missionaries began to multiply very rapidly after 1830. The missionary schools with their compulsory teaching of the Bible were able to attract the upper classes who desired to study English for the worldly advantages it brought. The missionaries believed that once they were attracted to the teachings of the Bible, they would embrace Christianity and would go to the people for further conversion in the Gospel. This, however, never happened though there were indeed a few cases of conversion of students from upper classes as in the cases of Madhusadhan Dutta and Krishnamohan Banerjee in the Bengal Presidency.

Opening up of India to the Non-English Missionaries

The Charter Act of 1833 "opened up" India to the missionary activity of other nations as well. It was in this year that the missionary activities of the non-English missionary societies began in India. The German and the American missions were the most prominent among them. In 1834 the Basel Mission Society began its work at Mangalore followed by the Protestant Lutheran Missionary Society founded at Dresden in 1836 and the Women's Association of Education of Females in the Orient, founded in Berlin in 1842. Among the "well-manned and richly financed" American societies were the American Baptist Union, the American Board and the American Presbyterian Mission Board North.

Among the most famous of the colleges which were established in rapid succession in various parts of India under the direct influence and inspiration of Duff were the one founded by Dr. John Wilson in Bombay in 1832 which later bore his name, the General Assembly's School in Madras founded by Anderson and Braidwood in 1837 (which later under Dr. Miller became the Christian College) and the Hislop College at Nagpur by Stephen Hislop in 1844. In 1841 Robert Noble founded the Noble College at Masulipatam and in 1853 the Church Missionary Society founded St. John's College at Agra. These colleges were in addition to those built by the Church of Scotland at Calcutta, Bombay and Madras.

Growth and Development of Missionary Enterprise

Richter has described the quarter century, 1830-57, as "the age of the mission school". As he observes, "During the period the Government, inspite of the good intentions of Bentinck, lay really in an apathy, which we find it hard to understand; for three years Lord Ellenborough was Governor-General, a man who regarded the political ruin of the English power as the inevitable consequence of the education of the Hindus! Hence at that time the mission school exercised a dominating influence over Indian thought which it is difficult to estimate nowadays". The growth of missionary enterprise in education was greatly facilitated by the cordial relations that existed between the missionaries and the Company officials, among whom were many utilitarians with an evangelical outlook. For example, Duff was a very close associate of Bentinck who encouraged him to establish the General Assembly's Institution in Calcutta in 1830. Secondly, the apprehension that interference with the religious institutions of the Hindus and the Muslims would be greatly resented by them gradually began to disappear as the Company officials were often required to manage Hindu temples and Hindu religious fairs. The abolition of *Sati* by Bentinck's Government in 1829 led to no revolt as the opponents of this reform had earlier pointed out, and the Company officials became bolder than before in their support for missionary causes now that the East India Company had firmly established itself politically after outwitting the Indian powers and its European rivals.

The missionary activities in education varied from province to province and were most remarkable in areas like Madras where the Company's initiatives in the field were negligible. By 1853 the missionary activity in education was almost equal to official enterprises which had 1,474 institutions with 67,569 pupils. If, however, the work of the Roman Catholic Mission were added to those of the Protestant organisations, missionary work in education certainly exceeded the official enterprise. The missionaries resented the Company schools which did not include the teaching of the Bible and were more popular with the Indians. They were therefore clamouring either for the inclusion of the Bible in the Company schools or for direct withdrawal of the Company from education, leaving the field entirely to missionaries. The Company would be indirectly involved through a system of grants-in-aid.

Enlightened Indians

Prevalent Prejudices against the Western Education

Indian private enterprise in the new education was confined to those who believed it to be an effective agent of modernising Indian society or those who had been trained in the new education and had found it to be a passport to new jobs which at once brought them money, status and power. The prevalent opinion in most areas was against the new system. Most parents initially refused to send their children to English schools because they were afraid that English education would anglicise them and make them lose faith in the religious beliefs and practices of their forefathers. They were also afraid of the spread of Western ideas through vernaculars as they thought the new education to be a part of some secret plan to tamper with their age old religion. Therefore, the few Indians who wanted to set up schools for imparting new education had to work under this limitation and in most cases their schools, as in the case of the Hindu School in 1817, were the results of active collaboration with and support from European officials or non-officials.

Hindu School Model

Hare, who was one of the founders of the Hindu School, had realised that all the education enterprises of the time were dominated by religion and had been keen on setting up one, whose main object would be to emphasise the study of English language and literature. The model of the Hindu School came to be generally adopted by the Company as well as by private enterprises and the principle of secularism enabled the Company to maintain its policy of religious neutrality while the emphasis on the study of English language and literature enabled it to obtain servants for the government departments where English was being adopted as the official language. Indians also found it convenient to follow the model of the Hindu School because a policy of secular education involved no administrative problems and a subordination of scientific studies made the functioning of the institutions less costly and difficult.

Rammohan Roy who was associated with the establishment of the Hindu School but had to withdraw his name from the management of the school under objection from the orthodox Indians, himself set up a school at Suripara in Calcutta for the free education of Hindu boys there. In 1822, he purchased a plot of land at Simla in Calcutta where he started another school known as the Anglo-Hindu School which was later named the Indian Academy in 1834. In 1818, Jainarain Ghosal started a school in Benares for the teaching of English, Persian, Hindustani and Bengali. Schools for teaching English were also started at different places in Calcutta and at some other places like Hughli, Burdwan, Midnapur, Dacca, Barisal,

Santipur, Murshidabad, Rangpur, Allahabad, Agra and Delhi. As Charles Travelyan observed: "In 1831 the Committee [of Public Instruction] reported that a taste for English had been widely disseminated and independent schools, conducted by young men reared in the Vidyalaya [Hinu School] are springing up in every direction. This spirit gathering strength from time to time, and from many favourable circumstances had gained a great height in 1835. Several rich natives had established English schools at their own expense; associations had been formed for the same purpose at different places in the interior similar to the one to which the Hindu College owed its origin".

Thus in 1831 Rasik Krishna Mallick, a brilliant product of the Hindu College started the Hindu Free School at Simla (Calcutta) where 80 students received education. In 1832 two wealthy persons Kalinath Ray Chaudhuri and Baikunthanath Ray Chaudhuri of Taki started a local school for teaching English, Arabic, Persian and Bengali to the boys and placed its entire management under the control of Duff. Five hundred students attended this school daily and many who wanted to study there could not be accommodated. In 1834 Govinda Chandra Basak started the Hindu Free School which was attended by some 130 students in six classes and were examined by David Hare in March 1835. In 1837, one more institution providing free coaching, named the Benevolent Institution, was started at a village called Amarpur in Hooghly.

Performance of the Hindu School Students

The students of the Hindu College, whose number rose from 70 in 1819 to 400 in 1830, and of many other schools established for English education were quite serious about studies, and in the examinations occasionally held for them they acquitted themselves creditably. Commenting on the performance of the students at one such annual examination of a school at Bhowanipore, a contemporary Bengali newspaper observed on 7 March 1829: "The students of Hindu College and of the schools founded by Rammohan Roy and Jagmohan Basu have recently been examined by Englishmen in English language. If we repeat the praises we have heard from these examiners we may be accused of flattery. But we may say that the Englishmen have been very pleased with the results of these examinations and it is their desire that the English education may be further spread in this country". Some of the students did really attain a remarkable proficiency in the English language and literature. Five talented young men of the Dutt family of Rambagan in Calcutta wrote English verses by 1848 which in the opinion of a contemporary reviewer were "distinguished by a grace and strength". A "gifted daughter" of this "gifted family" was Toru Dutt, the famous Indian poetess, who was born in Calcutta in 1856 and died at the early age of twenty one.

27

The Age of Dalhousie, 1848-1856

The age of Dalhousie is the most significant age in the history of education in modern India. For the foundations of a modern system of education were actually laid during the administration of Dalhousie as the Governor-General of India between 1848 and 1856. It will be seen that the Education Despatch of 1854, popularly, and perhaps incorrectly, known as Wood's Despatch, which laid the foundations of this system did really emerge out of the various experiments and steps taken in education by Dalhousie's predecessors and by Dalhousie himself till 1853. We shall study this chapter under four heads: First, the educational experiments of Dalhousie till 1853, second, the making of the Education Despatch of 1854; third, the main provisions of the Education Despatch of 1854 and finally, the implementation of the Education Despatch of 1854 and its later endorsement.

Educational Experiments of Dalhousie Till 1853

Dalhousie recommended Thomason's Scheme of Vernacular Education to the Court of Directors

When Dalhousie received Thomason's scheme for vernacular education in the North-Western Provinces, he had not formed any definite policy on the educational problems in India. He was still new to India and was yet to acquaint himself with the conditions prevailing there. Nevertheless, he had assured the Indian people at the very beginning of his administration that he would "afford every encouragement for the development of native talent". Since English

had already been decided upon as the right language for administrative work, it was now 'worse than a heresy' to argue for Arabic,
Sanskrit or Persian for this purpose. He, however, knew the defects of
such a system and the departures already made from it. And so he
admitted, "whether the Education of India should be based exclusively on English, rejecting the vernacular or not" was a question
which might admit of controversy as well as of experiment. Since
Thomason's scheme provided such an opportunity, he did not
hesitate to recommend it to the Court of Directors for their sanction
which was readily given in their despatch of 3 October 1849.

Dalhousie agreed to set up a School instead of a College at Amritsar

When Thomason was busy with his experimental scheme of
education in the North-Western Provinces, Dalhousie received a
proposal from the Board of Administration of the Punjab, to set up in
the newly acquired territory an experimental school or college at
Amritsar. He accepted the suggestion to found an institution at
Amritsar, "the Shrine of the Sikh religion and deeply reverenced by
the Hindus, the chief seat of the manufacturers of the Punjab, the
leading mart of its trade and the great repository of its learning", but
pointed out that the institution should be a school and not a college
since much more general enquiries and fuller information about the
state of education in the Punjab were needed before any general and
leading institution, as would be indicated by the title 'college', could
be founded. He suggested that simultaneously with instruction in the
vernaculars, English could be taught there if a strong desire for
learning it was felt among the very large population of Amritsar.

Success of Thomason's Scheme of Vernacular Education in Eight Districts

Meanwhile within three years after its introduction in the
North-Western Provinces, Thomason's scheme for vernacular
education proved extremely successful. Since 1850, a considerable
number of youths had been brought under instruction, the character
of the instruction raised and a vernacular school literature had been
created. The number of schools were raised from 2,014 in 1850 to
3,469 in 1852, the number of scholars had increased from 17,169 in
1850 to 36,884 in 1852. Elated with the success of his scheme in the
eight districts of the North-Western Provinces, Thomason now
requested Dalhousie to permit him to extend it to the other 23

districts where a population "no less teeming, and a people as capable of learning" existed, "the same want prevailed", and therefore "the same moral obligation" rested upon the government to dispel the ignorance.

Dalhousie extended Thomason's Scheme of Vernacular Education to Bengal and the Punjab

Dalhousie was fully convinced of the success of Thomason's scheme and therefore recommended "in the strongest terms" to the Court of Directors that full sanction be given to the scheme of vernacular education to all the districts within the jurisdiction of the North-Western Provinces. At the same time he felt that he would not be discharging the obligations as Head of the Government of India if he were to remain content with this recommendation only. In Bengal, Bihar and other Presidencies too "the same moral obligations" rested upon the government to exert itself for the purpose of dispelling the present ignorance. He referred to Dr. Mouat's report on the vernacular schools in the North-Western Provinces, where he had spoken about "the utter failure" of the scheme of vernacular education adopted in Bengal, "among a more intelligent, docile and less prejudiced people than those of the N.W.P.", as well as to his assurance that the scheme which had been best adopted to dispel the ignorance of the agricultural people of the N.W.P. was also "the plan best suited for the vernacular education of the mass of the people of Bengal and Bihar". Dalhousie therefore, extended the scheme of vernacular education for the North-Western Provinces to Bengal and Bihar on the recommendation of "the experienced authority" of Dr. Mouat and went further in extending it to the "new subjects beyond Jumna" the people of the Punjab. He also asked for the views of the Governor of Bengal and the Board of Administrators on the subject while awaiting the Court's sanction to the scheme of vernacular education.

Dalhousie reformed the Hindu College and made it the Presidency College at Calcutta

At the same time he carried out elaborate educational reforms in Calcutta – he converted the senior department of the Hindu College into an institution called "the Presidency College" in order to distinguish it by name from all other local and private institutions and threw it open to all youths of every caste, class or creed and hoped to see it "expand itself into something approaching to the dignity and proportions of an Indian University". He similarly reorganised the Madrasah by converting its senior department into the Arabic College as proposed by Mouat and suggested that if the Muslims did not object to the admission of the non-Muslims to the junior department and if there was any special reason for admitting them to it, they might be admitted.

Dalhousie thus laid the foundations of an efficient system of instructions for all sections of the community in Bengal. Hindu boys were to have learnt vernacular and English education at the junior department of the Hindu College and at its branch at Colootollah. Muslim boys would have similar facilities at the junior department of the Madrasah and at its branch at Collinga. Hindu boys would continue their higher studies in Hindu learning at the Sanskrit College while the Muslim youths, would follow up their studies in the Arabic College. And young men from both the communities, and of every community and class, would have an institution in the new Presidency College where they might obtain the instruction they desired in every branch of general acquirement offered to them. It was as such to be in reality what its name implied, a college, and not what all the establishments so called that he had seen in India were - "a compound of College and dames' school".

Dalhousie provided the First Official Support for Female Education in British India

While Dalhousie was thus supporting Thomason's system of vernacular education in the North-Western Provinces, the Punjab and Bengal, he was also developing Bethune's idea of female education as well as Thomason's plan for technical education in Bengal. Official support for female education in India was unknown before him though many like Elphinstone shared Dalhousie's conviction that the "diffusion of knowledge" among men and women would sound the death-knell of many social evils which degraded the condition of women in India. It was believed that the scheme of female education would be unpopular and would be "looked upon by the mass, with fear and dread, whether Hindus or Mahommedans". In his report on vernacular education Adam pointed out that a feeling allegedly existed in the majority of Hindu females, principally cherished by the women and not discouraged by the men, that a girl taught to read and write would become a widow soon after marriage and the idea was also generally entertained that intrigue was facilitated by a knowledge of letters on the part of females. The Mohammedans shared all the prejudices of the Hindus against education of their female offspring. The Eastern ideal of female life was one of strict purity, seclusion and quiet domestic duty, and the literature of the classical languages of India was far too corrupt, according to this ideal, to allow of any teaching of it. Besides, it was also believed that the natives would rise against any attempt to "submit their women folk to the equalising and emancipating influence of public instruction". The government therefore "purposely abstained from acting towards its female subjects as it acted towards male" in the field of education. This is evident from the fact that in none of the general dispatches relating to educational matters submitted to or received from the Court of Directors during the first half of the century is there any reference to the education of Indian girls and women.

Under these circumstances, the few institutions for female education that existed in the first three decades of the nineteenth century were owing particularly to the efforts of a few energetic missionaries and philanthropic private individuals. In 1821, Miss Cooke (later Mrs. Wilson) was deputed by the British and the Foreign School Society to open a school for female children at Calcutta. In 1826 she had 30 schools and 600 pupils under her charge, and these merged in 1828 into a Central School under a Committee called the Ladies Society for Native Female Education. Other similar schools had also been established by the London and the Church Missionary Society but the state of female education in India was not very encouraging except in the Punjab. The first report of the Board of Administration in the Punjab pointed out that female education which was "almost unknown in other parts of India" was to be found in all parts of the Punjab. There were also female teachers and female pupils who where drawn from all the communities – Hindu, Muslim, and Sikh.

It was Dalhousie who by supporting J.E.D. Bethune's female school in Calcutta closed the era of official non-interference, and marked "the beginning of that of open encouragement" in "the annals of female education in India." Bethune had founded this school in May 1849 with a view to imparting secular education to girls from higher families who were conspicuous by their absence in the missionary schools. Bethune who was a member of Dalhousie's Council and President of the Council of Education, wanted to discover whether the time had come "when this important step in the system of education of the Native can be taken with a reasonable hope of success. I wished the discredit of failure to rest with myself alone, if my expectation had proved abortive and that the credit of the Government should not be pledged to the measure until its success was assured". Dalhousie approved of the course Bethune had adopted and even encouraged him to preserve the institution in the face of the strong local opposition by saying: "I truly believe that you have planted the grain of mustard seed; and that it will one day be a great tree which you and those whom we serve may be proud to look upon".

Dalhousie's belief was not unfounded. After one year Bethune came forward with a successful and encouraging report of his institution. In a long letter to Dalhousie on 29 March 1850 he said: how, despite all intimidations to his institution, the number of its pupils had risen from 11 to 30 and how it had encouraged the Indians to found girls' schools at Uttarpara, Barasat, Neebudhia, Sooksagar, and Jessore. The school at Barasat was attended by more than 20 girls primarily of Brahminical caste, two of them married. At the Government Vernacular School at Chota Jagooleah in the Barasat district, students were offered a silver medal for the best Bengali essay on the benefits to be expected from "Female Education". Since these schools were always facing intimidation (which he had to face at Calcutta), frequent applications were made to him for constant support and encouragement as the position he had assumed naturally marked him out as the patron of all such undertakings. He, therefore, suggested to Dalhousie that "the time is come when all that is needed to secure their complete success is a declaration on the part of Government that it looks on them with a favourable eye".

Dalhousie took up the suggestion from Bethune and acted promptly. He circulated Bethune's letter among the members of his Council for their views on the subject, making it clear that female education in Calcutta had his "full and unreserved approval". Bethune had indeed done a "great work in the first successful introduction of Native Female Education in India, on a sound and solid foundation" and had earned "a right not only to the gratitude of the Government but to its frank and cordial support". Both Currie and Lowie agreed with Dalhousie about the importance of the subject but Litter submitted a dissenting judgment: "Will it not involve a dereliction of the principle of neutrality to which the Government (I have always understood) is pledged in like cases?" Despite Litter's views, Dalhousie regarded the support of Currie and Lowie on the subject of female education as "the beginning of a great revolution in Indian habits". The Council authorised him to issue necessary instructions to the Council of Education to supervise and support female education in India which was approved by the Court of Directors in their letter of 4 September 1850. The Court of Directors, however, declined Bethune's suggestion that Her Majesty the Queen Victoria should be the patroness to his school at Calcutta on the ground that the present state of female education did not warrant "such unusual proceedings".

In August 1851 Bethune died after suffering for a while from an abscess of the liver, speaking of "his female school as the anxiety that lay nearest to his heart". His original plan was to make over the school to Dalhousie later but changed his plans due to the critical state of his health and wanted to do so immediately "as, otherwise in the case of my death the whole must have been sold under the general powers of my will for the benefit of my sisters". Dalhousie who was grieved by the untimely death of Bethune realised that the experiment of his school was most likely to be rendered thoroughly successful if carried on for sometime longer, "as a private work watched with the closer care" and so he requested his wife, Lady Dalhousie, to take it for the present "under her charge". Since the number of girls in the school was likely to increase from 40 and since the monthly expenditure was likely to increase from the existing expense of Rs 650 – Rs 700, Dalhousie was, however, anxious that the Court of Directors should support it after his departure from India. The Court wanted to do so immediately but Dalhousie declined saying that he would look after the institution as long as he remained in India and only after his departure, it would go to the care of the Court.

Dalhousie developed Thomason's Scheme of Technical Education

While Dalhousie was thus supporting Bethune's idea of female education, he was simultaneously developing Thomason's plan for technical education in Bengal. In November 1847, Thomason had established a Civil Engineering College at Roorkee with Lieutenant R. Maclagan as its principal. It was designed to give theoretical and practical instructions in civil engineering to Europeans and Indians, with a view to their being employed on the public works of the country, according to their qualifications and the requirements of the service. Within a year of its foundation, Dalhousie realised that much good would result from training a certain number of youths annually in a well instructed class rather than a college for filling vacancies as they arose, and to meet the increasing demands of the department of public works. The establishment of such a class at each of the Presidencies would not be attended with great expense. Since the Court appeared to have sanctioned it to a certain extent at Madras and at the North-Western Provinces, he would request them to extend their approval for such a system to Bengal and Bombay. However, the introduction of railways and electric telegraph, as well as the construction of roads and irrigation works created such a great demand for civil engineers in the recently organised departments of public works in Bombay and Madras that Dalhousie changed his idea of establishing a civil engineering class to that of a civil engineering college in each of the Presidencies. Its primary object was to be the training of civil engineers of all classes employed in the departments of public works, and which was to be open to Europeans, Eurasians as well as Indians. In the Bengal Presidency though the Thomason College at Roorkee, where he had founded a scholarship in memory of Thomason who had died in 1853, was contributing a great deal, yet one college was not sufficient for the purpose. More so, because the college could not supply the lower grades of persons required in the departments of public works. They were supplied by the school founded by Major Maitland in the Madras Presidency. Dalhousie decided that in its junior department the proposed Bengal College should be based on the model of Major Maitland's school at Madras and in its senior department on that of the Thomason College at Roorkee. He asked the Lieutenant Governor of Bengal to submit details of such a scheme.

Dalhousie waited for the Court of Directors' Sanctions to the various Proposals he had sent to them

By the end of July 1854, Dalhousie was planning to set up a civil engineering college in each of the Presidencies in India to meet the increasing demand of civil engineers. He was thus on the way to share with Thomason the paternity of Technical Education in India. Again by supporting Bethune's school for girls at Calcutta he became the pioneer of Female Education in India. He had reformed the Madrasah, reorganised the Hindu College, both at Calcutta, and had founded there the Presidency College, open to all classes, creeds and castes, and which he fondly hoped would one day become an "Indian University" after "having elevated itself by its reputation and scholar-ships" and being "strengthened by the most distinguished scholars from other cities". He had picked up from Thomason, after his successful experiment, the idea of a vernacular education in India, "by means of Tehsildaree schools with Pergunnah and district visitors and with the Visitor-general to direct the whole", aided by the state. He had recommended to the Court of Directors for an extension of Thomason's scheme to the rest of the North-Western Provinces and to Bengal, Bihar and the Punjab. He had already received the report on the application of Thomason's scheme of vernacular education in the Punjab and had supported the principle stated by the Punjab Judicial Commissioner of grants-in-aid to the missionary schools in India. Dalhousie patiently waited for the approval of the Court of Directors to all these proposals he had submitted for sanction.

Dalhousie received Court of Directors' Reply

The Court of Directors' reply came quickly. It contained not a sanction to Dalhousie's proposals but a detailed policy regarding education in India which the Governor-General-in-Council must follow. Dalhousie's reaction to this was not only of shock and surprise but also one of satisfaction, as recorded by him in his *Diary* on 12 October 1854 and in his official minute on 19 October 1854. He entered the following observation in his *Diary* on 12 October:

> At the close of last year a despatch was sent to the Court proposing the immediate extension of Mr. Thomason's system of Vernacular Education to all the districts in the North West Provinces. At the same time a similar educational system was proposed for the Punjab, and the whole of the Lower Provinces. The Court have never up to this time thought proper even to acknowledge this despatch, and in the meantime they have sent out a mission, laying down a complete scheme of general education for all India; in which they not only do not enquire what the Government of India has effected, but actually represent what they have done as still left undone.

The Making of the Education Despatch of 1854

Charles Wood, President of the Board of Control, was requested to frame a General Scheme of Education for British India

A study of the Wood Papers at the India Office Library, London, simultaneously with a study of the Dalhousie Papers at the Scottish Record Office, Edinburgh, reveals that Charles Wood, the President of the Board of Control, was requested by the Court of Directors to frame a general scheme of education applicable to the whole of British India in a "proposed P.C." – a practice ultimately leading to the formation of a despatch to India. The occasion for this arose from the discussions that took place in Parliament relating to the Act for the future Government of India when great interest was shown expressed on the subject of education and a strong desire for its extension and improvement. "With a view to give effect to these feelings and wishes", the East India House supplied Wood with all the necessary materials to frame a comprehensive policy on education but told him that for this purpose it was not necessary that "the system hitherto acted on differing greatly as it does in detail in the several Presidencies, should undergo any great or violent change, but rather than the object should be sought by an extension of that system, in some directions, and by the use and encouragement of those Educational Establishments, unconnected with Government which have found much favour with the general community, but which have hitherto received no countenance or support from the state." In this connection the East India House which had already received by November 1853, Dalhousie's proposal for extension of Thomason's system of vernacular education to the rest of the North-Western Provinces, Bengal and the Punjab, drew Wood's attention to it: "With regard to the village schools the plan already acted on with success in the N.W. Provinces and in Bombay assisting and encouraging in the efforts of the people themselves for the improvement of existing schools should be adhered to; and there seems no reason to doubt that this mode of proceeding will be found adequate to the end in view".

Wood's Secretary summarised the Main Points for him and wrote the Despatch

Wood's Secretary, who later became Governor-General of India as Lord Northbrook, went through the materials supplied by the East India House and jotted down the following main points:

The general result of the information showed that in the North-Western Provinces alone was there anything approaching to a systematic scheme for educating or improving the education of the people.

That in Bengal and in the neighbourhood of the other Presidency Towns there was a considerable demand for English which has been responded to by the Government.

That wherever practical education had been attempted, it had been most successful and that a very considerable private agency might be taken advantage of, if grants-in-aid were sanctioned.

There was ample information from which to draw up a general scheme - and to make Native Education an integral part of the ordinary administration in India.

It was Northbrook who drafted the Education Despatch of 1854 which was submitted to the Court of Directors for onward transmission to India. Many years later when Northbrook was consulted by Curzon on the eve of his passing the Indian Universities Act of 1904-5, he wrote to Curzon: "It is I who wrote the Education Despatch". Needless to say, the handwriting in the draft Despatch of 1854, confirms this – it was certainly not Wood's.

Wood took the Credit for the Despatch

Yet the credit goes to Charles Wood because he, as the President of the Board of Control, was requested by the East India House to prepare a general scheme of education for "the whole of British India". Wood who had written to Dalhousie on 19 August 1853 "to desire somebody to prepare a report showing existing matters as they are ... and also what is feasible in the way of extension" and to Marshman, the editor of the *Friend of India* on 22 November 1853 "how we could embark on so gigantic an undertaking" consulted many others in the preparation of the Education Despatch of 1854. In a letter to Dalhousie he named the persons whom he had consulted: "Macaulay, Lord Glenelg, Bayley and Prinsep, Marshman, the Church Missionaries, Berry, Mouat, Beadon, and everybody we could think of here, as having an authority on the subject, have been consulted and have cordially approved the scheme". In the face of this admission it would seem surprising that Wood should take the whole credit for the Education Despatch of 1854 for himself. In a letter to

Colvile, Dalhousie's Legislative Councillor and Law Commissioner, he boasted: "I hope to have laid the foundation of a great improvement in the condition of the natives of our Indian territories".

Dalhousie's Reaction to Wood's Claim and his Contributions to the Despatch

It was as a reaction to such statements made by Wood that Dalhousie recorded rather bitterly in his *Diary:* "The education despatch ... is a mere clap-trap put forth to the House of Commons by Sir Charles Wood; whereby he seeks to filch for himself the whole credit of all that has been, or is to be, done; thus unduly detracting from the credit which fairly belongs to the Government of India and to the local administration". Indeed, besides adopting Thomason's plan for vernacular education in India, the Despatch developed many of Dalhousie's own ideas with regard to technical and female educations in India as well as his ideas of grants-in-aid and of the Indian universities, a model of which he hoped to see in the Presidency College. Dalhousie therefore could easily say: "the scope of the present despatch from the Honourable Court is more than sufficient to include within its sanction ... projects, which have been submitted by the Government of India". In short, the Education Despatch of 19 July 1854 is not a negation to, but an expansion of the educational policy pursued by Dalhousie and his predecessors in India.[1]

The Education Despatch of 1854

The Education Despatch of 1854 is divided into 100 paragraphs and occupies in print some 29 pages in J. Richey's *Selections from Educational Records 1840-59* (Part 2) first brought out in 1922.

Objects of a General System of Education

What are the factors that led the East India House or the Court of Directors to frame a comprehensive education policy for the whole of British India? The introductory paragraphs of the Despatch provide the answer:

> Among many subjects of importance, none can have a stronger claim to our attention than that of education. It is one of our most sacred duties, to be the means, as far as in us lies, of conferring upon the natives of India those vast moral and material blessings which

flow from the general diffusion of useful knowledge, and which
India may, under Providence, derive from her connexion with
England.... We have, moreover, always looked upon the encouragement of education peculiarly important, because calculated not
only to produce a higher degree of intellectual fitness, but to raise
the moral character to those who partake of its advantages, and so
to supply you with servants to whose probity you may with
increased confidence commit offices of trust....

Nor, while the character of England is deeply concerned in the
success of our efforts for the promotion of education, are her
material interests altogether unaffected by the advance of European
knowledge in India. This knowledge will teach the natives of India
the marvellous results of the employment of labour and capital,
rouse them to emulate us in the development of the vast resources
of their country, guide them in their efforts, and gradually, but
certainly, confer upon them all the advantages which accompany
the healthy increase, of wealth and commerce; and at the same time
secure to us a large and more certain supply of many articles
necessary for our manufacturers and extensively consumed by all
classes of our population as well as an almost inexhaustible demand
for the produce of British labour.

Nature of Education and Medium of Instruction

What was to be the nature of education the Despatch wanted to
impart to the Indians? It "emphatically" declared that the nature of
education was to be the "improved arts, sciences, and literature of
Europe" and categorically stated that the eastern systems "abound
with grievous errors". Since the Oriental institutions were valuable
for "historical and antiquarian purposes" and since the cultivation of
the Oriental languages was necessary for the study of Hindu and
Muslim laws and for the improvement of the vernaculars, the authorities had no desire to abolish them. On the other hand, the authorities
suggested that they should be improved and rendered useful. The
medium of higher education was to be English, but it was not to be
substituted for the vernaculars. As the Despatch pointed out, "It is
indispensable that in any general system of education, the study of
them should be assiduously attended to, and any acquaintance with
improved European knowledge which is to be communicated to the
great mass of the people whose circumstances prevent them from
acquiring a higher order of education, and who cannot be expected to

overcome the difficulties of a foreign language – can only be conveyed to them through one or other of these vernacular languages". The Despatch thus abandoned the filtration policy of 1835. The Despatch emphasised that vernaculars should be cultivated in the Anglo-Vernacular colleges and English in the Vernacular and Oriental institutions with a view to "that general diffusion of European knowledge which is the main object of education in India".

Department of Education

The Despatch replaced the provincial boards and councils of education by creating departments of public instruction in each of the five provinces into which the territory of the Company were divided at that time – Bengal, Madras, Bombay, the North-Western Provinces and the Punjab. This department was to be headed by an important officer called the Director of Public Instruction who was to be assisted by an adequate number of inspectors with the special responsibility of reporting on the state of inspected schools and colleges. The Director was required to submit to the government an annual report on the progress of education in his province.

Establishment of Universities

The progress of education as well as the requirements of the European and the Anglo-Indian communities led the Court of Directors to believe that the time had come for the establishment of universities in India. They, therefore, agreed with the earlier recommendation of the Council of Education and suggested that universities should be established at Calcutta and Bombay and also at Madras and other places if there were sufficient institutions suitable to be affiliated to them. These universities were to be modelled on the University of London "as being best adapted to the wants of India". They were to confer degrees on candidates from affiliated institutions. The examinations were not to include any religious subjects but institutions conducted by any religious denomination could be affiliated if they imparted a sufficiently high degree of education in the subjects examined. Professorships were to be created especially in Law and Civil Engineering and "in various branches of learning, for the acquisition of which, at any rate in advance degree, facilities do not exist in other institutions in India". The Despatch also pointed out that creation of Chairs in vernaculars and classical languages would greatly encourage the study of the former. The Chairs in the latter were, however, not to be used for the study of religious subjects.

Grants-in-aid

Since the filtration policy was being given up, the Court of Directors considered how best "useful and practical knowledge suited to every station in life" could be made available to the great mass of people. Such expansion was not possible by government effort alone because of the vastness of the task and the enormous expenses necessary. Therefore, it was resolved to resort to the grants-in-aid system which had been so successfully adopted in England. This aid was to be given on the basis of complete religious neutrality to all schools imparting a good secular education under satisfactory local management and government inspection. The Despatch also decided to levy fees from the students to encourage greater exertion and regularity in attendance, and the fees thus collected, it was decided, could be utilised for the benefit of the schools concerned. The Court of Directors hoped that in this way education provided entirely by government would ultimately stop and government institutions, especially of a higher type, could be transferred to local management while receiving aid from the government. It was also decided to carry out more fully Auckland's scheme of connecting the Zillah schools with the Central colleges by a system of scholarships and to further extend it to the schools of lower description in order to encourage talented students. Below the Anglo-Vernacular and Vernacular schools came the indigenous elementary schools which the Directors proposed to encourage by suitable grants-in-aid. They drew the attention of the Government of India to the particular plan of Thomason for encouraging indigenous schools in the North-Western Provinces, and recommended its adoption as largely as possible.

Trained School Teachers and Text-Books

The Despatch also paid attention to the question of providing trained teachers and suitable text-books in the schools. It was decided to establish normal schools and classes in each Presidency, as soon as possible, on the model existing in England. On the question of the nature of text-books, the Despatch approvingly quoted the view of Adam that the aim was to be "not to translate the words and idioms of the native languages but so to combine the substance of European knowledge with native forms of thought and sentiment as to render the school books useful and attractive".

Professional Education

Finally, the Despatch appreciated the drawbacks of a purely literary course of instruction and recommended professional training in Law, Medicine and Civil Engineering. It stressed the urgent need to establish vocational colleges and schools of industry and the urgency of spreading education among women. As it observed in paragraph 83, "The importance of female education in India cannot be overrated and we have observed with pleasure the evidence which is now afforded of an increased desire on the part of many of the natives of India to give a good education to their daughters. We have already observed that schools for females are included among those to which grants-in-aid may be given; and we cannot refrain from expression our cordial sympathy with the efforts which are being made in this direction. Our Governor-General in Council has declared, in a communication to the Government of Bengal, that the Government ought to give to the native female education in India its frank and cordial support; and in this we heartily concur...". The Despatch visualised that the progress of education would not only provide the government with able, efficient and faithful servants but that the possibility of such appointments would also act as an incentive to the progress of education in India.

A Critique of the Despatch

Richter has described the Education Despatch of 1854 as the "Magna Carta of Indian education" in his, *A History of Missions in India*. It is true that the Despatch did not bestow on the Indian people certain rights and privileges in education, but some of the concepts of the Despatch like cultivation of Indian languages, use of the mother tongue as the medium of instruction at the school stage, institution of university professorships in some subjects including vernaculars and classical languages, Law and Civil Engineering, concept of mass education and that of secular education in a plural society like India were the concepts which are significantly valid in an independent India. The Despatch realised that the goal of education was primarily employment and as such vocational education as well as absorption of qualified Indians in government services was emphasised. It hoped that Indian private enterprise would gradually replace the government in education through grants-in-aid and would help develop an education rooted in Indian soil.

It is not the fault of the framers of the Education Despatch that some of the provisions were never carried out and that some were given effect to in a mutilated form, while some others, the institution of teaching posts in universities, were implemented after a considerable lapse of time. It is however too much to expect that the Despatch, meant for the education of a colonialised people by an imperial power, would visualise concepts in education which are the products of recent changes in the socio-economic and political structure in the world. As M.R. Paranjpe has observed in his *Progress of Education* in 1941, which has received wide endorsement from educationists like J.P. Naik and S. Nurullah: "The Despatch does not even refer to the ideal of universal literacy although it expects education to spread over a wider field through the grants-in-aid system: it does not recognise the obligation of the state to educate every child below a certain age; it does not declare that poverty shall be no bar to the education of deserving students; and while it may be admitted that employment in government offices was not the object of English education as visualised in the Despatch, the authors did not aim at education for leadership, education for the industrial regeneration of India, education for the defence of the motherland, in short, education required by the people of a self-government nation". Was India a self-government nation in 1854? In the hey-days of British imperialism, it was not possible for the Despatch to visualise all these.

The most valid criticism about the Despatch was the one made by Dalhousie. As noted earlier the Despatch which "left nothing to be desired" did not recognise the various developments in education during the governor-generalship of Dalhousie and his predecessors which were given shape to in the various provisions of the Despatch, and as such "calculated to lead the world to infer an inactivity in the part of Government of India in the promotion of General Education with which it is not justly chargeable". As Dalhousie described it in one of his letters to his very old friend, Couper, it was "the shabbiest injustice to the Government of India".

Despite its drawbacks, the Education Despatch of 1854 offers us a platform to measure the changes in education in response to the changes in our society over the years since 1854. As H.R. James has correctly observed about the Despatch in his *Education and*

Citizenship in India: "What goes before leads up to it; what follows, flows from it".

Implementation of the Education Despatch of 1854 and its Endorsement in 1859

Dalhousie, however, did not allow his personal feelings to stand in the way of the implementation of the provisions of the Despatch, which opened an era of "Anglo-Vernacular educational epoch" in the history of Indian education. He realised that "it contained, a scheme of education for all India, far wider and more comprehensive than the Local or the Supreme Government would have ventured to suggest. It left nothing to be desired". In January 1855, Dalhousie laid the proposals for working out the Despatch of 1854 before his Council and by February, he was able to report to Wood about the launching of the scheme. He expressed his hope that if he lived, he would see "the whole organised and in complete operation (so far as this can be affected at once)".

And he did not hope in vain. By the end of 1855 a distinct department for the superintendence of education was constituted and a Director of Public Instruction had been appointed in each of the five provinces with inspectors and others appointed in each of them. Provisional rules for regulating grants-in-aid had been sanctioned for the guidance of the local governments. And finally, a Committee had been appointed for the purpose of framing a scheme for the establishment of universities at the Presidency towns of Calcutta, Bombay and Madras. By the time Dalhousie retired from India in March 1856 it was still engaged on that difficult task.

Need for an Endorsement of the Education Despatch after the Revolt of 1857

In 1857, the British empire in India was badly shaken by the outbreak of the Revolt of the Sepoys and in a despatch next year Lord Ellenborough, the President of the Board of Control wanted to withdraw the education policy enunciated by the Education Despatch of 1854 on the ground that some of the provisions like mass education, female education and financial help to mission schools might have contributed to the catastrophe of 1857. Hardly had there been any time to act on the recommendations of Ellenborough when the British Government in India changed. By Queen's Proclamation of 1858, the power was transferred from the Company to the Crown.

The post of the President of the Board of Control was replaced by the post of the Secretary of State for India who, with his Council, was made ultimately responsible for the British administration in India. Such a major change in administration required that the new authorities should review the existing policies including those in education and either confirm or amend them as early as possible.

The Education Despatch endorsed

Lord Stanley, the first Secretary of State, wanted to ascertain how far it would be right for him to pursue the education policy enunciated by the Despatch of 1854. Stanley's Despatch in 1859, following a review of the Education Despatch of 1854 did not make any drastic change in it but after admitting that prior to 1854 nothing was done seriously for the cause of elementary education, it observed that the grants-in-aid system hitherto in force in spite of its success with English and Anglo-Vernacular schools was not suitable for providing elementary education to the masses. It suggested that the government should itself run and establish elementary schools and should, if necessary, levy a compulsory local rate for defraying expenses. There was no doubt that Stanley was influenced by contemporary events in England, where the movement for the imposition of local taxes and the establishment of a system of public school had just begun as well as in India, Thomason's successful plan of levying one per cent on land revenue for defraying the expenditure of village schools. In doing so, Stanley missed the golden opportunity of combining the efforts of two agencies in the field of elementary education - voluntary effort and local organisation; and elementary education after becoming a sole responsibility of the government remained stunted in growth for many years to come.

Note

1. For fuller details, see my article, "Dalhousie Charles Wood and the Education Despatch of 1854" in *History of Education,* London, Summer 1975, Vol. 4, No. 2. pp. 37-40.

28

Expansion of Education Till 1882

The year following the Education Despatch of 1854 saw the growth and development of education at all levels – higher, secondary and elementary. We shall now analyse this growth and development of education under three heads: higher education, secondary and elementary education, in the following pages.

Higher Education

Establishment of Universities at Calcutta, Bombay and Madras

In January 1857, Lord Canning, Dalhousie's successor, passed the Acts of Incorporation which provided for the establishment of universities in Calcutta, Bombay and Madras on the model of the University of London (as provided by the Education Despatch of 1854). The preambles in these Acts of Incorporation establishing the three universities were identical. They defined the objects of the universities to be "ascertaining by means of examination the persons who have acquired proficiency in different branches of Literature, Science and Art and of rewarding them by Academic Degrees as evidence of their respective attainments". There was to be a Chancellor, a Vice-Chancellor and fellows, both *ex-officio* and ordinary, who together would constitute the "Body Politic and Corporate" for each of the three universities. The number of the fellows excluding the Chancellor and Vice-Chancellor was to be not less than 30. While the fellows ex-officio were to hold their fellow-ships during their official tenure only, the ordinary fellows were to be appointed by the government for life-vacancies in their ranks which could arise only by death, resignation or permanent retirement from India in the case of European officials, or by cancellation of the appointment by the government. Among these fellows, "the teachers were present as it were by accident, not by right; and many of the colleges, especially those in the mofussil were never represented at all". Thus, most of the fellows who were public men and administrators had little experience of teaching and knowledge of the problems they had to deal with. The university administration was run by a syndicate which was not mentioned in the Acts of Incorporation but its origin could be traced to an interpretation of Clause VIII of these acts which gave to the Chancellor, Vice-Chancellor and fellows, powers to control the university affairs as well as to make and alter by laws and regulations in general, touching on all matters regarding the university.

Nature of the Universities established

The universities established in 1857 by the Acts of Incorporation were affiliating universities and no geographical limits to the areas of the affiliation were indicated. Calcutta University, for example, functioned not merely for Bengal, but for Burma, Assam, the Central Provinces and Ceylon, and the affiliated colleges were dispersed from Simla and Mussorie to Indore and Jaipur, and from Jaffna and Batticaloa to Sylhet and Chittagong. A large number of colleges – government, aided and unaided were affiliated to each of the three universities, but the rules for affiliation framed by the university were not very strict. Indeed, the first rules for affiliation prepared by Calcutta University in February 1857 demanded, for example, only that the college seeking affiliation submit a declaration, countersigned by at least two members of the university senate, enumerating the staff and courses of study for the previous two years and of the institution's ability to impart education up to the standard of the degree of B.A. Managed by their own governing bodies, the affiliated colleges were not part of the university. They had no control over their required courses of study and their only function was to prepare students for examinations conducted by the university. They were created mostly through the generosity of the government and philanthropic societies, missionary bodies, or wealthy Indians interested in spreading enlightenment.

Affiliated Colleges

The number of such affiliated colleges had risen from 27 in 1857 to 72 by 1881-82. The government colleges among them included the Presidency College at Calcutta, developed from the Hindu College in 1853 by Dalhousie; the Presidency College at Madras developed from the Madras High School; the University College at Lahore (1869) where European education was imparted through the medium of the mother tongue and the study of Oriental languages was encouraged; and the Muir Central College at Allahabad, the foundation stone for which was laid by Lord Northbrook in 1873. The last two colleges later developed into Punjab and Allahabad Universities in 1882 and 1886 respectively.

It is interesting to note here that by 1881-82 Indians, were conducting five aided colleges – two in the North-Western Provinces and three in the Madras Presidency. The two colleges in the North-Western Provinces were the Canning College established by the Oudh Talukdars at Lucknow (1864) and the Mahomedan Anglo Oriental College established by Syed Ahmed Khan at Aligarh (1875) for spreading Western education among the Muslims – both of which developed into universities later. The three colleges in the Madras Presidency were the Pachaiyappa's College and the Hindu College at Vizianagram (1857) and Tninevelly (1861).

It was during this period that Rajkot College (1870), Mayo College, Ajmer (1872) and Daly College, Indore (1876) were established for the education of the Princes in the Indian States. Some notably missionary colleges were established during 1855-1882 : St. Xavier's Colleges of Calcutta (1860) and Bombay (1869), Forman College of Lahore (1864), Reid College of Lucknow (1877) and St. Stephen's College of Delhi (1882). As these colleges, except the Civil Engineering College at Shibpur in Bengal were opened to impart education in liberal arts, in 1876 Mahendra Lal Sircar founded the Indian Association for Cultivation of Science in Calcutta.

Students

The material advantages that were then attainable by the holders of university degrees attracted many Indians to higher education. In 1857 the number of students who successfully passed the first matriculation examinations of the universities was only 219 (Calcutta-162, Madras-36, Bombay-21) but by 1881-82 it had risen to 2,778 out of the

7,429 candidates who had appeared. The standard of examination was very high and in the 1858 examination for the B.A. degree of Calcutta university, 11 out of 13 who took the examination failed. Bankim Chandra Chatterji and Jadu Nath Bose were the first two graduates of Indian universities.

Neglect of the Modern Indian Languages

In these universities the study of the modern Indian languages was neglected, though in Bombay University a modern Indian language could be taken up as a subject from the matriculation to the B.A. examinations. In 1862, Alexander Grant, Director of Public Instruction in Bombay argued for the abolition of all modern Indian languages from all university examinations except the matriculation where its use would be optional, as no standard textbooks were available in them, and suggested greater attention to the study of the classical languages in their places. The acceptance of this proposal led to the discontinuance of the teaching of the Indian languages in the colleges and since their study was optional at the secondary stage, the schools also began to neglect them.

Secondary Education

Increase in the Number of Schools and Students

The creation of the departments of education in the five provinces of British India and the provision for a liberal grants-in-aid in each province led to a tremendous increase in the growth of secondary schools in all the five provinces. In 1854, the number of government schools was 169, attended by 18,335 students. In 1882, it rose to 1,362, attended by 44,605 students. Before 1857, the missionaries were the main non-government agent in the educational field but soon the Indians began to show a keen interest. Supported by the government aid they began opening schools for their children and by 1882 out-distanced the missionary enterprise in the field. In 1882, the Indians controlled 1,341 institutions while the missionaries had under their management 757 schools. In Bengal, the number of institutions under Indian management was quite large because they in most cases met the expenditure of their institutions from the fees charged on the students and did not have to depend upon the education department for grants-in-aid.

Medium of Instruction

Contrary to the suggestion of the Despatch of 1854, English came to be adopted as the medium of instruction. The schools prepared the students for the matriculation examination of the universities and the universities at Bombay and Madras followed the example of the Calcutta University which had since 1862 made use of English as the compulsory medium of answering papers in such subjects as Geography, History, Arithmetic and Science. There was no provision for vocational education except in one school at Bombay (1882) where students were awarded a scholarship of Rs 4 per month while obtaining training in agriculture. The students were mostly interested in obtaining matriculation certificates either to qualify for clerical jobs in government establishments or for entering colleges where the medium of instruction was English - not merely because the department of education insisted on English as the medium but also because most of the colleges were either staffed or managed by Europeans - to earn degrees which would fetch them highly paid jobs. In many cases school managers themselves were willing to instruct their pupils through the medium of English so that they had the best opportunities of reading, speaking and writing in English. Thus except in the Punjab, the highest education that could be obtained through vernaculars was limited to the middle stage only. By 1882 there were nearly 181 high schools teaching through English as against four imparting instruction through the vernaculars.

Teachers' Training Institutions

The absence of trained teachers in these schools aggravated the situation - there were only two training institutions for secondary school teachers – one at Madras (1856) and the other at Lahore (1880). In 1882 there were 8 graduates, 3 FAs and 18 matriculates at the Madras College while the Lahore College admitted 20 students of any qualification higher than that of a first year's examination in Arts (FAs). There was no practice school and all the students, despite their differences in attainments, were required to go through the same course. In any case only a small number of teachers could avail themselves even of this imperfect training. Thus, the three most important instructions of the Education Despatch of 1854 – vernaculars, vocational education and trained teacher – did not characterise the developments of secondary education during 1855-1882.

Elementary Education

Stanley on Elementary Education

In elementary education it was the missionary organisations rather than the Company which held the field. By 1854 while only 36,000 pupils were educated in government elementary schools, the mission schools were instructing almost twice the number. The Education Despatch of 1854 had rightly therefore urged the spread of mass education through grants-in-aid but five years later Stanely's Despatch reversed the order and directed that local rates should be levied for the spread of mass education through government efforts. The Despatch observed: "The grants-in-aid system, as hitherto, in force, is unsuited to the supply of Vernacular Education to the masses of the population; and it appears to them, so far as they have been able to form an opinion, that the means of elementary education should be provided by the direct instrumentality of the officers of Government, according to some one of the plans in operation in Bengal and the North-Western Provinces, or by such modification of those schemes as may commend itself to the several local Governments as best suited to the circumstances of different localities". The Despatch also suggested that "in order to avoid the difficulties experienced in obtaining voluntary local support, an education rate should be imposed, from which the cost of all schools throughout the country should be defrayed".

Dilemma for the Provincial Governments

Stanley's Despatch which reflected contemporary opinion on the development of elementary education in England created a sort of dilemma among the various provincial governments in India. While some provinces like Madras and Bengal, and Assam, which was a part of Bengal till 1874, attempted improvement of indigenous schools, encouraged local efforts through grants-in-aid and created some government schools as models, others like Bombay, North-Western Provinces, Punjab and Coorg solely neglected indigenous schools.

Progress of Elementary Education

As observed before, it was the success of Thomason's scheme for a levy of one per cent on land revenue, which was shared equally between the government and the landlords and devoted its proceeds to the maintenance of elementary schools in rural areas, that inspired

Stanley's idea of an 'education rate'. In the decade between 1861 and 1871 this suggestion was carried out in all the provinces except Bengal where no cess on land revenue could be imposed even as late as 1881, owing mainly to the existence of the Permanent Settlement of land revenue which was held to be a legal bar for the levy of any cess on land. Elementary education had made good progress by 1871 and by 1881-82 there were as many as 82,916 schools with 20,61,541 pupils as against 16,473 schools with 6,07,320 pupils in 1870-71.

Low Literacy Level

Inspite of such a growth, however, out of a total population of 195,875,127 in the whole of British India, only 20,61,541 attended elementary schools in 1881-82. These figures only reveal that the literacy level in India was considerably low compared to the growing population of British India in 1881-82. The indifference of the government officials to elementary education, provision of inadequate funds, and frequent diversion of money raised through local cess for educational purposes to other channels were some of the factors hindering the growth of elementary education between 1854 and 1882.

29

The Hunter Commission

A careful perusal of the developments in education in British India since 1855 reveals that many of these were not in accordance with the provisions of the Education Despatch of 1854. Contrary to the expectations of the Despatch, the government did not only withdraw from the field of education but also failed to build up a system of mass education through grants-in-aid. As a matter of fact, elementary education was much neglected at the expense of secondary and higher education. All these were certainly grounds for a review of the educational developments in the country since 1855 but the matter was actually hastened by the Christian missionaries.

Missionary Agitation for Leadership in Education

The Christian missionaries were particularly sore when they found that they could no longer reach the masses through an education system built upon grants-in-aid. They were further irked by the Queen's Proclamation of 1858 following the Revolt of 1857 which assured the Indian people of the British Raj's non-interference in religious matters. The government officials who adopted an unsympathetic attitude to mission schools and followed a line of direct competition by creating rival schools added further to their difficulties.

The missionaries therefore started an agitation both in India and in England complaining that, (a) the educational administration in India was not carried out in accordance with the provisions of the Education Despatch of 1854 which had recommended withdrawal of government from the field of education, (b) that the government officials were competing with missionary educational endeavour to such an extent that the mission schools were now threatened with extinction and (c) that the secular education imparted in government institutions was Godless. In England they formed "the General Council of Education in India" which included among its members important personalities such as Lord Lawrence, and Lord Halifax (Charles Wood). When Lord Ripon's name was announced as the Viceroy of India in 1882, a delegation of this Council waited upon him and requested him to institute an enquiry into the state of Indian education. Ripon observed: "The Despatch lays down clearly and forcibly the broad lines of the true educational policy for India, and upon these lines it will be my desire to work. It will be my duty when I get out to India to examine all such matters carefully in the light of the information which will then be at my disposal; but I do not think I shall be guilty of any indiscretion if I tell you even now how much I sympathise with your desire to promote the extension of elementary education among the poorer classes. This has been a special object of interest for many years in England, it will not be less so in India".

Appointment of Hunter Commission and its Terms of Reference

In February 1882, Ripon appointed the first Indian Education Commission with William Hunter, a member of his Executive Council, as its Chairman. Among its 20 members, Indians were represented by Anand Mohan Bose, Bhudev Mukherjee, Syed Mahmud and K.T. Telung, and the missionaries by Rev. Dr. Miller of Madras. B.L. Rice, the Mysore Director of Public Instruction, was appointed its secretary. The Commission was asked "to enquire particularly into the manner in which effect had been given to the principles of the Despatch of 1854 and to suggest such measures as it might think desirable with a view to the further carrying out of the policy therein laid down". The Commission was also asked to keep the enquiry into the primary education in the forefront, partly because of an agitation alleging its neglect in India, and partly because a national system of compulsory elementary education was built up in England two years ago with the passing of the Elementary Education Act in 1880. The Commission was further asked to enquire into the position of the government institutions in a national system of education, the position of the missionary institutions in it and the attitude of the government towards private enterprise. The Commission was also asked to offer suggestions on secondary education – European, and university education being excluded from the purview of the Commission.

The Commission submitted its Report

The Commission first started at Calcutta for nearly seven weeks and thereafter toured India for eight months examining witnesses and collecting materials, and finally submitted its voluminous report of more than 600 folio pages and 222 resolutions in 1883.

The most notable part of the Commission's recommendations was that it freed the government from the responsibilities of mass education by entrusting these to the local boards and suggested a gradual transfer of government colleges and secondary schools to efficient private bodies. Indians were thus required to raise funds for their own education and their efforts were to be assisted by a liberal grants-in-aid system. In this context the Commission reviewed the system of grants-in-aid prevalent in different provinces – the salary Grant System of Madras, the Payment-by Results System of Bombay and the Fixed Period System of Northern and Central India – and suggested that each state should be left free to adopt any system which would best suit its local conditions. There was to be no discrimination between government and non-government institutions while applying the rules of grants-in-aid to them.

Support for Indigenous Education

The Commission supported the indigenous system of education which had been waning for want of patronage. According to its definition, indigenous education was one "established or conducted by natives of India on native methods" and it observed that by surviving "a severe competition", these indigenous schools had proved both their vitality and popularity. The Commission recommended that they should be developed, patronised, and assisted to "fill a useful position in the state system of national education". The management of these schools was left to district and municipal boards and they were left free to develop its curricula, method of teaching and mode of examination. It forbade the government officials to interfere with their affairs and suggested encouragement of the teachers of these schools by training them properly. However, the natural growth of these schools was checked by the adoption of the

System of Payment by Results, which had been regarded as detrimental to secondary and collegiate education.

Elementary Education with Vocational Overtones

As per the Resolution of the Government of India, 1882, "the principal object of the enquiry of the Commission" was "the development of elementary education" which was "one of the main objects contemplated by the Despatch of 1854". The Commission therefore boldly admitted that, "while every branch of education can justly claim the fostering care of the state, it is desirable, in the present circumstances of the country, to declare the elementary education of the masses, its provision, extension and improvement to be that part of the educational system to which the strenuous efforts of the state should now be directed in a still larger measure than heretofore". The Commission recommended that primary education should be closely related to the practical aspect of the masses and so while allowing considerable "catholicity of views in allowing all the provinces to adopt a curriculum suited to their needs, they recommended that such curriculum should include certain subjects of practical utility, such as, book-keeping, mensuration, arithmetic and natural and physical sciences with their application to agriculture, health and industrial arts. The government should encourage primary education by throwing appointments at a lower level to merely literate persons – persons who can read and write – and should provide liberal grants-in-aid to primary education in tribal regions and educationally backward districts.

Management

The management of primary education was left to the local boards introduced in India by Lord Ripon's Local Self-Government Act. These boards modelled on the County Councils which managed primary education in England were responsible for the management and expansion of primary education of a particular locality. The Commission suggested that accounts of rural and urban primary institutions be separated so that the funds of rural institutions were not misappropriated by urban primary schools. Every district and municipal board was asked to keep a separate fund for education which should be exclusively used for the purpose for which it was meant. The Commission also asked the provincial governments to contribute to the local funds by a suitable system of grants-in-aid preferably at the rate of half the local assets or one-third of the total expenditure.

Normal Schools

The Commission which emphasised the need for establishing normal schools for the training of teachers, preferably at least one in each division, suggested that the provision of normal schools along with the cost of direction and inspection of primary education should be "the first charge on provincial funds".

Finance

The Commission thus pressed the claims of primary education on different types of funds but the funds placed at the disposal of the local boards were insignificant in view of the vast population of the country. Further the mode of grants-in-aid adopted for primary education in India, that is, Payment-by-Results introduced in England two years ago had already proved a failure, wherever it was tried and the Commission should have been more liberal in providing funds to the local boards. Finally, the government was able to shift responsibility for primary education entirely to the local bodies recently introduced in India, and much depended on the strength of such bodies to discharge their obligation towards the development of primary education. The history of primary education in India would have been different, had the government itself taken full responsibility for its development at this stage.

Bifurcation of Courses at Secondary Level

In secondary and collegiate education, as has been said earlier, the Commission recommended gradual withdrawal of the government from direct enterprise through a liberal and judicial use of the system of grants-in-aid. It however, suggested that the government should maintain some secondary schools, at least one model high school, in such districts "where they may be required in the interests of the people, and where the people themselves may not be advanced or wealthy enough to establish such schools for themselves with a grants-in-aid". The Commission also allowed the managers of these institutions to charge less fees than those of the government institutions and recommended bifurcation in the curricula to maintain a high standard in secondary and collegiate education. It suggested an 'A' course which was meant for the entrance examination of the universities and a 'B' course which was meant for commercial and non-literary studies. However, the commission kept silent on the medium of instruction, thereby implying the use of English.

Grants-in-aid for Collegiate Education

As far as college education was concerned, the Commission suggested that "the rate of aid to each college be determined by the strength of the staff, the expenditure on its maintenance, the efficiency of the institution and the wants of the locality". The Commission made valuable recommendations on the subjects of providing jobs, higher studies abroad and introduction of a wide and comprehensive curricula in different colleges of India to suit the needs of various students. However, as in the case of secondary schools, the Commission's permission to the private institutions to charge a lower rate of fees compared to the government institutions led to an undesirable and unhealthy growth of rivalry among institutions many of which were inefficient. Yet the Commission was far ahead in time in respect of measures which are now engaging the attention of our educational planners.

Provision for Educationally Backward Classes: Muslim and Women

While the Commission was anxious to extend the benefits of primary education to the backward classes, including aboriginal tribes and low castes through an exemption of fees, the disparity in the educational progress of the Hindu and Muslim communities as well as of males and females also attracted the attention of its members. The Commission recommended special educational facilities to the Muslims for encouragement of indigenous Muslim schools like the establishment of Muslim High, Middle and Primary Schools and normal schools as well as institution of scholarship and studentship from primary to college level. For girls it suggested liberal grants to girls' schools, establishment of normal schools, institution of a simple curriculum for the primary education of girls, award of grants to the zenana teachers, and a separate inspectorate for girls' education as in the case of Muslims' education.

Other Recommendations

The Commission also pointed out the need for establishing special schools and colleges for the education of princes and children of the royal families. The need for adult education was also discussed and it was suggested that night schools wherever practicable be started for them. Finally, the Commission acknowledged that much depended on the teachers and their proper training. It suggested an examination in the principles and practice of teaching for teachers and permanent employment of the successful candidates as teachers in the secondary schools, aided or government. For graduates it suggested a shorter duration of such courses in a normal school.

Missionary Hope of Dominance frustrated by the Commission

The Commission however, threw cold water to the missionary hope of dominating the field of education in India after the withdrawal of the government from direct involvement in it. It observed: "The private effort which it is mainly intended to evoke is that of the people themselves. Natives of India must constitute the most important of all agencies of educational means.... In a country with such varied needs as India, we should deprecate any measure which would throw excessive influence over higher education into the hands of any single agency; and particularly into the hands of an agency which, however, benevolent and earnest, cannot on all points be in sympathy with the mass of the community .... At the same time we think it well to put on record our unanimous opinion that withdrawal of direct departmental agency should not take place in favour of missionary bodies and the departmental institutions of the higher order should not be transferred to missionary management". The only concession the Commission seemed to have taken to rectify the missionaries' charge of 'Godless education' was to instruct the principal or one of the professors in the college to deliver a series of lectures on the duties of a man and a citizen in each session. It further suggested that an attempt be made to prepare a moral text-book based on the fundamental principles of human and natural religions.

The Hunter Commission while making many valuable recommendations such as those on vocational and adult education, still valid today, suggested withdrawal of government support from the field of secondary and collegiate education. Recent research has established beyond doubt that there was a stronger political reason for this withdrawal. By the end of 1870s it was realised that the system of Western education introduced by the British Raj was "raising a number of discontented and disloyal subjects" and the gradual extension of the use of Western method of agitation and organisation acquired through the universities and colleges by the educated Indians was posing a "real danger to our rule in India" as Hamilton, the Secretary of State for India pointed out several decades later to Curzon. As a matter of fact, Sir William Hunter himself thought the government supported education was producing, among educated Indians, a sense of revolt against the three principles which represented "the deepest wants of human nature – the principle of discipline, the principle of religion, the principle of contentment". Ripon who appointed the Hunter Commission observed in his Convocation Address at the University of Bombay in 1884, rather sympathetically to the Indian cause: "It is little short of folly that we should throw open to increasing numbers the rich stores of Western learning; that we should inspire them with European ideas, and bring them into the closest contact with English thought, and that then we should as it were, pay no heed to the growth of those aspirations which we have ourselves created, and the pride of those ambitions we have ourselves called forth".

30

Developments in the Post-Hunter Commission Years

Elementary Education

The Government of India accepted the recommendations of the Hunter Commission, and transferred primary education to the charge of the Municipalities and District Boards, created on the pattern of the County Councils of England by the two Acts – the Municipal Act and the Local Self-Government Act – introducing self-government in India. However, the extent of the transfer of control and of financial support varied from state to state. While Bombay agreed to pay half as much as the local boards assigned to primary education, Madras and Central Provinces agreed to pay 5 per cent of their total revenues on education to it, and Bengal and North-Western Provinces took upon themselves the entire responsibility of supporting primary education financially. However, the progress of primary education was not satisfactory. Between 1885-86 and 1901-02, the increase in the number of pupils was only 66,00,000 as compared to nearly 2,00,000 between 1870-71 and 1885-86. The slow progress may be explained partly by the inability of the government to carry primary education to inaccessible areas inhabited by a people indifferent to education and partly by the lack of adequate finances – the expenditure on primary education by the government rose by a negligible thousand rupees per year from Rs 16.77 lakhs in 1881-82 to Rs 16.92 lakhs in 1901-02.

Secondary Education

However, secondary education showed considerable progress. The number of secondary schools rose from 3,916 in 1881-82 to 5,124 in 1901-02 and the number of students rose from 2,14,077 in 1881-82 to 5,90,129 in 1901-02. Following the recommendation of the Commission, almost all the provincial governments had included practical education under course 'B'. In 1888, Madras started an Upper Secondary Course which included technical subjects; in 1897 Bombay started a School Final Course which prepared the students for government posts of certain grades; in 1900 Bengal started a scheme for practical course – course B which led to technical schools and colleges and course C which prepared boys for clerical and commercial career and in 1901, Punjab started two courses for clerical and commercial examination and science entrance examination. But these new courses were not very popular – Madras for example could only get some 210 candidates for its course till 1901-02 though the Bombay course which prepared candidates for clerical posts in public services was to some extent popular. The secondary education was completely dominated by matriculation courses and thus while in 1901-02 some 23,000 candidates took the Matriculation examination, only 2,000 examinees sat for the examination of the B course of the Hunter Commission.

Higher Education

It was in the field of higher education that the Commission's recommendation on withdrawal of government support led to a phenomenal growth of private enterprise. Among the colleges, many of which grew out of high schools, were the Fergusson College at Poona which was founded up by B.G. Tilak, V.K. Chiplonkar and G.G. Agarkar, the Ripon College at Calcutta by Surendra Nath Banerjee, and the Dayanand Anglo-Vedic College at Lahore in 1886 by the Arya Samaj. Annie Besant founded the Central Hindu College at Benares in 1889 and among the colleges set up by the missionaries were the Indian Christian College at Sialkot in 1889, Christ Church College at Hapur in 1892 and Gordon College at Rawalpindi in 1893. However, the Christian missionaries aggrieved by the Commission's recommendation did not show much interest in higher education and the colleges remained mainly in the hands of the Indians. By 1901-02 the number of colleges had risen from 68 in 1881-82 to 179 including 9 in Ceylon and 2 in Burma.

Punjab University

In 1882 the Punjab University was established by a Special Act of Incorporation. It grew out of the college at Lahore which included a Faculty of Oriental Learning and later developed a Faculty of Law. Thus, unlike the older universities at Calcutta, Bombay and Madras, it carried on teaching work. The medium of instruction was Urdu in the Oriental Faculty which conferred degrees and the diplomas in Oriental languages, that is, Arabic, Persian and Sanskrit.

Allahabad University

After the establishment of Punjab University in 1882, it was thought necessary to set up a separate university in the North-Western Provinces to "stimulate local progress" as Calcutta University was "too far distant" to suitably aid the development of higher education in Northern India. So by another Special Act of Incorporation Allahabad University was created in 1887. The Act imposed no limitations on the scope and activity of the university but, as the Quinquennial Review of the Progress of Education in India, 1897-1902, pointed out, Allahabad conformed to the practice of the three original universities and "confined itself to conferring degrees on candidates" who passed its examinations after following a prescribed course of study in an institution affiliated to it as per the system introduced by the Acts of Incorporation in 1857. Thus, by the end of 1901-02 there were five universities in India conferring degrees and diplomas on candidates who had successfully gone through a prescribed course of learning in an affiliated college.

31

Towards a Control of Higher Education

The expansion of higher education in India in the decades following the Hunter Commission recommendations aggravated the existing problem of unemployment among the educated Indians. The annual output of the graduates had increased with the growing years and by 1883, as Henry Maine estimated, there were already some 25,000 BAs and MAs out of an estimated population of 25,00,00,000. Having received a good secondary school education up to the Matriculation level and having attended a university, these men were certainly very educated compared to the illiterate town-dwellers or village ryots.

Prospects for the Educated Indians

What was the prospect open to the large number of students who were thus able to receive higher education in the country? For one thing, careers in India were virtually never open to talent, though the principle had been asserted time and again in the Charter Act of 1833 and the Queen's Proclamation of 1858 after the Mutiny to allay fear, suspicion and distrust. Again some avenues like army and politics were closed altogether. In those days agriculture offered little temptation and so did manufacturing and commerce, for the latter was almost impossible without skill, capital and equality of terms with which it could compete with European industry. As a matter of fact, the very nature of the courses with their "unique and disproportionate attention" to literature and philosophy compared with physical and cognate branches of practical instruction tended to limit the choice of a career to either government service or analogous employment. "What else can he do but qualify himself", lamented a Calcutta newspaper, *Indian Mirror*, "or, if he is a father, train his son for the public service or one of the learned professions".

In theory, the covenanted civil service was open to Indians since 1853 but in practice every difficulty stood in their way – the very early age-limits for the examination, the nature of the syllabus, the expense of going to London where the examination was held, the prejudice against crossing the "black water" and the official reluctance to admit Indians into this vital service. The only posts open to the Indians were at the lower level of the uncovenanted service. Here, the salaries were very poor, prospects for promotions nil and service conditions extremely bad.

The non-availability of suitable openings in the public service naturally compelled many to turn to independent professions such as teaching, law, journalism and medicine. Unlike the government servants who were dependent on the goodwill of their employers, these professionals had greater incentive for taking part in public life. By the end of 1870s and the beginning of 1880s there was hardly any important town in India which did not possess a sprinkle of teachers, lawyers, journalists and doctors who took a very lively and keen interest in social, political, economic and religious questions of the day.

Growing Unemployment among the Educated Indians

The professionals were fortunate but for the majority of the young Indians who went to schools and colleges, higher education brought no solace and as Sir Richard Temple, the Lieutenant Governor of Bengal, observed in a minute on 5 January 1877, it was "melancholy to see men, who once appeared to receive their honours in the university convocation now applying, for some lowly-paid appointment, almost begging from office to office, from department to department, or struggling for the practice of petty practitioner". Nevertheless, even with these examples before their eyes, "hundreds, perhaps thousands of young men persist in embarking on the same course which can lead only to the same sad ending", so lamented the Lieutenant Governor Richard Temple. By January 1889, the problem of unemployment among the educated Indians reached such a dimension that Lord Lansdowne, the Governor-General of India, drew pointed attention to it at his Calcutta Convocation Address as

Chancellor: "I am afraid we must not disguise from ourselves that if our schools and colleges continue to educate the youth of India at the present rate, we are likely to hear even more than we do at present of the complaint that we are turning out every year an increasing number of young men whom we have provided with an intellectual equipment admirable in itself but practically useless to them on account of the small number of openings which the professions afford for gentlemen who have received this kind of education".

The growing unemployment among the educated Indians and the latter's disillusionment with the British Raj's policy towards the problem increasingly added fuel to the nationalistic sentiments that had been growing ever since the middle of the nineteenth century. Bound together by common backgrounds, common occupations, and common grievances against the official system, the new educated class began to write in English dailies and to meet in associations to demand rights of the Indians especially those of representation and employment. In 1885 when the Indian National Congress, which Hume saw as a safety-valve to the growing discontent with the alien rule, was formed, it adopted "wider employment of the people in the public service" as one of "the three important questions" constituting "the chief planks in the Congress platform". Hardly any annual session of the Indian National Congress took place without a discussion on the subject of employment– "the most important key to our material and moral advancement" as Dadabhai Naoroji described it in the very first session, passing resolutions on it. In the session in 1900, Surendra Nath Banerjea quoted figures for Bengal to show how the Government of India was deliberately evading the various pledges and principles made in the Charter Act of 1833 and the Queen's Proclamation of 1858 regarding the employment of Indians in the public service. "If you look at the statistics...," Banerjea observed, "you will find that the higher offices, the bulk of the higher offices – I should not be guilty of the smallest exaggeration if I say that at least 90 per cent of the higher offices – are filled by Europeans and Anglo-Indians ... Imperialists, somebody says; they may be imperialists or not but at any rate these Departments constitute the close preserve, the absolute monopoly of these gentlemen. We are excluded. And why? Because of our race. Our colour is our disqualification".

Rise of Militant Nationalism and the Reaction of the British Raj

While the "discontended BAs and MAs" must have shared Banerjea's views on the policy of the Government of India with regard to the appointment of Indians to the Indian Civil Service and lesser services, some of them were becoming advocates of a more militant nationalism. The latter became adherents of the new generation of leaders like B.G. Tilak, Lajpat Rai and Bipin Chandra Pal, more "extremist" than the previous leadership. In Bengal, the extremist challenge began with Aurobindo's fierce attack on the Congress in 1893. Next year, Alfred Croft reported in his Convocation Address at Calcutta that lack of any suitable openings for those who had just been able to take their degrees as well as those who had failed was posing a grave problem. Quoting from Bacon's *Of Seditions and Troubles,* he underlined the danger by warning that one of the chief causes of discontent was "when more are bred scholars than preferment can take off".

In 1897, in the last year of Lord Elgin's viceroyalty when Bombay was threatened with an outbreak of plague, two educated young men, Damodar and Balkrishna Chapekar murdered Rand, the Collector and Plague Officer of Poona and his associate, Lt. Ayerst. As a reaction to the Poona murders, in 1898, the Government of India enacted the "Sedition Law". After going through the papers leading to the Poona murders, Hamilton found it impossible to dissociate these young men's ideas and hatred of England from the course of education and training through which they had passed. Hamilton and his advisers regarded the Fergusson College at Poona where Damodar and Balkrishna had studied as the mainspring of a small but deep rooted political conspiracy in the Deccan.

Hamilton's views on the Poona murders thus brought to a head the sentiments of those British officials who had since the early 1870s been pondering over the utility of spreading English education in India. Gustave LeBon, a French publicist and social scientist who visited India in the early 1880s, commented that English education was not at all suitable for the Indians' who had a strong traditional culture. The latter could not satisfy the wants created by English education and so the English-educated wrote to the Indian press with bitter attacks on the Raj. The "Babus", as he called the English-educated Indians in Bengal, were the enemies of British rule and it was silly to rule the country through them.

In the decades following the birth of the Indian National Congress, the feeling spread that the decision to promote education in English, ever since the days of Macaulay, was a "short story of grave political miscalculation" containing a lesson "that has its significance for other nations which have undertaken a similar enterprise". English education which was identified with higher education in India had given birth to a tone of mind and to a type of character that was "ill-regulated, averse from discipline, discontented, and in some cases actually disloyal". In short, it had raised a "fighting cock" while it was expected to raise "an innocuous hen". As Curzon later declared in connection with his scheme for education reform at the Conference at Simla, "When Erasmus was reproached with having laid the egg from which came forth the Reformation, 'Yes', he replied: 'but I laid a hen's egg, and Luther had hatched a fighting cock'. This, I believe, is pretty much the view of a good many critics of English education in India".

Schemes for Checking the Spread of Higher Education

Curzon himself fully subscribed to this view. Five weeks after landing at Calcutta, while delivering the Calcutta University Convocation Address as its Chancellor on 11 February 1899, he observed '*that our system of higher education in India is a failure; that it has sacrificed the formation of character upon the alter of cram; and that the Indian University turn out only a discontented horde of office seekers, whom we educated for places which are not in existence for them to fill*'.[1] Since it was not too late to undo Macaulay's or Bentinck's decisions to offer English education in India, the best that could be done at that moment was to devise means to restrict its disadvantages.

One of the means could have been to divert the attention of the young Indians from Western education to Oriental education which Annie Besant's Hindu College in Benares proposed to impart now "by undertaking the task of giving religious and moral education on Hindu lines to its Youths". Hamilton was willing to "encourage" Besant's scheme of education. As he wrote to Curzon in connection with Besant's Hindu College, "I think the real danger to our rule in India, not now but say 50 years hence, is the gradual adoption and extension of Western agitation and organisation; and if we could break the Hindu party into two sections holding widely different views, we should, by such a division strengthen our position against the subtle and continuous attack which the spread of education make upon our present system of Government".

Another means would be, as had been unsuccessfully done by the government before in the 1870s and in 1882, to give more attention to primary and secondary education and less to higher education. Anything, Hamilton remarked rather gloomily, would be better than expansion of purely literary education, "joy of the Babu and anglicised Brahmin" which "produces a wholesale mass of discontented individuals who, if they cannot find government employment spend their time in abusing the government which has educated them".

Curzon Opted for Control of Higher Education

Curzon was not too happy with Besant's scheme because it was associated with "not merely active, but disloyal politicians" though Besant "herself had no political motives"; he thought, however, that the best course to slow down what Hamilton later described in his *Reminiscences* as the "educational juggernaut" was to bring higher education under effective governmental control.

Note

1. Italics are mine.

32

The Age of Curzon, 1899-1905

Curzon's university reform became the pivot upon which his other reforms in education revolved. The most important fallout of his reform of the Indian universities was the first official announcement of the future education policy of the Government of India to reduce the tension created among the educated Indians by the process of his university reform. We shall study Curzon's age in education in British India under two heads, first, Curzon's university reform and second, the White Paper on Indian education announced on 4 March 1904 – a few days before the passing of the Indian Universities Act.

Curzon's University Reform

Curzon revealed his Plan for University Reform to Hamilton

As mentioned earlier, Curzon gave top priority to his reforms of higher education from the very beginning of his term as the Viceroy and Governor-General of India in January 1899. He allowed himself sufficient time to study the university question and took one important step when he appointed his friend, Raleigh, as the Vice-Chancellor of the University of Calcutta, then the largest among the five existing universities in India. In August 1901, he wrote to Hamilton: "I think it very likely that in the case of the universities for the reform of which we shall almost inevitably be compelled to resort to legislation, I shall have to appoint a small preliminary commission to go round and take evidence at Calcutta, Madras and Bombay, and allow the instructed MAs and BAs who swarm at these capitals to have their say in advance.... Such a situation as the present with a

Chancellor and a Vice-Chancellor of the Calcutta University in the persons of myself and Raleigh who are both Fellows of an Oxford College and strongly imbued with the university feeling is probably not likely to occur again for a long time in India. It would be a pity not to take advantage of it to carry out reforms which everyone admits to be essentials, which nobody hitherto has dared to touch; but which I think that I have the strength of position to carry through. If left alone to develop upon the present lines the Indian universities will ere long develop into nurseries of discontented characters and stunted brains. There are many, many indeed who say, that the effect has already been produced".

Defects of the Indian Universities as set up in 1857

There is no doubt that the five universities in India suffered from a series of defects. Majority of the ills which had plagued these universities could be traced to the Acts of Incorporation passed by the Governor-General and Viceroy, Lord Canning in January 1857, which provided for their establishment at Calcutta, Bombay and Madras.

As we have already seen in one of the preceding chapters, the preambles in the Acts of Incorporations establishing the three universities were identical – they defined the objects of the universities as "ascertaining by means of examination the persons who have acquired proficiency in different branches of Literature, Science and Art and of rewarding them by Academic Degrees as evidence of their respective attainments". There was to be a Chancellor, a Vice-Chancellor and fellows, both ex-officio and ordinary who together would constitute the "Body Politic and Corporate" for each of the three universities. The number of the fellows excluding the Chancellor and Vice-Chancellor was to be not less than thirty. While the ex-officio fellows were to hold the fellowship during their official tenure only, the ordinary fellows were to be appointed by the government for life – vacancies in their ranks were caused only by death, resignation and cancellation of appointment by the government, permanent retirement from India in the case of European officials.

In 1882, the Punjab University was established by a Special Act of Incorporation and in 1887, another Special Act of Incorporation established the fifth Indian university at Allahabad. The general framework of these two Special Acts of Incorporation was similar to the Acts of 1857, though power was given to the Senates of the Punjab and the Allahabad Universities "to appoint or provide for the appointment of Professor and Lecturers" – a privilege which was denied by the Acts of Incorporation to the first three universities at Calcutta, Bombay and Madras in 1857. The first three universities were deliberately intended to be examining universities only, in the same manner and on the same model as the then University of London. Thereby it ignored an important suggestion of the Education Despatch of 1854 which suggested possible institution of "professorships for the purpose of the delivery of lectures in various branches of learning for the acquisition of which, at any rate in an advanced degree, facilities do not now exist in other institutions in India". When Lahore and Allahabad got this privilege in 1882 and 1887 respectively, the Indians had asked for its extension to Calcutta, Bombay and Madras but European officials closely connected with the university contested it on two grounds: first that the demand for constitutional expansions was fictitious in as much as the place of a teaching university had in reality been taken by the collegiate system which had sprung into existence since 1857, and second that it would be vain and foolish to constitute professorships or lectureships for higher students than those who attended the college lectures because of the absence of such students, courses and any funds forthcoming for the endowment. In the case of the Punjab University only, the endowment came in the form of a grant of Rs 12,000 a year from the Government of India for maintaining the Oriental institutions and the classes in Oriental learning.

However, the most glaring defect of the Acts of Incorporation was in the appointment of the, fellows to the Senates of these universities. These fellows were appointed for life and not for a special period. There was also no upper limit to the number of the fellows to be appointed, though the minimum was fixed at 30. The minimum was the same at Allahabad but at Lahore it was raised to 50. The number of fellows steadily rose at Calcutta from 40 in 1857 to a maximum of 220 in 1890. Lord Lansdowne, in his Convocation Address on 18 January 1890, recognised the anomaly and proposed gradually to bring about its reduction, but how small an advance had been made in this direction could be seen from the fact that when Curzon came to India in the last week of December 1898, the number still stood at 200. Helped by "natural causes" and by his refusal to exercise the right of nomination, Curzon had been able to bring it to a little over 180 in 1901. As regards the composition and qualifications of the 180 fellows, excluding those who had been returned by election, the practice had been for the Chancellor to invite recommendations from the Lieutenant Governor of Bengal, the Vice-Chancellor of the University and from such representative persons as he might care to consult. The result had been that the fellowship came to be regarded as a sort of a titular reward, conferred without much reference to the academic qualifications of the recipient, but rather as a stage of promotion in an Indian career. Prominent English officials and prominent Indians had been thus honoured though the former as a rule recognised no answering obligations. A good many drifted away from Calcutta into other provinces and posts although their names continued to block the list. Of those who continued in Bengal, a large number never attended. The list actually included the name of the Lieutenant Governor of the North-Western Provinces, although he was the Chancellor of his own university at Allahabad, and that of the Lieutenant Governor of the Punjab, though he was similarly the Chancellor of his University at Lahore. From time to time names had been recommended by the local government and accepted by the Chancellor for the special object of giving due recognition of special interests such as medicine and engineering. The result had been that the list of the nominated fellows was on the whole a distinguished list but as Curzon later pointed out "it is largely an absentee list: and the distinction that it reflects is official or professional rather than academic".

In 1891, Lord Lansdowne conceded the privilege of election on a limited scale to the graduates of the university on an experimental basis and there was no pledge of its continuance. The qualifications laid down both for the electoral body and the elected were MA (BA before 1867) and higher degrees in any faculty – in other words the electorate could choose only from among themselves. This restriction was imposed on a reluctant Senate to prevent election of political agitators from outside. However, the slack and precipitated standard of qualification formulated in 1891 had resulted in the creation of a large and heterogeneous electorate scattered throughout Burma, Assam, Bengal, the Central Provinces and Ceylon, a cleverly organised system of canvassing, and a thoroughly undistinguished list of nominees. Of the 24 fellows elected since 1891, two had died. Of these, four had been chosen on specific grounds in exercise of a power by the government in 1892 to reserve occasional vacancies for the

Faculties of Medicine and Engineering or for eminence in education and literature. Of the remainder, 16 are practising lawyers and none of them was qualified for election by his degree in the Faculty of Law, that is, none was a D.L. They were all nominally elected by reason of their attainments in the Faculty of Arts, but only three of them had obtained a First Class in Arts, several only a Second and some even a Third. All of the lawyers came from unaided colleges where there had been no government supervision. Of the 22, only two or three were engaged in bonafide educational work and these were elected only in the reserved categories. Secondly, election was held through systematic and elaborate canvassing. Lists were kept by "the Vakils of the Elections" who having taken their degrees, had dispersed throughout India. Agents were employed to hunt them out and canvass for them; which involved considerable expense. Candidates who did not resort to these methods and was not supported by "the Vakils' Party" had no chance of being returned. The system whether looked at from the point of view of methods or of men seemed to stand equally condemned. It was felt that any Chancellor who "acquiesces in its continuance is shutting his eyes while a weapon is being forged which will ultimately extrude European standards and influence from the Senate altogether, and will hand over its government to a clique of political *frondeurs* who have no interest in Education".

The Senate was the nominal and statutory governing body of the university. The Syndicate of the Calcutta University, which was the real governing body of the Senate, was in the anomalous position of having no statutory origin. No mention was made of it in the Act of 1857 but its origin could be traced to an interpretation of clause VIII of the Act of Incorporation which gave the Chancellor, Vice-Chancellor and fellows powers to control university affairs as well as to make and alter any by-laws and regulations in general, touching all matters whatsoever regarding the university. The Senate had not only most completely abdicated its functions to the Syndicate but its own annual meeting for purposes of business was also held at the most inconvenient season of the year – on the third Saturday in April – when the majority of the Europeans were absent from Calcutta, as Maclean, the Vice-Chancellor of the Calcutta University later reported to Curzon.

No geographical limits to the areas of affiliation were indicated and the universities, thus set up by the Acts of Incorporation in 1857 were affiliating universities from distant geographical areas. The Calcutta University, for example, functioned not merely for Bengal, but for Burma, Assam, the Central Provinces, and Ceylon and the affiliated institutions spread over from Simla and Mussorie to Indore and Jaipur and from Jaffna and Batticaloa to Sylhet and Chittagong. Managed by their own governing bodies, the affiliated colleges were not a part of the university. Not all of them were residential institutions with a history of tradition, created through the generosity of some philanthropic societies, missionary bodies or wealthy Indians, interested in spreading the light of enlightenment, but for most part were collections of lecture rooms, and class rooms, and laboratories. They had no control over the courses of study which were prescribed by the affiliating university and their only function seemed to be to prepare students for the examinations which were again conducted by the university. Since a large number of colleges – government, aided and unaided – were affiliated with each of the three universities, it follows the rules for affiliation framed by the university were not very strict. And indeed the first affiliation rules prepared by the Calcutta University in February 1857, for example, only demanded from the college seeking affiliation with it, a declaration, counter-signed by at least two members of the Senate, of the staff and courses of study for the previous two years and of the institution's ability of imparting education up to the standard of B.A. degree. Despite the Hunter Commission's attempt in 1882 to follow a stricter application of rules relating to affiliation, the growth in the number of affiliated colleges continued unabated so that by the time Curzon came to India, the total number of affiliated colleges in the whole of British India was 191, of which 145 were Arts Colleges and the rest Professional Colleges including Law (30), Teaching (5), Agriculture (3), Medicine (4) and Engineering (4).

It would seem then that these universities were not merely examination bodies as their influences were extended far beyond examinations by their practical power to refuse or admit the affiliation of colleges. They were independent of the education departments set up in the provinces of British India as per the direction of the Education Despatch of 1854. While an education department could exercise control over the government and aided colleges, it had no control over the private colleges which had "the chief part in the education of undergraduates" of the universities. The education departments were unable to banish politics from the unaided colleges where the managers and professors were likely to educate their pupils "in all the political and financial fallacies" antagonistic to the British connection. The number of such unaided colleges imparting legal education was particularly high in Bengal where the Law students perhaps more than any other class of students were prone to politics and, it was feared that the government had made a mistake "to let the control of legal education go entirely out of its hands" by not providing a properly recognised Government Law College in Calcutta as in Madras and Bombay.

It is obvious that the affiliated colleges in different parts of British India could not be expected to maintain a uniform and high academic standard as there was no separate education department in case of the Government of India as in England, with an organisation and a staff of its own to supervise higher education in the whole of British India. As a matter of fact, Madras normally turned out considerably greater number of graduates than Calcutta and many more than Bombay, Allahabad and Punjab put together arousing doubts about the standard at Madras. Many of the new affiliated colleges that came into existence as a result of the local and private efforts, before Curzon's Viceroyalty, were "weak, understaffed and incapable of affording the individual attention either to the needs of the student or of providing the varied courses of study, practical as well as literary", as reported by the Calcutta University Commission almost more than a decade and a half later in 1917.

Curzon's Minute on University Reform on 23 February 1901

By 23 February 1901, Curzon's scheme for university reform was ready when he recorded an extremely long minute on the subject, revealing his tremendous capabilities for hard work, for which he had a great reputation at Oxford, and, for which he almost impaired his health in India just as Dalhousie had actually done before him. The main thrust of his arguments in the minute was that, legislation was necessary to *(a)* extended the functions of the Indian universities from examination to teaching, *(b)* regulate the number, tenure and qualifications of the fellows as well as to maintain a proper balance between Europeans and Indians, officials and non-officials, and between the various faculties or professions, *(c)* reconstitute the electorate by adding residential qualifications among the graduates just as the Convocation of Oxford then consisted of resident MAs or rather such graduates as were capable of coming to the Senates to vote, as well as by laying down some academic or educational standard which was necessary for election to a fellowship at Oxford, as a qualification for election here, *(d)* provide a statutory status to the Syndicate which was the real executive body of the university, *(e)* narrow the geographical limits or areas of each university, *(f)* strengthen the law relating to the recognition and affiliation of colleges as well as withdraw recognition or affiliation in cases in which discipline had been relaxed and the standard too much lowered, *(g)* curtail power of the boards of studies which prescribed textbooks for the colleges as well as regulate the courses of instruction of the candidates reading for the university examination; and finally, to revoke the university degrees in cases where the holder had been convicted by a criminal court. After listing the areas for legislation to tighten control over the universities, Curzon felt that the plate was still not full:

> There are doubtless other subjects affecting the case for or against legislation which have not occurred to me, or of which I am ignorant.... There also remains the question as to the competence of the Government of India to reform (either by legislative or by executive action) the University of Calcutta without reference to the case of the Universities of Madras and Bombay; and even if the competence be indisputable, the expedience or desirability of the same.

Conference at Simla

It was, therefore, necessary to consult a body of expert opinions, and six months after he had drafted the proposals for the university reform, he summoned a Conference at Simla to look for the light at the end of the tunnel. The first Educational Conference in India, started on 2 September 1901, was attended by the Vice-Chancellors of the Universities of Calcutta, Bombay and Madras, the Directors of Public Instruction in Bengal, Bombay, and Madras, the North-Western Provinces and the Punjab, Inspector-General of Education in the Central Provinces, Principal of the Deccan College at Poona, Principal of the School of Arts in Madras, Reporter on Economic Products to the Government of India and finally Risley besides Curzon and the members of his Council. The character of the Conference was "both official and private" and did not include any representative of the Indian people. Curzon opened the proceedings with a statement which was intended to be communicated to the press. In it he outlined all the flaws of "our system" and indicated the line upon which, tentatively at any rate, reform would proceed. Curzon presided over the Conference for 16 days and himself drafted each one of the 150 resolutions on education which were passed unanimously by the twenty people attending the Conference.

The proceedings of the Conference were never published and the secrecy with which Curzon enveloped the Conference at Simla earned for it such names as Secret Conclave and Star Chamber. As Surendra Nath Banerjea later remarked rather sarcastically: "The Conference met in secret, deliberated in secret, resolved in secret, and I presume dispersed in secret".

Out of the 150 resolutions drafted by Curzon and unanimously passed by the Conference no fewer than 45 were on the subject of university education. The delegates to the Conference emphatically voted in favour of a thorough constitutional reform of the universities in India. They also recommended that the powers of the government in respect of affiliation, recognition and textbooks be strengthened; that a Director-General of Indian education be appointed; that the rules for examinations and degrees be coordinated and improved, and that the establishment of hostels be encouraged and that a minimum rate of fees be fixed. The Conference also endorsed the decision taken by Curzon before it met at Simla that it was desirable to appoint a Commission to examine the question of university education in all its aspects.

Appointment of Indian Universities Commission

In a telegram to Hamilton on 13 January 1902, Curzon proposed to appoint six persons as permanent members of the Commission including Raleigh who was to be the Chairman. The other five were Hewett, Pedler, Bourne, Mackichan and Syed H. Bilgrami, last being the only Indian representative. When the appointment of the Commission was made public after obtaining Hamilton's approval, the absence of a Hindu among the six permanent commissioners created a great stir since the Hindus had "the largest interest in the educational problems that were to be considered". Surendra Nath Banerjea, a dismissed member of the Indian Civil Service on flimsy grounds, who had earlier led the Civil Service Agitation in 1876-77, raised "a vigorous protest" in the editorial columns of the *Bengalee* against "this ostracism of the Hindu element".

The Indian public opinion supported Banerjea's view and
Curzon had no other alternative but to send a private telegram to
Hamilton seeking his approval on the nomination of Gooroodas
Banerjee, a former Vice-Chancellor of the Calcutta University and
now a prominent judge of the Calcutta High Court. In their
assignment of collecting evidences from "the disgruntled MAs and
BAs", the permanent members of the Commission were to be assisted
by five local commissioners – Ashutosh Mukliopadhyaya for Bengal,
Sankaran Nair for Madras, Chandavarkar for Bombay and Lewis and
Bell for the North-Western Provinces and the Punjab respectively.

Appointment of the Director-General of Education

While announcing the appointment of the Indian Universities
Commission, Curzon also made an appointment to the newly created
post of the Director-General of Education discussed at the
Conference at Simla and latter approved by Hamilton. Orange, who
had two first classes from Winchester and Oxford and was then
working in the Department of Education as an Examiner in the
White Hall, was appointed to the post on the recommendation of
Sadler who was first offered the post but declined to accept it.

The Indian Universities Commission submitted its Recommendations

The Indian Universities Commission started its work at Madras on 18
February and after examining 156 witnesses including only 63 Indians
at different places, the Commission submitted its recommendations
on 9 June to Curzon who in a delightful mood wrote to Northbrook,
"My Universities Commission had just reported". It is not necessary
to enter here into details about the various recommendations of the
Commission, nor to Gooroodas Banerjee's disagreement with them
in his Note of Dissent as the Commission's recommendations faith-
fully reflected Curzon's views on the reform of the Indian
universities, first elaborately delineated in his minute on 23 February
1901 and later discussed and endorsed at the Conference at Simla.
What is interesting to note here is the Commission's views on legislation to implement the changes suggested in its recommendations.
The Commission felt since the changes did not "involve repeal of the
existing Acts of Incorporation" the legislature could "give effect to
our proposal by passing a General Indian University Act, which

would be construed as supplementing and amending the Acts of Incorporation".

Recommendations leaked out and a Storm blew

Curzon never wanted to make the recommendations of the Indian Universities Commission public just as he had earlier prevented the proceedings of the Conference at Simla from becoming public. However, a local newspaper got hold of a copy of the report "probably through the agency of some clerk" and began in his words, "publishing a series of daily denunciations of the Government or rather of myself, for having rung the death-knell of higher education in India". "You are certain to be attacked", consoled Hamilton,

> "If you attempt to in any way purify University Education and to free if from its existing excrescences. The Babu believes that one of the main objects for which British Rule was established in India was to enable him to get university degree; and any attempt to heighten the standard is sure to meet with violent abuses. But I have been so long the subject of almost universal abuse and misrepresentation by the Indian Press, that I am compelled to attach little importance to what they say".

A fortnight after Hamilton had dispatched his letter to Curzon from London, Curzon wrote to Sir Henry Cotton on 31 August, "The Bengalis are denouncing me like fury because the University Commission has reported in a sense that they dislike. They seem to think that I both dominated the enquiry and wrote the Report. What a strange people! They take the heart of one". Ten days later, he wrote to Hamilton, "the Town Hall and the Senate Hall of the university have been packed with shouting and perspiring graduates, and my name has been loudly hissed as the author of the doom of higher education".

Curzon's Reactions to the Agitation against University Reform

Curzon psychologically reacted to the "fierce agitation" as he described it in one of his letters to Hamilton, put up by the Indians not only in Bengal, but also in Bombay and Madras and decided to consult the local governments before drafting the Indian Universities Bill based on the recommendations of the Commission. As there had not been much differences in the views offered by them, he went ahead with the drafting of the Indian Universities Bill.

State Paper on Education

At the same time he asked Ibbetson, Risley and Organge to help him prepare a State Paper on education "to assuage the ill feeling that may be aroused in some quarters by the Universities Bill, and that the public may be more inclined to accept reforms which are shown to be part of a great scheme, conceived on liberal principles and directed towards raising the standard of every aspect of education".

Financial Provision

In the same vein and acting on the same principle Curzon also added a provision to the Indian Universities Bill for financially assisting the Indian universities for a period of five years "to gild as much as we can, that somewhat unpalatable pill that we are offering to the native patient, and the greater the generosity that we can show at the present juncture, the more likely are we to disarm antagonism and to succeed".

The State Paper on Indian education was issued on 11 March 1904, and the Indian Universities Bill was passed, despite stiff resistance by G.K. Gokhale and Asutosh Mukhopadhyaya, and became an Act on 21 March 1904 marking the end of "a long and arduous struggle conducted for five years in the face of every discouragement and of bitter opposition". Two days after the Bill had been passed, Curzon privately sent an identical letter to the Governors of Bombay and Madras and the Lt. Governors of the North-Western Provinces and Bengal. It read, "The Universities Bill is now passed into Law; and the various Chancellors of the universities will before long be called upon to take action under it". Next day he wrote to Godley in a very relaxed mood, "Here I have had the stiffest session on record, and have carried the Universities Bill, *which was my child*".[1]

The Indian Universities Act

The Indian Universities Act introduced radical changes into the five existing universities at Calcutta, Bombay, Madras, Lahore and Allahabad. Among these were, an enlargement of the functions of the university; reduction in the size of the University Senates; introduction of the principles of election; statutory recognition of the Syndicates where university teachers were to be given an adequate representation; stricter conditions for the affiliation of colleges to a university; definition of the territorial limits of the universities;

provision for a grant of Rs 5 lakh a year for five years for implementing these changes to the five Indian universities and finally powers to the government to make additions and alterations while approving of the regulations passed by the Senates.

The Validating Act of February 1905

The Act, which had not found favour with the educated Indians, created problems when the government set about to carry it out. The validity of the directions issued by the Chancellor of the Bombay University to the effect that the election should be held by the faculties, was challenged in the Bombay High Court immediately after the provisional Syndicates had been chosen. It was soon clear that similar action was going to be taken at Calcutta also and that the controversy would soon "extend to Madras, Allahabad, and Lahore and that litigation may become general". Curzon wanted to put a speedy end to the doubts raised about the interpretation of the Indian Universities Act. He wanted to straighten matters regarding the validity of some of the directions issued under it by the Chancellors by legislation, as suggested by the Governor of Bombay, and introduce a bill in his Legislative Council validating the action of the Chancellors as well as the constitution of the senates and the syndicates. The validating bill was passed into law on 10 February 1905. It provided that all directives purporting, to have been constituted under the Indian Universities Act of 1904 had been duly issued and constituted.

State Paper on Education

We have already noted how Curzon wanted to project the reform of university education as a part of his attempt to reform the entire system of education in India to assuage public feelings. The State Paper on education was prepared with that end in view. It was formulated out of the 150 resolutions taken on the different aspects of Indian education at the Conference held in Simla in September 1901, and was issued as a Resolution of the Governor-General in Council on Indian education on 11 March 1904 – a few days before the passing of the Indian Universities Act on 21 March 1904. Needless to say, this is the first comprehensive document on Indian education policy ever issued by the Government of India since the emergence of a modern system of education in the country in 1854.

Extent of the Education System in 1904 and its Merits and Defects

The document which consists of some 46 paragraphs extending over nearly 50 pages, begins with a brief sketch of the educational developments in the country till 1854, and then critically analysed the system created in 1904. The system included five universities which prescribed courses and examined some 23,009 students of the 191 affiliated colleges, scattered throughout the country. Provision was made for studies in Arts and Oriental learning, and for professional courses of Law, Medicine, Engineering, Teaching and Agriculture. Below the colleges were secondary schools, to the number of 5,498, with an attendance of 5,58,378 students and primary schools numbering 98,538 with 32,68,726 pupils. Including the special schools, the technical and industrial schools of art, and the normal schools for teachers, the total number of colleges and schools amounted to 1,05,306 with 38,87,493 pupils. If 'private institutions' which did not conform with departmental standards were added to these, the total number of schools under the Education Department reached about 4.5 million. There was no doubt that this education system had substantially benefited the people in many respects – in the spread of knowledge, in opening up new avenues of employment and in recording a "marked improvement" in the character of the public servants now chosen from the educated Indians. However, its shortcomings in point of quality needed no demonstration. As the document pointed out, "Four villages out of five are without a school; three boys out of four grow up without education and only one girl in forty attends any kind of school".

The main charges brought against the system could be generally grouped under five heads: First, the higher education was pursued with too exclusive a view to entering government service, which unduly narrowed its scope, and those who failed to obtain employment under government were ill fitted for other pursuits. Second, excessive importance was given to examinations. Third, the courses of study were too literary in character. Fourth, the schools and colleges exercised the intelligence of the students too little, and taxed their memory too much, so that mechanical repetition took the place of sound learning. And finally, in the pursuit of English education the vernaculars were neglected, with the result that the hope expressed in the Despatch of 1854 that they would become the vehicle for diffusing Western knowledge among the masses was far from realisation.

The Governor-General in Council reviewed the existing methods of instruction closely and came to the conclusion that it stood in need of a substantial reform. With the object in view the Resolution of 11 March 1904 reviewed the whole subject of education in its various aspects, indicating the defects that required correction in each of its branches and the remedies which ought to be applied now.

Education and Government Service

The Resolution referred to the suggestion that the higher interests of education in India were injuriously affected by the prevailing system of basing selection for government services on the academic attainments of the candidates; and that separate examinations for the public service be organised on the model of the English Civil Service Commission under the control of a special board. However the Government of India could not accept this suggestion. It stressed that in fixing the educational standards which qualified individuals for appointments, the natural division of primary, secondary and university education should be followed – school and college certificates of proficiency should be accepted as full evidence of educational qualifications, regard being paid, within the limits of each standards, to their comparative value. Due weight was also to be attached to the recorded opinions of collegiate and school authorities regarding the proficiency and conducts of candidates during their period of tuition.

The Abuses of Examinations

The Resolution then dwelt on the abuses of the examinations which had in recent years grown to extravagant dimension – confining the instruction within the rigid framework of courses and neglecting all forms of training which did not admit of being tested by written examinations. These demoralising tendencies had been further encouraged by the practice of assessing grants to aided schools upon the results shown by examination which was based on a similar practice, now condemned in England. This was to be replaced now by more equitable tests of efficiency, depending on the number of scholars in attendance, the buildings provided for their accommodation, the circumstances of the locality, the qualifications of the teachers, the nature of the instruction given, and the outlay from other sources such as fees and private endowments or subscriptions.

In future, there was to be only two examinations – the first of these to mark the completion of the lowest stage of instruction, testing the degree of proficiency attained in the highest classes of primary schools and the second was to take place at the end of the secondary, usually an Anglo-Vernacular course, recording the educational attainments of all those who had completed this course. In both the stages of instruction special provision was made for the award of scholarships.

Government Control and Private Enterprise

The Resolution accepted the progressive devolution of primary, secondary and collegiate education upon private enterprise and the continuous withdrawal of government from competition, as recommended by the Hunter Commission in 1883. It also recognised the utmost importance of limiting the number of institutions in each branch of education by the government both as models for private enterprises to follow as well as in order to uphold *a* high standard of education. In withdrawing from direct management, it was further essential that the government retain a general control by means of efficient inspection over all public educational institutions.

Primary Education

The Resolution asserted that the Government of India fully accepted the proposition that the active extension of primary education was one of the most important duties of the state as recommend by the Hunter Commission in 1883. It undertook the responsibility not merely on general grounds but because, as Lord Lawrence observed in 1868, "among all the sources of difficulty in our administration and of possible danger to the stability of our Government, there are few so serious as the ignorance of the people". The extension of railways had helped commercialisation of agriculture in India. The cultivator had been brought into contact with the commercial world, and involved in transactions in which an illiterate man was at a great disadvantage. The Census of 1901 revealed that only one in ten of the male population, and seven in a thousand of the female population were literate (when the population of British India was over two hundred, and forty million). These figures exhibited the vast dimensions of the problem and showed how much remained to be done before the proportion of the population receiving elementary instruction could approach the standard recognised as compulsory in more advanced countries.

The Government of India realised that primary education had till then received insufficient attention and an inadequate share of the public funds. They acknowledged that it possessed a strong claim to the sympathy both of the Supreme Government and of the Local Governments, and that it should be made a leading charge upon provincial revenues. In those provinces where primary education was in a backward condition, its encouragement should be a primary obligation. In order to ensure that the claims of primary education received due attention, it was essential that the education authorities be heard when resources were being allotted and that they should have the opportunity of carrying their representations to a higher authority in the event of their being disregarded. In future, so much of the budget estimates of District or Municipal Boards as related to educational charges was to be submitted through the Inspector to the Director of Public Instruction before sanction. Secondly, the Government of India, looked with favour upon the extension of kindergarten methods and object lesson as practised in Madras and Bombay in order to correct some of the inherent defects of the Indian intellect, to discourage exclusive reliance on the memory, and to develop a capacity for reasoning from observed facts. Physical exercises, it held, should as far as possible be made universal in the primary schools. In the case of rural schools, the aim should be not to impart definite agricultural teaching but to give to the children a preliminary training which would make them intelligent cultivators, would train them to be observers, thinkers, and experimenters in however humble a manner, and would protect them in their business transactions with the landlords to whom they paid rent and the grain dealers to whom they disposed of their crops. The books prescribed should be written in simple language, not in unfamiliar style, and should deal with topics associated with rural life. This and other reforms in primary schools would involve some revision of the pay of primary teachers which varied greatly, and in some provinces was too small to attract or to retain a satisfactory class of men.

Secondary Education

The Resolution admitted that the growth of secondary instruction was "one of the most striking features in the history of education in India" though the progress had been accompanied by a substantial increase in the number of inefficient institutions as had no capable teachers, sufficient furniture, adequate library, proper building and adequate sports and hostel facilities. The document stressed the need for applying stringent conditions while recognising these schools, making them eligible for grants-in-aid and for preparing students for admission to universities and public service. The Resolution noted the "too literary" character of the courses pursued in the schools and also the attempts made to introduce alternative courses, following the recommendations of the Hunter Commission, in order to meet the needs of the boys who were destined for industrial or commercial pursuits that had not till then met with success. However, the Government of India would try to promote diversified types of secondary education, corresponding with the varying needs of practical life, in the present stage of social and industrial development.

The problems of choice of subjects to be taught and the means by which proficiency in them was tested could be solved by adopting the system of no examinations, at the conclusion of the secondary course, which had been tried with success in other countries, to Indian conditions. They would be of a more searching character than the present Entrance Test and the certificate given at the end would be evidence that the holder had received a sound education in a recognised school, that he had borne a good character, and that he had really learnt what the school professed to have taught him – it would then deserve recognition not only by government and universities but also by a large body of private employers who were in need of well-trained assistants in their various lines of activity.

The Resolution stated that the secular character of the government institutions where no scriptures were taught had stimulated tendencies unfavourable to discipline and had encouraged the growth of a spirit of irreverence in the rising generation. The remedy lay not so much in any formal methods of teaching conduct by means of moral text-books or primers of personal ethics as in the influence of carefully selected and trained teachers, the maintenance of a high standard of discipline, the institutions of well-managed hostels, the proper selection of text-books such as biographies which taught by example, and above all in the association of teachers and pupils in the common interests of their daily life. The Resolution announced the framing of rules to regulate the admission of scholars to government and aided schools and their promotion on transfer from one school to another so as to secure that a record of their conduct was maintained and that irregularities and breaches of discipline not passed unnoticed. These rules would now be extended to all unaided schools which desired to enjoy the benefits of recognition.

Medium of Instruction

The Resolution made significant observations on the medium of instruction. As a general rule, a child should not be allowed to learn English as a language until he had made some progress in the primary stages of instruction and had received a thorough grounding in his mother tongue. While the dividing line between the use of vernacular and of English should be drawn at a minimum age of 13, no scholar in a secondary school should be allowed to abandon the study of his vernacular, which should be kept up until the end of the school course. "If the educated classes neglect the cultivation of their own languages, these will assuredly sink to the level of mere colloquial dialects possessing no literature worthy of the name, and no progress will be possible in giving effect to the principle, affirmed in the Despatch of 1854, that European knowledge should gradually be brought, by means of the Indian vernaculars, within the reach of all classes of people", the Resolution observed.

Female Education

Despite the fact that the government agreed with the view that a "far greater proportional impulse is imparted to the educational and moral tone of the people than by the education of men" alone, and had accordingly treated this branch of education liberally in respect of scholarships and fees, female education as a whole was still in a very backward condition. The number of female scholars in public schools in the year 1901-02 was 4,44,470 or less than a ninth of the number of male scholars. The Resolution expressed the hope that with the increase of the funds assigned in aid of education the recommendations of the Hunter Commission for the extension would now be fruitful. The measure taken for further advance included establishment in important centres model primary girls' school, an increase in the number of training schools with more liberal assistance to those already in existence, and a strengthening of the staff of inspectresses. The Government of India also desired to encourage missionary efforts and *zenana* teaching in promoting female education by grants-in-aid.

University Education

The Resolution referred to the recent changes in the character of the London University which had acted as a model to the universities in India earlier and had now set an example of expansion that could not "fail to react upon the corresponding institutions in India". It referred to the defects of university education and to the appointment of a Commission with Raleigh as President to report upon the constitution and working of the universities, to recommend measures for elevating the standard of university teaching and promoting the advancement of learning. After full consideration of the report of the Commission and of the criticisms which it called forth, the Government of India came to the conclusion that certain reforms in the constitution and management of the universities were necessary. It outlined these reforms and mentioned the financial aid it proposed to give in order to carry out the necessary improvement in the universities and their affiliated colleges. This included more than 400 schools and colleges for Europeans and Eurasians in India with nearly 30,000 scholars costing annually Rs 42.5 lakhs (of which Rs 8.5 lakhs came from public funds) as well as for the improvement of Chief's Colleges set up at Ajmer, Rajkot and Lahore where some of the features of the English public school system had been reproduced.

Technical Education, Schools of Art, Industrial Schools, Commercial and Agricultural Education

After having referred to the measures including liberal financial support for the improvement of the universities, the Resolution turned its attention to technical education in India. The Resolution mentioned about the attempt of the government hitherto directed to train men for government service as engineers, mechanicians, electricians, overseers, surveyors, revenue officers or teachers in schools, and for employment in railway workshops, cotton-mills, and mines, through the Engineering Colleges established at Rurki, Sibpur and Madras, the Colleges of Science at Poona, the Technical Institute at Bombay and the Engineering School at Jubulpur. It stressed the need for developing a technical course which could be imparted "in schools of ordinary type". In fixing the aim of the technical schools, the supply or expansion of the existing Indian markets was to be of superior importance to the creation of new export trades. As a step towards providing men qualified to take a leading part in the improvement of Indian industries, the Government of India had decided to give assistance in the form of scholarships to selected students in order to enable them to pursue a course of technical education in Europe or America.

Regarding the Schools of Art and Industries in British India, at Madras, Bombay, Calcutta and Lahore, the Resolution pointed out that these institutions gave training on subjects like designing, painting, illumination, modelling, photography and engraving as the pupil intended to pursue when he had left the school. It was suggested that free admission and scholarship should be discouraged and should gradually be replaced by payment of fees.

The Government of India did not expect a large immediate increase in the number of industrial schools, the number, of which stood at 123 with 8,405 pupils in attendance, and the number of different trades taught as 48 but it desired rather to confine their institutions to boys belonging to the specialised caste or occupational groups who were likely to practise the crafts taught in the schools. The courses of study were to be so ordered as not to tend themselves to the manufacture of clerks, but to bear exclusively upon carefully selected industries.

The Resolution which spoke of the attempts to provide commercial education at Bombay, Lucknow, Calcutta, and Amritsar and the encouraging response it had met asserted that increased attention would now be given to the extension of such teaching adapted to Indian needs in large centres of commerce and population. In this context the Resolution indicated a great deficiency in agricultural technology for a country like India where two-thirds of the population were dependent for their livelihood on the produce of the soil.

There was no institution capable of imparting "a complete agricultural education". The existing schools or colleges at Poona (Bombay), Saidapet (Madras), Cawnpore (U.P.), Nagpur (M.P.) and at Sibpur (Bengal) "have not wholly succeeded, either in theory or in practice. They have neither produced scientific experts, nor succeeded in attracting members of the landholding classes to qualify themselves as practical agriculturists". The Resolution spoke of a scheme of establishing an Imperial Agricultural College in connection with an Experimental Farm and Research Laboratory under the supervision of the Inspector General of Agricultural Science combined with constant practice in farm work and estate management.

Training Institutions for Teachers

The Resolution accepted the Hunter Commission's recommendation that an examination in the principles and practice of teaching should be made a condition for permanent employment as a teacher in any secondary school, "if, in a word, European knowledge is to be diffused by the methods proper to it". There existed at Madras, Kurseong, Allahabad, Lahore and Jubulpur institutions in which teachers were trained for service, and the time had come to extend the system to the provinces where it did not exist, notably in Bombay. The Resolution spoke in favour of developing training institutions for secondary school teachers which should be as well-equipped as Arts Colleges, with good practising schools attached to each one of them. The period of training for students in a Training College must be at least two years, except in the case of graduates, for whom one year's training might suffice. It should be a university course, culminating in a university degree or diploma. The scheme of instruction should be determined by the authorities of the Training College and by the Education Department and the examination at the close of it should be controlled by the same authorities. This was to be followed by an orientation programme for the trained teachers for better impact on secondary school teaching.

The Resolution felt that there should be an increase in the number of normal schools for primary teachers particularly in some provinces like Bengal, with an increase in the salaries paid to primary teachers to induce them to undergo a course of training which should in future be of a duration "not less than two years". For the rural schools the object of courses should be to serve the more limited and practical purpose of supplying them with teachers whose stock-in-trade was not mere book learning, and whose interests had been aroused in the study of rural activities, so that they might be able to connect their teaching with the objects which were familiar to the children in the country or village schools.

Hostels

The Resolution attached great importance to the provision of hostels or boarding houses, under proper supervision, in connection with colleges and secondary schools. These institutions protected the resident students from the moral dangers of life in large towns; provided common interests and created a spirit of healthy companionship, and they were in accord not only with the usage of English public schools and colleges, but also with the ancient Indian tradition that the pupil should live in the charge of his teacher. The returns for the year 1901-02 showed that there were then 1,415 hostels with 47,302 boarders. The Government of India desired an extension of the system which under direct supervision by the teachers exercised a profound influence on student life in India.

Administration

The Resolution suggested an increasing stringency in inspection and a substantial strengthening of the inspecting staff who should not only judge the results of teaching but guide and advise as to its methods and courses taught in view of the reduction in the numbers of examinations which was being carried out and the general raising of educational standards which was contemplated. Their assistance could only be enlisted by increasing the cadre of the Indian Educational Service then consisting of two branches superior and subordinate. The Resolution decided to add four posts of officers to the Indian Educational Service in order to provide the Directors of Public Instruction in Madras, Bombay, Bengal and the United Provinces with assistants, upon whom part of their duties of making themselves acquainted with the educational conditions of their provinces and the circumstances of the numerous schools under their control might be devolved. Members of the Indian Educational Service when on furlough would be provided with facilities to keep themselves abreast of the advances which were now being made in England and other countries of Europe.

Conclusion

Thus, the Education Resolution of 1904 reviewed the history and progress of Western education under British rule in India: the objects it sought to accomplish and the means which it employed. The Resolution showed how the principles accepted since 1854 were consistently followed and affirmed by the Education Commission of 1882 and how they were now being further extended and developed, in response to the growing needs of the country by the combined efforts of the Government of India and the Provincial Governments.

"The system of education thus extended", observed the Resolution, "makes provision in varying degrees for all forms of intellectual activity that appeal to a civilised community. It seeks to satisfy the aspirations of students in the domains of learning, and research; it supplies the Government with a succession of upright and intelligent, public servants; it trains workers in every branch of commercial enterprise that has made good its footing in India; it attempts to develop the resources of the country and to stimulate and improve indigenous arts and industries; it offers to all classes of society a training suited to their position in life; and for these ends it is organised on lines which admit of indefinite expansion as the demand for education grows and public funds or private liberality afford a large measure of support". It now rested with the people themselves to use wisely the opportunities thus offered by the labours of the Government of India in framing the Resolution on Indian Education Policy. "Those labours", the Resolution pointed out, "have been undertaken in the hope that they will command the hearty support of the leaders of native thought and of the great body of workers in the field of Indian Education. On them the Governor-General Council relies to carry on and complete a task which the Government can do no more than begin".

Note

1. Italics are mine. For details about the role of Curzon, see my article, "The Genesis of Curzon's University Reform, 1899-1905" in *Minerva*, London, December 1988, Vol. XXVI, No. 4, pp. 463 – 492.

33

National Education Till 1912

Curzon's university reform not only provided a comprehensive document on the Government of India's education policy but also activated Indian intellectuals' attempt at generating a parallel system of education, called national education, which received a shot in the booster when the movement against Curzon's partition of Bengal started in 1905. National education became one of the issues on which the Swadeshi Movement which grew out of the Anti-Partition Movement was built up and in 1906 it was also one of the issues on which the Moderates and the Extremists failed to agree – leading to a split the following year of the Indian National Congress at Surat.

Genesis of National Education before Curzon

However, the idea of a national system of education, more appropriately Indian education in spirit and substance, did not suddenly emerge as a reaction to the passing of the Indian Universities Act in 1905. In 1890-92, in his Convocation Address as the Vice-Chancellor of the Calcutta University, Gooroodas Banerjee had drawn attention to some of the most glaring defects from the point of view of intellectual training and of discipline of the system set up by the Education Despatch of 1854. He suggested, among others, the urgent introduction of the mother tongue as the medium of instruction, university fellowships for the promotion of original researches and adequate arrangement for technical education. About the same time Rabindranath Tagore in his paper on *Shikshar Her Fer,* published in December 1892 – January 1893 issue of *Sadhana,* pointed out clearly the inadequacy of the prevailing system of education under the British Raj and pleaded for acceptance of Bengali as the medium of instruction. Tagore's views on education in *Sadhana* were fully supported by Bankim Chandra Chatterjee, Gooroodas Banerjee, Ananda Mohan Bose and Lokendra Nath Palit. Far away from Bengal at Lucknow was established in 1898 Darul-Uloom, Nadwatul Ulema which attracted students from all parts of India and Islamic countries outside India. This residential institution was not certainly as orthodox as the one set up much earlier at Deoband in 1864 which was regarded as the fourth Muslim University of the World offering instruction in Arabic, Persian, Taiveid (reciting of the Holy Quran), Tybb (Unani Medicine) and Tabligh (missionary activity).

Indian Universities Commission and the Indian Universities Act

In 1898, immediately before the arrival of Curzon on the scene, Satish Chandra Mukherjee as the editor of the *Dawn* observed how the prevalent system of university education had failed to satisfy all the parties concerned. When therefore, Curzon spoke of a faulty and rotten education system being in need of reform in his first Convocation Address at Calcutta in 1899, he was profoundly applauded by the audience present there. Despite the exclusion of an Indian educationist from the Conference at Simla, the proceedings of which were kept secret, and the omission of a Hindu representative at first on the Indian Universities Commission, the intelligentsia in Bengal and elsewhere had shown great enthusiasm in Curzon's proposed university reform as could be seen from the article entitled, "An Examination into the Present System of University Education in India and a Scheme of Reform" written by Satish Chandra Mukherjee in the April, May, June 1902 issues of the *Dawn*. However, the report of the Indian Universities Commission shattered their hopes and aspirations when they found that Curzon's main aim was to restrict the area of higher education and to deprive them of the control of their universities. Besides writing in his own paper, Satish Chandra Mukherjee offered the most uncompromising opposition to the Commission's report through the editorial columns of the *Amrita Bazar Patrika* and the *Bengalee* edited by Surendra Nath Banerjea. Not content with a mere theoretical discussion in these papers, Mukherjee founded in July 1902, a society named after the paper he edited, to continue to focus attention on the subject.

Partition of Bengal

In the wake of the Indian Universities Act which reflected the recommendations of the Indian Universities Commission, came the partition of Bengal in October 1905. The British Raj felt the preponderance of the Bengalis in provincial politics was "most desirable" to diminish and this could best be achieved by dividing them: "Bengal united is a power. Bengal divided will pull several different ways". The partition of Bengal was an insult to the sense of unity and of pride developed among the Bengalees ever since the beginning of the nineteenth century Bengal Renaissance. When the partition of Bengal was effected on 16 October 1905, the day was observed as a day of national mourning for the whole of Bengal. The people of Bengal rose like one man to resist, to suffer and to sacrifice. A new tone, a new perspective, a new dimension hitherto unknown was added to the national movement in India and for all this, as Gokhale acknowledged in his presidential address at the December Benares Congress which condemned the partition of Bengal emphatically, "India owes a deep debt of gratitude to Bengal". Spearheaded by the students who represented youth and dream, vigour and selfless dedication and joined by the workers and the peasants, the clerks and the teachers who had been affected most by the rising prices since 1904, the Anti-Partition Movement soon broke away from traditional moorings and after transcending its rather limited and immediate objective broadened into a struggle for *Swaraj*.

National Council of Education

In Bengal, British crackdown on student picketers through the Carlyle Circular on 22 October 1905, which threatened to withdraw all grants, scholarships and affiliations from the nationalist dominated institutions climaxed into the urge for the boycott of government controlled education – an urge which had been growing in Bengal ever since the appointment of the Indian Universities Commission in 1902, the creation of the Dawn society by Satish Chandra Mukherjee, and the passing of the Indian Universities Act in 1904. Within a month of the Carlyle circular, on 4 November 1905, the Anti-Circular Society presided over by Krishna Kumar Mitra of the *Sanjivani* and sympathised critically by Tagore was born. The Moderates like Banerjea, Bhupendranath Basu and Ashutosh Chauduri combined with the Extremists like Bipin Chandra Pal,

Motilal Ghosh and Brahma Bandhav, who described the government controlled Calcutta University as the house of slaves at Goldighi, in organising a National Council of Education which was financed by the Zamindars of Mymansingh and leading lawyers like Subodh Chandra Mallick and formally inaugurated the Bengal National College on 14 August 1906.

Aurobindo became the principal of the college. The young followers of Satish Chandra Mukherjee formed the nucleus of its teaching staff. Vernacular was to be the chief medium of instruction but foreign languages were not to be neglected. Scientific and technical education were calculated to develop the material resources of the country and to satisfy its pressing needs. Unfortunately, the National Council of Education could not retain its unity for long and the Moderates headed by Taraknath Palit set up a rival organisation called the Society for the Promotion of Technical Education which founded a college, the Bengal Technical Institute, and a large number of national high schools numbering more than 50 (11 in West Bengal and 40 in East Bengal) as estimated by the *Quinquennial Review of Education* for the period 1907-12. Managed by Indians who were inspired by a love for their motherland, these institutions included courses on religion and culture, emphasised the importance of vocational education and urged the development of modern Indian languages by adopting one of them as the medium of instruction. However, these institutions were often sectarian in character and to that extent less national. They had also to submit themselves to governmental inspection for recognition, for without recognition they would not be able to receive grants-in-aid and therefore survive, as the financial support from the patriotic Indians was not often adequate.

Gokhale's Attempts at introducing Compulsory Primary Education

In December 1911, Hardinge who succeeded Minto annulled the partition of Bengal to stem the tide of rising nationalism. Bihar, and Orissa were taken out of Bengal and Assam was created as separate province. The Anti-Partition Movement which provided the framework for national education died and with that also the zeal for national education, but its spirit was kept alive by the Congress leaders like G.K. Gokhale. Gokhale believed that "an illiterate and ignorant nation can never make any solid progress and must fall back in the race for life". Influenced by the example in England which introduced a new era in primary education in 1902 and by the act of the Baroda State of making primary education compulsory in 1906, he moved a resolution in the Imperial Legislative Council on 19 March 1910. It stated, "That this Council recommends that a beginning should be made in the direction of making elementary education free and compulsory throughout the country, and that a mixed commission of officials and non-officials be appointed at an early date to frame definite proposals". The Bill suggested that free and compulsory education for boys between the age of 6 and 10 especially in those areas where 33 per cent of the male population was already at school be introduced. The expenditure was to be shared between the local bodies and the government in the proportion of 1: 2 and a separate post of the level of a Secretary be created to look after the implementation of the scheme. However, the motion was withdrawn when the Government of India promised to look into the matter carefully. A Department of Education was created at the Centre to devise a scheme for a better extension of primary education and a policy of creating an Imperial Grant was recommended.

When within the next one year nothing tangible was done for the progress of primary education in British India, Gokhale introduced a private Bill "to provide for the gradual introduction of the principle of compulsion into the elementary educational system of the country" on 16 March 1911. First, the Bill when passed into an Act would apply to those areas of local bodies where certain specific percentage of boys and girls to be decided by the Government of India was already attending the schools. Second, the local bodies were fully empowered to enforce the Act with the prior consent of the government concerned to the whole or any specified area within their jurisdiction. It was incumbent on the parents to send their boys and later girls, between 6 and 10 years of age to schools and any one failing to do so was to be liable to punishment. Finally, local bodies were permitted to levy an educational cess supplemented by the grants-in-aid from the governments concerned. Since the financial aspect of the Bill was to decide its acceptance or rejection in the Council, Gokhale thus explained: "It is obvious that the whole working of this Bill must depend, in the first instance, upon the share, which the Government is prepared to bear, of the cost of compulsory education, wherever it is introduced. I find that in England, the Parliamentary grants cover about two-thirds of the total expenditure on elementary schools. In Scotland, it amounts to more than that proportion whereas in Ireland it meets practically the whole cost. I think that we are entitled to ask in India, that at least two-thirds of the total expenditure should be borne by the state".

The Bill was circulated for opinion and came up for discussion on 17 March 1912. The debate lasted for two days and in course of the debates it was clear that the Government of India was not willing to accept the Bill. The official members who were in a clear majority in the Imperial Legislative Council as well as the non-official members consisting of the landed classes were opposed to the passing of the Bill despite the eloquent pleading of Gokhale. It was argued that there was no popular demand for compulsory primary education, that the local bodies as well as the provincial governments were against this measure as this would involve them in many a difficulty in respect of organisation and administration of this subject and finally the step was premature and unnecessary as the cause of primary education in India could well be attended by the system of grants-in-aid in vogue. So when the motion to refer the Bill to the Select Committee was put to vote, it was rejected by 38 votes to 13.

However, as Gokhale had observed in his concluding speech in the Imperial Legislative Council, "we, of the present generation in India, can only hope to serve our country by our failures". Primary education began to receive increasing attention from the Government of India which now sanctioned a recurring grant of Rs 50 lakhs and a non-recurring grant of Rs 84 lakhs for the purpose. While free compulsory primary education was engaging the attention of the Indian National Congress and the Muslim League, it was made free in the North-Western Provinces in 1912, and in the United Provinces, the Punjab, Assam and in the Central Provinces nominal fees were charged.

Significance

With the annulment of the partition of Bengal in 1911, enthusiasm for national education certainly ebbed but it must be said to the credit of this movement that it did create an awareness among the people of the need for a system of education which was to be Indian in spirit and substance. Most secondary schools adopted modern Indian languages as the medium of instruction, replaced photographs of the British monarch with those of the Indian national leaders. The song "God Save the King" was replaced by *Bande Mataram* except on a few tense occasions, when the singing of the latter and other national songs became a common practice in most school assemblies. Thus the movement for national education was at least able to create an environment of patriotism in secondary and collegiate institutions though it failed to achieve any substantial progress either in the number of institutions or of students.

34

The Government of India Resolution on Indian Education

While Gokhale's Bill on primary education was pending with the Imperial Legislative Council, King George V and his wife Queen Mary visited India. Addressing the Delhi Durbar on 12 December 1911, he announced an additional grant of fifty lakhs of rupees for primary education and expressed a desire that "there may be spread over the land a network of schools and colleges". After the rejection of Gokhale's Bill in March 1912, the Under Secretary of State for India admitted in the House of Commons in course of his discussion on the Indian budget, the need for paying greater attention to Indian education, allotted £ 330,000 annually to education and proclaimed that the number of primary schools would be increased by 75 per cent, with their pupils doubled. This coupled with administrative changes brought about by the Government of India Act of 1909, led the Government of India to review the whole field of education and to issue the Government of India's Resolution on Indian Education Policy on 21 February 1913.

Higher Education

This Resolution unlike the Resolution on 11 March 1904 is not an authoritative declaration of a bold policy in education but a review of the developments in education that had taken place since 1904. However, like the Resolution of 11 March 1904, it indicated defects in the system and suggested measures to rectify them. Echoing the development in the organisation of British universities which were fast becoming unitary, teaching and residential institutions, the Resolution declared that there would be a university for each province of British India, that teaching activities of universities would be encouraged and that mofussil colleges would be developed into teaching universities with provision for research in due course. It may be mentioned here that by 1912, there had been only 5 universities and 185 colleges and the need for the increase in their number for a growing population could hardly be exaggerated.

Secondary Education

The Resolution criticised the complete withdrawal of government from the field of secondary education and suggested that state schools should be retained as model institutions. While encouraging private enterprise by suitable grants-in-aid, the Resolution stressed the need for adequate inspection. It advocated the introduction of vocational courses at the secondary stages, which would be free from the domination of Matriculation requirements. In the case of girls, it suggested a special curriculum of practical utility for them, not much importance to the examination of girls' education and increase of women teachers and inspectresses.

Primary Education

Thirdly, the Resolution stressed the need for expanding primary education – starting lower primary schools where only three R's were taught and upper primary schools at suitable places as well as by creating local board schools in place of private aided schools. Its suggested that maktabs and patshalas should be adequately subsidised and the teachers should be drawn from the same class to which the primary school students belonged. It was only by expanding primary education "that illiteracy must be broken" and though the Government of India was unable to recognise "the principle of compulsory education", it desired the widest possible extension of primary education on a voluntary basis and hoped to see in near future some 91,000 primary public schools added to the existing 1,00,000 and the doubling of 4¼ millions of pupils who now received instructions in them.

The Resolution also spoke about the need for giving proper training to primary and secondary school teachers improving their salaries and retirement benefits, giving moral and religious instruction to students – a departure from the Education Resolution of 1904 – and emphasised proper supervision of students' hostels. Thus, as said before, the 1912 Resolution was more for improving the standard of existing institutions than for increasing their number.

Implementation

The Resolution was immediately implemented and by 1917 almost the entire primary education in Bombay, the Punjab, the United Provinces, the Central Provinces, the North-West Frontier Province, and Assam was monopolised by board schools. However, in other provinces the government could not oust the private schools on which it had relied so long to spread elementary education, though in Bengal it started the "Panchayati Union Scheme" by which the government provided at its own cost one model lower primary school with 3 classes in each "union" (of about 14 square miles) and entrusted its management to the district board. These model schools were models only in terms of having better buildings than private maktabs and pathsalas; their curriculum was not useful, their teachers were ill-paid and often their management was neglected by the boards. By 1917 there was on an average one boys' school to every 8 square miles, and the number of boys attending primary schools of some sort was less than 33 per cent of the number of boys of school age in British India.

35

The Calcutta University Commission

Appointment of the Commission

While issuing the Education Resolution of 1913, the Government of India planned to appoint a Commission on university education under Lord Haldane who had presided over a similar Commission on London University earlier. However, it could not materialise partly because of the outbreak of the First World War in 1914 and partly because of the reluctance on his part to accept the assignment. However, after the conclusion of the War in 1917, the Government of India appointed the Calcutta University Commission under the Chairmanship of Michael Sadler, the Vice-Chancellor of Leeds University, who had earlier declined Curzon's offer of the newly created post of Director-General of Education in India in 1904. The Commission was asked "to inquire into the condition and prospects of the University of Calcutta and to consider the question of a constructive policy in relation to the question it presents". Among other members of the Commission were Dr. Gregory, Professor Ramsay Muir, Philip Hartog, the Director of Public Instruction in Bengal, Asutosh Mukhopadhyaya and Zia-Ud din Ahmad. After a hard labour of 17 months during which it visited other universities in British India, the Commission submitted its report in 13 volumes giving a critical account of the working of the Calcutta University and indicating the lines on which higher education in Bengal should develop in future. The report investigated the problems which were common to the other four universities in India as well, and its recommendations provided the basis for the future development of university education in India.

Problems of Secondary Education

The Commission first studied the problems of secondary education because it held the view that improvement of secondary education was an essential foundation for the improvement of university education. The Commission therefore recommended "a radical reorganisation of the system of secondary education" after a close and critical study – it suggested the formation of a Board of Secondary and Intermediate Education consisting of representatives of government, university, high schools and intermediate colleges with full power of managing secondary and intermediate education; the separation of the intermediate classes from degree colleges by instituting separate intermediate colleges providing instruction in arts, science, medicine, engineering, education, agriculture, commerce and industry and finally the admission test for universities should be the passing of an examination from the intermediate colleges. The Commission hoped that by this arrangement the division of authority between the university and the Department of Education, that had plagued secondary education, would disappear and the university would be free from the responsibilities of secondary education to devote its full time to higher education alone. The Commission further recommended use of mother tongue in the intermediate colleges except for the teaching of English and mathematics.

Problems of the Calcutta University

The Commission then thoroughly examined the problems of the Calcutta University and found that the size of the university had become too large and the number of students and colleges affiliated to it too great to be effectively dealt with by a single institution. It therefore recommended: (a) creation of a teaching and residential university in Dacca; (b) pooling of teaching resources in Calcutta in order to create a real teaching university and finally, (c) development of mofussil colleges in such a way as to make it possible for the gradual rise of new university centres at a few places by concentrating all possible resources for higher education on them.

The Commission also wanted to free the university from the rigid governmental control imposed on it by Curzon's Indian Universities Act of 1904-05. It recommended the formation of a widely representative Court and an Executive Committee in place of the Senate and the Syndicate respectively. It suggested that teachers should be entrusted with more powers over academic affairs and recommended the formation of Academic Council with full powers over courses of study, examinations and degrees, of various faculties, boards of studies and other statutory bodies. It also recommended the organisation of teaching work in each department under the headship of a faculty member, discussed the case of appointment of a full-time and salaried Vice-Chancellor to head the university and recommended appointment to professorships and readership through special selection committees including external experts.

The Commission found the courses of instruction "too predominantly literary in character and too little varied to suit various needs" and commented on the inadequate provision for "training in technical subjects". It urged the inclusion of applied science and technology in its courses and asked the university to make provision for the efficient training of personnel needed for the industrial development of the country. The Commission recommended introduction of various courses of instruction in this context, instituted a three-year degree course after the intermediate stage, Honours courses as distinct from the Pass courses of abler students and recommended inclusion of Indian languages among subjects for Pass and Honours degrees. In this context the Commission stressed the need for establishing a link between the university and institutes of Oriental learning. The Commission emphasised the need for increasing the number of trained teachers, recommended the creation of a Department of Education and inclusion of Education as a subject for the intermediate, B.A. and M.A. degree examinations. The commission also recommended the organisation of *purdah* schools for Hindu and Muslim girls whose parents were willing to extend their education up to 15 or 16, a special board for women's education to look after courses particularly suited for women and to organise cooperative arrangements for teaching in the women's colleges and suggested every encouragement for the education of the Muslims. The Commission did not overlook the welfare of the students and suggested creation of a board of students' welfare and of a post of Director of Physical Education with the rank and salary of a professor. And finally, the Commission recommended the establishment of an Inter-University Board for coordinating the activities of various Indian universities.

Recommendations influenced by the Haldane Commission on the London University

Most of the recommendations of the Calcutta University Commission were influenced by the Haldane Commission which enquired into the organisation and functions of the London University earlier – some of the Calcutta University Commission's recommendations were therefore unsuitable to Indian conditions prevailing at that time. For example, development of mofussil colleges into future university centres and pooling together of the teaching resources in Calcutta to create a real teaching university on the pattern of Oxford or Cambridge were really beset with great difficulties and complications. Secondly, the recommendation to free the Calcutta University from the burden of secondary education by creating intermediate courses and instituting a Board of Secondary and Intermediate Education was excellent no doubt but was far ahead in times and as such liable to failure when implemented. So also was the suggestion of transferring the control of government colleges to non-official governing bodies.

Significance

Despite these limitations inherent in the recommendations of all commissions appointed in India, which had always looked to the British model for guidance, there is no doubt that the recommendations of the Calcutta University Commission not only reshaped the character of the existing universities in India but showed the lines on which future universities in India would develop. The Calcutta University Commission revolutionised the character of university organisation in India by creating statutory bodies like the Board of Studies and the Academic Council, reshaping the Senate and the Syndicate as the University Court and the Executive Council and by adding new Faculties to make university education more dynamic and more real. It emphasised the selection of the right persons through selection committees with external experts to the posts of Readers and Professors and mooted the question of appointing a full time salaried Vice-Chancellor to head the university organisation in India. It provided for the further development of modern Indian languages by including them in university courses while keeping in touch with institutions of classical studies. While introduction of new types of courses and research work improved the tone of university education in India, the suggestion to set up an Inter-University Board provided an unique opportunity to coordinate the activities of various universities in India. The greatest contribution of the Calcutta University Commission to university education in India, however, lay in freeing it from the governmental shackles imposed on it by Curzon's Indian Universities Act of 1904-05. Henceforth, the universities in India were to enter an era of freer growth and development – the process of university autonomy and democratisation of higher education in India may be said to have begun with the recommendations of the Calcutta University Commission.

36

Education Under Dyarchy

The Government of India Act of 1919

The year which saw the Calcutta University Commission submit its report also saw the passing of the Government of India Act of 1919 by the British Parliament. Based on the reform proposals of Montagu, the Secretary of State, and Chelmsford, the Viceroy, first announced in the House of Commons on 20 August 1917 by Montagu against the background of the Home Rule Movement in India led by B.C. Tilak and Annie Besant, the Act set up a Council of State and a Legislative Assembly with elected majorities but no control over the ministers at the Centre. It introduced dyarchy in the Provinces where departments with less political weight and little funds like education, health, agriculture and local bodies were transferred to ministers responsible to the Provincial Legislatures. Officials were given control of more vital department like law and order or finance, and the Provincial Governors like the Viceroy at the Centre were given powers to veto plus "certificate" procedure of pushing through rejected Bills. Revenue resources were divided between the Centre and the Provinces and despite some criticism of the separate electorates made in the Report in 1918, the Act of 1919 not only retained communal representation and reservations first announced in the Act of 1909 to appease the demand of the Muslim League formed in 1906 but also extended them by conceding the justice Party demands for non-Brahmin reservations in Madras.

Education in the New Set-up

As mentioned earlier, education was transferred to the Indian ministers but since there was considerable opposition to the idea of a total transfer from the Anglo-Indians, the resident Europeans in India and some provincial governments, the following reservations were made: First, institutions of higher learning including universities with an all-India character; second, colleges for Indian princes and similar institutions for members of His Majesty's armed forces and public services, their children, and finally, the education of the Anglo-Indians and the resident Europeans were to be looked after by the Government of India. The Government of India also reserved the right to legislate on university education including establishment, constitution and functions of new universities to give effect to the recommendations of the Calcutta University Commission.

Limitations

The new set-up worked under many limitations. In the first place, the Government of India stopped spending its own revenues on any transferred subject and discontinued the practice of helping provincial governments with a part of its revenues in education. Second, besides the veto power of the Governors, the Indian ministers had to encounter stiff opposition on many an occasion from the members of the Indian Education Service who were recruited in England and were responsible to the Secretary of State for India through the Governor-General-in-Council. The Indian ministers had little or no control over them and disagreements between the two often created a lot of ill-feeling, which hampered work including education. Ultimately, recruitment to the Indian Education Service stopped in 1924 with the recommendation of the Lee Commission on Superior Civil Services in India to the effect that "for the purposes of Local Governments, no further recruitment should be made to the All-India Services which operate in transferred fields". Third, the Government of India ceased to take interest in provincial matters including education which were transferred to Indian ministers. It refused to perform even those of its functions where an element of control was not involved, though it continued to publish quinquennial reviews of education concerning different parts of British India. Finally, the provincial governments not only drifted from the Central subjects but also created a gulf amongst themselves in the administration of transferred subjects including education. The new set-up doubtless encouraged an exaggerated form of parochialism, overlapping of various experiments and wastage of energy and money. Henceforward, there was to be no uniform development of education for the different parts of British India.

Need for Coordination in Education

In these circumstances there was a genuine need for a coordinating agency and the Government of India responded to it by setting up the Central Advisory Board of Education in 1921, to offer expert advice on important educational matters referred to it. However, within two years, on the recommendations of the Inchape Committee it was abolished and with it was abolished the Bureau of Education and its publication programme of the selections from educational records, owing to the financial crisis faced by the Government of India. The Department of Education at the Centre was amalgamated with that of Revenue and Agriculture.

Reaction of the Indian National Congress

The Indian National Congress which had denounced the Montagu-Chelmsford reform proposals when published in 1918 as unsatisfactory, was persuaded by Gandhi who emerged as the unquestioned leader of the national movement in December 1919 at Amritsar to give the Act of 1919 a fair trial. However, the Hunter Commission Report of 1 May 1920 which absolved the British officials of all blame for the Punjab atrocities including the Jallianwalla Bagh massacre by General Dyer on 13 April 1919,[1] followed by the publication of the harsh terms of the Treaty of Sevres with Turkey on 14 May 1920, changed Gandhi's stand. In the first week of June 1920, the Central Khilafat Committee meeting at Allahabad decided to begin a Non-Cooperation Movement against the British Raj including boycott of titles, Civil Services, police and the army and the movement started on 1 August – a day also memorable for the death of Tilak. In the December 1920, session of the Nagpur Congress, Gandhi pressed the Congress to adopt a similar plan of campaign around the three issues of the Punjab wrong, the Khilafat wrong and the *Swaraj* which was left deliberately undefined.

National Education

The Non-Cooperation Resolution passed by the Nagpur Congress in 1920 advised "the gradual withdrawal of children from schools and colleges owned, aided or controlled by government, and, in place of such schools and colleges, the establishment of national schools and colleges in the various provinces" was encouraged. Within a short period of time national schools and colleges were established throughout the country at Ahmedabad, Benares, Calcutta, Lahore, Patna and Poona. The courses offered by these schools and colleges did not differ much from those offered by government controlled institutions, though the medium of instruction was invariably the mother tongue and the object was to breed a race of Indians to provide leadership to the national movement with a national outlook.

Among the national universities thrown up by the national education movement during this period were the Jamia Millia Islamia, the Viswa-Bharati and the Gurukul which now adorn the scene of our higher education in the country. A section of the Muslim community opened a number of Azad Schools in Uttar Pradesh and led by Maulana Mohammad Ali in 1920 established the Jamia Millia Islamia or Muslim National University at Aligarh. The university which preferred "the hardships and ordeals of an honourable independence to the enervating security of a permanent grant which would frustrate its noblest ambitions" was transferred to Delhi in 1925. In 1921 Tagore founded the Viswa-Bharati without any financial support from the government, with the object of understanding the diverse cultures of the East and the West and building up a platform for world fellowship, peace and harmony. The Gurukul University which grew out of the *Arya Pratinidhi Sabha* in the Punjab in 1902 was shifted in 1924 to Kangri where it continued to conduct its work in "sylvan solitude ... free from the un-educational influence of city life".

The establishment of national schools and colleges, which functioned with a number of handicaps such as a lack of suitable buildings, trained personnel, equipment and finances certainly led to a decline in the number of pupils attending government recognised schools and colleges. "In 1921 the percentage of decrease in attendance – for the whole country was 8.6 (colleges), 5.1 (high schools), and 8.1 (middle schools)" involving great financial loss to the institutions owing to decrease in income through tuition and examination fees.

However, the national school movement came to a sudden end when Gandhi stopped the Non-Cooperation Movement following the *Chauri Chaura* incident, on 5 February 1922. Although short-lived, the movement was significant in formulating the principles of national education, preparing alternative courses suited to national needs and aspirations and in adopting modern Indian languages as the medium of instruction. As the *Quinquennial Review of the Progress of Education* for the period 1917-1922 observed, "In short, the crisis had left behind the conviction that our educational aims need restatement .... The political and economic conditions of India have been undergoing change and the national school movement can at least claim that it lent strength to the advocates of educational reform".

Appointment of the Hartog Committee as an Auxiliary Committee of the Simon Commission

On 8 November 1927, the British Government announced the appointment of a Commission to enquire into, and report on the working of the Montagu-Chelmsford reforms as a basis for further action. As per the provision of the Act of 1919, the first such enquiry was to be held after ten years in 1929 when British elections would be held. Since there was a growing probability that the Labour Party would return to power, it was considered safer to forestall the Labour Government by advancing the date by two years. The Commission was to consist of seven British Members of Parliament, including Attlee, under Sir John Simon. The Simon Commission was also asked to submit a report on education and for this purpose an Auxiliary Committee with Philip Hartog as President was formed. Hartog was a former member of the Calcutta University Commission under Sadler as well as an ex-Vice-Chancellor of the newly formed Dacca University.

The Hartog Committee submitted its Report

However, the Simon Commission was boycotted by all political leaders, irrespective of their party affiliations mainly on the ground of exclusion of Indians from a body which was to prepare the future constitution of India. Despite the hostility of the Indian political leaders, the Hartog Committee was able to submit a comprehensive report on Indian education in September 1929. The Committee admitted in its report that during the decade between 1917 and 1927, education had made considerable progress. As the report observed:

> Education has come to be regarded generally, as a matter of primary national importance, an indispensable agency in the difficult task of 'nation building'. The attention given to it by legislative councils is both a symptom and evidence of this recognition. The transfer of

the Department of Education to popular control, as represented by a Minister, has both increased the public interest in it and made it more sensitive to the currents of public needs and public opinion. Nor is it only the authorities and the well-to-do classes that have welcomed and encouraged the spread of education. Communities which had for long been educationally backward, as for example the Muslim community, have awakened to the need and possibilities of education for their children. The movement has spread to the depressed classes and even to the tribal aborigines, and has stirred a much larger proportion of the people than before to demand education as a right.

Primary Education: Wastage and Stagnation

However, the Hartog Committee was not satisfied with the progress of literacy during the same period. Out of every hundred boys admitted in class 1 in 1922-23, only 19 were found studying in class IV in 1925-26. "Primary education", the Committee observed, "is ineffective, unless it at least produces literacy. On the average, no child who has not completed a primary course of at least four years will become permanently literate". The gradual decrease in number was ascribed to wastage, that is, premature withdrawal of children from any stage before the completion of the primary course and stagnation, that is, retention of a child in a class for more than one year.

Wastage and stagnation were attributed to: (a) the absence of a systematic organisation of adult education, (b) difficulty of providing schools in villages with a population under 500, (c) uneven distribution of schools and inadequate utilisation of existing schools, (d) shortage of separate boys' and girls' schools or separate schools on communal or religious ground, (e) ineffective teaching, unsuitable curricula, and inadequate inspecting staff and (f) unsatisfactory provision of compulsory primary education. The Committee felt that the problem of primary education was mainly a problem of the villages, as nearly 87 per cent of the people lived in villages. Poverty, illiteracy and conservatism of the parents, coupled with lack of communication, particularly in hilly and backward areas or deserts and deltas, seasonal diseases, barriers of caste, religions, communal and linguistic differences, and finally premature engagement of children in agricultural occupations aggravated the problem.

The Committee, therefore, condemned a policy of expansion and recommended one of consolidation in primary education. It recommended: (a) fixing up of the minimum duration of the primary course to a period of four years, (b) liberalisation of school curricula and adjustment of school hours and holidays to seasonal and local requirements, (c) special attention to the lowest class to prevent wastage and stagnation, (d) provision for suitable training, refreshers courses and conferences, and salaries for teachers, (e) rural reconstruction work in the village primary schools, (f) strengthening of the inspecting staff, and finally, (g) introduction of compulsion after a careful preparation of the ground by the government which should not feel complacent by handing over the charge of primary education to local bodies but keep an active interest in its expansion.

Secondary Education

In the sphere of secondary education, the Committee noted "an advance in some respects", but found the whole system of secondary education "still dominated by the ideal that every boy who enters a secondary school should prepare himself for the university; and the immense number of failures at the matriculation and in the university examinations indicate a great waste of efforts'. It attributed this wastage of time, effort and money of the pupils to: (a) the laxity of promotions in the secondary schools from class to class and (b) the absence of a reasonable selective system of courses which would never have permitted a large number of students to prepare themselves for matriculation examinations with an eye to admission to colleges.

The Committee made the following recommendations to reduce the domination of the matriculation: First, introduction of a more diversified curricula in the middle vernacular schools and admission of a large number of boys in them intended for rural pursuits; and second, diversion of more pupils to industrial and commercial careers at the end of the middle school stage and provision for alternative courses in the high school stage preparatory to special instruction in technical and industrial schools. The Committee also observed that as in the case of primary schools, the average quality of the teacher and of the teaching depended to a considerable extent on the pay and conditions of service, which though still far from satisfactory, had improved in recent years. In no province was the pay of the teacher sufficient to give him the status which his work demanded and in some provinces, for example, Bengal and Bihar, the pay of the teacher was often woefully low. But the most serious difficulty facing the teacher in the great majority of privately managed schools and schools managed by local bodies was "insecurity of tenure". In spite of what had been done in recent years, the conditions of service of the teacher must be greatly altered before the quality of secondary education could become satisfactory.

University Education

The Committee felt satisfied at the growth of university education but found a "too large acceptance" in India of the theory that "a university exists, mainly, if not solely, to pass students through examinations". One of the primary functions of any university was "the training of broad-minded, tolerant and self-reliant citizens" but the universities in India had been "hampered in their work by being overcrowded with students who are not fitted by capacity for university education". The Committee, therefore, observed: "In the interests of university education itself and still more in the interests of the lower educational institutions which feed the universities and of the classes from which university students are drawn, the time has come when all efforts should be concentrated on improving university work, on confining the university to its proper function of giving good advanced students who are fit to receive it, and, in fact, to making the university a more fruitful and less disappointing agency in the life of the community". In this context, the Committee recommended the need for enriching college libraries, concentration of Honours Course at selected centres and organisation of tutorial and research work in the universities.

Women's Education

In women's education, the Committee noted a great disparity existing in the figures of school going boys and girls. It found primary education of girls in villages inefficient and restricted and at the secondary stage it was quite inadequate. It stressed the need of prescribing a curricula that would suit the requirements of girls, of appointing a large number of women teachers and inspectress on good salaries as well as of appointing official of the rank of a Deputy Director to look after the programme of women education. The Committee also recommended a gradual introduction of compulsion for the education of girls, the future mothers of the country.

On the aspect of educational administration the Committee observed that the transfer of control of education from the Central to the Provincial Governments was not a wise step and that the

Government of India could not absolve itself of the responsibilities in this manner. It pointed out the need for establishing a centralised educational agency at Delhi, increasing the inadequate staff of the Directors of Public Instruction in the provinces, relieving the Educational Commissioner of the responsibility of the centrally administered areas by appointing an Education Secretary, and finally, for holding regular conferences of senior education officials on current matters of educational importance.

Thus, the Hartog Committee report revealed how quality had been scarified at the altar of quantity and so the need of the hour was to improve quality rather than strive to increase the numbers still further. In other words, consolidation rather than expansion. "We have no doubt", concluded the Hartog Committee report, – "that more and more money will be gladly voted for education by the legislatures of India .... Money is no doubt essential, but even more essential is a well-directed policy carried out by effective and competent agencies, determined to eliminate waste of all kinds. We were asked to report on the organisation of education. At almost every point that organisation needs reconsideration and strengthening; and the relations of the bodies responsible for the organisation of education need readjustment".

Impact

The Hartog Committee report was warmly welcomed by the bureaucrats and acted as a guide to their activities in education till 1937. The reports of the Provincial Directors of Public Instruction show a general uniformity of ideas emphasising such defects as the prevalence of wastage and stagnation, extreme devolution of authority to local bodies, and inadequacy of the inspecting staff. As the Director of the Public Instruction in the Madras Presidency summed up the situation in the *Quinquennial Review of the Progress of Education* between 1932 and 37: "The policy of expansion which was in full swing between 1920 and 1930, countenanced the establishment of a large number of inefficient, uneconomic and superfluous schools which proved worse than useless. This policy of expansion has led to the recent reaction in favour of concentration and elimination, which is partly responsible for the reduction in the number of elementary schools". Yet many of the recommendations of the Hartog Committee including an increase in the salary of the teachers, and of the staff in the inspectorate and improvement of curricula remained as mere pious hopes.

The world-wide economic depression which began in 1929 was another factor which helped indirectly Hartog Committee's recommendation on consolidation rather than expansion in education. The Central and Provincial Governments had to make ruthless curtailment in the budget assigned to education which in the eyes of the Hartog Committee was a "nation-building" force. Government expenditure was gradually reduced from 1,361 lakhs in 1930-31 to 1,184 lakhs in 1935-36.

Private Enterprises remained unaffected

However, Hartog Committee report which aimed at raising the standard of education and consolidating it did not affect private enterprise in the field of education. Despite the curtailment of government efforts on account of financial stringency, a comparison of the following statistics of 1936-37 with those of 1921-22 shows an unprecedented increase in the number of institutions and of scholars under instruction:

Institutions	1921-22	1936-37	1921-22	1936-37
	Number	Number	Scholars	Scholars
Universities	10	15	N.A.	9,697
Arts Colleges	165	217	45,418	86,273
Secondary Schools	64	75	13,662	20,645
Primary Schools	7,530	13,056	11,06,803	22,87,872
Special Schools	1,55,017	1,92,244	61,09,752	1,02,24,288
Total Recognised	3,344	5,647	1,20,925	2,59,269
Institutions	1,66,130	2,11,308	73,96,560	1,28,88,044
Total unrecognised Institutions	16,322	16,647	4,22,165	5,01,530
Total for all Institutions	1,82,452	2,27,955	78,18,725	1,33,89,574

The Hartog Committee's explanation of the progress of education during the decade before its appointment in 1927 is also applicable to the decade after it despite the fact that following the Lahore Congress resolution of December 1929 the Indian National Congress had started a Civil Disobedience Movement under the leadership of Gandhi for the attainment of *purna swaraj* or complete independence and British India had been in turmoil.

Progress of Education

The Quinquennial Review of the Progress of Education in India between 1922 and 1937 throws a flood of light on the developments in education in British India. They may be briefly noted here: In higher education, following the recommendations of Sadler Commission five new universities were set up at Delhi (1922), Nagpur (1923), Andhra (1926), Agra (1927) and Annamalai (1929).

As per recommendations of the Conference of Indian Universities held in Simla in 1924, an Inter-University Board with its headquarters at Bangalore was established to coordinate the activities of various universities while changes in the constitutions and functions of the older universities at Calcutta, Bombay, Madras, Punjab, Allahabad and Patna were brought about by passing Acts, amending the Acts of Incorporation of these universities. The number of affiliated colleges also rose from 207 in 1922 to 446 in 1937 and that of students from 66,258 to 1,26,228 in the two years respectively.

In secondary education, the number of recognised schools rose from 7,530 in 1921-22 to 13,356 in 1936-37 with a corresponding rise in the number of students from 11,06,803 to 22,87,872. In elementary education the number of primary schools rose from 1,55,016 in 1921-22 to 1,84,829 in 1926-27 with a corresponding rise in expenditure from Rs 3,94,69,080 to Rs 6,75,18,802 following the enactment of compulsory primary education to a certain extent in Bengal, U.P., Punjab, Bihar and Orissa in 1919, Madras in 1920, Bombay in 1923 and Assam in 1926. However, after the Hartog Committee report, primary education rose very slowly. By 1937 the number of schools rose to 1,92,244, that of pupils to 1,02,24,288 and the direct expenditure involved came to Rs 8,13,38,015 only.

Note

1. Should not be confused with the Hunter Commission Report of 1882-83. The 1882-83 Commission was presided over by Sir William Hunter who died in 1900. This one was presided over by Lord (also William) Hunter, formerly Solicitor-General of Scotland and at the time of the submission of the Report, Senator of the College of Justice in Scotland.

37

Education Under Provincial Autonomy

The Government of India Act of 1935

The British Prime Minister, Ramsay MacDonald, summoned the third and final session of the Round Table Conference at London on 17 November which lasted till the end of December 1932. It was largely a small gathering of 46 delegates compared to the second session in 1931 which was attended by 112 delegates including Gandhi. This time the Congress which was then staging Civil Disobedience Movement in India did not attend the session. The Conference was followed by the issue of a White Paper in March 1933 and setting up of a joint Select Committee of Parliament under Linlithgow with a provision merely for consulting Indians. Quite naturally and expectedly, many of the admittedly restricted concessions offered in 1930-31 under pressure of Civil Disobedience Movement were now reduced through this process. And in August 1935, the Government of India Act emerged after a long and tortuous process which started eight years earlier with the appointment of the Simon Commission in 1927.

We are already acquainted with the recommendations of the Hartog Committee which was an auxiliary committee of Simon Commission on education and we need not enter here into the details of the provisions of the Government of India Act except those which affected the development of education in the country. It is sufficient here to say that the Government of India Act of 1935 put an end to the diarchical system of administration set up by the Act of 1919, abolished the distinction between reserved and transferred subjects, and placed the whole field of provincial administration under a Ministry responsible to a legislature which had an overwhelming majority of elected members. The new system of governance, popularly known as Provincial Autonomy, came into operation in 1937 in eleven provinces of British India.

Impact of the Act on Education

How did this Act affect the administration of education in India? As we have already seen, the Act of 1919 made education a subject which was "partly all-India, partly reserved, partly transferred with limitations and partly transferred without limitations". But the Act of 1935 improved upon this anomalous position considerably and divided the educational administration into two categories only – Federal or Central and State or Provincial and included under the first head the following subjects: Imperial Library, Indian Museums, Imperial War Museum and Victoria Memorial Hall – all in Calcutta and any similar institution controlled or financed by the Federal Government, Benares Hindu University and Aligarh Muslim University; Archaeology; Education in Centrally Administered Areas and finally Education for the Defence Forces. In the State or Provincial subjects the Act included all matters regarding education other than those included in the Federal or Central list.

Central Advisory Board of Education revived

Following the recommendations of the Hartog Committee the Central Advisory Board of Education (CABE) was revived in 1935 and at its first annual meeting held in December 1935, the Board adopted the following resolutions: a radical readjustment of the present system of education in schools, to be made in such a way as not only to prepare students for professional and university courses but also to enable them to be diverted to occupations or separate vocational institutions after completion of appropriate stages. The separate stages mentioned by the CABE resolution consisted of three stages: Primary, Lower Secondary and the Higher Secondary. While the aim at the Primary Stage was to ensure permanent literacy by providing at least a minimum of general education and at the Lower Secondary Stage to prepare students for higher education or specialised practical courses by providing a self-contained course for general education, the Higher Secondary Stage was to aim at preparing students for admission to arts and science courses of the universities. It also aimed at raising a number of trained personnel in agriculture as well as teaching in rural areas, in selected technical subjects in consultation with prospective employers and in the clerical works which might be available in government and non-government establishments. The CABE resolved in this context that the first public examination should take place at the end of the Lower Secondary Stage and decided to seek expert advice in connection with its resolution to reconstruct education in British India, as outlined in its first resolution.

Wood Abbott Report

As per the last resolution of the CABE, the Government of India invited S.H. Wood, Director of Intelligence, and A. Abbott, formerly Chief Inspector of Technical Schools of Board of Education, England to advise the Government of India in connection with the CABE resolution on the proposed reconstruction of education in British India. Wood and Abbott toured India during the winter of 1936-37 and submitted their report in June 1937. The first part of the report concerning general education and its administration was written by Wood and the second part on vocational education by Abbott, which became known as the Wood-Abbott Report.

In the first part, Wood recommended that provision should be made for trained teachers in primary or infant schools and for this purpose education of girls and women was of paramount importance. There was a great need for change in the curricula of elementary education – and as such, it should be based more upon the natural interests and activities of children concerned than upon book-learning. In rural areas the curricula of middle schools should be related to rural needs and requirements. In such schools, he observed, the medium of instruction should be the mother tongue and teaching of English should be avoided as far as possible. If it was ever taught, it must not result in an excessive amount of linguistic grind. However, English should be a compulsory language in high schools while the mother tongue should be the medium of instruction as far as possible. The high schools should obtain a supply of qualified teachers in Fine Arts to teach the subject and, there should be a training course of three years' duration for the teachers of primary and middle schools immediately after they had completed the middle school course.

The second part of the report concerning vocational education was written by Abbott. Observing that vocational education should keep pace with the industrial development of the country to check all

the earlier and latter phases of a continuous process. Admission to

vocational education should not be below the standard reached at the

end of the middle school and pupils from this stage could be admitted

VIII course and offering a 3-year course till vocational education,

would be parallel to the higher secondary school, while the senior

course and opting a course of two years in vocational education

Abbott observed that there was the need for training of three

They were managers, supervisors and operators. There should be a

Commerce should be offered as an optional subject in secondary

Polytechnic School to separate individual schools for each vocation,

where training in many vocations could be given. The report also

Delhi. Finally, Abbott recommended the establishment in each

curricula for each one of the vocations should, he noted, rest with the

Congress Ministries in Seven Provinces

As said before, Wood and Abbott submitted their report to the
Government of India in June 1937. By the time provincial autonomy

as per the provisions of the Government of India Act of 1935 had come into operation in eleven provinces of British India. With a radical agrarian programme the Congress was able to sweep the polls in elections held at the beginning of 1937 as far as the predominantly or general Hindu seats were concerned. The Muslim League desired to form a coalition government in each province but the Congress refused to admit into the ministry anyone who did not subscribe to its creed. In seven out of eleven provinces the Congress formed Ministries. Most of the difficulties like the worldwide economic depression and the consequent financial stringency, the holding of the finance portfolio by a member of Governor's Executive Council who was not amenable to the influence of Indian ministers, Indian Educational Service whose European members had a final say in educational matters and absence of popular support as the ministers were not represented by the Congress, then the most influential political organisation in the country which the Indian ministers had to face earlier in the nation-building task of education had disappeared with the abolition of the diarchical system of administration. It was naturally expected that the new provincial governments would be able to work on education more vigorously than before in the changed circumstances.

Gandhi's Scheme of Basic Education

In the meantime, Gandhi who had spoken strongly in 1920 against the present system of education, now, having got the opportunity of influencing the ministers in the seven provinces who had been fellow workers in the struggle for freedom of the country, felt "an irresistible call", as he later wrote in *Educational Reconstruction,* "to make good the charge that the present mode of education is radically wrong from top to bottom". He wrote a series of articles in the *Harijan* about his ideas on educational reconstruction in India, suggesting a scheme of universal compulsory education for all children in the age group of 13-16 through the medium of mother tongue which would be self-supporting, leading to all-round development of the pupils. In other words, industrial vocations such as the processing of cotton, wool and silk, paper-making and cutting, book-binding, cabinet-making, etc., taught at the primary schools should serve a double purpose. They should help the pupils to pay for their tuition through the products of their labours while developing the human qualities in them through the vocations learnt at these schools. This primary education which Gandhi later described as Basic Education should equip the boys and girls to earn their bread with some support from the state.

Wardha Conference

Gandhi's ideas on self-supporting aspect of the scheme which he described as "basic education" (basic because it was expected to form the basis of our national culture), published in the *Harijan* created a great public stir. However, they came to be "unfortunately mixed up with the disappearance of drink revenues" which the Congress Ministries in the seven provinces were committed to enforce. It was, therefore, thought desirable to get the scheme examined by expert educationists and with that end in view the First Conference on National Education was called at Wardha on and 23 October 1937 with Gandhi in the chair. While the Conference was attended by the Education Ministers of the seven provinces with Congress Ministries, the number of delegates was limited to national workers, particularly workers in national education. Gandhi himself placed his scheme of national education through rural handicrafts before the Conference and after a serious discussion on it for two days the Conference adopted the following four resolutions:

1. That in the opinion of this Conference free and compulsory education be provided for seven years on a nation-wide scale.
2. That the medium of instruction be the mother tongue.
3. That the Conference endorses the proposal made by Mahatma Gandhi that the process of education throughout this period should centre round some form of manual productive work, and that all the other abilities to be developed or training to be given should, as far as possible, be integrally related to the central handicraft chosen with due regard to the environment of the child.
4. That the Conference expects that this system of education will be gradually able to cover the remuneration of teachers.

Zakir Husain Committee Report

The Conference then appointed Dr. Zakir Husain, Principal of Zamia Millia Islamia, Delhi, as Chairman of a Committee entrusted with the task of preparing a detailed syllabus on the lines of the four resolutions mentioned above and asked him to submit a report to the Chairman of the Conference as early as possible. Within a short period of two months, Zakir Husain Committee submitted its report. It pointed out that modern educational thought was practically unanimous in commanding the idea of educating children through some suitable form of productive work. While psychologically it relieved the child from the tyranny of a purely academic and theoretical instruction against which its active nature was always making a healthy protest, socially it would tend to break down the existing barriers of prejudice between manual and intellectual workers, harmful alike for both and economically it would increase the productive capacity of our workers and would also enable them to utilise their leisure advantageously. From the strictly educational point of view greater concreteness and reality could be given to the knowledge acquired by children by making some significant craft the basis of education – knowledge would thus become related to life, and its various aspects would be correlated with one another. The object of this new educational scheme was not primarily the production of craftsmen able to practise some craft mechanically, but rather the exploitation for educational purposes of the resources implicit in craftwork. This demanded that productive work should not only form a part of the school curriculum – its craftside-but should also inspire the method of teaching all other subjects.

As a matter of fact, in the course of the report, the Committee explained the principles and objectives of the scheme in terms of recognised doctrines of education and psychology, worked out detailed syllabuses for a number of crafts, and made valuable suggestions regarding such important aspects of the scheme as the training of teachers, supervision and examination, administration and even worked out a few possible correlations with basic craft of spinning and weaving. It also warned against an obvious danger of stressing the economic aspect in the working of the scheme at the sacrifice of the cultural and educational objectives. As the report observed: "Teachers may devote most of their attention and energy to extracting the maximum amount of labour from children, while neglecting the intellectual, social and moral implication and possibilities of craft training. This point must be constantly kept in mind, in the training of teachers as well as in the direction of the work of the supervisory staff and must colour all educational activity". The report thus emphasises the educational aspects of the scheme more than its self-supporting aspect which is a radical and significant departure from Gandhi's ideas on Basic Education.

Gandhi who had very humbly described the writings on Basic Education as the writings of "a layman for the lay reader" was happy to find that his views were now endorsed by the Zakir Husain Committee consisting of educational experts. The Indian National Congress which met at Haripura in February 1938 under the presidentship of Subhas Chandra Bose accepted Gandhi's scheme and it was immediately implemented in the seven provinces with Congress Ministries.

Kher Committee Report

Gandhi's scheme on basic education aroused considerable interest in the provinces of British India with non-Congress Ministers as well and the Central Board of Education which was then discussing Wood-Abbott report, decided to go through the Zakir Husain Committee's report on Gandhi's scheme. In 1938 it appointed B.G. Kher, then Prime Minister of the Bombay State who went through it and made the following observations: the scheme should first be introduced in rural areas and made compulsory for the children between 6 and 14 years of age, and it was after completing Class V or attaining the age of 11 that they should be allowed to leave basic school for other kinds of schools with a school leaving certificate. While the medium of instruction should be the mother tongue, there would be no external examinations, and school leaving certificates based on internal examinations should be given to the pupils after the completion of the course of the basic school.

After going through the report submitted by the Kher Committee the CABE asked it to consider it further whether the scheme could be conveniently split into two parts, each part complete in itself, while preserving its essential unity. At this the Kher Committee suggested that it could be conveniently split at class V which might be the first stage and might be called junior stage and it was only after the completion of the junior stage that children could be allowed to join other forms of post-primary education offering a variety of courses extending over a period of at least five years after the age of eleven. The courses offered by the other forms of post-primary schools should be so designed as to prepare the pupils for entry to industrial and commercial vocations as well as to universities, while preserving an essentially cultural character.

Congress Ministries resigned

The Kher Committee submitted its second report but by that time the Congress Ministries in the seven provinces were increasingly facing the problem of alienation of workers, *kisans* and all left elements within the party. At the same time, they were unable to please the landlords or business groups when in the face of tight financial constraints of provincial autonomy they took recourse to measures like Bombay urban property tax. Such was the hopeless nature of the financial position of the Congress Ministries that in July 1939, Vallabhbhai Patel hinted that the Ministries might have to be dissolved unless the provinces received a greater share of income tax. Finally, they were also realising the embarrassing possibility of having to use the new emergency powers against demonstrations by their own party men if the war broke out soon. The war was declared on 2 September 1939, by Britain on Germany and India as a colony of Britain was automatically committed to belligerency, by Linlithgow, the Viceroy, without bothering to consult the Provincial Ministries or any Indian leader. When the Congress Working Committee meeting on 14 September invited the British Government to declare in unequivocal terms their war aims in regard to democracy and imperialism and how they were going to be applied to India, Linlithgow took more than a month to tell the Congress about his inability to elaborate the war aims of Britain further than the British Prime Minister. The Congress Working Committee found Linlithgow's reply far from satisfactory and asked the Congress Ministers in the seven provinces to resign on 29-30 October, which they did.

Sargent Plan

With the resignation of the Congress Ministers any hopes of an educational reconstruction under Provincial Autonomy were lost. The caretaker governments that now succeeded the popular governments in the provinces were too preoccupied sorting out the problems created by the war as well as by the freedom movement led by Gandhi to have any time and money for education in British India. However, as the victory of the Allied Powers was in sight by 1943, the Government of India asked all provincial governments to chalk out plans of post-war developments in India and as a part of the general scheme, Sir John Sargent, the then Education Adviser with the

Government of India, was also asked by the Reconstruction Committee of the Government of India to prepare a memorandum on post-war educational development in India for submission to the Viceroy's Executive Council for consideration. At their meeting in October 1943 and January 1944, the Central Advisory Board of Education accepted Sargent's memorandum and under his guidance, was able to prepare a report which was compiled from the materials in the forms of reports on different aspects of education in India then lying with it. The report, popularly known as Sargent Report, was entitled "Postwar Educational Development in India", and aimed at attaining the educational standard of contemporary England in India, within a minimum period of forty years. We may now have a look at the main recommendations for post-war educational development in British India.

First, the report recommended for the first time a reasonable provision of pre-primary education for children between 3 and 6 years of age, covering some ten lakh places in nursery schools or classes.

Second, there should be a provision of universal free and compulsory primary education for all children between the ages of 6 and 14, divided in two stage – Junior Basic (6-11) and Senior Basic (11-14). While Junior Basic would be compulsory for all, Senior Basic would be meant for those who would not join high schools.

Third, high school education should be meant for selected children (including twenty per cent from Junior Basic Schools) between the ages of 11 and 17. There would be two types of high schools – Academic High Schools providing instruction in Arts and Sciences and Technical High Schools providing instruction in applied sciences, industrial and commercial subjects. Girls were to be additionally instructed in Home Sciences. For all high schools, the medium of instruction was to be the mother tongue.

Fourth, Intermediate courses were to be abolished – first year of the intermediate course was transferred to the high schools while the second year of it to the universities. Only one out of every 10 or 15 matriculates were to be given admission to universities meant for post-graduate teaching and research. There should be an all-India body on the model of the University Grants Committee of Great Britain for co ordinating activities of the various universities.

Fifth, the requirements of industry and commerce would determine the amount, type and location of each type of institutions, namely, Technical, Commercial and Art Education. Generally speaking; four types of institutions would be required: (I) Junior Technical, Industrial or Trade School with a two-year course after the Senior Basic Stage; (II) Technical, Industrial or Trade School with a six-year course after the Junior Basic Stage; (III) Senior Technical, Industrial or Trade School with a programme of course in consultation with employers and finally, (IV) University Technological Departments providing facilities for research and teaching. Over and above this, the report also emphasised the need for instituting part-time courses for students who could be working in factories, and other industrial or commercial concern as paid workers for improving their knowledge and efficiency.

Sixth, there should be proper arrangements for the education of the adult illiterates between the ages of 10 and 40 (approximately 9 crores) through visual and mechanical aids such as pictures, illustrations, artistic and other objects, magic lanterns, cinema, gramophone, radio, folk dances, music – both vocal and instrumental – and dramatic performance. In adult education, the report observed that though the main emphasis would be on literacy, there should be some provision for those turned literate to have "an inducement as well as an opportunity to pursue their studies". There should be separate classes for boys and elderly persons while special attention should be devoted to women adult illiterates.

Seventh, there should be full provision for the training of teachers. It was estimated that implementation of the scheme would need nearly 2,21,733 teachers – 20,00,000 non-graduate teachers, including 23,333 for the pre-primary stage, 11,96,200 for the Junior Basic Stage and 6,25,560 for the Senior Basic Stage and 1,81,320 graduate teachers for high schools. In the Pre-Basic and Junior Basic Schools there should be one teacher for every 30 children, in Senior Basic Schools one for every 25 students and in high schools one teacher for every 20 students. While the graduates would be trained for one year in training colleges, non-graduates would be given three kinds of training – Pre-Basic and Junior Basic Stages teachers (2 years), Senior Basic Schools (3 years) and non-graduate teachers for high schools (2 years). There should be refresher courses for trained teachers at different intervals. As far as the training of technical and commercial teachers was concerned, they would acquire it in technical and, industrial institutions. The report also proposed a revision of a scale of pay for all grades of teachers.

Eighth, there should be provision for compulsory physical education, medical inspection and treatment of students in order to keep them physically fit and a thorough medical test of the students should be made at the age of six, eleven and fourteen years.

Ninth, there should be special institutions for the education of physically and mentally handicapped children including imbecile, blind, deaf and dumb.

Finally, the report suggested provision for an Employment Bureau advising students about various employment possibilities and also for social and recreational activities of the institutes on a very large scale.

The report emphasised the creation of education departments both at the Centre and in the States to supervise education in the country. Provinces would look after the entire education except university and higher technical education which would be coordinated on all-India basis. It would also be necessary for the provincial governments to resume all powers in education from local bodies which were not functioning efficiently.

A Critique of Sargent Plan

The whole plan covering a period of forty years in which the contemporary educational standard of England was to be achieved had further been divided into five-year programmes. "The first five", the report pointed out, should be devoted to planning propaganda and particularly to the provision of the institution necessary for training teachers, and that thereafter the actual carrying out of the scheme should be divided into seven five-year programmes, during each of which an area or areas should be fully dealt with. "The size of these areas in the case of each Province will be determined during each programme period by various factors of which the supply of teachers available will be the most important". The total cost of the scheme, it was estimated, would be Rs 31,260 lakhs, out of which Rs 27,700 lakhs would have to come from public funds.

K.G. Saiyidain who was associated with the working of the Sargent Plan has thus appreciated it:

> What is the wider significance of this scheme? It is the first comprehensive scheme of national education; it does not start with the

assumption, implicit in all previous Government schemes, that India was destined to occupy a position of educational inferiority in the comity of nations, it is based on the conviction that what other countries have achieved in the field of education is well within the competence of this country. The mere formulation of such a scheme ensures that no other scheme which proposes any half-hearted, piecemeal changes or merely tinkers with the idea of expansion can ever be seriously entertained. Secondly, it is inspired by the desire to provide equality of opportunity at different stages of education. At the primary stage it envisages not merely the provision of free schooling but also of other facilities without which the poorer children cannot fully avail themselves of the education opportunities -- mid-day meal, books, scholarships, medical inspection and treatment. At higher stages, free places and scholarships are proposed for all bright and deserving students. This is by no means that full measure of educational equality which an enlightened sense of social, justice demands but it is certainly a welcome step forward towards that goal and would be a great improvement on the existing situation. Thirdly, it stresses in clear terms the importance of the teaching profession and makes proposals for increasing its miserable standard of salaries and poor conditions of service. It lays down a minimum national scale of salaries, and provides for its adjustment in accordance with the rise in the cost of living.

Sargent Plan had been criticised on the ground that "it placed a very tame ideal before the country. As the Report itself admitted, India would reach the educational standard of the England of 1939 in a period of not less than 40 years: In other words, even assuming that the plan were fully implemented, the India of 1984 would still be nearly 50 years behind England". Secondly, "the only ideal held up by the Report is that of the educational system of England, while, as a matter of fact, England is the one country which could not very well serve as a model, to India, because the social, political and economic conditions in the two countries are so vastly different. If India had to have a model, she could look for it elsewhere in eastern countries like China or Egypt or Turkey or in Western agricultural countries like Denmark or Soviet Russia – all of which had many problems similar to those of India, and which have been able to achieve splendid results in a very short time".

It must be remembered that the main reason for fixing the period for implementing the plan at forty years was the impossibility of obtaining resources in terms of men and money within a short period after the conclusion of a devastating World War. The reason why England was accepted as a model was partly because India was a British colony and partly because all educational innovations in India since 1854 had always been inspired by the examples in England and when Sargent drew his plan he had little inkling that India would achieve freedom soon. If social, political and economic conditions in England and India were different, they were not similar either between India and China or Egypt or Turkey or Denmark or Russia despite the fact that they might have many similar problems. It is futile to argue that what Russia could achieve within fifteen years, India could have achieved within the same period. The character of development of a country depends upon the character of the people and, even after independence, if India could have achieved an educational standard which would have been lower than the standard in England by 40 years, that would have been indeed a tremendous achievement for us.

Implementation of Sargent Plan

Immediately after the publication of the Sargent Plan in 1944, the Central Government asked the Provincial Governments to draw up their five-year programmes on the basis of the plan. In 1945, a separate Education Department was established at the Centre and in the following year the University Grant Committee was established. Thus by 1946, the Central Government which had accepted the major recommendations of the Sargent Plan was trying to give shape to many of them.

India achieved Independence

By 1946, the Congress had returned to power by winning in the general constituencies in the elections held in the 1945-46 winter, routing its rivals – the Hindu Mahasabha and the Communists. In the Central Assembly the Congress captured 57 out of 102 seats against 36 in 1937 and in the provinces it won majorities everywhere except Bengal, Sind and the Punjab. On 24 March, the Cabinet Mission came to India "to promote, in conjunction with the leaders of Indian opinion, the early realisation of full self-government in India". However, this was as usual stalled on the rock of Jinnah's insistence on Pakistan. Because of the post-war difficulties facing the country, Britain did not want to continue to hold on to India and the British Prime Minister Attlee replaced Wavell by Mountbatten who came as the Viceroy of India on 24 March 1947, to arrange for transfer of power which was done in August 1947. Jinnah, as President of the Pakistan Constituent Assembly created on 11 August, was to become the Governor-General of the Dominion of Pakistan comprising Sind, Baluchistan, the North-West Frontier Province, the West Punjab and the East Bengal. The Congress requested Mountbatten to continue to act as the Governor-General of the Dominion of India which included "a truncated" Bengal as well as "a truncated" Punjab.

Let us now have a look at the extent of education in British India immediately before August 1947. We shall however, keep in mind the approximate total number of population which according to Sargent's estimate in 1944 was 400 million. If we make an allowance for an increase of 2 million per year, then immediately before August 1947, the British India had a population of nearly 406 million.

Elementary Education

Immediately after Hartog Committee's recommendation which argued for quality rather than quantity, elementary schools declined in number from 1.89 lakhs in 1936-37 to 1.67 lakhs in 1944-45 and then rose to 1.72 lakhs in 1946-47. Despite the decline in the number of elementary schools, there was an increasing enthusiasm among the growing population for primary education and this could be seen in the ever increasing number of pupils attending elementary schools. Thus, the number of pupils increased from 1.05 crores in 1936-37 to 1.14 crores in 1944-45 and by 1946-47 it had reached 1.30 crores. By 1946-47 the total expenditure on primary education had also shot up from 6.98 crores in 1936-37 to 15.48 crores.

Secondary Education

In secondary education there was a steady increase in the number of institutions – from 13,410 in 1937-38 to 16,017 in 1943-44 and by 1946-47 the number had reached 17,258 mark. From the statistics of high schools and middle schools we can also detect a steady increase in enrolment – the number of students rose from 23.93 lakhs in 1937-38 to 36.06 lakhs in 1946-47. The expenditure on secondary education also increased from Rs 9.6 crores in 1937-38 to Rs 17.9 crores in 1946-47 – almost a double increase.

Higher Education

In higher education by 1946-47, two more universities had been added to the existing 15 universities in British India and the number of Arts and Science Colleges increased from 174 in 1937-38 to 297 in 1946-47. The number of students studying in universities rose from 10,000 in 1937-38 to 16,000 in 1946-47, while the number of students in Arts and Science Colleges increased from 53,000 in 1937-38 to 96,000 in 1946-47. The expenditure on universities increased from Rs 1.10 crores in 1937-38 to Rs 2.03 crores in 1946-47 while in that on Arts and Science Colleges it rose from Rs 1.64 crores to Rs 3.53 crores in 1946-47. However, Engineering and Technical Colleges could not show much progress in their number which increased from 9 in 1937-38 to 16 in 1946-47, while other professional colleges increased from 47 in 1937-38 to 82 in 1946-47. Corresponding to the expenditure on these colleges which increased from Rs 1.20 crores in 1937-38 to Rs 2.75 crores in 1946-47, the number of students in these institutions increased from 53,697 in 1937-38 to 71,897 in 1946-47 – a healthy sign that despite inadequate facilities of professional education in the country, professional education was attracting a good number of students immediately before independence.

38

Independent India: Towards a National Policy on Education

Independence for India meant not only a vivisection of her body but also a vivisection of her soul. Education, both Western and Indian, which was an aspect of her soul also got vivisected. If a part of the Western system of education built up by the British Raj went to Pakistan, a substantial part of education developed in the Indian States[1] which opted for merger with India did fill in the gap and became henceforward a part of Indian education. It must be stated here that apart from the Chiefs' Colleges, education in the Indian States depended upon the whims and caprices of the Indian Princes, many of whom were educated abroad and no uniformity either in standard or in instruction (the medium varied from State to State according to its regional dialect) could be expected as was the case with the education in British India.

When India achieved her independence, newly emergent nations in Asia, Africa and Latin America were preoccupied with the task of renovating their educational structures to suit national needs and national aspirations. We have seen how the concept of national education was born as a side product of freedom movement beginning with the Anti-Partition Movement in 1905-11. We have also noted how there was a continuous effort to clarify the concept and to set up some experimental institutions outside the official system financed and controlled by the British Raj as in the 1920s and the 1930s. The earlier national institutions could now become a part of the general system and the effort now made was to convert the entire system of education to the national pattern. Thus, in January 1948 in his inaugural address to the All India Educational Conference convened by the Union Education Minister, Jawaharlal Nehru, the first Prime Minister of India, observed: "Whenever conferences were called to form a plan for education in India, the tendency, as a rule, was to maintain the existing system with slight modification. This must not happen now. Great changes have taken place in the country and the educational system must also be in keeping with them. 'The entire basis of education must be revolutionised".

Nehru's observation was quite in keeping with the forces of the time which saw emergent nations in Asia, Africa and Latin America preoccupied with the task of renovating their educational structures to suit national needs and national aspirations. But the promised revolution in education system in India was not so easy to materialise. India after independence was plagued with a host of pressing problems. The Partition had brought to India refugees from East and West Pakistan – they had to be rehabilitated. The Princely States had to be integrated with the Indian Union. The bureaucracy and the army had to be reorganised as the departure of British officials had left these services depleted. India had to be granted a constitution and made a republic. Plans had to be drawn up for developing the country.

Radhakrishnan Commission

In the midst of all these the utmost that could be done in education was to appoint in 1948 a University Commission under the Chairmanship of Dr. S. Radhakrishnan as reconstruction of university education was considered essential to meet the demand for scientific, technical and other manpower needed for the socio-economic development of the country.

The recommendations of the Commission in 1949 were wide, covering all aspects of university education in India. They emphasised the 10+2 structure at the pre-university stage, correction of the "extreme specialisation" in the courses, development of research to advance the frontiers of knowledge and of professional education in agriculture, commerce, law, medicine, education, science and technology including certain new areas such as business and public administrations and industrial relations and suggested reform of the examination system by assessment of the student's work throughout the year and introduction of courses on the central problems of the philosophy of religion. They also emphasised the importance of student's welfare by means of scholarships and stipends, hostel, library and medical facilities and suggested that they should be familiar with three languages – the regional, federal, and English – at the university stage and that English be replaced as early as possible by an Indian language. The Commission was also in favour of the idea of setting up rural universities to meet the need of rural reconstruction in industry, agriculture and various walks of life. The universities should be constituted as autonomous bodies to meet the new responsibilities, a Central University Grant Commission be established for allocating grants, and finally, university education be placed in the Concurrent List.

Education in the Constitution

Earlier, in the same year when the Radhakrishnan Commission submitted its recommendations, on 26 January 1949, Independent India had adopted a constitution finalised by the Constituent Assembly and the following year on the same date India proclaimed herself a Republic. The Constitution made Education a State Subject and divided the educational responsibility between the Government of India and the State as reproduced below:

List I: List of Union Functions

63. The institutions known at the commencement of this constitution as the Benares Hindu University, the Aligarh Muslim University and the Delhi University and any other institution declared by Parliament by Law to be an institution of national importance.
64. Institutions for scientific or technical education financed by the Government of India wholly or in part and declared by Parliament by law to be institutions of national importance.
65. Union agencies and institutions for:
    (a) professional, vocational or technical training, including the training of police officers; or
    (b) the promotion of special studies or research; or
    (c) scientific or technical assistance in the investigation or detection of crime.
66. Co-ordination and determination of standards in institutions for higher education or research and scientific and technical institutions.

List II: List of State Functions

11. Education including universities, subject to provision of entries 63, 64, 65, and 66 of List I and entry 25 of List III.

List III: List of Concurrent Functions

25. Vocational and technical training of labour.

The Constitution provided statutory recognition (Part XVII, Article 343) to the demand for the use of Hindi in Devnagri script as the official language of the Indian Union replacing English. It was further provided that the transition from English to Hindi be gradual and acceptable to all, that English should continue to be used till 1965 for all official purposes of the Union for which it was being used immediately before the adoption of the Constitution while States were authorised to adopt Hindi or any other modern Indian language for their official purposes. The Constitution also provided for the appointment of a Language Commission five years after the adoption of the Constitution. The recommendations of the Language Commission were to be considered by a Parliamentary Committee and the decision about the use of Hindi as the official language was to be taken on the basis of the recommendations of the Official Language Committee. While providing adequate safeguards for the educational and cultural interests of minorities, the Constitution realised the importance of universal primary education for the proper development of democracy. Thus, Article 45 of the Constitution, also one of the important Directive Principles of State Policy, observed that "the State shall endeavour to provide within a period of ten years from the commencement of this Constitution, for free and compulsory education for all children until they complete the age of 14 years.

Planning Commission

In the same year when India was proclaimed a Republic, a decision to develop the country in a planned way was taken. With that end in view, a Planning Commission was created at the Centre and was entrusted with the task of drawing five-year plans covering all aspects of national development including education. The First Five-Year Plan began in 1950-51 with Rs 153 crores as an outlay on education, which represented 7.8 per cent of the total Plan outlay.

Mudaliar Commission

One of the most significant recommendations of the Radhakrishnan Commission was on the reorganisation of secondary education as a prerequisite condition for the development of university education. In 1952, the Secondary Education Commission was appointed under the Chairmanship of Dr. A.L. Mudaliar which submitted its report in 1953. It reduced the total duration of the school course from 12 to 11 years and transferred the control of secondary school leaving examination from the universities to the specially constituted Boards of Secondary Education. While developing the curricula of the higher secondary course, the Commission sought to diversify it by the establishment of Multipurpose Schools which would provide terminal courses in technology, commerce, agriculture, fine arts and home science. The obvious object was to divert students from university education into different walks of life according to their aptitudes and capabilities.

It is clear from the above that the Mudaliar Commission as well as the Radhakrishnan Commission which met before it dealt exclusively with two areas of education in which the ruling elite groups were interested. Both these sections received large allocations of funds and underwent rapid unplanned and uncontrolled expansion, resulting in deterioration of standards and creation of severe problems of educated unemployment. On the other hand, the programmes of adult education and liquidation of illiteracy continued to be neglected as in the past. In elementary education, the evils of wastage and stagnation continued unabated as no structural changes like multiple-entry or part-time education were introduced. A perfunctory attempt at introducing basic education on Gandhian ideas was made but it was not successful and practically given up soon. In the context of all these developments, the aim of constitutionally providing free and compulsory education for all children up to 14 years of age by 1960 seemed a distant dream now.

Kothari Commission

It is also clear from the earlier developments in education that the country was only interested in retaining the colonial set-up and was mostly engaged in dealing with education in a piece-meal fashion. The vision of a national system of education seen in 1947 thus got blurred within two decades. Yet, the demand by the electorates for such a system continued to be made so persistently that in 1964, M.C. Chagla, the Union Education Minister, appointed the Education Commission under the Chairmanship of Dr. D.S. Kothari, to advise the government on the general principles and policies for the development of education at all stages and in all its aspects so that a national system of education could emerge.

In 1966, the Commission in its voluminous report suggested a drastic reconstruction, almost a revolution in education, to meet the problems facing the country in different sectors. It suggested an internal transformation in education to relate it to life, the needs and aspirations of the people, a qualitative improvement to raise its standards and a quantitative expansion of educational facilities on the basis of manpower needs and equalisation of educational opportunities. The internal transformation could be achieved by making science education an integral part of school education and improving its teaching at the university stage. Similarly, work experience should be an integral part of all general education. Vocational education was emphasised both at the lower (11-16 years) and the higher (17-18 years) secondary stage while in higher education about one-third of the total enrolment was expected to be in vocational courses. A common school system with equal access to children from all social strata was suggested and some form of social service was made obligatory for students at all stages. Development of fundamental, social, moral and spiritual values including a provision for some instruction on different religions was emphasised. National consciousness as well as a sense of belonging to the country was sought to be promoted through the adoption of a curricular programme which was both dynamic and elastic at all stages. While retaining the three language formula of the Radhakrishnan Commission with some modifications, the Kothari Commission recommended the development of all modern Indian languages for use in education as well as in administration in their respective States. While all the three languages should be studied at the lower levels, only two of these were to be compulsory at the higher secondary stage.

The qualitative improvement could be achieved by a maximum utilisation of the existing facilities. Since resources for upgrading all the institutions were not available, the Commission suggested that at least ten per cent of them should be upgraded to adequate standards during the next ten years – the model would be one secondary school in every community development block, one college in each district and five or six universities at the national level. The Commission accepted 10+2 at the secondary and the higher secondary stages followed by a first degree course of a duration of not less than three years. The Commission also made various recommendations including uniform pay-scales to improve the service conditions of teachers so that the best persons coming out from the education system could be attracted to teaching. It felt that the education facilities could be expanded on a selective basis at the secondary and the higher secondary stages while effective primary education should be provided to all. Adult illiteracy should be liquidated on a mass or selected scale and part-time courses of about one year's duration for the drop-outs in the 11-14 age group. The Commission visualised that total enrolment would rise from 70 million in 1965 to 170 million in 1985 and educational expenditure from Rs 6,000 million in 1965 to Rs 47,000 million in 1985, representing an increase in the proportion of national income devoted to education from 2.9 per cent in 1965 to 6 per cent in 1985.

Implementation

Since education was then a State subject, the usual procedure would have been to refer those recommendations concerning States to them but the public demand for the education was so great that the Government of India decided to depart from the procedure followed earlier. After a wide circulation through its own organs and the press, the government referred them to a Committee of Members of Parliament for consideration. The recommendations along with the report of the Parliamentary Committee were then discussed in both the Houses of Parliament, followed by a discussion in Cabinet. Out of these discussions emerged the first national policy in independent India in the form of a resolution on education in July 1968. Needless to say, the recommendations of the Kothari Commission were progressively diluted at every stage of the discussions. Yet the policy that was born out of them remained the basic framework for all governmental action despite an attempt by the Janata Government to revise it in 1979 after it came to power in 1977, till the coming of "the New Education Policy" in May 1986.

1986 New National Policy on Education

In January 1985, the Government of India announced that "a New Education Policy" would be formulated soon. In August 1985 after making a careful assessment of the existing developments, the proposals were submitted to the public for a countrywide debate and discussion, and in May 1986 emerged the National Policy on Education after its approval by Parliament.

The document on the National Policy on Education is divided into twelve parts. After some preliminary observations in the first two parts, it discusses in some detail about some of the essential characteristics of a national system of education providing scope for equal access to education to all irrespective of class, caste, creed or sex, and areas including backward, hilly and desert. It envisages a common educational structure like 10+2+3, a common core in the curricular programme at some level, an understanding of the diverse socio-cultural systems of the people while motivating the younger generations for international cooperation and peaceful coexistence.

"The New Policy" therefore stresses the need for removal of disparities and emphasises the steps to be taken to equalise educational opportunity by attending to the specific needs of those who have been denied equality so far – women, Scheduled Castes and Scheduled Tribes, the handicapped and certain minority groups who are either educationally deprived or backward. People belonging to rural areas, hill and desert districts, remote and inaccessible areas and islands need special care and incentives. "The whole Nation", observes the National Policy on Education, "must pledge itself to the eradication of illiteracy, particularly in the 15-35 age group". The document seeks to organise programmes on adult education linked with national goals to enable the beneficiaries to participate in the development programme of the country.

While the local community will be fully involved in early childhood care and education, "the new thrust" in elementary education will be on (a) universal enrolment and retention up to 14 years and (b) attempt to substantially improve the quality of education. This effort will be fully coordinated with the network of non-formal system so that by 1990, all children attaining the age of 11 years will have had five years of schooling and by 1995 all children up to 14 years of age will be provided free and compulsory education. In secondary education, talented children will be provided opportunities to proceed at a faster pace by means of pace-setting schools with full scope for innovation and experimentation. Courses on vocational education will ordinarily be provided after the secondary stage, but keeping the scheme flexible, these may also be made available after class VIII. Vocational education will be a distinct stream, intended to prepare students for identified occupations spanning several areas of activity. By 1990, vocational courses are to cover 10 per cent, and by 1995, 25 per cent of the higher secondary students. In higher education the most urgent need is "to protect the system" consisting of 150 universities and 5,000 colleges from "degradation". Autonomous colleges are to be developed to gradually replace the affiliating system while the creation of autonomous departments within universities on a selective basis are to be encouraged. Research in Science and Technology and interdisciplinary research in Social Sciences as well as setting up of national research facilities with proper forms of autonomous management are to be encouraged. The Open University system will be initiated in order to augment opportunities for higher education while Rural University, on the lines of Mahatma Gandhi's revolutionary ideas on education, is to be set up to transform rural India. Technical and Management Education curricula was targeted on current as well as the projected needs of industry or user system and were to relate to the changes in the economy, social environment, and knowledge. Delinking degrees from jobs will be made in selected areas where candidates despite being equipped for a given job are unable to get it because of an unnecessary preference for graduate candidates.

The document makes a series of observations on cultural perspective, value education, languages, books and libraries, media and educational technology, work experience, education and environment, mathematics teaching, science education, sports and physical education, the role of youth, and proposes to recast the examination system so as to ensure a method of assessment that is a valid and reliable measure of a students' overall development and a powerful instrument for teaching and learning. Since these and many other "new tasks" of education cannot be performed in "a state of disorder" the first task is to make the system "work". "All teachers should teach and all students study". The strategy of the New Education Policy in this respect consists of (a) better deal to teachers with greater accountability; (b) provision of improved students' service and insistence on observance of acceptable norms of behaviour; (c) provision of better facilities to institutions; and (d) creation of a system of performance appraisals of institutions according to standards and norms set at the National or State levels.

How is this system going to be managed? Since Education is a Concurrent Subject now as per the Constitutional Amendment of 1976, it is expected that a meaningful partnership will be formed between the States and the Union Government in managing it. The guiding considerations will be: (a) evolving a long-term planning and management perspective of education and its integration with the country's development and manpower needs; (b) decentralisation and the creation of a spirit of autonomy for educational institutions; (c) giving pre-eminence to people's involvement, including association of non-government agencies and voluntary effort; (d) inducting more women in the planning and management of education; and finally, (e) establishing the principle of accountability in relation to given objectives and norms. As far as the financial aspect of the system is concerned, the government proposes to gradually increase the expenditure on education till it "uniformly exceeds, 6 per cent of the National Income". Additional sources, to the extent possible, will be raised partly by mobilising donations from the beneficiary communities and partly by raising fees at the higher levels of education while effecting some saving by the efficient use of facilities. And finally, implementation of the various parameters of "the New Policy" will be reviewed "every five years".

Reviewing of the educational policy "every five years" was a decision taken by the British Government as a sequel to the Report of the "Indian Education Commission" in 1882 and was first implemented in 1886, exactly hundred years ago from the date of the promulgation of the New Education Policy. While this aspect of the New Education Policy is not certainty new, the question may now be asked as to how new are the contents of the New Education Policy? The answer to the question can only be provided by reviewing the past developments in education and for this purpose we need not go beyond 1947 – the year when India achieved her independence. India's educational policy, immediately after her independence, was based on the structure provided by Sir John Sargent, Educational Adviser to the British Government, in his Post-War Plan of Educational Development in India in 1944. The object of the Plan was to achieve for India in 1984, the same educational standard as it had then existed in England. It had provided for the liquidation of illiteracy, universal elementary education and higher education for students out of every twenty that completed the secondary school and a certain amount of vocational, technical and professional education. It also provided for compulsory physical education, milk and mid-day meals for under-nourished children and special education for the physically and mentally handicapped.

Extent of Newness

How new is this New Education Policy? It is interesting to note that the framers of the New Education Policy have never cared to answer this question. They have never bothered to explain anywhere in the long policy statement in what sense the present policy is new or how different it is from the 1968 policy resolution. A comparative study of the New Education Policy with that of the 1968 National Policy on Education reveals that the former has directly borrowed many of its ideas from the recommendations of the Kothari Commission which provided the basis for the 1968 National Policy on Education. In some places there are also direct acknowledgements of its indebtedness to the 1968 policy. For example, on the subject of the languages which always remains one of the most sensitive issues in any education policy in India, the New Education Policy observes: "The Education Policy of 1968 had examined the question of the development of languages in great detail; its essential provision can hardly be improved upon and are as relevant as today". Similarly on the subject of raising resources or making investments in education, the New Education Policy says: "The National Policy on Education, 1968, had laid down that investment on education be gradually increased to reach a level of expenditure of 6 per cent of the National income as early as possible .... It will be ensured that from the Eighth Five Year Plan onwards it will uniformly exceed 6 per cent of the National Income".

The New Education Policy thus does not appear to be new in many aspects of its policy. Its indebtedness goes beyond the 1968 National Policy on Education, as for example, the idea of setting up rural universities is directly taken from the Radhakrishnan Commission of 1948-49. It may be mentioned here that the subject of Model School or pace setting school of the New Education Policy which has been seen as undesirably favouring a privileged few against many students by its critiques is not a new concept at all. The idea of the Model School is older than the education system itself which emerged in Modern India in 1854. It is an idea which first found favour with James Thomason, the Lt. Governor of the North-Western Provinces in 1849, when he decided to introduce a scheme of vernacular education by means of establishing a school in every village and every district to remove the appalling ignorance of the people in understanding the new revenue settlement in the North-Western Provinces. The scheme was successful – it was extended to the rest of British India before it finally became a part of the plan of the Education Despatch of 1854. Similarly, the idea of autonomous colleges which has been in the air since the days of the Kothari Commission and is now an important aspect of the new policy is also older than the structure of the Indian education system itself. Colleges like the Hindu College, Sanskrit College, Agra College, Delhi College and the Presidency College which grew out of the Senior Department of the Hindu College in 1853 were all autonomous colleges. They were brought under the jurisdiction of the Education Department which emerged in 1855 and were later affiliated with the three universities that came into existence at Calcutta, Bombay and Madras in 1857.[2]

If the New Education Policy is not "new" in themes and ideas, it is certainly "new" in the emphasis it has placed on its implementation and the directions it has issued for the purpose. Immediately after its approval in the Budget session in 1986, a "Programme of Action" was prepared and presented for approval in the Monsoon session of the Parliament. The 1968 National Policy on Education was taken so half heartedly and its implementation was made so casually that a decade after the policy had been promulgated, J.P. Naik, a Member-Secretary of the Kothari Commission, was led to remark: "The stresses and strains of the [education] system have continued to grow so that the educational scene in the country in 1978 is not certainly better and is probably a little more complicated and difficult than in 1966". It is also new in the way it has emerged. The 1968 policy was based on the recommendations of the Kothari Commission which took nearly two years to finalise them. Whereas the formulation of the proposals of the New Education Policy was not preceded by the appointment of an expert Commission on the subject. The proposals were formulated by the concerned Ministry officials under guidance from the ruling party immediately after its coming to power in December 1984/January 1985 with a massive majority in Parliament. They were ready by August 1985 and were then submitted to the politicians, academicians and administrators for their reactions. The final policy emerged, out of the discussions that followed, in May 1986 – the shortest possible time that has ever gone into the making of a policy in education while the first announcement of such a policy on the subject, Indian Educational Policy, in March 1904, took nearly three years after the proposals were first mooted in a secret Conference at Simla in September 1901, as we have already seen.

Genesis

Since the secret files of the government are not open to us, it is difficult to say at this stage how the proposals for the New Education Policy came to be formulated. Yet from a study of the developments that had taken place in India in the last three decades before 1986 as well as from a careful study of some of the observations made in the 1986 policy documents, it is possible to guess that the reasons for promulgating the New Education Policy are more political than educational. In the past few decades, the education scene has been in turmoil in most of the developing countries which have recently emerged independent but in India it has a peculiar dimension because of the vastness of the country with a huge, almost exploding population now,[3] who speak different languages, follow different religions and cultures, and practise different social norms and behaviours. Since early 1950s, a Planning Commission has been set up to chalk out a planned development of India and education has become part of the planned programme. Unfortunately it has not received the attention it deserves "whether in absolute terms or relatively to investment in other sectors", and the Planning Commission has never bothered to develop educational programmes after a careful assessment of the educational needs of the country. Since education is a catalyst in one's development, everybody asks for it and the political party which seeks its mandate from the public to rule has normally accepted such demand. The result is that within three decades after independence we have a tremendous but unplanned expansion of education, particularly in higher education which is too academic in nature. For example, in 1947, there were only 19 universities, 277 Arts and Science Colleges, 199 Intermediate Colleges and 140 colleges of professional and technical education – in 1974, there were 100 universities and about 4,000 colleges. The enrolments in higher education which stood at 2.5 lakhs in 1947 were estimated in 1974 at 34 lakhs.

What were the prospects open to these educated youngmen and women whose parents made considerable investment in their education? The Indian economy did not in those years expand sufficiently to absorb the output of an unplanned expansion in education. Most of them remained unemployed or underemployed. In 1974 the Register of the Directorate General of Employment and Training reveals that there were some 54.58 per cent educated unemployed at the Matriculation, 26.01 per cent at the under graduate, 17.87 per cent at the graduate and 1.53 per cent at the post-graduate levels. In other words out of a total population of nearly 600 million, approximately 41,74,000 remained unemployed. Underemployment and unemployment which may differ in their consequences for individuals have many social consequences in common, especially the monopolising of issues of social conflict in the political arena. The incidence of unemployment among the educated added to the stresses of the society already suffering from communalism, casteism, linguism and sectionalism. What could be the attitude of these young educated unemployed towards the government that had helped them to get education but no employment after it? It is one of discontent, as Bacon's *Of Seditions and Troubles,* observes that one of the chief causes of discontent is "when more are bred scholars than preferment can take off". This also saps student motivation, creates unrest on the campus, and leads to further deterioration of standards. As a matter of fact, higher education converts on a large scale the uneducated underemployment or unemployment, which is mute, unorganised, and without a nuisance value into educated, urban unemployment which is vocal and organised and has a great nuisance value.

And what could be the attitude of the government towards them? One which could possibly be best described in words used by Curzon in 1901 more than eighty years ago while commenting on the spread of English education in India since 1835: When Erasmus was reproached with having laid the egg from which came forth the Reformation, "Yes", he replied: "But I laid a hen's egg, and Luther had hatched a fighting cock".

It is not therefore surprising to see that the educated unemployed spilled into the political arena. Many regional political parties began to exploit the discontent of the educated unemployed against the government to strengthen their grip over the people, while leadership and recruits as cadre members of the Naxalites and other radical groups in Indian politics came largely from the ranks of the educated unemployed. Until 1967, the Congress Party held power both at the Centre and in the States but since 1967 election it not only began to loose its hold over the States, particularly in Kerala, Tamil Nadu, West Bengal, Tripura, Andhra Pradesh, Karnataka, Jammu and Kashmir, Punjab, Assam and Haryana but also mauled itself by a split in 1969. Also, new political parties have emerged demanding the creation of separate States for them such as Uttarakhand in the Uttar Pradesh, Gorkhaland in West Bengal, and Jharkhand in parts of Bihar, West Bengal, Orissa and Madhya Pradesh which have posed a serious challenge to the government at the Centre. However, it is the militants' demand of Khalistan, in the Punjab, a State fully independent of India that has taxed the nerves of the Centre to the utmost and the government had to pull all its resources to fight these forces of disintegration. In all these developments where the involvement of the educated, both employed and unemployed has been quite large, there has been no evidence of patriotism, no sense of belonging to one country and even no recollection of the past suffering and sacrifices of their ancestors for the freedom of the motherland. It seems they have not got the correct education since independence and the government therefore is determined to introduce an education policy which while contributing to the national development will rectify these defects. As the document of National Policy on Education, 1986 observes in the concluding part of its Introductory Chapter: "India's political and social life is passing through a phase which poses the danger of erosion to long accepted values. The goals of secularism, socialism, democracy and professional ethics are coming under strain. The rural areas, with poor infrastructure and social services, will not get the benefit of trained and educated youth, unless rural-urban disparities are reduced and determined measures are taken to promote diversification and dispersal of employment opportunities. The growth of our population needs to be brought down significantly over the coming decades .... Besides, a variety of new challenges and social needs make it imperative for the Government to formulate and implement a new Education Policy for the country. Nothing short of this will meet the situation". The same sentiment is also echoed by *Programme of Action* when it observes: "Time is of essence, and unless we act now, we stand in the danger of once again missing the opportunity of educational reform, so critical not only for the development of our nation, but for our very survival".

Prospect

What is the prospect of success for this new National Policy on Education? In Part XII of the document it speaks highly of the prospect it visualises "........ given our tradition which has almost always put a high premium on intellectual and spiritual attainment, we are bound to succeed in achieving our objectives". However, the success of such a scheme in a democratic country like India with many political parties with different ideologies assumes that all the political parties at least hold similar or common views on the subject of education. Unfortunately, this is not the case and there is a feeling in the States with non-Congress governments that some of the programmes in the New Education Policy like Model Schools, Autonomous Colleges, Open University, De-Linking degrees will further widen the gulf between the rich and the poor, the privileged few and the non-privileged many. Already, some Marxist teachers organisations in India have begun to view the New Education Policy with suspicion and distrust. The recent[4] month long university and college teachers' strike on the subject of the revision of teachers' salaries has further added cynicism to suspicion and distrust.

If the political parties in India fail to hold similar or common views on the New Education Policy, it still has chances of success provided the party that frames it rules both at the Centre and in the States and is assured of its return to power in the succeeding elections. But this is not only the case now, as there are many non-Congress governments in the States, but also seems to be a remote possibility. In the Assembly Elections between 1985-1986, non-Congress governments were returned to power in Kerala, Andhra Pradesh, Assam, Karnataka, West Bengal and Tripura. In Tamil Nadu the Congress was able to share power with AIADMK but in Haryana, a traditional seat of power for the Congress, it was badly mauled by Devi Lal's Lok Dal. The corruption charges in the country's defence deals involving high Congress dignitaries and government officials which have begun to surface in the media since June 1987 has considerably eroded the image and credibility of the ruling party at the Centre and there are now[5] frequent demands from the opposition parties for a Mid-term Poll.

In view of the facts stated above, the prospect of the New Education Policy does not appear to be very bright at the moment,[6] despite the fact that the government is pumping huge amount of money in implementing some of its programmes like operation black-boards, Open University and teachers training. There is no doubt that the document on the New Education Policy does possess many valid, sound and relevant proposals to do away with many of the existing problems in Indian education. It is imperative that these should be implemented to substantially alter the inherited colonial set-up in our education to suit national needs and aspirations. The only way out seems to be a Central Act embodying all the proposals of the New Education Policy and binding upon all governments, present and future, both at the Centre and in the States. If this is not done immediately, the fate of the New Education Policy will not be much different from the 1968 National Policy on Education. Let us thank God that Nostradamus' prediction about the end of the World by 1999 has proved wrong and the New Education Policy of 1986 has helped us to land in India of the Twenty-first Century smoothly without any broken limbs![7]

Notes

1. At the time of independence, there were more than five hundred Indian states which varied enormously from each other in its size, importance and status.
2. We have already been acquainted with these educational developments in colonial India in the preceding chapters.
3. 1987.
4. Immediately before 1987.
5. Ibid.
6. Ibid.
7. This chapter is based upon a paper on the 1986 National Policy on Education written in November 1987 and delivered at an International Conference at Atlanta as well as at the School of Education, Indiana University, in USA in March 1988.

39

The Critical Years Till 1998

In the preceding chapter we have expressed a hope that the New National Education Policy formulated in 1986 would help us with a smooth sailing in education for the rest of the years before we enter a new millennium. However, the events of the last twelve years have belied our hopes and expectations and only confirmed the fear and misgivings expressed earlier about the success of the 1986 Policy.

In August 1997, India completed fifty years of independence and began a year long celebration of the golden jubilee of its independence but the celebration was rather dim because not only the year of celebration but also those preceding it were extremely critical for its survival as a nation, not because of any external aggression but because of the development of inner conflicts within it, which are always found to be inherent in the death and the decay of an old civilisation. These years were marked not only by an acute political instability but also by a violent form of social disorder. The resurrection of the ghost of the Mandal Commission on reservation, signifying the rise of the Dalit and other backward classes in national administration in 1990 and the demolition of the Babri Masjid, reflecting the rise of Hindu fundamentalism in national politics, in 1992 added fuel to the fire by releasing disintegrating social forces that threatened the very fabric of Indian society. While a sagging and dying economy was brought back to life by injecting a dose of globalisation into its veins, its side-effects adversely affected the poor and the downtrodden. The situation was further aggravated by the economic sanctions flowing from many developed countries following India's second nuclear explosion in May 1998, at Pokharan where "the Buddha smiled again". When the people were suffering from inflation and the rising high prices, the news of a multitude of scams of high dimensions involving high political dignitaries before which the 65-crore Bofors' scandal paled into insignificance, were making almost daily rounds in the media. For most of the developments like corruption and disintegrity, violence and lawlessness, communal passion and tension in these years, education was singled out, as in the past, as the whipping boy needing a dose of reforms at the hands of its political masters.

Implementation of the New Education Policy

However, the years immediately after the formulation of the New Education Policy in 1986 saw the start of a vigorous implementation of many of its important programmes and paradoxically enough all seemed to be well with education in the country. Thus, after intensive discussion with various agencies, schemes like Operation Blackboard, District's Institutes of Education and Training (DIET), Vocationalisation of Education and Technical Education were finalised. While the Navodaya Vidyalaya Scheme was implemented by opening 205 model schools in several important places of the country, a national core curriculum was finalised by the National Council of Educational Research and Training in consultation with the State Governments. Schemes on Non-Formal Education were also finalised and the summer of 1986 saw nearly two lakh college students involved in functional literacy programmes on a voluntary basis. With financial help from the Centre, various State Governments and Union Territories implemented the scheme of free education for girls up to the higher secondary stage. In higher education centralised agencies like National Assessment and Accreditation Council, National Council of Higher Education, National Council of Teacher Education, All India Council of Technical Education were set up to improve its tone and quality while a National Eligibility Test (NET) was introduced by the University Grants Commission to regulate the entry of candidates into the teaching profession at institutes of higher learning. Academic Staff Colleges were set up at important universities in the country to refresh and reorient the knowledge of university and college teachers and in the two summers of 1986 and 1987, a massive Teacher Orientation Programme was organised to cover nearly ten lakh teachers.

Replacement of the Congress Government by the National Front Government and the Appointment of the Ramamurti Committee

However, the implementation of the New Education Policy received a severe jolt when the Congress Government that had fathered it was replaced by the National Front Government under the Janata Dal leader V.P. Singh in 1989. As the name of V.P. Singh's government suggests, it was a coalition government consisting of many political parties representing various sections of society. And since many of its constituent parties had not earlier viewed with favour some of the programmes of the 1986 Policy, a revision of the education policy became imperative and with that end in view a review committee was appointed under Acharya Ramamurti in May 1990.

The scheduled time for the review of the New Education Policy was five years after its introduction, that is, in 1992. In a resolution appointing the Ramamurti Committee on 7 May 1990, the Government of India attempted an explanation for hastening the review so much before the expiry of the stipulated period of five years:

"Despite efforts of social and economic development since attainment of independence, a majority of our people continue to remain *deprived of education*. It is also a matter of grave concern that our people comprise *50 per cent of the world's illiterate*, and large sections of children have to go without *acceptable level of primary education*. Government accords the highest priority to education both as a *human right* and as the *means* for bringing about a *transformation* towards *a more humane and enlightened society*. There is need to make education an *effective instrument* for securing a status of *equality for women*, and persons belonging to the *backward classes and minorities*. Moreover, it is essential to give a *work and employment orientation* to education and to exclude from it the *elitist aberrations* which have become the glaring characteristic of the educational scene. Educational institutions are increasingly being influenced by *casteism, communalism and obscurantism* and it is necessary to lay special emphasis on struggle against this phenomenon and to move towards a genuinely *egalitarian and secular order*. The National Policy on Education (NPE), 1986, needs to be reviewed to evolve a *framework* which would enable the country to move towards *this perspective of education*".[1]

It will be seen that the concerns expressed in the government resolution appointing the Ramamurti Committee were also the concerns earlier expressed by the New Education Policy in 1986, except the right to work which was then sought to be enshrined in the constitution. While the *Challenge of Education* felt that "the present scenario is an indication of the failure of the education system", the *Education Policy* stressed the need to make education "a forceful tool" for its two roles "combative and positive". However, the events during the four years since 1986 had shown that it had failed in its missions as "the situation has grown much worse. Everywhere there is economic discontent, cultural decay, and social disintegration. The youth are in revolt. Violence is fast becoming a way of life... The nation is faced today with a crisis of many dimensions. Its very survival is threatened. In the total crisis of the nation, along with Politics, Business, and Religion, Education has its full share."

Recommendations of the Ramamurti Committee

Thus "the nation is in peril" at the moment[2] and the only way to save it from an impending disaster was to make education an integral part of national development through participation which "must go beyond government departments and reach the people in villages and muhallas. While there should be understanding and coordination among departments, there should be active participation among the people themselves." This could be achieved by treating the village itself as a unit for an integrated programme of education, democracy and development.

"The Panchayati Raj Bill, 1990", so observes the Ramamurti Committee, "proposes that each village will have a Gramsabha composed of all the adults in the village, male and female. It will have wide powers and functions. As a representative of the village this Gramsabha may be asked to prepare a plan of development including education for the village with its own priorities. As part of the village plan, each family will have its own small plan. The Gramsabha plan provides for each family means of livelihood – land for agriculture, cattle for dairying, tools for crafts, or other means of gainful employment. The Gramsabha itself will be responsible for implementing the plan. As for resources, the funds available for all the different development and education schemes may be pooled and placed at the disposal of the Gramsabha which may form its own committees to look after different activities... As the work progresses

The Critical Years Till 1998

and development mindedness grows and problems arise the village people will realise that without education and training, progress is not possible. Writing the muster rolls, keeping records, handling money, measuring dug earth, calculating wages, repairing the pumping set or implements, protecting crops, increasing the yield of milk, first-aid to simple injuries, and a lot of other problems will create a situation in which there will be a compelling demand for know-how, for information, for literacy, functional and general, and training in a number of skills". And thus the village would become a school where "those who are educated will teach; those who have skill will train; those who have experience will guide and train" – and in such a scheme correlated to productive work in a natural and social environment, the engineer, the doctor, the accountant and mechanic, the social worker and others, retired or serving, "all have their place and will create an example of participatory education for life through life".

The Ramamurti Committee also delineated how the children of the villagers would be educated. They would have formal education in a regular village school called Gramshala. The children while assisting their parents in their work could easily take a few hours off to attend a formal and graded education at the Gramshala according to their convenience. The Gramshala would hold separate classes for young men and adults in the evening, devoted to a discussion of their common problems and the acquisition of literacy. The nearest high school should be equipped with a science laboratory and a workshop for special courses in subjects like mechanical skills, functioning of the Gramsabha and Panchayat, development planning, Anthyodaya, mobilisation and use of resources, accounting, and a number of other related subjects.

An Analysis of the Recommendations

In the Ramamurti committee's scheme of education villages have been assigned a pivotal role, for India lives in its villages and no vision of future India can be greater than to rebuild its half-a-million villages. It is the villages that hold the key to the country's problems. It is here that "our producers live, voters live, the poor and the illiterate live". And so the first step in any educational reconstruction in the country should begin with few selected homogeneous scheduled caste, scheduled tribe and other backward villages in the first phase.

The whole thrust of educational reforms as suggested by the Ramamurti Committee has rested on evolving a policy of planned decentralisation. For the Ramamurti Committee, decentralisation does not mean merely the devolution of certain functions from the Centre to the lower levels of administration. It means a clear transfer of power from the former to the latter and is concerned with the role of the State vis-a-vis the Civil Society. As a matter of fact, the three key-points in the Ramamurti Committee's thinking on education have been universalisation, vocationalisation and decentralisation drawn from the "great tradition of India, the experiences and experiments of pioneers in our own country and abroad and great thinkers like Gandhi, Tagore and others".

The most redeeming feature of the recommendations of the Ramamurti Committee is the implication that an educational programme should develop on the requirements of the society as has been evident in the participatory education in the village. However, such a concept is not original with the Committee as we have already seen how in the mid-nineteenth century Thomason developed his concept of vernacular education on the reforms in the land revenue in the North-Western Provinces. Similarly Dalhousie transferred his idea of instituting classes in technical education to the concept of establishing technical colleges in each of the three presidencies of Bombay, Bengal and Madras in the wake of the introduction of railways, electric telegraph, uniform postage and the creation of the department of public works involved in the construction of irrigation canals and roads.

The second most important redeeming feature is the implication that educational activity of the government could not be an isolated programme – it must be interrelated to other departments of the government to be a successful one. One reason why our educational reforms in the past have failed is the sectoral activities of the government where its different activities such as in education, agriculture, forest, industry, and a host of other areas do not only not relate to each other but are often mutually contradictory. As the Ramamurti Committee says, "In a country like ours, with vast areas of backwardness, economic, social, educational, development, democracy, and education have to go together. They have to be woven in an integrated programme of transformation and reconstruction. Peaceful transformation is an organic process in which economy and education cannot work in isolation with each other. Take, for example, the right to work. Even if it is enshrined in the constitution, it is the economy alone that can create opportunities for employment, education can only empower people for work. This is the principal reason why, despite growing unemployment, vocational education has not become popular. The economy failed to create jobs so vocational training became useless".

Thirdly, this also means by implication from the preceding paragraph that educational activity could not be left to the initiative and judgment of specialists at the desk, controlled and guided by those far removed from where people live and work. Education co-related to life has to be linked to clearly defined social objectives and comprehensive strategies and this can only be done by decentralising educational administration to such an extent that each village and muhallas could participate in it. And this way it could not only reduce the dependence of the people upon the State alone to bring about the much needed educational and social transformation but also would reduce the "growing alienation between the masses and the elite in all spheres of national life".

A Critique of the Recommendations

As said before, villages have been the pivot on which have revolved the Ramamurti Committee's recommendations and are heavily influenced by the concept of the village school in Ancient and Medieval India. From time immemorial the village school existed in some form or other to meet the educational requirements of people other than the priestly classes who monopolised the Vedic schools where studies in Sanskrit religious scriptures were imparted. In Ancient India there had been since the days of the Mauryas, village assemblies or functionaries under the village pradhan or headman who managed the affairs of the village. In the post-Gupta period such a village assembly often consisted of the whole adult population or of Brahmanas or of a few greatmen of the village selected by a kind of ballot. The assembly whose work was supervised by royal officers or Adhikaris appointed committees to look after specific departments including tanks, temples, justice and provided for the appointment of a teacher to instruct in regional prakrits the children of the villagers who were usually peasants, artisans, craftsmen, small traders and merchants. The village teacher who imparted instruction in the three R's to them and usually received his fees in kind, kept his school open in all seasons of the year to admit them according to their convenience to his school which they left after they had picked up the necessary elementary knowledge either to start their own work or to join their family professions. The children came mostly from the classes of the people who were generally debarred from joining the Vedic schools monopolised by the Brahmins and other higher castes who often distinguished themselves in the political, military, medical and economical activities of the kingdom.

In Medieval India which saw the rule of Islam, large tracts of land had of necessity to be left in the hands of old Hindu chieftains, who were not interfered with in the ruling of their ancestral territories so long as they sent their tributes and presents to Delhi and Agra and so the village communities with their village schools remained unaffected. As the Islamic rule penetrated into the remote villages and as more and more converts from Hinduism began to join its ranks numerous mosques with maktabs began to appear on the scene, where the new converts began to receive their elementary education in a medium which was neither Arabic nor Persian though certainly they were required to learn these languages, particularly Arabic, to study the Quran. The maktab which was endowed and supported by a rich Muslim not only institutionalised the concept of education in a village but inspired others from the Hindu communities in the villages to similarly come forward in support of the education of their children. Thus, Islam boosted to some extent the elementary education in the villages.

However, with the destruction of the economic resources of the villages including village arts and crafts and large scale migration of the people from the villages to earn their livelihood in the metropolitan cities, in the wake of the establishment of the British rule, the prosperity of the villages which sustained the village schools began to decline. Since the fifty years of our independence have not been able to restore these villages to their old prosperous position and since villages today are increasingly losing their own identities in the wake of the vast technological revolutions affecting our daily lives and recent globalisation of Indian economy, one wonders how the villages in India could act as the spring board for meaningful educational reforms in the country.

Another flaw in the Ramamurti Committee's recommendation is the neglect of higher education in the country despite its recommendation for a structured UGC. In view of the fact that the share of elementary education has decreased from 56 per cent in the First Plan to 29 per cent in the Seventh Plan while that of higher education has increased from 18 to 44 per cent some serious discussion on its problems including quality and relevance would have been most

appropriate. Instead, the bulk of the report is given to issues like
equality, social justice and education, early childhood care and
education, universalisation of elementary education, adult and
continuing education and education and the right to work. There is
no doubt that each one of these issues is an important one but at the
same time nobody would deny that we need higher education to
sustain our economic, political and social development and that
without higher education there could not be any onward march
towards progress and civilisation.

The entire recommendations of the Ramamurti Committee are
obsessed with the Macaulayan idea of education from classes to the
masses, which characterises the present system of education and is
thought to be responsible for all the ills of our society: "the erosion of
social and moral values, weakening of democracy, the partisan
character of our development, corruption and a number of elitist
aberrations". And so the Committee suggests an education which
should be not for classes but for masses: "The need of the hour is a
people's movement for a New Education, not for a few but for all".
This is no doubt an excellent idea underlying social justice, equality
and uniformity. But who are to educate the masses? We certainly need
teachers first – they are to be imparted the lessons first. In Ancient
India in the Vedic schools and the Buddhist Viharas it was the Gurus
and the Acharyas who imparted education to the students respectively. In Medieval India, it was the Sufi Saints, the Ulemas and the
Maulavis who did it to their students. In other words, education has
always flowed from the classes to the masses keeping in view the
needs and requirements of administration and the society at large. To
do it otherwise would be to presuppose a prior change in the society.
Is it possible now? As the Ramamurti Committee admits: "It will be a
challenging situation. Our present day administrators and teachers
are not equipped to meet it... The present entrenched system is not
likely to respond except under the relentless pressure of public
opinion and peaceful people's action".

Taking a holistic view of education, the Committee holds that
each stage of education should be complete in itself and that the same
values should permeate all the stages. The present system in which the
lower stage was a preparation for the higher should be given up and it
would be easier to do so if degrees were delinked from jobs. There
should be only one stream of education both vocational and general:
"Universal education upto the matriculation standard[3] plus a sound

grounding in a vocation is a goal we should work for". Since all the basic reforms recommended by the Committee could not be introduced at once, it divides them into three categories – immediate, intermediate, and ultimate and decides to lay stress on elementary education up to class VII – "the minimum level every boy and girl in India should be enabled to attain".

National Front Government replaced by the Congress Government

The Ramamurti Committee submitted its report on 26 December 1990 but soon after that the National Front Government which had appointed it had to resign and a minority government under the leadership of Chandrashekhar with Congress support came into existence. And the Report of the Ramamurti Committee went into cold storage. However, with the withdrawal of support by the Congress Party, the Minority Government of Chandrashakar fell. And in the resultant General Election marked by the tragic assassination of Rajiv Gandhi, the Congress returned to power riding on the sympathy wave for Rajiv and formed the next government under the leadership of P.V. Narasimha Rao in 1991.

Since the 1986 Policy was the handiwork of another Congress Government under the leadership of Rajiv Gandhi, the Narasimha Rao Government immediately switched back to it but decided to have a look at it before resuming its implementation in the light of the Ramamurti Committee's recommendations.

The Government indeed took steps to review the 1986 Policy – in July 1991 a Central Advisory Board of Education on policy with six Education Ministers belonging to the major political parties and eight educationists under the Chairmanship of the Chief Minister of Andhra Pradesh was constituted to review the implementation of the various parameters of the 1986 Policy. In its report in January 1992 the Committee pointed out that the policy framework outlined in the National Policy on Education in 1986 "is robust and can guide the educational development of the country for a long time to come". The Committee further stated that "while very little of the NPE, 1986 required reformulation, the Programme of Action needed to be revised considerably" in many areas such as adult literacy where involvement of people on "a large scale", and educational administration where establishment of linkages between education and other related services such as child care, nutrition be emphasised.

The Revised Programme of Action, 1992 which was prepared keeping in mind the resource availability as indicated for it in the Eighth Five-Year Plan (1992-1997) guided the educational activities of the Congress Government at the Centre as well as of the States and the Union Territories till the next 'General Election in 1996. One such important activity was the initiation of the District Primary Education Programme (DPEP) to reaffirm the national commitment to the universalisation of elementary education before the dawn of the twenty-first century. By May 1995, education projects were prepared in 42 districts spreading over the seven States of Assam, Haryana, Madhya Pradesh, Karnataka, Maharashtra, Tamil Nadu and Kerala followed by the initiation of education planning in the districts in West Bengal and Andhra Pradesh. At the same time it was decided to extend the coverage to all the districts gradually satisfying one of the twin criteria: (a) educationally backward districts with female literacy below the average and (b) districts where Total Literacy Campaigns (TLCs) have been successful leading to an enhanced demand for primary education.

The United Front Government succeeds the Congress Government and appoints the Saikia Committee

In the 1996 General Election the Congress Party failed to return to power and following a 13-day stint of the BJP Government at the Centre, a United Front Government with Congress support from outside was formed under Deve Gowda. The United Front Government went a step further towards universalisation of elementary education by appointing a Committee of State Education Ministers under the Chairmanship of the Minister of State for Education, Muni Ram Saikia, in August 1996 to report on it.

The Saikia Committee which submitted its report in January 1997 pointed out that compulsion was not the only answer to achieve universalisation of elementary education and the Government had to motivate both parents and children, involve communities and build up public opinion in its favour so that elementary education could be universalised by 2000 A.D. With that end in view the Committee unanimously endorsed the proposal of the United Front Government to amend the Constitution through legislation to make elementary education up to 14 years of age a Fundamental Right. Simultaneously, an explicit provision should be made in the Constitution to make it a Fundamental Duty of every citizen who was a parent to provide opportunities for elementary education to all children upto 14 years of age.

The United Front Government not only prepared the Bill on the subject but introduced it in Parliament for debate and approval. However, the United Front Government did not last long to ensure the passage of the Bill though as a token beginning it allocated Rs 35 crore out of Rs 40,000 crore needed over a period of five years to implement the legislation when passed to make the right to free and compulsory elementary education a Fundamental Right.

A Critique of the Saikia Committee's Recommendations

We are not certain whether such a step would facilitate the task of universalising elementary education in the country as we have already seen how the Constitutional provision in the form of Article 45 on the subject made at the time of the inauguration of our country as a republic in the Directive Principles of States Policy has failed to achieve the desired object. Yet, there can be no doubt that such a measure is likely to face difficulties at every stage besides the huge and staggering costs involved in its implementation.

The government can enforce the Fundamental Right on the subject if it has already provided the access to schooling for children everywhere in the country. Since this is not the actual position and since the socio-economic compulsions of families concerned often keep the children away from schools, the legislation will likely to result in a situation where there may be more parents in jails than children in schools. Besides, the parents could take the States to the courts if they feel that their children are being denied the right to education as the States have not made adequate arrangements for their access to schooling. This explains why the Compulsory Education Acts already enacted by the 14 States and 4 Union Territories many years ago have been allowed to remain in abeyance till now.

In the ultimate analysis, the government by declaring elementary education as a Fundamental Right will be shifting the responsibility of universalising elementary education from the States to the parents – a move which cannot be justified under any circumstances despite the fact that such a legislation is likely to check the growing problem of child labour and its exploitation by unscrupulous persons in India.

The United Front Government is replaced by the BJP-led Government

As said before, the United Front Government did not survive long enough to enact the safe passage of the Bill and the task was handed down to the BJP-led government which replaced it in April 1998. However, despite making some financial provision on the subject, it did not seem to have much interest in reviving legislation as it had its own ideas on educational development to pursue in the country. It had already been attempting to mould its ideas on the subject in the BJP States like Rajasthan and Uttar Pradesh through a chain of Vidya Bharati Schools run by RSS.

The Conference of the Education Ministers of the States and of the Education Secretaries

With the BJP's elevation to the centre stage as lead partner in the national government, it realised the time had come to play a national role in education. And with that end in view, within six months of its coming to power, the BJP-led government summoned in 22-24 October 1998 a Conference of the State Education Ministers and Education Secretaries to discuss the Agenda Notes prepared by the HRD Ministry as well as the Recommendations of the Groups of Experts enclosed with them.

An Analysis of the Agenda Notes and the Recommendations of the Group of Experts

A careful perusal of the Agenda Notes called the National Agenda for Governance (NAG) in education indicated that most of the items in the 1992 Revised Programme of Action have been taken up both for endorsement as well as for further expansion. Thus, the Agenda Notes proposed to provide free and compulsory education upto 5th standard and total eradication of illiteracy under Education for All; included girls, scheduled castes, scheduled tribes and other backward classes and educationally backward minorities under Education of Prioritised Groups; assured equal access and opportunity for all up to school stage and improvement of quality at all levels under Access and Quality and an increasing government and non-government spending under Financing of Education. The Agenda Notes also proposed to expand the involvement of youth power in the total eradication of illiteracy, undertake necessary constitution and legal reforms to give effect to the targeted educational reforms as well as to carefully nurturing the vast potentiality of India to emerge as a superpower in software information technology. Among the innovations mentioned are the setting up of a National Elementary Education Mission (NEEM), appointment of a Commission on Elementary Education, development of a National Information System on Education to sustain decentralised planning and management of education in the country.

Thus, the Agenda Notes appear innocuous enough to reveal a sustained educational development in the country according to the 1992 Programme of Action revised in the light of the three key principles of the recommendations of the Ramamurti Committee, that is, universalisation, vocationalisation and decentralisation.

However, the Recommendations of the Group of Experts which have suggested the setting up of a High Power Autonomous National Mission for Education Reforms sound disturbing for a country like India consisting of a population of diverse races, religions, and cultures. The Group of Experts whose identities had not been revealed in the Conference Papers but were certainly linked to the BJP think-tank recommended that "the curricular from the primary to the highest education should be Indianised, nationalised and spiritualised" by making Sanskrit a compulsory subject from Class III to X and establishing Sanskrit Universities in four zones of the country; by providing a course on Indian philosophy in all higher education programmes and finally by assigning a place for the Vedas and the Upanishads in the curriculum from primary to higher level courses in the light of the Supreme Court's definition of "Hindutva" as a way of life. While such recommendations certainly suit the interests of educational institutions run by particular religious organisations like the RSS, they certainly do not fit in with the image of a National Government at the Centre and were further aggravated by the decision to start the meeting of the Conference with the Saraswati Vandana – a practice followed mostly in RSS-run schools.

And so the meeting of the Conference started on a stormy note with protests not only from within the allies of the government but also from the media and the enlightened public including minorities. Under such a pressure the Conference decided to temporarily shelve these recommendations and proposed to start work at the moment on more generally agreed vital issues like the universalisation of elementary education in the country.

A Redeeming Feature of the Recommendations of the Group of Experts

It must however be said that not all recommendations of the Group of Experts can be dubbed as an attempt to "saffronise" India as the media did. For example, the proposal to establish Sanskrit Universities in the four zones of the country is quite in keeping with the interest shown by the developed countries in the West in our past culture and civilisation. The Sanskrit Universities could have been assigned the task of rejuvenating our knowledge in our past culture and civilisation in Ancient India, almost eclipsed by more than six hundred years of Islamic rule in Medieval India and finally came to life in Modern India with the establishment of the Asiatic Society at Calcutta in 1783-84. Needless to say, it is through the works of William Jones, Charles Wilkins, Horace Hayman Wilson, Anquetil-Duperron, Alexander Hamilton, Friedrich Schlegel, Leonard de Chezy, Franz Bopp, James Prinsep, Friedrich Max Muller, Alexander Cunningham and John Marshall that Ancient India was unlocked not only to us but also to the world. While there would have been certainly no Rammohan Roy in the last couple of years of the twentieth century to object to the establishment of Sanskrit Universities in India, an extremely blunt and casual approach to the proposal by the Group of Experts seems to have almost fractured a genuine attempt to share a knowledge of the wonder that was India.

Appointment of a Committee on Fundamental Duties for Inclusion in the Educational Curriculum

An interesting fallout of the October 1998 Conference of Education Ministers and Secretaries was the appointment of a Committee under a retired Chief Justice, J.S. Verma to explore the possibility of including the subject of Fundamental Duties as laid down in Article 51A of the Constitution in the curriculum of the schools and the colleges. However, the significance of the appointment of such a Committee towards the understanding of citizenship values seems to have been almost lost in the wake of the stir created by the October 1998 Conference.

Notes

1. Italics are the Ramamurti Committee's.
2. May 1990.
3. It is really surprising that the Ramamurti Committee which is so much against the present system of education as an extension of the one set up by the British Raj have used a colonial concept 'Matriculation Standard' to describe the higher secondary stage in school education in Independent India.

40

A Post-Mortem

Absence of a Balanced, Sensible and Realistic Approach in Education

If the Recommendations of the Group of Experts at the Conference of Education Ministers and Education Secretaries included such proposals as to make the simplified essence of all the existing religions in India a compulsory course as well as elementary Sanskrit, Arabic and Persian an optional course at some stage in the school education, there would have been probably less stir than witnessed recently. However, such a balanced and sensible approach to education in the country was rarely seen in the past and whenever a new political party either singly or in alliance formed a government at the Centre, the first thing it tried to do was to stamp its own views on education irrespective of the fact whether or not they were going to ultimately benefit the people at large. Irrespective also of the fact that each time when such a thing happened, the new government at the Centre felt that it had the last word on education in the country. As the Ramamurti Committee observed:

"All the basic reforms recommended in this report cannot be introduced at once. So the reforms may be divided into three categories: immediate, intermediate and ultimate. There are still questions that require fuller consideration. A thousand practical details have to be worked out. Innovations will have to be made and extensive experiments carried out. But a beginning in the right direction brooks no delay, and a total transformation of our education system should be brought about in *a period not longer than ten years.*[1] The 1990s are going to be crucial for us as a nation. What we do in the next ten years will determine how we shall face the challenge of the next century".

Similarly the 1992 Programme of Action (POA) while revising the 1986 Education Policy in the light of Ramamurti Committee's recommendations observed about its implementation:

"In the ultimate, resources and management would define implementation. In developing this document the resource availability indicated for the 8th Five-Year Plan (1992-97) was kept at the back of the mind; but at the same time long term perspective has not been lost sight of. Many actions envisaged by the POA, 1992 span *not only the 8th Five-Year Plan but also the 9th and even beyond.*[2] *Phasing has, therefore, to be left somewhat flexible so that the pace of implementation can match the mobilisation of resources*".

When the Congress Government was replaced by the BJP and its allies in April 1998, the new government also spoke in the same vein at the October 1998 Conference of Education Ministers and Secretaries:

"The Experts reached an overall conclusion that there was a dire need to institute a National Commission on Educational Reforms with a mission approach and where the participation of educational thinkers and practitioners is considered as a first step. Secondly, representation from various sections such as industrialists, technologists, management experts, man-power specialists, social education in a way that it has its roots in the glorious cultural heritage on the one hand and pragmatic curricula and activities imbibed with scientific outlook on the other. It should be given the mileage and futuristic vision for the *next twenty to thirty years.*[3] The Commission should have the capability to assess and estimate educational needs and provisions from the decentralised rural/tribal habitations to regional and national levels. It should be able to complete its work in a definite time frame so that the reforms and reconstruction of Indian Education is synchronised with the cycle of National and State level Five Year Plans".

Seen in the background of past failures in education and of the recent instability in the political situation in the country such hopes certainly appear to be not only presumptuous but also boisterous.

Genesis of Change in Education Policy

We may now ask the question – why such things involving abrupt changes in education policy happen whenever a new government formed by an opposition party and its allies takes over at the Centre? The answer to this question may be found in the hybrid nature of our society, composed as it is of a fast expanding population which now exceeds the nine hundred million mark, speaking different dialects and languages, following different religions and cultures, and practising different social norms, customs and behaviours often regulated by their castes, and classes. In a plural society like India, different social groups and classes, including minorities, develop and articulate policies, and indeed a general outlook reflecting their own needs and aspirations. Societies all over the world, not to speak of India alone, are riven by contradictions and divisions between opposing social forces. Such divisions, and the conflicts to which they give rise, are necessarily reflected in the world of education sometimes directly. The result is that education becomes and is best seen as, the site of a struggle between what are often opposing, or at least, antagonistic, social forces. Such conflicts can often become acute, as the historical record shows very clearly, and· characterises the very beginning of the history of education in Modern India. The Anglo-Oriental controversy was not merely a controversy between the two groups of British officials over the nature of education to be imparted to the Indians but a controversy where the segments of the contemporary Indian society were involved as opponents of each other. With the dawn of independence, the gradual spread of enlightenment among the masses and the rise of socially backward castes and classes in national politics and administration, such conflicts on education have become more acute and confused than before, as reflected in the views often expressed on education by a host of political parties consisting of heterogeneous elements from the different segments of our society. As a result, educational reforms when initiated by a political party or parties representing various segments of Indian society which have formed the government at the Centre, they are often resisted at various levels when pushed for implementation. And this partly explains the failure of most of the educational reforms initiated since our independence.

Domination of Elite Social Groups in Education

The retention after independence of the British colonial administrative system as well as of many of the numerous rules, regulations and acts including such draconian ones as the Official Secrets Act,[4] introduced by the British Raj to govern India, obviously favour the domination in national politics and national administration, of the elite social groups of diverse castes and creeds brought up and nurtured in the colonial educational traditions. The domination of these social groups was almost complete in the first few decades of our independence till they were increasingly challenged by the weaker sections of the society including the dalits, the scheduled castes, scheduled tribes and other socially backward classes whose leadership had the benefits of a liberal and progressive education in the country. Since that time the Indian political scene was never the same as before and had been increasingly marked by a growing confrontation on various socio-economic and political issues often resulting in an acute political instability in the country.

In view of the extremely fluid political situation in the country it seems that the golden period for any meaningful educational reforms was the first three decades immediately after independence when the Congress Party held power both at the Centre and in the States, provided the ruling elite classes were prepared to shed a part of their selfish interests for the larger interests of the nation. Imbued with a vision of building up a new and dynamic India, the latter could have vigorously pushed reforms, universalise elementary education, vocationalise secondary education and reorganise higher education in such a way as to be able to answer to the unspoken needs and requirements of a developing nation. Further, while an introduction of courses on our past cultural heritage would have certainly inspired the young school-goers with pride and honour, introduction of courses on the different Indian States and the Union Territories and their people as well as on different practising religions in historical perspectives in India would have to a large extent freed the minds of the future citizens of India from the evils of parochialism and communalism respectively, which now plague us often. The ruling classes should have been prepared to share their responsibility in the educational regeneration of India with the indigenous business and industrial houses as well as with a variety of private and non-governmental socio-religious organisations. Following the examples of excellence in education created by the Tatas and the Birlas, other business and industrial houses should have been invited to set up institutes and design courses to train their manpower requirements.

Unfortunately all these did not happen as the elite social groups who dominated the Indian political and administration scene, almost without any challenge, failed to look behind their own selfish preoccupations. Had all these educational reforms stated in the preceding paragraph materialised, we should not have to declare elementary education as a Fundamental Right or witness the panic in our education scene created in the last decade of the present century by throwing India open to world market – while a series of meeting was hurriedly convened by the University Grants Commission and the universities to take steps in designing courses and curricula to meet the challenge of liberalisation, professional institutes with varied standard mushroomed overnight all over India to attract students to their programmes to take advantage of the employment opportunities created by investment from abroad. However, there were may who could not obtain admissions not only in the sophisticated professional institutes subsidised by the government but also in privately run organisations and they fell an easy prey to the nets cast by foreign universities through attractive advertisements in the daily newspapers, thereby causing a great strain not only to middle class parents but also on the national exchequer causing a huge drain of wealth from the country.

However, the silver lining in all these developments following globalisation of Indian market had been the diversion of students from pursuing a stereotyped course at our universities which have little relevance to our developmental needs and consequently to the prospects of the students concerned. Since 1947, there has been no change in the curricula for higher education mostly in social sciences and the result has been disastrous for a developing country like India. The number of unemployed educated increased as they could not find a suitable opening to suit their qualifications. There had been discussions to check students' entry to universities since the days of the Mudaliar Commission in 1953-54, which suggested diversification of courses at the higher secondary stage but as nothing substantial happened in this direction, the New Education Policy in 1986, as well as the Ramamurti Committee in 1990, advised delinking degrees from jobs to ease pressure on higher education. However, this strategy of delinking degrees from jobs failed to click as it went against the colonial psyche of Indian parents and students while a single act of an economic reform worked wonders.

Impact of Elite Domination: Failures are more than Successes in our Education

Standing on the threshold of a new millennium and looking back at the past six decades of our independence, we find that our failures in our educational reforms are more than our successes. Our first and foremost failure is our inability to translate the constitutional pledge contained under Article 45 of the Directive Principles of State Policy of providing free and compulsory education for all children up to 14 years of age into a reality. The second important failure is our inability to provide an expenditure on education to exceed 6 per cent of our National Income by the end of the Seventh Five-Year Plan, that is, by 1992, as suggested by the Kothari Commission in 1963-64. We have often deplored cramming by students at all levels without being able to provide a suitable alternative to the acquisition of learning by all. We have become alarmed at the rapid and unplanned expansion of higher education and an enormous increase in the number of the unemployed educated persons without being able to put a stop to it. We have suggested the privatisation of higher education to ease financial pressure on the government but the draft Bill on the subject is yet to become an Act. In vocational education we have often failed to reach our targets as we have targeted schemes on vocational education to those areas where there are no vocations to follow. And finally, in elementary education the Operation Blackboard and many other schemes including National Literacy Campaigns could not fully be implemented as the grants assigned by the Centre to the States often remain either unspent because of the inertia of the States or become misappropriated in the process of their implementation.

Development of a Negative Approach in Education

What is, however, disturbing at the moment is the development of a negative approach to the solution of our continuing educational problems. Thus, we have tried to solve the pressure on higher education and on employment opportunities by delinking degrees from jobs, the phenomenon of enormous illiteracy among the masses by declaring elementary education as a Fundamental Right and poor allocation for expenditure on education at less than 6 per cent of National Income by computing private expenditure on education with governmental one to show that it nearly reaches the estimated goal on expenditure as has been done in the Agenda Notes of the October 1998 Conference of State Educational Ministers and Secretaries:

"The expenditure by the government on education currently amounts to about 3.5 per cent of GDP. If one includes the expenditure incurred by households on education and the expenditure incurred by the management bodies of the private schools to the government expenditure on education, the total expenditure forms nearly six per cent of GDP".

Development of a Fundamentalist Outlook in Education

Added to the development of a negative approach in the government educational policy is the growth of a fundamentalist outlook which seeks to divert our attention from the major and vital educational problems of the day in the country. While the framers of our Constitution have provided the minorities with the right to develop and mould their own educational institutions and programmes according to their own needs and interests, such right could possibly be extended, by amending the Articles 29 and 30 of the Constitution, to every section of citizens, irrespective of their religion or language, to set up and administer educational institutions of their choice, where *Saraswati Vandana* or singing of *Vandenwntram* will not perhaps raise any eyebrows. However, to do so in governmental institutions which are attended by students with varied socio-religious and cultural backgrounds is not perhaps a wise decision to take since in a democracy, a government represents the interests of all classes and religions. And it should not therefore act in a partisan and communal manner to hurt the sentiments and feelings of the people who may not like such practices in educational institutions as they are contrary to their socio-religious beliefs and ideas. Such actions indeed hasten to contribute further to the existing stresses and tensions among the various social groups in the country.

Silver Linings in Education

In the midst of these dismal and gloomy developments, when we are about to enter the next millennium with one of the world's largest illiterate populations, there are certain silver linings in education in the country, which merit greater publicity and are worthy of emulation in other areas. One of them is the District Education Guarantee Scheme in Madhya Pradesh, one of the country's largest and poorest States with 44.20 per cent literacy rate as per 1991 Census. In Madhya Pradesh, with the help of local communities, schools are provided within one kilometre of any village which have sought them and this has led to a phenomenal increase in enrolment in primary education, particularly among girls. Another extremely positive scheme started in the same State in 1992, has been the teacher empowerment programme which involves the teacher not merely in its design and development but also in the curriculum. This scheme of "Joyful Learning" where a child's interest in education is sustained by incorporating songs and dances into lessons with the help of local teaching aids has been quite successful and has since been adopted by a number of States in the country. Again, across the borders of Madhya Pradesh, in Andhra Pradesh an NGO has initiated an innovative programme where families of child workers are motivated to send them to schools. And so successful has been this innovation that the very employers who have earlier utilised their labour have come forward to sponsor their education. And finally, Andhra Pradesh's neighbour in the South, Tamil Nadu is not also lagging behind in attracting children to schools and has increased the enrolment in elementary education by an effective mid-day meal programme.

These schemes are successful because they involve community participation and are able to capture the imagination and attention of the children. With a degree of flexibility built into them, these schemes exhibit a greater readiness to adapt to local conditions so as to meet the needs and requirements of different sections of children. The States and Union Territories which have not yet implemented these innovative schemes should be encouraged to do so as they benefit the people at the grass-root level, who have for centuries remained in the darkness of ignorance. And finally, as these schemes are neither expensive nor labour intensive; no governments either at the Centre or at the States should be allowed to discontinue them either from lack of finance or dearth of man power.

Notes

1. Italics are mine.
2. Ibid.
3. Ibid.
4. The Official Secret Act was passed by Curzon in the wake of the leakage of a part of the Report of the Indian Universities Commission of 1902 to prevent such occurrence in the future. see p. 395.

A Retrospection

I

The Rig Veda is the nucleus of the education system in Ancient India. Composed orally by the priestly tribes among the Aryans between 1500 and 1000 B.C., it is followed by the composition of three more Vedas – Sam, Yajur and Atharva. These four Vedas with six Vedangas or auxiliary sciences formed the core subjects of study in Vedic schools. These Vedic schools were managed by the priestly class now known as the Brahmanas as they were the persons who had the supreme knowledge of the Brahma or the universe through their mastery over the Vedas. With the expansion of the Aryans eastwards and transformation of their tribal organisations into monarchical ones, the influence of these Brahmins extended beyond the Vedic schools. The Brahmins became the advisers and guides of the kings and emperors as Purohitas. The kings and emperors could perform no Yajnas or sacrifices without them and so did their subjects who needed the presence of priests in all religious functions including birth, marriage and death. The dominance of the Brahmins was reflected in the creation of a new set of religious scriptures called Brahmanas. A section among the Brahmins soon found asceticism rather than elaborate ritualism as the means to salvation and still another found realisation of the supreme knowledge preached by the Rig Veda by merging Atman or soul with Brahman or universe as the key to obtain freedom from the transmigration of soul. Aranyakas and Upanishads were added to the Brahamanas and by 600 B.C. they together with the four Vedas and their six Vedangas were studied in the Vedic schools by the Brahmins, the Kshatriyas and the Vaishyas. For the last two classes, study of the Vedas or the first three Vedas was compulsory before they could acquire their professional knowledge which brought them their livelihood. For Shudras in the Aryan society, study of the Vedas was forbidden and they learnt their professional knowledge in agriculture and animal husbandry, spinning and weaving, fine arts and crafts through the expertise of their own families.

By 600 B.C. the religion in the Aryan society which had been dominated by the Brahmins had become too ritualistic, dogmatic and complex to attract the simpler folks. A formidable reaction in the form of Jainism and Buddhism came from the Kshatriyas who were next to the Brahmins in the societal hierarchy. Both Mahavira and the Buddha preached the simplest way to reach salvation but it was Buddhism more than Jainism that posed a challenge to the Brahmanism. The Buddhist Viharas threw their doors open to all classes of the Aryan society and taught the inmates who had now become Bhikkhus, how to achieve Nirvana through the teachings of the Buddha codified as Vinayak, Sutta and Abidhamma. Brahmanism tried to meet the challenge by compiling, codifying and simplifying the existing religious literatures through the works of the Sutrakaras and was able to hold the field till the arrival of Ashoka on the scene when Buddhism and the Buddhist Viharas or the centres of learning became dominant in the most parts of the Ashokan empire.

. However, the Buddhist Viharas did not possess the inherent vitality of the Vedic schools. This inherent vitality consisted in making the Aryan society completely dependent on the learning imparted by the Vedic schools. The Vedic schools not merely taught the religious scriptures but also various arts and crafts including medicine and other useful sciences to meet the various requirements of the society while the services of the Brahmins or teachers of the Vedic schools were always required by the people at large for various religious observances. This cannot, however, be said about the Buddhist Viharas where its inmates had renounced the world to achieve Nirvana and depended solely for their existence and survival on the charity of the laity. The Buddhist monks in the Buddhist Viharas may well be compared to the last ashram or stage of the four ashrams where a person having lived his life fully took to sannyas to achieve salvation or liberation from rebirth. Because of the absence of this inner strength, the Buddhist Viharas had often suffered reverses at the hands of the reactionary monarchs like Pushyamitra Sunga after the downfall of the Mauryas or like Mihirgula when the fortunes of the Guptas were on the decline. They faced, however, no problems when the monarchs though practising a different religion as were the Guptas who were followers of Vaishnavism or Harsha who was a devotee of Saivaism, were tolerant and sympathetic to them.

Added to this, was an inherent weakness in the Buddhist system of learning. The Buddhist Viharas were composed of heterogenous elements; some of them were there simply to escape the problems of life. Coming as they were from the existing Brahminical religion, they brought with them the influences of their old religion when they joined the Buddhist Viharas as monks. And the Buddhist Viharas exposed as they were to a variety of non-Indian influences through their foreign patrons like Meanander or Kanishka, soon developed subtle cracks within them in the forms of the Greater and Lesser Vehicles as well as the Vehicle of the Thunderbolt which brought Buddhism closer to Hinduism. The Buddha soon became one of the Avatars or Gods in the Hindu Panthenon and his religion was almost devoured by the vociferous Hinduism.

The Buddhist Viharas thus, almost died a natural death in India before the final blows were delivered to them by the Islamic invaders. The latter certainly did not exempt the Hindu temples from the fire and the fury of the Islamic arms but Hindu learning survived as it did not thrive through temples as the Buddhist learning did through Buddhist Viharas, but through generations of priestly families and Guru-Shishya Paramparas in different parts of India, especially in the South in the Middle Ages. There is no doubt that the Brahminical learning was imprisoned by the Sutrakaras and creativity almost became a thing of the past since then, yet it left behind, when Islam came to rule India, a rich legacy in poetry and prosody, grammar and phonetics, anatomy and astronomy, mathematics and philosophy as well as in various arts and crafts, some of which still survive. While a Buddhist Vihara with its specialised departments of learning and of administration, organised libraries, residential complexes for the monks and a Council of Elders to advise the chief abbot in running it, resembles very much a modern university anywhere in the world, the Brahminical system of learning throws up features including those adapted by the Buddhist Viharas such as debates and discussions at conferences and assemblies held on sacrificial occasions, at a king's court and at a local parishad, which characterise our modern learning.

However the greatest contribution of the Vedic schools and of the Buddhist Viharas is not only its search for the truth, for the supreme knowledge of the Brahman and the Atman and of the liberation of the souls or the Nirvana through enlightenment but also its help in the formation of the nucleus of a civilisation which has survived the onslaughts of the Islamic invaders in the Middle Ages as well as of the British rule in Modern India.

II

In Brahminical and Buddhist India, education was religion, and religion, education but in Muslim India education was the fulfilment of religion as emphasised by the Prophet Muhammad in his various utterances on the acquisition of knowledge which he considered to be the nectar of life. The Muslim rulers of Medieval India who owed their allegiance to the Caliphs of Baghdad and Egypt, the successors of the Prophet and studied and followed the Quran were all pious Muslims who strove towards the fulfilment of their religion by regularly constructing maktabs and madrasahs attached to mosques, the places of worship. In the hey-days of the Muslim rule in India there was hardly a village, town or city without any of these institutions as in the glorious days of Buddhism when the Buddhist Viharas dotted the various parts of the Mauryan empire.

However, the fate of these institutions was extremely ephemeral as it entirely depended on their patrons, be they rulers or not, for their sole existence. The moment their patrons went into oblivion either through death or through dynastic changes or through any other catastrophe that might have befallen them, they began to wither for want of care and support. Much depended often on the personality of the rulers who in their attempt to resist the influence of the Ulemas by putting state before religion could do things which often threatened their survival as Ala-ud-din did when he deprived these institutions of their endowments. Finally, there was no guarantee that the descendants of their patrons would continue to financially support such institutions – instead they would probably like to build new maktabs or madrasahs with mosques to prove their piety and devotion to Islam. In such cases the old educational institutions became deserted and dilapidated and turned into abodes of animals and birds. And we already know from the recorded observation of Firuz Shah in his *Futuhat-i-Firuz Shahi* that he repaired, and rebuilt quite a few of these institutions which had been earlier built by his predecessors, Iltutmish and Ala-ud-din.

The fate of such institutions also suffered particularly when the imperial rulers were weak and sensuous and unable to control the operation of centrifugal tendency among the provincial rulers which asserted itself through secession of provinces from the former's control or when there were invasions from outside India. In all such cases there was no peace and stability so vitally needed for the flourishing of learning as it exactly happened in the days when the Delhi Sultanate disintegrated or when the Mughal empire declined to a fall. In the former case, the succeeding rulers were the Mughals who were also followers of Islam – so the Muslim educational institutions survived and prospered to meet the needs and requirements of the Mughal administration but not so in the case of the latter, when the Mughals were replaced by the British who were followers of Christ and gradually built up the Western system of education in British India to meet their imperial needs and requirements.

Despite the ephemeral existence of maktabs and madrasahs, a continuous line of succession of Muslim rulers for nearly six centuries was able to provide the necessary patronage for the sustenance of the Islamic system of education and was able to push into the background the Hindu system of learning which flourished only in the few existing and struggling Hindu kingdoms. The Islamic system of education met the needs and requirements of Muslim administration by providing it with qualified personnel in civil, military, law and religion while many among them went to the educational institutions as teachers. The Islamic system of education in Medieval India consisting of maktabs and madrasahs was the same as it was in other parts of the Islamic word, particularly in the Central and Western Asia and consequently there was a constant flow of learned men from these areas to the Muslim Courts in India and many of them were appointed as teachers in imperial capitals, cities and towns. Since the medium of instruction was Persian and a study of Arabic was compulsory as it was the language of the Quran the system made the Muslims in Medieval India not only homogeneous and compact despite occasional religious differences between the Shias and the Sunnis among them. The use of common languages for official purposes and religious needs, certainly contributed to a feeling of brotherhood among the Muslims in their conquered territories in Europe and Asia in the Middle Ages.

The dominance of Persian in maktabs, madrasahs and royal Courts gave birth to a crop of Persian literature, mainly history and *belles lettres*. There was hardly a Muslim Court which was without its quota of learned men and as the Muslim rulers loved history and *belles lettres*, they patronised Muslim chroniclers and writers of prose and verses. The Persian which drove away Sanskrit from the royal Courts also helped further development of vernaculars or regional languages which got their nourishment from religious reformers and patronisation from the provincial Muslim rulers. Muslim rulers' interest in Indian language and literature coupled with an increase in the number of Muslim communities, partly through conversions and partly through marriages, produced a cultural synthesis in the linguistic sphere in the birth of a new language called Urdu, which by the end of our period was largely spoken by the Muslims in India. As far as the arts and crafts were concerned, the Islamic system of education brought no or little innovation except in tastes and ideas, designs and forms and they continued on traditional lines either through family connexions or through apprenticeships. The interests of the various arts and trades in Medieval India were looked after by numerous guilds as in Ancient India.

Finally, the Islamic system of education not only democratised education but also institutionalised it further, not only emphasised the growth and development of libraries and literary societies but also encouraged residential or domestic teaching which was largely confined to the members of the royal families, wealthy Muslims and urban females. In all these one could easily discover a continuity from the past. There is no doubt that in the Brahminical system of learning the priestly class dominated the scene and though its vocational education was mainly class and caste based it was possible for a member of family following a particular vocation to opt for one usually followed by another class or caste. The Buddhist system of learning not only threw its doors open to all castes, classes and creeds but also highly institutionalised education by concentrating it in Viharas with its organised departments of teaching and administration as well as with its residential complexes for its students and teachers under the Chief Abbot elected by the suffrage of all the monks in the monastic parish assisted by a committee of elder monks. The organisation of the Buddhist Viharas later influenced Brahminical learning to institutionalise it in the form of a temple colleges, particularly in South India. In one sense the Buddhist Vihara was more secular than the Islamic system of learning as the former admitted to its Order students from other sects and religions, say, Hinduism and Jainism while the Islamic system of learning was mainly confined to the followers of Islam till the days of Akbar, who threw the doors of the maktabs and madrasahs open to non-Muslims. Secondly, as the Brahminical learning was orally transmitted, its diffusion was limited and could not be the proud possession of a king or a monarch unless he became a teacher or a student like the kings Janaka or Ajatasatru. However, it will not be unjust to think that as literature in Sanskrit began to grow up steadily and was gradually put to writing, and as the kings began to adorn their Courts with learned scholars since the days of the Guptas, there could be an accumulation of manuscripts in the royal palaces. The Buddhists were the first to put their religious scriptures to writing and by the time of Hiuen-Tsang's visit in the early seventh century most of the Buddhist Viharas in Ancient India possessed valuable collection of manuscripts on various subjects and in Nalanda a large building called Dharmaganj or Abode of Religion was erected to serve as library. It was divided into three departments – Ratna Sagar, Ratno Dadhi and Ratna Ranjaka, which were named after its collection of rare manuscripts on classified subjects. And as far as the literary societies of Medieval India were concerned, these could be seen in Ancient India in the Courts of kings, Sabhas and Parishads as well as in the organised meetings at the Buddhist Viharas where regular learned discussions and discourses took place often by scholars from distant parts of India.

Yet, with all these apparent continuities from the past the Islamic system of education was more practical than spiritual. If it had failed to provide the people of Medieval India with a probe into the mysteries of the universe which the Brahminical system of learning had done in the past with its Vedas and Upanishads, it had provided them with a lust for life, and with a zeal for living both of which had been so vividly portrayed by the royal Courts of Muslim kings and emperors who now live in the pages of Indian history. As a matter of fact, more than 650 years of Islamic rule in Medieval India with its maktabs and madrasahs, mosques and khanqahs embossed upon the heart and the mind of the country an imprint of a civilisation that was largely Persian in nature and content and that was almost dominant till it was challenged by the new rulers who replaced the Islamic education with the Western education ushering in a new set of norms and values to further transform our civilisation in modern times.

III

We have seen in Modern India how the officials of the East India Company which came to India for trading purposes became interested in Oriental learning and literature but after the transformation of the Company from merchants to rulers, they had no other alternative but to import their own system of education as the existing systems of education in India, both Brahminical and Islamic, could not meet the needs and requirements of a growing British administration. In an alien climate and environment, the British administration, though manned at the top by officials recruited in England, had to look for support at the base among Indians through the New Education imported into the country. The importation was, of course, followed by important debates among British officials, statesmen and philosophers about the impact of Western education in ridding Indian society of many of its evils such as *Sati* and Infanticide which shocked the conscience of the contemporary Western mind.

However, true to the fears expressed by many among the advocates of Western education in India about its destabilising impact as had been recently experienced in the New World in the birth of the United States of America in 1776, the Indians educated in the New Education, from 1870 onwards, became hostile critics of the British Raj which could not fulfil the hopes and expectations raised by the acquisition of new qualifications. As a result, the British Raj had to reverse gears in education through a series of Education Commissions beginning with the Hunter Commission of 1882 and climaxing with the Indian Universities Commission of 1902, the report of which not only led to the passing of the Indian Universities Act of 1904-05, but also to the issue of the first White Paper on Indian Education Policy to camouflage the ulterior motives behind the reform of the five existing Indian Universities of Calcutta, Bombay, Madras, Punjab and Allahabad. The Indian Universities Act which sought to bring higher education in the country under effective governmental control and the partition of Bengal which followed it, led to the beginning of a national movement widely participated in by the Indian people which succeeded in overthrowing British rule finally in 1947.

The educated Indians who provided the leadership to this movement held the reins of government after independence. In the heydays of the freedom movement they had the opportunity to discuss, particularly at the Wardha Conference in 1937, the evolution of an education system which would be Indian in name, spirit and content but they soon found that the inherited colonial system of education was not only best suited to govern a vast country like India but to further their own dominance in the country. There had been indeed occasionally some talks and attempts at renovating the colonial structure and contents of education till 1968, when independent India had her first education policy, more than twenty years after the achievement of freedom.

However, by that year new social forces had emerged on the Indian political scene in the rise of the dalits, the scheduled castes, scheduled tribes and other backward classes whose leadership had the benefits of a liberal and progressive education in the country as well as in an increasing number of young unemployed educated Indians whose qualifications and skills did not find any place in the development of their own country. And together they formed a formidable challenge to the existing leadership in national politics and administration. In 1986, based upon past experience in education, current realities in the situation as well as upon future outlook, the New Education Policy was formulated to recover lost ground but it was too late to have a substantial impact on the existing system of education and it soon became a victim of an acute political instability in the country.

However, what the New Education Policy of 1986 and the Revised Programme of Action of 1992 could not achieve in education was achieved by a single economic act of liberalisation, bringing in its wake not only huge investment from multinational companies but also a host of technological innovations, particularly in software and information technology, affecting our daily lives, needs and deeds in metropolitan cities and towns. Here again it is the elite social groups with their public school background, where the medium of instruction is English, who stand to gain by liberalisation and reap its benefits. As in the past decade, they are not only able to obtain through rigorous written tests and interviews admissions in prestigious professional institutes in the country but also to capture the lucrative jobs here and abroad after completion of their courses. Many among those who come from rich families and are unable to join professional institutes in the country spread their wings abroad to earn professional degrees and diplomas at the cost of the country's wealth and a sizeable portion of them always prefer to stay abroad. On the other hand, the fate of those who are educated in regional languages in their own States and Union Territories does not seem to be as bright. They are not only confronted with fewer job opportunities, but also remain handicapped by their inability to settle down in a job in a State other than their own because of a different educational background in a different language. They indeed have chances of employment in all India or national organisations and services but here again they are likely to be outsmarted by the elite social groups with English school backgrounds.

In the ultimate analysis, taking everything into consideration including the forces of liberalisation, we can assert that the early years of the new millennium will be characterised by increasing social tensions and conflicts affecting not only the formation of governments at the Centre and the States but also the formulation, articulation and execution of its policies in all matters including education.

Bibliography

Part I
Ancient India, C. 3000 B.C. - 1192 A.D.

Primary Authorities
This part is mainly based on the religious scriptures and non-religious literature of the Aryans as well as works of Chinese travellers and authors as
available in English translations. They are as follows:

Acharya, (ed.), *The Isadivimsottarasalopanisadah*, Bombay, 1928.

Aiyar, K.N., *Thirty Minor Upanishads*, Madras, 1914.

Aung, S.Z., and Rhys Davids, T.W., *Compendium of Philosophy*, London,
1910.

Beal, S., *Life of Hiuen Tsiang* (by Shaman Hwuili), London, 1911.

Benfey, Th., *Sama Veda*, Leipzig, 1848.

Bloomifield, *The Atharvaveda*, Strassburg, 1899.

Brough, J., *Selections from Classical Sanskrit Literature*, London, 1951.

Buhler, G., *The Laws of Manu*, Oxford, 1886.

Chalmers, R., *Further Dialogues of the Buddha*, 2 Vols. Oxford, 1926-27.

Cowel, E.B. et al., *The Jataka*, 6 Vols. Cambridge, 1895-1907.

Eggeling, J., *The Satapatha Brahmana*, 5 Vols. Oxford, 1882-1900.

Geiger, W., *The Mahavamsa*, London, 1912.

Giles, H.A., *The Travels of Fa-Hien*, Cambridge, 1923.

Griffith, R.T.H., *The Ramayana*, Benares, 1915.

—, *The Rig Veda*, 2 Vols. Benares, 1896-97.

Hume, R.A., *Thirteen Principal Upanishads, Oxford, 1921.*

Jacobi, H., *Jaina Sutras*, 2 Vols. Oxford, 1894-95.

Jha, Ganganath and Sastri Sitarama, S., (ed.), *The Upanishads*, 5 Vols., Madras, 1898-1921.

Jolly, J., *The Minor Law Books of Narada and Brihaspati*, Oxford, 1889.

—, *The Institute of Vishnu*, Oxford, 1880.

Kaegi, A., *The Rigveda*, Boston, 1886.

Kasi Sanskrit Series, *Susruta Samita*, Varanasi, 1973.

Keith, A.B., *Rig Veda Brahmanas, The Aitareya and the Kausitaki Brahmanas*, Cambridge (USA), 1920.

Legge, J., *Record of Buddhist Kingdoms* (by Fa-Hien), Oxford, 1886.

Macnicol, N. et al., *Hindu Scriptures*, London, 1938.

Madhavananda, Swami, *Brihadaranyaka Upanishad*, Calcutta, 1950.

MacCrindle, J.W., *Ancient India as described by Megasthenes and Arrian*, Calcutta, 1877.

—, *Ancient India as Described in Classical Literature*, London, 1901.

Majumdar, S.N., (ed.), *Ancient India as Described by Ptolemy*, Calcutta, 1927.

Müller, Friedrich Max., *The Upanishads*, 2 Vols. Oxford, 1879-82.

—, (ed.), *Sacred Books of the East*, 50 Vols. Oxford, 1879-1900.

—, *The Six Systems of Indian Philosophy*, London, 1899.

Oldenberg, H., *Rig Veda*, 2 Vols. Berlin, 1909-12.

Raghunathan, N., *Srimad Bhagavatam*, 2 Vols. Madras, 1974.

Roy, P.C., *The Mahabharata*, 11 Vols., Calcutta, 1919-35.

Rhys, Davids, T.W., *The Questions of King Milinda*, 2 Vols., Oxford, 1890-94.

—, *Psalms of the Sisters*, Oxford, 1908.

—, *Psalms of the Brethren,. Oxford, 1913.*

—, and Oldenberg, H., *The Vinaya Texts*, 3 Vols. Berlin, 1881-85.

Ryder, A., *Shakuntala and Other Writings of Kalidasa*, London, 1912.

—, *The Little Clay Cart*, Cambridge (USA), 1905.

—, *The Ten Princes*, Chicago, 1927.

Shamasastry, R., *Kautilya's Arthashastra*, Mysore, 1929.

Shree Gulabkanvorba Ayurvedic Society, *Caraka Samhita*, Jamnagar, 1949.

Takakusu, A., *Record of the Buddhist Religion* (by I-tsing), Oxford, 1896.

Thibaut, G., *The Vedanta Sutras of Badarayana*, Oxford. 1890-1904.

Thomas, E.J., *Early Buddhist Scriptures*, London, 1935.

Vasu, S.C., *The Astadhyayi of Panini*, Allahabad, 1891-98.

Von Schroeder, L., (ed.), *Kathaka Samhita, Leipzig. 1910-11.*

—, (ed.), *Maitrayani Samhita*, Leipzig, 1881-86.

Watters, Thomas, *On Yuan Chwang's Travels in India*, 629 A.D. – 645 A.D. 2 Vols. London, 1904-05.

Weber, A., (ed.), *Taittriya Samhita*, Berlin, 1871-72.

Whitney, W.D., *The Atharva Veda,. Cambridge (USA), 1905.*

Williams, A., *Tales from Panchatantra*, Oxford, 1930.

Wilson, H.H., *Rigveda Sanhita*, London, 1850.

Woords, J.H., *The Yoga System of Patanjali*, Cambridge (USA), 1914.

Woodward, F.L. and Rhys Davids, T.W., *The Book of the Gradual Sayings*, 5 Vols. London, 1932-36.

—, *The Book of the Kindred Sayings*, 5 Vols., London. 1917-30.

Besides Translations of the above religious and non-religious works, the following authoritative works are consulted:

Altekar, A.S., *The Position of Women in Hindu Civilisation*, Benares, 1938.

—, *Education in Ancient India*, Benares, 1934.

Apte, V.M., *Social and Religious Life in the Griha Sutras*, Bombay, 1954.

Bannerjee, G.N., *Hellenism in Ancient India*, Calcutta, 1920.

Barnett, L.D., *The Heart of India*, London, 1908.

Basham, A.L., *The Wonder that was India*, London, 1953.

Barkh, Auguste, *Religions of India*, London, 1892.

Bentlay, J., *A Historical View of Hindu Astronomy*, London, 1825.

Brown, P., *Indian Architecture, Buddhist and Hindu,. Bombay, 1949.*

Chatterjee, Mitali, *Education in Ancient India*, New Delhi, 1999.

Chattopadhyaya, D.P., *Science and Society in Ancient India*, Calcutta, 1977.

Chopra, P.N, Puri, B.N. and Das, M.N. (eds.), *A Social, Cultural, and Economic History of India*, 3 Vols. Madras, 1990.

Das Gupta, S.N., *History of Indian Philosophy*, 4 Vols., Cambridge, 1923-49.

—, *Yoga as Philosophy and Religion*, London, 1924.

Deussen, Paul, *Philosophie des Veda, Leipzig, 1894.*

—, *Das System des Vedanta*, Leipzig, 1893.

—, *The Philosophy of the Upanishads,. Edinburgh, 1906.*

Elliot, C., *Hinduism and Buddhism*, 3 Vols. London, 1922.

Farquhar, J.N., *Outline of the Religious Literature of India*, Oxford, 1920.

Gruber, R. Elmar and Kersten, Holger, *The Original Jesus*, Shaftesbury, 1995.

Hill, W.D.P., *The Bhagvad Gita*, Oxford, 1928.

Hopkins, E.W., *The Religions of India,. Boston, 1895.*

Kane, P.V., *History of Dharmasastra*, 5 Vols. Poona, 1930.

Keith, A.B., *The Religion and Philosophy of the Vedas and Upanishads.* Cambridge (USA), 1925.

—, *History of Sanskrit Literature*, Oxford, 1928.

—, *Indian Logic and Atomism*, Oxford, 1921.

Kaye, G.R., *Indian Mathematics*, Calcutta, 1915.

Keay, F.E., *Indian Education in Ancient and Later Times*, London, 1938.

Kramrisch, S., *Indian Sculpture*, Calcutta, 1933.

Macdonell, A.A., *History of Sanskrit Literature*, London, 1900.

—, and Keith, A.B., *Vedic Index of Names and Subjects*, 2 Vols. London, 1912.

Majumdar, R.C., *Ancient India*, Benares, 1952.

—, (ed.), *The History and Culture of the Indian People*, 9 Vols. Bombay, 1965. The first five volumes cover our period.

—, R.C., Raychaudhuri, H.C., and Datta, Kalikinkar, *An Advanced History of India. London, 1953.*

Maeterlinck, Maurice, *The Great Secret* London, 1922.

Marshall, J. and Others, *Mohenjo Daro and the Indus Civilisation*, 3 Vols. London, 1931.

Mortimer Wheeler, *The Indus Civilization*, Cambridge, 1953.

Mookerji, R.K., *Ancient Indian Education*, London, 1947.

—, *Hindu Civilisation*, Bombay, 1970 (Fifth Edition).

Nath, Pran, *A Study in the Economic Condition of Ancient India*, London, 1929.

Oldenberg, H., *Ancient India*, Chicago, 1898 (Second Edition).

—, *Die Religion des Veda*, Berlin, 1894.

—, *Buddha – His Life, His Doctrine, His Order*, London, 1927.

Olivelle, Patrick, *The Asrama System*, Oxford, 1993.

Pillai, Puranlingam, M.S., *Tamil Literature*, Tinnevelly, 1929.

Radhakrishnan, S., *Indian Philosophy*, 2 Vols. London, 1923-27.

—, *The Hindu View of Life*, New York, 1928.

—, et al. (ed.), *The Cultural Heritage of India*, 4 Vols. Calcutta, 1937-56.

Ray, P.C., *A History of Hindu Chemistry*, 2 Vols. Calcutta, 1907-25.

Raychaudhuri, H.C., *Political History of Ancient India*, Calcutta, 1972 (Seventh Edition).

—, *Studies in Indian Antiquities*, Calcutta, 1958 (Second Edition).

Renou, L., *Religions of Ancient India*, London, 1953.

—, *La Civilisation de l'Inde Ancienne*, Paris, 1950.

Rhys Davids, T.W., *Buddhism, its History and Literature*, London, 1926.

Saletore, R.N., *Life in the Gupta Age*, Bombay, 1943.

Sharma, R.S., *Material Cultures and Social Formations in Ancient India. Madras, 1990.*

Sigerist, H., *A History of Medicine*, 2 Vols. New York, 1961.

Sinha, Nandalal, *The Vaisashika Sutras of Kanada*, Allahabad, 1923.

Stevenson, S., *The Heart of Jainism*, Oxford, 1916.

Tibault, G., *Astronomie, Astrologie und Mathematik*, Strassburg, 1899.

Valavalkar, P.H., *Hindu Social Institutions*, Baroda, 1942.

Warmington, E.H., *Commerce between the Roman Empire and India*, Cambridge, 1928.

Weber, Max, *The Religions of India*, Glencoe, 1958.

Whitney, W.D., *A Sanskrit Grammar*, Leipzig and London, 1879.

Winternitz, M., *History of Indian Literature*, 2 Vols. Translation from German Version of 1909-20 into English by S. Ketkar, Calcutta, 1927-33.

Zimmer, H.R., *Philosophies of India*, New York, 1951.

—, *Hindu Medicine*, Baltimore, 1948.

Journals and Periodicals
(Relevant Volumes Consulted)

Bulletin of the School of Oriental and African Studies, London.

Epigraphia Indica, Calcutta and Delhi.

Journal Asiatique, Paris.

Journal of the Royal Asiatic Society of Great Britain and Ireland, London.

Journal of the Royal Asiatic Society of Bengal, Calcutta.

Journal of the American Oriental Society, Baltimore.

Part II
Medieval India, 1192 A.D. – 1757 A.D.

Primary Authorities

This part of the work has been exclusively based on contemporary Arabian, Turki and Persian works as available either in full or in part translations in English by European scholars. Complete translations of the following works, as available in Calcutta and Delhi, with the years indicating their editions, are consulted:

Akham-i-Alamgiri by Hamid-ud-din Khan. English translation by Jadunath Sarkar, Calcutta, 1912.

Ain-i-Akbari by Abul Fazl Allami. Translated into English in 3 Vols. Vol.1 in 1893 by H. Blochaman and Vols.2 and 3 in 1894 by H.S. Jarret.

Akbarnama by Abul Fazl Allami. English translation in 3 Vols. by H. Beveridge, London, 1907-12.

Babarnama by Zahir-ud-din Muhammad Babar. Written in Turki, Persian translation by Abdur Rahim Khan-i-Khaman, son of Bairam Khan. English translation from Turki by Mrs. A.S. Beveridge in 2 Vols., London 1922. English translation from Persian by J. Leyden and W. Erskine, Oxford, 1826.

Burhan-i-Ma'asir by Ali bin Azizullah Tabataba. English translation by J.S. King, London, 1900.

Futuhat-i-Alamgiri by Ishwardas Nagar. English translation by Tasneem Ahmad. Delhi, 1978.

Futuh-al-Buldan by Ahmad bin Yahya Baladhuri. English translation in two parts – Part I by P.K. Hitti, New York, 1916 and Part II by F.C. Murgotten, New York, 1924.

Futuhat-i-Firuz Shahi by Firuz Shah Tughluq. English translation by S.A. Rashid, Aligarh, 1943.

Humayunnama by Gulbadan Begam. English translation by Mrs. A.S. Beveridge, London, 1902.

Kashf-ul-Mahjub by Shaikh Ali bin Usman al-Hujwiri. English translation by R.A. Nicholson, London, 1939.

Khazain-ul-Futuh by Amir Khusrau. English translation by M. Habib, Madras, 1931.

Kitab-ul-Hind by Abu Raihan Alberuni. English translation by E.C. Sachau, London, 1910. Also translated by J.N. Sarkar.

Ma'asir-i-Alamgiri by Saqi Mustad Khan. English translation by Hidayat Husain, Calcutta, 1924. Also translated by J.N. Sarkar.

Ma'asir-i-Jahangiri by Khawaja Kamgar Husaini. English translation by Azra Alavi. Bombay, 1978.

Masalik-ul-Absar by Sahibab-ud-din-al-Umari. English translation by O. Spies, I.H. Siddiqi and Qazi Muhammad Ahmad, Aligarh, 1971.

Mirat-i-Ahmadi by Ali Muhammad Khan. English translation in parts by J. Bird in his *Political and Statistical History of Gujarata*, London, 1835.

Mirat-i-Sikandari by Sikandar bin Muhammad. English translation by E.C. Bayley, London, 1886.

Mutakhab-ul-Tawarikh by Mulla Abdul Qadir Badauni. Translated into English in 3 Vols. – Vol.1 by Ranking in 1898, Vol.2 by Lowe in 1924 and Vol.3 by Haig in 1925. All the volumes were published in Calcutta.

Padshahnama by Abdul Hamid Lahori. English translation by Wheeler Thackhton, New York, 1997

Qanoon-i-Humayuni by Khwandamir. English translation by B. Prasad, Calcutta, 1910.

Rihla by Ibn Batuta. English translation in 2 Vols. by A.M. Husain, Baroda, 1953.

Riyaz-us-Salatin by Ghulam Husain Salim. English translation by A. Salam, Calcutta, 1912.

Ruka'at-i-Alamgiri by Hamid-ud-din Khan. English translation by Jamshid H. Bilmoria, Bombay.

Shah Jahan Nama by Inayat Khan. English translation by W.E. Begley and Z.A. Desai. Delhi, 1990.

Siyar-ul-Mutakherin by Ghulam Husain Salim. English translation in 3 Vols. by Charles Stewart, London 1826. Also by Briggs, London, 1832.

Tabaqat-i-Akbari by Nizam-ud-din Ahmad. Translated into English in 3 Vols. Vol.1 by B. De and Vols.2 and 3 by B. De and Prasad, Calcutta, 1913-40.

Tabaqat-i-Nasiri by Minhaj-ud-din Siraj. English translation by H.G. Raverty in 2 Vols. Calcutta, 1897.

Tarikh-i-Mubarak Shahi by Yahya bin Ahmad Sirhindi. English translation by K.K. Basu, Baroda, 1932.

Tarikh-i-Firishta by Muhammad Qasim Firishta. English translation in 3 Vols. by J. Briggs, Calcutta, 1829.

Tarikh-i-Firuz Shahi by Shams-i-Siraj Afif. English translation in parts by Vilayat Husain in 1891.

Tarikh-i-Firuz Shahi by Zia-ud-din-Barani. English translation in parts by Syed Ahmad Khan in 1869-70.

Tarikh-i-Guzidah by Hamdullah Mustaufi. English translation by E.G. Browne, London, 1913.

Tarikh-i-Jahan Gusha by Ala-ud-din Ata Malik Juwaini. English translation by J. Boyle in 2 Vols. Manchester, 1958.

Tarikh-i-Rashidi by Mirza Muhammad Haider Dughlat. English translation by N. Elias and E. Denison Ross, London, 1895.

Tarikh-i-Yamini by Abu Nasr Muhammad al-Jabbar al-Utbi. English translation from the Persian version of the Arabic text by James Reynolds, London, 1858.

Tazkirat-ul-Waqiyat by Jauhar. English translation by Charles Stewart, London, 1832.

Tazkirat-uk-Muluk by Rafi-ud-din Sirazi. English translation by J.S. King, London, 1900.

Tazkirat-ul-Ulema-e-Jaunpur by Maulana Khair-ud-din Muhammad Jaunpuri. English translation by Muhammad Sanaullah, Calcutta, 1934.

Tuzuk-i-Baburi by Zahir-ud-din Muhammad Babar. See *Babarnama*.

Tuzuk-i-Jahangiri by Jahangir. Jahangir himself wrote his memoirs till the seventeenth year of his reign (1622-23) and Mutamad Khan, his court historian, continued his memoirs till the nineteenth year of his reign under his direction. English translation by Alexander Rogers and edited by H. Beveridge in 2 Vols. Vol.1 published in 1909 and Vol.2 in 1914 at London. Major David Price's translation was published earlier at Calcutta in 1904.

Zafar-ul-Walih bi Muzaffar wa Alih by Abdullah Mohammad bin Umar-al-Makki. English translation by E.D. Ross in 3 Vols., London, 1910-29.

The extracts from the following Persian works which have been translated into English and cited in the various standard authorities on Medieval India including Elliot and Dowson's have also been utilised to interpret history of education during our period:

Alamgirnama by Muhammad Kazim.

Badshahnama by Mirza Aminai Qazwini.

Futuh-us-Salatin by Isami.

Iqbalnama-i-Jahangiri by Muhammad Sharif Mutamad Khan.

Khulasat-ut-Twarikh by Sujan Rai Khattri.

Laila Majnun by Amir Khusrau.

Lubalo-ul-Albab by Muhammad Awfi.

Ma'asir-i-Rahimi by Mulla Abdul Baqi in 3 Vols.

Mirat-ul-Alam by Bakhtawar Khan.

Mutakhab-ul-Lubab by Muhammad Hashim Khafi Khan in 3 Vols.

Subh-i-Sadiq by Muhammad Sadiq.

Tadhkira-Khusnavisan by Gulam Ali Haft Qalam.

Tafrih-ul-Imarat by Lala Shilchand.

Tarikh-i-Daudi by Abdullah.

Tarikh-i-Haqqi by Abdul Haqq Muhaddis Dihlawi.

Tarikh-i-Jan Jahan by Jan Jahan Khan.

Waqiat-i-Mustaqi by Rizqulla Mushtaqi.

Contemporary Travellers' Accounts, Memoirs, Diaries, Letters, Pamphlets and Other Polemical Works

Batuta, Ibn, *Voyages*, 1325-1354. Edited by C. Defremery and B.R. Sanguinetti in 4 Vols, Paris, 1853-58.

—, *Travels in Asia and Africa 1324-1354*, Edited by H.A.R. Gibb, London, 1929.

Bernier, Francois, *Voyages de Francois Bernier, 1656-88*, 2 Tomes, Amsterdam, 1699, Archibald Constable's English translation was published at London in 1894.

Beruni, Al, *Al Beruni's India: An Account of the Religion, Philosophy, Literature, Geography, Chronology, Customs, Laws and Astrology of India of 1030 A.D.*, Edited by Edward C. Sachau, Delhi Edition (2 Vols. in I), 1964.

Catrou, F.F., *The General History of the Mogol Empire from its Foundation by Tamerlane to the late Emperor Orangzeb*, London, 1709.

De Laet, *Empire of the Great Mogul, 1630-32*, Edited by J.S. Hoyland, Bombay 1928.

Della Valle, Pietro, *Travels of Pietro Della Valle in India, 1623-24*, Edited by Edward Gray, London, 1892.

Frayer, John, *A New Account of the East Indies and Persia, 1672-81*. Edited by William Crooke in 3 Vols., London, 1909.

Frayer, John, and Thomas Roe, *Travels in India in the Seventeenth Century*, London, 1873.

Hamilton, Alexander, *A New Account of the East Indies, 1688-1723* in 2 Vols., Edinburgh, 1726.

Hawkings, William, *Voyages during the Reign of Henry VII, Queen Elizabeth and James 1608-13*, Edited by C.R. Markham, London, 1883.

Hedges, William, *The Diary of William Hedges, 1681-87, Edited by Henry Yule in 2 Vols, London, 1877*.

Huyghen, Von John, *The Voyage to the East Indies, 1583-88*, Edited by A.C. Burnel and P.A. Tiele in 2 Vols., London, 1875-85.

Manucci Niccolao Venetian, *Storia Do Mogor*, Edited by William Irvine in 4 Vols., London, 1907-08.

—, *Memoirs of the Mogul Court*, Edited by Michael Edwardes, London, 1960.

Manrique, Fray Sebastien, *Travels of Fray Sebestian Manrique, 1629-43*, Edited by C.E. Luard and Rev. H. Hosten in 2 Vols. London, 1926-27.

Marshall, John, *John Marshal in India, 1668-72*, Edited by Shafat Ahmad Khan, Oxford, 1928.

Mundy, Peter, *Travels of Peter Mundy in Asia and Europe, 1628-33*, Edited by R. Temple in 2 Vols. London, 1914.

Monserrate, S.J., *The Commentaries, 1580-82*, Edited by J.S. Hoyland, Oxford, 1922.

Ovington, J., *A Voyage to Surat in the year 1689*, London, 1696.

Martin, Francois, *India in the Seventeenth Century, 1670-94*, Edited by Lotika Varadarajan in 2 Vols., Delhi, 1981.

Palsaert, Francois, *The Voyage of Francois Palsaert to the East Indies, 1620-27*, Edited by Albert Gray and H.C.P. Bell in 2 Vols. London, 1898.

Pierre, Du Jarric, *Akbar and the Jesuits*, Edited by Denison Ross and Eileen Power, Delhi, 1979.

Polo, Marco, *The Travels of Marco Polo (1254-1323)*, Translated by Aldo Ricci. London, 1931.

Pyrad, Francois, *The Voyage of Francois Pyrad of Laval, 1608-09*, Edited by Albert Gray in 2 Vols., London. 1878.

Roe, Sir Thomas, *The Embassy of Sir Thomas Roe, 1615-19*, Edited by William Foster in 2 Vols., London, 1899.

Tavernier, Jean Baptiste, *Travels in India, 1640-66*, Edited by V. Ball in 2 Vols., London, 1889.

Terry, William, *A Voyage to the East Indies in 1622*, London, 1655.

Thevenot and Careri, *Indian Travels of Thevenot in 1677 and of Careri in 1695*, Edited by S.N. Sen, Delhi, 1949.

English Factory Records (manuscripts as well as printed) were consulted earlier at the India Office Library, London. They are as follows:

Europeans in India, Vols. 1 and 2.

Letters to and from India, Vols. 1 and 2.

W. Foster, (ed.), *English Factories in India, 1618-1669*, 13 Vols. Oxford, 1906-27.

Secondary Authorities

(Year of publication indicates, as before, the edition consulted)

Books and Monographs

Afonso, J.C. (ed.), *Letters from the Mughal Court; 1580-1583*, Bombay, 1980.

Ahmed, Aziz Muhammad, *Political History and Institution of the Early Turkish Empire of Delhi*, Lahore, 1949.

—, Muhammad, *An Intellectual History of Islam in India*, Edinburgh, 1969.

Aiyangar, S.K., and Sewell, Robert, (ed.), *Historical Inscriptions of Southern India (Collected till 1923) and Outlines of Political History*, Madras, 1983.

Ali, Syed Amir, *The Spirit of Islam*, London, 1964.

Arberry, A.J., *The Koran Interpreted*, 2 Vols. London, 1955.

Arnold, T.W., *The Preaching of Islam*, London, 1913.

Ashraf, K.M., *Life and Conditions of the People of Hindustan, 1200-1500,*. Delhi, 1959.

Atkinson, J., *The Shah Namah*, London, 1832.

Banerjee, A.C., *Guru Nanak and His Times*, Patiala, 1972.

Binyon, L., *Akbar*, London, 1939.

Browne, E.G., *A Literary History of Persia*, 4 Vols, Cambridge, 1928.

Browne, Percy, *Indian Painting under the Mughals, 1550-1750*, London, 1924.

Burn, Richard, (ed.), *The Cambridge History of India*, Vols. IV, Cambridge, 1937.

Carpenter, J.R., *Theism in Medieval India*, London, 1921.

Chand, Tara, *Influence of Islam on Indian Culture*, Allahabad, 1946.

Chandra, Satish, *Historiography, Culture and the State in Medieval India*, Delhi, 1996.

—, *Parties and Politics at the Mughal Court*, 1707-40, Delhi, 1959.

Day, U.N., *Mughal Government, 1556-1707*, Delhi, 1970.

Dow, Alexander, *The History of Hindostan*, 3 Vols, London, 1768-72.

Elliot, H.M. and Dowson, William. *The History of India as told by its own Historians*, 8 Vols, London, 1867-1877.

Erskine, William, *History of India under Babur and Hamayun*, Karachi, 1974.

Farquhar, J.N., *Outline of the Religions Literature of India*, London, 1920.

—, *Modern Religious Movements in India*, London, 1929.

Foster, William, *Early Travels in India*, Oxford, 1921.

Gibb, H.A.R., *Studies in the Civilisation of Islam*, London, 1962.

Gladwin, F.A., *The Institutes of the Emperor Akbar*, 2 Vols, London, 1800.

Grewal, J.S., *Muslim Rule in India*. Calcutta, 1970.

Grierson, G.A., (ed.), *Linguistic Survey of India*, 11 Vols, Calcutta, 1921.

—, *Languages of India*, Calcutta, 1903.

—, *The Modern Vernacular Literature of Hindustan*, Calcutta, 1889.

Haig, Wolsey, (ed.), *The Cambridge History of India*, Vol.III, Cambridge, 1928.

Habib, Irfan, *The Agrarian System of Mughal India*, Bombay, 1963.

Habib, M., *Life and Works of Hazarat Amir Khusrau*, Aligarh, 1927.

Habibullah, A.B.M., *The Foundation of Muslim Rule in India*, Allahabad, 1961.

Hardy, Peter, *Historians of Medieval India*, London, 1960.

Hasan, Ibn, *The Central Structure of the Mughul Empire*, London, 1936.

Havell, E.B., *Handbook of Agra and the Taj, Sikandra, Fathpur-Sikri and the Neighbourhood with illustration*, London, 1904.

—, *Indian Architecture, its Psychology, structure and History from the first Muhammadan Invasion to the Present day*, London, 1913.

Hitti, Philip K., *History of the Arabs*, London, 1949.

Hunter, W.W., *Indian Musalmans*, London, 1871.

Husain, Agha Mahdi, *Rise and Fall of Muhammad-bin-Tughluq*, London, 1938.

Jaffar, S.M. *The Mughal Empire from Babar to Aurangzeb*, Peshwar, 1936.

—, *Some Cultural Aspects of Muslim Rule in India*, Delhi, 1972.

—, *Medieval India under Muslim Kings*, Delhi, 1973.

—, *Education in Muslim India, 1000-1800*, Peshwar, 1936.

Jaiswal, Suvira, *Origin and Development of Vaisnavism*, Delhi 1981.

Kaur, Kuldeep, *Madrassa Education in India: A Study of its Past and Present.* Chandigarh, 1990.

Kennedy, Pringle, *History of the Great Moghals*, 2 Vols. Calcutta, 1905-11.

Keay, F.E., *Kabir and His Followers*, London, 1931.

Keene, H.G., *Fall of the Moghul Empire*, London, 1876.

—, *History of Hindustan from the First Muslim conquest to the Fall of the Moghul Empire*, London, 1885.

Khaldun, Ibn, *Muqaddima Tarikh*, Translated into English by Franz Rosenthal, London, 1959.

Lal, K.S., *History of the Khalijis*, Delhi, 1980.

Lanepoole, Stanley, *Mohammedian Dynasties*, London, 1894.

—, *Moors in Spain*, London, 1888.

—, *History of the Mogal Emperors of Hindustan*, London, 1892.

—, *Medieval India under Mohammadan Rule, 712-1764*, London, 1917.

—, *Aurangzib and the Decay of the Mughal Empire*, Oxford, 1930.

—, *Babar*, London, 1899.

Law, N.N., *Promotion of Learning in India during Muhammadan Rule*, Calcutta, 1915.

Leitner, G.W., *History of Indigenous Education in the Punjab since Annexation and in 1882,. Delhi, 1982 [1882].*

Major, R.H., (ed.), *India in the Fifteenth Century,. London, 1857.*

Majumdar, R.C., (ed.), *History and Culture of the Indian people*, Vols. VI and VII, Bombay, 1960.

Malcolm, John, *Memoirs of Central India.* London, 1832.

Martin, F.R., *Miniature, Painting and Painters of Persia, India and Turkey*, Quaritch, 1912.

Mehta, J.L., *Advanced Study in the History of Medieval India*, Delhi, 1983.

Moreland, W.H., *The Mughal Empire from Akbar to Aurangzeb*, Delhi, 1990.

—, *The Agrarian System of Moslem India*, Cambridge, 1929.

Mukhia, Harbans, *Perspectives on Medieval History*, Delhi, 1993.

Nizami, K.A., *On History and Historians of Medieval India*, Delhi, 1983.

—, *Studies in Medieval India History and Culture*, Allahabad, 1966.

—, *Some Aspects of Religion and Politics in India during the Thirteenth Century Delhi*, 1978.

Prasad, Ishwari, *History of the Qaraunah Turks*, Allahabad, 1936.

—, *History of the Medieval India*, Allahabad, 1952.

Qanungo, D.R., *Sher Shah and His Times*, Bombay, 1965.

—, *Dara Shukoh*, Calcutta, 1952.

Qureshi, I.H., *The Administration of the Sultanate of Delhi*, Lahore, 1942.

—, *The Administration of the Mughul Empire*, Karachi, 1966.

Rai, Krishnadasa, (ed.), *Mughal Miniatures*, Delhi, 1955.

Sahay, B.K., *Education and Learning under the Great Mughals, 1526-1707*, Bombay, 1968.

Salatore, B.A., *Social and Political Life in the Vijayangar Empire, 1346-1646*, 2 Vols., Madras, 1934.

Salimova, Kadriya, (ed.), *Why Should We Teach History of Education*, Moscow, 1993.

Sardesai, G.S., *Main Currents of Maratha History*, Bombay, 1933.

Sarkar, Jadunath, *Fall of the Mughal Empire*, 4 Vols, Calcutta, 1947-52.

—, *Mughal Administration*, Calcutta, 1952.

—, *Shivaji and His Times*, Calcutta, 1952.

—, *History of Aurangzeb*, 5 Vols, Calcutta, 1930.

—, *History of Bengal*, Dacca, 1948.

—, *Studies in Mughal India*, Calcutta, No Date.

—, *Chaitanya's Life and Teachings*, Calcutta, 1922.

Sen, Dinesh Chandra, *History of Bengali Language and Literature*, Calcutta, 1954.

Sewell, Robert, *A Forgotten Empire*, London, 1924.

Sircar, D.C., *Studies in the Society and Administration of Ancient and Medieval India*, Calcutta, 1967.

Sinha, N.K., *Rise of the Sikh Power*, Calcutta, 1933.

Sleeman, W.H., *Rambles and Recollections of an Indian Officials*, 2 Vols., London, 1844.

Smith, V.A., *Akbar, the Great Mughal*, Oxford, 1919.

Srivastava, A.L., *The Sultanate of Delhi, 711-1526*, Agra, 1989.

Thomas, Edward, *Chronicles of the Pathan Kings of Delhi*, London, 1871.

Tod, James, *Annals and Antiquities of Rajasthan*, 2 Vols., London, 1914.

Tripathi, R.P., *Some Aspects of Muslim Administration*, Allahabad, 1964.

Tripathi, R.S., *History of Kanauj to the Moslem Conquest of Delhi*, Delhi, 1959.

Williams, J.A., *Themes of Islamic Civilisation*, Berkeley, 1971.

Relevant volumes of the following learned journals and periodicals are also consulted:

Epigraphica Indica, Calcutta and Delhi.

Journal of the Royal Asiatic Society of Great Britain and Ireland, London.

Journal Asiatique, Paris.

Journal of the Asiatic Society of Bengal, Calcutta.

Muslim Education, Cambridge.

Paedagogica Historica, Gent (Belgium)

III
Modern India, 1757 A.D. – 1998 A.D.

This part is substantially based on my own research done at different times
on different occasions in India and U.K. as well as on my lectures delivered to
M.Phil/Ph.D. students in history of education in JNU.

Unpublished Sources

These sources include the Private Papers of Warren Hastings, Auckland,
Alexander Duff, Bentinck, Dalhousie, Charles Wood, Curzon and
Hamilton. While the Private Papers of Hastings and Auckland were
consulted at the British Museum, London, of Duff at the National Library of
Scotland, Edinburgh, of Bentinck at the Nottingham University Library, of
Dalhousie at the Scottish Record Office, Edinburgh, and of Wood at the
India Office Library, London. The microfilm copies of the Private Papers of
Curzon and Hamilton were seen at the National Archives, New Delhi. The
unpublished sources also include a study of the East India Company Records:
Letters from Bengal (1793-1833) and Letters from India and Bengal (1834-54)
as well as Despatches to Bengal (1793-1833) and Despatches to India and
Bengal (1834-54) at the India Office Library, London.

Published Sources

(A)   The official publications come first under this head. They include
*Papers relating to the renewal of the Charter of the East India Company in
1813 and 1833; Reports of the General Committee of Public Instruction
(1831-42) and of the Council of Education (1842-54); Papers connected with
the establishment of Universities in India in 1857; Report of the Hunter
Commission, 1882-83; Quinquennial Reviews of the Progress of Education
since 1886; Report of the Indian Universities Commission, 1902; Indian
Educational Policy, 11 March 1904; Report of the Calcutta University
Commissions, 1917; Report of the Hartog Committee 1929; Post-War Plan
for Educational Development in India, 1944-84; Report of the
Radhakrishnan Commission, 1948-49; Report of the Mudaliar
Commission, 1952-53; Report of the Kothari Commission, 1964-66;
National Policy on Education, 1968; the Draft National Policy on*

Education, 1979; the Challenge of Education, 1985; the National Policy on Education, 1986; Programme of Action, 1986; Report on Implementation of National Policy on Education-1986; Report of the Committee for Review of National Policy on Education 1986, December, 1990; Revised Programme of Action, 1992; DPEP Guidelines, May 1995; Report on the Committee of State Education Ministers on Implications of the proposal to make Elementary Education a Fundamental Right, January 1997, and finally Conference of State Education Ministers and Education Secretaries: Agenda Notes, October 22-24, 1998. While these publications deal exclusively with education, there are others like the Report of the Public Service Commission, 1886-87; Moral and Material Progress Reports since 1859; Statistical Abstracts; Reports of the Committees and Conferences on Women since 1947; Register of the Directorate General of Training & Employment; National Sample Survey (NSS), 1997; Five Year Plans including the Ninth Five Year Plan (1998-2003); UNICEFs Report on State of World's Children, 1999 and finally, Jean Dreze et. al., Public Report on Basic Education, New Delhi, 1999 throws a flood of light on the development of education in India. Relevant volumes of Hansard's Parliamentary Debates and Papers are also consulted.

(B) Select newspapers published from Calcutta as well as from Bombay and Madras till 1947 and the Times of India published from Delhi for the Post-independence period are consulted while the proceedings of the Indian National Congress are extremely useful for public reactions during the Curzon era, 1899-1905.

(C) Books, Memoirs, Diaries, Pamphlets and Selections from Records and Reports.

Adam, William, Three Reports on the State of Education in Bengal and Behar, ed. by Long. Calcutta, 1868.

Aggarwal, J.C., Landmarks in the History of Modern Indian Education, New Delhi, 1984.

Arberry, A.J., Asiatic Jones, London, 1946.

Ashby, Eric, Universities: British, Indian, African, London, 1966.

Auber, P., An Analysis of the Constitution of the East India Company, London, 1826.

Baird, J.G.A., Private Letters of the Marguess of Dalhousie, Edinburgh, 1910.

Banerjea, Surendranath, A Nation in Making, Calcutta, 1925.

Basu, A.N., Education in Modern India, Calcutta, 1947.

Basu, Aparna, The Growth of Education and Political Development in India, 1898-1920. Delhi, 1974.

—,Essays in the History of Indian Education. New Delhi, 1982.

Bearce, G.D., *British Attitudes Towards India, 1784-1858*, Oxford, 1961.

Bowring, J., (ed.), The *Works of Jeremy Bentham*, 11 Vols, London, 1843.

Briggs, Asa, *Victorian People.* London, 1954.

—, *The Age of Improvement.* London, 1959.

Broughton, Lord, *Recollections of a Long Life,* 6 Vols, 1909-11.

Buchanan, C., (ed.), *The College of Fort William in Bengal,* London, 1805.

Cannon, G., *Oriental Jones,* London, 1964.

Chapman, Priscilla, *Hindoo Female Education,* London, 1839.

Chatterjee, K.K., *English Education in India,* Delhi, 1976.

Chintamani, C.Y., *Indian Social Reform,* Bombay, 1901.

Chirol, V., *Indian Unrest,* London, 1910.

Collet, S.D., *Life and Letters of Raja Rammohan Roy,* London, 1900.

Coupland, R., *Wilberforce.* London, 1945.

Das, M.N., *Studies in the Economic and Social Development of Modern India, 1848-56.* Calcutta, 1959.

Datta, K.K. *A Social History of Modern India,* New Delhi, 1975.

Delors, Jacques, *Learning: The Treasure Within,* Paris, 1996.

Desai, A.R., *Social Background of Indian Nationalism,* Bombay, 1948.

Dhar, T.N., Ilchaman, A.S. and W.F., *Education and Employment in India.* Calcutta, 1976.

Di Bona, Joseph, (ed.), *One School, One Teacher,* New Delhi, 1983.

Dubois, Abbe, *A View of Hindoo Manners, Customs and Ceremonies,* London, 1897.

Embree, A.T., *Charles Grant and British Rule in India,* London, 1962.

Ganguly, B.N., *Dadabhai Nauroji and the Drain Theory,* New Delhi, 1965.

Ghosh, J., *Higher Education in Bengal under British Rule,* Calcutta, 1926.

Ghosh, S.C., *The Social Condition of the British Community in Bengal,*1757-1800, Leiden, 1971.

—, *Dalhousie in India, 1848-56,* New Delhi, 1975.

—, *Indian Nationalism,* New Delhi, 1985.

—, *Education Policy in India since Warren Hastings,* Calcutta, 1989.

—, *Freedom Movement in India,* New Delhi, 1991.

—, (ed.), with Shri J.P. Naik, The *Development of Educational Service, 1859-79,* New Delhi, 1977.

—, (ed.), *Educational Strategies in Developing Countries,* New Delhi, 1977.

—, (ed.), *Development of University Education, 1916-20,* New Delhi, 1977.

Copal, S., *British Policy in India, 1858-1905.* Cambridge, 1965.

—, (ed.), *Selected Works of Jawaharlal Nehru* (Second Series), Vol, 5.New Delhi, 1987.

Halevy, Elie, *La Formation du Radicalism Philosophique*, 3 tomes. Paris, 1991-04.

—, *Histoire du Peuple Anglais au XIX Siecle*, 5 tomes. Paris, 1912-32.

Hamilton, G., *Parliamentary Reminiscences and Reflections*, 2 Vols., London, 1916-24.

Heimsath, C.H., *Indian Nationalism and Hindu Social Reform*, Calcutta, 1964.

Howell, A., *Education in British India*. Calcutta, 1872.

Hundred Years of the University of Calcutta. Calcutta, 1957.

Jaeger, M., *Before Victoria*. London, 1956.

Jenks, L.H., *The Migration of British Capital to 1875*, New York, 1927.

Karve, D.K., *Looking Back*, Poona, 1936.

—, *My Twenty Years in the Cause of Indian Women*, Poona, 1915.

Kaye, J.W., *The Administration of the East India Company*, London, 1853.

Keith, A.B., *Constitutional History of India*, Oxford, 1937.

Kopf, David, *British Orientalism and the Bengal Renaissance*, Berkeley-Los Angeles, 1969.

Laird, M.L., *Missionaries and Education in Bengal, 1793-1837*, London, 1972.

Le Bon, Gustave, *Les Civilisation de L'Inde*, Paris, 1887.

Leon, Antoine, *The History of Education Today*, Paris, 1985.

Mangan, J., (ed.), *The Imperial Curriculum*, London, 1993.

Marshman, J., *Carey, Marshman and Ward*, London, 1864.

Mathur, Y.B., *Women's Education in India, 1833-1966*, Delhi, 1973

Martin, Briton, Jr., *New India, 1885*, Bombay, 1970.

Mayhew, A., *The Education of India*. London, 1926.

Misra, B.B., *The Indian Middle Classes*. London, 1961.

McCully, B.T., *English Education and the Origins of Indian Nationalism*, New York, 1940.

Mehrotra, S.R., *The Emergence of the Indian National Congress*, Delhi, 1971.

Mitra, Peary Chand, *A Biographical Sketch of David Hare*, Calcutta, 1877.

Mukheree, Haridas and Uma, *The Origins of the National Education Movement, 1905-10*, Calcutta, 1957.

—, *The Growth of Nationalism in India*, Calcutta, 1957.

Nag, Kalidas, (ed.), *Bethune School and College Centenary Volume*, Calcutta, 1949.

Naik, J.P., and Nuruilah, S., *A History of Education in India*, New Delhi, 1974 [19431.

Naik, J.P., (ed.), *Development of University Education, 1860-87,* Delhi, 1963.

—, *Some Aspects of Post-Independence Development in India.* Sambalpur, 1974.

Nanda, B.R., *Cokhale,* Delhi, 1977.

Narain, Prem, *Press and Politics in India, 1885-1905.* Delhi, 1970.

Narayan, J.P., *Education for Our People.* New Delhi, 1978.

O'Malley, L.S.S., *Modern India and the West,* London, 1941.

—, *The Indian Civil Service,* London, 1931.

Philips, C.H., *The East India Company, 1784-1834,* Manchester, 1940.

Plumb, J.H., *England in the Eighteenth Century,* London, 1961.

Rehman, A., et. al., *Scientific Societies in India,* Delhi, 1965.

Richter, *J., History of Missions in India,* London, 1908.

Salimova, Kadriya, (ed.), *Why Should We Teach History of Education?* Moscow, 1993.

Sarkar, Susobhan, *Bengal Renaissance and Other Essays,* Bombay, 1970.

Seal, Anil, *The Emergence of Indian Nationalism,* Cambridge, 1968.

Sengupta, K.P., *Christian Missionaries in Bengal, 1793-1833,* Calcutta, 1971.

Sharp, H. and Richey, J.A., (eds.), *Selections from the Educational Records of the Government of India,* 2 Vols, Calcutta, 1920-22.

Shore, F.J., *Memoirs of the Life and Correspondence of John Lord Teignmouth,* 3 Vols. London, 1843.

Sinha, D.P., The *Educational Policy of the East India Company in Bengal.* Calcutta, 1964.

Siqueria, T.N., *Modern Indian Education,* Calcutta, 1960.

Steven-Watson, J., *The Reign of George III,* Oxford, 1957.

Stokes, Eric, *The English Utilitarians and India,* Oxford, 1959.

Strachey, J., *India: Its Administration and Progress,* London, 1903.

Temple, Richard, *Men and Events of my Time in India,* London, 1882.

Thomas, F.W., *The History and Prospects of British Education in India* London, 1891.

Trevelyan, C.E., *On the Education of the People of India,* London, 1838.

Trevelyan, G.O., *Life and Letters of Lord Macaulay,* 2 Vols, London, 1876.

Tripathi, Amales, *The Extremist Challenge,* Calcutta, 1967.

University of Calcutta Convocation Addresses, 3 Vols, Calcutta, 1914.

Ward, W., *A View of the History, Literature and Religion of the Hindoos,* 2 Vols, Serampore, 1818.

Young, C.M., *Victorian England,* London, 1936.

(D) Periodicals and journals. (Relevant volumes consulted)

Bengal: Past and Present, Calcutta.

Calcutta Review, Calcutta.
Cambridge Historical Journal, London.
English Historical Review, London.
History of Education, London.
Journal of Indian History, Trivandrum.
Minerva, London.
Modern Asian Studies, Cambridge.
Paedagogica Historica, Ghent (Belgium).
St. Anthony's Papers on South Asian Affairs, London.

Other Works (Relevant volumes consulted)

Economic and Political Weekly, Bombay.
The Times of India Year Book, Bombay.
Education File (NIEPA), New Delhi.

Index